*The Great
Republic*

VOLUME TWO

# The Great Republic

## A History of the American People

FOURTH EDITION

~

### Bernard Bailyn
*Harvard University*

### Robert Dallek
*University of California,*
*Los Angeles*

### David Brion Davis
*Yale University*

### David Herbert Donald
*Harvard University*

### John L. Thomas
*Brown University*

### Gordon S. Wood
*Brown University*

D. C. HEATH AND COMPANY
LEXINGTON, MASSACHUSETTS  TORONTO

*Address editorial correspondence to:*

D. C. Heath
125 Spring Street
Lexington, MA 02173

Cover:   Dan Budnik/Woodfin Camp & Associates.

For permission to use illustrations, grateful acknowledgment is made to the copyright holders listed on pages xxvii–xxviii, which are hereby considered an extension of this copyright page.

Published simultaneously in Canada.

Printed in the United States of America.

International Standard Book Number: 0-669-20987-2

Library of Congress Catalog Number: 91-71285

**GHIJ-CRW-03 02 01**

# PUBLISHER'S FOREWORD

$\int$INCE it was first published in 1977 *The Great Republic* has held an honored place in the small company of truly distinguished and pathbreaking textbooks in American history. The work's authoritative scholarship, interpretive richness, and elegant style have been widely recognized and admired, not only among teachers of United States history courses but among historians in general. As Bernard Bailyn recently stated, "Every historian—however technical—has an obligation to reach out to a broad public because the purpose of the whole effort is to make a culture aware of its origins and development." D. C. Heath is proud to be the publisher of this work in which these distinguished historians have set out to reach that wider public.

Those familiar with earlier editions will find all the original qualities still here: a supple literary style; sufficient detail to provide supporting evidence and memorable examples; special attention to the colonial- and Revolutionary-era origins of the American experience; a dedication to tracing the subtle interconnections of social, economic, and cultural strands with the history of public events; and a consistent commitment to explaining the importance of ideas—whether formally articulated or unspoken—in the shaping of history. But over the years *The Great Republic* has been refined in response to classroom experience and the evolution of historical scholarship, and we believe that this fourth edition is the finest version yet. Throughout the book, of course, the authors have drawn upon recent research to keep the interpretation up-to-date. For example, contemporary historians' fruitful work on the history of native Americans has enriched this account of our history. In the antebellum chapters, previous limitations of space have been slightly relaxed, allowing for more contemporary quotations and anecdotes that render the analysis less abstract, and the role of the 1857 depression in shaping the decade's disastrous political crisis receives more attention. The treatment of Reconstruction has been reorganized for greater clarity and to eliminate overlapping coverage of post–Civil War economic and political issues at the end of Part Four and the beginning of Part Five. Chapters 22 and 23 have been thoroughly rewritten, not only to achieve a more concentrated focus on Gilded Age economic and political topics, but also for greater interpretive clarity. And Part Six, which traces American history since 1920, has been expanded and rewritten. Readers will now find its central thread—the reshaping of progressivism into modern liberalism in the New Deal era, the liberal triumph in the 1960s, and the subsequent crisis of liberal ideas and policies—much more clearly described.

An even more dramatic change in the fourth edition is the book's format. As a publisher, D. C. Heath is acutely aware of the rapidly rising cost of producing elaborate full-color textbooks. Clearly, such a format has pedagogical as well as aesthetic justifications. But many instructors object to the higher price that their students must inevitably pay for a full-color textbook. We believe that *The Great Republic* will have a particularly strong appeal to those history teachers for whom the sacrifice of color illustrations is worth a substantial reduction in the net cost of the book. With this edition we have striven for a clean, elegant appearance, well illustrated with crisply reproduced black-and-white photographs chosen for their quality as visual documents. At the same time we have retained color where it is most necessary—in the book's broad array of maps.

Instructors should also welcome another feature of the fourth edition: the extensive set of supplements that they can add to the textbook, mostly at little or no cost. Neal Stout of the University of Vermont has written a stimulating student's guide to the study of history, *Getting the Most Out of Your U.S. History Course,* that is available free of charge to every student who purchases a new copy of either volume. A challenging workbook in historical geography, *Surveying the Land* by Robert Grant of Framingham State University, is also available to student readers at their instructor's request. So are two documentary anthologies that focus on American regional history: *Document Sets for the South in U.S. History* by Richard Purday of North Georgia College and *Document Sets for Texas and the Southwest in U.S. History* by J'Nell L. Pate of Collin County Community College. The *Study Guide* that accompanies *The Great Republic,* revised for this edition by Patrick Reagan of Tennessee Technological University, offers students a wealth of practical aids. Instructors may also order for their students' use a menu-driven computerized version of the *Study Guide,* available for Macintosh, IBM, and IBM-compatible computers.

For instructors' use, Heath also makes available an *Instructor's Guide and Test Item File,* revised for this edition by Herbert Lasky of Eastern Illinois University, offering a great many classroom-tested suggestions for teaching the survey course with *The Great Republic,* as well as over a thousand questions for quizzes and examinations. These questions are also available on disk—for IBM computers in both 3½- and 5¼-inch formats, and for the Macintosh computer. All the book's maps are reproduced on acetate transparencies. Ivan Steen of the State University of New York, Albany, has created for Heath a cassette tape of recordings of speeches, songs, and other aural documents from American history, which many instructors will find an important and intriguing supplement to their lectures.

For further information about these supplements and to arrange to receive them, instructors should contact their D. C. Heath campus or telemarketing representative, or telephone D. C. Heath toll-free at 1-800-235-3565.

Publisher and authors alike owe a deep debt of gratitude to the historians who reviewed the book, in whole or in part, specifically: **Carl Abbott,** Portland State University; **Guy Alchon,** University of Delaware; **Charles Alexander,** Ohio University; **David Bernstein,** California State University, Long Beach; **Iver Bernstein,** Washington University; **W. Roger Biles,** Oklahoma State University; **Bernard Burke,** Portland State University; **David Burner,** State University of New York, Stony Brook; **Paul Bushnell,** Illinois Wesleyan University; **Dorothy Brown,** Georgetown University; **David Colburn,** University of Florida; **John Milton**

Cooper, University of Wisconsin, Madison; **David Danbom,** North Dakota State University; **Michael Ebner,** Lake Forest College; **Leon Fink,** University of North Carolina, Chapel Hill; **Larry Gerber,** Auburn University; **David Hammack,** Case Western University; **Michael W. Homel,** East Michigan University; **Bruce Kuklick,** University of Pennsylvania; **Allan Lichtman,** American University; **Norman Markowitz,** Rutgers University; **Alan Matusow,** Rice University; **George McJimsey,** Iowa State University; **Anne McLaurin,** Louisiana State University, Shreveport; **Samuel T. McSeveney,** Vanderbilt University; **Thomas Mega,** University of St. Thomas; **Keith Olson,** University of Maryland, College Park; **Richard Pohlenberg,** Cornell University; **Carroll Pursell,** Case Western Reserve University; **James Rawley,** University of Nebraska, Lincoln; **Patrick Reagan,** Tennessee Technological University; **Leo Ribuffo,** George Washington University; **Judith Riddle,** Jefferson College; **Donald Rogers,** University of Hartford; **Nick Salvatore,** Cornell University; **Robert D. Schulzinger,** University of Colorado, Boulder; **June Sochen,** Northeast Illinois University; **Robert Thomas,** University of Washington; **Charles Tull,** Indiana University, South Bend; **Jules Tygiel,** San Francisco State University; and **William Wagnon,** Washburn University.

Many members of D. C. Heath's staff assisted ably in producing this edition. Special thanks are due to Andrea Cava and Martha Wetherill for long hours of painstaking work as production editors, to Henry Rachlin for design, to Martha Friedman and Martha Shethar for photo research, to Charles Dutton for overseeing the manufacturing process, and to Irene Cinelli for expertly producing the supplements.

James Miller
Senior Editor, History

# INTRODUCTION

$\mathscr{T}$HIS book is a history of the American people, from the earliest European settlements in the New World to the present. We call our book "The Great Republic," adopting a phrase that Winston Churchill used to describe the United States. No one can doubt the greatness of the American Republic if it is measured by the size of our national domain, the vastness of our economic productivity, or the stability of our governmental institutions. Less certain has been its greatness in the realm of culture, in the uses of power, and in the distribution of social justice. Our purpose has been to present a balanced story of American development—a story of great achievement, of enormous material success, and of soaring idealism, but also one of conflict, of turbulent factionalism, and of injustice, rootlessness, and grinding disorder.

Three general themes unify the six sections of this book. The first is the development of free political institutions in America. Understanding the United States today requires knowledge of conditions in the colonial period that made popular self-government at first possible, then likely, and in the end necessary. In the American Revolution the longings of provincial Britons for a total reformation of political culture were implemented in American political institutions. During the first half of the nineteenth century, democratic institutions and practices expanded to the limits of the continent, and they received their crucial testing in the American Civil War. By the twentieth century, urbanization and industrialization profoundly changed American society, but our democracy survived all of these changes, as well as depressions, international crises, and world wars. To understand why today, in the last decade of the twentieth century, no significant groups of Americans question our free institutions requires an understanding of how these institutions evolved from eighteenth-century republicanism to modern mass democracy.

Our second theme is the tension that has always existed in America between the interests of groups with special goals and needs and those of the society as a whole. From the beginning the New World, with its abundant resources, stimulated ambitions among the shrewd, the enterprising, and the energetic that often conflicted with the shared needs of the entire populace. The enormous expanse of the country and the admixture of peoples from every quarter of the world encouraged social fragmentation and fostered cultural diversity. But from colonial times to the present, there have been countervailing forces working for social stability and cultural homogeneity.

The Founding Fathers of the Republic were aware that there would be no automatic harmonizing of regional, economic, and social interests, and they worried that minorities might become subject to the tyranny of majorities. At the same time, they feared a centralized government powerful enough to impose order on these conflicting and local interests and active enough to defend the weak against the powerful. In the national and state constitutions they devised a mechanism for the mediation of struggles and for the protection of human rights. In the years since, the balance between the general welfare and the welfare of regions, states, and economic and social groups has often been precarious, and our book shows how, from time to time, that balance has tipped, sometimes in the direction of social order and stability, sometimes in favor of minority interests and individual rights. Much of our story deals with successive attempts, never fully satisfactory, to reconcile the needs of the whole country with the interests of the parts.

Our third theme reflects our recognition that the history of the United States has always been part of a larger history. Except for the native Americans, who had developed a complex and diverse indigenous civilization, the early settlers in America were all immigrants who brought with them the beliefs, values, and cultural legacy of the European and African societies in which they had been born. Naturally, then, developments in America have been closely and inextricably related to those abroad. We believe that the American Revolution, for all of its distinctiveness, needs to be viewed as one in a series of great democratic revolutions that swept the Western world. We think the leveling of social distinctions and the democratization of political life in Jacksonian America are closely related to similar contemporary movements in Europe. And we have stressed that the urbanization, mechanization, and bureaucratization of the United States by the end of the nineteenth century paralleled, copied, and influenced like transformations in the other modernizing nations.

By the twentieth century the connections between developments in the United States and those in the world at large became even closer, and the final sections of our book trace the emergence of the United States as a world power. We have told the story of our involvement in two devastating world wars, in addition to other, smaller conflicts all over the globe, from Korea to Vietnam to the Persian Gulf. We have shown how, in recent decades, the president of the United States has become the most influential political leader in the world, how variations in the American economy have affected the well-being of all other nations, and how, for better or worse, American popular culture has reached a global audience. At the same time, we have emphasized that changes in other parts of the world have profoundly affected American political life, economic growth, and social organization. In short, we have written an American history that is part of world history.

In presenting these three themes, the authors have started from a shared view of the nature of history. We all believe that history is a mode of understanding, not merely a collection of information about the past. Our obligation is not simply to describe what happened, but to explain it, to make clear why things developed as they did. We share, too, an aversion to any deterministic interpretation of history. At certain times economic and demographic forces are dominant, but they are themselves shaped by cultural forces. Great political events are sometimes triggered by economic drives, but at other times they are responses to ideologies.

We do not believe, then, that the course of American history was predetermined. The present condition of our national life has to be explained historically, stage by stage. In the pages that follow, we present both a narrative and an analysis of how the United States has come to be what it is today—a great power, but still a Great Republic, where freedom and equality are dreams that can become realities.

B. B.     D. H. D.
R. D.     J. L. T.
D. B. D.   G. S. W.

# CONTENTS

# MAPS AND CHARTS

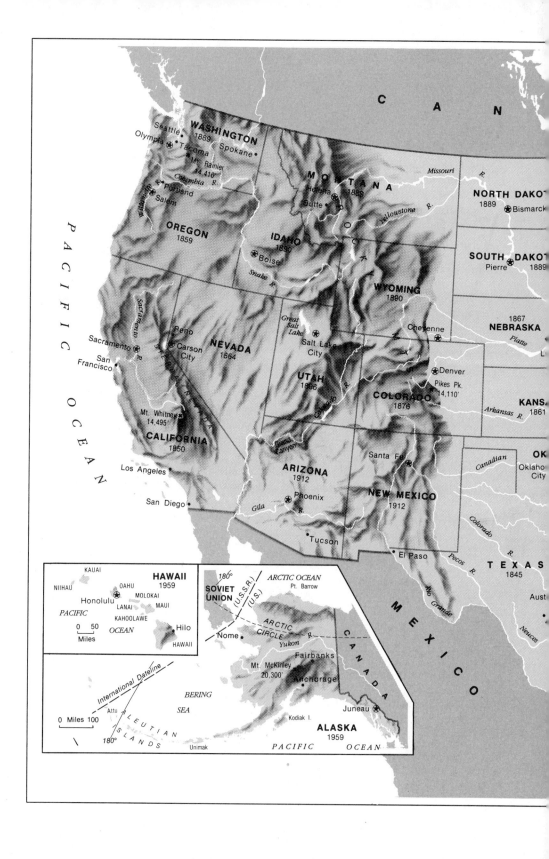

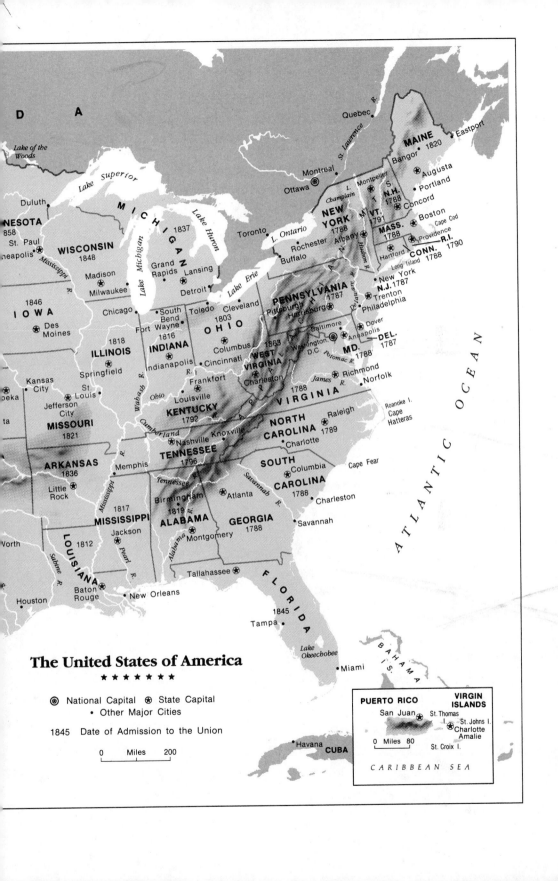

# The United States of America

★ ★ ★ ★ ★ ★ ★

◉ National Capital  ⊛ State Capital
• Other Major Cities

1845  Date of Admission to the Union

0     Miles     200

**PUERTO RICO**         **VIRGIN ISLANDS**

San Juan ⊛     St. Thomas
          I.   St. Johns I.
          ⊛ Charlotte
             Amalie
0  Miles  80     St. Croix I.

CARIBBEAN SEA

PART FOUR

# Uniting the Republic

## 1865–1877

David Herbert Donald

*W*AS THE Civil War a turning point in American history? Obviously in some important ways it was. It established beyond question the integrity and perpetuity of the American union. Never again did a state attempt to secede from the nation. It marked the end of Southern dominance of the national government. Not until the inauguration of Woodrow Wilson in 1913 was there another Southern-born president. It ended slavery. As Charles and Mary Beard have said, the emancipation, without compensation to the owners, of black slaves valued at about $4 billion was "the most stupendous act of sequestration [of property] in the history of Anglo-American jurisprudence." The Civil War era witnessed a shift in the balance of power in American government. After the ratification of the Fourteenth Amendment, in 1868, there was no question that the nation was superior to the state and that local governments could not abridge the privileges and immunities of citizens of the United States.

But in another sense the changes brought about by the Civil War were neither radical nor revolutionary. Although some Republicans desired a complete transformation of the social and economic system of the conquered Confederacy, there were relatively few, and only limited, social experiments or political innovations during the Reconstruction years after the war. In both the North and the South, shared beliefs in limited government, in economic laissez-faire, and in the superiority of the white race blocked drastic change. Meanwhile shared economic interests and national political parties pulled the sections back into a common pattern of cooperation.

What the union victory in the Civil War did do was to allow the emergence of new social and economic issues that were to become the central concerns of Americans during the last decades of the nineteenth century. During the long period of sectional controversy, when both the North and the South had had to maintain a facade of unity, internal dissensions within these sections had largely been ignored or suppressed. Now in the postwar years antiexpansionists were free to clash with those who desired to add further territory to the American domain. Native Americans tried to defend their tribal lands from white encroachers. Small businesses fought to keep from being swallowed up by monopolies. Farmers struggled to break the power of the railroads and grain elevators that controlled their access to markets. Seeking fairer wages, hours, and conditions of work, labor came into conflict with capital.

The emergence of these postwar issues helped place the old controversies between North and South in better perspective. Thoughtful observers came to realize that the Civil War had not been so much a conflict between two separate nations. It had instead been just one of the many continuing struggles within the American nation to define a boundary between the centralizing, nationalizing tendencies of American life and the opposing tendencies toward localism, parochialism, and fragmentation.

# 20

# *Reconstruction*

## *1865–1869*

*A*HOUSE divided against itself cannot stand," Abraham Lincoln prophesied in 1858. The Civil War proved that the United States would stand, not as a loose confederation of sovereign states but as one nation, indivisible. Never again would there be talk of secession. The war also ended slavery, the most divisive institution in antebellum America. Weakened by the advances of the Union armies and undermined by Lincoln's Emancipation Proclamation, slavery received its deathblow in February 1865, when Congress adopted the Thirteenth Amendment, outlawing slavery and involuntary servitude. After three-fourths of the states had ratified it, the amendment became part of the Constitution in December 1865.

But the Civil War did not settle the terms and conditions on which the states, sections, races, and classes would live in the firmly united "house." Those problems formed the agenda of the Reconstruction era, one of the most complex and controversial periods in American history. During these postwar years some basic questions had to be answered. What, if any, punishment should be imposed on Southern whites who had supported the Confederate attempt to break up the Union? How were the recently emancipated slaves to be guaranteed their freedom, and what civil and political rights did freedmen have? When and on what conditions were the Southern states, so recently in rebellion, to be readmitted to the Union—that is, entitled to vote in national elections, to have senators and representatives seated in the United States Congress, and, in general, to become once more full-fledged, equal members of the United States?

The initial moves to answer these questions came from the president, whose powers had grown significantly during the war years. In December 1863 President Lincoln announced a generous program of amnesty to repentant rebels and inaugurated a plan for reorganizing loyal governments in the South when as few as 10 percent of the voters in 1860 were willing to support them. After Lincoln's assassination in April 1865, President Andrew Johnson, his successor, continued the process of Reconstruction under a similar plan. Johnson, like Lincoln,

3

expected Southern whites to take the lead in establishing new state governments loyal to the Union. To begin the process, the president appointed a provisional governor for each of the former Confederate states (except those in which Lincoln had already initiated Reconstruction). Johnson directed these provisional governors to convene constitutional conventions, which were expected to adopt the Thirteenth Amendment ending slavery, to nullify or repeal the ordinances of secession, and to cancel state debts incurred for the prosecution of the war. By early 1866 each of the states that had once formed the Confederacy had completed most of these required steps, and the president viewed the process of Reconstruction as concluded. He recommended that the senators and representatives chosen by these reorganized governments promptly be given their rightful seats in Congress.

Presidential Reconstruction drew criticism from the outset. Having jealously watched executive power grow during the war, Congress was ready to reestablish its political equality with the presidency, and even to reassert its superior influence. Unlike President Lincoln, Andrew Johnson had no popular mandate. Johnson, a Tennessee Democrat and former slaveholder, was an inflexible and aggressive man who did not understand that politics is the art of compromise.

After an initial attempt to cooperate with the new president, Republican leaders in 1866 began to draw up their own plans for Reconstruction. The first congressional plan was embodied in the Fourteenth Amendment to the Constitution, which made it clear that blacks were citizens of the United States and tried to define the rights and privileges of American citizens. When the Southern states refused to ratify this amendment, congressional Republicans moved in 1867 to a tougher program of reorganizing the South by insisting that blacks be allowed to vote. Under this second plan of congressional Reconstruction, every Southern state (except for Tennessee, which had been readmitted to the Union in 1866) received a new constitution that guaranteed to men of all races equal protection of the laws. Between 1868 and 1871, all these states were readmitted to the Union. Republican governments, which depended heavily on black votes, controlled these states for a period ranging from a few months in the case of Virginia to nine years in the case of Louisiana.

## Paths Not Taken

Contemporaries called this the period of Radical Reconstruction—or, very often, Black Reconstruction. It is easy to understand why many Americans viewed these changes as little short of revolutionary. No amendments had been added to the Constitution since 1804; but within the five years after the Civil War, three new and far-reaching amendments were adopted. The Thirteenth Amendment ended slavery, the Fourteenth Amendment defined the rights of citizens, and the Fifteenth Amendment (1870) prohibited discrimination in voting because of race or color. The national government, which so recently had tottered on the edge of defeat, was now more powerful than at any previous point in American history.

The Southern ruling class of whites, lately in charge of their own independent government, now had to ask for pardon. More than 3 million blacks, slaves only a few months earlier, were now free and entitled to the same privileges as all other citizens. Americans fairly gasped at the extent and the speed of the changes that had occurred in their society, and it is hardly surprising that most subsequent historians accepted this contemporary view of the Reconstruction era as one of turbulent disorder.

Without denying that real and important changes did occur during the Reconstruction period, it might help to put these changes into perspective by inventing a little counterfactual, or imaginary, history—a recital of conceivable historical scenarios that never in fact occurred. For example, it would be easy to imagine how the victorious North might have turned angrily on the defeated South. In 1865 Northerners had just finished four years of war that had cost the Union army more than 360,000 casualties. Americans of the Civil War era and subsequent generations had to pay at least $10 billion in taxes to destroy the Confederacy. Northerners had reason to believe, moreover, that their Confederate opponents had conducted the war with fiendish barbarity. Sober Union congressmen informed their constituents that the Confederates had employed "Indian savages" to scalp and mutilate the Union dead. Reliable Northern newspapers told how in April 1864 General Nathan Bedford Forrest and his Confederates overran the defenses of Fort Pillow, Tennessee, manned by a black regiment and, refusing to accept surrender, deliberately beat, shot, and burned their prisoners. The influential *Harper's Weekly Magazine* carried apparently authentic drawings of a goblet that a Southerner had made from a Yankee soldier's skull and of necklaces fashioned of Yankee teeth that Southern ladies wore. When Union armies liberated Northern prisoners from such hellholes as Andersonville, Georgia, pictures of these half-starved skeletons of men, clad in grimy tatters of their Union uniforms, convinced Northerners that Jefferson Davis's policy had been "to starve and freeze and kill off by inches the prisoners he dares not butcher out-right."

After the murder of President Lincoln by the Southern sympathizer John Wilkes Booth, an outraged North could easily have turned on the conquered Confederacy in vengeance. The victorious Northerners might have executed Jefferson Davis, Alexander H. Stephens, and a score of other leading Confederates and might have sent thousands more into permanent exile. The triumphant Union might have erased the boundaries of the Southern states and divided the whole region into new, conquered territories. Northerners might have enforced the confiscation acts already on the statute books and seized the plantations of rebels, for distribution to the freedmen.

But nothing so drastic happened. No Confederate was executed for "war crimes" except Major Henry Wirtz, commandant of the infamous Andersonville prison, who was hanged. A few Southern political leaders were imprisoned for their part in the "rebellion," but in most cases they were promptly released. To be sure, Jefferson Davis remained in prison for two years at Fort Monroe, and he was under indictment for treason until 1869, when all charges were dropped. His case was, however, as unusual as it was extreme. One reason for the long delay in bringing him to trial was the certainty that no jury, Northern or Southern, would render an impartial verdict. There was no general confiscation of the property of Confederates, and no dividing up of plantations.

Another scenario—this time featuring the Southern whites—is equally conceivable, but it too did not happen. For four years Confederate citizens had been subjected to a barrage of propaganda designed to prove that the enemy was little less than infernal in his purposes. Many believed the Southern editor who claimed that Lincoln's program was "Emancipation, Confiscation, Conflagration, and Extermination." According to the North Carolina educator Calvin H. Wiley, the North had "summoned to its aid every fierce and cruel and licentious passion of the human heart"; to defeat the Confederacy it was ready to use "the assassin's dagger, the midnight torch, . . . poison, famine and pestilence." Charges of this kind were easy to credit in the many Southern families that had relatives in Northern prison camps, such as the one at Elmira, New York, where 775 of 8,347 Confederate prisoners died within three months for lack of food, water, and medicine. The behavior of Union troops in the South, especially of Sherman's "bummers," members of raiding forces who plundered indiscriminately in Georgia and the Carolinas, gave Southerners every reason to fear the worst if the Confederate government failed.

It would therefore have been reasonable for Confederate armies in 1865, overwhelmed by Union numbers, to disband quietly, disappear into the country-side, and carry on guerrilla operations against the Northern invaders. Indeed, on the morning of the day when Lee surrendered at Appomattox, Confederate General E. P. Alexander advocated just such a plan. He argued that if Lee's soldiers took to the woods with their rifles, perhaps two-thirds of the Army of Northern Virginia could escape capture. "We would be like rabbits and partridges in the bushes," he claimed, "and they could not scatter to follow us." The history of more recent wars of national liberation suggests that Alexander's judgment was correct. At least his strategy would have given time for thousands of leading Southern politicians and planters, together with their families, to go safely into exile, as the loyalists did during the American Revolution.

But again, no such events occurred. A few Confederate leaders did leave the country. For example, General Jubal A. Early fled to Mexico and from there to Canada, where he tried to organize a migration of Southerners to New Zealand. But when he found that nobody wanted to follow him, Early returned to his home and his law practice in Virginia. A few hundred Confederates migrated to Mexico and to Brazil. But most followed the advice of General Lee and General Wade Hampton of South Carolina, who urged their fellow Southerners to "devote their whole energies to the restoration of law and order, the reestablishment of agriculture and commerce, the promotion of education and the rebuilding of our cities and dwellings which have been laid in ashes."

Still another counterfactual historical scenario comes readily to mind. Southern blacks, who for generations had been oppressed in slavery, now for the first time had disciplined leaders in the thousands of black soldiers who had served in the Union army. They also had weapons. The blacks could very easily have turned in revenge on their former masters. Seizing the plantations and other property of the whites, the freedmen might have made the former Confederacy a black nation. If the whites had dared to resist, the South might have been the scene of massacres as bloody as those in Haiti at the beginning of the nineteenth century, when Toussaint L'Ouverture drove the French from that island.

Many Southern whites feared, or even expected, that the Confederacy would become another Haiti. They were frightened by reports that blacks were joining the Union League, an organization that had originated in the North during the war to stimulate patriotism but during the Reconstruction era became the stronghold of the Republican party in the South. The secrecy imposed by the league on its members and its frequent nighttime meetings alarmed whites, and they readily believed reports that the blacks were collecting arms and ammunition for a general uprising. Fearfully, Southern whites read newspaper accounts of minor racial clashes. Indeed, whites were told, racial tension was so great that blacks "might break into open insurrection at any time."

But no such uprising occurred. Although the freedmen unquestionably hoped to obtain the lands of their former masters, they did not seize them. Indeed, black leaders consistently discouraged talk of extralegal confiscation of plantations. Nor did freedmen threaten the lives or the rights of whites. One of the earliest black political conventions held in Alabama urged a policy of "peace, friendship, and good will toward all men—especially toward our white fellow-citizens among whom our lot is cast." That tone was the dominant one throughout the Reconstruction period, and in many states blacks took the lead in repealing laws that disfranchised former Confederates or disqualified them from holding office.

The point of these three exercises in counterfactual history is, of course, not to argue that the Civil War brought no changes in American life. The preservation of the Union and the emancipation of the slaves were two consequences of tremendous importance. Instead, these exercises suggest that conventional accounts of the Reconstruction period as a second American Revolution are inadequate. During these postwar years there were swift and significant changes in Southern society, but the shared beliefs and institutions of the American people—North and South, black and white—set limits to these changes.

## Constitutionalism as a Limit to Change

One set of ideas that sharply curbed experimentation and political innovation during the Reconstruction period can be labeled constitutionalism. It is hard for twentieth-century Americans to understand the reverence with which their nineteenth-century ancestors viewed the Constitution. Next to the flag, the Constitution was the most powerful symbol of American nationhood. Tested in the trial of civil war, the Constitution continued to command respect—almost veneration—during the Reconstruction era.

**States' Rights**      Among the most unchallenged provisions of the Constitution were those that separated the powers of state and national government. Although the national government greatly expanded its role during the war years, Americans still tended to think of it as performing only the specific functions delegated to it in the Constitution. These functions allowed the national government virtually no authority to act directly on individual citizens. For example, the national government could neither prevent nor punish crime; it had no control over public education; it could not outlaw discrimination against racial minorities; and it could not even intervene to maintain public order unless requested to do so by the state government. Virtually everybody agreed, therefore, that if any laws regulating social and economic life were required, they must be the work of state and local, not of national, government.

Consequently, nobody even contemplated the possibility that some federal agency might be needed to supervise the demobilization after Appomattox. Everybody simply assumed that after some 200,000 of the Union army volunteers bravely paraded down Pennsylvania Avenue on May 23–24, 1865, and received applause from President Johnson, the cabinet, the generals, and members of the diplomatic corps, the soldiers would disband and go back to their peaceful homes. This is precisely what they did. Of the more than one million volunteers in the Union army on May 1, 1865, two-thirds were mustered out by August, four-fifths by November. The United States government offered the demobilized soldiers no assistance in finding jobs, purchasing housing, or securing further education. It paid pensions to those injured in the war and to the families of those who had been killed, but assumed no further responsibility. Nor did anyone think of asking the national government to oversee the transition from a wartime economy to an era of peace. By the end of April 1865, without notice the various bureaus of the army and navy departments simply suspended requisitions and purchases, government arsenals slowed down their production, and surplus supplies were sold off.

Hardly anybody thought that the national government might play a role in rebuilding the warworn South. The devastation in the South was immense and ominous. The Confederate dead totaled more than a quarter of a million. In Mississippi, for example, one-third of the white men of military age had been killed or disabled for life. Most Southern cities were in ruins. Two-thirds of the Southern railroads were totally destroyed; the rest barely creaked along on worn-out rails with broken-down engines. But none of these problems was thought to be the concern of the United States government.

**Ruins of Richmond**
*When the Confederate government evacuated Richmond on April 3, 1865, orders were given to burn supplies that might fall into the enemy's hands. There were heavy explosions as ironclads, armories, and arsenals were blown up. The next morning, as the fires spread, a mob of men and women, whites and blacks, began to plunder the city.*

The national government's failure to come to the rescue was not caused by vindictiveness. To the contrary, Union officials often behaved with marked generosity toward Confederates. After Lee's hungry battalions surrendered at Appomattox, Grant's soldiers freely shared their rations with them. All over the South, federal military officials drew on the full Union army storehouses to feed the hungry. But the federal government did not go beyond these attempts to prevent starvation, and very few thought that it should. Not until the twentieth century did the United States make it a policy to pour vast sums of money into the rehabilitation of enemies it had defeated in war.

Rebuilding therefore had to be the work of the Southern state and local authorities, and this task imposed a heavy burden on their meager resources. In Mississippi one-fifth of the entire state revenue in 1866 was needed to provide artificial limbs for soldiers maimed in the war. The resources of the South were obviously inadequate for the larger tasks of physical restoration. Drawing on antebellum experience, Southern governments did the only thing they knew how to—namely, they lent the credit of the state to back up the bonds of private companies that promised to rebuild railroads and other necessary facilities. These companies were underfinanced, and the credit of the Southern states after Appomattox was questionable, to say the least. Therefore these bonds had to be sold at disadvantageous prices and at exorbitant rates of interest. In later years, when many of these companies defaulted on their obligations and southern state governments had to make good on their guarantees, these expenditures would be condemned as excessive and extravagant. Democrats blamed them on the Republican regimes established in the South after 1868. In fact, however, immediately after the war the need for physical restoration was so obvious and so pressing that nearly every government—whether controlled by Democrats or Republicans—underwrote corporations that promised to rebuild the region.

**The Freedmen's Bureau**

Even in dealing with the freedmen—the some 3 million slaves emancipated as a result of the war—the United States government tried to pursue a hands-off policy. In North and South alike, few influential leaders thought that it was the function of the national government to supervise the blacks' transition from slavery to freedom. Even abolitionists, genuinely devoted to the welfare of blacks, were so accustomed to thinking of the black man as "God's image in ebony"—in other words, a white man in a black skin—that they had no plans for assisting him after emancipation. In 1865 William Lloyd Garrison urged the American Anti-Slavery Society to disband because it had fulfilled its function, and he suspended the publication of *The Liberator.* Sharing the same point of view, the American Freedmen's Inquiry Commission, set up by the Union War Department in 1863, unanimously opposed further governmental actions to protect the blacks. "The negro does best when let alone," argued one member of the commission, Samuel Gridley Howe, noted both for his work with the deaf, dumb, and blind and for his hostility to slavery. "We must beware of all attempts to prolong his servitude, under pretext of taking care of him. The white man has tried taking care of the negro, by slavery, by apprenticeship, by colonization, and has failed disastrously in all; now let the negro try to take care of himself."

But the problem of caring for the freedmen could not be dismissed so easily. Wherever Union armies advanced into the South, they were "greeted by an irruption of negroes of all ages, complexions and sizes, men, women, boys and girls . . . waving hats and bonnets with the most ludicrous caperings and ejaculations of joy." "The poor delighted creatures thronged upon us," a Yankee soldier reported, and they insisted: "We'se gwin wid you all." "What shall be done with them?" commanders in the field plaintively wired Washington.

**A Group of Freedmen in Richmond, Virginia, 1865**
*A central problem of Reconstruction years was the future of the freedmen. Nobody had made any plans for a smooth transition from slavery to freedom. Consequently, when emancipation came, as one former slave recalled, "We didn't know where to go. Momma and them didn't know where to go, you see, after freedom broke. Just like you turned something out, you know. They didn't know where to go."*

The administration in Washington had no comprehensive answer. Initially it looked to private humanitarian organizations to rush food, clothing, and medicine to the thousands of blacks who thronged in unsanitary camps around the headquarters of each Union army. The New England Freedmen's Aid Society, the American Missionary Association, and the Philadelphia Society of Friends [Quakers] promptly responded, but it was soon clear that the problem was too great for private charity.

Gradually sentiment grew in the North for the creation of a general Emancipation Bureau in the federal government—only to conflict directly with the even stronger sentiment that the national government had limited powers. Out of this conflict emerged the Freedmen's Bureau Act of March 3, 1865. Congress established the Bureau of Refugees, Freedmen, and Abandoned Lands under the jurisdiction of the War Department. It entrusted to the new agency, for one year after the end of the war, "control of all subjects relating to refugees and freedmen." To head the new organization, Lincoln named Oliver O. Howard, a Union general with paternalistic views toward blacks.

At first glance, the Freedmen's Bureau seems to have been a notable exception to the rule that the national government should take only a minor, passive role in the restoration of the South. Howard had a vision of a compassionate network of "teachers, ministers, farmers, superintendents" working together to

**The Freedmen's Union Industrial School, Richmond, Virginia**
*Freedmen were eager to learn, and both the old and the young flocked to schools sponsored by the Freedmen's Bureau. Most of these schools taught only reading, writing, and arithmetic, but this one, in Richmond, gave instruction in sewing, cooking, and other domestic skills.*

aid and elevate the freedmen; and, under his enthusiastic impetus, the bureau appointed agents in each of the former Confederate states. The bureau's most urgent task was issuing food and clothing, mostly from surplus army stores, to destitute freedmen and other Southern refugees. This action unquestionably prevented mass starvation in the South. The bureau also took the initiative in getting work for freedmen. The bureau agents feared on the one hand that Southern landlords would attempt to exploit and underpay the freedmen, but they were also troubled by the widespread belief that blacks, once emancipated, would not work. The agents therefore brought laborers and landlords together and insisted that the workers sign labor contracts.

The bureau's most successful work was in the field of education. The slow work of educating the illiterate Southern blacks had already begun under the auspices of army chaplains and Northern benevolent societies before the creation of the bureau. Howard's bureau continued to cooperate with these agencies, providing housing for black schools, paying teachers, and helping to establish normal (teachers') schools and colleges for the training of black teachers. The freedmen enthusiastically welcomed all these educational efforts. During the day, black children learning the rudiments of language and arithmetic crowded into the classrooms; in the evenings, adults "fighting with their letters" flocked to the schools, learning to read so that they would not be "made ashamed" by their children. "The progress of the scholars is in all cases creditable and in some remarkable," reported one of the teachers condescendingly. "How richly God has endowed them, and how beautifully their natures would have expanded under a tender and gentle culture."

Even more innovative was the work of the bureau in allocating lands to the freedmen. During the war many plantations in the path of Union armies had been deserted by their owners, and army commanders like Grant arranged to have these lands cultivated by the blacks who flocked to their camps. The largest tract of such abandoned land was in the Sea Islands of South Carolina, which Union troops had overrun in the fall of 1861. Although speculators bought up large amounts of this land during the war, many black residents were able to secure small holdings. When General W. T. Sherman marched through South Carolina, he ordered that the Sea Islands and the abandoned plantations along the river-banks for thirty miles from the coast be reserved for black settlement and directed that the black settlers be given "possessory titles" to tracts of this land not larger than forty acres. The act creating the Freedmen's Bureau clearly contemplated the continuation of these policies, for it authorized the new bureau to lease confiscated lands to freedmen and to "loyal refugees." The bureau could also sell the land to these tenants and give them "such title thereto as the United States can convey."

But if the Freedmen's Bureau was an exception to the policy of limited federal involvement in the reconstruction process, it was at best a partial exception. Although the agency did extremely valuable work, it was a feeble protector of the freedmen. Authorized to recruit only a minimal staff, Howard had to rely heavily on Union army officers stationed in the South—at just the time when the Union army was being demobilized. Consequently, the bureau never had enough manpower to look after the rights of the freedmen; toward the end of its first year of operation, the bureau employed only 799 men, 424 of whom were soldiers on temporary assigned duty. Important as the work of the bureau was in black education, its chief function was to stimulate private humanitarian aid in this field. In providing land for the freedmen, the bureau was handicapped because it controlled only about 800,000 acres of arable land in the South, at best enough for perhaps one black family in forty. Moreover, Congress and the president repeatedly undercut its efforts to distribute land to the blacks. The very wording of the act creating the bureau suggested congressional uncertainty about who actually owned deserted and confiscated lands in the South. When President Johnson issued pardons to Southerners, he explicitly called for the "restoration of all rights of property." In October 1865 the president directed Howard to go in person to the Sea Islands to notify blacks there that they did not hold legal title to the land and to advise them "to make the best terms they could" with the white owners. When blacks bitterly resisted what they considered the bureau's betrayal, Union soldiers descended on the islands and forced blacks who would not sign labor contracts with the restored white owners to leave. Elsewhere in the South the record of the bureau was equally dismal.

In short, belief in the limited role to be played by the national government affected the rehabilitation of the freedmen, just as it did the physical restoration of the South and the demobilization in the North. The United States government was supposed to play the smallest possible part in all these matters, and its minimal activities were to be of the briefest duration.

It is certain that most whites in the North and in the South fully approved of these strict limitations on the activities of the national government. It is harder to determine what the masses of freedmen thought. On the one hand stands the protest of the Sea Island blacks when they learned they were about to be dispossessed: "Why, General Howard, why do you take away our lands? You take them from us who have always been true, always true to the Government! You give them to our all-time enemies! That is not right!" On the other is Frederick Douglass's reply to the question "What shall we do with the Negroes?" The greatest black spokesman of the era answered: "Do nothing with them; mind your business, and let them mind theirs. Your doing with them is their greatest misfortune. They have been undone by your doings, and all they now ask and really have need of at your hands, is just to let them alone."

## Laissez-Faire as a Limit to Change

Along with the idea of limited government went the doctrine of laissez-faire ("let things alone"), which sharply limited what the government could do to solve the economic problems that arose after the Civil War. Except for a handful of Radical Republicans, such as Charles Sumner and Thaddeus Stevens, most congressmen, like most academic economists, were unquestioning believers in an American version of laissez-faire. Although they were willing to promote economic growth through protective tariffs and land grants to railroads, they abhorred government inspection, regulation, and control of economic activities. These matters, they thought, were ruled by the unchanging laws of economics. "You need not think it necessary to have Washington exercise a political providence over the country," William Graham Sumner, the brilliant professor of political and social science, told his students at Yale. "God has done that a great deal better by the laws of political economy."

**Reverence for Private Property**    No violation of economic laws was considered worse than interference with the right of private property— the right of an individual or group to purchase, own, use, and dispose of property without any interference from governmental authorities. There was consequently never a chance that most congressmen would support Thaddeus Stevens's radical program to confiscate all Southern farms larger than two hundred acres and to divide the seized land into forty-acre tracts among the freedmen. "An attempt to justify the confiscation of Southern land under the pretense of doing justice to the freedmen," declared the *New York Times,* which spoke for educated Republicans, "strikes at the root of all property rights in both sections. It concerns Massachusetts quite as much as Mississippi."

Experts in the North held that the best program of Reconstruction was to allow the laws of economics to rule in the South with the least possible inter-ference by the government. Obsessed by laissez-faire, Northern theorists failed to consider the physical devastation in the South caused by the war, and they did not recognize how feeble were the South's resources to rebuild its economy. Even excluding the loss of slave property, the total assessed property evaluation of the Southern states shrank by 43 percent between 1860 and 1865.

**Southern Economic Adjustments**
Northern experts also failed to take into account the psychological dimensions of economic readjustment in the South. For generations Southern whites had per-suaded themselves that slavery was the natural condition of the black race, and they truly believed that their slaves were devoted to them. But as Union armies approached and slaves defected, these Southerners were compelled to recognize that they had been living in a world of misconceptions and deceits. So shattering was the idea that slaves were free that some Southern whites simply refused to accept it. Even after the Confederate surrender, some owners would not inform their slaves of their new status. A few plantation owners angrily announced that they were so disillusioned that they would never again have anything to do with blacks, and they sought, vainly, to persuade European immigrants and Chinese coolies to work their fields.

Even those whites who on the surface accepted emancipation betrayed the fact that, on a deeper emotional level, they still could only think of blacks as performing forced labor. "The general interest both of the white man and of the negroes requires that he should be kept as near to the condition of slavery as possible, and as far from the condition of the white man as is practicable," announced one prominent South Carolinian. "Negroes must be made to work, or else cotton and rice must cease to be raised for export." The contracts that in 1865 planters signed with their former slaves under pressure from the Freedmen's Bureau were further indications of the same attitude. Even the most generous of these contracts provided that blacks were "not to leave the premises during work hours without the consent of the Proprietor," that they would conduct "them-selves faithfully, honestly and civilly," and that they would behave with perfect obedience" toward the landowner.

Nor did the advocates of laissez-faire take into account the blacks' difficulties in adjusting to their new status. *Freedom*—that word so often whispered in the slave quarters—went to the heads of some blacks. A few took quite literally the coming of what they called Jubilee, thinking that it would put the bottom rail on top. Nearly all blacks had an initial impulse to test their freedom, to make sure that it was real. Thus during the first months after the war there was much movement among southern blacks. "They are just like a swarm of bees," one observer noted, "all buzzing about and not knowing where to settle."

Much of this black mobility was, however, purposeful. Thousands of former slaves flocked to the Southern towns and cities where the Freedmen's Bureau was issuing rations, for they knew that food was unavailable on the plantations. Many blacks set out to find husbands, wives, or children from whom they had been forcibly separated during the slave days. A good many freedmen joined the general movement of the Southern population away from the coastal states, which had been devastated by war, and migrated to the southwestern frontier in Texas. Most blacks, however, did not move so far but remained in the immediate vicinity of the plantations where they had labored as slaves.

The freedmen's reluctance in 1865 to enter into labor contracts, either with their former masters or with other white landowners, was also generally misunderstood. Most blacks wanted to work—but they wanted to work on their own land. Freedmen knew that the United States government had divided up some abandoned plantations among former slaves, and many believed that on January 1, 1866—the anniversary of their freedom under Lincoln's Emancipation Proclamation—all would receive forty acres and a mule. With this prospect of having their own farms, they were unwilling to sign contracts to work on plantations owned by others.

Even when the hope of free land disappeared, freedmen resisted signing labor contracts because, as has been noted, so many white landowners expected to continue to treat them like slaves. The blacks were especially opposed to the idea of being again herded together in the plantation slave quarters, with their communal facilities for cooking and washing and infant care, and their lack of privacy. Emancipation did much to strengthen the black family. Families divided by slave sales could now be reunited. Marital arrangements between blacks, which had not been legally valid during slavery, could be regularized. Freedmen's Bureau officials performed thousands of marriage ceremonies, and some states passed general ordinances declaring that blacks who had been living together were legally man and wife and that their children were legitimate. This precious new security of family life was not something blacks were willing to jeopardize by returning to slave quarters. Before contracting to work on the plantations, they insisted on having separate cabins, scattered across the farm, each usually having its own patch for vegetables and perhaps a pen for hogs or a cow.

When these conditions were met, freedmen in the early months of 1866 entered into labor contracts, most of which followed the same general pattern. Rarely did these arrangements call for the payment of wages, for landowners were desperately short of cash and freedmen felt that a wage system gave landowners too much control over their labor. The most common system was sharecropping. Although there were many regional and individual variations, the system usually called for the dividing of the crop into three equal shares. One of these went to the landowner; another went to the laborer—usually black, although there were also many white sharecroppers in the South; and the third went to whichever party provided the seeds, fertilizer, mules, and farming equipment.

**The Same Georgia Plantation in 1860 and 1880**
*Before the Civil War, slave quarters were located close together, all near the white master's house, so that he could impose order and prevent secret meetings of the blacks. After emancipation, freedmen insisted upon scattering out over the plantation, so that each family could have its own house and some privacy.*

This system had several advantages for the landowner. At a time when money was scarce, he was not obliged to pay out cash to his employees until the crop was harvested. He retained general supervision over what was planted and how the crop was cultivated, and he felt he was more likely to secure a good harvest because the freedmen themselves stood to gain by a large yield. Blacks too found the sharecropping system suited to their needs. They had control over how their crops were planted and when they were cultivated and harvested. They could earn more money by working harder in the fields.

**The "Breakup" of the Plantation System**

To some observers the disappearance of the slave quarters and the resettling of families in individual, scattered cabins seemed to mark a revolution in the character of Southern agriculture. According to the United States census, the number of Southern landholdings doubled between 1860 and 1880, and their average size dropped from 365 acres to 157 acres. But these figures are misleading, because the census takers failed to ask farmers whether they owned their land or were sharecroppers. An examination of tax records, which show landownership, in the representative state of Louisiana helps correct the census distortion. Between 1860 and 1880 in Louisiana, the number of independently owned farms of less than one hundred acres actually dropped by 14 percent, while during the same period the number of plantations increased by 287 percent. By 1900 plantations of one hundred acres or more encompassed half the cultivated land in the state, and more than half the farmers were not proprietors.

If the postwar period did not see the breakup of large plantations, it did bring some significant changes in ownership and control of the land. Hard hit by debt, by rising taxes, and by increasing labor costs, many Southern planters had to sell their holdings, and Northern capital flowed into the region after the war. More tried to cling to their acres by going heavily into debt. Since the postwar Southern banking system was inadequate, the principal source of credit was the local merchant, who could supply both the landowner and his sharecroppers with clothing, shoes, some food, and other necessities to tide them over the lean months between the planting of the tobacco or cotton crop and its harvest. On each sale the merchant charged interest, to be paid when the crop was sold, and he also charged prices ranging from 40 percent to 110 percent higher for all goods sold on credit. It is hardly surprising that those landowners who could afford to do so set up their own stores and extended credit to their own sharecroppers— and quite soon they discovered they were making more profits from mercantile enterprises than from farming. Planters who could not make such arrangements frequently had to sell their lands to the neighborhood merchant. It is not accidental that in William Faulkner's twentieth-century series of novels that constitute a fictional saga of Southern history, the power of landowning families like the Compsons and the Sutpens diminished during the postwar years, while the Snopes family of storekeepers—hard-trading, penny-pinching, and utterly unscrupulous—emerged prosperous and successful.

It would be a mistake, however, to accept without reservation the novelist's hostile characterization of the Southern merchant. The storekeeper insisted on the crop-lien system, which required the farmer legally to pledge that the pro-ceeds from his crop must go first to pay off his obligations to the merchant, because he knew that crops could fail throughout the South, as they did in both 1866 and 1867. And if the merchant urged farmers to forget about soil con-servation, diversification, and experimentation with new crops, he did so because he realized that the only way to pay his own debts was to insist that his debtors raise cotton and tobacco, for which there was a ready cash market.

Thus merchants, landowners, and sharecroppers—white Southerners and black Southerners—became locked into an economic system that, at best, prom-ised them little more than survival. At worst, it offered bankruptcy, sale of lands, and hurried nighttime migrations in an attempt to escape from a set of debts in one state but with little more than the hope of starting a new set in another.

By the 1880s, then, the South had become what it remained for the next half-century—the nation's economic backwater. In 1880 the per capita wealth of the South was $376, compared with per capita wealth outside the South of $1,086. Yet this impoverished region had to deal with some of the most difficult political and racial problems that have ever confronted Americans. In attacking these problems, Southerners, black and white, could expect no assistance from the government, because such intervention would violate the unchanging laws of laissez-faire economics.

## Political Parties as a Limit to Change

The most influential institutions that blocked radical change during Reconstruction were the national political parties. The fact that both parties were conglomerates of different and often competing sectional and class interests meant that parties had to decide on their policies through compromise and concession. That process nearly always screened out extreme and drastic measures.

Nationally the Democratic party was torn by two conflicting interests during the postwar years. On the one hand, Democrats sought the immediate readmission of the Southern states under the governments President Johnson had set up. Controlled by whites hostile to the Republican party, these states would surely send Democrats to Congress and support Democratic candidates in a national election. Even during the 1850s the South had increasingly become a one-party region; now the goal of a solidly Democratic South appeared within reach. On the other hand, too-enthusiastic advocacy of the Southern cause could hurt Democrats in the North by reviving talk of disloyalty and the Copperhead movement during the war. To blunt such attacks, Democrats had no choice but to urge restraint on their colleagues in the former Confederacy.

Among Republicans, similar constraints dampened any ideas of taking vengeance on the South or of encouraging blacks to seize control of that region. From its beginnings the Republican party had been an uneasy alliance of antislavery men, former Whigs, dissatisfied Democrats, and Know-Nothings. The factional disputes that racked Lincoln's administration showed the weakness of the ties that bound these groups together. It was a bad omen for the party that Republicans disagreed most sharply over Lincoln's plan to reorganize the Southern state governments.

**Presidential Reconstruction**

During the first year after Lincoln's death, quarrels among Republicans were somewhat muted because practically all members of the party joined in opposing President Johnson's program of Reconstruction. Followed by only a handful of Conservative Republicans, including Secretary of State Seward and Navy Secretary Gideon Welles, Johnson began to work closely with the Democrats of the North and South. He announced that the Southern states had never been out of the Union, and he insisted that, under the provisional governments he had set up, they were entitled to be represented in Congress.

It is easy to understand why almost all Republicans—whether they belonged to the Radical or Moderate faction—rejected the president's argument. Members of both these wings of the party were outraged when the Southern elections of 1865, held at the president's direction, resulted in the choice of a Confederate brigadier-general as governor of Mississippi, and they were furious when the new Georgia legislature named Alexander H. Stephens, the vice-president of the Confederacy, to represent that state in the United States Senate.

Republicans had even more reason to fear these newly elected Southern officials because, although many of the Southerners had been Whigs before the war, they clearly contemplated allying themselves with the Democratic party. However much Republicans disagreed among themselves, they all agreed that their party had saved the Union. They believed, with Thaddeus Stevens, "that upon the continued ascendancy of that party depends the safety of this great nation." Now this ascendancy was threatened. The threat was the more serious because once the Southern states were readmitted to the Union they would receive increased representation in Congress. Before the Civil War, only three-fifths of the slave population of the South had been counted in apportioning representation in the House of Representatives; but now that the slaves were free men, all would be counted. In short, the Southern states, after having been defeated in the most costly war in the nation's history, would have about fifteen more representatives in Congress than they had before the war. And under the president's plan all Southern Congressmen unquestionably would be Democrats.

Republicans of all factions were equally troubled by the fear of what white Southerners, once restored to authority, would do to the freedmen. The laws that the Southern provisional legislatures adopted during the winter of 1865–66 gave reason for anxiety on this score. Not one of these governments considered treating black citizens just as they treated white citizens. Instead the legislatures adopted special laws, known as the Black Codes, to regulate the conduct of the freedmen. On the positive side, these laws recognized the freedmen's right to make civil contracts, to sue and be sued, and to acquire and hold most kinds of property. But with these rights went restrictions. The laws varied from state to state, but in general they specified that blacks might not purchase or carry firearms, that they might not assemble after sunset, and that those who were idle or unemployed should "be liable to imprisonment, and to hard labor, one or both, . . . not exceeding twelve months." The Mississippi code prevented blacks from renting or leasing "any lands or tenements except in incorporated cities or towns." That of South Carolina forbade blacks from practicing "the art, trade or business of an artisan, mechanic or shopkeeper, or any other trade, employment or business (besides that of husbandry, or that of a servant)." So clearly did these measures seem designed to keep the freedmen in quasi-slavery that the *Chicago Tribune* spoke for a united, outraged Republican party in denouncing the first of these Black Codes, that adopted by the Mississippi legislature: "We tell the white men of Mississippi that the men of the North will convert the state of Mississippi into a frogpond before they will allow any such laws to disgrace one foot of soil over which the flag of freedom waves."

**The Fourteenth Amendment**

For these reasons, all Republicans were unwilling to recognize the regimes Johnson had set up in the South; when Congress reassembled in December 1865, they easily rallied to block seating of the Southern senators and representatives. All agreed to the creation of a special joint committee on Reconstruction to handle questions concerning the readmission of the Southern states and their further reorganization. In setting up this committee, congressional Republicans carefully balanced its membership with Radicals and Moderates. Its most conspicuous member was the Radical Stevens, but its powerful chairman was Senator William Pitt Fessenden, a Moderate.

Congressional Republicans found it easier to unite in opposing Johnson's plan of Reconstruction than to unite in devising one of their own. Congressional leaders recognized that it would take time to draft and adopt a constitutional amendment and then to have it ratified by the required number of states. Therefore, early in 1866 they agreed on interim legislation that would protect the freedmen. One bill extended and expanded the functions of the Freedmen's Bureau, and a second guaranteed minimal civil rights to all citizens. Contrary to expectations, Johnson vetoed both these measures. Refusing to recognize that these measures represented the wishes of both Moderate and Radical Republicans, the president claimed that they were the work of the Radicals, who wanted "to destroy our institutions and change the character of the Government." He vowed to fight these Northern enemies of the Union just as he had once fought Southern secessionists and traitors. The Republican majority in Congress was not able to override Johnson's veto of the Freedmen's Bureau bill (a later, less sweeping measure extended the life of that agency for two years), but it passed the Civil Rights Act of 1866 over his disapproval.

While relations between the president and the Republicans in Congress were deteriorating, the joint committee on Reconstruction continued to meet and consider various plans for reorganizing the South. With its evenly balanced membership, the committee dismissed the president's theory that the Southern states were already reconstructed and back in the Union, as well as Thaddeus Stevens's view that the Confederacy was conquered territory over which Congress could rule at its own discretion. It also rejected Charles Sumner's more elaborate argument that the Southern states had committed suicide when they seceded, so that their land and inhabitants now fell "under the exclusive jurisdiction of Congress." More acceptable to the majority of Republicans was the "grasp of war" theory advanced by Richard Henry Dana, Jr., the noted Massachusetts constitutional lawyer who was also the author of *Two Years Before the Mast.* Dana argued that the federal government should hold the defeated Confederacy in the grasp of war only for a brief and limited time, during which it must act swiftly to revive state governments in the region and promptly to restore the constitutional balance between national and state authority. Dana's theory was an essentially conservative one: it called for only a short period of federal domination and looked toward the speedy restoration of the Southern states on terms of absolute equality with the loyal states.

Finding in Dana's theory a constitutional source of power, the joint committee after much hard work produced the first comprehensive congressional plan of Reconstruction—the proposed Fourteenth Amendment to the Constitution, which Congress endorsed in June 1866 and submitted to the states for ratification. Some parts of the amendment were noncontroversial. All Republicans accepted its opening statement: "All persons born or naturalized in the United States, and subject to the jurisdiction thereof, are citizens of the United States and of the State wherein they reside." This provision was necessary in order to nullify the Supreme Court's decision in the *Dred Scott* case (1857), which had denied citizenship to African Americans. There was also no disagreement about the provision declaring the Confederate debt invalid.

All the other provisions of the amendment, however, represented a compromise between Radical and Moderate Republicans. For example, Radicals wanted to keep all Southerners who had voluntarily supported the Confederacy from voting until 1870. Indeed, the arch-Radical Stevens urged: "Not only to 1870 but 18,070, every rebel who shed the blood of loyal men should be prevented from exercising any power in this Government." Moderates favored a speedy restoration of all political rights to former Confederates. As a compromise, the Fourteenth Amendment excluded high-ranking Confederates from office, but it did not deny them the vote.

Similarly, the Fourteenth Amendment's provisions protecting the freedmen represented a compromise. Radicals like Sumner (who was considered too radical to be given a seat on the joint committee) wanted an outright declaration of the national government's right and duty to protect the civil liberties of the former slaves. But Moderates drew back in alarm from entrusting additional authority to Washington. The joint committee came up with a provision that granted no power to the national government but restricted that of the states: "No State shall make or enforce any law which shall abridge the privileges and immunities of citizens of the United States; nor shall any State deprive any person of life, liberty, or property, without due process of law; nor deny to any person within its jurisdiction the equal protection of the laws."

Finally, another compromise between Radicals and Moderates resulted in the amendment's provision concerning voting. Although Sumner and other Radicals called black suffrage "the essence, the great essential," of a proper Reconstruction policy, Conservatives refused to give the national government power to interfere with the state requirements for voting. The joint committee thereupon devised a complex and, as it proved, unworkable plan to persuade the Southern states voluntarily to enfranchise blacks, under threat of having their representation in Congress reduced if they refused.

The Fourteenth Amendment's feasibility as a program of Reconstruction was never tested because of the outbreak of political warfare between President Johnson and the Republican party, which had elected him vice-president in 1864. During the summer of 1866, Johnson and his friends tried to create a new political party, which would rally behind the president's policies the few Conservative

Republicans, the Northern Democrats, and the Southern whites. With the president's hearty approval, a National Union Convention held in Philadelphia in August stressed the theme of harmony among the sections. The entry into the convention hall of delegates from Massachusetts and South Carolina, arm in arm, seemed to symbolize the end of sectional strife. The president himself went on a "swing around the circle" of leading Northern cities, ostensibly on his way to dedicate a monument to the memory of another Democrat, Stephen A. Douglas. In his frequent public speeches Johnson defended the constitutionality of his own Reconstruction program and attacked Congress—and particularly the Radical Republicans—for attempting to subvert the Constitution. In a final effort to consolidate sentiment against Congress, he urged the Southern states not to ratify the proposed Fourteenth Amendment. With the exception of Tennessee, which was controlled by one of Johnson's bitterest personal and political enemies, all the former Confederate states rejected the congressional plan.

**The Second Congressional Program of Reconstruction**

When Congress reassembled in December 1866, the Republican majority therefore had to devise a second program of Reconstruction. Cheered by overwhelming victories in the fall congressional elections, Republicans felt even less inclined than previously to cooperate with the president, who had gone into political opposition, or to encourage the provisional regimes in the South, which had rejected their first program. Republican suspicion that Southern whites were fundamentally hostile toward the freedmen was strengthened by reports of a race riot in Memphis during May 1866, when a mob of whites joined in a two-day indiscriminate attack on blacks in that city. An even more serious affair occurred four months later in New Orleans, when a white mob, aided by the local police, attacked a black political gathering with what was described as "a cowardly ferocity unsurpassed in the annals of crime." In New Orleans, 45 or 50 blacks were killed, and 150 more were wounded.

Once again, however, the Republican majority in Congress found it easier to agree on what to oppose than on what to favor in the way of Reconstruction legislation. Stevens urged that the South be placed under military rule for a generation and that Southern plantations be sold to pay the national debt. Sumner wanted to deny the vote to large numbers of Southern whites, to require that blacks be given the right to vote, and to create racially integrated schools in the South. Moderate Republicans, on the other hand, were willing to retain the Fourteenth Amendment as the basic framework of congressional Reconstruction and to insist on little else except the ratification of the amendment by the Southern states.

The second congressional program of Reconstruction, embodied in the Military Reconstruction Act of March 2, 1867, represented a compromise between the demands of Radical and Moderate Republican factions. It divided

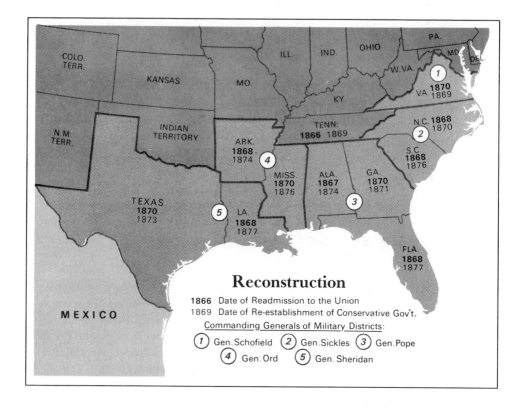

**Reconstruction**

1866 Date of Readmission to the Union
1869 Date of Re-establishment of Conservative Gov't.
Commanding Generals of Military Districts:
(1) Gen. Schofield   (2) Gen. Sickles   (3) Gen. Pope
(4) Gen. Ord   (5) Gen. Sheridan

the ten former Confederate states that had not ratified the Fourteenth Amendment into five military districts. In each of these states there were to be new constitutional conventions, for which black men were allowed to vote. The task of these conventions was to draft new state constitutions that provided for black suffrage, and they were required to ratify the Fourteenth Amendment. When thus reorganized, the Southern states could apply to Congress for readmission to the Union.

It was easy to recognize the radical aspects of this measure, which Democrats pointed out during the congressional debates and President Johnson denounced in his unsuccessful veto of the act. In particular, the requirement of black suffrage, which Sumner sponsored, seemed to Radicals "a prodigious triumph."

In fact, however, most provisions of the Military Reconstruction Act were more acceptable to Moderate than to Radical Republicans. The measure did nothing to give land to the freedmen, to provide education at national expense, or to end racial segregation in the South. It did not erase the boundaries of the Southern states. It did not even sweep away the provisional governments Johnson had established there, although it did make them responsible to the commanders of the new military districts. So conservative was the act in all these respects that Sumner branded it as "horribly defective."

Intent on striking some kind of balance between the Radical and Conservative wings of the Republican party, the framers of the Military Reconstruction Act drafted the measure carelessly. As Sumner had predicted, the act promptly proved to furnish "Reconstruction without machinery or motive power." Having to choose between military rule and black suffrage, the Southern provisional governments chose the former, correctly believing that army officers generally sympathized with white supremacy. To get the Reconstruction process under way, Congress therefore had to enact a supplementary law (March 23, 1867), requiring the federal commanders in the South to take the initiative, when the local governments did not, in announcing elections, registering voters, and convening constitutional conventions. During the summer of 1867, as the president, the attorney general, and Southern state officials tried by legalistic interpretations to delay the Reconstruction program, Congress had to pass two further supplementary acts, explaining the "true intent and meaning" of the previous legislation.

With these measures, the congressional Reconstruction legislation affecting the South was substantially completed. Both the first and the second congressional plans of Reconstruction were compromises between the Radical and the Moderate factions in the Republican party. The Radicals' insistence on change was essential in securing the adoption of this legislation, but the Moderates blocked all measures that would have revolutionized the social and economic order in the South.

**Impeachment**  The same need to compromise between the factions of the Republican party dictated Congress's policy toward the president during the Reconstruction years. Almost all Republicans were suspicious of President Johnson and feared that he intended to turn the South over to Confederate rule. Johnson's repeated veto messages, assailing carefully balanced compromise legislation as the work of Radicals and attacking Congress as an unconstitutional body because it refused to seat congressmen from all the states, angered Republicans of both factions. Therefore, most Republicans wanted to keep a close eye on the president and sought to curb executive powers that had grown during the war. In 1867, fearing that Johnson would use his power as commander in chief to subvert their Reconstruction legislation, Republican factions joined to pass an army appropriations bill that required all military orders to the army—including those of the president himself—to go through the hands of General Grant. Suspecting that Johnson wanted to use the federal patronage to build up a political machine of his own, they enacted at the same time the Tenure of Office Act, which required the president to secure the Senate's consent not merely when he appointed officials, but also when he removed them.

The Republicans in Congress were prepared to go this far in impressive unanimity—but no farther. When Radical Republican James M. Ashley in January 1867 moved to impeach the president, he was permitted to conduct a half-serious, half-comic investigation of Johnson's alleged involvement in Lincoln's

**"Awkward Collision on the Grand Trunk Columbia Railroad"**
*This cartoon depicts presidential and congressional Reconstruction as two engines going in opposite directions on the same rails. Andrew Johnson, driver of the locomotive "President," says: "Look here! One of us has got to [go] back." But Thaddeus Stevens, driver of the locomotive "Congress," replies: "Well, it ain't going to be me that's going to do it, you bet!"*

assassination, his purported sale of pardons, and other trumped-up charges. But when Ashley's motion reached the House floor, Moderate Republicans saw that it was soundly defeated.

A subsequent attempt at impeachment fared better, but it also revealed how the Radical and Moderate factions blocked each other. In August 1867, President Johnson suspended from office Secretary of War Edwin M. Stanton, who was collaborating closely with the Radicals in Congress. As required by the Tenure of Office Act, he asked the Senate to consent to the removal. When the Senate refused, the president removed Stanton anyway and ordered him to surrender his office. News of this seemingly open defiance of the law caused Republicans in the House of Representatives to rush through a resolution impeaching the president, without waiting for specific charges against him to be drawn up.

The trial of President Johnson (who was not present in court but was represented by his lawyers) was a test of strength not merely between Congress and the chief executive, but also between the Radical and the Moderate Republicans. Impeachment managers from the House of Representatives presented eleven charges against the president, mostly accusing him of violating the Tenure of Office Act but also censuring his repeated attacks on Congress. With fierce joy Radical Thaddeus Stevens, who was one of the managers, denounced the president: "Unfortunate man! thus surrounded, hampered, tangled in the meshes of his own wickedness—unfortunate, unhappy man, behold your doom!"

But Radical oratory could not persuade Moderate Republicans and Democrats to vote for conviction. They listened as Johnson's lawyers challenged the constitutionality of the Tenure of Office Act, showed that it had not been intended to apply to cabinet members, and proved that, in any case, it did not cover Stanton, who had been appointed by Lincoln, not Johnson. When the critical vote came, Moderate Republicans like Fessenden voted to acquit the president, and Johnson's Radical foes lacked one vote of the two-thirds majority required to convict him. Several other Republican Senators who for political expedience voted against the president were prepared to change their votes and favor acquittal if their ballots were needed.

Nothing more clearly shows how the institutional needs of a political party prevented drastic change than did this decision not to remove a president whom a majority in Congress hated and feared. The desire to maintain the unity of the national Republican party, despite frequent quarrels and endless bickering, overrode the wishes of individual congressmen. Throughout the Reconstruction period Moderate Republicans felt that they were constantly being rushed from one advanced position to another in order to placate the Radicals, who were never satisfied. More accurately, Radical Republicans perceived that the need to retain Moderate support prevented the adoption of any really revolutionary Reconstruction program.

## Racism as a Limit to Change

A final set of beliefs that limited the nature of the changes imposed on, and accepted by, the South during the Reconstruction period can be labeled racism. In all parts of the country, white Americans looked with suspicion and fear on those whose skin was of a different color. For example, in California white hatred built up against the Chinese, who had begun coming to that state in great numbers after the discovery of gold and who were later imported by the thousands to help construct the Central Pacific Railroad. White workers resented the willingness of the Chinese to work long hours for "coolies" wages; they distrusted the unfamiliar dress, diet, and habits of the Chinese; and they disliked all these things more because the Chinese were a yellow-skinned people. Under the leadership of a newly arrived Irish immigrant, Dennis Kearney, white laborers organized a workingman's party with the slogan "The Chinese must go."

**Anti-Chinese Agitation in San Francisco: A Meeting of the Workingman's Party on the Sand Lots**
*Racism in postwar America took many forms. In California its strongest manifestation was in the hostility toward the Chinese immigrants stirred up by Dennis Kearney's workingman's party.*

The depression that gripped the nation in 1873* gave impetus to the anti-Chinese movement. Day after day thousands of the unemployed gathered in the San Francisco sandlots to hear Kearney's slashing attacks on the Chinese and on the wealthy corporations that employed them. In the summer of 1877, San Francisco hoodlums, inspired by Kearney, burned twenty-five Chinese laundries and destroyed dozens of Chinese homes. The movement had enough political strength to force both major parties in California to adopt anti-Chinese platforms, and California congressmen succeeded in persuading their colleagues to pass a bill limiting the number of Chinese who could be brought into the United States each year. Because the measure clearly conflicted with treaty arrangements with China, President Rutherford B. Hayes vetoed it, but he had his secretary of state initiate negotiations leading to a new treaty that permitted the restriction of immigration. Congress, in 1882, passed the Chinese Exclusion Act, which suspended all Chinese immigration for ten years and forbade the naturalization of Chinese already in the country.

---

*For the Panic of 1873, see chapter 21, p. 55.

**Northern Views of the Black Race**

If white Americans became so agitated over a small number of Chinese, who were unquestionably hard-working and thrifty and who belonged to one of the most ancient of civilizations, it is easy to see how whites could consider blacks an even greater danger. There were more than 3 million blacks in the United States, most of them recently emancipated from slavery. The exploits of black soldiers during the war—their very discipline and courage—proved that blacks could be formidable opponents. More than ever before, blacks seemed distinctive, alien, and menacing.

Most American intellectuals of the Civil War generation accepted black inferiority unquestioningly. Although a few reformers like Charles Sumner vigorously attacked this notion, a majority of philanthropic Northerners accepted the judgment of the distinguished Harvard scientist Louis Agassiz concerning blacks. He held that while whites during antiquity were developing high civilizations, "the negro race groped in barbarism and never originated a regular organization among themselves." Many adopted Agassiz's belief that blacks, once free, would inevitably die out in the United States. Others reached the same conclusion by studying Charles Darwin's recently published *Origin of Species* (1859), and they accepted the argument put forward by Darwin's admirers that in the inevitable struggle for survival "higher civilized races" must inevitably eliminate "an endless number of lower races." Consequently, the influential and tenderhearted Congregational minister Horace Bushnell could prophesy the approaching end of the black race in the United States with something approaching smugness. "Since we must all die," he asked rhetorically, "why should it grieve us, that a stock thousands of years behind, in the scale of culture, should die with few and still fewer children to succeed, till finally the whole succession remains in the more cultivated race?"

When even the leaders of Northern society held such views, it is hardly surprising that most whites in the region were openly antiblack. In state after state whites fiercely resisted efforts to extend the political and civil rights of blacks, partly because they feared that any improvement in the condition of blacks in the North would lead to a huge influx of blacks from the South. At the end of the Civil War only Maine, New Hampshire, Vermont, Massachusetts, and Rhode Island allowed blacks to have full voting rights; in New York only blacks who met certain property-holding qualifications could have the ballot. During the next three years in referenda held in Connecticut, Wisconsin, Kansas, Ohio, Michigan, and Missouri, constitutional amendments authorizing black suffrage were defeated, and in New York voters rejected a proposal to eliminate the property-holding qualifications for black voters. Only in Iowa, a state where there were very few blacks, did a black suffrage amendment carry in 1868, and that same year Minnesota adopted an ambiguously worded amendment. Thus at the end of the 1860s, most Northern states refused to give black men the ballot.

In words as well as in votes, the majority of Northerners made their deeply racist feelings evident. The Democratic press constantly cultivated the racial fears of its readers and regularly portrayed the Republicans as planning a "new era of miscegenation, amalgamation, and promiscuous intercourse between the races." From the White House, denouncing Republican attempts "to Africanize the [Southern] half of our country," President Andrew Johnson proclaimed: "In the progress of nations negroes have shown less capacity for self-government than any other race of people.... Whenever they have been left to their own devices they have shown an instant tendency to relapse into barbarism." Even Northern Republicans opposed to Johnson shared many of his racist views. Radical Senator Timothy O. Howe of Wisconsin declared that he regarded "the freedmen, in the main... as so much animal life," and Senator Benjamin F. Wade of Ohio, whom the Radical Republicans would have elevated to the presidency had they removed Johnson, had both a genuine devotion to the principle of equal rights and an incurable dislike of blacks. Representative George W. Julian of Indiana, one of the few Northern congressmen who had no racial prejudice, bluntly told his colleagues in 1866: "The real trouble is that *we hate the negro*. It is not his ignorance that offends us, but his color.... Of this fact I entertain no doubt whatsoever."

Both personal preferences and the wishes of their constituents inhibited Northern Republicans from supporting measures that might have altered race relations. When Sumner sought to remove from the books federal laws that recognized slavery or to prohibit racial discrimination on public transportation in the District of Columbia, his colleagues replied: "God has made the negro inferior, and ... laws cannot make him equal." Such congressmen were hardly in a position to scold the South for racial discrimination or to insist on drastic social change in that region.

**Southern Views of the Black Race**   If racism limited the innovation that northerners were willing to propose during the Reconstruction period, it even more drastically reduced the amount of change that white southerners were prepared to accept. Racial bigotry runs through both the private correspondence and the public pronouncements of Southern whites during the postwar era. "Equality does not exist between blacks and whites," announced Alexander H. Stephens. "The one race is by nature inferior in many respects, physically and mentally, to the other. This should be received as a fixed invincible fact in all dealings with the subject." A North Carolina diarist agreed: "The Anglo-Saxon and the African can never be equal ... one or the other must fall." Or, as the Democratic party of Louisiana resolved in its 1865 platform: "We hold this to be a Government of white people, made and to be perpetuated for the exclusive benefit of the white race; and ... that people of African descent cannot be considered as citizens of the United States, and that there can, in no event, nor under any circumstances, be any equality between the white and other races." The Black Codes were the legal embodiment of these attitudes.

These racist views shaped the attitudes of most Southern whites toward the whole process of Reconstruction. White Southerners approved of President

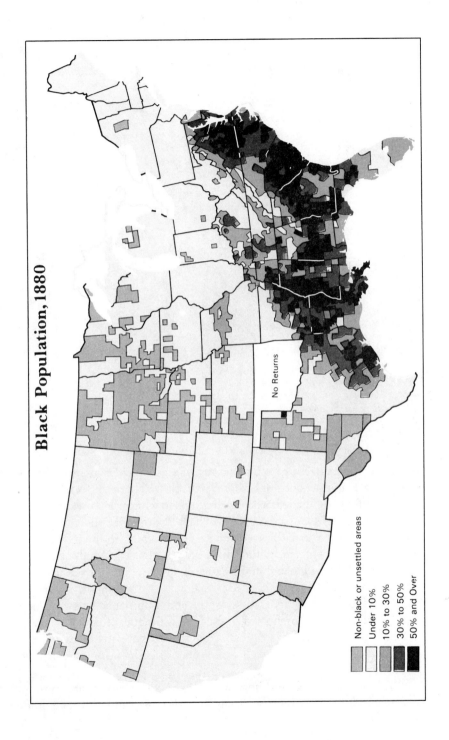

Black Population, 1880

No Returns

Non-black or unsettled areas

Under 10%

10% to 30%

30% to 50%

50% and Over

**Blacks in the South Carolina Legislature**
*Blacks voted and were elected to office under the Radical Reconstruction program. In South Carolina they briefly formed a majority in the House of Representatives. Hostile observers noted that some black members engaged in idle chatter, read the newspapers, and put their feet on their desks while the legislature was conducting business.*

Johnson's plan of Reconstruction because it placed government in the Southern states entirely in the hands of whites. They rejected the Fourteenth Amendment primarily because it made blacks legally equal to whites. They watched with utter disbelief as Congress passed the 1867 Military Reconstruction Act, for they simply could not imagine that the freedmen were to vote. Stunned, they saw army officers supervise voter registration—a process that excluded many prominent whites who had participated in the Confederate government but included more than 700,000 blacks, who formed a majority of the eligible voters in South Carolina, Florida, Alabama, Mississippi, and Louisiana. Knowing that these black voters were well organized by the Union League, often with the assistance of agents of the Freedmen's Bureau, whites were more apathetic than surprised when the fall elections showed heavy majorities in favor of convening new constitutional conventions.*

With hostile and unbelieving eyes, most Southern whites observed the work of these conventions, which between November 1867 and May 1868 drafted new

---

*The Texas election was not held until February 1868. Tennessee had no election, because it had already been readmitted to the Union.

**Blacks Voting**
*Under the congressional plan
of Reconstruction, Southern
states were required to give
blacks suffrage. This drawing
from* Harper's Weekly *shows
how both old and young
flocked to the polls to exercise their new right. Notable
is one young black who is
still wearing his US Army
uniform.*

constitutions for the former Confederate states. To Southern whites unac-
customed to seeing blacks in any positions of public prominence, the presence of
freedmen in these conventions meant that they were black-dominated. In fact,
except in the South Carolina convention, in which blacks did form a majority,
only between one-fourth and one-ninth of the delegates were blacks. Whites
ridiculed the black members' ignorance of parliamentary procedures, and they
laughed sarcastically when they read about how the "coal black" temporary
chairman of the Louisiana convention put a question by asking those who favored
a motion "to rise an stan on der feet" and then directing "all you contrairy men to
rise."

Racial prejudice also determined Southern whites' reactions to the constitutions produced by these conventions. Generally the whites denounced these new
charters as "totally incompatible with the prosperity and liberty of the people."
In reality the constitutions, often copied from Northern models, were generally
improvements over the ones they replaced. Besides giving blacks the right to vote
(as Congress had directed), they promised all citizens of the state equality before
the law. They reformed financial and revenue systems, reorganized the judiciary,
improved the organization of local government, and, most important of all,
instituted a state-supported system of public education, hitherto notably lacking
in most Southern states.

**The Reconstruction Governments in the South**

Because these constitutions guaranteed racial equality, Southern whites tried, without great success, to block their ratification. In Alabama whites boycotted the ratification election; in Mississippi they cast a majority of votes against the new constitution. In Virginia ratification was delayed because the conservative army commander of that district discovered that there was no money to hold an election, and in Texas all moves toward the creation of a new government lagged several months behind those in the eastern states. But despite all the foot dragging, new governments were set up, and in June 1868 Congress readmitted representatives and senators from Alabama, Arkansas, Florida, Georgia, Louisiana, North Carolina, and South Carolina. Two years later the Reconstruction of Virginia, Mississippi, and Texas was completed, and in early 1870 these states were also readmitted. Meanwhile Georgia experienced one further reorganization after its state legislature attempted to exclude blacks who had been elected to it. But by 1871, when the Georgia senators and representatives again took their seats in Congress, all the states of the former Confederacy had undergone Reconstruction and had been readmitted to the Union.

Most Southern whites were bitterly hostile to this reorganization of their state governments. The name "Black Reconstruction," as they called the ensuing period of Republican domination in the South, reveals the racial bias behind their opposition. In fact, these Southern state governments were not dominated by blacks, and blacks held a smaller proportion of offices than their percentage of the population. Blacks dominated the state legislature only in South Carolina. No black was elected governor, although there were black lieutenant governors in South Carolina, Louisiana, and Mississippi. Only in South Carolina was there a black supreme court justice. During the entire Reconstruction period only two blacks served in the United States Senate—Hiram R. Revels and Blanche K. Bruce, both from Mississippi and both men of exceptional ability and integrity. Only fifteen blacks were elected to the House of Representatives.

Even to the most racist Southern whites, it was obvious that most of the leaders of the Republican party in the South, and a large part of the Republican following as well, were white. Racists called the Northern-born white Republicans carpetbaggers because they allegedly came South with no more worldly possessions than could be packed into a carpetbag (a small suitcase), ready to live on and exploit the conquered region. The term, with its implication of corruption, was applied indiscriminately to men of Northern birth who had lived in the South long before the war, as well as to newly arrived fortune hunters, many of them recently discharged Union army officers.

Southern-born white Republicans were called scalawags, a term that cattle drivers applied to "the mean, lousy and filthy kine [cattle] that are not fit for butchers or dogs." Again the term was used indiscriminately. Southern racists applied it to poor hill-country whites, who had long been at odds with the plantation owners in states like North Carolina and Alabama and now joined the Republican party as a way of getting back at their old enemies. But other scalawags were members of the plantation-owning, mercantile, and industrial classes of the South. Many were former Whigs who distrusted the Democrats, and they felt at home in a Republican party that favored protective tariffs, subsidies for railroads, and appropriations for rebuilding the levees along the Mississippi River. A surprising number of Southern-born white Republicans were former high-ranking officers in the Confederate army, like General P. G. T. Beauregard and General James Longstreet, who knew at first hand the extent of the damage caused by the war and were willing to accept the victors' terms promptly.

Bitterly as they attacked these white Republicans, Southern Democrats reserved their worst abuse for blacks. They saw in every measure adopted by the new state governments evidence of black incompetence, extravagance, or even barbarism. In truth, much that these state governments did supplied the Democrats with ammunition. The postwar period was one of widespread political corruption, and there was no reason to expect that newly enfranchised blacks would prove any less attracted by the profits of politics than anybody else. Petty corruption prevailed in all the Southern state governments. Louisiana legislators voted themselves an allowance for stationery—which covered purchases of hams and bottles of champagne. The South Carolina legislature ran up a bill of more than $50,000 in refurbishing the statehouse with such costly items as a $750 mirror, $480 clocks, and two hundred porcelain spittoons at $8 apiece. The same legislature voted $1,000 to the speaker of the House of Representatives to repay his losses on a horse race.

But these excesses angered Southern Democrats less than the legitimate work performed by the new state governments. Unwilling to recognize that blacks were now equal citizens, they objected to expenditures for hospitals, jails, orphanages, and asylums to care for blacks. Most of all they objected to the creation of a public school system. There was considerable hostility throughout the South to the idea of educating any children at the cost of the taxpayer, and the thought of paying taxes in order to teach black children seemed a wild and foolish extravagance. The fact that black schools were mostly conducted by Northern whites, usually women, who came south with a reforming mission, did nothing to increase popular support. Too many of the teachers stated plainly and publicly their intention to use "every endeavor to throw a ray of light here and there, among this benighted race of ruffians, rebels by nature." Adding to all these hostilities was a fear that a system of public education might someday lead to a racially integrated system of education. These apprehensions had little basis in reality, for during the entire period of Reconstruction in the whole South there were significant numbers of children in racially mixed schools only in New Orleans between 1870 and 1874.

**The Ku Klux Klan**     Not content with criticizing Republican rule, Southern Democrats organized to put an end to it. They made a two-pronged attack. On the one hand, they sought to intimidate or to drive from the South whites who cooperated politically with the Republican regimes. On the other hand, they tried to terrorize and silence blacks, especially those active in

**Ku Klux Klan Broadside**
*A terrorist organization, the Ku Klux Klan pictured itself as a defender not merely of white supremacy but of the nation itself against incendiary blacks.*

politics. Much of this pressure was informal and occasional, but much was the work of racist organizations that sprang up all over the South during the postwar years. The most famous of these was the Ku Klux Klan, which originated in 1866 as a social club for young white men in Pulaski, Tennessee. As the Military Reconstruction Act went into effect and the possibility of black participation in Southern political life became increasingly real, racists saw new potential in this secret organization with its mysterious name and its bizarre uniforms of long flowing robes, high conical hats that made the wearers seem unnaturally tall, and white face masks.

In 1867 the Klan was reorganized under a new constitution that provided for local dens, each headed by a Grand Cyclops. The dens were linked together into provinces (counties), each under a Grand Titan, and in turn into realms (states), each under a Grand Dragon. At the head of the whole organization was the Grand Wizard—who, according to most reports, was former Confederate General Nathan Bedford Forrest. Probably this elaborate organizational structure was never completely filled out, and certainly there was an almost total lack of central control of the Klan's activities. Indeed, at some point in early 1869 the Klan was officially disbanded. But even without central direction its members, like those of the Order of the White Camellia and other racist vigilante groups, continued in their plan of disrupting the new Republican regimes in the South and terrorizing the blacks who supported these administrations.

Along with other vigilante organizations, the Klan expressed traditional Southern white racism. White Southerners were willing to accept the defeat of the Confederacy and were prepared to admit that slavery was dead. But they could not bring themselves to contemplate a society that would treat blacks and whites as equals. As a group of South Carolina whites protested to Congress in 1868: "The white people of our State will never quietly submit to negro rule.... We will keep up this contest until we have regained the heritage of political control handed down to us by honored ancestry. That is a duty we owe to the land that is ours, to the graves that it contains, and to the race of which you and we alike are members—the proud Caucasian race, whose sovereignty on earth God has ordained."

The appeal was shrewdly pitched, for the Southern racist knew how to reach his Northern counterpart. Joined together, their fears of men with darker skins helped to undercut the Reconstruction regimes in the South and to halt any congressional efforts at further innovative Reconstruction legislation.

## CHRONOLOGY

**1865**  Lincoln assassinated; Andrew Johnson becomes president.
Johnson moves for speedy, lenient restoration of Southern states to Union.
Congress creates Joint Committee of Fifteen to supervise Reconstruction process.
Thirteenth Amendment ratified.

**1866**  Johnson breaks with Republican majority in Congress by vetoing Freedmen's Bureau bill and Civil Rights bill. Latter is passed over his veto.
Congress approves Fourteenth Amendment and submits it to states for ratification.
Johnson and Republicans quarrel. Republicans win fall congressional elections.
Ku Klux Klan formed.

**1867**  Congress passes Military Reconstruction Act over Johnson's veto. (Two supplementary acts in 1867 and a third in 1868 passed to put this measure into effect.)

Congress passes Tenure of Office Act and Command of Army Act to reduce Johnson's power.

**1868**  Former Confederate states hold constitutional conventions, in which freedmen are allowed to vote, and adopt new constitutions guaranteeing universal male suffrage.
Alabama, Arkansas, Florida, Georgia, Louisiana, North Carolina, and South Carolina readmitted to representation in Congress. Because of discrimination against black officeholders, Georgia representatives are expelled. (State is again admitted in 1870.)
President Johnson impeached. Escapes conviction by one vote.
Republicans nominate Ulysses S. Grant for president; Democrats select Governor Horatio Seymour of New York. Grant elected president.

**1869**  Congress passes Fifteenth Amendment and submits it to states for ratification.

## Suggested Readings

*Reconstruction: America's Unfinished Revolution* (1988), by Eric Foner, is a full, eloquent account. Three shorter interpretations are John H. Franklin, *Reconstruction After the Civil War* (1961); Kenneth M. Stampp, *The Era of Reconstruction* (1965); and Rembert W. Patrick, *The Reconstruction of the Nation* (1967).

The best account of steps taken during the Civil War to reorganize the Southern states is Herman Belz, *Reconstructing the Union* (1969). William B. Hesseltine, *Lincoln's Plan of Reconstruction* (1960), argues that Lincoln had not one but many approaches to Reconstruction, all of them unsuccessful. LaWanda Cox, *Lincoln and Black Freedom* (1981), is an important study. Peyton McCrary, *Abraham Lincoln and Reconstruction* (1978), is the authoritative account of developments in Louisiana, where Lincoln's approach to Reconstruction was most fully tested.

*The Presidency of Andrew Johnson* (1979), by Albert Castel, is a balanced account, and Hans L. Trefousse's *Andrew Johnson* (1989) is the best biography of that president. Favorable versions of Johnson's Reconstruction program include George F. Milton, *The Age of Hate* (1930), and Howard K. Beale, *The Critical Year* (1930). The following accounts are critical: Eric L. McKitrick, *Andrew Johnson and Reconstruction* (1960); LaWanda Cox and John H. Cox, *Politics, Principle, and Prejudice* (1963); and W. R. Brock, *An American Crisis* (1963).

On constitutional changes in the postwar period, see Harold M. Hyman, *A More Perfect Union* (1973); Hyman and William M. Wiecek, *Equal Justice Under Law* (1982); Stanley I. Kutler, *Judicial Power and Reconstruction Politics* (1968); and Charles Fairman, *Reconstruction and the Union* (1971).

George R. Bentley, *A History of the Freedmen's Bureau* (1955), is a standard work, but it should be supplemented by William S. McFeely, *Yankee Stepfather: General O. O. Howard and the Freedmen* (1968). Claude F. Oubre, *Forty Acres and a Mule* (1978), discusses the abortive efforts of the bureau in land distribution.

Leon Litwack, *Been in the Storm So Long* (1979), is a masterful account of the transition from slavery to freedom. See also Peter Kolchin, *After Freedom* (1972), on Alabama; Willie Lee Rose, *Rehearsal for Reconstruction* (1964), and Joel Williamson, *After Slavery* (1965), on South Carolina; and Vernon L. Wharton, *The Negro in Mississippi* (1947).

Fred A. Shannon, *The Farmer's Last Frontier* (1945), and E. Merton Coulter, *The South During Reconstruction* (1972), give good general accounts of economic changes in the postwar South. Recently historians and economists using sophisticated quantitative methods have reexamined these changes: Stephen J. DeCanio, *Agriculture in the Postbellum South* (1974); Robert Higgs, *Competition and Coercion: Blacks in the American Economy* (1977); Roger Ransom and Richard L. Sutch, *One Kind of Freedom: The Economic Consequences of Emancipation* (1977); and Gavin Wright, *Old South, New South* (1986). On the alleged breakup of the plantation system, see Roger W. Shugg, *Origins of Class Struggle in Louisiana* (1939), and on the continuing dominance of the planter class, see Jonathan M. Wiener, *Social Origins of the New South* (1978).

On Radical Reconstruction, see Michael L. Benedict, *A Compromise of Principle* (1974); David Donald, *The Politics of Reconstruction* (1965); and Hans L. Trefousse, *The Radical Republicans* (1969). The best account of Grant's Southern policy is William Gillette, *Retreat from Reconstruction* (1980). Among the fullest biographies of Reconstruction politicians are Fawn M. Brodie, *Thaddeus Stevens* (1959); David Donald, *Charles Sumner and the Rights of Man* (1970); William S. McFeely, *Grant* (1981); and Benjamin P. Thomas and Harold M. Hyman, *Stanton* (1962).

David M. DeWitt, *Impeachment and Trial of Andrew Johnson* (1903), remains the standard account, but it should be supplemented with Michael L. Benedict's book of the same name (1973) and with Hans L. Trefousse, *Impeachment of a President* (1975).

On American racial attitudes, George M. Fredrickson, *The Black Image in the White Mind* (1971), is excellent. On Northern racism, see V. Jacque Voegeli, *Free But Not Equal* (1967), and Forrest G. Wood, *Black Scare* (1967).

Dan T. Carter, *When the War Was Over* (1985), ably traces the failure of presidential reconstruction in the South. For a favorable view of the Reconstruction governments in the South, see W.E.B. DuBois, *Black Reconstruction* (1935). Some excellent accounts of Reconstruction in individual states are Francis B. Simkins and Robert H. Woody, *South Carolina During Reconstruction* (1932); Jerrell H. Shofner, *Nor Is It Over Yet: Florida in the Era of Reconstruction* (1974); James W. Garner, *Reconstruction in Mississippi* (1901); and Joe G. Taylor, *Louisiana Reconstructed* (1974).

On the education of blacks after the war, see Henry A. Bullock, *A History of Negro Education in the South* (1967); William P. Vaughn, *Schools for All* (1974); and Roger A. Fischer, *The Segregation Struggle in Louisiana* (1974). Two useful accounts of the educational work of the Freedmen's Bureau are Ronald E. Butchart, *Northern Schools, Southern Blacks, and Reconstruction* (1980), and Robert C. Morris, *Reading, 'Riting, and Reconstruction* (1981).

Southern white resistance to the Reconstruction process is the theme of Michael Perman, *Reunion Without Compromise* (1973). Allen W. Trelease, *White Terror* (1971), is a harrowing recital of white vigilantism. *The Road to Redemption* (1984), by Michael Perman, traces southern politics from 1869 to 1879.

# 21

## *Compromises*

### *1869–1877*

*A*N EXCLUSIVE focus on the Southern states during the postwar years obscures the fact that Reconstruction was a national, not just a sectional, process. In the North as well as the South the impulses unleashed by the Civil War portended revolutionary consequences. With nationalism at high tide, many Northerners favored an expansionist foreign policy. Just as some Radical Republicans wished to overturn the entire Southern social system, so other postwar leaders hoped to change the North. Some reformers wanted to expand the role of the federal government in the economy. Civil service reformers sought the end of the spoils system and the professionalization of governmental bureaucracy. Other advocates of change wanted to improve the lot of labor, of women, and of native Americans. But many—perhaps most—Northerners objected to all these changes. To them the reforms proposed for their section were almost as objectionable as Radical Reconstruction was to most white Southerners.

This tension between those who opposed change and those who favored it became a central theme of American history in the decades following the Civil War. When the advocates of change were politically powerful and vigorously led, supporters of the status quo found it necessary to accept compromises. Thus by the 1880s a series of loose, informal, and frequently tacit understandings had evolved, between Democrats and Republicans, between supporters and opponents of expansion, between friends and enemies of the high tariff and "sound" currency. But where the innovators were politically inexperienced, like the leaders of the women's movement in the 1860s, or poorly organized, like the members of the early national labor unions, the powerful conservative majority found it possible to ignore or overrule their wishes.

## Compromises Between Equal Forces

**Nationalism**     In the years after the Civil War one major compromise reconciled divergent views as to the nature and direction of America as a nation. The war strongly encouraged nationalist sentiments among Northerners. The primary Northern war aim was not to guarantee equal rights to all men nor even to end slavery; it was to preserve the Union. By that often repeated phrase, men and women of the war years meant something more than merely maintaining the country as a territorial unit. The idea of union implied an almost mystical sense of the wholeness of the American people. Americans viewed themselves as a chosen people, selected to conduct an experiment in self-government, to be a test case of the viability of democratic institutions. As Lincoln declared, the United States was nothing less than "the last, best hope of earth."

That faith in the special destiny of the United States gave courage and hope to Northerners during the darkest hours of the war. Defeats on the battlefield, properly understood, seemed to them the fire that burned away the impurities in American life. As the Reverend Marvin R. Vincent of Troy, New York, announced: "God has been striking, and trying to make us strike at elements unfavorable to the growth of a pure democracy; and . . . he is at work, preparing in this broad land a fit stage for a last act of the mighty drama, the consummation of human civilization." A similar inspiration moved Julia Ward Howe to draw on the imagery of the Book of Revelation in composing the most powerful and popular battle hymn ever written:

> *Mine eyes have seen the glory of the coming of the Lord:*
> *He is trampling out the vintage where the grapes of wrath are stored;*
> *He hath loosed the fateful lightning of His terrible swift sword:*
> *His truth is marching on.*

Northerners believed that the Union would emerge from the war more powerful, more firmly united, than ever before. They expected that the United States would no longer be a confederation, or union of states, but rather a nation in the fullest sense. A small shift in grammar tells the whole story. Before the Civil War many politicians and writers referred to the United States in the plural— "the United States *are*"—but after 1865 only a pedant or the most unreconstructed Southerner would have dreamed of saying anything but "the United States *is.*"

The word *nation* now came easily to American lips. Unlike his predecessors, who generally avoided the term, Lincoln regularly referred to the United States as a nation. For example, he used the word no fewer than five times in his brief Gettysburg Address, most eloquently in the concluding pledge: " . . . that this nation, under God, shall have a new birth of freedom." In 1865, when Republicans agreed to establish a weekly journal that would reflect their views, they called it, as a matter of course, *The Nation,* and it became, as it has remained, one of the most influential periodicals in the country. When Charles Sumner, in 1867, took to the lecture circuit to supplement his senatorial salary, he chose for his topic, "Are We a Nation?" The answer, he believed, was obvious. Americans were "one people, throbbing with a common life, occupying a common territory, rejoicing in a common history, sharing in common trials." Never again should any "local claim of self-government" be permitted "for a moment [to] interfere with the supremacy of the Nation." He concluded: "Such centralization is the highest civilization, for it approaches the nearest to the heavenly example."

Political theorists as well as public men in the postwar generation exalted American nationalism. In 1865 Orestes Brownson, once a spokesman for Jacksonian ideals, published the first book-length contribution to the bibliography of American nationalism, *The American Republic: Its Constitution, Tendencies, and Destiny.* "Nations are only individuals on a larger scale," Brownson argued. His book was designed to resolve the identity crisis of the Civil War by persuading the American nation to "reflect on its own constitution, its own separate existence, individuality, tendencies, and end." Even more soaring were the claims of the Reverend Elisha Mulford's *The Nation: The Foundations of Civil Order and Political Life in the United States* (1870). Mulford's argument derived from the views of the early-nineteenth-century German philosopher Hegel: the nation was a mystic body, endowed with a spirit and a majesty of its own. "The Nation," he concluded, "is a work of God in history. . . . Its vocation is from God, and its obligation is only to God."

It would be easy to conclude from such statements that Americans of the post–Civil War generation, rejoicing in the newly restored unity of their country, were swept into an ultranationalistic frenzy comparable to that of the Germans, who almost simultaneously achieved national unity under Bismarck, or of the Italians, who were being reunited under Cavour. But a moment's reflection shows the weakness of these historical parallels. After all, the federal structure of the American government survived the Civil War. The government in Washington continued to coexist with the governments of the several states. If there was no further talk of secession, there was frequent invocation of states' rights, and regionalism and localism remained strong forces in American life.

American political theorists sought a formula to express the proper relationship between the nation and its constituent sections and groups. The most influential of these attempts was that of Professor Francis Lieber of Columbia University, whose book *On Civil Liberty and Self-Government,* published before the war, became a bible for statesmen of the postwar era. Lieber understood the power of nationalistic feeling; as a youth in Prussia he had wept when the armies of Napoleon overran his native land, and he had fought against the French at Waterloo. But he also was acquainted with the dangers of excessive nationalism, for the Prussian government had arrested him for harboring dangerous, liberal ideas and he had been obliged to flee to the United States. In this country he realized that nationalism was essential for "the diffusion of the same life-blood through a system of arteries, throughout a body politic." But he sought to check excessive centralization through organically related institutions—the family, the churches, the scientific community, the business community, and the like—which could provide "the negation of absolutism" by supporting "a union of harmonizing systems of laws instinct with self-government." Thus Lieber's theory simultaneously exalted American nationalism and encouraged autonomy for local and particularistic interests. It upheld the Union but sought to prevent its powers from becoming despotic. Lieber's political theory was, in short, typical of the compromises of the postwar period. His formulation allowed Americans to eat their cake and have it too.

**American Foreign Policy**

American diplomacy during the post–Civil War generation fell into a pattern that Lieber heartily approved. On the one hand, it was vigorously nationalistic, even at times bellicose; on the other, it drew back from conflict with foreign powers, and it refrained from pursuing goals strongly opposed by influential interest groups.

In the decade after the Civil War hardly a year passed without some significant American diplomatic move, either to assert the dominance of the United States in the Western Hemisphere or to annex new territory. These foreign policy

**"The Stride of a Century"**
*Buoyed with nationalist sentiment, the United States celebrated at the Centennial Exposition at Philadelphia of 1876. This Currier and Ives print shows a boastful Uncle Sam bestriding the Western Hemisphere.*

initiatives received considerable popular support. After Appomattox there was a general feeling that the United States, with a million seasoned veterans under arms, was in a position to humiliate the French emperor Napoleon III, to have a showdown with Great Britain, and to pick up any adjacent territory that it pleased. The expansionist spirit of Manifest Destiny, which had flourished in the 1840s but had languished during the war, sprang to life again. Even those who feared expansionism expected its triumph. The more optimistic rejoiced in the prospect. Advocating the annexation of both Haiti and the Dominican Republic, and hoping for the future acquisition of the Kingdom of Hawaii, President Johnson concluded in his 1868 annual message to Congress: "The conviction is rapidly gaining ground in the American mind that with the increased facilities for intercommunication between all portions of the earth the principles of free government, as embraced in our Constitution, if faithfully maintained and carried out, would prove of sufficient strength and breadth to comprehend within their sphere and influence the civilized nations of the world."

Even if the accomplishments of American foreign policy did not live up to Johnson's predictions, they were, nevertheless, considerable. From the point of view of national security, the most important feat was Seward's success in getting French troops out of Mexico. Introduced into Mexico during the Civil War, ostensibly to compel the bankrupt Mexican government of President Benito Juarez to pay its debts, French troops in 1864 provided the support for installing Archduke Maximilian of Austria as emperor of Mexico. While the war was going on, Seward could do no more than protest against this violation of the Monroe Doctrine's principle that European powers must not extend their "system" to the New World. But he adopted a more vigorous tone after Appomattox. Yet, knowing that the French emperor was a proud and volatile man, Seward refrained from direct threats and allowed Napoleon to discover for himself how expensive, unpopular, and unsuccessful his Mexican adventure was proving. By 1867 Napoleon finally decided to cut off further financial support for Maximilian's shaky regime and, under steady American pressure, withdrew his troops. Captured by Juarez's forces, Maximilian was shot by a firing squad on June 19, 1867.

A second diplomatic achievement of the Reconstruction years was the settlement of the *Alabama* claims—claims of American shippers against the British government for damages that British-built Confederate raiders had inflicted during the war. Immediately after the war it probably would have been possible to clear up this controversy speedily and inexpensively, had not the British government haughtily denied that it had violated international law by permitting Confederate raiders to be built in its shipyards. American grievances deepened with delay. Sumner, the powerful chairman of the Senate Committee on Foreign Relations, began to argue that the British not only owed repayment for actual damages done by the *Alabama* and other vessels; they also were responsible, he said, for prolonging the war—for the "immense and infinite" cost of the entire last two years of the conflict. Americans were further embittered by the failure of Reverdy Johnson, Seward's special envoy to Great Britain, to secure an apology or an expression of regret from the stubborn British government. A settlement was worked out only when Grant put Hamilton Fish in charge of the American State Department and a new cabinet came to power in Great Britain.

In the Treaty of Washington of 1871, Great Britain admitted negligence in permitting the Confederate cruisers to escape and expressed regret for the damages they had caused; and the United States quietly abandoned the extravagant claims put forward by Sumner and agreed that the amount of damages should be assessed by an arbitration commission representing five nations. Ultimately, damages to American shipping were estimated at $15.5 million, and the British government paid this amount. However, the precedent of settling international disputes by arbitration was more important than any monetary settlement, and the Treaty of Washington paved the way for an improvement in relations between the two greatest English-speaking nations. Not until the two world wars of the twentieth century would the full consequences of this development emerge.

Apart from the almost unnoticed American occupation of the Midway Islands in August 1867, the United States' sole territorial acquisition during the Reconstruction era was the purchase of Alaska. Seward's 1867 treaty to buy Russian America for $7.2 million brought under the American flag new territory one-fifth as large as the entire continental United States, a land of obvious strategic importance for the future of the United States in the Pacific. Nevertheless there was little popular enthusiasm for the purchase. Newspapers called Alaska "a national icehouse" consisting of nothing but "walrus-covered icebergs." Congressmen were equally unenthusiastic. Yet after much grumbling the Senate finally ratified the treaty and the House reluctantly appropriated the money for the purchase. Seward's success in part reflected his ability to convince senators that Alaska had vast hidden natural resources. It was also in part the result of the judicious payment of money to American congressmen by the Russian minister in Washington. The most important factor, however, was the general feeling that rejecting the treaty would alienate Tsar Alexander II, who alone of the leading European rulers had been sympathetic to the Union cause during the Civil War.*

Nothing came of other postwar plans for expansion. Each of them ran into snags that made American diplomats draw back. For example, the desire of many United States politicians, including Grant, Fish, and Sumner, to annex Canada had to be abandoned when it became clear that the British would not withdraw without a fight. Grant's plan to acquire the Dominican Republic aroused the

---

*The tsar's pro-Union policy resulted in part from unrest in the Russian-ruled Polish territories, which revolted in 1863 and were reconquered by military force. Like the Union, Russia feared European intervention in what both regarded as internal matters. After the Civil War, the tsar concluded that Alaska was vulnerable to seizure by the British in the event of a future conflict and that it would be better to sell the territory to the United States.

opposition of Sumner, who considered himself the blacks' senatorial voice and wanted the island to become not an American possession, but the center of "a free confederacy [of the West Indies], in which the black race should predominate." Seward's proposal for the purchase of the Danish West Indies (now the Virgin Islands) was pigeonholed by the Senate when those unfortunate islands were visited by a hurricane, a tidal wave, and a series of earthquake shocks.

It would, however, be a mistake to put too much stress on these special factors that stopped American expansionism. Broader forces were also at work. The American people were exhausted by four years of fighting, and they were not prepared to support a vigorously nationalistic foreign policy if it threatened another war. Northern businessmen felt that it was more important to reduce taxes and to return to a sound monetary policy than to engage in foreign adventures. The difficulties of racial adjustment in the South made increasing numbers of politicians hesitate before agreeing to annex additional dark-skinned populations. During Johnson's administration many Republicans opposed all Seward's expansion plans because they might bring credit to the unpopular president. During Grant's tenure alienated Republicans had similar motives for blocking the president's diplomatic schemes; by 1872, these dissidents had joined the Liberal Republican party and were opposing Grant's reelection. Most important of all, the American people were generally aware that they had plenty of room for expansion closer to home, in the lands still occupied by the Indians.

American foreign policy during the Reconstruction generation, then, was the result of compromise. On issues that clearly touched the national security, such as the presence of French troops in Mexico, there was a consensus sufficiently strong to allow the national government to act. But where there was no clear, overriding national interest, objections to expansion prevailed. Although presidents and secretaries of state often fumed, local, sectional, racial, and class objections blocked expansion.

**Politics of the Gilded Age**

A similar deadlock marked the politics of the Gilded Age—so called after the novel of that title by Mark Twain and Charles Dudley Warner, which depicted the boom-and-bust mentality of businessmen of the post–Civil War era and the willingness of politicians to serve the needs of these speculators. The two major parties were almost equally balanced during the entire era. Most of the presidents of the period barely squeaked into office. Grant's success in 1868 was a tribute to a great military leader, not an endorsement of the Republican party that nominated him. Even so, he received only 53 percent of the popular vote. Grant's reelection by a huge popular margin in 1872 was due chiefly to his opponents' willingness to commit political suicide. Dissatisfied members of Grant's own party joined the Liberal Republican movement, which agitated for lower tariffs and for reconciliation with the South—and then proceeded to nominate for president the erratic *New York Tribune* editor Horace Greeley, famed as a protectionist and hated for his prewar denunciation of slaveholders. Holding its nose, the Democratic party also endorsed Greeley, but thousands of Democrats and Liberal Republicans stayed away from the polls. In 1876 Republican Rutherford B. Hayes received a minority of the popular vote and was inaugurated only after a prolonged controversy.

Even had these presidents been elected by overwhelming majorities, they would have been frustrated in attempting to implement any programs because their political opponents usually controlled Congress. To be sure, Grant started with safely Republican majorities in both houses of Congress, but Carl Schurz, Charles Sumner, and other leading Republicans soon defected to the Liberal Republican movement, voted with the Democrats, and blocked the administration's favorite measures. In the congressional elections of 1874 the Democrats for the first time since the Civil War won a majority in the House of Representatives which, except for two years, they continued to control until 1889. Given these conditions, it is easy to understand that the few measures enacted by the politicians of the Gilded Age had to be compromises.

**Economic Issues of the Gilded Age**
For the most part the national government had little to do with the basic economic problems of the Gilded Age. In dealing with economic issues, just as in dealing with those relating to the South and the freedmen, Americans were constrained by the doctrines of constitutionalism—by the belief that the government had only the fixed powers set forth in the Constitution. In the area of economics, only the tariff and the currency seemed to be clearly under the control of the national government. Therefore during the postwar years disagreements over economic issues were usually voiced in connection with these two endlessly troublesome, highly technical questions, so complex that only a handful of congressmen fully understood them.

**The Tariff Problem**
Debates on the tariff involved basic questions as to whether the industrial sector of the economy should be favored at the expense of the exporting agricultural sector and whether the factories of the Northeast should benefit at the expense of the farmers of the South and West. But these questions did not surface clearly, and during the debates in Congress the issue was rarely put in terms of free trade versus protection. Almost everybody during the Gilded Age recognized that some tariff barrier was needed to protect American industries from cheap foreign imports. The debates in Congress revolved around which industries and how much protection.

By 1865 most informed Americans recognized the need to modify the high tariffs that had been enacted during the Civil War to protect heavily taxed American industry from untaxed foreign competition. A bill intended to make a reasonable adjustment was drafted by the New England economist David A. Wells, who was appointed Special Commissioner of the Revenue in 1866. Wells's bill proposed to reduce duties on imported materials such as scrap iron, coal, and lumber; eliminated arbitrary and unnecessary duties on items like chemicals and spices; and made slight reductions in duties on most manufactured articles. Most lawmakers admitted the theoretical excellence of Wells's bill—and most opposed the provisions that lessened or removed protection from their own constituents' businesses. Consequently, Congress rejected Wells's bill, and during the next fifteen years there was no general revision of the tariff legislation.

The absence of general tariff acts did not mean that discussion of tariff rates had ended. To the contrary, throughout the period there was constant pulling and hauling between economic interests that stood to gain or lose from changes in duties on specific imported items. For example, during the war Boston and Baltimore had developed a considerable copper industry that smelted and refined Chilean ore, which paid a very low tariff duty. But in the late 1860s the great copper mines around Lake Superior began to be worked on a large scale, and their owners asked Congress to protect their product by raising duties on imported ore. After sharp disagreement, in which President Johnson supported the refiners and most congressional Republicans sided with the ore producers, the tariff on copper ore was increased in 1869 to a point at which most of the eastern smelting firms had to go out of business.

Other tariff changes were the consequence of combined efforts by the producers and processors of raw materials. An 1867 act revising the duties on raw wool and on woolen cloth was drafted at a convention of wool producers and manufacturers at Syracuse, and it was lobbied through Congress by the tireless and effective secretary of the Wool Manufacturers' Association, John L. Hayes.

Some of the minor adjustments made in the tariff during the postwar years reflected political pressures. In a general way Republicans, with some notable exceptions, tended to favor high protective tariffs, and Democrats, especially those in the South who needed foreign markets for their cotton, wanted to reduce duties. But the issue was rarely clear-cut, for Democrats in manufacturing states like Pennsylvania were high-tariff men. Moreover, both parties tinkered with the tariff issue at election time. In 1872, for instance, the Republican party faced a split. Many tariff reformers in the Liberal Republican movement were preparing to join the Democrats. Attempting to check the bolt, the Republican-dominated Congress rushed through a bill reducing all duties by 10 percent.

The complex history of tariff legislation during the Gilded Age demonstrates the continuing strength of the highly nationalistic impulse toward protectionism that had manifested itself during the war. At the same time it shows that powerful regional and economic interests adversely affected by high duties were able to secure relief without overturning the general protective framework.

**Debates over Currency**   The controversies over currency during the post–Civil War generation were more complex, but in general they illustrate the same tension between the needs of a national economy and the desires of local and special economic interests.

Unless a historian is prepared to write a book about these monetary issues, perhaps he ought to confine his account to two sentences: During the generation after the Civil War there was constant controversy between those who wished to continue, or even to expand, the inflated wartime money supply and those who wanted to contract the currency. Most debtors favored inflation because it would allow them to pay debts in money that was less valuable than when they had borrowed it; and creditors favored contraction, so that the money they received in payment of debts would be more valuable than it had been when they lent it.

But these two sentences, accurate enough in a general way, fail to convey the full dimensions of the controversy. They make the whole issue seem a purely economic question of profit and loss. In fact, for many people the resumption of specie payment—that is, the redemption in gold, at face value, of the paper money that had been issued by the United States government—involved the sanctity of contracts, the reliability of the government's pledges, and the rights of private property. Indeed, the return to the gold standard seemed to have an almost religious significance. Probably most economists of the period shared the conviction of Hugh McCulloch, Johnson's secretary of the treasury, that "gold and silver are the only true measures of value.... I have myself no more doubt that these metals were prepared by the Almighty for this very purpose, than I have that iron and coal were prepared for the purposes for which they are being used." On the other hand, the advocates of so-called soft, or paper, money argued that it was downright un-American to drive greenbacks out of circulation and return to the gold standard. "Why," asked the promoter Jay Cooke, "should this Grand and Glorious Country be stunted and dwarfed—its activities chilled and its very life blood curdled—by these miserable 'hard coin' theories, the musty theories of a bygone age?"

That two-sentence summary also ignores the fact that the currency controversy involved economic interests falling into categories more sophisticated than debtors and creditors. Merchants in foreign trade were ardent supporters of resumption because fluctuations in the gold value of United States paper money made the business of these importers and exporters a game of chance. On the other hand, many American manufacturers, especially iron makers, staunchly resisted resumption because they needed an inflated currency to keep their national markets expanding.

Finally, that two-sentence summary does not indicate that attitudes toward these monetary policies changed over time. Throughout the postwar period farmers were mostly debtors, but they were primarily concerned with such issues as railroad regulation and until 1870 showed little interest in the currency. Creditor interests of the Northeast were indeed mostly supporters of resumption, but when a depression began in 1873 they unsuccessfully urged President Grant to sign the so-called Inflation Bill of 1874, which would have slightly increased the amount of paper money in circulation. In other words, they preferred mild inflation to economic collapse. Moreover, by the late 1870s, inflationists were no longer calling for additional greenbacks; instead they joined forces with western mining interests to demand that the government expand the currency by coining silver dollars. When they discovered that, partly by oversight and partly by plan, the Coinage Act of 1873 had discontinued the minting of silver, they were outraged. Protesting the "Crime of '73," they demanded a return to bimetallism (both gold and silver being accepted in lawful payment of all debts) and the free and unlimited coinage of silver dollars.

With so many opposing forces at work, it is scarcely surprising that the history of currency policy and financial legislation in the postwar years is one of sudden fits and starts. Right after the war, Secretary McCulloch assumed that everybody wanted to return to specie payments promptly, and, in order to raise the value of the paper currency, he quietly held back greenbacks paid into the United States treasury for taxes and for public lands. His mild contraction of the currency restricted business expansion, and Congress forced him to stop. Subsequently, the greenbacks that had been taken out of circulation were reissued, and they remained in circulation for the next decade in the total amount of $382 million.

Indirectly the currency became an issue in the presidential election of 1868. During the previous year, what became known as the Ohio Idea gained popularity in the Middle West. Critics of hard money objected to the government's practice of paying interest on the national debt in gold—which was, of course, much more valuable than greenbacks. The critics argued that since the bonds had been purchased with greenbacks, it would be entirely legal and proper to pay their interest in the same depreciated currency. In this way the crushing burden of the national debt on the taxpayer would be reduced. This argument was so attractive that the Democratic national convention incorporated a version of the Ohio Idea in its 1868 platform. However, the party negated the move by nominating Governor Horatio Seymour of New York, an earnest hard-money man, for president. The Republican national convention sternly rejected the Ohio Idea— against the wishes of many western delegates—and nominated Grant with a pledge to reject "all forms of repudiation as a national crime."

Despite this commitment, Grant's administration witnessed the completion of a series of compromises on currency. The new president announced that he favored a return to the gold standard; but at the same time he warned: "Immediate resumption, if practicable, would not be desirable. It would compel the debtor class to pay, beyond their contracts, the premium on gold... and would bring bankruptcy and ruin to thousands." But lest anyone think that this last statement meant that he desired further issues of paper money, Grant vetoed the Inflation Bill of 1874, against the wishes of many of his advisers.

It was within this broad policy of affirmation checked by negation that John Sherman, the Senate expert on finance, persuaded Congress in 1875 to pass the Resumption Act. This law announced the United States government's intention to redeem its paper money at face value in gold on or after January 1, 1879. On the surface this legislation was a victory for hard-money interests, but in fact it was a brilliant compromise. It did commit the United States to resumption—but only after four years' delay. Sherman sweetened this pill for the silver-mining interests by providing that "as rapidly as practicable" silver coins would be minted to replace the "fractional currency"—notes of postage-stamp size in 3-, 5-, 10-, 15-,

25-, and 50-cent denominations—issued during the war. To placate the green-back interests in the South and West, Sherman's measure made it easier to incorporate national banks in those regions and thus increased their supply of treasury notes.

Although efforts were made after 1875 to repeal the Resumption Act, it was such a carefully constructed compromise that all these attempts failed. Sherman, who became secretary of the treasury in President Hayes's cabinet, skillfully managed the transition in 1879 so that resumption took place without fanfare and without economic disturbance. The whole controversy over currency during the Gilded Age thus illustrates the kind of compromises that Americans of this generation hammered out. The national policy of resumption, desired by most businessmen and needed if the United States was to play a part in world trade, was sustained; but local business interests were able to delay and modify implementation of the policy so that it did not impose too sudden or heavy a burden on groups adversely affected by hard money.

**Scandals and Corruption**

During the Gilded Age neither the Democrats nor the Republicans were able to take a decisive stand, whether on issues relating to the South or those connected with the national economy, and the principal means of cementing party loyalty became patronage and favoritism. As a result the Gilded Age was a period of low political morality in the United States, and many public officials were stained by charges of fraud, bribery, and subservience to special interests. During the 1870s reformers and crusading newspaper editors started to expose shocking scandals. The earliest revelations concerned New York City, which had fallen under the control of "Boss" William Marcy Tweed, who proceeded joyfully to loot the taxpayers. Tweed's ring began construction of a new county courthouse, on which $11 million was spent. Nearly $3 million went to a man named Garvey for plastering; after the amount of his fees leaked out, he became known as the "Prince of Plasterers." Tweed approved the purchase of so many chairs, at $5 each, that if placed in a line they would have extended seventeen miles. In 1871, when the *New York Times* began to expose the ring's padded bills, faked leases, false vouchers, and other frauds, the entire nation's attention was attracted, and when *Harper's Weekly* started carrying Thomas Nast's devastating caricatures of the Boss, Tweed's face became more familiar to Americans than that of any other man except Grant.

Soon revelations about the national government began to make equally fascinating reading. Shortly before the 1872 election, the *New York Sun,* a Democratic paper, exposed the workings of the Crédit Mobilier, the construction company that the Union Pacific Railroad Company paid to build its transcontinental route. Investigation proved that members of the Crédit Mobilier were also members of the board of directors of the Union Pacific, who were thus paying themselves huge profits. Even more damaging was the revelation that, in order to prevent public inquiry, the Crédit Mobilier offered stock to Vice-President

Schuyler Colfax, Representative (and future President) James A. Garfield, and other prominent politicians. They were allowed to "purchase" the stock on credit, the down payment being "earned" by the high dividends that the stock began to pay.

Although Republicans found it advisable to drop Colfax from their ticket in 1872, scandal did not seriously touch the Grant administration until after the election. Then, in short order, stories of fraud began to appear about practically every branch of the executive offices. In the Treasury Department unscrupulous customhouse officers, especially in New York, preyed on importers. Merchants who failed to pay off the thieves had their shipments delayed; their imported goods subjected to minute, time-consuming inspection; and their crates and boxes that were not immediately removed from the docks stored at exorbitant rates. Corruption was rampant in the Navy Department, where political favoritism dictated everything from the employment of workers in the shipyards to the contracts for the construction of new vessels. Secretary of War William W. Belknap was proved to have accepted bribes from Indian traders, who had the exclusive and well-paying franchise to sell goods to Indians and soldiers at frontier posts. He resigned to avoid impeachment.

Of all these scandals, the closest to the White House was the Whiskey Ring. In order to avoid heavy excise taxes, first levied during the war, whiskey distillers, especially those at St. Louis, had for years been conspiring with officials of the Internal Revenue Service. During Grant's administration the dealers secured the cooperation of none other than Orville E. Babcock, the president's private secretary, who warned the swindlers whenever an inspection team was sent out from Washington. In return for his assistance, Babcock received such favors as a $2,400 diamond shirt stud—which he found defective and asked to have replaced with another, more expensive one—and from time to time the services of a prostitute. When Grant first learned of the scandal, he urged, "Let no guilty man escape." But as it became clear that his close friends and his personal staff were involved, he did everything he could to block further investigation. When Babcock went on trial, the president of the United States offered a deposition expressing "great confidence in his integrity and efficiency." Babcock was acquitted, and Grant retained him on the White House staff.

**Civil Service Reform**     The desire to reduce political corruption led to the emergence of the civil service reform movement during the Gilded Age. Although the spoils system had been criticized long before the Civil War, an organized reform drive did not appear until after Appomattox. Knowledge of widespread corruption among government officials, fear that President Johnson might convert the government bureaucracy into a tool to promote his renomination, and the example of the British system of appointing civil servants after competitive examinations gave strength to the movement. Early efforts to require federal appointees to pass competitive examinations failed in Congress, but the reformers, led by the politically ambitious George

William Curtis, editor of *Harper's Weekly,* and by E. L. Godkin of *The Nation,* hoped for success under Grant's administration.

The reformers were doomed to disappointment, for on this, as on all other controversial topics, Grant perfectly understood that compromise was the mood of the age, and he straddled. He made no mention of civil service reform in his first message to Congress. The future historian Henry Adams—the son of Lincoln's minister to Great Britain and the grandson and great-grandson of presidents—remarked in his snobbish way that Grant was inaugurating "a reign of western mediocrity." But when angry civil service reformers began to talk loudly about joining the Liberal Republican movement, Grant moved swiftly to head them off. In 1871 he pressured Congress into creating the Civil Service Reform Commission, and he neatly co-opted his chief critic by naming Curtis its chairman. Although the commission had little power and achieved less success, the move kept Curtis and a sizable number of reformers as supporters of Grant's reelection. Once the election was over, Grant lost interest in the commission and so blatantly violated its rules that Curtis had to resign.

Strengthened by news of the scandals that rocked Grant's second administration, civil service reformers claimed some of the credit for the nomination of Rutherford B. Hayes in 1876. But they found him as difficult to manage as Grant had been. On the one hand, the new president did take on the powerful political machine of New York's Senator Roscoe Conkling, and he succeeded in ousting some of Conkling's supporters—a group called Stalwarts, which included the future president Chester A. Arthur—from the New York customhouse. On the other hand, at election time the president wanted his own appointees to contribute to Republican campaign funds and to help organize Republican state conventions, much as their predecessors had done. "I have little or no patience with Mr. Hayes," exclaimed the reforming editor of the *New York Times.* "He is a victim of . . . good intentions and his contributions to the pavement of the road to the infernal regions are vast and various."

Hayes's successor, James A. Garfield, gave civil service reformers little more satisfaction. With cruel accuracy one Massachusetts reformer characterized the new president as a "grand, noble fellow, but fickle, unstable, . . . timid and hesitating." Civil service reform advocates noted suspiciously that Garfield's vice-president was Arthur, named by the Republican national convention in a vain attempt to placate Conkling. Consequently, reformers felt no special sense of victory when Garfield began to remove more of Conkling's Stalwarts from the New York customhouse. Conceited and arrogant, Conkling resigned from the Senate in a huff and rushed to Albany seeking vindication through reelection. To his surprise, the removal of his friends from federal office undercut his support, and the New York legislature failed to send him back to the Senate. Shortly afterward, a crazed office seeker named Charles Guiteau assassinated Garfield, shouting that he was a Stalwart and rejoicing that Arthur was now president. Shocked by Garfield's assassination, Congress in 1883 passed the Pendleton Act, which required competitive examinations of applicants for many federal jobs.

The measure was typical of the compromises of the period. It was a genuine measure of civil service reform and encouraged the emergence of a professional government bureaucracy, but it covered only a fraction of all government employees and permitted the spoils system to continue in the distribution of most federal patronage.

## Where Compromise Did Not Work

Thus compromise was usually the outcome of struggles in the post–Civil War era when the rivals for the control of policy and power were relatively evenly balanced. But when the rival forces were unevenly matched, the outcome was very different, as the story of labor, women, and Indians reveals.

**Labor Organization in the Gilded Age**    Industrial laborers in the United States were slow to organize. Factory workers came from many national backgrounds and spoke many languages. In the decade after the Civil War, more than 3.25 million immigrants, mostly from northern Europe, poured into the United States, and from these the labor force was largely recruited. By 1880, 87 percent of the inhabitants of Chicago, 84 percent of those in Detroit and Milwaukee, and 80 percent of those in New York and Cleveland were immigrants or the children of immigrants. Divided along ethnic and religious lines, they had little sense of workers' solidarity. Many members of the work force, moreover, regarded their status as transient. They hoped, unrealistically, to move west as homesteaders or, having made their fortunes, to return to their European homelands.

It was almost impossible for a meaningful national labor movement to emerge from such a fractured work force. One of the earliest efforts was the eight-hour movement, led by Ira Stewart, a Boston machinist who sought legislation to limit the workday to eight hours without reduction of wages. Under this pressure the United States established an eight-hour day for its employees in 1868, and legislatures in six states passed acts to make eight hours a legal day's work. In private industry these laws proved ineffectual because they instituted the eight-hour restriction only "where there is no special contract or agreement to the contrary." Consequently, most businessmen required employees to agree to work longer hours as a condition of employment.

The National Labor Union, created in 1866 at a Baltimore conference of delegates from various unions, proved little more effective. It was headed by William H. Sylvis, a dedicated propagandist and a superb speaker, whose interests, however, were not in conventional labor issues like hours and wages, but rather in cooperatives and currency reform. Sylvis recruited many members for the National Labor Union—it claimed 640,000 in 1868—but whether these were actual workingmen is questionable. A scornful observer remarked that the National Labor Union was made up of "labor leaders without organizations, politicians without parties, women without husbands, and cranks, visionaries, and agitators without jobs." After Sylvis's death in 1869, the organization began to decline, and it disappeared during the depression of 1873.

An ultimately more successful labor movement was the Knights of Labor, founded in 1869 by Uriah Stephens and other garment workers of Philadelphia. It grew slowly at first and, like the National Labor Union, received a serious setback in the depression. By the 1880s, however, its membership increased spectacularly as it attempted to create a broad union of all workingmen, skilled and unskilled.*

Neither the National Labor Union nor the Knights of Labor organized a large segment of the nation's industrial labor forces, and the tactics of both organizations did little to relieve the day-to-day problems of working men and women. Hours were long, wages were miserably low, regular employment was uncertain, health or accident insurance was absent, and there were no pension or retirement programs. Child labor was exploited, and employees who dared to speak out against such abuses found themselves blacklisted by employers.

**The Panic of 1873**   These labor organizations were even less able to help in the severe depression that followed the Panic of 1873, precipitated by the failure of the financial firm of the Civil War financier Jay Cooke, who had subsequently become deeply involved in speculative ventures. Between 1873 and 1879 business activity in the United States declined by about one-third, and bankruptcies doubled. Thousands of workers lost their jobs. During the winter of 1873–74 about one-fourth of all laborers in New York City were unemployed, and during the following winter the number increased to one-third. In this time of crisis, the National Labor Union virtually collapsed, and many local unions disappeared as well. In New York City, for example, membership in all unions dropped from 45,000 in 1873 to 5,000 in 1877.

Private charities did what they could to relieve distress. But nobody seemed to know how to end the depression. Experts tended to view the panic and the subsequent unemployment and suffering as part of the natural workings of the national economic order, necessary to purge unsound businesses and speculative practices. Economists warned that "coddling" laborers would only retard this inevitable and necessary process. Blaming the depression on the wartime habit of looking to the federal government for leadership, Democratic Governor Samuel J. Tilden of New York called for a return to "government institutions, simple, frugal, meddling little with the private concerns of individuals . . . and trusting to the people to work out their own prosperity and happiness."

Those labor leaders who remained active were little more helpful. Many sought panaceas for the economic crisis. A writer in the *Radical Review* found the cause of the depression in private landownership which, in his words, "begets . . . ground rent, an inexorable, perpetual claim for the use of land, which, like air and light, is the gift of Nature." Later, in 1879, Henry George made that idea the basis for the economic system proposed in his book *Progress and Poverty.*

---

*For the Knights of Labor in the 1880s, see chapter 22, p. 121.

**Baltimore and Ohio Railroad Strike**
*The 1877 strike on the Baltimore and Ohio Railroad led to the worst labor violence the
United States had experienced. President Hayes called upon federal troops to break the strike
and to restore order.*

Other labor voices supported the Socialist Labor movement, founded in 1874,
which foresaw the ultimate overthrow of the capitalist system through a socialist
revolution. As interim measures to combat the depression, the movement advocated federal aid for education, industrial accident compensation, and women's
suffrage. It attracted only a tiny following.

Some labor spokesmen sought the way out of the depression by supporting
independent political parties pledged to protect labor's position in the national
economy. There was considerable labor support for the Greenback, or National
Independent, party, which was organized in 1874 at Indianapolis. The party's
national program opposed the resumption of specie payments and advocated
further issues of paper money to relieve the country's depressed industries. But
the Greenback party was not exclusively a labor movement: its presidential
candidate in 1876 was the eighty-five-year-old New York iron manufacturer Peter
Cooper. The 80,000 votes Cooper received came mostly from middle western
farm states. In the congressional elections two years later, however, more laborers
supported the National Independent party because it campaigned for governmental regulation of the hours of labor and for the exclusion of Chinese immigrants. Like other advocates of inflation, the party by this time had moved beyond
favoring greenbacks and urged expansion of the currency through silver coinage.
Candidates endorsed by the National Independent party received more than a
million votes in the 1878 congressional elections.

With the collapse of the trade union movement, other laborers during the depression rejected politics in favor of strikes and terrorism.* In July 1877, the worst year of the long depression, labor unrest reached its peak in the Great Railroad Strike, a spontaneous and violent outburst that spread throughout the East and to some of the roads beyond the Mississippi and into Canada. Local and State governments proved unable or unwilling to cope with the crisis. To protect the national system of transportation so essential to the United States economy, President Hayes sent in regular army troops. This action marked the first time in American history that the army had been used on any extensive scale to crush a labor disturbance. The army promptly restored order, and the strike collapsed. Deeply disturbed members of the business community took steps to prevent any recurrence of such labor violence. State legislatures began passing conspiracy laws directed against labor organizations, and the courts began to invoke the doctrine of malicious conspiracy to break strikes and boycotts. Throughout the North the state militia, which had so often proved untrustworthy during the 1877 crisis, was reorganized and given stricter training. The inventor and manufacturer Cyrus Hall McCormick personally purchased equipment for the Second Regiment of Illinois militia because it had, he said, "won great credit for its action during... [labor] disturbances and can be equally relied on in the future."

**The Women's Movement**

The fate of the women's rights movement during the postwar era offers another illustration of how the conservative forces in society dealt with advocates of change who lacked political power and effective leadership. During the Civil War years the central concern of most women was to house and clothe their families after the men had gone into the army. Great numbers of women entered the teaching profession, and for the first time the number of women workers in the federal bureaucracy—mostly on lower, clerical levels—became significant. Others found new fields of usefulness by becoming army nurses. Dorothea Dix, famed as an advocate of reform of prisons and insane asylums, began a new career as head of the nursing service in the Union hospitals, and Clara Barton, who worked closely behind the lines of the Union armies, distributing medical supplies and nursing the wounded, gained the experience that later led her to found the American Red Cross.

During the war the leaders of the women's suffrage movement reluctantly put aside their crusade in order to give their wholehearted support to the Union cause. Critical of the Lincoln administration for its slowness in moving toward emancipation, both Susan B. Anthony and Elizabeth Cady Stanton sought to rally loyal women in support of a constitutional amendment abolishing slavery. With the motto "Let none stand idle spectators now," they organized the National Woman's Loyal League to secure signatures on a gigantic petition to Congress.

---

*Labor unrest in the 1870s is discussed in detail in chapter 22, pp. 121–123.

Ultimately, nearly 400,000 women and men signed the document, which contributed to the adoption of the Thirteenth Amendment.

Quite reasonably, the leaders of the women's rights movement expected their services be recognized when the war was over. They were appalled to discover that in the proposed Fourteenth Amendment to the Constitution, which Congress began debating in the summer of 1866, only males were to be guaranteed the right to vote. Furious, Anthony pledged, "I will cut off this right arm of mine before I will ever work for or demand the ballot for the Negro and not the woman." Women were further outraged when the Fifteenth Amendment prohibited discrimination against voters "on account or race, color, or previous condition of servitude"—but not sex.

They looked for support from their former allies in the antislavery movement, only to be rebuffed. Horace Greeley's reformist *New York Tribune* had no good word for their complaints, and Charles Sumner, while admitting that women's suffrage was "obviously the great question for the future," refused to have the Reconstruction amendments "clogged, burdened, or embarrassed" by provisions for women's suffrage.

Angry, Stanton and Anthony in 1869 formed the National American Woman's Suffrage Association, to promote a proposed Sixteenth Amendment to the Constitution that would provide for women's suffrage, but their movement had little chance against the powerful conservative interests in society. Senator George Williams of Oregon announced that the proponents of women's suffrage were displaying "a spirit which would, if able, convert all the now harmonious elements of society into a state of war, and make every home a hell on earth," while Senator Theodore Freylinghuysen of New Jersey unctuously pronounced that women possessed "a milder, gentler nature, which not only makes them shrink from, but disqualifies them for the turmoil and battle of public life." By invoking women's higher and holier mission of domesticity, conservatives ended hopes for women's suffrage for the next fifty years.

**Indian Problems**     Equally unsuccessful in bargaining with the dominant forces of society were the Native Americans. Whites called all these diverse peoples Indians—meaning, really, "wild Indians." President Lincoln voiced the general paleface view of the redskin. To leaders of several western Native American nations who visited the White House in March 1863, just after the bloody battle of Fredericksburg, the president announced, with no intentional irony: "We are not, as a race, so much disposed to fight and kill one another as our red brethren."

Union leaders took advantage of the opportunities presented during the Civil War to limit the rights of native Americans and to restrict their territories. The loyalties of the Five Civilized Nations were divided between the Union and the Confederacy, and after the Union victory the treaties governing the Indian Territory were renegotiated. As a result the native Americans were forced to give up huge tracts of land and to grant a right of way to railroads crossing the territory.

## Westward Expansion and Indian Wars
## 1864-1876

*The first date indicates the establishment of the territory with the boundaries shown. In several instances earlier territories were formed with the same names but with different boundaries.*

Far to the north, wartime inefficiency and delay, along with the endemic corruption of the federal Indian Bureau, which regulated white–Indian relations, kept promised supplies from reaching the Santee Sioux. In desperation, the Indians took to the warpath and threatened white settlements in Minnesota. Lincoln appointed John Pope, fresh from his defeat at the second battle of Bull Run, to command the armed forces in the Northwest, and the general announced that he would deal with the Sioux "as maniacs or wild beasts, and by no means as people with whom treaties or compromises can be made." When the Sioux surrendered in September 1862, about 1,800 were taken prisoner and 303 were condemned to death. Against the strong objections of local authorities, Lincoln commuted the sentences of most, but he authorized the hanging of 38—the largest mass execution in American history.

In 1864 warfare spread to the Central Plains after the discovery of gold in Colorado and the opening of the Pike's Peak trail led to an influx of whites. Because the regular army was fighting the Confederacy, maintaining the peace was the job of the poorly trained Colorado territorial militia. On November 29, 1864, a group of Colorado volunteers, under the command of a former minister, Colonel John M. Chivington, fell on Chief Black Kettle's unsuspecting band of Cheyennes at Sand Creek in eastern Colorado, where they had gathered under the protection of the governor. "As an act of duty to ourselves and civilization," the militia slaughtered about 150 native Americans, mostly women and children.*

## The Restoration of "Home Rule" in the South

The final adjustment of the relationship between the triumphant Union and the conquered South provides yet one more illustration of the process of compromise in the Gilded Age. In this case there were three parties to the compromise: the victorious Northerners, eager to restore the Union but uncertain what constraints to impose on the South; the Southern whites, who had been conquered but not stripped of their economic power; and the Southern blacks, who had been emancipated and enfranchised but not given land.

Within eighteen months after Appomattox, Northern interest in Southern problems began to wane. In the fall elections of 1867, when many Northern states chose governors and legislators and filled vacancies in the House of Representatives, the Democrats made impressive gains. Responding to the popular mood of conservatism, the Republican party in 1868 passed over Radical presidential candidates like Benjamin F. Wade and nominated Ulysses S. Grant, who had only recently affiliated with the Republicans but whose broad popular appeal as a military hero was unrivaled. Shrewdly sizing up the country's changing attitude toward Reconstruction, Grant used his inaugural address to announce his policy: "Let us have peace."

Just what he meant was not immediately clear. Some thought the new president was appealing to the white Ku Kluxers who were trying to overthrow the Reconstruction governments in the South; others believed that he was speaking to Northern Radicals who wanted to bring about further changes in Southern society. As it proved, Grant had both extremes in mind. On the one hand, the president warmly supported the immediate and unconditional readmission of Virginia to the Union, even though Radicals like Sumner warned that the Virginia legislature was "composed of recent Rebels still filled and seething with that old Rebel fire." On the other hand, Grant was outraged by the terrorism rampant in the South, and he insisted that Congress pass a series of Enforcement Acts (1870–71) enabling him to crush the Ku Klux Klan. Under this legislation the president proclaimed martial law in nine South Carolina counties in which white

---

*Further outrages against the native Americans are discussed in chapter 22, pp. 103–107.

**"One Vote Less"**
*Thomas Nast's drawing picked up on a statement in the Richmond* Whig *that the death of a black man meant one vote less for the Republican ticket in 1868.*

**Anti–Ku Klux Klan Propaganda**
*Thomas Nast, the celebrated Republican cartoonist, suggested that Democrats and the Ku Klux Klan wanted to return African Americans to a condition worse than slavery.*

terrorists were most active, and federal marshals arrested many suspected Klansmen in North Carolina, Mississippi, and other Southern states. In brief, then, Grant's policy was to warn Southern whites that the national government would not tolerate open violence and organized military activity—but to let them understand that at the same time they would not be harassed if they regained control of their state governments through less revolutionary tactics.

**The "Redemption" of the South**  Southern whites quickly accepted the hint. They promptly undertook the restoration of what they called home rule—the rule of native white Democrats. Aware of Northern sensitivities, they now downplayed, when possible, the more brutal forms of terrorism and outright violence. White Republicans had to face social pressure and economic boycott; many fled the South, and others joined the Redeemers (as the advocates of home rule and white supremacy liked to call themselves). Redeemers exerted economic pressure on blacks by threatening not to hire or extend credit to those who were politically active.

In several states whites organized rifle clubs that practiced marksmanship on the outskirts of Republican political rallies. Usually blacks were cowed by these tactics. In a few cases, however, they organized and tried to defend themselves. On such occasions there occurred what Southern newspapers called race riots— a better term would have been "massacres," for the more numerous and better-armed whites overpowered the blacks and slaughtered their leaders. In state after state, Republican governors appealed to Washington for additional federal troops, but Grant refused, convinced that the public was tired of "these annual autumnal outbreaks" in the South.

In consequence of Grant's policy, the Redeemers quickly seized power in Virginia, North Carolina, Tennessee, and Georgia. In 1875 they won control of Alabama, Mississippi, Arkansas, and Texas, and early in 1877 they ended Republican rule in Florida. By the end of Grant's second administration, South Carolina and Louisiana were the only Southern states with Republican governments.

**The Election of 1876**  The fate of these two remaining Republican regimes in the South became intricately connected with the outcome of the 1876 presidential election. The Democratic nominee, Samuel J. Tilden, undoubtedly received a majority of the popular votes cast—although, equally undoubtedly, thousands of blacks who would have voted for his Republican rival, Rutherford B. Hayes, were kept from the polls. But Tilden lacked one vote of having a majority in the electoral college unless he received some of the votes from South Carolina, Florida, and Louisiana, all of which submitted to Congress competing sets of Democratic and Republican ballots. (There was also a technical question of the eligibility of one Republican elector from Oregon.)

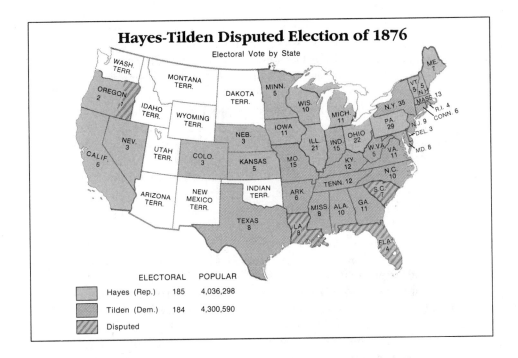

## Hayes-Tilden Disputed Election of 1876

Electoral Vote by State

| | ELECTORAL | POPULAR |
|---|---|---|
| Hayes (Rep.) | 185 | 4,036,298 |
| Tilden (Dem.) | 184 | 4,300,590 |
| Disputed | | |

Congress therefore confronted a crisis when it assembled in December 1876. If it decided to accept the disputed Democratic electoral votes, Republican control of the White House would be broken for the first time in a quarter of a century and the Reconstruction of the South would be ended. If Congress accepted the Republican electoral votes, that decision would run contrary to the will of a majority of the voters in the country.

Thus to resolve the impasse a compromise was needed—and not just a single compromise, but a complicated, interlocking set of bargains. After elaborate and secret negotiations, several agreements were reached. First, Congress decided that the disputed electoral votes should be referred to a special electoral commission, which should consist of five members from the House of Representatives, five members from the Senate, and five associate justices of the Supreme Court. This body was composed of eight Republicans and seven Democrats, and on every disputed ballot the commission ruled in favor of Hayes by the same 8-to-7 vote. In consequence of these decisions, Tilden's electoral vote remained at 184, while Hayes's slowly mounted to 185. In March 1877, for the fifth time in succession, a Republican president was inaugurated.

Democrats reluctantly accepted Hayes's election because of some other bargaining that took place while the electoral votes were being counted. One set of compromises came to be known as the Wormley agreement because it was negotiated in the luxurious Washington hotel owned by the black restaurateur

James Wormley. Representing Hayes at these sessions were Senator John Sherman, Representative James A. Garfield, and other prominent Republicans. Across the table sat Southern Democratic leaders, including Senator John B. Gordon, the former Confederate general who now represented Georgia in Congress, and L. Q. C. Lamar, once the Confederate envoy to Russia and now a senator from Mississippi. The Republicans promised the Southerners that, if Hayes was allowed to be inaugurated, he "would deal justly and generously with the South." Translated, this statement meant that Hayes would withdraw the remaining federal troops from the South and allow the overthrow of the Republican regimes in South Carolina and Louisiana. The Southerners found the terms acceptable, and they promptly leaked the news of the agreement, so as to protect themselves from charges that they had betrayed their section.

Behind the Wormley agreement lay other, less formal, compromises. Hayes's backers promised that the new president would not use federal patronage in the South to defeat the Democrats. They further pledged that he would support congressional appropriations for rebuilding levees along the flood-ridden Mississippi River and for construction of a transcontinental railroad along a Southern route. In return, Southerners agreed to allow the Republicans to elect Garfield Speaker of the new House of Representatives—a position that gave him the power to determine the membership of congressional committees. More important, the Southerners promised to protect the basic rights of blacks, as guaranteed in the Thirteenth, Fourteenth, and Fifteenth amendments to the Constitution.

Virtually all these informal agreements were ignored by both sides once Hayes was inaugurated. For his part, Hayes did order the removal of federal troops from the South and appointed a Southerner and former Confederate colonel, David M. Key, to his cabinet as postmaster general. But two-thirds of the federal officeholders in the South remained Republicans. Hayes changed his mind about supporting a Southern transcontinental railroad, alleging that federal funding would lead to corruption.

Southern Democrats likewise went back on their promise to support Garfield for Speaker. They eagerly joined in an investigation of alleged fraud in Hayes's election once the House was organized under Democratic leadership. Only a very few Southern Democratic politicians, among them Governor Wade Hampton of South Carolina, remembered their promise to respect the rights of blacks. Instead almost all took the final withdrawal of federal troops from the South as a signal that blacks, already put in a position of economic inferiority, could also be excluded from Southern political life.

**Disfranchisement of Blacks**　　Southern whites moved steadily and successfully to reduce black voting, although they had to act cautiously, so as not to offend public opinion in the North or to invite renewed federal intervention. One of the simplest devices was the poll

**A Southern Chain Gang**
*Unwilling to spend much of their revenues to build penitentiaries, state governments instead turned black convicts over to railroads and other businesses, who leased the prisoners for cheap manual labor under brutal and degrading conditions.*

tax, adopted in Georgia in 1877 and quickly copied by other Southern states. To Northerners the requirement that a voter pay $1 or $2 a year did not seem unreasonable. Yet because three-fourths of the entire Southern population had an average income of only $55.16 in 1880, the poll tax was a considerable financial drain, especially to poverty-stricken blacks. More imaginative was the "eight box" law adopted by South Carolina in 1882 and imitated by North Carolina and Florida. Under this system ballots for each contested race had to be deposited in separate boxes—one for governor, one for sheriff, and so forth. The system frustrated the illiterate black voter, who could no longer bring to the polls a single ballot, marked for him in advance by a Republican friend. To make the task of semiliterate voters more difficult, election officials periodically rearranged the order of the boxes. Still another device, which did not become popular until the late 1880s, was the secret ballot, also called the Australian ballot. The secret ballot was supposedly introduced in the South, as in the North, to prevent fraud. But actually it discriminated heavily against blacks, for as late as 1900 the number of illiterate black males ranged from 39 percent in Florida to 61 percent in Louisiana.

Despite all these obstacles, Southern blacks continued to vote in surprising numbers. In the 1880 presidential election, for example, more than 70 percent of the eligible blacks voted in Arkansas, Florida, North Carolina, Tennessee, and Virginia, and between 50 percent and 70 percent voted in Alabama, Louisiana, South Carolina, and Texas. These black voters posed a double threat to the Redeemers. Black voters were numerous enough that ambitious Northern Republicans, hoping to break the now solidly Democratic South, might be tempted again to try federal intervention in state elections. Even more dangerous was the possibility that Southern poor whites, whose needs for public education and welfare were consistently neglected by the business-oriented Redeemers, might find common cause with the poor blacks.

The Redeemers saw both these dangers materialize after 1890. Shortly after the Republicans gained control of the House of Representatives in 1889, Representative Henry Cabot Lodge of Massachusetts introduced a strong bill for federal control of elections, which promptly became known as the Force Bill. Although Democrats in the Senate defeated Lodge's bill in January 1891, Redeemers saw in it a threat to renew "all the horrors of reconstruction days." Their fear was doubtless greater because the almost simultaneous rise of the Populist movement threatened, as never before, to split the white voters of the region.* The Populist party appealed to farmers and to small planters and was the enemy of lawyers, bankers, and the rising commercial and industrial spokesmen of the so-called New South. Some of the Populist leaders, like Thomas Watson of Georgia, openly criticized the Redeemers' policy of repressing the blacks and seemed to be flirting with the black voters.

Faced with this double threat, Southern states moved swiftly to exclude the blacks completely and permanently from politics. Mississippi led the way with a constitutional convention in 1890 that required voters to be able to read and interpret the Constitution to the satisfaction of white registration officials. It is not hard to imagine how difficult even a graduate of the Howard University Law School would have found this task. In 1898 a Louisiana constitutional convention improved on the Mississippi example by requiring that a literacy test be passed by all voters except the sons and grandsons of persons who had voted in state elections before 1867. Because no Louisiana blacks had been permitted to vote before that date, this provision allowed illiterate whites to vote, while the literacy test excluded most black voters.

State after state across the South followed, or elaborated on, these requirements. South Carolina held a disfranchising convention in 1895. North Carolina amended its constitution to limit voting in 1900. Alabama and Virginia acted in 1901–02, and Georgia adopted a restrictive constitutional amendment in 1908. The remaining Southern states continued to rely on the poll tax and other varieties of legislative disfranchisement. When opponents of these measures accused their advocates of discriminating against blacks, Senator Carter Glass of

*For the rise of the Populist movement, see chapter 22.

# WHITE SUPREMACY!

### Attention, White Men!

## Grand Torch-Light Procession

### At JACKSON,

On the Night of the

## Fourth of January, 1890.

**The Final Settlement of Democratic Rule
and White Supremacy in Mississippi.**

GRAND PYROTECHNIC DISPLAY!
Transparencies and Torches Free for all.

**All in Sympathy with the Grand Cause
are Cordially and Earnestly Invited to be
on hand, to aid in the Final Overthrow of
Radical Rule in our State.**

Come on foot or on horse-back; come any way, but
be sure to get there.
  Brass Bands, Cannon, Flambeau Torches, Transparencies, Sky-rockets, Etc.

**A GRAND DISPLAY FOR A GRAND CAUSE.**

"White Supremacy!"
*In 1890, when the Mississippi
constitutional convention
devised a way to disfranchise
virtually all blacks, whites held a
"grand pyrotechnic display" to
celebrate.*

Virginia replied for his entire generation: "Discrimination! Why that is precisely what we propose; that exactly is what this convention was elected for."

It took time, then, for the complete working out of the political compromises of the Reconstruction era. Not until the end of the nineteenth century did white Southerners receive the full price they had demanded in permitting the election of Rutherford B. Hayes. But by 1900 that payment had been made in full. The black man was no longer a political force in the South, and the Republican party was no longer the defender of black rights.

## CHRONOLOGY

**1866** National Labor Union formed.

**1867** Maximilian's empire in Mexico falls. Purchase of Alaska.

**1868** Ulysses S. Grant elected president in contest with Democrat Horatio Seymour.

**1869** Knights of Labor organized.

**1871** Treaty of Washington, settling differences between United States and Great Britain, signed. Tweed Ring scandals in New York City exposed.

**1872**  Crédit Mobilier scandals revealed. Grant names G. W. Curtis to head Civil Service Commission.
Grant reelected over Horace Greeley, candidate of Liberal Republicans and Democrats.

**1873**  Coinage Act demonetizes silver in so-called Crime of '73.
Panic of 1873 begins long depression.

**1874**  Grant vetoes Inflation Bill.

**1875**  Specie Resumption Act provides for return to gold standard by 1879.

**1876**  Exposure of Whiskey Ring reveals further corruption in Republican administration.
Republicans nominate Rutherford B. Hayes for president; Democrats nominate Samuel J. Tilden. Disputed returns leave outcome in doubt.

**1877**  Congress creates electoral commission, which rules that all disputed ballots belong to Hayes, who is inaugurated president.
Nationwide railroad strike and ensuing violence lead to first significant use of federal troops to suppress labor disorders.

## Suggested Readings

The best general treatment of social and economic change during the post–Civil War period is Allan Nevins, *The Emergence of Modern America, 1865–1878* (1927). Ellis P. Oberholtzer, *History of the United States Since the Civil War,* vols. 1–4 (1929–31), contains an enormous amount of unassimilated data.

Foreign affairs during the Reconstruction era are treated in Glyndon G. Van Deusen, *William Henry Seward* (1967); Allan Nevins, *Hamilton Fish* (1936); and David Donald, *Charles Sumner and the Coming of the Civil War* (1970). Adrian Cook, *The Alabama Claims* (1975), is authoritative. Thomas D. Schoonover, *Dollars over Dominion* (1978), examines Mexican-American relations. On expansionism the standard work is A. K. Weinberg, *Manifest Destiny* (1935).

For a spirited, irreverent, and not entirely accurate account of the politics of the Gilded Age, read Matthew Josephson, *The Politicos, 1865–1896* (1938). Morton Keller, *Affairs of State: Public Life in Late Nineteenth Century America* (1977), is much more judicious and analytical. For balanced studies of three Republican presidents, see William S. McFeely, *Grant* (1981); Harry Barnard, *Rutherford B. Hayes and His America* (1954); and Allan Peskin, *Garfield* (1978). Two full studies of corruption in New York City are Alexander B. Callow, *The Tweed Ring* (1966), and Seymour Mandelbaum, *Boss Tweed's New York* (1965). Ari A. Hoogenboom, *Outlawing the Spoils* (1961), is a model history of the civil service reform movement.

Three modern, sophisticated analyses of the currency controversy are Robert P. Sharkey, *Money, Class, and Party* (1959); Irwin Unger, *The Greenback Era* (1964); and Walter T. K. Nugent, *The Money Question During Reconstruction* (1967).

Wilcomb E. Washburn, *The Indian in America* (1975), and Robert F. Berkhofer, Jr., *The White Man's Indian* (1978), are superior works. On governmental policy toward the Native Americans, see David A. Nichols, *Lincoln and the Indians* (1978); Francis P. Prucha, *American Indian Policy in Crisis* (1975); and Loring B. Priest, *Uncle Sam's Stepchildren* (1942).

Labor organization and unrest are treated in depth in John R. Commons et al., *History of Labor in the United States,* vol. 2 (1918). Norman J. Ware, *The Labor Movement in the United*

*States* (1929), is especially valuable on the National Labor Union. On the changing character of work and laborers' responses to industrialism, see Herbert G. Gutman, *Work, Culture and Society in Industrializing America* (1976), and Daniel T. Rogers, *The Work Ethic in Industrial America* (1978).

Eleanor Flexner, *Century of Struggle* (1975), is the standard account of the woman's suffrage movement. For two excellent general accounts of the role of women, see Mary P. Ryan, *Womanhood in America* (1979), and Carl Degler, *At Odds: Women and the Family in America* (1980).

Many of the works cited in the previous chapter are also helpful in understanding the restoration of "home rule" in the South. C. Vann Woodward, *Reunion and Reaction* (1951), is an original reexamination of the compromise of 1876–77. Keith I. Polakoff, *The Politics of Inertia* (1973), is a more recent interpretation. For an analysis of the Redeemer regimes, see Woodward's *Origins of the New South* (1951). The best study of the disfranchisement of blacks is J. Morgan Kousser, *The Shaping of Southern Politics* (1974).

PART FIVE

# Nationalizing
# the Republic
## 1877–1920

John L. Thomas

*A*s THE American people completed their industrial revolution in the half-century following the Civil War, they continued to celebrate unprecedented growth even as they were driven to experiment with new ways of regulating it. In 1900 as in 1850, most Americans saw a reason for national self-congratulation in the numerous signs of prosperity all around them. The standard of living was improving, the population was growing rapidly, great cities were rising, and the stock of consumer goods was steadily increasing. More thoughtful observers, however, noted that a high social price had been paid for all these achievements. A rural people had been suddenly uprooted and their communities disrupted, new masses of underprivileged persons had been forced into mobility, too many Americans worked under deplorable conditions, and a conspicuously unequal distribution of wealth persisted. Still, for most people caught up in America's industrial transformation, the benefits of rapid material growth clearly outweighed its costs.

Economic growth continued to verify earlier predictions of unlimited betterment, and most Americans continued to believe in the cherished ideal of progress. Freedom from external restraints on individual ambitions was the key concept in the doctrine of progress, and this concept had survived the Civil War—if not unscathed, at least largely intact. In 1900 a majority of Americans continued to maintain a simple faith in the individual, just as it had a generation earlier.

Yet despite the country's optimistic mood, by 1880 reform-minded citizens in all walks of life were beginning to note the signs of mounting social disorder. Industrialization, modernization, and urbanization forced a growing number of leaders in all parts of the national community to recognize the need for controls and systems in order to make American society efficient and stable. To improve their operations and increase their profits, businessmen sought consolidated power within their firms. Farmers quickly discovered an urgent need for better credit facilities and marketing mechanisms. Social theorists and urban reformers began to adjust their vision to the requirements of systematic planning. By 1890 the American way of life, which had once seemed a self-regulating device for producing happiness automatically, had come to be seen as a machine badly in need of repair, if not of a complete overhaul.

These would-be reformers of American society after 1890 did not always agree on priorities and means. But the thrust of their ideas and programs pointed unmistakably toward the construction of a new national order. In historical terms this new vision seemed to reject the libertarian philosophy of Thomas Jefferson and to revive the nationalist model of Alexander Hamilton. In the fields of law and constitutional theory, formal definitions of rights and duties were replaced by more flexible concepts of social utility, requiring new roles for lawyers and legislators alike. In social reform there was a new emphasis on training, expertise, and the predictive functions of science. In politics an organizational revolution brought new styles of leadership and new approaches to the workings of government.

The distance the nation had traveled by 1920 could be measured in two widely different assessments of American politics and society. The first assessment was that of the individualist prophet Ralph Waldo Emerson at the height of moral reform before the Civil War. Emerson located the essence of the American spirit in the "wise man" with whose appearance "the state expires." "The tendencies of the times," Emerson predicted, "favor the idea of self-government, and leave the individual . . . to the rewards and penalties of his own constitution which works with more energy than we believe whilst we depend on artificial restraints." But three-quarters of a century later, the progressive sociologist Charles Horton Cooley dismissed Emerson's self-enclosed individual as a moral abstraction unknown to history. "In a truly organic life the individual is self-conscious and devoted to his work, but feels himself and that work as part of a large joyous whole. He is self-assertive, just because he is conscious of being a thread in the great web of events." The story of the years separating Emerson, the sage of Concord, from the progressive social scientist Cooley is the account of the American discovery of the great social web and the multitude of connecting threads that composed it.

# 22

## *Stabilizing the American Economy*

~

*I*N THE first years of the Republic, Alexander Hamilton predicted that industry and agriculture would advance together in the American march toward abundance. Hamilton's promise was echoed a few years later by Henry Clay in his prophecy of the eventual triumph of his American System, and it was repeated again and again in the years before the Civil War by businessmen and promoters eager to exploit the country's resources. While in power, Hamilton, and later Clay and John Quincy Adams, had tried to build a framework for industrial growth. But not until the last decades of the nineteenth century did the American people make good on Hamilton's initial promise. At the end of the Civil War, the United States still stood on the threshold of the modern industrial world—as did France, Germany, Japan, and Russia. Thus in 1865 the United States continued to be a hungry importer of capital, labor, and most of its technology. Thirty years later the nation had transformed itself into a major exporter of foodstuffs and the producer of a mammoth stockpile of industrial and consumer goods. Within a generation it had joined Great Britain and Germany as one of the world's leading industrial powers.

Statistics, with which Americans were beginning to measure their success, told a story of unprecedented economic growth. The value of American manufactured products soared from $3 billion in 1869 to more than $13 billion at the turn of the century. Between the Civil War and 1900 industrial output tripled. The national labor force rose sharply too, from 13 million to 19 million, and the percentage of the national income that went to pay wages increased from 37 percent to 47 percent.

Figures like these led Charles E. Perkins, president of the Chicago, Burlington, and Quincy Railroad, to ask his fellow citizens: "Have not great merchants, great manufacturers, great inventors, done more for the world than preachers and philanthropists? . . . Can there be any doubts that cheapening the cost of necessities and conveniences of life is the most powerful agent of civilization and progress?" Some Americans had little love for great merchants and great manufacturers, whom they tended to blame for the period's economic disruptions and recurrent hard times. But most of them probably also agreed that material progress came first because the intellectual and cultural achievements of their civilization depended on such progress. In turn, material progress resulted from an industrial revolution that had changed the face of American society in less than a generation. What was this revolution? How did it happen? What forces accounted for it? How did it affect the nation's various regions—the Northeast and Midwest, the South and West—and the farming and industrial labor populations? And behind it was there any guiding plan? Did it have any goal?

## The Foundations of the American Industrial Revolution

The search for an answer to these questions begins with the rapid settlement of the new lands across the Mississippi River—the Great Plains stretching westward from the tier of states along the river across the hundredth meridian to the foothills of the Rockies. Only a generation earlier this huge area had been marked the "Great American Desert" on the most up-to-date map, but now it was being billed by land speculators and railroad promoters as the "Great Breadbasket of the World." On the eve of the Civil War, settlement hugged the banks of the Missouri River where fifteen years earlier the historian Francis Parkman had stood scanning "level plains, too wide for the eye to measure, green undulations, like motionless swells of the ocean" before jumping off to follow the Oregon Trail westward toward "those barren wastes, the haunts of the buffalo and the Indian, where the very shadow of civilization lies a hundred leagues behind." In 1860 only the centuries-old Spanish town of Santa Fe and the new Mormon communities in Utah broke the emptiness of the High Plains. Yet by the time Parkman died in 1893, hordes of new settlers from the East and recent arrivals from California across the mountains formed clusters of settlement in an almost unbroken chain. In 1890 the superintendent of the United States census announced—a bit prematurely—the closing of the frontier. "Up to and including 1880 the country had a frontier settlement," he reported, "but at present the unsettled area has been so broken into by isolated bodies of settlement that there can hardly be said to be a frontier line."

A phenomenal growth of the national population kept pace with increasing western settlement. In the years between Appomattox and the centennial celebration in 1876, the population of the United States rose by 30 percent from 35.7 million to 46.1 million on a wave of immigrants, mostly from Europe, who flooded the nation. Their numbers were matched by massive increases in production in all sections of the economy. In these same years the American corn harvest increased by 100 percent. Railroad mileage grew by 111 percent; the production of bituminous coal, by a whopping 163 percent.

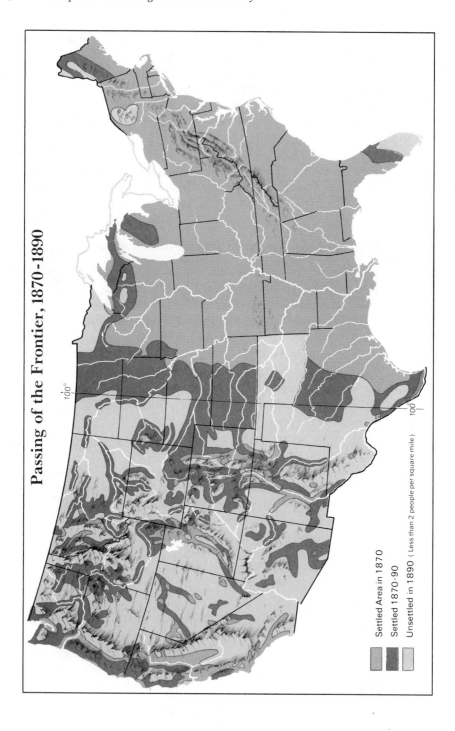

**Passing of the Frontier, 1870-1890**

Settled Area in 1870

Settled 1870-90

Unsettled in 1890 ( Less than 2 people per square mile )

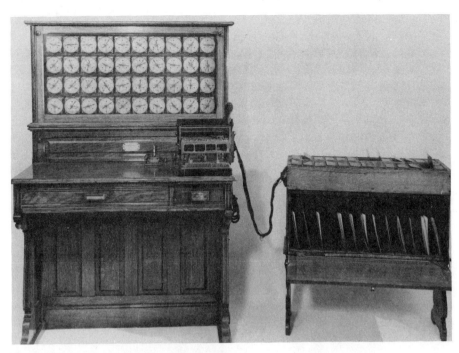

**Herman Hollerith Census Tabulating Machine**
*New inventions made tabulating and storing needed statistics easier and more efficient.*

## Origins of National Economic Consolidation

The Gilded Age, as the immensely productive period following the Civil War was called, witnessed the rise to wealth and prominence of new industrial and financial leaders who began to apply the lessons learned from their wartime experience in developing and perfecting innovative technology and systems of large-scale management. For example, Andrew Carnegie, who arrived from Scotland as a poor but ambitious young immigrant, trained himself to become a skilled telegraph operator and served as an aide to Thomas Scott, the assistant secretary of war in charge of government railroads and transportation lines. From his vantage point at the managerial center of the Union war effort, Carnegie saw clearly the coming of a postwar expansion and reorganization of the nation's railroads, and he invested his savings in the company that owned the patents for Pullman sleeping cars. Soon these sleeping cars became standard equipment on the railroads, and Carnegie had acquired the necessary investment funds with which to build his steelmaking empire.

Another sharp-eyed entrepreneur who seized the opportunities provided by the Civil War was John D. Rockefeller, a pious young Baptist from Cleveland, Ohio, who got his start handling wartime contracts for hay, grain, meat, and other commodities. Rockefeller, like Carnegie, recognized the advantages of order and

**Pioneer Run, 1865**
*The discovery of petroleum in western Pennsylvania led to its rapid and wasteful exploitation.
Not more than one well out of twenty was properly sunk and carefully managed.*

system as the means to increased efficiency with which to drive competitors from the field. In the early 1860s he began to apply these principles with a vengeance to the petroleum industry in western Pennsylvania, concentrating on gaining control of the refining process, and by 1863 he owned the largest refinery in Cleveland, which he used as a base to seize control of an oil industry that once had been openly competitive but also inefficient and wasteful. Within a decade Standard Oil of Ohio, as his company was called, made its own barrels for shipping oil, built and maintained its own warehouses, and owned an entire fleet of tankers.

Rockefeller's methods, although highly effective, violated the accepted norms of small-scale competition. With his suddenly increased volume of business, he succeeded first in convincing the railroads to give him lower shipping rates, and then in forcing on the carriers secret agreements for "drawbacks," or a percentage of the payments made by his competitors. By 1880, using more sophisticated variations of such methods, Standard Oil controlled 95 percent of the oil refining business in the country and nearly all of the transporting of oil, whether by railroad or pipeline. Casting up Standard Oil's accounts for the 1870s in his *Wealth Against Commonwealth* (1894), the muckraking journalist Henry Demarest Lloyd pronounced judgment on Rockefeller as an ignorant and irresponsible *arriviste:*

> Our barbarians come from above. Our great moneymakers have sprung in one
> generation into seats of power kings do not know. The forces and the wealth are

new and have been the opportunity of new men. Without restraints of culture, experience, the pride, or even the inherited caution of class or rank, these men, intoxicated, think they are the wave instead of the float, and that they have created the business which created them.

Lloyd's indictment of the new "American Pasha" was also directed to the predatory Jay Gould, the "greatest mouse-catcher in America" and the original model for the Gilded Age robber baron. To those observers like Lloyd, schooled in the ways of financial probity, Jay Gould seemed a demonic Horatio Alger, the sharp-eyed trickster who teaches costly lessons in wariness to Americans by bilking the stockholders of the Erie Railroad, bribing judges, cornering the Gold Market on Black Friday in 1869, draining the treasury of New York City's elevated railroad companies, arranging a hostile takeover of Western Union, and finally gaining control of the Texas and Pacific Railroad and breaking the Knights of Labor strike in 1886 with wholesale discharges, blacklists, scabs, and spies. The prince of financial pirates who learned his buccaneering in the war years, Gould died in 1892 in his Fifth Avenue mansion encased in tapestries, huge frescoes, and gilt ceilings, probably the most hated public figure in the country. "Ten thousand ruined men will curse the dead man's memory," declared the *New York World* in its obituary.

## Growth of Cities

Cities—Rockefeller's Cleveland, Carnegie's Pittsburgh, Jay Gould's New York— furnished the stage on which the industrial transformation of late-nineteenth-century America was played out. The nation's big cities acted as magnets drawing native-born Americans and newly arrived immigrants off worn-out agricultural lands into new urban cores packed with factories and offices, stores and warehouses, tenements and apartments. The novelist Theodore Dreiser gave to his character Sister Carrie, as her train nears Chicago, the emotions experienced by millions of real-life new arrivals in the Gilded Age city. As Carrie sits gazing in wonder out of the window, other trains flash by and telegraph poles suddenly appear nearby to point the way to big smokestacks thrusting high into the air. Soon two-story frame houses in the suburbs give way to giant office buildings and warehouses until at last, Carrie realizes, "they were under a great shadowy train shed, where the lamps were already beginning to shine out."

> To the child [Dreiser comments], the genius with imagination, or the wholly untravelled the approach to a great city for the first time is a wonderful thing. Particularly if it be evening—that mystic period between the glare and gloom of the world when life is changing from one sphere or condition to another.... Though all humanity be still enclosed in the shops, the thrill runs abroad. It is in the air. The dullest feel something they may not always express or describe. It is the lifting of the burden of toil.

In the half-century after 1860 the number of people living in cities of more than 8,000 rose tenfold. By 1880 over a quarter of the American people lived in urban areas. In the remaining years of the century, the urban population grew at the phenomenal rate of 6 percent per decade, until by 1900 a full 40 percent of the people lived in cities. This huge demographic shift had actually begun in the years before the Civil War as the forces of commercial development began to alter the appearance of the older walking cities, filling up downtown residential zones with new financial and retailing establishments, sweatshops, and wholesale houses, and pushing middle-class residents out to the streetcar suburbs along the metropolitan periphery. By mid-century, canals, railroads, and the steam engine had already built the basic structure of the modern industrial city, segregating zones of work from wealthy residential neighborhoods and connecting them with rudimentary transit systems. After the Civil War this push-pull movement quickened, centripetal forces collecting large pools of willing workers—new ethnic groups from Europe, rural whites, and African Americans from the South—in the center of cities while centrifugal forces propelled older inhabitants out to the margins. The reciprocal "flow" of people and goods in, out, and through metropolitan centers quickly became a distinguishing characteristic of Gilded Age American life.

The largest cities were to be found in the Northeast and the Midwest where urban concentration proceeded most rapidly. Here in the new metropolis industrialization was already well advanced, and financial resources, transportation and communications links, and an army of eager workers were readily available. Big cities were increasingly segregated by wealth and work into zones of affluence and abject poverty, walled off but still within walking distance of each other. In the 1870s, in the depths of a severe depression, New York City's Fifth Avenue north of Twenty-sixth Street sported recently built monuments to conspicuous consumption in Renaissance palaces and French chateaus while immigrant families in the noisome Five Points neighborhood converted dark twelve-by-ten living rooms into sweatshops where they sewed precut garments or rolled cigars.

Here too in the industrial city were millions of anonymous consumers who furnished vast markets for a bewildering variety of new products—basic necessities like food, clothing, and furniture, and newly developed products like sewing machines, typewriters, and cigarettes. Inhabitants of the city quickly became dependent on a steady supply of consumer goods provided by manufacturers, processors, and distributors. "We cannot all live in cities," Horace Greeley, the aging editor of the *New York Tribune,* complained to a younger generation headed toward the metropolis, "yet nearly all seem determined to do so.... 'Hot and cold water,' baker's bread, the theater, and the streetcars... indicate the tendency of modern taste."

As these burgeoning cities expanded the boundaries of old commercial centers after the Civil War, they too became giant municipal consumers of the heavy industrial goods with which to modernize—electrical dynamos, telephone wire, lead piping and copper tubing, streetcars and the motors to run them.

Whether they subsidized huge public constructions like John and Washington Roebling's Brooklyn Bridge or encouraged massive private ventures like Henry Hobson Richardson's Marshall Field Warehouse in Chicago, big cities provided an insatiable appetite for all the products of the American industrial machine.

The railroad lines that tied cities together in an interurban corridor in the Northeast were joined at midwestern terminals by new roads that ran straight across the Great Plains and over the Rocky Mountains to the Pacific Coast, collecting on their several strands clusters of central-place cities and towns like beads on a string. The growth of western cities matched those east of the Mississippi: nationwide, the number of cities with populations of over 100,000 in the closing decades of the nineteenth century increased from 9 to 50, while the number of those cities with populations from 25,000 to 100,000 jumped from 26 to 178 and that of smaller cities with populations under 25,000 skyrocketed from 58 to 369. Major western cities straddled the transcontinental railroad lines that crossed the Great Plains and the Rockies, the northern tier stretching from Minneapolis to Spokane and on to Tacoma, Seattle, and Portland; a central urban band running from Chicago and St. Louis through Kansas City, Omaha, Cheyenne, to San Francisco; and a southern route sprouting cities, many of them new. All these instant cities served as distributing centers for surrounding regions and as producing centers for specialized regional products like beer, flour, meat products, and cotton oil. Already by 1880 the fabled West of the covered wagon and the cowboy was receding into history before the advance of mechanization and modernization.

The Civil War had devastated a number of major southern cities, among them Columbia and Charleston, South Carolina; Atlanta, Georgia; and Richmond and Petersburg, Virginia, all of which undertook rebuilding programs during Reconstruction. As in the trans-Mississippi West, railroads throughout the South opened up new inland cities like Houston and Dallas and rehabilitated old river ports like Memphis and Natchez for commercial and industrial development. The pattern of urban growth in the New South differed in scale and pace from metropolitan expansion in the Northeast and Midwest. Most southern cities continued to depend on the marketing of regional staple-crop agricultural products until late in the century, when commercial activity began to give way to industrial development.

The cityscape in the New South presented a lower profile than its urban counterparts in New York or Chicago, where tall office buildings with steel frames and curtain walls were beginning to create steep city canyons at the bottom of which pedestrians and vehicles of all kinds crawled and knotted. Nashville and Montgomery boasted two- and three-story commercial blocks fronting on miles of wide thoroughfares, a marked contrast to Chicago's Loop with its compact mix of banks, retail houses, business offices, city hall, library, museum, and opera house.

The emergence of new southern industrial cities like Birmingham was accompanied by the mushroom growth of smaller market towns that sprang up everywhere in the postwar years. Before the Civil War planters had invested in slaves at the expense of land and commercial development. Now, as Reconstruction drew to a close, new money, much of it initially from the North but increasingly local, began to flow into town-building, improved roads, and urban development all across the South. Urbanization in the South depended more and more heavily after 1880 on local enterprise and crash programs for building new markets in interior towns and financing cotton and lumber mills. Mill-building and town-building combined to connect outlying rural districts with regional cities and to extend the effects of rapid urbanization into the farthest reaches of the South.

## Railroads Provide an Organizational Model

Railroads played a crucial role in America's industrial revolution by helping to develop a powerful national economy and dominating the American technological imagination for a generation. Railroads were giant consumers that fed heavy industry with ever-larger orders for steel rails, machines, and equipment. Railroading was the nation's first big business, and it provided the model for Gilded Age big businessmen—raising large amounts of capital, integrating operations, building distribution systems, and managing the movement of goods and people with regular timetables and systematic purpose.

Plans for a transcontinental railroad, which date from the 1840s, had been repeatedly shelved because of mounting sectional controversy, but in 1862 Congress lent its support to railroad promoters by incorporating the Union Pacific Railroad Company and financing it together with the Central Pacific with grants and huge tracts of public lands. Construction work began in earnest in 1865 with the Union Pacific pushing rapidly west across a thousand miles of Great Plains through Evans Pass in Wyoming to link up with the Central Pacific tunneling eastward through the Donner Pass. A reporter from the East described in amazement the construction of the Union Pacific: "Five men to the 500-pound rail, 28 to 30 spikes to the rail, three blows to the spike, two pair of rails to the minute, 400 rails to the mile, and half a continent to go. . . ." On the western end, reaching 700 miles eastward, the Central Pacific sent some 10,000 Chinese "coolies" swarming over the canyons of the Sierras, boring through 1695 feet of solid rock, and blasting their way with a new untested explosive, nitroglycerine. Charles Crocker, one of California's Big Four merchant investors and the hard-driving construction boss of the Central Pacific, accepted a $10,000 bet that his men could not lay ten miles of track in a single day. On April 18, 1869, Crocker won his bet, and his colleague Leland P. Stanford drove the golden spike uniting the two lines at Promontory Point, Utah, as news flashed by telegraph to an awaiting nation.

The transcontinental railroads' achievements in conquering space and standardizing and compacting time caught the American imagination and quickly changed the image of the West from the Great American Desert with unknown

**Promontory Point, Utah Territory, 1869**
*Joining the tracks of the Union Pacific and Central Pacific railroads.*

**Dining in Splendor While Heading West**
*By the 1870s dining cars were a regular feature on express trains to the West Coast.*

potential into a scrambling economic region marked by large-scale industrialization and urbanization. All too quickly, the 160-acre homestead gave ground before the forces of corporate development. Railroads also altered the visual landscape of the West by imposing new rectilinear grids on once-open country and by fostering farm-supply towns and building huge grain elevators all along their lines.

Less dramatic than the accomplishments of the transcontinental lines but of greater immediate economic significance was the coordinating and consolidating of railroads east of the Mississippi. Before the Civil War there had been eleven different rail gauges in use on northern roads. President Lincoln's selection of the 4-foot 8½-inch gauge for the Union Pacific soon established that width as standard for all lines. Then came standardization of time with the mandating of time zones and successful experiments in cooperation between competing lines with bills of lading that facilitated easy transfer of goods. Before the Civil War passenger travel from New York to Chicago involved using eight to ten independent, hastily constructed lines and repeated time-consuming transfers. In 1869 Commodore Vanderbilt consolidated the New York Central and Hudson River railroads to provide continuous service from New York to Buffalo and five years later was able to provide through service to Chicago. At the same time the Pennsylvania Railroad, the Erie Railroad, and the Baltimore and Ohio Railroad completed connections and were offering competing service.

The completion of a modern communications network kept pace with the construction of railroads. As early as 1861 it was possible to send a telegram from San Francisco to Washington, D.C., even though the service was sporadic. But by 1866 the Western Union Telegraph Company, thanks to its wartime contracts with the military, had driven out its competitors and secured a virtual monopoly. Western Union made it possible for the first time for people in virtually every part of the country to communicate almost instantaneously with people in any other part of the nation. Then came the telephone, invented by Alexander Graham Bell and successfully demonstrated at the Centennial Exhibition in Philadelphia in 1876, which provided a second communications network. By the 1880s most doctors in major cities had telephones, and during President Hayes's administration an instrument was installed in the White House. The telephone was still such a novelty that, when it rang, the president himself was likely to answer it.

In the last three decades of the nineteenth century, railroads, supplied with instant communications, a uniform gauge, standard time zones, and improved bridge designs, managed to link the cities and their surrounding regions together, first in a loose network and then in a tighter web that composed a national design. Financiers and construction chiefs seldom looked beyond the problems involved in laying the next mile of track. As one investor explained, "We must get a cheap line and a safe road, but at the outset we must in grades and curves try to *save*— and trust to the future for higher finish." Time was money, and railroading an expensive business.

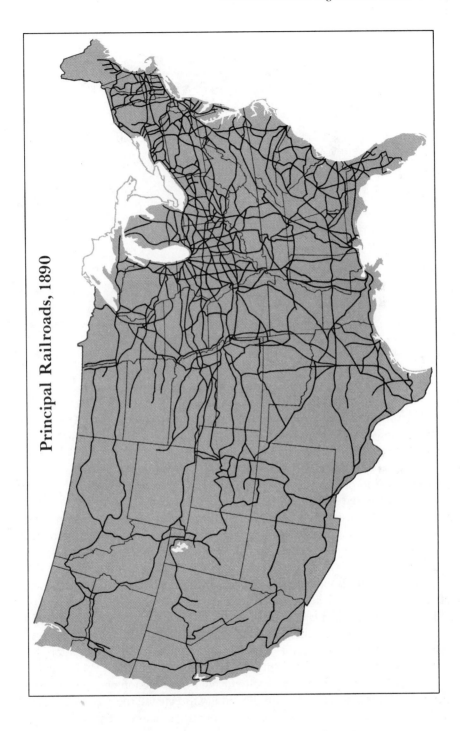

Principal Railroads, 1890

**Wreck on the New York Central at Batavia, New York, 1885**
*Passenger safety was not always a top priority for the nation's railroads.*

Still, statistics again told Americans what they wanted to hear: 35,000 miles of track in 1865 had become 242,000 by 1897. At the end of the Civil War railroads reached the end of the line just across the Mississippi in Iowa and Missouri. By century's close there were no fewer than five transcontinental lines. East of the river by 1890 railroad transportation had come to be dominated by a small group of integrated systems like the New York Central and the Pennsylvania roads. In the Midwest the Burlington line dominated as did the Union Pacific, Northern Pacific, and Great Northern with their routes to the West Coast. Here was a lesson in system-building that all American business would seek to learn and apply.

Financing and building the railroads involved massive financial chicanery and fraud, and they quickly acquired unsavory reputations, initially well deserved and subsequently difficult to overcome. "We...do not claim to be immaculate, beyond expediency," admitted one railroad executive, "[but] are content with right intentions and good results obtained on the whole." An investigation of the Crédit Mobilier scandal in 1872 caught the directors of the Union Pacific Railroad in the act of diverting huge sums to their own construction company of which they were the managers. When public inquiry threatened the continued success of this scam, the construction company sought to quash the investigation by offering stock on credit to Vice-President Schuyler Colfax and future President James A. Garfield. When he was discovered distributing railroad shares among

**Commodore Vanderbilt
Riding One of His Trains**
*A cartoonist's version of "The
public be damned."*

his fellow congressmen, Representative Oakes Ames brashly defended his actions: "I think a member of Congress has a right to own property in anything he chooses to invest in." His colleagues in the House disagreed and voted to "absolutely condemn" him. For the next twenty years the railroads continued to be accused (frequently with ample proof) of disregarding the safety and comfort of their passengers, watering their stock, jerry-building their roads as purely speculative ventures, and rigging rates that discriminated against farmers, merchants, and small shippers. When Commodore Vanderbilt consolidated the New York Central and Hudson River lines with a stunning increase in unsecured stock, Wall Street brokers paid him a backhanded compliment by unveiling a statue of him holding a gigantic watering can. "It is the use of water," a spokesman quipped, "not as a beverage but as an element of public wealth, which has been the distinguishing characteristic of Commodore Vanderbilt's later years." Charles Francis Adams, Jr.'s, verdict on the behavior of railroaders was more severe: "They exact success and do not cultivate political morality."

To their critics the railroad managers replied that as private enterprises they were accountable first and foremost to their stockholders, who demanded profits above all else. They also admitted to running their roads as *regional* systems that escaped regulation by crossing state boundaries—large operational units in which individual farmers and shippers were only cogs in their wheels. Rather than being forced to meet particular demands for rate regulation and warehousing rules, railroad spokesmen insisted, they should be left free to manage their own enterprises with an eye to eliminating competition and increasing efficiency. If, then, it cost twice as much to ship wheat from Fargo, North Dakota, to Duluth, Minnesota, where there was no competition, than it did to ship the same wheat from Minneapolis to Chicago, where competition was intense, this discrepancy could be explained as the workings of a free-market system.

Despite their growing unpopularity with farmers, shippers, and small merchants, railroads continued to compile an impressive record in establishing new traffic patterns. In 1865 the railroads were a collection of local systems without standard gauge or equipment and lacking even a common timetable. Twenty-five years later, railroad magnates, who gave less thought to acceptable public policy than to their own needs, had nevertheless supplied the country with an immense transportation system composed of regional units. In their attempt to keep their cars full, railroads necessarily gave rate preferences to large producers, and they both encouraged and took advantage of regional specialization. Along their tracks moved wheat, corn, and hogs from the Midwest, cotton and sugar from the Mississippi Delta, lumber from the Lakes states, oil products from Pennsylvania to seaboard terminals, and coal from West Virginia to Pittsburgh's steel mills. With improvements in refrigeration came meat from Chicago, Kansas City, and Omaha, and fruit and vegetables from California and Florida. In the pioneer achievements of these carriers, American business could recognize a national model of ever-larger firms practicing economies made possible by huge volume—economies of scale—and passing these savings along to consumers in a nation-wide market in the form of lower prices. As both an organizational ideal and a promise of abundance, railroads dominated the growth of the American economy for a generation and seized the American public's technological fancy.

**Technology**        Another powerful stimulant to late-nineteenth-century economic growth was swiftly developing technology. Even before the Civil War, the modern science of metallurgy had been born with the discovery in the 1850s first of the Bessemer process and then of the open-hearth method, which together made possible the production of high-grade steel in large amounts. Like many industrial improvements in the nineteenth century, these breakthroughs in steel technology originated in Europe but were quickly adapted to American conditions. Thus by the mid-1870s Bessemer mills in this country were producing 50 percent more steel than their British counterparts—and the margin widened every year as homegrown technological geniuses like Carnegie Steel's Captain "Bill" Jones designed more efficient layouts and found better ways of moving hot steel through them.

The American public could see for itself the countless new uses of steel when it visited Machinery Hall at the Philadelphia Centennial Exhibition in 1876 and examined firsthand all the productions deemed worthy of a Centennial Medal by the judges. Among the many American award-winning technological exhibits were Sharps rifles and Gatling guns; Midvale Steel's axles and shafts; Yale locks and Otis elevators; the Westinghouse air brake; Roebling's steel suspension bridge; Fitts road steam engines; and Pullman sleeping cars. Scattered in between these major exhibits were displays of hundreds of machine tools manufactured by Pratt and Whitney of Hartford, Connecticut, and Brown and Sharpe of Providence, Rhode Island.

In the center of the gigantic hall, dominating the other displays as both active presence and potent symbol stood the majestic Corliss engine designed by George Corliss of Providence—a double-acting, duplex vertical high-pressure steam engine standing on a platform fifty-six feet in diameter and supplying the power for all the machinery throughout the cavernous building. Visitors to the fair likened the Corliss engine to the human heart as a way of comprehending it as a system for generating power and sending it to its destination through metal arteries and leather capillaries. The massive engine rose forty feet in the air, weighed 680 tons, was powered by twenty boilers and equipped with cylinders forty-four inches in diameter with ten-foot strokes. The engine's massive flywheel—some thirty feet in diameter—made thirty-six revolutions per minute meshing with cogs on a pinion that turned an underground line geared to eight secondary shafts running along the ceiling the full length of the hall. All the machines beneath ran from belts attached to the 650-foot-long shaft that transmitted 180 horsepower. Here made visible for millions of onlookers stood the meaning and the promise of system for a dawning industrial age.

The number of inventions in post–Civil War America mounted steadily until the annual total of patent applications reached 25,000 in 1891. Thus the Hoe printing press and the Ingersoll air drill were invented in 1871; three years later came the third rail for subways and elevated lines. In the centennial year Alexander Graham Bell demonstrated the telephone at the Exposition in Philadelphia, and the next year the phonograph appeared. The year 1878 saw the installation of the first switchboard in New Haven, Connecticut, and in 1886 George Westinghouse perfected his system for transmitting alternating current over long distances. In every branch of industry and manufacturing, new inventions raised productivity, reduced man-hours of labor, and by competitive processes forced down the cost of finished goods.

American technology proved remarkably flexible in borrowing and improving foreign designs. Sometimes it provided lighter and faster machinery, as in the textile industry; at other times it developed bigger and more powerful equipment, like the mammoth steam shovels needed for heavy construction. In the oil industry the "cracking" process, which was developed in the 1870s, allowed refiners to control various yields by altering the molecular structure of the petroleum.

In the beginning inventors tended to work alone or in small unsubsidized groups, and frequently stumbled on their inventions by trial and error. The discovery of the Bessemer converter is an example. Only after some clever guesswork and haphazard experimenting did Sir Henry Bessemer in England and (working independently in the United States) William Kelly learn to force blasts of air into molten pig iron to burn out the carbon.

Soon after the Civil War, however, inventors like Thomas A. Edison came to understand the necessity of *system* rather than trial and error. An inveterate self-promoter, Edison always billed himself as a lone independent who required freedom from interference by combination or confederacy. "If you make the coalition," he warned the organizers of General Electric consolidation, "my usefulness as an inventor is gone. My services wouldn't be worth a penny. I can invent only under powerful incentive. No competition means no invention." Yet no one understood better than Edison the advantages of organization and order in the experimental process itself. His new approach to technological development and improvement took the forms of systematic organization of research in large independent or corporate-funded laboratories like his consortium at Menlo Park, New Jersey, and of the systematic application of a series of inventions—a process today called *innovation*—to a productive or extractive process conceived as a whole. Often invention and innovation combined to break a technological bottleneck that had blocked an entire process, as in the case of George Westinghouse's system for transmitting alternating current over long distances. In the same way, the rapid perfection of measurement devices, cutting tools, and lathes in the machine tool industry triggered a chain reaction of development of machine tools to make other machine tools to make tools.

This multiplier effect could be seen most clearly in the development of the combine harvester, patented before the Civil War but brought to Minnesota's wheat fields during and after the war. The combined reaper-thresher, to which was added a twine-binder by 1880, sold like the hotcakes it made possible throughout the 1880s, and together with the disc harrower and the wheeled gangplow quickly revolutionized wheat farming on the Great Plains, as mechanization spread from Minnesota's Red River Valley to California's interior valley bonanza farms. Mechanization on a rapidly expanding scale tripled American agricultural output between 1860 and 1920 and drastically reduced the farmer's labor costs. This new system of large-scale production and distribution of foodstuffs—which the twentieth century would call "agribusiness"—was being put firmly in place in the 1890s in a geographically segmented set of specialized farming regions extending in huge horizontal bands across the nation: a northern strip of hay and dairying land stretching from New England to Minnesota; spring wheat country pushing out through the Dakotas into eastern Montana; an expanding zone of "breadbasket" agriculture of wheat, corn, and hogs from Illinois out into the High Plains; a cotton belt running from South Carolina to the Texas and Oklahoma panhandles; and a Gulf Coast fringe of market-garden agriculture, by the turn of the century reaching up into California and the Pacific Northwest.

Equally impressive was the effect of technological system on American industry in fostering vertical integration—that is, the building of huge industrial firms that connected and controlled all the successive stages of manufacturing from the marshaling of natural resources to the marketing of the finished product. A good example of the accomplishments of vertical integration was provided by Judge Elbert H. Gary in his testimony before a congressional investigating committee. Gary, who was president of the Federal Steel Company and Andrew Carnegie's chief competitor, vehemently denied that he presided over any sort of "trust" or that he sought "monopoly." The key to Federal Steel's success, he explained, was vertical integration. "It takes the ore from the ground, transports it, manufactures it into pig iron, manufactures pig iron into steel, and the steel into finished products, and delivers these products." With its control of supplies of ore and the management of its own railroads, together with an efficient plant for making vast amounts of steel, Gary's company by the 1890s produced 30 percent of the steel rails in the country.

In the Mountain West, innovation in the extractive industries—logging and mining—made a similar impact with new systems devised to meet enormously expanding demands for lumber and metals of all kinds. In the silver, lead, copper, and iron mines across the country, the introduction of dynamite and then nitroglycerine led to more efficient, if highly dangerous, methods of getting out the ore. The depths of mine shafts sank from 3,000 feet to double that figure. Mining engineers employed by large syndicates found ways to straighten mine shafts to accommodate mechanized lifts and hoists. Air pumps and mining lamps to replace candles, arc lights and automatic drills, steam-driven regrinders and concentrators—all operated in concert within a new integrated system of production, altering the face of the American landscape and the lives of those who worked in that system.

A final example of rapid innovation and industrial system-building is the heavy construction industry in the cities, where giant steam shovels and steam-driven piledrivers, pneumatic drills, and electric cranes built the tall office buildings designed by newly integrated architectural firms in New York and Chicago.

Technology and a new science of management worked together to train the labor force in new skills and work patterns that were needed for industrialization. In celebrating the centenary of the Patent Office in 1891, one participant in the ceremonies listed the necessary ingredients for a successful policy of invention: individual enterprise; schools and universities; learned societies and professional organizations; and government aid. "To the modern investigator," he concluded, "leisure and opportunities are necessary . . . apparatus and laboratories are indispensable; and few men working alone can command either the needful time or the bare material necessities. During this century nine-tenths of the great discoveries have been made by men with institutions back of them." A huge pool of unskilled labor was still considered essential to American economic expansion, but the long-term trend pointed toward mechanization and, in the end, automation. Despite the willingness of native-born boys fresh from the farm, and young immigrants just off the boat, to feed the furnaces and work the lathes, it was machinery that sent American productivity soaring and consumption with it.

**Capital Investment**   Technology bred great expectations and a mounting hunger for capital. In the early years of the oil business just after the Civil War, John D. Rockefeller was able to acquire a small refinery for $10,000 and a large one for $50,000. By 1910 the market value of Rockefeller's Standard Oil was $600 million. Technology promised greater productivity and increased efficiency but also required ever-larger amounts of investment capital, which was readily forthcoming in the last three decades of the century. In 1860 a total of $1 billion was invested in the nation's manufacturing plants, which turned out a collective product worth $41.8 billion and employed 4.3 million workers. By 1900 the size of the work force had grown fivefold, and the total value of products nearly tenfold; at the same time, the amount of invested capital had multiplied twelvefold.

The sudden availability of large amounts of capital represented one of the most striking features of the American industrial revolution. The rate of savings, which had hovered around the 15 percent mark before the Civil War, suddenly shot up to 24 percent in the 1870s and 28 percent in the 1880s (compared, for example, to the present rate of savings by Americans, which is approximately 5 percent). Americans with money were turning to investment of their savings in the workings of the great industrial machine. The last half of the nineteenth century was a period of what economists call "capital deepening." Standard Oil and the Carnegie Steel Company regularly plowed back sizable portions of their mounting profits into the business; and individual investors, who in the Jacksonian years tended to buy land and mortgages, had been taught by the financial entrepreneur Jay Cooke during the Civil War to switch to government bonds as "the ready, *present* and *required* means to strike the death blow at rebellion," a preference for stocks and bonds they retained after the war.

The positive results of this process of accumulating savings could be seen in plant modernization, growing research and development programs, expanding product lines, and more efficient systems of distribution. The debit side of the ledger could be read in the growing disparity in income dividing well-to-do Americans from their less fortunate fellow citizens—a result in part of regressive federal tax policies (a small wartime income tax had been jettisoned after the war) that allowed wealthy people to keep their money for investment purposes. The earnings of the less wealthy—recent immigrants, unskilled workers, growing numbers of working women—increased over the last three decades of the nineteenth century, but not enough to close the gap in income and economic power.

To put this new money to work a host of new financial institutions appeared: commercial banks, savings banks, life insurance companies, and investment houses. These new institutions served as intermediaries between the eager investor and the needy business firm. By 1900 the stock market, now over a hundred years old, had established itself as the main mechanism for exchanging securities and mobilizing the vast funds required by new industrial firms. By the time of World War I, Wall Street had succeeded in creating a genuine national market for investment capital.

The pace of the American Industrial Revolution was unregulated and hence uneven. Boom-and-bust has historically been a flaw in free-market economies together with marked disparities in the distribution of income, and the economy of the Gilded Age was no exception. For the first time in American history a combination of potent forces was at work—a huge urban market, an efficient distribution system, a highly motivated work force, and vast amounts of capital. All that was lacking was a public policy that recognized the need for regulation and direction. Without such a program the transformation of the American economy was destined to be disorganized and at times chaotic.

**Economic Instability**   The gains made by the American Industrial Revolution were real. Per capita income grew by 2 percent a year; between 1870 and 1910 it tripled. The workweek declined from sixty hours to fifty in these same years. A declining death rate outstripped a falling birthrate, and an improved diet and better health care raised the life expectancy for white males from thirty-seven to forty-six years in this period. (The average life span of black males, however, was sixteen years shorter.) Most important for American businessmen and consumers was a steady drop in prices of food and manufactures and the increasing availability of both to consumers. Recalling for a congressional investigating committee in 1883 his early years in the Manchester, New Hampshire, mills, the former governor of the state attributed his greatly improved standard of living to his frugality as a young man:

> I got $125 [a year].... Now, how did I get my clothes? I clothed myself. I mended my own stockings; my employer used to give me a pair of socks sometimes. We had no new clothes as boys have nowadays. During the whole year that I was first in this place I never paid one dollar for a carriage; spent no money for cigars; no money for rum; we had no amusements, no holidays. I never heard of such a thing as a vacation for ten years. This is the way we grew up here—by constant labor. Labor is the foundation of prosperity.

If these long-term improvements in the standard of living were real, so too in the short term were the severe deprivations stemming from economic instability, particularly the decline in status among formerly independent artisans and mechanics. Testifying before the same congressional committee, a textile worker and union organizer from Fall River, Massachusetts, described working conditions in the city's mills:

> The condition of operatives in our city is a very unenviable one. The work there is very hard and the wages are very low—low in proportion to what they used to be some ten years ago, before the financial depression [of 1873–78] set in. Our females in particular are overworked; their strength is entirely overtaxed by the labors they have to perform. I have often argued myself that if our manufacturers would give over preaching so much about temperance and other things and try

to bring about a reform in the condition of their operatives, it would be better than all the many thousand temperance lectures and temperance tales.

The American economy after the Civil War swung like a pendulum between good times and hard times, and back again. The Panic of 1873 plunged the country into six years of depression, with massive unemployment, wage cuts, and price declines. Following a short season of recovery, a second recession buffeted the economy in 1884, and again sent prices skidding and workers into the ranks of the unemployed. Once more after a brief respite, the Panic of 1893 brought four more years of economic paralysis from which the country recovered only at the end of the century.

Satisfactory explanations of the causes of depressions were hard to come by. American observers compared depressions to a swing of the pendulum, the breaking of a wave, or the onset of a fever, but the experts despaired of controlling business cycles or erasing the effects of periodic slumps. Despite the recent lessons in the need for economic planning that the Civil War had suggested, the great majority of middle-class Americans still believed devoutly in the self-regulating market. And conventional wisdom declared that government should never interfere with this market. "Money-getters," the great showman P. T. Barnum warned the politicians, "are the benefactors of our race." Stand aside and let them do their work!

The result of this popular belief in unlimited business opportunity and citizen autonomy was a national government that frequently subsidized business but seldom regulated it. Politicians, professionals, and educators alike predicted marvelous achievements for a new industrial statesmanship left to its own devices. Big corporations, the wealthy ironmaster and mayor of New York City, Abram S. Hewitt, advised the Chicago Board of Trade, were the "best friends" the American people had. Far-seeing industrialists, having dispensed with the strictures of the Founders, were now busy "doing the work which was done by Jefferson and Madison in the early days of the Republic." William Graham Sumner, Yale's crusty sociologist and the great defender of American rugged individualism and self-help, amended this judgment only slightly: "The great leaders in the development of the industrial organization need those talents of executive and administrative skill, and fortitude, which were formerly called for in military affairs and scarcely anywhere else." Academicians and professionals chimed in. "I believe in general that that government is best which governs least," Francis A. Walker, president of the Massachusetts Institute of Technology, warned Congress, "and that interference with trade or manufactures is very undesirable."

As Gilded Age politicians deferred to business leadership and praised business values, the directive force of government tended to disappear in misty hopes for automatic prosperity. The great steel manufacturer and self-made man Andrew Carnegie explained the terms of this new social contract in a language that a business civilization instinctively understood. It would be a serious mistake

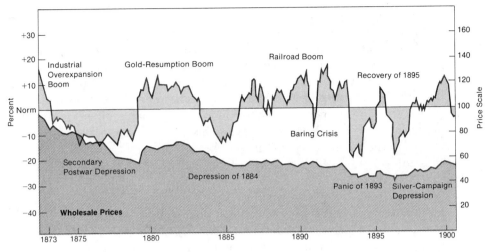

The U.S. Economy, 1873–1900

he joked, for the American community to shoot its millionaires because, after all, they were the "bees" that made the most honey: "Under our present conditions the millionaire who toils on is the cheapest article which the community secures at the price it pays for him, namely, his shelter, clothing, and food." Carnegie need not have worried: there would never be an open season on American millionaires.

## Business Fills a Vacuum

Because the federal government was reluctant to assert its control over the economy—and because state governments responded only gradually with piece-meal and often ineffective legislation—the job of providing a measure of eco-nomic stability fell to American businessmen themselves. Only the application of system could manage the national economy efficiently and fairly, assuring all Americans a measure of financial security and personal well-being. Blessed with organizational talent and boundless energy, American businessmen were the first to respond to the challenge of disorder, even though they tended to concentrate on the specific problems confronting their own businesses rather than on the creation of an equitable national market system. In most businessmen's views, their needs did not require public policy; rather, they could be met by a series of limited private strategies designed to protect their own firms. Slowly a general pattern of self-regulation of business and industry emerged in response to threats to continued prosperity.

What were those threats? First of all, businessmen knew that their costs of production were rising as they took advantage of new technologies and expensive machinery to meet a mounting consumer demand. Throughout the last quarter of the century these capital costs, as they called them, kept increasing. To compound their problem, the same machinery that made mass production possible also attracted new investors and entrepreneurs eager to seize their share of a new national mass market. This competition drove prices inexorably downward toward cost: the wholesale price index sank from 100 in 1880 to 82 in 1890.

Thus the businessman faced the problem of how to break out of a circle of rising production costs, increasing competition, and tumbling prices. He could cut production, lay off his workers, and close his factory, but as the steelmaker Andrew Carnegie soon discovered, it was cheaper and more efficient for big business to "run full," even at a short-term loss, than to close down. The manufacturer could meet competition by slashing his prices, but not below the long-run break-even point. Faced with recurrent slowdowns and slumps, menaced by competitors, and confronted with shrinking profits, the nation's businessmen began to experiment with various ways of gaining greater control over their enterprises. The day of the small businessman attempting to solve the problem all by himself was over. "We live in an atmosphere of organization," one keen observer commented. "Men are learning the disadvantages of isolated action. Whether we approve of trusts and trades-unions and similar combinations, and whatever their motives, they rest on a foundation which is sound alike from the business and religious standpoint; namely, the principle of union and cooperation."

The first experiments in securing industrial order through the imposition of a system were improvised attempts made by a business community that was suddenly faced with severe problems but left to its own devices to find solutions. In deciding to demolish a small-business economy with its unregulated market forces and to replace it with new combinations, American business leaders played—often without realizing it—a genuinely revolutionary role.

**Cartels and Trusts**     The earliest forms of consolidation—those requiring the least amount of change—were *cartels.* These were loose trade associations, or *pools,* of independent business firms voluntarily joined together to dominate and hopefully direct an industry. With disarming candor, the organizer of the Wire Nail Association explained his case for forming a pool:

> There is nail machinery enough in this country to produce four times as many nails as can be sold. When there is no pool the makers simply cut each other's throats. Some people think there is something wicked about pools. When we were trying to get up the nail pool, I talked with directors of companies who held up their hands against going into any sort of combination. I said to them, "How much did you make last year?" "Not a cent." "Are you making anything now?" "No." "Well, what do you propose to do? Sit here and lose what capital you have got in the business? . . . " There is only one way to make any money in a business like the nail business, and that is to have a pool.

Pools attempted to meet the problem of overproduction and falling prices through gentlemen's agreements: competitors, while maintaining their independence, agreed among themselves to accept production quotas and refrain from price cutting. For example, the whiskey distillers agreed that "only 28 per cent of the full capacity shall be operated, and no stocking up beyond this amount under any circumstances." To tighten sagging steel prices, the steel rail manufacturers in 1887 formed a pool, the Steel Rail Association, which established a strict quota system and provided for a series of stiff fines for uncooperative members. Although the Steel Rail Association continually denied charges of price fixing, it nevertheless enjoyed a period of remarkable price stability thereafter.

Yet cartels had their drawbacks. They flourished in good times but collapsed under the pressure of recessions. Their agreements could not be enforced in the courts, and American consumers regarded them as an undue restraint of trade. Recognizing these limitations and sensitive to an aroused public opposition to secret agreements, pioneer organizers, among them John D. Rockefeller, turned to "horizontal" combinations, or *trusts.* The trust was the brainchild of a member of Standard Oil's legal staff, the affable and shrewd Samuel C. T. Dodd, who patiently explained its advantages to hesitant colleagues. Because state laws prohibited a company's outright ownership of another company's stock, there was no foolproof way of consolidating, holding, and managing a string of separate companies, Dodd admitted.

> But you could have a common name, a common office, and a common management by means of a common executive committee. . . . If the Directors of one of the companies and their successors shall be made Trustees of all such stock, you thus procure a practical unification of all the companies.

The idea worked. In 1882 forty-one stockholders in the Standard Oil Company of Ohio signed an agreement creating a board of nine trustees to whom they transferred all the properties and assets of their companies in exchange for trust certificates. The visible signs of this financial feat were 700,000 hundred-dollar certificates, the price of consolidated control over the American oil industry. The corporate spirit had worked its first miracle.

Once they acquired formal control over production and prices, many trusts and *holding companies* (similarly integrated firms that were allowed to hold stock in other corporations) were content to operate as loose cartels, simply parceling out shares of the market without trying to impose a centralized system or authority. The hoped-for efficiency and economies were not always forthcoming in such cases of partial consolidation, and soon the largest and most powerful businesses began to follow the examples of Carnegie Steel and Federal Steel by achieving "vertical" integration of their industries through control of the entire industrial process from raw materials to sales. In his annual report to stockholders in 1901 the president of a vertically integrated concern explained why his company looked inward for success rather than buying out the competition:

We turned our attention and bent our energies to improving the internal management of our business, to getting the full benefit from purchasing our raw materials in large quantities, to economizing the expense of manufacture, to systematizing and rendering more effective our selling department, and above all things and before all things to improve the quality of our goods and the condition in which they should reach the customer.

More and more frequently after 1890, big business tried to secure control "backward" to resources and transportation, as well as "forward" to control of the market through research departments and central business offices. From the last years of the nineteenth century through World War I, even more intensive consolidation would finish the demolition of Gilded Age capitalism and clear the ground for new twentieth-century giants.

The business drive toward a national economy in the Gilded Age did not go unopposed. For every gain there was a corresponding loss: for every winner, a disgruntled loser. Not all business in the Northeast, for example, welcomed every change made by integration. If New York City flourished as the new center of the nation's financial and transportation networks, its growth was at the expense of such former rivals as Boston and Philadelphia. If Standard Oil profited handsomely from Rockefeller's nationalizing of the oil business, a large part of the cost was ultimately borne by hundreds of small independents driven from the field. Andrew Carnegie's J. Edgar Thompson steel mill mass-produced nails, which made building cheaper and more efficient, but it also cost blacksmiths, ironmongers, and older artisans their livelihood.

And for what ends was the American financial and industrial order being transformed? The builders of the new corporate America, like their many admirers, were never entirely clear about their ultimate aims. Heavy investment capital, rapid plant expansion, increased production and reduced overhead, economies of scale and mass distribution systems—all to what greater good? For huge profits, surely, and for rising quantities of consumer goods for more and more people. But beyond that? What did mass advertising and the constant manipulation of consumer demand mean for individual freedom of choice? How were Americans to balance rising standards of living with loss of control over the workplace? Could big business be made to deliver on its promise of economic security for all citizens? Were huge industrial and financial combinations compatible with political democracy and social responsibility? In short, was big really better? Neither the corporate revolutionists nor their uneasy admirers could quite answer these questions, which posed a dilemma that would persist throughout the twentieth century.

**The Counter-revolution Fails** These same questions troubled the opponents of big business, who called themselves "antimonopolists" and whose numbers and influence swelled in the late nineteenth century, beginning with the farmers' and workingmen's fight against the railroads and culminating in the Populist movement in the 1890s. If these critics of monopoly and enemies of the Money Power finally failed to prevent economic concentration or to check its political influence, it was not for lack of numbers. The antimonopoly army in the last quarter of the century recruited at one time or another farmers and artisans with strong beliefs in equality and community; small businessmen with limited capital but limitless faith in individual initiative; and liberal publicists, country lawyers, clergymen, and educators determined to protect the claims of the "little people" against the incursions of monopoly. Stronger and fiercer than the party loyalties of Republicans and Democrats, the faith of the antimonopolists exhibited all the fervor of a civic religion promising spiritual renewal as well as economic restoration and political purity.

Many of the antimonopolists' complaints were pointed and direct. Monopolies, some charged, were the source of a prodigious waste of natural resources. In planning only for increased profits, big business misdirected investment, misallocated manpower, and thus kept the total output of American goods lower than it should have been. Others argued that the trusts behaved unfairly, tying the people's hands and then picking their pockets. If pools and trusts and all the other instruments of business collusion did not immediately raise prices, they had the power to do so and would soon invoke it. And that power, all the antimonopolists agreed, had been acquired by driving out honest competitors and seizing the citadels of power. The harshest indictment of monopolies was directed at their *political* influence. This was the charge leveled against Standard Oil by Henry Demarest Lloyd in his famous exposé *Wealth Against Commonwealth* (1894):

> Monopoly cannot be content with controlling its own business. . . . Its destiny is to rule or ruin, and rule is but a slower ruin. Hence we find it in America creeping higher every year up into the seats of control. Its lobbyists force the nomination of judges who will construe the laws as Power desires, and of senators who will get passed such laws as it wants for its judges to construe.

At the heart of the antimonopoly appeal lay a belief in a law of "natural development," which, left to operate as divine providence intended, would ensure steady, measured economic growth. Natural growth, critics like Henry Demarest Lloyd and Henry George insisted, would be accompanied by full employment, fair wages, and widespread abundance. In this alternative reading of American prospects, the United States had enjoyed a "normal" pace of economic development until monopolies played havoc by unduly accelerating the growth rate and encouraging speculation. If trusts, pools, and holding companies could simply be dismantled and their special privileges annulled, the country would return to a healthy state of "real growth" and a fairer distribution of wealth to all its citizens. The social reformer and antimonopolist Henry George described this future America for his fellow opponents of economic concentration. Without massive engrossment of land by railroads and absentee owners, and without the forced migration of the nation's yeomen to city slums where they became the new proletarians, the national future would bring utopia:

There would be no necessity for building costly railroads to connect settlers with a market. The market would accompany settlement. No one would have to go out into the wilderness to brave all the hardships and discomforts of the solitary life; but with the foremost line of settlement would go the church and the school-house and lecture room. The ill-paid mechanic of the city would not have to abandon the comforts of civilization, but where there would be society enough to make life attractive, and where the wants of his neighbors would give a product for his surplus labor. . . .

Behind such a vision stood a set of democratic-republican convictions whose history ran back to the middle of the eighteenth century and the American colonists' "country party" opposition to the commercial revolution and the British Empire. First of all, there was the view of history as an unending struggle between the virtue of the people and the dark forces of corruption lurking in the halls of state. Only the unsleeping vigilance of all citizens could stem the onslaught of predatory wealth and power bent on their destruction. Next came the distinction, still a vital one for the antimonopolists after the Civil War, between the true producers of the world—farmers, workingmen and -women, small businessmen—and the parasites who lived off their honest labor—bankers, lawyers, gamblers, and speculators. Finally, the opponents of big business held firm to the belief in the whole people organized in their communities and practicing a moral economy based on cooperation as well as competition. All these assumptions had survived the American Revolution to help direct the Jeffersonian opposition to the Federalists, and later, to inform the Jacksonians' attack on the Bank and to shape the abolitionist indictment of slavery. Now it was the turn of the Gilded Age antimonopoly forces to invoke them in their fight against economic concentration. Now, however, they had to learn the uses as well as the abuses of government: their ideal community of true producers and participatory democracy could be saved only by actions of the federal government to which they would have to appeal.

Public opposition to monopoly accomplished little in terms of legislation before 1890. In the 1870s the national farmers' organization, the Grange, and its allies among local businessmen pressured various midwestern state legislatures into passing laws regulating the rates that railroads charged for hauling freight and storing grain.* Although the Supreme Court originally upheld these so-called Granger Laws in *Munn* v. *Illinois* (1877), nine years later in *Wabash, St. Louis & Pacific Railway Co.* v. *Illinois* a more conservative minded majority declared that individual states could not regulate rates for interstate carriers.

On the federal level the Interstate Commerce Act (1887) was not much more successful in bringing the railroads to heel. The act prohibited pools, rebates, and rate discrimination, and it set up a commission to investigate and report viola-

---

*For the Granger movement as an expression of rural discontent, see pp. 111–112.

tions. But the commission's findings could be enforced only by the courts, a costly and cumbersome procedure. The Interstate Commerce Act marked the beginning of the American public's acceptance of the principle of government intervention, but it did not provide effective regulation. For that the country had to await Theodore Roosevelt's Square Deal.

By the time Congress responded to the public clamor to "do something about the trusts" by passing the Sherman Antitrust Act in 1890, more than a dozen states had already attempted some kind of antitrust legislation aimed at making restraint of trade illegal. Big business, however, deftly countered these attempts at control by moving into more permissive states like New Jersey, where they quickly secured favorable laws. Henry Demarest Lloyd, perhaps the severest critic of monopoly, complained that Standard Oil, in its bid for special favors, had done everything to the legislature of Pennsylvania except refine it.

The Sherman Act was designed to address concerns like Lloyd's, but it failed to destroy monopolies. The bill that Ohio senator John Sherman introduced in the Senate was quickly rewritten by the Judiciary Committee before the full Senate passed it by a vote of 52 to 1. The House in turn passed the measure unanimously. The result was an honest, although confused, attempt to regulate the trusts. But the long list of unanswered questions involving enforcement of the act showed that big business still had ample leeway. The act declared illegal "unreasonable restraint" of trade—but what did "unreasonable" mean? What was "trade"? What constituted a monopoly? How much power over an industry spelled "control"? How, in short, was the federal government to proceed with the job of breaking up the trusts?

The Sherman Act left these questions to government attorneys and judges, who, at least during the administrations of Grover Cleveland (1885–89, 1893–97) and William McKinley (1897–1901), were not disposed to stop the merger movement. Labor unions, on the other hand, seemed to capitalists and their subservient allies in the government thoroughly objectionable conspiracies against trade. When Eugene Debs's American Railway Union, in its momentous battle with the Pullman Company in Chicago in 1894, refused to move the trains with Pullman cars, President Grover Cleveland's attorney general Richard Olney drew up an injunction declaring the union in restraint of trade and successfully prosecuted Debs for contempt of court in violating the injunction. On appeal, the Supreme Court upheld the application of the Sherman Act to labor unions.

During the first ten years following its passage in 1890, only eighteen cases were initiated under the Sherman Act. It was successfully applied in only two railroad cases, in 1897 and 1898. But in the crucial *E. C. Knight* case of 1895, a poorly drafted government brief allowed a conservative majority on the Supreme Court to declare the American Sugar Refining Company—a trust controlling 98 percent of the sugar industry—not technically in restraint of trade. On this occasion the waspish Olney spoke for big businessmen everywhere when he declared: "You will observe that the government has been defeated in the

Supreme Court on the trust question. I always supposed it would be, and have taken the responsibility of not prosecuting under a law I believed to be no good."

The early twentieth century would see some apparent improvement in antimonopolists' fortunes. Presidents Theodore Roosevelt, William Howard Taft, and Woodrow Wilson, together with Congress, would all pursue trustbusting with varying degrees of enthusiasm. In 1904, in the *Northern Securities* case, the Supreme Court would apply the Sherman Act to end J. P. Morgan's dream of merging the Northern Pacific, Union Pacific, and Burlington railroads. Yet presidential, congressional, and judicial efforts to curb monopoly coincided with an unprecedented surge in business consolidation.* On balance, the counterattack against big business failed.

## Rural Structure

Although individual American farmers, confronting a hostile nature and declining prices, were slow to acknowledge the change, their world too was being revolutionized by the forces of new technology, financial consolidation, and the corporate system. These new forces left their imprint on the nation's agriculture just as clearly as on its industry. Mechanical reapers, harrowers, spreaders and harvesters, steam plows, scientific agriculture—all these inventions and innovations spelled massive increases in productivity. And with increased production of staple crops—corn, wheat, sugar, cotton—came new systems of financing, organizing, and regulating farm work. A new arrangement of farm space, for example, began to alter the landscape of the Great Plains with rectilinear fencing, huge octagonal or circular barns, and towering grain elevators, symbols of the corporate revolution transforming the provinces just as skyscrapers and elevated trains marked its triumph in the metropolis. Huge twenty-five-ton steam engines crisscrossed the prairies of the trans-Mississippi West, dragging heavy disk plows, harrows, and harvesters. The largest of these steam-driven contraptions, encased in steel frames, could pull thirty plows and till a hundred acres in a single day. As early as 1880 some 80 percent of American wheat was being harvested by machine.

Soon new ideas for making farm work more systematic and scientific were being extended and applied to other aspects of farm management, such as improved storage facilities, double-entry bookkeeping, and better roads. By the opening of the new century American agriculture was already beginning to look like agribusiness. The rural equivalent of the industrial trust was the bonanza wheat farm, like the 55,000-acre spread owned by the California wheat baron Hugh J. Glenn, who employed an army of migratory Mexican and Chinese workers to plant and harvest his crop. Better known was the famous Dalyrumple operation in Cass County, North Dakota, incorporated by directors of the Northern Pacific Railroad and equipped with professional managers, 200 harrows, 125 seeders, 25 steam threshers, and 600 men to harvest the hundreds of

---

*See chapters 24 and 25.

thousands of bushels of wheat grown each year. Although there were increasing numbers of such large enterprises in the wheat belt by 1890, the bonanza farm was more a portent of the future than an immediate reality for hundreds of thousands of small and medium-sized farmers struggling, often blindly, within this new impersonal system to make a crop and turn a profit.

**Indian Defeat on the Last Frontier**    The key to agricultural surplus was the new land across the Mississippi River—the Great Plains stretching westward to the Rockies. In the 1870s and 1880s the Great Plains furnished a gigantic stage for the clash of four different civilizations, each with its own frontier, which was receding before the advance of corporate capitalism. First to be invaded and decimated were the native American tribes who formed the family of Plains Indians. In 1850 an estimated 250,000 Indians roamed the Great Plains, together with millions of buffalo that provided them with food, shelter, and clothing. The native American frontier on which an expanding capitalism imposed its system was first a killing ground and then a holding pen for those survivors deemed ready for assimilation. By 1885 the Indians' defeat and the destruction of the buffalo herds were virtually complete. Indian resistance was determined, fierce, and ultimately futile. The story of their defeat at the hands of mechanized white predation is a sordid one of broken promises, governmental corruption, and senseless massacre, already presaged by the slaughter at Sand Creek, Colorado, in 1864.*

With the end of the Civil War the whole of the Great Plains became a battlefield. For nearly two decades scarcely a year passed without significant clashes between United States soldiers, recently released from action in the South, and Indian warriors. With their hit-and-run tactics the native Americans were frequently victors in sharp skirmishes, for the United States army, dragging heavy supply trains, was unused to the ways of guerrilla war. For example, in 1866, when the army attempted to build and maintain a string of forts along the Bozeman Trail, which linked the North Platte with the recently opened mines in Montana, the Sioux fought them every step of the way, and in December wiped out a contingent of eighty soldiers.

More familiar is the legendary fate, ten years later, of George Armstrong Custer, the golden-haired boy-general of the Civil War, who had won several victories over the Southern Plains Indians. The discovery of gold in the Black Hills and the survey of the route of the recently chartered Northern Pacific Railroad brought whites swarming into ancestral lands that the Sioux considered the sacred dwelling place of their gods, and they fiercely resisted the advance of the white man. General Philip H. Sheridan, now the commander of the United States army in the West and Custer's superior officer, planned to force concessions of land from the Sioux by seizing the large Indian encampment on the Little Bighorn River (which the native Americans called Greasy Grass). Custer's

---

*See chapter 21.

column was part of a three-pronged attack, but when he reached the Indian encampment first, he ordered his men to charge without waiting to coordinate his attack with those of the other commanders. As Custer's soldiers advanced, Chief Low Dog called out to his warriors: "This is a good day to die; follow me." They did and within an hour on June 25, 1876, Custer and every one of his men had been killed.

But such short-lived Indian victories scarcely slowed the march of white settlers following in the tracks of the United States Army. Soon the Sioux were forced to give up their grazing lands to the horde of gold-seekers who rushed into the Black Hills in search of instant fortune. Farther west in Idaho, Chief Joseph of the peaceful Nez Percé, refusing to cede the tribal lands along the Salmon River, was forced to fight for them and, having lost, to undertake a heroic 1,500-mile retreat northeastward toward Canada. Chief Joseph and his depleted band of warriors were finally captured thirty miles from the border and confined to a reservation. In the Southwest it was much the same story with the last stand of Geronimo, a leader of the Chiricahua Apaches, who after a fifteen-year running war with white America was finally defeated and disarmed in 1886. Soon thereafter the Apache, Hopi, and Comanche were forced onto reservations in the Southwest; in the North the same fate befell the Sioux, Blackfeet, and Cheyenne.

In part the defeat of the Indians was the result of superior white force and fire power. The twenty-year war, it was estimated, cost $1 million and the lives of twenty-five soldiers for each native American warrior killed. In the long run, however, it was the completion of two transcontinental railroads—the Union Pacific and the Northern Pacific—that did more to defeat the Indians and destroy their way of life than all the military campaigns. The railroads and the towns strung along them disrupted traditional patterns of migration, and the slaughter of hundreds of thousands of buffalo intentionally stripped a nomadic people of their means of subsistence. Professional hunters boasted of killing two hundred animals a day, some for sport but many more for their hides, worth an average 25 cents apiece. Once more technology in the form of the railroad and repeating rifles made a design on the land described by one of the professional hunters:

> I have seen their bodies so thick after being skinned, that they would look like logs where a hurricane had passed through a forrest [sic]. . . . The buffalo would lie in this way until warm weather, drying up, and I have seen them piled fifty or sixty in a pile where a hunter had made his stand. As the skinner commenced on the edge, he would have to roll it out of the way to have room to skin the next, and when he finished they would be rolled up as thick as logs around a sawmill.

The final act in this saga of annihilation was played out at Wounded Knee in South Dakota on December 29, 1890. Two years earlier the Ghost-dance religion, promising a return to sacred ways and the recovery of ancestral lands, had spread rapidly among the remnants of the Sioux, but there had been no Indian raids on

**A Buffalo Hunter and Skinner at Work**
*This scene of a buffalo hunt in Taylor County, Texas, in the 1870s shows how the Indians' means of subsistence was eliminated.*

white settlements when the Seventh Cavalry—George Custer's old unit—fell upon the village at Wounded Knee and methodically slaughtered men, women, and children, some of whom they pursued for miles outside the village. American Horse, one of the surviving chiefs who returned to Wounded Knee following the massacre, reconstructed for the Commissioner of Indian Affairs the act of butchery by identifying the spots where bodies had lain from the track of blood:

> There was a woman with an infant in her arms who was killed as she almost touched the flag of truce, and the women and children of course were strewn all along the circular village until they were dispatched. Right near the flag of truce a mother was shot down with her infant; the child not knowing that its mother was dead was still nursing.

As the proud nations that had once dominated the West were defeated by white technology, driven from their lands by rapid settlement, and degraded by the white man's alcohol, reformers and humanitarians across the United States began to realize that they were witnessing what Helen Hunt Jackson called *A Century of Dishonor.* This was the title of her book, published in 1881, which

**End of the Ghost Dance, January 1, 1891**
*Burying the victims of the Wounded Knee Massacre.*

reviewed the history of the government's underhanded and brutal treatment of the native American. But how could this record of inhumanity be reversed? What should well-meaning Americans propose as a measure of justice? Most Americans, it was clear, were prepared to go on confining the Indians to smaller and smaller reservations on poorer and poorer lands. The only alternative that humanitarian reformers could suggest was to transform the Indians through assimilation into, they hoped, independent citizens by breaking up the tribes and teaching the individual native American to fend for himself in a world made over. This process of incorporation was accomplished in the Dawes Severalty Act of 1887, which provided for nominal citizenship at the cost of native customs, language, and religion; an inferior vocational training; dissolution of tribal units and division of Indian lands into individual 160-acre plots that could not be sold for twenty-five years. Of the 187 million acres constituting the original reservations, only a third of them went to settled Indian families; the remainder—usually the best land—fell to land-hungry white settlers and speculators.

Even well-intentioned humanitarians and supporters of Indian rights viewed assimilation or extermination as the only options. Thus President Merrill E. Gates of Amherst College in 1887 told the Lake Mohonk Conference of the

Friends of the Indians that the answer to the native American's plight was incorporation as rapidly as possible into the capitalist market system:

> To bring him out of savagery into citizenship we must make the Indian more intelligently selfish before we can make him unselfishly intelligent. We need to awaken in him wants.... Discontent with the teepee and the starving rations of the Indian camp in winter is needed to get the Indian out of the blanket and into trousers—and trousers with a pocket in them, and with a pocket that aches to be filled with dollars.

As Indian resistance collapsed, miners, cattlemen, and farmers poured into the West, vying for mastery of this new frontier of capitalism.

**The Indians' Successors**     Miners were the first white Americans since the antebellum fur trappers to exploit the West's natural wealth. In the years following the Civil War the miners' frontier moved rapidly eastward as nomadic California "placer" miners from the gold fields armed with pick, shovel, and sluicebox scrambled over the mountains into Colorado to work "the poor man's mines" as loners or partners. But with the discovery of rich deposits of lead, copper, and iron to compete with silver, the mining frontier spread rapidly northward into Idaho and Montana and southward as far as Arizona. In mining as in farming, technological improvements and innovative practices accelerated the growth of the industry: the use of mercury to separate the gold in huge retorts; steam-driven "stamp" mills to crush the ore; heavy machinery to sink deeper shafts; and the development of hydraulic mining with flumes and sluices, high-pressure hoses, and cannonlike nozzles that could skin a whole hillside in a day. Mining became more elaborate and expensive. "Quartz" mining, as it was called to distinguish it from surface "placer" mining, required ever-greater amounts of capital, which was readily forthcoming, first from regional investors like the "Comstock Millionaires" in San Francisco who cashed in and reinvested in the "Big Bonanza" at Comstock in the 1870s, and increasingly from eager eastern investors. Work grew specialized, and the new mining syndicates began to hire trained engineers to devise ways of getting the ore out more cheaply, accounting departments to balance the books and manage the payroll, and lawyers to keep an eye on compliant courts and legislatures. The more expensive mining technology became, the greater its destructive powers. Typical practices involved skimming the best and leaving the rest, moving out, and leaving behind open mine shafts and piles of tailings to pollute ground and surface water for over a century. By the mid-1880s the "Wild West" mining frontier with its boomtowns and vigilance committees, saloons, and brothels celebrated by Mark Twain in *Roughing It,* was disappearing into myth before the advance of mechanization and corporate managers.

The cattlemen's frontier had opened in the 1840s and 1850s when American settlers began drifting into Texas and the New Mexico territory, where they found a hardy breed of cattle, descendants of Mexican longhorns, that grazed on the open ranges. The early settlers promptly began to breed these cows for sale, branding the calves at yearly roundups and selecting the strongest steers for the long drive to the market. One of these pioneers, Richard King, owner of the famed King Ranch on the Gulf Coast south of Corpus Christi, built an empire that by 1870 consisted of 15,000 acres and employed 300 Mexican cowboys to handle 65,000 head of cattle, 10,000 horses, 7,000 sheep, and 8,000 goats. The early Texas cattle barons shipped their steers by cattle boat to regional markets in Galveston, New Orleans, and Mobile until the opening of the Great Plains by the railroads after the Civil War provided access to larger markets with links to eastern cities. In the beginning the huge herds were driven northward to Sedalia, Missouri, but when the Kansas Pacific Railroad reached Abilene, Kansas, in 1867, cattlemen discovered a shorter and better route to market. This was the Good-night-Loving Trail, the first of a series of legendary cattle trails to new railhead towns—first Abilene, then Ellsworth, Wichita, Dodge City, and Cheyenne. Rough, primitive, and dirty, these railhead towns nevertheless served a basic economic function by connecting the cattle industry to the growing national economy.

Between 1866 and 1884 more than 5 million head of cattle were driven north from Texas, but by this time the entire cattle industry was heading northward on a sweeping arc of semiarid land a thousand miles long paralleling the mining frontier. Already by 1882, 7.5 million cattle grazed on the High Plains, and the cattle industry was valued at $187 million, a big enough sum to entice greenhorns like the young Theodore Roosevelt to the Dakota hills and corporate investors from across the Atlantic. The Swan Land and Cattle Company, incorporated in Edinburgh, Scotland, claimed control of a strip of grazing land in Wyoming 130 miles long and 42 miles wide. Like manufacturing, farming, and mining, the cattle business soon declared itself big business even as ex-rancher Roosevelt nostalgically described a lost way of life for eastern tenderfeet:

> The great free ranches, with their barbarous, picturesque, and curiously fascinating surroundings, mark a primitive stage of existence as surely as do the great tracts of primeval forests, and like the latter must pass away before the onward march of our people. . . .

In the absence of effective federal law, the management of the cattle kingdom fell to local groups of the cattle barons themselves. The most powerful of these was the Wyoming Stock Growers Association, widely acknowledged as the "unchallenged sovereign" of its vast grazing domain. While they struggled to maintain high beef prices and discourage rustling, the stock growers associations did little to prevent overgrazing or to check the ensuing soil erosion. Beef prices peaked in 1882 and plunged soon thereafter. Then nature took revenge on a wasteful industry, imposing many of the same conditions that unchecked competition brought to industrialists in the East and forcing ranchers to make man-

**Wagon Train Resting in a Western Town**
*A common sight on the High Plains in the 1870s and 1880s.*

agerial adjustments that emphasized greater capital investment and further consolidation. A severe winter in 1885 was followed the next year by a brutal blizzard that wiped out nearly 75 percent of the herds. The infamous Blizzard of '88 signaled the end of open-range grazing as the cattle business turned to raising smaller herds, improving stocks, sinking wells, building windmills, and settling down to the practice of scientific management.

The farmers' frontier was the last to close. Development of the Great Plains reached its peak in the 1880s and 1890s, when the total amount of improved land in the United States more than doubled from 189 million to 414 million acres. Railroad agents, boasting of bonanza farms and abundant crops, and local chambers of commerce, promising everything from a cure-all for the sickly to husbands for young women, seized developmental control of the Great Plains through a land policy tailored to mythical yeoman farmers and a homestead law written for an earlier generation.

Settlers lured across the ninety-eighth meridian with the promise of bountiful crops found an environment different from any they had ever experienced. John Wesley Powell, the geologist and explorer of the High Plains, spent much of his career after the Civil War trying to tell Americans what it was like to farm land where fewer than twenty inches of rain fell annually. The choice, he explained, was between organizing what he called "this new industry of agriculture by irrigation" in the Arid Regions as a voluntary cooperative community of small

**John Wesley Powell's "Arid Regions and Invaders"**
*Wagon train crossing the High Plains in the 1870s.*

landholders, on the one hand, or by an outside monopoly of "a few great capitalists" on the other. Few of Powell's contemporaries, least of all the individualistic farmers and their representatives in Washington, heeded his predictions of an emerging exploitative agribusiness.

The peopling of the trans-Mississippi West began in earnest with the passage in 1862 of the Homestead Act, which granted 160 acres of public lands free to any citizen over twenty-one or the head of a family who agreed to reside on his land for five uninterrupted years. Or, alternatively, a homesteader could buy his land outright from the government for $1.25 an acre after living on it for six months. Between 1862 and the turn of the century about 400,000 families took up homesteads under this act, although the old Jacksonian dream of free land as a safety valve for industrial discontent never materialized. Not many urban artisans and mechanics possessed the money or the skills to move west and make a go of farming. The vast majority of the new settlers were men and women who were already living on the land but hoped to improve their lot by relocating. But even experience could not ensure success: fully two-thirds of all homesteaders before 1900 failed at the venture.

Nor did all settlers in the New West take up their lands under the Homestead Act. Most of them either purchased land directly from the government or bought it from the railroads, which had received handsome grants from state and national governments with which to finance their construction. Congress, for example, gave the Union Pacific and the Central Pacific ten square miles of public land for every mile of track laid in the states, and twice that amount for each mile built in the territories.

**Rural Discontents**  The farmers soon became part of the national market system emerging from the Civil War. For a few years immediately after the war they enjoyed flush times as a mounting demand for grain in eastern cities and the growing dependence of Great Britain on American harvests provided a booming market for staple crops.

Encouraged by rapidly rising prices, farmers in the Midwest and Plains states began to expand their operations to keep pace. Reaping machines and new and bigger plows were expensive, and small farmers, who were chronically short of funds, could not afford them. The future belonged to large producers who were willing and able to go into debt in order to buy the needed machinery. Now success depended not simply on the land and weather but on the workings of an international economic system. But the new national economy created severe problems for farmers, who suspected, often with good reason, that they were not getting their fair share of the growing national abundance.

Even in the prosperous years after the war, life on the Great Plains could be lonely and bleak. "I shall never forget the black prairie as I saw it in 1872, just after a prairie fire had swept over it," recalled one woman of her arrival at her new home in Adams County, Nebraska:

> To me, coming from southern Michigan with her clover fields, large houses and larger barns, trees, hills, and running streams, the vast stretches of black prairie never ending—no north, south, east, or west—dotted over with tiny unpainted houses—no I can't say barns—but shacks for a cow, and perhaps a yoke of oxen—that picture struck such a homesick feeling in my soul it took years to efface.

The Norwegian-born novelist Ole Rölvaag, drawing from immigrant accounts for his famous novel *Giants in the Earth* (1929), sketched the classic figure of the suffering pioneer woman in Beret, wife of Per Hansa, the vigorous and congenitally optimistic Norwegian immigrant who triumphs over droughts, blizzards, and plagues of grasshoppers in building a profitable farm. But Beret is driven mad by the solitude and the emptiness of life on a land without trees and neighbors. She falls victim to an overmastering fear: *"Something was about to go wrong."* Staring out across the flat plains that seem to have no horizon, she thinks: "Why, there isn't even a thing that one can *hide behind!"* Beret regains her sanity but at the price of religious fanaticism: she sends her hapless husband out into a blizzard to fetch the minister for a dying neighbor. He never returns, and his body is discovered the following spring in the shelter of a haystack, "his eyes set towards the west."

In an attempt to overcome the problems of loneliness and rural isolation, Oliver Hudson Kelley, who had lived in Massachusetts, Iowa, and Minnesota and traveled widely in the postwar South, founded the Patrons of Husbandry in 1867. In the beginning the Grange, as each local unit in Kelley's society was called, was primarily a social organization with a secret ritual, an educational program, and

**Nothing to Hide Behind**
*The Sod House Frontier, Miller, Dakota Territory, 1885.*

high hopes for communal solidarity. By the mid-1870s there were some 800,000 members of the Grange, most of them living in the Middle West and the South. The constitution of the Patrons of Husbandry prohibited members from engaging in politics under its name, but discussion of issues and candidates grew more heated as the economy cooled following the Panic of 1873.

Agrarian grievances were numerous and increasingly widespread. Farmers in Iowa, Nebraska, and Kansas complained bitterly that it took one bushel of corn to pay the shipping charges on another, a complaint echoed by wheat farmers in Minnesota and Dakota. Midwestern farmers, in particular, were incensed by the practices of the owners of the grain elevators who intentionally misgraded their grain, offering them only the lowest-grade price for superior produce. And everywhere in the West and South farmers complained about limited and expensive bank credit and the shortage of national banks in rural areas. Farmers in the Midwest were joined in their indictments of the railroads and grain elevator operators by shippers and businessmen who also objected to discriminatory rates and high-handed storage practices. Out of this shared discontent came state legislation, somewhat misleadingly called Granger laws because lawyers in Illinois, Wisconsin, Iowa, and Minnesota drafted legislation at the behest of businessmen, setting maximum charges for grain elevators and railroads and establishing state regulatory commissions with broad powers of enforcement. Farmers enthusiastically supported such laws even though they did not always initiate them. The Granger laws, however, were quickly challenged in the courts by the railroads and grain elevator companies, and soon were declared unconstitutional and modified or repealed. By 1880 it was clear that state regulation of interstate carriers and their facilities would not work.

After 1870 agricultural surpluses mounted steadily. Both a cause and a result of these surpluses were increasing crop specialization and the rise of single-crop agriculture—corn and wheat in the Midwest; wheat on the Plains; dairy products in the Old Northwest; and cotton in the South and Southwest. A rising demand for staples acted much like the growing demand for industrial goods in the nation's cities. In fact, the two developments were related. As American staples flooded Europe, prices for foodstuffs fell sharply there and land prices collapsed. The agricultural depression in Europe, beginning in the 1870s, drove millions of peasants and small farmers out of the countryside and into seaports, the first stopping point en route to American cities. In both Europe and America, cheaper food hastened industrial transformation. In the United States, however, farmers paid a large part of the price for this transformation by ensuring the nation a favorable balance of trade with mass exports of staple crops at declining prices. Nor could the individual farmer effectively cut production but, instead, was driven to produce even more in an already glutted market simply to get his share. Overproduction posed a conundrum the average farmer could not solve.

On the one hand the American farmer could consider the move from subsistence farming to specialized commercial farming as progress toward a higher standard of living. But this advantage was soon offset by the staple-crop farmer's suspicions that he had become the prisoner of the market, locked into a price structure from which there was no ready means of escape. With the onset of world agricultural depression in the 1870s, the price curve for staple crops plummeted, and the farmer's income slid with it. Wheat fell from $1.19 a bushel in 1881 to a low of 49 cents in 1894. Corn slipped in these same depression years from 63 cents a bushel to 18 cents. Buying in a market that was protected by tariffs, and selling in an unprotected market, the staple-crop farmer saw himself as the victim of an absurd situation: he was forced to grow more and more in order to earn less and less. Why, he asked himself, as the producer of the largest share of the nation's abundance, should he sink deeper into the mire each year? A Kansas farmer in 1891 summed up these feelings of betrayal:

> At the age of 52 years, after a long life of toil, economy, and self-denial, I find myself and family paupers. With hundreds of hogs, scores of good horses, and a farm that rewarded the toil of our hands with 16,000 bushels of golden corn we are poorer by many dollars than we were years ago. What once seemed like a neat little fortune and a house of refuge for our declining years, by a few turns of the monopolistic crank has been rendered valueless.

Conditions for staple-crop farmers were worst in the South, where a cotton monoculture fastened on the region an exploitative system of tenancy and sharecropping as a replacement for the antebellum plantation. Southern planters emerged from the Civil War with their landholdings intact but confronting an acute shortage of capital and credit. The freedmen, for their part, refused to work under the old gang system and preferred the promise of economic independence, however illusory. In agreeing to provide credit and "furnishings" at necessarily high but sometimes exorbitant rates, planters and country merchants were simply taking the advice of a veteran planter who urged: "Let each family work by itself, in separate fields or farms. This is much easier and I think far better than the old plantation style of all working together."

Sharecropping, tenancy, and crop liens (mortgages) formed interlocking parts of yet another system, this one constructed like an economic ladder with each of the rungs supporting a victim of exploitation. On the bottom rung stood the landless wage laborer with neither mule nor harness but standing ready to sell his labor for the subsistence wage paid him once he had made the owner's crop. Ranged on the intermediate rungs were the "croppers" working for varying shares of the cotton crop, usually from a third to a half depending on the ownership of a mule. A step higher on the ascending ladder came the full-fledged tenant, who rented the land outright for a sizable part of his crop. On the top rungs stood the planter and the furnishing merchant (often the same person), who supplied land, tools, seed, and furnishing at prohibitive rates of interest sometimes exceeding 40 percent.

Designed originally for the freedmen, sharecropping spread quickly across racial barriers so that by 1900 two-thirds of the share tenant farmers in the South were white. The system, which survived until World War II, devastated lives as well as the land by confining the exploited cropper—as it were—in a debtor's prison from which there was no escape. His debts mounted from one year to the next. He lacked all incentive to care for land that was not his own. Thrift was impossible; frequently he could not even read the contract that bound him. As one observer explained in describing how the malevolent system worked: "The debts of the people...have been no small factor in bringing about the overproduction of the great staple crop. Men in debt want money. Farmers know that cotton is the only crop that will bring in money...cotton brings money, and money pays debts. This will deliver the man from his trouble. Thus reasons the average farmer."

**The Alliance and Populism**

Independent farmers in the Midwest and Great Plains suddenly realized that, like their city cousins, they too were businessmen but that their business was always unpredictable and sometimes hazardous. To increase their output and cut their costs many staple-crop farmers borrowed heavily to buy more land, improve their farms, and purchase machinery—only to find themselves saddled with a crushing load of mortgage payments made all the heavier by falling prices and high interest rates. When the farmer hunted for money to renew his loan or make a payment, he was told by local bankers that credit was scarce because the pipeline of capital from the East had been turned off. Farmers reasoned that tight money lay at the root of their troubles: the rising value of the dollar could be traced directly to the decline in the actual number of dollars in circulation after the Civil War. The dollar, like the farmer himself, was being overworked. Bankers and eastern creditors could assure him that his problem was overproduction, but he knew it was "underconsumption" and cursed the restrictionist "gold bugs" and their minions on Wall Street.

Then, in 1887, a series of drought years and poor harvests tumbled the farmers into a deep agricultural depression. Local mortgage companies folded; interest rates soared; foreclosures mushroomed. The targets of the farmers' resentment were local bankers and the railroads, but increasingly they blamed a distant "price-fixing plutocracy"—which, they were sure, had rigged the system against them. "There are three great crops raised in Nebraska," a disgruntled small-town editor complained in 1889. "One is a crop of corn, one a crop of freight rates, and one a crop of interest. One is produced by farmers who by their sweat and toil farm the land. The other two are produced by men who sit in their offices and behind their bank counters and farm the farmers." Then there were the greedy trusts—the barbed wire trust and the plow trust in the West, the cottonseed oil trust and the jutebagging trust in the South—all of them gouging the small independent farmer. And behind all these oppressors stood state and federal governments that appeared to do their bidding. At the height of the agrarian distress in 1889, the still-unknown but aspiring writer Hamlin Garland found his neighbors caught up in a social crisis and engaged "in a sullen rebellion against government and against God":

> Every house I visited had its individual message of sordid struggle and half-hidden despair. . . . All the gilding of farm life melted away. The hard and bitter realities came back upon me in a flood. Nature was as bountiful as ever . . . but no splendor of cloud, no grace of sunset, could conceal the poverty of these people; on the contrary, they brought out, with a more intolerable poignancy, the gracelessness of these homes, and the sordid quality of the mechanical routine of these lives. I perceived bountiful youth becoming bowed and bent.

The only answer, farmers and their advocates like Garland realized, was to organize to fight the bankers, the railroads, and the trusts—to wrest control of government away from the plutocracy and return it to the people. The 1880s saw the rapid growth of farm organizations in both the South and the West. The most powerful of them was the National Farmers Alliance and Industrial Union, or the Southern Alliance as it came to be called, which was originally formed in Texas in the late 1870s but which, during a decade of recruitment, education, and experimentation, had been fashioned into a mass democratic movement made more broadly reformist than the faltering Grange largely because of the vision and organizational genius of Dr. Charles W. Macune. By 1889 Macune had succeeded in uniting a group of regional societies into a cooperative crusade consisting of 3 million white farmers in the South and another 1.2 million black members organized separately as the National Colored Farmers Alliance. Meanwhile, in the West, hard-pressed farmers in Kansas, Iowa, and Nebraska also began to seek safety in numbers as early as 1880, but a six-year spell of good weather and bountiful crops dampened their organizational ardor until 1887, when another cycle of drought slashed yields and tipped the entire trans-Mississippi West into a prolonged depression. Two years later, in 1889, the Northern Alliance, as the federated state groups were called, merged with the larger and more adventurous Southern Alliance as farmers in both regions prepared to enter the political arena and challenge an unresponsive two-party system in the midterm elections of 1890. Here was the beginning of the Populist revolt that swept across agrarian America in the next six years.

In joining the Alliance movement and the People's party that grew out of it, farmers were responding to the same need for order and system that was driving American business toward consolidation and cooperation. But unlike their counterparts in business and industry the farmers professed a deep faith in the folk—the common people living in rural and small-town America and organizing in their several communities to build a program of mutuality and cooperation. American farmers' basic insight throughout the nineteenth century was the moral primacy of agriculture over all other ways of life. This enduring view was stated most eloquently by William Jennings Bryan in his famous "Cross of Gold" speech at the Democratic party convention in 1896. "You come to us and tell us that the great cities are in favor of the gold standard," Bryan thundered. "We reply that the great cities rest upon our broad and fertile prairies. Burn down your cities and leave our farms and your cities will spring up again as if by magic; but destroy our farms and grass will grow in the streets of every city in the country." Bryan confirmed the average farmer's deep-seated belief, borne out by the record, that the yeoman farmer had indeed built America—clearing and cultivating the land, pioneering in lonely isolation, raising the foodstuffs, feeding his own people and other people throughout the world, and laying the material base on which a modern industrial society now rested. Despite the damage methodically done to it, the land remained foremost in the American moral imagination. "On the land we are born, from it we live, to it we return again—children of the soil as truly as is the blade of grass or the flower of the field," Henry George wrote. And his message reached millions of already converted farmers who now sought government endorsement of their faith.

The farmers' fervent belief in an agrarian way of life was matched by an acute sense of their immediate practical needs and the role of the federal government in meeting them. Farmers were following the same route to effective organization taken by their business and industrial counterparts. As a first step they established member-financed Alliance stores and cooperatives, which offered discounts and provided affordable credit. In acknowledging their need for cooperatives farmers were responding to the impulse that was also driving businessmen to experiment in risk-pooling and to design new marketing and bargaining instruments. The pioneer Alliance cooperatives, however, were weakened by inadequate financing and falling staple-crop prices. It quickly became clear to farmers in both the South and the West that voluntary cooperatives, which lacked federal funding, were not enough; they needed federal support for a concerted plan for limiting risk and ensuring price stability. That plan, designed by Macune, was the "subtreasury system" in which the federal government would provide warehouses and elevators to hold the farmers' crops for the best price, meanwhile issuing them certificates of credit worth up to 80 percent of the crop. For a very modest rate of interest the average farmer would obtain cheap credit for fertilizer, machinery, and furnishings, together with government help in marketing his crop. The subtreasury system, quickly accepted by the Populists, was designed to eliminate the middleman in his various roles as furnishing merchant, local banker, mortgage company manager, and eastern investment-house promoter, all of whom joined forces to defeat the plan.

Out of this Alliance proposal for government-subsidized cooperation came the grassroots politics of Populism. Populism was the last stand of the republican producerist army against advancing corporate capitalism. The Populist creed consisted of the time-honored values and principles that marked workingmen's societies and land-reform leagues in the Age of Jackson. These made a blend of secular prescriptions and Christian ethics that defined a moral economy and a system of justice by making the distinction between the many who lived by the sweat of their brows and the selfish few who knew not the dignity of labor. The real workers of the world, in the view of the farmers and urban workingmen who voted the Populist ticket, were those men and women who, whether in the field or in the factory, actually built the nation, while the nonproducers "with no knowledge of frugality and without legitimate skill achieve a fortune in a day" and then look on in idleness and luxury. The true producers, Populists insisted, were responding to the universal instinct of workmanship with its spiritual as well as material rewards. Every citizen had a God-given right to a job, and held a just claim on society to provide one. Meaningful work, in the Populist creed, meant an entitlement to a birthright stake in a system that guaranteed the individual "the fruits of his toil." Labor came first in the providential scheme of things, and capital, if earned in reasonable amounts, constituted the proper reward for hard work. In a just economic system the natural and proper workings of the market ensured a balance between energy expended and wealth acquired. It was only when this equilibrium was upset by greed or privilege that the natural system broke down and producers suffered. Then it fell to the "plain people" of the country to enter politics and set matters right. "I believe that it is not God's fault that we are in this bad condition," the Populist leader Leonidas Polk told his listeners. "Congress could give us a bill in forty-eight hours that would relieve us, but Wall Street says nay." The task, then, was to rescue Congress from the "bold and aggressive plutocracy" that had usurped power and used it as a policeman "to enforce its insolent decrees."

Populists wanted the federal government to stand sponsor to their producerist way of life by encouraging invention, stimulating industry and cooperation, guaranteeing private property, and only occasionally stepping in to help the little man by redressing the political and economic balance in his favor. They explained their second-class status under the rule of the Money Power by resorting to a highly charged moral language as old as the American Revolution. Government, they asserted, had fallen prey to the "plutocracy" that filled public offices with "corrupt rulers" whose chief business was "robbing the honest yeomanry." These "money Kings" monopolized the "bounties of nature" once reserved by "Divine Providence" for the "sons of toil." Thus, while the "idle rich" continued to hoard their "blood money," the poor people in field and factory were being reduced to "servitude." Soon all American society would stand fatally divided between "masters and slaves."

When the cheering delegates of the People's party put forward their presidential candidate in the election of 1892, they were determined to save not simply the country's farmers but industrial workers and the whole nation from impending moral as well as material ruin. Populism declared itself a redemptive grassroots movement of the American folk, resolved to take their fellow citizens along an alternative route to the just society across the roadblocks put in their path by a selfish minority of plutocrats. "A vast conspiracy against mankind has been organized on two continents and is taking possession of the world," the Populist platform of 1892 declared. "If not met and overthrown at once, it forebodes terrible social convulsions, the destruction of civilization, or the establishment of an absolute despotism." With the coming of Populism in the 1890s, the American farmers' crusade organized by the Grangers twenty years earlier became a political war.

## Workers and the Challenge of Organization

Of all the groups caught up in the late-nineteenth-century American economic revolution, industrial workers depended least on statistics to confirm what they already knew: that their rewards for tending the national industrial machine hardly matched their services. Real wages rose 25 percent in the 1880s, but in 1882 male Fall River textile workers could not support their families unless their wives also worked. As late as the turn of the century the workweek for the average worker was a little less than sixty hours, and the average wage for skilled workers was 20 cents an hour—and only half that amount for unskilled workers. Annual wages for most factory workers in 1900 came to an average of $400 to $500, from which a working family saved an average $30 per year. Nearly half the remainder went for food, another quarter for rent, and the balance for fuel, light, and clothing. There was not much left for luxuries.

Earnings for industrial workers continued to go up 37 percent between 1890 and 1914, but between 1897 and 1914 the cost of living climbed 39 percent. Despite growing national wealth, most American workers managed on the slimmest of margins. Their share of the pie, although larger than it had been a half-century earlier, was still comparatively small. The richest tenth of the population received 33.9 percent of the nation's income; the poorest tenth collected 3.4 percent. The rich were certainly getting richer, while American workers, if not absolutely poorer, were still not enjoying much of the wealth they were busy creating.

But despite these growing disparities in wealth between the well-to-do and the workers, the paramount considerations for industrial laborers were the conditions under which they were forced to work and the routines that the new impersonal system was pressing on them. At best, factory work was exhausting, repetitious, and boring—ten hours a day, for example, standing before a noisy mechanical loom in the half-light of an ill-ventilated factory. A mule spinner in one of New England's many cotton mills estimated that tending the four "stretches" made by his four "long mules" each minute meant walking some thirty miles a day. Children provided a pool of cheap, if inefficient, labor for the region's cotton and woolen mills, tying broken threads and scrambling in and out of the machinery despite state child labor laws. "Poor, puny, weak little children," complained a female spinner in one of Rhode Island's mills, "are kept at work the entire year without intermission of even a month for schooling. The overseers are to them not over kind and sometimes do not hesitate to make them perform more work than the miserable little wretched beings possibly can." The effect of the 1885 Rhode Island ten-hour law in giving her more free time was explained with unintentional irony by an "Irish widow" to a state factory inspector:

> Why, the extra quarter hour at noon gives me time to mix my bread; an' then when I comes home at night at six o'clock, it is ready to be put in the pans, an' I can do that while Katie sets the table; an' after supper, an' the dishes are washed, I can bake; an' then I am through an' ready to go to bed, mebbe, afore it's quite nine o'clock. Oh, it's splendid, the best thing as ever 'appened.

**Making Steel**
*Work in the steel mills was hot, dirty, and dangerous.*

Industrial labor was harsh, closely supervised, and often punitive in its sanctions: fines, docked pay, time clocks, bullying bosses and distant superintendents, blacklists and yellow-dog contracts forbidding workers to join a union— all combined to make mills and factories seem like prisons from which tired men and women contrived to escape at the end of the day. For the common unskilled laborer on the docks, a construction site, or a steel mill, work was not only backbreaking but extremely dangerous. The steel plant at Homestead shut down just twice a year, running "straight out" around the clock the rest of the time with steelworkers taking the swing shift—an uninterrupted twenty-four hours—every other week. Hamlin Garland, visiting Homestead, saw "pits gaping like the mouth of hell and ovens emitting a terrible heat, with grimy men filling and lining them. One man jumps down, and works desperately for a few minutes, and is then pulled up exhausted. Another immediately takes his place...." Under such conditions accidents were common and frequently fatal. In a single year in Pittsburgh's iron and steel mills there were 195 fatalities—22 from hot metal explosions, 10 from rolling accidents, and 5 from asphyxiation.

**Workers Organize**    For a number of reasons workers were slower to organize than businessmen or farmers. In the first place, most business leaders were implacably opposed to unions and spared no efforts to prevent their formation or break them up. With the help of lobbyists and their trade associations, industrialists were able to prevail on governors of states to send in troops nearly five hundred times between 1875 and 1910 to quell what middle-class Americans persisted in calling "labor unrest." Often direct recourse to state or federal courts was enough to prevent or break strikes. Then there was the huge diversity of the work force and the barriers of ethnicity and race that militated against feelings of labor solidarity. In the decade after the Civil War some 3.5 million immigrants, most of them from northern Europe, poured into this country and formed a vast labor pool in the industrial cities. By 1880, 87 percent of the inhabitants of Chicago, 84 percent of those in Detroit and Milwaukee, and 80 percent of those in New York and Cleveland were immigrants or the children of immigrants. Organizing such a diverse population speaking dozens of different languages and possessing a wide variety of skills proved a formidable task. Native-born Americans tended to hold the skilled jobs; immigrants found themselves relegated to the growing ranks of unskilled or semiskilled workers. Craft unions—the "aristocracy" of labor—were apt to be exclusive, shutting out women, blacks, and menial workers from their organizations. Then too the workplace in industrial America was growing in size and impersonality. Machines replaced hand tools. Older artisans and master craftsmen saw their jobs disappear.

Despite these mounting odds against them, workers attempted in increasing numbers to unionize on a national scale. One early effort was William Sylvis's National Labor Union, which lasted only from 1866 to the Panic of 1873.* Only

---

*See chapter 21, p. 54.

slightly more successful in the immediate postwar years was the Knights of Labor, founded in 1869. Its ranks were also decimated by the depression of the 1870s, and not until 1879, with the election of Terence V. Powderly as General Master Workman, did the union acquire a truly national spokesman. Powderly, mercurial, dictatorial, and an ineffectual organizer, was a teetotaling labor evangelist who saw himself first and foremost as a teacher of the toiling masses in the ways of respectability and cooperation with employers. "Our order," he explained again and again to restive members of local assemblies of the Knights, "is above politics." The national leadership also opposed strikes. "Not once," he recalled proudly, "during my fourteen years in office of Grand Master Workman did I order a strike." It was the decisions of hundreds of local assemblies in the Great Upheaval of the mid-1880s to strike, even without the support of the national leadership, that accounted for the meteoric rise of the Knights of Labor, whose membership in 1886 topped three-quarters of a million.

Still, only a tiny fraction of the nation's work force belonged to any union before 1880. Some workers turned instinctively to politics and attempted to organize an independent political party pledged to support its demands for paper money and the free coinage of silver, an eight-hour day, and the exclusion of Chinese immigrants. This was the Greenback, or National Independent, party, organized in 1874, which fielded a presidential candidate in 1876 and whose congressional candidates two years later won more than a million votes. Greenbackers, however, enjoyed little success in achieving their goal of economic security.

Other workers in the throes of hard times in the 1870s turned to direct action—terrorism and the strike. In the anthracite coal fields of western Pennsylvania the so-called Molly Maguires, a secret cabal that controlled the Irish fraternal society, the Ancient Order of Hibernians, were accused and on flimsy evidence convicted of launching a crime wave against the coal bosses and their superintendents. Twenty-four Mollies were swiftly convicted and hanged, the last of them in 1878, and violence in the coal field subsided.

Even more frightening to middle-class Americans was the Great Railroad Strike of 1877, a spontaneous labor protest in the depths of a punishing economic depression. The Panic of 1873, triggered by the collapse of the financial firm of Jay Cooke, tipped the country into a six-year depression. Between 1873 and 1879 the national economy shrank by one-third. Thousands of workers lost their jobs, and unemployment in cities like New York ran as high as 33 percent. Caught in an unprecedented economic squeeze and faced with unresponsive politicians, industrial workers abandoned their newly formed unions in droves. In New York City, for example, union membership plummeted from 45,000 in 1873 to 5,000 in 1877.

The massive railroad strike that paralyzed business and struck terror into the hearts of American businessmen began in the small railhead town of Martinsburg, West Virginia, where workers learned of sharp wage cuts ordered by management and in retaliation stopped all trains and shut down the yards. When the local police failed to get the trains rolling again, troops were called in. Then a switchman attempting to derail a cattle train was shot and killed by the militia, and a crowd that had gathered to protest was dispersed with force. The incident at Martinsburg was just the beginning of a week of violence that spread from one major city to another, as wage cuts and layoffs were met by angry workers bent on sabotage and looting. In Baltimore, a regiment dispatched to protect Baltimore and Ohio Railroad property retreated before a hail of rocks, while the rest of the militia took refuge in a local armory, then broke out, panicked, and fired into the crowd, killing ten onlookers. In Pittsburgh the militia proved wholly unreliable until reinforcements from Philadelphia managed to clear a railroad crossing by killing twenty workers. Fighting back, strikers burned railroad yards, overturned cars, looted storehouses, and penned up the soldiers in a roundhouse into which they continued to pour rifle fire until they were finally driven off. In Buffalo, another mob, infuriated by the wanton killing of eleven of its members, tore up track and broke into an arsenal for the guns with which to defend themselves. In Chicago, striking switchmen roamed through the shops calling out their comrades and moving on to the stockyards and the packinghouses for support. Suddenly the city came to a standstill, and for the first time in American history middle-class citizens all over the country understood the power of workers to disrupt their lives.

American businessmen and industrialists quickly responded to these perceived threats to their welfare in what they continued to call the "labor problem" by resorting to corrective and punitive action, which only made relations with their workers worse. State legislatures, prodded by the business community, passed conspiracy laws designed to break up unions and prevent strikes. The courts, both state and federal, could be relied on to narrow the rights of workers to protest and organize in their own defense. State militias, which had proved unreliable in the Great Railroad Strike, were reorganized and given training in riot control. Thus, when another economic recession in the mid-1880s drove industrial workers in all sections of the country to strike in an attempt to recoup lost wages and regain control of working conditions, their attempts were met with the determined resistance of management backed now by a resentful middle-class public increasingly disposed to identify labor protest with the presence of "foreigners" and to denounce both as unpatriotic. The secretary of the Southern Industrial Convention, a trade association representing heavy industry in the South, spoke for an aroused consuming public in denouncing labor unions as "the greatest menace to this government that exists. . . . [A] law should be passed that would make it justifiable homicide for any killing that occurred in defense of any lawful occupation." Thus, when the Haymarket Square Riot occurred in May 1886, there were millions of Americans prepared to agree with the advocates of severe repression.

A few minutes after ten o'clock on the night of May 4, 1886, in Chicago's Haymarket Square, a crowd of some 2,000 workingmen, many of them members of a small German-speaking anarchist contingent, were listening to a denunciation of police brutality in dispersing a demonstration the day before at the

McCormick Harvester Company, when 180 uniformed policemen came rushing out of a nearby police station intent on breaking up the protest. Suddenly from out of nowhere a dynamite bomb came spiraling; it exploded, killing one policeman instantly and wounding sixty others, eight of whom subsequently died along with another eight onlookers. Three weeks later eight of the anarchists—the presumed ringleaders of a "conspiracy"—were charged with sixty-nine counts as accessories before the fact and with general conspiracy to murder. The verdict at the trial, presided over by the bitterly prejudiced Judge Joseph E. Gary, was a foregone conclusion: all eight defenders were found guilty, and within eighteen months four of them had been hanged, a fifth had committed suicide in his jail cell, and the remaining three were serving long sentences in the penitentiary (until they were pardoned in 1893 by Governor John P. Altgeld).

Overnight the shock waves of the Haymarket bombing went rolling across the country as an outraged middle-class public denounced the anarchist workers as "vipers" and "curs," "hyenas" and "serpents." "The only good anarchist is a dead anarchist," a Cincinnati newspaper declared. Haymarket broke the force of direct labor resistance to the new industrial order for nearly a decade. "A single bomb," wrote Samuel Gompers, the organizer of the fledgling American Federation of Labor, "had demolished the eight-hour movement."

Native-born Americans in the so-called comfortable classes, although they were quite wrong in attributing working-class agitation to recently arrived immigrants, nevertheless correctly noted the predominance of the new arrivals in the ranks of the nation's unskilled labor force. Throughout the post–Civil War decades the proportion of immigrants tending machines and performing unskilled tasks in the heavy industries mounted steadily. Where only one in three workers immediately after the Civil War was foreign-born, by the first decade of the new century four out of five steelworkers in Pittsburgh had come from southern or eastern Europe and were entering the work force at the bottom. Wages dipped from $22 a week for native-born white skilled workers to just half that for unskilled "Slavs," a broad category that covered Magyars and Italians, as well as such actual Slavic peoples as Slovaks, Croats, and Russians. Separation by ethnic origin, race, religion, or color divided workers and their families into tight urban enclaves and neighborhoods, each with its own churches, schools, and saloons—French Canadians on the floodplains of New England's mill cities, Slovaks on the cinder piles of Pennsylvania steel towns, African-Americans south of Chicago's teeming stockyards. The urban reformer Jacob Riis (himself Danish-born) described the social surface of New York's Lower East Side as having "more stripes than the skin of a zebra, and more colors than any rainbow." Ethnic neighborhoods were little cities within cities, havens from the impersonality and animosity of the outside world.

Work was being rapidly deskilled by the new forces of technology and new systems of industrial management as machine labor replaced skilled hand work and operatives found themselves at the mercy of the machines they tended. An older artisanal culture of skilled craftsmen who once considered themselves the backbone of America was being shattered by the systematic destruction of their skills and the division of their work routines by efficiency-minded managers. Still, friendship on the shop floor sometimes made work bearable and communication across language barriers possible, as a native-born "greenhorn" from the mid-western countryside learned on his first day on the floor of a steel mill:

> When I started in I figured I'd keep going as long as I could and loaf after I was played out. First the little Italian boy tapped me on the shoulder and advised, "Lotsa time! Take easy!" I slowed down a notch or two. A little later the Russian, wiping off the sweat as he sat for a moment on a pile of bricks, cautioned: "You keel yourself. Twelve hours long time." Finally, after every one had remonstrated, I got down to a proper gait—so you'd have to sight by a post to see if I was moving. But at that I guess they knew better than I—I'm certainly tired enough as it is.

With the huge increase in industrial scale that accompanied the shift from village workshop to urban factory came a new system of organization similar to that being applied to staple-crop agriculture and business and finance by the forces of consolidation and concentration. This new industrial system—impersonal, bureaucratic, mechanized—was designed to run according to the principles of *hierarchy*, which capitalists were beginning to recognize as the key to stable and efficient large-scale industrial operations. Hierarchy built a huge pyramid of productive forces with management at the apex and descending layers of middle managers and superintendents, shop-floor supervisors, foremen, and section bosses, all of them resting on a wide base of unskilled workers. Here, first in the imagination of planners and increasingly in actual fact, was an industrial army whose workings Edward Bellamy described in his utopian novel *Looking Backward* (1888): a gigantic national work force organized along military lines for increased productivity and efficiency with orders passed down the chain of command from the general staff at the top to the lowliest industrial recruit. More a goal than a reality until the twentieth century, this regimen recommended by pioneer scientific managers like Frederick Winslow Taylor promised to make American workers more efficient by fixing "scientifically" what managers considered "an honest day's work" performed by a "first-class man." Scientific management offered business leaders the hope of making the worker over into a human machine whose efficiency could be measured with a stopwatch, and Taylor himself described the ideal industrialist as a supervisor who insists on and gets from his workers discipline, obedience, proper motivation, and hard work. "If a man won't do right, *make* him," he urged.

Here was the view, still on the distant horizon in 1900, of the factory as a moral gymnasium complete with a "military system" to encourage what Taylor called "actual hard work" performed "under careful and constant supervision." In spelling out its logic for the new managers of the industrial work routine, Taylor insisted:

It is only through *enforced* standardization of methods, *enforced* adoption of the best implements and working conditions, and *enforced* cooperation that this faster work can be assured. And the duty of enforcing the adoption of standards and enforcing this cooperation rests with *management* alone.

Even partial implementation of scientific efficiency awaited the twentieth century and the further consolidation of big business, and in the meantime the battle between management and their workers for control of the shop floor continued to rage.

Many businessmen's attitude toward their "labor supply" before 1900 was likely to be that of the steelmaker who admitted to a congressional committee that "if I wanted boiler iron I would go out on the market and buy where I could get it the cheapest, and if I wanted to employ men I would do the same thing." The views of independent shop owners were often more pronounced. "While you are in my workshop," one manufacturer told his workers, "you must conform to my rules.... You must not attempt to take the control of the workshop out of my hands." As for American workers' well-known preference for "lager and leisure," Joseph Medill, publisher of the Chicago *Tribune,* warned his readers that the indulgence of the workers must be stopped by teaching them that their "impecunious condition" was the direct result of their "improvidence and misdirected efforts.... The wage-classes cannot support in idleness a quarter of a million saloon keepers...and at the same time hope to prosper themselves."

To correct such benighted attitudes Terence V. Powderly, who was elected president of the Knights of Labor in 1879, proposed a mass educational campaign to hasten the arrival of the "cooperative commonwealth" when American workingmen and women and their bosses would arbitrate their differences and securely establish the "nobility of toil." The Knights inherited their artisanal faith and consensual politics from the original workingmen's parties in Jacksonian America: a solid grounding in republican institutions; firm belief in the centrality of the local community; the cultivation of a hearty "manliness"; and the sustaining powers of home and hearth. These time-honored values of skilled craftsmen were now being threatened by the impersonality and the exploitation of the new industrial system, and the Knights were determined to organize in self-defense. Their organizational strategies in many cases looked forward rather than backward—to internal coordination among different groups of workers, common presentation of demands, shop committees of representatives from all trades in a mill or plant, and executive boards to handle grievances. Far from seeking to overthrow capitalism, as various groups of American socialists hoped to do after 1880, the Knights of Labor wanted simply to prevent "wage slavery" and to secure "personal dignity" within a more equitably arranged capitalist system. Theirs was a program of mass organization of all workers, education, voluntary cooperation, arbitration with employers, and, only as a last resort, moderate economic sanctions. The Knights shared with the Farmers Alliance and the Populists, with whom they made common cause and fashioned a movement culture, a moral economy that rewarded hard work and honest intentions. At the center of this collective dream stood the "new commonwealth" in which mere wealth would give way to standards of honorable work. In appealing to solidarity across class and occupational lines and in assigning government a limited mediational role, the Knights called for moderate production and equitable distribution of wealth, and an ultimate reliance on the community in which so many of its members lived, worked, and organized their local assemblies for fellowship as well as protection.

Matching the Knights of Labor in their sudden rise to prominence in the 1880s and 1890s were the Working Girls Clubs, which managed to outlive their male counterparts. In 1881 the first clubs were organized when women were inducted into the Knights as members. Women workers in the carpet, box, jute, and cigarette factories in the Northeast provided most of the original membership of the clubs, whose organization and growth were encouraged by wealthy philanthropists like Grace Dodge and Josephine Shaw Lowell. Like the local assemblies of the Knights of Labor, the Working Girls Clubs were social as well as labor organizations, and they offered their members classes in dressmaking, sewing, typing, and physical culture, and held evening discussions at which, as one participant explained, "we learn to speak quickly and think readily." The "master workman" who headed Chicago's 50,000-member District 24 was Elizabeth Rodgers, wife of an iron molder and mother of ten children. Like their brother Knights, too, these women sought "cooperation, self-government, self-support" and celebrated a "womanliness" that complemented the Knights' invocation of manly virtue. An anonymous poem in their *Journal of United Labor* put the case for all women who worked:

> *We ask not your pity, we charity scorn,*
> *We ask but the rights to which we were born,*
> *For the flag of freedom has waved o'er the land,*
> *We justice and equality claim and demand.*
> *Then strive for your rights, O sisters dear,*
> *And ever remember in your own sphere,*
> *You may aid the cause of all mankind*
> *And be the true woman that God designed.*

The Knights of Labor's educational campaign was aimed at converting employers to acceptance of arbitration and voluntary cooperation and at convincing their membership of the "folly of strikes." But education convinced neither businessmen, who considered union leaders as bad as Civil War secessionists, nor the local assemblies across the country, which began to retaliate against industrial management's attempt to wrest control of hours and wages away from them. With or without union help, workers began to turn to the strike in the mid-1880s as their chief defensive weapon against their employers. There were 477 work stoppages in 1881, nearly 2,000 a decade later, and more than 1,800 at the turn of the century. Strikes were usually responses to sharp wage cuts. The

Great Railroad Strike of 1877, the so-called Great Upheaval on Jay Gould's Southwestern system in 1886, and the rash of railroad strikes culminating in the Pullman Strike of 1894 were all triggered by management's determination to slash wages. The pattern was the same in nearly every industry: strikes followed employers' attempts to increase hours by "grinding" or "driving" workers beyond agreed-on limits or, more frequently, to cut wages during recessions. It was the policy of retaliatory strikes undertaken by local assemblies that broke the power of the Knights of Labor in their disastrous contest with Jay Gould's Texas Pacific Railroad in 1886. Soon thereafter the Knights entered a period of sharp decline—victims of mounting business antagonism, craft-union fears of industrial unionism, and their own decentralized organizational structure.

The American Federation of Labor (AFL), a flexible but conservative organization of craft unions formed in 1886, represented a new generation's coming to terms with the corporate revolution. Workers too could learn the lessons of consolidation. Samuel Gompers, the founder and longtime president of AFL, and his lieutenant, Adolph Strasser, readily confessed that their sole concern was for the skilled trades—carpenters, iron-molders, railroad engineers, and other affiliates—that they represented and for the immediate welfare of their members. When Strasser was asked to define the "ultimate ends" of his organization's "pure and simple unionism," he replied at once that the two terms were contradictory. "We have no ultimate ends. We are going on from day to day. We are fighting for immediate objects—objects that can be realized in a few years."

The new union leaders reminded businessmen that they too were "practical men"—not closet theorists or soft-headed dreamers, but pragmatists and opportunists. Like their employers, the new union leaders were tough-minded organizers with their eyes on the main chance. The distance the AFL had come from the cooperative industrial unionism and the republican hopes of the Knights of Labor could be measured in Gompers's reply to Socialist Morris Hillquit. Bent on discrediting his rival, Hillquit demanded to know whether Gompers really believed that American workers received the "full product" of their labor. Gompers brushed aside the question as meaningless. "I will say," he replied, "that it is impossible for anyone to definitely say what proportion the workers receive as a result of their labor, but it is the fact that due to the organized labor movement they have received and are receiving a larger share of the product of their labor than they ever did in the history of modern society." Irate socialists and labor radicals, many of them friends and mentors from the 1870s and early 1880s, could accuse Gompers of having sold out the movement by refusing to implement a genuine social philosophy. But Gompers had weighed the prospects of a socialist future as well as the promises of a united labor party and found both wanting. Now he and his fellow craft-unionists cheerfully admitted to a chastened belief in half a loaf and a willingness to follow "the lines of least resistance."

"Least resistance" for organized labor as the twentieth century opened meant accepting industrial consolidation and financial concentration, holding government at arm's length, calling for immigration restriction, and bargaining closely with big business—altogether a conservative strategy worthy of the most stalwart corporation head. The trusts, Gompers conceded, "are our employers, and the employer who is fair to us, whether an individual, or a collection of individuals in the form of a corporation or a trust, matters little to us so long as we obtain fair wages." Little, he felt, could now be gained by quarreling with the wage system on which an integrated capitalism rested or by dreaming up pie-in-the-sky substitutes. "The hope for a perfect millennium," Gompers told the United States Industrial Commission, "well, it don't come every night."

**Working-Class Life**     Workers, packed in slums and ghettos of center cities, knew precisely how far they stood from the margins of the millennium. The quality of life in the working-class districts of most American cities was appalling. For new arrivals from Europe and the American countryside, urban housing—whether three-story wooden firetraps in South Boston or dumb-bell tenements on New York's Lower East Side or dilapidated single-family shanties in Cincinnati, St. Louis, or Chicago—was generally deplorable and, worse still, expensive. Gas, water, electricity, sanitation, and transportation—all the services that were needed to make the life of city workers and their families tolerable—were in short supply and of poor quality as late as 1914. Jacob Riis's *How the Other Half Lives* (1890), an exposé of tenement life on the Lower East Side, described the onset of summer and hot weather along Mulberry Street Bend as the "time of greatest suffering among the poor":

> It is in hot weather, when life indoors is well-nigh unbearable with cooking, sleeping, and working all crowded into the small rooms together, that the tenement expands, reckless of all restraint. Then a strange and picturesque life moves up on the flat roofs.... In the stifling July nights, when the big barracks are like fiery furnaces, their very walls giving out absorbed heat, men and women lie in restless, sweltering rows, panting for air and sleep.

The main surge in urban rehabilitation began with the new century, and within a decade municipal services improved, giving cities a public face-lift and a new vitality. But housing and personal standards of living improved much more slowly. The public life of American cities responded to the work of urban reformers with their vision of revived democratic purpose; yet blighted neighborhoods, fractured communities, crumbling apartments, and stunted lives continued as a stark reality for too many American workers.

Recently arrived immigrants who endured these conditions and made up by far the largest portion of the industrial labor force by 1900 faced still another and more subtle kind of exploitation: the cultural drive to "Americanize" them as quickly and thoroughly as possible. All the ethnic groups arriving in such great numbers after 1880—Italians, Greeks, Poles, Russian Jews—were viewed at one time or another as potential bomb throwers who required the saving word and the restraining hand from "100 Percent Americans." Earlier generations had

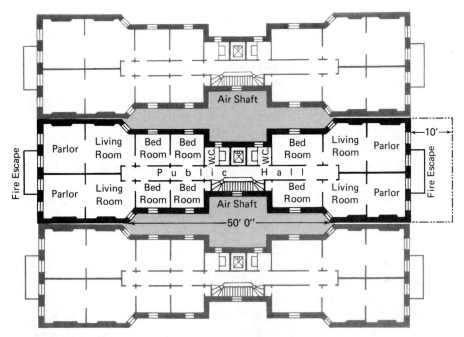

**Dumbbell Tenement**
*In New York City's teeming Lower East Side, most families were crowded into the notorious "dumbell" tenements, seven or eight stories high. Only one room in any apartment in these wooden firetraps received direct sun or air. All the families on each floor shared a toilet in the hall, while in the oppressive heat of July and August people fled to fire escapes and roofs to sleep.*

singled out the political party as the chief agent of cultural adjustment; reformers after 1880 emphasized the school as the chief agency of assimilation. As one observer explained to the readers of *World's Work* in 1903, "There are many things in which, as a rule, the public consider that the public schools fail, but one thing that cannot be denied—and it is the greatest—is that these boys and girls of foreign parentage catch readily the simple American ideas of independence and individual work and, with them, social progress." "Social progress" in the half-century after 1880 meant vigorous Americanization: widespread literacy, technological education, elimination of child labor, cultural conformity, and, last but not least, stimulating an aspiring working class's appetite for all the consumer goods produced by the huge American industrial machine.

Just as American businessmen after 1900 continued to form monopolies and oligopolies, and farmers launched their own organizational revolution, so the nation's industrial workers began to adjust their roles to the demands of corporate capitalism. By 1900 a majority of American workers had seemingly come to accept their assignments—and thus they added their weight to the impression of inevitability that the production statistics had created.

But were these impressions of inexorability accurate? Were American workers—both those inside and outside unions—content with their lot and satisfied with their share of the pie? The rising number of strikes, walkouts, work stoppages, and slowdowns after 1900 indicated the contrary, as did the continuing repressive tactics against labor employed by the business community. Were there, then, alternative routes open to the good society that American workers sought— roads not taken or paths only provisionally explored which, had they been followed, might have carried them there? One option was organizing a national labor party much like those being formed in Europe in these same years. For some American workers hopes for a united labor party persisted—the challenge of building their own platform of equity, lifting up committed comrades as candidates from the rank and file, and going to the people to capture control of the political as well as the industrial machinery of the nation. And in fact such partisans of labor politics—alone or in concert with other like-minded reform groups—did succeed periodically throughout the Gilded Age, on the local or state level, in electing a mayor, winning a majority on a city council, or sending a spokesman to a state legislature. But all too often labor's success at the polls was measured in near misses and second-best, as Henry George learned with his United Labor party in New York City's mayoral election of 1886, when he lost to Democrat Abram S. Hewitt while running ahead of the Republican silk-stocking candidate, young Theodore Roosevelt. Local hopes for a genuine national labor contender waxed and waned throughout the Gilded Age, but the road to Washington and the White House seemed a long one.

A second alternative to Gompers's course of least resistance was socialism with its calls for political action or trade-union agitation. These hopes would burn brightest for a minority of American industrial workers after the turn of the century when a loosely organized Socialist party led by Eugene Debs succeeded in winning an increasing number of votes and garnering new recruits. But those achievements lay in the future in 1900 when the obstacles in the road to socialist unity still seemed formidable. First there was the intransigence of an American business community that continued to identify socialism with dangerous "foreigners" and to tell the "reds" to go back where they came from if they didn't like it here. An equally strong set of constraints lay within the American labor movement itself, both native-born workers in whom republican radicalism and Protestant evangelicalism ran deep, and the new immigrant working class— divided by race, ethnicity, and religion and united chiefly in the hope of individual advancement. A majority in both groups in 1900 still shared the promise of achieving success inside a reformed, humanized, and more equitable capitalist system.

The American dream of 1900 remained what it had been a half-century earlier: a vision of a chosen people uniquely equipped to create and enjoy abundance. Economic integration and hugely increased production themselves seemed convincing proof of the near approach of what the journalist Herbert Croly called "the promise of American life." A national market had been built and the nation's shelves stocked with an incredible variety of goods. In this sense the economic well-being of the United States appeared to be exactly what the new corporation heads pronounced it—a single bountiful system binding producers and consumers, citizen and nation, together in a network of mutual obligations and benefits.

But beneath the surface, as the new century began, lay not unity, but multiplicity; not a single all-encompassing national purpose, but competing and even warring interests; not pressures unifying American society, but social forces threatening to fling it apart; not the conservation of national energies, but their diffusion in politically volatile forms. Americans in 1900 thus confronted a paradox capping a half-century of growth: the rapid integration that had seemingly saved them from the waste of competition and economic disorder had set in motion cultural and political counterforces that now threatened fragmentation and isolation. To cope with these threats to national order, Americans would need new and more sophisticated concepts of social change and political organization, and the capacity somehow to use them.

## CHRONOLOGY

**1873** Panic of 1873 begins six years of depression.

**1876** Alexander Graham Bell invents the telephone.

**1877** Great Railroad Strike.

**1879** Henry George's *Progress and Poverty* published.
Thomas Alva Edison perfects the electric light bulb.

**1880** Farmers' Agricultural Wheel and National Farmers' Alliance join together to form Southern Alliance.

**1882** John D. Rockefeller's Standard Oil of Ohio consolidates American oil industry under Standard Oil Trust.

**1883** Chicago builds first elevated electric railway.
Brooklyn Bridge completed.

**1884** Recession and unemployment jar the economy.

**1886** AFL (American Federation of Labor) founded.
The "Great Upheaval" stops work on Jay Gould's Texas Pacific Railroad.
George Westinghouse founds Westinghouse Electric Co. and subsequently perfects use of alternating current.

**1887** Interstate Commerce Act passed to control railroads.

**1888** Edward Bellamy's *Looking Backward* published.

**1890** Sherman Antitrust Act passed in attempt to regulate monopolies in restraint of trade.
Sherman Silver Purchase Act passed, resulting in depleted gold reserves.
At "Battle" of Wounded Knee, South Dakota, federal troops massacre 200 Indians.

**1891** Hamlin Garland's *Main-Travelled Roads* describes hardships of

midwestern farmers' lives.
Louis Sullivan's Wainwright
Building completed in St. Louis.

**1892**  Populists organize; nominate
General James B. Weaver for
president at a national
convention in Omaha.
Grover Cleveland elected
president.
Homestead Strike in Carnegie steel
mills.

**1893**  Financial panic sends U.S.
economy into four years of
depression.
Repeal of Sherman Silver Purchase
Act.
Historian Frederick Jackson
Turner, in "The Significance of
the American Frontier,"
announces closing of the
frontier.

**1894**  Pullman Strike broken by federal
troops; Eugene V. Debs jailed.
Henry Demarest Lloyd's *Wealth
Against Commonwealth,* exposé
of Standard Oil Company,
published.

**1895**  In *U.S.* v. *E. C. Knight Co.,*
government defeated in antitrust
suit against sugar monopoly.

**1896**  William McKinley elected
president, defeating William

Jennings Bryan and "Free
Silver."

**1900**  McKinley reelected president,
defeating Bryan once again.
National Civic Federation
established by labor leaders and
industrialists.
Theodore Dreiser's *Sister Carrie,*
naturalistic novel, causes literary
stir.

**1901**  Theodore Roosevelt becomes
president after McKinley
assassinated.
United States Steel Corporation
formed.

**1903**  Wright brothers make their first
flight.
National Association of
Manufacturers (NAM) formed.
Citizens Industrial Association
formed to secure open shop in
American industry.

**1904**  Case of *Northern Securities Co.* v.
*U.S.* upholds government's case
against railroad mergers.

**1911**  Triangle Shirtwaist Factory fire in
New York City's East Side kills
146 women; investigation and
revision of state factory codes
follow.

## SUGGESTED READINGS

There are two outstanding general interpretations of the organizational revolution in American society in the half-century following 1870. A succinct account that remains the model for more recent interpretations is Samuel P. Hays, *The Response to Industrialism* (1957). Robert Wiebe, *The Search for Order* (1968), traces the shift from small-town America to modern mass society in terms of changing political outlooks and social values. Ray Ginger, *The Age of Excess* (1965), is a lively and impressionistic survey, and Howard Mumford Jones, *The Age of Energy: Varieties of American Experience, 1865–1915* (1970), explores Gilded Age manners and morals with sympathy and gusto.

Rodman Paul, *Mining Frontiers of the Far West* (1963), traces the opening of the Mountain West to modern mechanized mining, and Harry Sinclair Drago, *The Great Range Wars* (1985), recounts the stormy history of the early cattle industry. Sandra L. Myres, *Westering Women and the Frontier Experience* (1982), describes the activities of a variety of pioneer women. The literature on native Americans of the trans-Mississippi West is voluminous. Good overviews are Wilcomb E. Washburn, *The Indian in America* (1975), and Robert F. Berkhofer, *The White Man's Indian* (1978). Francis Paul Prucha, *The Great Father: The United States Government and the American Indians* (1984), is an informative and critical analysis of Indian policy.

The best recent overview of the American economy in these years is Stuart Bruchey's brief but perceptive essay, *Growth of the Modern Economy* (1975). The early chapters in Alfred D. Chandler, Jr., *Strategy and Structure: Chapters in the History of American Industrial Enterprise* (1966), provide a compact summary of the first phase of business concentration. Ralph L. Nelson, *Merger Movements in American Industry* (1959), gives a good account of the great merger movement at the end of the nineteenth century, and Hans B. Thorelli, *Federal Antitrust Policy: The Origination of an American Tradition* (1955), traces the course of the countermovement against monopoly. The industrial transformation of the United States is described as a success story in Edward C. Kirkland's survey, *Industry Comes of Age: Business, Labor, and Public Policy, 1860–1897* (1961), which can be read along with Thomas Cochran, *The Inner Revolution* (1965).

For a corrective account of the strategies of large corporations in the late nineteenth century, see Alfred D. Chandler, Jr., *The Visible Hand: The Managerial Revolution in American Business* (1977), and David Montgomery, *The Fall of the House of Labor: The Workplace, the State, and American Labor Activism, 1865–1925* (1987), which follows the attempts of organized labor to cope with the effects of rapid industrialization and new technology on the nation's labor force. For a highly informative account of women in the labor force, see Alice Kessler-Harris, *Out to Work: A History of Wage-Earning Women in the United States* (1982). Thomas P. Hughes, *American Genesis: A Century of Invention and Technological Enthusiasm* (1989), argues the centrality of technological innovation in the modernizing of the United States.

The connections between economic theory and public policy are explored in Sidney Fine, *Laissez-Faire and the General Welfare State* (1956). Richard Hofstadter, *Social Darwinism in American Thought* (1945), and Robert McCloskey, *Conservatism in the Age of Enterprise* (1951), are highly readable accounts of conservative thinking in the Gilded Age. Irvin G. Wyllie, *The Self-Made Man in America* (1954), scrutinizes a venerable American myth, and Edward C. Kirkland's lively essays in *Dream and Thought in the Business Community, 1860–1900* (1956) describe the musings of businessmen on the American social order. For an account of the careers of three notable critics of Gilded Age business practices, see John L. Thomas, *Alternative America: Henry George, Edward Bellamy, Henry Demarest Lloyd and the Adversary Tradition* (1983).

Urban growth and its accompanying problems are admirably summarized in Howard Chudacoff, *Evolution of American Urban Society* (1975), and Zane Miller, *Urbanization of America* (1973). The story of the mounting difficulties of the American farmer is well told in Fred Shannon, *The Farmer's Last Frontier* (1963). For an illuminating study of agrarian politics in the South in this period, see Theodore Saloutos, *Farmer Movements of the South, 1865–1933*. Grant McConnell, *The Decline of Agrarian Democracy* (1953), describes the rise of commercial farming. On American labor there are two useful surveys: Joseph G. Rayback, *A History of American Labor* (1959), and Henry Pelling, *American Labor* (1959). Herbert G. Gutman, *Work, Culture and Society in Industrializing America* (1976), points toward a new synthesis of cultural and labor history, and Daniel T. Rogers, *The Work Ethic in Industrial America, 1850–1920* (1975), examines shifting attitudes toward work that accompanied the industrial transformation of the United States. Daniel Walkowitz, *Worker City, Company Town: Iron and Cotton*

*Worker Protest in Troy and Cohoes, New York, 1855–1884* (1978), compares two different social and cultural settings as they determine the responses of industrial workers.

Biographies of leaders in the American industrial revolution are many. Among the best are monumental works: Joseph Wall, *Andrew Carnegie* (1970); Alan Nevins, *Study in Power: John D. Rockefeller, Industrialist and Philanthropist* (2 vols., 1953); Matthew Josephson, *Edison* (1940); and Maury Klein, *The Life and Legend of Jay Gould* (1986).

# 23

# *The Politics*
# *of Reform*

⌒

*I*N THE quarter-century after the Civil War, politics appeared to give Americans a sense of permanence and stability that their economic system lacked. The Jacksonian generation had first discovered in the political party the means of containing the disruptive forces of modern democracy until the moral issue of slavery upset their developmental plans, broke both Whig and Democratic parties wide open, and precipitated a bloody civil war. Now the Jacksonian generation's sons—the professionals who ruled the Republican and Democratic parties after 1870—repaired the political system, which they attempted to run with efficiency and assurance.

Their fragile creation—a new political equilibrium—depended, first of all, on restoring a regional balance of power. Throughout the Gilded Age the Republicans sought to include both northeastern workers and midwestern farmers in their plans for rapid business development, and until the 1890s they continued to dream of competing with the Democrats in the South for the votes with which to become for the first time a truly national party. The Democrats, for their part, were busy repairing the broad Jacksonian coalition of southern planters and northern city bosses, which had been badly shaken by the war. The calm that seemingly descended on both contestants with the close of Reconstruction was nevertheless deceptive. Both parties remained caught between agendas: the slavery issue, which had dominated the antebellum political scene, had disappeared but left in its place the vexing questions of political rights and social equality for black citizens that neither party was committed to solving. And it would be another quarter of a century before a younger generation of progressives in both parties acknowledged the need for a program to correct the ills resulting from rapid and uncontrolled industrialization. In the meantime both parties struggled with dissidents in their ranks—moral reformers and prohibitionists, women, farmers, industrial workers—whose loyalty they failed to hold and who periodically broke away to form splinter parties of their own. None of these third parties, however, proved broad or durable enough to permanently challenge the rule of the two major parties. It was the resilience and tenacity of Republican and Democratic managers that made both parties seem to their members more stable than they actually were.

Before the Populist revolt in the 1890s, the most serious challenges to the two major parties often came at the local level in municipal elections. In New York City in 1886, for example, the Knights of Labor and the city's trade union assemblies convinced the single-taxer Henry George to enter the mayoralty race against Democratic party stalwart Abram S. Hewitt and the Republican silk-stocking candidate, newcomer Theodore Roosevelt. Underfinanced and beset with severe organizational problems, George and his United Labor party conducted a "tailgate" campaign throughout New York. From early morning until late at night he dashed about the city in his horsecart, haranguing crowds of workers and passersby in neighborhood markets from his movable podium. On a typical day George addressed a group of Franco-Americans on the Lower East Side, met another ethnic gathering in Abingdon Square, spoke to a crowd of railway workers under the El, and closed the day with a huge rally at Sulzer's Harlem River Park at midnight. Told by Republican and Democratic party professionals that he would be "counted out," George proceeded to administer a lesson in popular campaigning by running a respectable second to Democrat Hewitt and garnering nearly 70,000 votes to Roosevelt's 60,000. Yet a year later the United Labor party disintegrated in a factional dispute between socialists and trade unionists, and in a second campaign for secretary of state of New York, George went down to ignominious defeat. Still, major party bosses could be taught a lesson when they ignored the interests of disaffected elements in their parties.

The smooth operation of American politics in the Gilded Age also depended on the mastery of a few basic rules. Chief among them was the principle, accepted by politicians in both parties, that their organizations did not differ in class or economic interests, which were often quite similar, or even in general policies, which were frequently fuzzy. Both Republicans and Democrats were now financed by wealthy citizens whose opinions party leaders carefully acknowledged while maintaining an egalitarian posture before the rest of the country. Party leaders realized that voters seldom approached political questions like the tariff and the currency as clear issues to be decided in reasoned terms. Instead the professionals considered these questions symbols and rallying cries with which to mobilize support for the party and its candidates. The skilled practitioners of Gilded Age politics had learned from the stormy debates of the Civil War years that most American voters' electoral behavior was ultimately determined by images and impressions, prejudices and preferences. Voters might consider themselves both rational and informed, but no office seeker could afford to ignore these vague but deeper forces at work in the political population.

Politicians at various levels of government seeking to instruct the American voter spoke in a variety of tongues and accents in explaining their purposes and setting their agendas. If Gilded Age politics was a search for a national political

**Unveiling a Statue**
*Patriotism and purity combined readily in the Gilded Age imagination.*

culture, the actual discovery awaited the arrival of a progressive generation at century's end. Meanwhile the American political language remained polyglot, a babble of competing voices defining the practice of politics in a variety of vocabularies and dialects according to particular interests and needs. Aging Boston Brahmins invoked a lost tradition in calling for the return to a pristine New England political community "during the first years of the century, before the coming of Jacksonian democracy and the invasion of the Irish." The now-triumphant Irish, secure in the fastness of Tammany Hall, listened to the practical advice dispensed by political boss George Washington Plunkitt from his rostrum at the New York County Courthouse bootblack stand concerning the indispensability of patronage. "Men ain't in politics for nothin'," Plunkitt reminded his admirers. "They want to get somethin' out of it. . . . Me and the Republicans are enemies just one day in the year—election day. Then we fight tooth and nail. The rest of the time it's live and let live with us."

> You see, we differ on tariffs and currencies and all them things, but we agree on the main proposition that when a man works in politics, he should get something

out of it. The politicians have got to stand together this way or there wouldn't be any political parties in a short time.

Many big businessmen approached politics and its professional practitioners in much the same spirit of candor with which the railroad buccaneer Collis P. Huntington instructed his lobbyist in Congress: "If you have to pay money to have the right thing done, it is only just and fair to do it. . . . If a man has the power to do great evil and won't do right unless he is bribed to do it, I think the time well spent when it is a man's duty to go up and bribe the judge."

It was the seemingly cozy partnership between businessmen and the politicians that outraged reformers who were determined to dry up the pools of patronage by passing a strong civil service law. Beginning with the Liberal Republican enemies of the Grant administration, who denounced its many scandals as "offensive to every right-thinking man," to the lamentations a decade later of the Mugwumps, those Republican bolters who could not stomach the presidential candidacy of James G. Blaine, "The Continental Liar from the State of Maine," reformers called for the return of the moral law, right reason, probity, and responsibility to the halls of state. Increasingly, as the century neared a close, the reform community invoked the language of medical science and public health in calling voters' attention to the "festering centers" of "urban corruption," the "moral contagions" and "plague spots" of city politics and statehouse rings.

The professionals in both parties responded to the reformers' complaints with open repugnance. Who were these namby-pambys and do-gooders, pursuing their "iridescent dream" of moral purity? demanded Senator John J. Ingalls of Kansas, his words dripping with vitriol. "Man-milliners," "carpet-knights," "dillettanti"—all of them eunuchs, "effeminate without being either masculine or feminine; unable to beget or bear; possessing neither fecundity nor virility, endowed with the contempt of men and the derision of women, and doomed to sterility, isolation, and extinction."

Both Republican and Democratic parties, in fact, were broad-based, non-ideological coalitions that appealed to businessmen, farmers, professionals, and workers. Wealth, political convictions, and social status did not separate Republicans and Democrats as much as did differing clusters of religious, racial, ethnic, and cultural values, which were often tied to older regional outlooks that ran deep into the American past. One way of describing these differences is to examine their roots in the antebellum party system. The Democratic party that Andrew Jackson and his political lieutenants assembled in the second quarter of the nineteenth century marched under the banner of states' rights, limited government, and laissez-faire in cultural as well as economic matters. From its beginnings, Jacksonian orators had preached what Gilded Age Democrats still honored as "the master-wisdom of governing little and leaving as much as possible to localities and individuals," a principle particularly appealing to the South, which was intent on protecting white supremacy against incursions from the North. Local autonomy also proved attractive to religious minorities like

Roman Catholics and Lutherans, as well as newly arrived immigrants intent on preserving their inherited customs and rituals. Throughout the Gilded Age most recent immigrants could be counted on to vote Democratic, a fact of political life wryly acknowledged by Mark Twain in his apocryphal account of an immigrant's first day in the United States. "When he first landed in New York," Twain joked, "he had only halted at Castle Garden for a few minutes to receive and exhibit papers showing that he had resided in this country two years—and then he voted the democratic ticket and went up town to hunt a house."

Democrats in Congress, which they dominated for most of the postwar period, generally followed the advice of one of the party's national spokesmen, Senator William L. Wilson of West Virginia, who insisted that "it is better for some things to be done imperfectly and clumsily than to set up a paternal and bureaucratic government to do them." Democrats generally favored lower tariffs and cheap money, limited government and the avoidance of "the unwholesome progeny of paternalism," by which they meant their Republican opponents. Democratic success in Congress and in the various states in the last thirty years of the century, their spokesmen boasted, was hardly accidental: "It can have no other rational explanation than that the party has been, from the beginning, the guardian and defender of some fundamental principle, or principles, of free government, in whose truth and permanence it has found its life and its growth."

Republicans also traced their antebellum ancestry across the Civil War, which had strengthened the party's nationalist proclivities. Like their Whig forebears, Republicans believed in energetic government charged with promoting growth and well-being, which they nurtured by admitting new states to the union in order to strengthen their political grip, underwriting a national railroad system, distributing public lands freely, enacting protective tariffs to favor a developing American industry, and regularly denouncing their do-nothing Democratic opposition (just as their Whig fathers had reviled the Jacksonians) as a "standing menace to the prosperity of the country." Before the Civil War, governmental activism had combined with a strong middle-class morality to give the Republican party a reformist thrust directed at the evils of slavery, intemperance, and personal immorality. Whig and Republican party members were primarily Protestant, predominantly of native stock or Anglo-Saxon descent, aggressively reform-minded, and eager to use government at all levels to impose their promotional schemes and behavioral standards on the rest of the community. George F. Hoar, the venerable Republican senator from Massachusetts, drew on all these moral resources after the war when he described his party as still composed of "the men who do the work of piety and charity in our churches, the men who administer our school systems, the men who own and till their own farms, the men who perform the skilled labor in the shops." The bitterly partisan Republican campaigner Robert Ingersoll was less charitable in naming the sins of the Democrats for an audience of midwestern farmers: "I believe in a party that believes in good crops. . . . The Democratic Party is a party of famine; it is a friend of the early frost; it believes in the Colorado beetle and the weevil."

**Women's Temperance Movement**
*A local demonstration in Ohio by women against the saloon.*

Business and financial interests steadily infiltrated the Republican party after 1880, but it continued to attract a broad range of social moralists—prohibitionists, sabbatarians, blue-law advocates, and moral reformers of every sort. Only at the end of the century had these evangelical types become marginal enough in the party as a whole for the managers to cast them aside as political liabilities in a new age of fund-raising and full campaign coffers.

Lacking the Republican concern with the mote in its neighbor's eye, the more permissive Democratic party seemed very different from its rival. It embraced Catholics as well as Protestants, and it claimed a tolerance of immigrants who lacked the compulsive morality of the native-born. Democrats continued to preach a "personal liberty" that was thought safest when government was kept minimal and local. The New York party organization expressed this viewpoint clearly when in 1881, harking back to the pronouncements of Andrew Jackson, it declared itself "unalterably opposed to centralization of power in either state or federal governments." While Republicans expected all government to be generous and active, Democrats hoped to keep it grudging and stingy, if only to check the Anglo-Saxon Republicans' "cultural imperialism" toward immigrants, as well as to curb the Republicans' appetite for patronage. Thus the differences between the two parties in 1880 were real, but they derived as much from ethnic origins, religious backgrounds, and cultural outlook as from strict class or economic interest.

This pattern of politics survived until the last decade of the century, when suddenly the very idea of party rule came under attack by a younger generation of political reformers. By 1890 rural Populists and urban progressives were challenging the code of business as usual and forcing the professionals in both parties to respond to new pressures. Out of their revolt came a transformation of politics that paralleled the revolution in the national economy and created new forms in the American political process, along with new ways of ordering it.

## The Politics of Equilibrium

The Civil War shaped the thinking and molded the political behavior of Americans for a generation. Gilded Age politicians succeeded in tapping the emotions that had been aroused by the war in both sections of the country. They were able, first of all, to inspire remarkably high levels of voting. In the six presidential elections between 1876 and 1896, an average of 78.5 percent of the country's eligible voters actually voted, and an equally impressive 62.8 percent turned out for off-year elections. (In the late twentieth century, even presidential elections bring slightly less than half the eligible voters to the polls.) If political democracy is measured by a high rate of voter participation, then the Gilded Age remained flamboyantly, defiantly democratic despite its glaring social and economic inequalities.

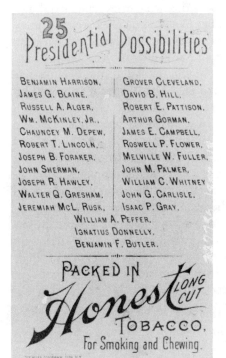

**Advertising the Product**
*An advertising card inside a package of chewing tobacco listed nearly all of the available candidates from three parties in the presidential election of 1892.*

The voting patterns remained strikingly consistent. Whether they marched to the polls behind candidates waving the "bloody shirt"—the Radical Republicans' vengeful rhetoric aimed at preserving northern hostilities toward the South—or stirred to memories of the Confederacy's Lost Cause, voters across the nation kept alive the Civil War even after the constitutional and ideological struggles of Reconstruction had ended. Joining enthusiastically in campaigns that came complete with mounted military troopers and fancy drill teams, they made national elections extremely close. Sixteen states could always be counted on to go Republican; fourteen just as regularly voted Democratic. Presidential elections were usually decided by the voters in five key states—Connecticut, New York, Indiana, Nevada, and California. Between 1872 and 1912 the Republicans held a grip on the presidency that was broken only by Grover Cleveland's two victories in 1884 and 1892. They appeared to be a well-established majority party. But in fact the Democrats controlled the House of Representatives with sizable majorities in seven out of ten congressional elections. In key states the margins of victory were perilously thin, particularly in New York and Indiana. With such intense competition and close contests, winners were not only lucky but often surprised. In the three presidential elections in the 1880s, the victor edged out his closest opponent by less than 1 percent. In the election of James A. Garfield in 1880 and of Cleveland in 1884, fewer than 25,000 votes separated the candidates. In 1888 the winner in electoral votes, the Republican Benjamin Harrison, received fewer popular votes than did Cleveland, the loser.

**Party Lines Drawn**    Throughout the 1880s the two parties remained drawn up against each other like two equally matched armies, their skirmishes resembling the engagements of the still-familiar Civil War. Political rhetoric featured famous military figures well into the decade—in songs, war whoops, and speeches by bewhiskered colonels "late of the Confederate Army" or beribboned commissary generals of the Grand Army of the Republic. The presidential election of 1880 pitted two former Union generals against each other—forty-eight-year-old James A. Garfield, Republican from Ohio, matched against General Winfield Scott Hancock, hero of Gettysburg and able military governor of Texas and Louisiana under congressional Reconstruction. Hancock's superb war record did not save him from sustained Republican attacks on his family as former Rebel sympathizers or canards on his supposed battlefield cowardice despite glowing tributes to his heroism from former President Grant. Then the Republicans shifted from slander to scare tactics, warning of the rise of a "Solid South" and the danger of a Democratic administration that would reimburse all Confederates for property damage done during the war and vote huge pensions for Confederate veterans. A Garfield campaign song singled out for ridicule black disfranchisement in the New South:

> *Sing a song of shotguns,*
> *Pocket full of knives,*
> *Four-and-twenty black men*

**Republicans Celebrate Patriotism**
*The Republican national convention at Chicago, June 2, 1880 invoked "Independent
America—The home of the freeman, where the humblest citizen can attain the highest honors
in the gift of her people."*

> *Running for their lives,*
> *When the polls are open*
> *Shut the nigger's mouth,*
> *Isn't that a bully way*
> *To make a solid South?*

Democrats countered with time-worn charges of corruption and the $329 bribe
presumably tendered Garfield in the Crédit Mobilier scandal in 1868, and by
exposing the misdeeds of Garfield's running mate, the notorious New York
custom house spoilsman Chester A. Arthur. A campaign long on personal
vituperation but short on issues still turned out the voters—three-quarters of all
those eligible—who provided "Boatman Jim" Garfield with a 10,000 popular
majority out of 9 million votes cast.

The median age of voters in the Gilded Age was thirty-seven, and so generally
they had arrived at political maturity under the guidance of fathers who had
fought to preserve the "glorious Union" or to rescue a "prostrate nation." Ticket
splitting suggested a lack of patriotism, and the voter who switched parties was
regarded as little better than a bounty jumper. Novelist Brand Whitlock remembered that in his youth being a Republican was "a fundamental and self-evident
thing. . . . It was merely a synonym for patriotism, another name for the

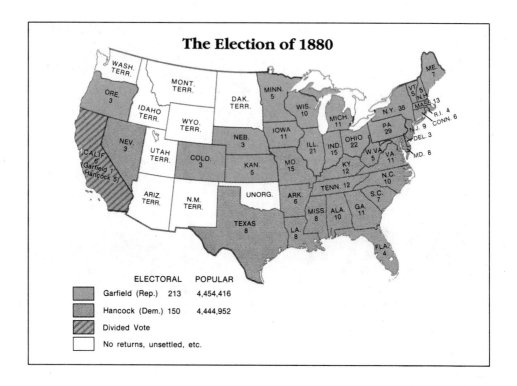

## The Election of 1880

| | ELECTORAL | POPULAR |
|---|---|---|
| ▨ Garfield (Rep.) | 213 | 4,454,416 |
| ▨ Hancock (Dem.) | 150 | 4,444,952 |
| ▨ Divided Vote | | |
| ▢ No returns, unsettled, etc. | | |

nation. . . . It was inconceivable that any self-respecting person should be a Democrat." Nor was it likely that in the South, increasingly solid in its support of the Democracy, a true gentlemen would require any greater comfort than the assurance given by Bourbon conservatives that "the nation as a nation, will have nothing more to do with the Negro."

Yet for all its apparent stability, politics in this era was in the process of transformation—the same stage of transformation that small-scale entrepreneurial capitalism was undergoing. Newly arrived immigrants were urban consumers in need of jobs, favors, and services. The political boss of Boston's South End, Martin Lomasney, once lectured the journalist Lincoln Steffens on the indispensability of the boss and his political machine: "There's got to be in every ward somebody that any bloke can come to—no matter what he's done—and get help. Help, you understand, none of your law and justice, but help." Here in crowded neighborhoods was a vast human market in which a wise investment of political capital could pay off handsomely. The new business of politics, unlike more established concerns, was open at the bottom to fresh talent and offered unlimited opportunity for making good and getting ahead. As an organizer and go-getter, the professional politician—ward heeler, precinct captain, county chairman, state assemblyman, or senatorial aspirant—was a salesman who had to know the buying habits of every prospective customer in his territory.

George Washington Plunkitt, one of the leaders of New York City's Democratic organization Tammany Hall, described the political district in terms familiar to every salesman out of New York or Chicago with a territory to cover, concluding: "If he holds his district and Tammany is in power, he is amply rewarded by a good office and the opportunities that go with it." The Gilded Age boss was the Horatio Alger rags-to-riches hero, in ward heeler's attire, sporting a campaign button. "Yes, many of our men have grown rich in politics," Plunkitt confided. "I have myself. I've made a big fortune out of the game, and I'm gettin' richer every day." The shortest route to success in the business of politics lay through the upstairs room at party headquarters, where the sign over the door read "Never closed."

**The Urban Political Boss**

From the city to the Senate, politics in the Gilded Age constituted a revitalized patronage society that in some ways resembled its eighteenth-century ancestor. Under the guiding hand and sharp eye of the boss, political power was organized vertically within the machine in a hierarchical system of patrons and clients. The style of the Gilded Age boss was new and coarse, more personalized and direct than that of his gentleman predecessor. To reform critics, among them Moisei Ostrogorski, whose *Democracy and the Organization of Political Parties* summed up the reformers' indictment of machine politics, the political boss was an all-powerful leader, unsleeping, devious, and ruthless, who commanded solely through "his strength of will, his cleverness, his audacity and his luck." In short, he was Niccolò Machiavelli's Renaissance prince come to life. As Ostrogorski described the political boss:

> To this one he lends a dollar; for another he obtains a railroad ticket without payment; he has coal distributed in the depth of winter; he makes gifts of other kinds; he sometimes sends poultry at Christmas time; he buys medicine for a sick person; he helps bury the dead by procuring a coffin on credit or half-price. He has a kind heart in virtue of his position and his position gives him the means of satisfying his need for kindness: the money which he distributes comes from the chest of the Machine; the latter has obtained it by the most reprehensible methods...but no matter. With this money he can also dispense an ample hospitality in the drinking saloons. As soon as he comes in, friends known and unknown gather round him, and he treats everybody, he orders one drink after another for the company; he is the only one who does not drink; he is on duty.

The urban machine's stock in trade was jobs and appointments, transit franchises, paving contracts, public construction bids, licenses, permits, and a hundred other salable items needed to conduct the business of the nation's cities. These were the methods perfected by Tammany boss Richard Croker in New York City after 1880. Croker maintained firm control over all municipal purchases by granting favors to friendly businessmen in whose concerns he took both a public interest and a handsome slice of honest graft for himself. Reformers forced Croker's resignation in the early 1890s following an investigation of police corruption, but soon he was back as head of Tammany, holding court at the Democratic Club on Fifth Avenue to thirty-five district leaders from whom he continued to exact tribute before being ousted by the reform forces of Mayor Seth Low in 1901.

In Philadelphia, Republican boss "King" James McManes ruled unopposed for two decades by controlling the city's finances through his adroit management of the board in charge of the municipal gas utility, which he used as a base for extending his power to the rest of the bureaucracy, collecting payoffs from contractors and kickbacks from city employees. Like many of the bosses, McManes grew rich on the spoils of office as he proceeded to increase the municipal debt by 350 percent. In Chicago, which lacked a strong boss with centralized authority, machine politics was more casual and confused with each ward the fiefdom of a highly visible ward boss: in the Nineteenth Ward, Johnny Powers came to be known as "The Chief Mourner" because of his unblemished record in attending the funerals of friends and supporters. Michael "Hinky Dink" Kenna and his colleague "Bathhouse" John Coughlin presided over the famous First Ward from his saloon, where he dispensed favors and a free lunch. "King" Michael McDonald's power in his bailiwick rested on a string of gambling houses, while the West Side belonged to the "Blond Boss" William Lorimer, the only Republican chieftain in the city.

Virtually every major city in the country experienced some form of boss rule—Democratic or Republican—in the half-century following the Civil War: Abe Ruef in San Francisco; Martin Behrman in New Orleans; Christopher Magee in Pittsburgh; the Pendergast brothers in Kansas City; and Edward Crump in Jersey City. The explanation for such concentrations of power is quite simple: city bosses with their machines were attempting to impose the same kind of order and system over their sprawling empires that businessmen sought in industrial and financial consolidation. The impulse motivating the city boss was essentially conservative: the need to bring a semblance of method and predictability in the running of his city. "Politics ain't bean bag," observed the Chicago Irish saloonkeeper Mr. Dooley, the fictional creation of the humorist Finley Peter Dunne. "Tis a man's game; an' women, childher, an' prohybitionists do well to keep out iv it." The reformer, bosses knew, always suffered from innocence and amateurism. "He hasn't been brought up in the difficult business of politics," Plunkitt of Tammany Hall complained, "and he makes a mess of it every time." Bosses in all the metropolitan centers of the nation watched the aimless spreading of their cities and understood the problem of managing them. Their domains, they realized, were fragmented like giant jigsaw puzzles. Only a professional could provide the liberal application of patronage to glue them together, even though his workmanship might be both slipshod and expensive. All the boss's accomplishments—from new courthouses to public parks, transit systems to street lighting—came at the price of widespread corruption, waste, and an astronomical increase in the city's bonded debt.

Yet bosses seldom achieved the efficiency they sought. At best they built oligarchies and presided over loose federations of wards and precincts. In the 1890s the bosses' failings in efficiency and accountability would give progressive reformers much ammunition in attacking the urban machines. Meanwhile, in the absence of a genuine science of administration and of a corps of professional managers to apply it, the bosses at least provided a minimum of order and services—however lavishly and corruptly they improvised with the materials at hand.

**Patronage Politics in the States**
In the years immediately following the Civil War state bosses like Roscoe Conkling in New York and James G. Blaine, the "plumed knight" from Maine, were highly visible and colorful figures who organized their state parties while cultivating the arts of demagoguery and personal invective in Congress. Both these leaders were practiced congressional showmen and consummate haters with long memories. In fact, Conkling, head of the "Stalwart" faction of the Republican party, and Blaine, chief of the "Half-Breeds," were bitter rivals for control of federal patronage and cordially hated each other. Throughout the 1870s members of the House witnessed a series of verbal skirmishes. When, for example, Blaine learned from colleagues that the domineering and conceited Conkling had announced that the mantle of the famed Civil War orator Henry Winter Davis had fallen on himself, Blaine rose to demolish the "Turkey Gobbler" from New York with masterful sarcasm:

> The resemblance is striking. Hyperion to a satyr, Thersites to Hercules, mud to marble, dunghill to diamond, a singed cat to a Bengal tiger, a whining puppy to a roaring lion. Shade of the mighty Davis, forgive the almost profanation of that jocose satire.

By the 1880s, however, a younger generation of political leaders was taking over and quietly seizing control in many states by recruiting loyal followers and building efficient organizations. In New York, Thomas C. Platt, known to his friends as the "Easy Boss" and to his Democratic opponents as "Mousy," replaced the flamboyant Roscoe Conkling. Platt conducted party business on the sabbath at his "Sunday School" at the Amen Corner of the Fifth Avenue Hotel in New York City, where, it was said, vigorous "amens" from the assembled congregation of the faithful ratified his various nominations for governor, state senator, supreme court judge, or member of Congress. Platt's specialty was the "arrangement" with eager business interests whose spokesmen in turn regarded him as eminently "safe" and "sound." He was also a master of careful preparation for elections—what he called his "subsoil" work—and dispensed campaign funds with an unerring sense of the political odds. The New York State Assembly regularly did Platt's undemonstrative bidding, bottling up unwanted bills in committee and tailoring requested legislation to the Easy Boss's specifications. Friends and foes alike widely recognized Platt as the model of the new party leader whom one of his protégés, Elihu Root, described as the supreme power broker, "elected by no one, accountable to no one, bound by no oath of office, removable by no one."

Next door in Pennsylvania the Republican state boss was the sad-eyed, cynical calculator of his own strengths and other people's weaknesses, Matthew Quay, a veteran party man who had worked his way to the top of the political heap after twenty-five years' service. Matt Quay ran his statehouse ring out of his office in Harrisburg, which held his voluminous card-index files—"Quay's coffins"—containing useful information on every political figure in the state. The secret of Quay's success, like that of Platt in New York, was the quiet accommodation reached with the Pennsylvania Railroad, the directors of the Iron and Steel Association, and public-utility company executives whose needs he tended carefully and who were the principal beneficiaries of his silent rule.

The key device for harmonizing party interests at the state level was the caucus, where local bosses, county chairmen, and state legislators gathered to consult friendly business interests and stamp approval on the state boss's choice of candidates. But the real work was often done in advance and on the sly. Michigan boss James McMillan explained to his followers how his rise to the Senate only proved "what quiet work and an active continuance of party organization can accomplish.... When party organization is perfect, campaigns are more easily conducted and victory more certain."

Democratic party bosses won control over their states more slowly than Republicans, and, particularly in the one-party South, kept a looser grip on the party reins. Yet southern Democratic, or "Bourbon," conservatism soon became the model for longtime Democrats who continued to invoke the name of Jefferson in deploring the "spirit of centralization" while silently employing just that principle in staffing and strengthening their county cliques and statehouse operations. In both parties, as in the business world after 1880, concentration was the order of the day.

**A New Breed of Professionals**　　As late as 1880, however, much remained to be done. Democrats in that election year were entering the third decade of their prolonged period as the opposition party, and they still suffered from unimaginative leadership, a negative program, and a philosophy of "go slow." The Republican party had also fallen on evil days. Republicans had spent the 1870s watching their share of the popular vote dwindle and their hopes for holding the South dim and then disappear. In 1880 the party was still torn by contending factions—Conkling's "Stalwarts" and Blaine's "Half-Breeds." These factional squabbles concerned patronage rather than matters of policy, but they were serious enough to deadlock the Republican convention in 1880 and send delegates scurrying for a compromise candidate, James A. Garfield. Having gone down to defeat with three civilian contenders since the Civil War, Democrats decided to follow their Republican rival's example and try their luck with the military by nominating General Hancock, the hero of Gettysburg. From now on a new note of caution and calculation could be heard in the deliberations of the two major parties, both of which recognized the need for prudence and forethought in the tending of their political gardens.

Nevertheless the veteran professionals of the Civil War era stood firm against innovation and reform, inveighing against the nefarious plots of would-be reformers who sought to put them out of business with a federal bureaucracy free from political influence and the taint of corruption. For the old professionals in both parties, politics could not be cut and trimmed by moral shears or patched together with the principles of reform. Dismissing reform as contrary to human nature, and ridiculing its champions as long-haired men and short-haired women, the bosses snarled their defiance in crude and unambiguous language. Let the civil service reformers remain in their well-furnished parlors, exchanging rumors of political misbehavior while sipping their lemonade, declared Kansas Senator John J. Ingalls. The real world, the Ingallses and Blaines and Conklings insisted, was their own world of full whiskey tumblers and cigar smoke, fifteen-dollar votes, rolling logs, and brimming pork barrels.

But the day of the spoilsmen was ending, a political fact acknowledged even by the once-irreconcilable Ingalls himself, who likened the new political age to the long-extinct pterodactyl—the winged reptile with feathers on its paws and plumes on its tail. A political system in the chain of evolution that accommodated both the party loyalist and the reformer, Ingalls scoffed, "can properly be regarded as in the transition epoch and characterized as the pterodactyl of politics. It is, like that animal, equally adapted to waddling and dabbling in the slime and mud of partisan politics, and soaring aloft with discordant cries into the glittering and opalescent empyrean of civil service reform." In any event politics as usual was doomed to extinction.

Thus as the presidential election of 1880 approached and neither party appeared to have a decided edge, the professionals' confidence in the robust style and principle-be-damned began to evaporate. In subsequent presidential contests down to the turn of the century the new cautionary political style and prudential approach to policy was unmistakable, and nowhere was it more evident than among a new breed of presidential contenders.

## The Lost Decade

The twentieth-century novelist Thomas Wolfe once observed that for most Americans the Gilded Age presidents from Hayes to Harrison have become irretrievably lost:

> their gravely vacant and bewhiskered faces mixed, melted . . . together in the sea-depths of a past, intangible, immeasurable, and unknowable. . . . For who was Garfield, martyred man, and who had seen him in the streets of life? . . . Who had heard the casual and familiar tones of Chester Arthur? and where was Harrison? Where was Hayes? Which had the whiskers, which the burnsides; which was which?

**Campaign Propaganda for the Custodial Presidency**
*The "Grand National Republican Banner" provides the answer to Thomas Wolfe's question: "Which had the whiskers, which the burnsides; which was which?"*

The limited concept of the presidential office in the Gilded Age, and the equally limited political imaginations of the men who filled it, consigned these shadowy figures to oblivion.

**The Shadow Presidents**

The principal task assigned to these presidents by party managers in Congress was to get themselves elected without compromising their reputations by saying anything provocative, and then to dispense patronage dutifully to the party worthies. Winning the presidency was not easy, especially when no clear-cut issues of public policy divided the two parties. James Bryce, the British minister in Washington who observed his first presidential election in 1884 in the heated contest between Blaine and Cleveland, was amazed to find that neither party had a distinctive platform: "Neither party has any principles, any distinctive tenets. Both have traditions. Both claim to have tendencies. . . . All has been lost, except office or the hope of it."

Once elected, the new president found that the first order of business was handing out jobs, a process that was complicated, time-consuming, and personally demeaning. Immediately following his nomination in the summer of 1880,

Garfield received his orders from Stephen Dorsey, field marshal of the Republican National Committee, who insisted imperiously on a hurried conference with Roscoe Conkling and the other eastern bosses as "an absolute essential to success in this campaign."

> They want to know whether the Republicans of the State of New York are to be recognized...or whether the "Scratchers" and Independents and "featherheads" are to ride over the Republican party of this state as they have for the last four years. They...can only be satisfied by a personal conference with you.

Garfield later claimed that he hadn't given out any "mortgages" at the conference. "No trades, no shackles," he noted in his diary, but wondered whether the New Yorkers had been properly mollified. "My letters indicate that the New York trip did no harm and much good." In his brief time in office, Garfield was exhausted by job hunters, although he had been chosen by Republican bosses precisely for his sensitivity to the patronage demands of the party's warring factions. Soon after his inauguration in March 1881, Garfield's mutterings about party office seekers swelled to a sustained wail: "My God! What is there in this place that a man should ever want to get into it?" He was not to remain in it long. In July 1881, as Garfield was boarding a train in Washington for a well-earned vacation, a crazed government clerk who had recently been dismissed shot him in the back. Garfield lingered through the summer and died in September. "I am a Stalwart," Charles Guiteau had shouted as he fired at Garfield, "and Arthur is President now."

"My God! Chet Arthur!" was the response of liberal Republicans and Democrats alike at the prospect of four years of boss rule by a veteran spoilsman. Chester A. Arthur, former head of the corrupt New York customhouse and loyal lieutenant of Roscoe Conkling, had been given second place on the ticket chiefly to placate New York's Stalwart faction, as Garfield was widely recognized as a protégé of Blaine and his Half-Breeds. Arthur was jovial, suave, accommodating, and thoroughly hardened to the work of dispensing patronage. He once explained his political philosophy to a fellow Republican as the honest brokerage of competing interests. Elections, he warned, are won only *"when all the men in politics* are pleased and satisfied and set to work with enthusiasm for the ticket. They bring out the votes, and if you trusted these elections to business men and *merely respectable influences,* the Democratic Party would get in every time." The new president genially oversaw the staffing of the federal bureaucracy with party hacks even as he signed the Pendleton Act (1883), which established the independent Civil Service Commission charged with classifying federal jobs and with administering examinations. In two notable respects Arthur surprised his critics: he urged the prosecution of those involved in the fraudulent Star Route postal contracts, and he vetoed an unprecedented $18 million rivers and harbors bill. The fact that the Star Route prosecutions failed and that Congress passed the pork-barrel appropriation over his veto in no way lessened the surprise and appreciation of liberals and reformers in both parties who agreed, on his retirement, that Chet Arthur "had done well...by not doing anything bad."

In 1885 it was Grover Cleveland's turn to suffer the demands both of Democratic bosses clamoring for jobs and of civil service hopefuls bent on cleaning up the spoils system. Cleveland, like Garfield before him, endured a "nightmare" and complained constantly about "this dreadful, damnable office seeking." Cleveland's discomfort was the sharper because he had made his political fortune out of reform, first as the so-called Veto Mayor of Buffalo, New York, where he got rid of corrupt street-cleaning and sewer contracts, and then in the governorship of New York, where he quickly became known as the "Great Obstructionist" of the special interests. The "Big One," as the young assemblyman Theodore Roosevelt called him, looked the part of the reform-minded man of integrity—a massive three hundred pounds of jut-jawed, rocklike imperturbability—who called for "the application of business principles to public affairs" and perfected the veto as his chief weapon.

The Republicans had chosen as their 1884 standard-bearer the perennial public favorite and scourge of the Democracy James G. Blaine. This move had made Cleveland the obvious "reform" preference of the Democrats along with those disaffected Republicans (called variously "Mugwumps," "Holy Willies," "Dudes," and "Goody-Goodies" by the party regulars) who could not stomach the unsavory Blaine and bolted their party in the hope of destroying both the "Plumed Knight" and the spoils system. Still, genuine issues dividing the two contenders were difficult to discern. Blaine concentrated on the tariff, a recently discovered bone of contention, and Cleveland stressed his leadership of a "far-reaching moral movement," which left the two candidates much like Tweedledee and Tweedledum. Both men, Lord Bryce noted with amusement, openly declared their unyielding enmity to monopolies, their love of the flag, and their determination to defend the rights of Americans around the globe. Neither was willing to venture beyond these patriotic pronouncements to the uncertain ground of policy, and it was only a question of time before the issues became highly personalized and cheapened into a contest, as one observer commented, between "the copulative habits of one and the prevaricative habits of the other."

The presidential campaign of 1884 was a comedy of errors that dramatized the poverty of ideas besetting both parties. Republican and Democratic national organizations were equally matched. With firm control over the South, the Democracy contended on even terms with its opponents in all the key northern states by avoiding discussion of the tariff issue wherever possible. For their part, Republicans had only recently discovered the tariff as a campaign issue with which they were nervously testing the political waters. With no genuine policy differences at stake, professional managers on both sides resorted to slander and character assassination. The Republicans led off with a report of Cleveland's early departure from the paths of righteousness in fathering a child out of wedlock with a young widow who seemingly had "loved too well." Partisan press and pulpit denounced Cleveland as a "moral leper," "a gross and licentious man,"

**"Magnetic" Blaine**
*This Democratic party cartoon ridicules James G. Blaine as a magnet for corruption and chicanery in the presidential election of 1884.*

and "a man stained with disgusting infamy." Stunned Democratic managers who brought the news to Cleveland were further astounded by the candidate's admission that the story, if exaggerated, was nevertheless true. "Above all," Cleveland instructed his lieutenants, "tell the truth."

Democrats, who needed something stronger than the truth with which to fend off Republican attacks, found their weapon in another batch of the Mulligan letters published by the Boston press and further implicating Blaine in the railroad scandals of the late 1860s. Among the telltale letters was one that Blaine himself had written, exonerating him from all charges of misconduct, which he had sent to Warren Fisher, a railroad attorney, to sign. "The letter is strictly true," Blaine explained, "is honorable to you and me, and will stop the mouths of slanderers at once. Regard this letter as strictly confidential." Blaine closed his instructions with the reminder that in signing the letter Fisher would be doing him "a favor I shall never forget" and a final command to "burn this letter." Here was the ready means of defending "Grover the Good," which Democrats so badly needed. Soon came a spate of songs, rallying cries, and chants:

> *Ma, Ma!*
> *Where's my pa?*
> *Gone to the White House*
> *Ha! ha! ha!*

and

> *Blaine! Blaine!*
> *The Continental Liar*
> *From the State of Maine!*
> *Burn this letter!*

By election eve it was clear that victory would hinge on New York's 36 electoral votes, and at the last moment Republican managers made two fatal miscalculations. The first was allowing the Reverend Samuel D. Burchard, a Presbyterian minister, to explain his reasons for voting for Blaine to a gathering of New York City clergymen: "We are Republicans, and don't propose to leave our party and identify ourselves with a party whose antecedents have been Rum, Romanism, and Rebellion." When Blaine neglected to disavow Burchard's unfortunate remark, Democrats seized the opportunity to secure the city's Irish-American vote by spreading thousands of handbills with the inflammatory statement throughout the city.

Blaine's managers only compounded his troubles by staging a lavish fundraiser for New York's millionaires in the glittering ballroom of Delmonico's restaurant where, following a sumptuous banquet, they listened to Blaine claim credit for "organizing and maintaining the industrial system which gave to you and your associates in enterprise the equal and just laws which enable you to make this marvellous progress." Again the Democratic press, led by Joseph Pulitzer's *New York World,* exploited the Republicans' mistake in bold headlines. Above a cartoon showing fat capitalists in diamond-studded boiled shirts gathered around the groaning board blazed the headline:

THE ROYAL FEAST OF BELSHAZZAR BLAINE AND
THE MONEY KINGS
BLAINE HOBNOBBING WITH THE MIGHTY MONEY KINGS
MILLIONAIRES AND MONOPOLISTS SEAL THEIR ALLEGIANCE
AN OCCASION FOR THE COLLECTION OF A REPUBLICAN
CORRUPTION FUND

Blaine lost New York by 1,149 votes out of more than a million cast, enough to give Cleveland the election in a national count, which provided the Democrats with a margin of 23,000 votes out of more than 9 million cast. Blaine explained his defeat as the result of an "intolerant and utterly improper remark," and added ruefully: "I should have carried New York by 10,000 if the weather had been clear on election day, and Dr. Burchard had been doing missionary work in Asia Minor or Cochin China."

As president, Cleveland attempted to play the role of the realistic reformer. He admitted, however, that the "boss system" survived in American politics, and because it did, it was a necessity—"a disagreeable necessity, I assure you"—for him to recognize it. Approached by a prominent Democratic senator with a complaint about his strict policy regarding appointments, Cleveland asked what he wanted the president to do. "Why, Mr. President, I should like to see you move more expeditiously in advancing the principles of the Democracy." "Ah," Cleveland shot back, "I suppose you mean that I should appoint two horse-thieves a day, instead of one." Cleveland managed to double the number of jobs covered under civil service from 14,000 to 28,000, at the same time appointing his own people to all the jobs left untouched by the Pendleton Act. He had not been elected "merely for the purpose of civil service," he reminded his reform critics, and asked to be saved from "the misguided zeal of impracticable friends." No one could accuse Grover Cleveland of pandering to reform!

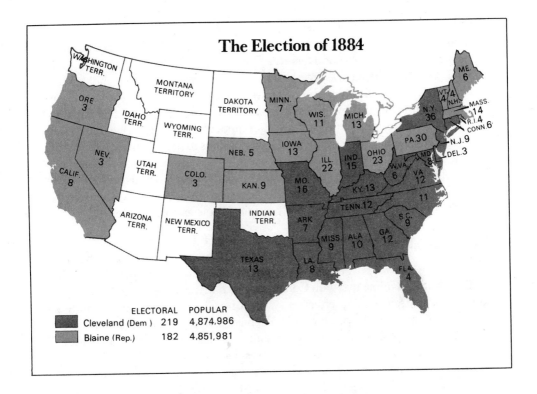

**The Election of 1884**

|  | ELECTORAL | POPULAR |
|---|---|---|
| Cleveland (Dem.) | 219 | 4,874,986 |
| Blaine (Rep.) | 182 | 4,851,981 |

Cleveland had greater success in checking the abuses in awarding veterans' pensions. "We are dealing with pensions, not with gratuities," he reminded Congress, but many of the pension claims were as specious as the one presented by a man who had hurt his ankle while *intending* to enlist. In 1866 there were 126,722 pensioners paid a total of $15.5 million. In 1885 there were 345,125 recipients of $65,171,937. Cleveland personally inspected each and every pension bill passed by Congress, and then resorted to his favorite weapon—the presidential veto. In his first administration he vetoed over one hundred such bills.

Benjamin Harrison, a prosperous railroad lawyer from Indiana and grandson of "Old Tippecanoe," President William Henry Harrison, narrowly defeated Cleveland in his bid for reelection in what was probably the most corrupt presidential election in American history. He then announced that "providence" had awarded his party a great victory. "He ought to know," snorted Matt Quay, the Republican boss of Pennsylvania, "that Providence hadn't a damn thing to do with it." Harrison, he added, would never know "how close a number of men were compelled to approach the gates of the penitentiary to make him President." The new president—whose personality, one observer noted, had all the warmth of a "dripping cave"—was scarcely the man to meddle in patronage matters. "When I came into power," he recalled for a group of Republican leaders, "I found that the party managers had taken it all to themselves. I could not name my own Cabinet. They had sold out every place to pay the election expenses." Harrison continued to leave patronage to congressional bosses, who quickly replaced some 30,000 Democratic postmasters with Republicans.

Yet by 1890 the civil service principle had taken root in the federal bureaucracy, and it continued to grow until by 1900 there were 100,000 positions subject to rules enforced by the Civil Service Commission. The gradual triumph of civil service affected the president's work quite directly. With fewer and fewer officeholders who could be dunned for contributions to party coffers, it fell to the president as party leader to seek out wealthy donors—for Republicans the Rockefellers and the Jay Goulds, for Democrats the Levi Mortons and Henry B. Paynes—who now contributed the lion's share to the party treasury. In this sense civil service reform strengthened the president's role as party leader.

**The Custodial Presidency**

In other respects, however, the Gilded Age presidents were content with their custodial role. The real power—to make budgets, authorize expenditures, and draft legislation—remained with Congress, which in the 1880s was just beginning to modernize itself with an effective system of chairmanships and committees. With the great political questions of Reconstruction now dead letters, there seemed no compelling demand for presidential leadership. To congressional Republicans and Democrats alike, their president seemed simply a first-among-equals in constant need of advice and direction.

Grover Cleveland clearly defined the custodial presidency by insisting on the "entire independence" of the executive power from the legislative branch. Cleveland's power lay in the veto, with which he sought to make Congress accountable and the federal government honest, impartial, frugal, and not very energetic. He used the veto sweepingly: in his first term (1885–89) he vetoed three times as many bills as had all his predecessors combined. His veto messages embodied a social as well as a legal conservatism. In the aftermath of a series of devastating crop failures in the Texas Panhandle, Congress passed the Texas Seed Bill, appropriating the modest sum of $10,000 for seed grain for needy farmers. But the assumption that in times of distress the federal government could lend a helping hand aroused Cleveland's ire:

> I do not believe that the power and duty of the General Government ought to be extended to the relief of individual suffering which is in no manner properly related to the public service or benefit. A prevalent tendency to disregard the limited mission of this power and duty should, I think, be steadfastly resisted, to the end that the lesson should constantly be enforced that though the people support the Government, the Government should not support the people.

Republican presidents tended to be less inflexible, but they agreed that drafting policies and programs was no part of their duties. None of the major pieces of Republican legislation that were passed during Harrison's administration (1889–93)—the Sherman Silver Purchase, the Sherman Antitrust Act, and the McKinley Tariff—bore the stamp of his design or the mark of his favor. Presidents of both parties were generally content with the narrow functions that had been assigned them by an antebellum tradition of legislative dominance.

Thus Congress was the most visibly active branch of the federal government, even though its pace, accelerating slightly, was still leisurely, and its sense of itself as a national lawmaking body was limited. The volume of congressional business had doubled from an average 37,000 public and private bills per session in the 1870s to 74,000 by the mid-1880s. Gradually both houses of Congress were organizing themselves, modifying an older deliberative style and adapting it to the routine of new and stronger committees like the House's powerful Ways and Means Committee. By 1890 an informal but highly organized clique of a half-dozen senators who controlled all committee appointments were managing a Republican-dominated Senate. In the House both parties reluctantly were beginning to agree on the need for tightening rules and procedures. The average length of congressional tenure increased. In the 1870s more than half the membership in each session was new. During the 1880s only one member in three was newly elected, and a decade later only one in four. By the end of the century Congress was filled with seasoned professionals.

Still, Congress was slow to break with its past. Senators and representatives still used the congressional floor as the forum for debate among elected agents whose connections with their local constituencies were all-important. Lawmaking under these circumstances tended to become an involved exercise in horse trading by representatives of competing interests. Nowhere was this process more in evidence than in the making of the tariff.

**Tariff Making**     The difficult and seemingly insoluble problem for Congress after the Civil War was not raising revenue but spending it. There was a surplus of federal revenue every year between 1866 and 1893, and the average annual surplus in the 1880s was $100 million, with more than half this amount coming from customs duties. To spend this enormous sum, legislators had only pork-barrel legislation and the patronage system that sluiced off some of the reserve into federal jobs (although for the latter the passage of the Pendleton Act restricted the use of federal funds). The tariff had become an embarrassment, and complaints multiplied against the principle of protection that took from the poor consumer and gave to the already-rich corporations. Republicans, suddenly in need of a strong defense of the tariff, took up James G. Blaine's cry that all the "wonders" of the previous twenty years were the result of high tariff schedules. Democrats gradually came to agree with Grover Cleveland that tariffs were "vicious, inequitable and illogical," in dire need of downward revision.

By the mid-1880s the tariff question had come to serve as a distinguishing symbol for Republicans and Democrats in much the same way that the race issue had functioned during Reconstruction and that the free-silver cause would operate in the 1890s. The tariff had a political as well as an economic significance. Combined imports and exports accounted for less than 10 percent of the gross national product. What kept the economy going, it was clear, was a burgeoning domestic market. The tariff, to be sure, was important for particular economic interests—wool growers, steel manufacturers, sugar refiners—who stood to gain directly from high import barriers. It was also true that as the decade of the 1880s opened, none of these interest groups had irrevocably tied itself to either the Republican or the Democratic party. Yet five years later "protection" had become the watchword of the Republican party, which increasingly catered to business and industry, and "a tariff for revenue only" was the war cry of the Democratic party, identified with farmers and urban consumers.

Tariff making defied science, reason, and all but the most tireless lobbyists. Enacting a new tariff—raising rates with Republicans or lowering them with Democrats—was an elaborate three-act drama. The opening act was filled with speeches concerning the dangers to civilization lurking behind higher or lower schedules—the babble of the innocents. Act Two was set in the legendary smoke-filled room where the lobbyists held court and the amendments were drafted. The final act contrasted the embarrassment of the bill's original sponsors with the quiet satisfaction of the special-interest groups who had rewritten it. This ritual began in 1882 when President Arthur appointed a blue-ribbon Tariff Commission and charged it with finding a way to lower the schedules for those American industries long past infancy and no longer in need of the paternal care provided by the tariff. The commission promptly obliged by drawing up a model bill that lowered the rates by an average 20 percent. When it was submitted to Congress, however, the carefully drafted bill lost whatever symmetry and harmony its draftees had originally claimed for it. The hammerings of the lobbyists and their representatives quickly reduced it to rubble. Still dissatisfied with their demolition work, both House and Senate wrote separate bills and then joined forces to pass a "compromise" that raised the schedules on almost every product.

In all the tariff contests between 1880 and 1900 the Republicans consistently frustrated the Democrats' attempts to lower schedules. Both the McKinley Tariff (1890) and the Dingley Tariff (1897) legislated sizable increases in protection, and the Democrats could not prevent their enactment. From 1880 until Woodrow Wilson's first administration more than thirty years later, Democrats failed to achieve a meaningful downward revision of the tariff schedules.

The real significance of the tariff debate lay in the rudimentary education in national policy planning it provided. In invoking Hamilton in support of an active government prepared to intervene in the economy, or in citing Jefferson in defense of limited government action, congressional debates slowly brought the outlines of national policy into focus across the country.

**Toward a National Policy**
The same recognition of the need for new national controls lay behind the Interstate Commerce Act (1887). In 1886 the Supreme Court in the *Wabash* case invalidated a state attempt to regulate rates for interstate railroads. In response the Senate appointed the Cullom Committee to investigate complaints against the railroads and to report on the feasibility of establishing a federal regulatory

commission. Conservatives from both parties dominated the Cullom Committee, and the Interstate Commerce Act was a conservative law, even though anguished reactionaries like Senator Nelson B. Aldrich cried out that any regulation amounted to revolution. The Interstate Commerce Commission, which the law established, was empowered to forbid collusive manipulation by the railroads in the form of rebates, rate discrimination, and railroad pools. But its supervisory powers were narrowly defined, and its decisions were subject to review by the courts. The Interstate Commerce Act was intended as a means of establishing national railroad policy, but the commission itself never achieved that goal.

Gilded Age politics produced the semblance rather than the substance of national policy. Neither the president nor Congress had a clear understanding of the powers needed by government to function effectively in national affairs. The concepts of a comprehensive national policy and executive leadership capable of carrying it out did not emerge until the twentieth century. Meanwhile rapid industrialization was producing severe economic and social disruption. Farmers were caught in a downward spiral of prices and credit. Industrial workers were locked in combat with management over wages, hours, and the right to organize. And small-town America, uneasy with the new political order, felt the stirrings of still another crusade for a Christian society. Ever since the Civil War, farmers, laborers, and moral reformers had been involved in third-party politics, but with scant success. Their main efforts—the Greenback Labor party and the Prohibition party—had never won more than 3.5 percent of the vote in a national election. Watching the repeated failures of these would-be reformers, the Republican and Democratic party bosses felt sure that the political stability they had achieved was permanent.

But there were deeper stirrings by 1890. In agrarian revolts in the countryside and civic campaigns in the cities, reformers were beginning to draw on the resources of two deep-lying traditions in American politics. The Populist movement in the trans-Mississippi West and in the South revived a spirit of social reform with strong ethical and religious overtones that had erupted repeatedly in the past in moments of crisis. And by 1895, in the nation's cities, progressive reformers were challenging boss politics by drawing on the fears of the established elite groups, on business notions of efficiency and economy, and on the scientific ideas of a new generation of professionals and academics. In the midst of industrial strife and rural discontent, these two sets of reformers—Populists and urban progressives—shattered the professional politicians' confidence by confronting them with new interpretations and promises of American life.

## Conditions Without Precedent: The Populist Revolt

The first reform effort to challenge the late-nineteenth-century political establishment was the Populist movement. The Populists had both political and social aims: they sought, first of all, to win elections and to send to Washington representatives who would repair the economic system, clean up political corruption, and return to "the plain people" the management of the social order. It was this combination of ambitions and aims that gave Populists the sense of being part of a great moral awakening rising from the "intellectual ferment" eagerly described by an early participant:

> People commenced to think who had never thought before, and people talked who had seldom spoken. On mild days they gathered on street corners, on cold days they congregated in shops and offices. Everyone was talking and everyone was thinking....Little by little they commenced to theorize upon their condition. Despite the poverty of the country, the books of Henry George, Bellamy, and other economic writers were bought as fast as the dealers could supply them. They were bought to be read greedily; and nourished by the fascination of novelty and the zeal of enthusiasm, thoughts and theories sprouted like weeds after a May shower....They discussed income tax and single tax; they talked of government ownership and the abolition of private property; fiat money, and the unity of labor;...and a thousand conflicting theories.

The great awakening that pointed the Populists toward a political course also raised two basic problems—defining ultimate economic ends and finding the necessary political means. They were going to have to organize quickly if they hoped to effect reforms. The preamble to the Omaha platform of July 1892 announced their grievances in the apocalyptic terms of an impending social crisis: "Corruption dominates the ballot box....The people are demoralized....The newspapers are largely subsidized or muzzled...our homes covered with mortgages; labor impoverished....The fruits of the toil of millions are boldly stolen to build up colossal fortunes for the few...." After excoriating the two major parties for neglecting these problems and indulging in a sham battle over the tariff, the Populists announced their own intentions. At first glance the economic program of Populism seemed to bear all the marks of an earlier small-scale entrepreneurial capitalism, with its hopes for the independent producer, steady growth rate, and voluntary cooperation. These hopes had once sustained the North and Lincoln's Republican party in their war against slavery. But instead of the promised millennium of small producers, the war had brought rapid business and financial consolidation and the rule of the spoilsmen. The original yeoman vision had dimmed until it guided only such marginal political groups as the prohibitionists and the Greenbackers. Thus the calls for a "new politics" of purification and participation came from the political margins—from Henry George's legion of "single taxers," and from the recruits to Edward Bellamy's "industrial army" and the converts to what was beginning to be called the Social Gospel who preached Christian cooperation. All the grievances stated in the Populist platform at Omaha were issues with social and cultural as well as political and economic meaning. The Populists saw the demonetization of silver and constricted bank credit as the handiwork of the "gold bugs"—parasites and plutocrats from the East—"to fatten usurers, bankrupt enterprise, and enslave industry." Monopolists and their hirelings in the halls of justice "despised the

**Salvation Army Meeting**
*"Soldiers" of the Salvation Army preach the gospel of social service and salvation.*

republic" and trampled on the people. These grievances underscored feelings of isolation and the insignificance of the beleaguered little man in an increasingly impersonal society. The social seedbed of Populism lay in the convictions of farmers and their neighbors in town that they were being dispossessed and in their fierce determination to reverse the course of history by returning power to the people.

**Regional Populism**    The Populist grievances were real enough, and so were their proposals. In the trans-Mississippi West their problems were the result of the hectic pace of unregulated economic development; in the South they were the product of a new feudal order complete with tenancy, a crop-lien system, and a large submerged class of dirt-poor farmers, both black and white. In the South and the Midwest alike, Populist leaders strove to overcome the sectional hatreds and racial prejudices that survived from the Civil War era and to unite farmers in both sections of the country in defense of their common interests. In both regions after 1887, exorbitant shipping charges, greedy middlemen, and extortionate mortgage rates were compounded by a series of crop failures that sent land prices and farm income skidding. Years of retrenchment and retreat followed, and destitute farmers trekked back eastward from the sod-house frontier, leaving behind ghost towns with gilded opera houses and empty stores.

In the trans-Mississippi West, western Kansas lost half its population between 1882 and 1892, and South Dakota's population shrank by some 30,000. In 1891 an estimated 18,000 prairie wagons lumbered back to Iowa from the Nebraska frontier. A sign on an abandoned farmhouse in Blanco County, Texas, in the drought year 1886 read: "200 miles to the nearest post office; 100 miles to wood; 20 miles to water, 6 inches to hell. God bless our home! Gone to live with the wife's folks." Populist Mary E. Lease put it this way:

> We were told two years ago to go to work and raise a big crop, that was all we needed. We went to work and plowed and planted; the rains fell, the sun shone, nature smiled, and we raised the big crop they told us to; and what came of it? Eight-cent corn, ten-cent oats, two-cent beef, and no price at all for butter and eggs—that's what came of it. Then the politicians said that we suffered from overproduction.

Populism in the South, while plagued by many of the same problems, showed distinctive features. Tenancy and crop liens exploited an underclass of black and white farmers, whose keen sense of their plight was limited by their fears of challenging an elite based on white supremacy. Western farmers risked little more than failure in organizing a third party. But in attacking their political establishment in Dixie, southern farmers put their personal security and sometimes their lives on the line. In some parts of the South, Populists made genuine attempts to appeal to both black and white farmers and to organize them, albeit separately.

In both regions Populism emerged rapidly from a nonpartisan background in 1890 and drew into politics groups that had previously been politically inarticulate and inert. Some of these new recruits were women: Mary Lease, who gave impassioned speeches on the power of monopolies; Annie L. Diggs, who was bent on saving the West from alcohol as well as Wall Street; Sarah Emery, whose tract *Seven Financial Conspiracies* traced the national decline along a descending curve of democratic participation. For every seasoned veteran of third-party politics such as Ignatius Donnelly, "the Sage of Nininger," there were three new converts, including Georgia's Tom Watson, fired by Populist speeches for campaigns "hot as Nebuchadnezzar's furnace."

The atmosphere at Populist meetings was heavy with the spirit of revivalism—"a pentecost of politics," according to one participant, "in which a tongue of flame sat upon every man." In South Dakota in 1892 the Populists staged a convention that was the largest ever held in the state. "It lasted one week, and partook of the good old-fashioned camp-meeting order," an observer commented. "I never saw men so filled with zeal and inspired by a cause." "From Forge and Farm; from Shop and Counter; from Highways and Firesides," ran an Ignatius Donnelly campaign broadside, "come and hear the 'Great Commoner' on the mighty issues which are moving mankind to the ballot box in the great struggle for their rights." Recruits, like converts, came from everywhere: farmers, hard-pressed local merchants, cattlemen, miners, small-town editors; men with

**Women Voting in Wyoming, 1888**
*Long before the Nineteenth Amendment enfranchising them (1920), women were voting in state elections, particularly in the West.*

chin whiskers, broad-brimmed hats, and muddy boots, accompanied by wives "with skin tanned to parchment by the hot winds, with bony hands of toil, and clad in faded calico." Quickly they became stereotypes to the rest of the world— comic hayseeds to the political opposition, heroic figures in the folklore of Populism with nicknames to match: "The Kansas Pythoness," "Bloody Bridles," "Sockless Socrates." Behind the mask appeared the original type, frequently a biblical figure like William A. Peffer, a Topeka editor elected to the United States Senate, who, with his full beard, steel-rimmed glasses, frock coat, and "habitual expression" of gravity on an otherwise inscrutable face, reminded Hamlin Garland of the Old Testament prophet Isaiah. "He made a peculiar impression on me, something Hebraic," Garland recalled, "something intense, fanatical."

The Populists, or People's party, drew a great variety of contrasting types into their reform movement. Southern Populists listened to the saving word not only from "Stump" Ashby, the Texas cowpuncher, and "Cyclone" Davis, toting his volumes of Jefferson, but also from the shrewd and hard-hitting country editor C. W. Macune, the professional North Carolina organizer Leonidas L. Polk, and Virginia patricians bearing the names of Page, Beverly, and Harrison. In the Midwest, Ignatius Donnelly's fiery campaign in Minnesota was offset by the sober advice of Charles H. Van Wyck, the party's candidate for governor in Nebraska, who singled out solid issues like railroad regulation for his campaign. For the most part, however, Populist rank and file were political newcomers, and they considered inexperience in the dubious practices of politicking a virtue. To eastern professionals in the two major parties, the Populists, gathered under banners urging the steadfast to vote as they prayed, presented the strange spectacle of an embattled interest group talking in tongues much like the early Christians. In fact, the Populists were followers of a social vision that had once guided the abolitionists before the Civil War—the dream of a redeemed society, honest, just, open, and equitable as the corrupt world of the moneybags and their political henchmen clearly was not.

**Building a National Party**   The Populists were new to the work of organizing a national political party and encountered formidable obstacles in building a platform designed to appeal to farmers, attract urban workers, and detach Republicans and Democrats from their former loyalties. They discovered that appeals for votes could be made in two distinct ways. First, they could explain their problems as staple-crop farmers and call on the federal government for help. Or they could transcend interest-group appeals and call on the "people"—all those who lived by the sweat of their brow—to join the crusade of "true producers" against the Money Power. Populism undertook both of these assignments at the same time. The Omaha platform, for example, called on "all men" to "move forward until every wrong is remedied, and equal rights and equal privileges [are] securely established for all the men and women of this country," and then proceeded to "demand a national currency, safe, sound, and flexible."

The interest-group program of the Populists grew out of the reasoning of political leaders who urged the federal government to respond to the specific needs of rural America—in effect, to come to the rescue. They demanded a graduated income tax to lift the financial burden from farmers and workers. They called for nationalizing the railroads, a postal savings bank system, and the free and unlimited coinage of silver. And they advocated a subtreasury plan for storing surplus crops and issuing loans that would circulate like money. The Populists could justify all these demands as protective measures for producers who lacked the security and the privileges that had been made available to the more favored industrial interests. Some of the Populist leaders who formulated these demands had a sophisticated grasp of what should be done to relieve the farmers' economic plight. And many of these demands would eventually be enacted into law in the twentieth century—an income tax, a paper currency freed from the gold standard and pegged to the strength of the national economy, and government price-support programs. Although the late-nineteenth-century Populists would have no role in carrying out these reforms, larger American society would ultimately recognize the logic of their demands.

Another set of Populist demands represented an attempt to reach out to urban workers by calling for reform of state and local taxation, the eight-hour day, limitation on the use of injunctions in labor disputes, immigration restriction, punitive legislation against monopolies, and farmer-labor cooperation in building a brotherhood of true producers. In defining the American land as "the heritage of all the people" and denying that the public domain could be monopolized "for speculative purposes," Populists anticipated the pioneer conservation efforts of President Theodore Roosevelt's administration. And in insisting on such basic changes in the political machinery as the direct election of senators, the Australian ballot, referendum and recall, Populism antedated many of the demands progressives would make twenty years later. Looking back in 1914 over her long career as a reform agitator, Mary E. Lease expressed satisfaction "that my work in the good old Populist days was not in vain":

> The Progressive party has adopted our platform clause by clause, plank by plank....Direct election of senators is assured. Public utilities are gradually being removed from the hands of the few and placed under the control of the people who use them. Woman suffrage is now almost a national issue....The seed we sowed out in Kansas did not fall on barren ground.

But Populism above all was an act of political rebellion and a promise of spiritual renewal—a new Declaration of Independence from alien rule. The Omaha platform called on all the people to seize power for themselves as their ancestors had in founding the nation: "Assembled on the anniversary of the birthday of the nation, and filled with the spirit of the grand general chieftain who established our independence, we seek to restore the government of the Republic to the hands of the plain people with whose class it originated.... We declare we must be in fact, as we are in name, one united brotherhood of freemen." In the ideal society that the Populists envisioned, honesty and integrity would infuse God's chosen people with high purpose and fierce determination. In the recesses of the Populist imagination lay dreams of a realm of harmony transcending partisan strife and economic exploitation—a haven where virtue and probity reigned supreme over a vast empire of rejuvenated yeomen. The triumph of American justice would finally come when the people had purified national life at the source. Only part of such a gigantic task involved the passage of "wise and reasonable legislation." A larger part involved a moral awakening "to bring the power of the social mass to bear upon the rebellious individuals who thus menace the peace and safety of the state."

Populism went beyond conventional politics in declaring itself "not a passing cloud on the political sky" nor a "transient gust of political discontent," but rather "the hope of realizing and incarnating in the lives of common people the fulness of the divinity of humanity." And with this shift in political perception came glimpses of social catastrophe should the people's courage fail—the swift approach of the "last days" before the final upheaval, nightmare visions of "men made beastlike by want, and women shorn of the nobility of their sex" pouring through the streets of Sodom past plutocrats who stand "grabbing and grinning" as the mob rushes to its destruction. Measured in the terms of a moral economy, the crisis facing the nation could be reduced to simple choices between justice and injustice, liberty and slavery. "The very fact of widespread suffering," a Nebraska Populist insisted, "is sufficient evidence that the whole system under which they have lived is a lie and an imposture." Once the people destroyed the Money Power, the old politics of individual greed and the selfish pursuit of wealth and power would die out. Like the abolitionists before the Civil War, the Populists emphasized issues that had symbolic resonance as well as practical import—above all the money question and, later, free silver.

It was unlikely that as political upstarts the Populists could immediately unseat the two major parties. Populists lacked the necessary funds with which to launch a national campaign, and, even more urgently they needed credible and attractive candidates. Populists sought to meet the first requirement with meager contributions from the faithful by passing the hat at midwestern whistle-stops. Even with the goodwill and support of local editors and the rural press, People's party candidates found it hard going against the organized and well-heeled major parties whose own editors scoffed at them as hayseeds and cranks, ne'er-do-wells and nincompoops:

> *Why should the farmer delve and ditch?*
> *Why should the farmer's wife darn and stitch?*
> *The government can make 'em rich,*
> *And the People's Party knows it.*
> *So hurrah, hurrah for the great P.P.!*
> *1 = 7, and 0 = 3*
> *A is B, and X is Z*
> *And the People's Party knows it!*

More serious as a liability was the lack of candidates with a national reputation and more than regional appeal. When their first choice as a contender, Leonidas Polk, died in the summer of 1892, his mantle fell on the veteran campaigner and former Greenbacker General James B. Weaver. Party leaders balanced the ticket with "General" James G. Field of Virginia, who was actually a former Confederate major. Field's southern credentials did not protect him from rough handling by Democratic party thugs who broke up Populist rallies throughout the South with rotten eggs, heckling, and physical intimidation. Southern voters, fearful of black suffrage and a possible Republican resurgence, held fast to the Democratic party, while Democrats in the West undermined the People's party campaign by offering fusion and promising future political considerations.

Cleveland won the election of 1892 with 267 electoral and 5,500,000 popular votes to 145 electoral and 5,180,000 for Harrison. The Populists polled over a million popular votes and 22 electoral votes for Weaver while carrying Kansas, Idaho, Nevada, and Colorado and sending a dozen congressmen to Washington. But the party had made few inroads in the South against an entrenched Democracy, and owed its support in the Mountain States chiefly to the appeal of free silver. Already fusion with the Democrats held increasing appeal for many Populist leaders. The year 1892, in fact, represented the high-water mark of Populist achievement. As the Panic of 1893 tipped the country into the deepest depression it had ever known, the Populists tried to reach into the industrial cities for support. But their party was still short of funds and attractive candidates, beset with organizational problems, and confronted with voter intransigence, particularly in the South, where Democratic regulars stuffed ballot boxes and threw out Populist votes. "We had to do it!" one Democratic party organizer later explained. "Those damned Populists would have ruined the country."

Although the People's party increased its total popular vote by nearly 50 percent in the elections of 1894, it lost control of several of the western states it had won two years earlier, and after 1894 there was not a state in either the South or the West that could be considered safe for Populism. The meaning of these disturbing statistics was clear: the third party would have to seek a formal alliance—"fusion"—with the Democrats. In addressing the thorny question of the best strategy for survival if not success, the Populists confronted the same problem that had plagued the Liberty party and the Free Soil party before the Civil War—whether to seek short-term gains in winning elections with a single issue at the expense of larger principles or, on the contrary, to cling to long-term reform objectives at the cost of continuing electoral defeat. Translated into the terms of future political campaigning, the question was a stark one: Should Populists unite with their former Democratic enemies on a "fusion" ticket of free silver even though they would be forced to relinquish much of the platform and many of their reform aims? Or, conversely, should the party retain its independence and steer an uncompromising course in "the middle of the road"?

The issue of fusion with the Democrats split the Populists into two warring camps. Henry Demarest Lloyd, a delegate to the Populist convention in St. Louis in the summer of 1896, most forcefully stated the case against uniting with the Democrats: "The Free Silver movement is a fake. Free Silver is the cow-bird of the Reform movement. It waited until the nest had been built by the sacrifices and labour of others, and then it laid its eggs in it. . . . The People's party has been betrayed. . . . No party that does not lead its leaders will ever succeed." Resistance to fusion was headed by diehard reformers like Lloyd and Ignatius Donnelly, who insisted that whereas the Democratic party had learned a few of its lessons, Populists ought not to "abandon the post of teacher and turn it over to [a] slow and stupid scholar." The diehards realized that the Democrats were not interested in any of the People's party reforms except the free coinage of silver in addition to gold—and that the free-silver movement largely reflected the interests of a powerful silver lobby mounted by wealthy mine owners. For southern Populists, moreover, fusion seemed suicidal, because it meant joining the Bourbon conservatives whose ranks they had so recently deserted—and whose response to the Populist challenge had often been intimidation, ballot-box stuffing, and appeals to white supremacy. But for a majority of the delegates at St. Louis, following the advice of silverite leadership, a "Demopop" ticket headed by

William Jennings Bryan seemed to offer the only sure route out of the political wilderness. As one of the "practical" fusionists explained:

> I do not want [my constituents] to say to me that the Populists have been advocates of reforms, when they could not be accomplished, but when the first ray of light appeared and the people were looking with expectancy and anxiety for relief, the party was not equal to the occasion; that it was stupid; it was blind; it "kept in the middle of the road" and missed the golden opportunity.

Following an angry debate in which it was charged by the losers that the People's party had become "more boss-ridden, gang-ruled, gang-gangrened than the two old parties of monopoly," the delegates agreed to unite with their former rivals under the banner of free silver.

## The Great Reversal: The Election of 1896

By 1896 the Democratic party was bitterly divided between agrarians and eastern business interests, and needed all the help it could get. Grover Cleveland's return to office four years earlier had been marked by the onset of a depression and a series of industrial strikes that seemed to many Americans the opening shots in a class war. In 1892 the first of these labor upheavals came outside Pittsburgh at Homestead, Pennsylvania, when Andrew Carnegie sailed for Scotland and left Henry Clay Frick, his hard-driving manager and an implacable enemy of labor unions, in charge of his steel company.

Frick took advantage of his chief's absence by attempting to break the Amalgamated Association of Iron and Steel Workers, whose eight hundred members at the Homestead plant were firmly supported by their unskilled comrades. The union's chief grievances were the reduction of a sliding scale, which amounted to a 20 percent cut in pay, and a matching reduction in tonnage rates at the steelworks, where new more efficient machinery had been installed. Frick countered the Amalgamated's demands by ordering a lockout, hiring strikebreakers, and erecting three miles of barbed-wire fence around Homestead. When his original plans for assembling a sheriff's posse of one hundred deputies yielded only twenty-three men, two of them on crutches and nineteen bearing doctors' certificates declaring them unfit to serve, Frick turned to the Pinkerton National Detective Agency, which supplied him with three hundred "watchmen" at $5 a day. The union retaliated by calling a strike, and prepared to repel the Pinkerton guards, who had been sent by barge up the Monongahela River with orders to seize the plant. A hail of bullets from the workers lining the shore met the invaders. In the pitched battle that followed, the Pinkertons were routed and their barges burned to the waterline. But final victory, as Frick and Carnegie had foreseen, lay with the company, which prevailed on the governor of Pennsylvania to send in the militia to open the plant. In July 1893 some 1,000 new workers entered the Homestead mill under military protection, and two months later a grand jury, following Frick's orders, indicted the union leaders on charges of murder, riot, and conspiracy. But when no jury could be found that would convict the defendants, charges were summarily dropped. Frick's unionbusting nearly cost him his life: in the course of the strike a young anarchist, Alexander Berkman, attempted to assassinate him but bungled the job. One of the soldiers stationed at Homestead was overheard to shout, after Berkman's failed attempt, "Three cheers for the assassin!" for which opinion his commanding officer had him strung up by his thumbs, ordered his head shaved and the miscreant drummed out of camp. The steel union fared little better. After five months out on strike, the Homestead workers were forced to accept the harsh new terms of the settlement, suffering a defeat that ended effective organizing in the steel industry for nearly half a century. Andrew Carnegie, who had kept in close touch with Frick throughout the strike from his sumptuous Skibo Castle in Scotland, cabled congratulations to his manager on a job well done.

**The Pullman Strike**    Cleveland threw his considerable weight on the side of management against the forces of organized labor in the Pullman Strike of 1894. The Pullman Strike, like the Homestead Strike, was a desperate response to the antiquated ideas of a big businessman whose sense of duty to his employees involved building them a model company town but did not extend to allowing them the right to negotiate their wages. The town of Pullman south of Chicago was widely hailed as a model workers' community with its substantial brick houses fronting on well-kept lawns and tree-lined streets, its library, meetinghouse, and public park. Living conditions at Pullman were vastly superior to housing available elsewhere in the region, but rents and taxes were high, and George Pullman's rules for property maintenance and personal behavior were arbitrary and irksome. Pullman's company town provided many of the amenities made possible by the new science of urban planning, but it also displayed all the unlovely features of industrial feudalism.

Worker protest stemmed from George Pullman's personal decision in the bitter depression winter of 1894 to reduce wages in his shops while at the same time keeping rents pegged at their current high level. Approached by a grievance committee of workers, Pullman announced that there was no connection between his two roles of town landlord and president of the Pullman Palace Car Company. He refused to hear the committee's complaints and instead summarily fired three of the delegates. When all requests for arbitration had failed, workers struck and Pullman closed his shops. As tensions mounted in the early summer of 1894, Pullman's workers appealed for help to the fledgling American Railway Union and its charismatic president, Eugene V. Debs. George Pullman turned to the General Managers Association, a tight-knit group composed of the chief executives of the twenty-four railroads entering Chicago. The General Managers promptly instructed their members to fire all workers who participated in the rapidly spreading strike. Debs's "one big union," flushed with its recent victory over James J. Hill's Great Northern Railroad, boasted 150,000 members in 465 locals. Although Debs was reluctant to commit his new union to an unequal contest with railroad management, the intransigence of the General Managers, whose members were spoiling for a fight, forced his hand. On the eve of the national boycott, the chairman of the General Managers Association was heard to admit that "we can handle the various brotherhoods, but we cannot handle Debs. We have got to wipe him out too." In his address "To the Railway Employees of America," Debs defined the issue squarely: "The struggle with the Pullman Company has developed into a contest between the producing classes and the money power."

When the Pullman Company, backed by the General Managers Association, rejected a final appeal for arbitration, Debs had no choice but to declare a boycott against all Pullman cars, even those carrying the mails. The company and the managers, turning this decision to their own advantage, sought an injunction from the federal courts and appealed directly to President Cleveland for the immediate dispatch of federal troops. Cleveland quickly obliged. Faced with a choice between the rights of labor and the rights of property, the president unhesitatingly sided with the men of property. The arrival of federal troops in Chicago triggered widespread protest and flaring violence as crowds of workers attacked a regiment that retaliated by firing at point-blank range, killing several participants and onlookers. By midsummer there were 14,000 troops in the city. Defeated and demoralized, workers were sullenly returning to work by the end of the summer, but George Pullman and the General Managers were still bent on revenge and punishment. A federal grand jury's indictment of Debs for conspiracy was dropped, but despite an able defense by his lawyer, Clarence Darrow, Debs was convicted of contempt in ignoring the injunction and sentenced to six months in jail.

**The Depression of 1893**

The American economy hit bottom in 1894. Five hundred banks closed their doors, 16,000 business firms collapsed, and unemployment reached nearly 20 percent. New issues on the New York Stock Exchange plummeted from $100 million to $37 million, and 2.5 million jobless workers tramped winter streets looking for work. Municipal governments and private charity organizations could not cope with the large numbers of destitute men who wandered aimlessly from city to city, finding factory gates closed everywhere and long lines at soup kitchens. Not since the dark days of the Civil War had the country seemed so threatened.

Workers met the depression and the savage wage cuts it brought with the only weapon they possessed—the strike. In 1894 alone there were more than 1,300 strikes. The mining industry was hit by a wave of strikes that rolled across the country from the coal fields of the East to Coeur d'Alene in Idaho, where besieged miners fought with sticks of dynamite, and Cripple Creek, Colorado, where armed deputies broke up demonstrations. For such acute economic suffering President Cleveland prescribed the heroic remedies of self-denial and sacrifice.

The specter of masses of starving men marching on the nation's cities to plunder and pillage in an uprising of the dispossessed turned into farce in the spring of 1894 with the arrival in Washington of Coxey's Army, a "petition in boots" that had come to the capital to ask for work. The leader of the few hundred jobless men who finally straggled into the city was the self-appointed "General" Jacob Coxey from Massillon, Ohio. Coxey simply wanted to present his plan for solving unemployment with a "good roads bill," which would finance public improvements with $500 million worth of government bonds. The Cleveland administration's reaction to this living petition was a measure of its fear of mass upheaval: Coxey's followers were dispersed and their leader jailed on a technicality, while rumors of revolution swept through the city.

Cleveland blamed the free-silver forces for the depression. In 1890 Congress had responded to the clamor of the silver interests and had passed the Sherman Silver Purchase Act, which required the government to buy 4.5 million ounces of silver each month and to pay for it with treasury notes redeemable in gold or silver. The Sherman Silver Purchase Act brought a sudden rush on the gold reserves of the United States by investors frightened by high imports and falling crop prices. The gold reserves plunged from $190 million to $100 million in just three years. As the depression deepened, Cleveland persuaded Congress to repeal the Silver Purchase Act. The purpose of repeal, he insisted, was to make the nation's currency "so safe . . . that those who have money will spend and invest it in business and enterprise instead of holding it." After a heated debate Congress complied in 1893, but the repeal seriously weakened Cleveland's control over his own party. He had succeeded in limiting the flow of silver from the mines at the behest of eastern bankers, but in so doing he had also lost support of the agrarian half of the Democratic party, as well as the senators representing western silver-mining interests. By 1895 the president was complaining that there was "not a man in the Senate with whom I can be on terms of absolute confidence."

**The Gold Standard: "A Crown of Thorns"?**  To stop the drain on American gold, Cleveland issued government bonds at a generous rate of interest to attract European investors. In calling on the banking syndicates of J. P. Morgan and August Belmont to market the bonds, the president only compounded his political difficulties. Working together, the administration and the bankers arranged the sale of government bonds for gold on terms that allowed the banking houses to manipulate exchange rates in their own favor. To the Populists and to irate Democrats in the South and West, Cleveland's deal with the bankers was powerful proof of a Wall Street conspiracy to rig the economy against them. Even Joseph Pulitzer's *New York World,* again serving as the watchdog of the little man's interests, denounced the "Bond Scandals" in boldface headlines:

SMASH THE BOND RING
GO TO THE PEOPLE
SAVE THE COUNTRY FROM THE MISCHIEF, THE WRONG,
THE SCANDAL OF THE PENDING BOND DEAL WITH THE
MORGAN SYNDICATE

The silverites proceeded to make the presidential election of 1896 a one-issue campaign. Silver and gold quickly became organizing symbols for diametrically opposed (and, to modern economists, equally misguided) strategies for economic recovery. Financial policy was treated as sacred truth, and the opposing view was inevitably denounced as utterly sinful. According to its defenders silver was the "people's" money—abundant, cheap, and flexible. To businessmen and bankers gold was sacrosanct and the sole "honest currency"—solid and time-tested. Cleveland chose "sound money," the gold standard, and currency restriction as the only ethical course, while William Jennings Bryan described gold as "a crown of thorns" for bankrupt farmers and western debtors, pressed on the brow of the honest laborer who was being crucified by the moneylenders. In fact Cleveland's monetary policy did worsen the effects of the depression. But more important, it gave farmers a highly visible target for their grievances. Addressing his backcountry constituents, South Carolina demagogue Ben Tillman denounced the president as a Judas who had thrice betrayed the Democracy: "He is an old bag of beef, and I am going to Washington with a pitchfork and prod him in his fat ribs."

With similar intentions Democrats gathered in Chicago for the convention of 1896. Southern and western Democrats quickly realized that by rejecting Cleveland's restrictionist policies and advocating the free and unlimited coinage of silver, they had an opportunity to upstage the Populists. The thirty-six-year-old Bryan, "strong-limbed, strong-lunged," immediately emerged as the choice of the agrarian wing of the party, "the wild crowd" ready to be stampeded for the Nebraskan. "Ear-splitting noises were heard; waves of scarlet fans danced in the galleries." The westerners ran roughshod over the "sound money" wing of the Democratic party and drove them out of the convention to form their own splinter organization. Bryan spoke the mood of his followers in sounding a new note of resistance:

> We have petitioned, and our petitions have been scorned; we have entreated, and our entreaties have been disregarded; we have begged and they have mocked when our calamity came. We beg no longer; we entreat no more; we petition no more. We defy them!

The eastern press, both Republican and Gold Democratic, replied with charges of anarchy and treason. "The Jacobins are in full control at Chicago," one editor announced, comparing Bryan and his supporters to the radicals of the French Revolution. "No large political movement in America has ever before spawned such hideous and repulsive vipers." Both the promise and the danger of a Democratic victory seemed greater after the Populists' convention in St. Louis also endorsed Bryan for president. Not since 1860 had the fate of the nation appeared to hang in the balance of a single election. In 1896, as in 1860, the differences were sectional and economic, but they were also social and cultural, as two fundamentally opposed views of politics competed for the American voter's allegiance. There were those Republicans, Bryan told the assembled delegates, "who believe that, if you only legislate to make the well-to-do prosperous, their prosperity will leak through on those below." The Democratic party's idea, on the contrary, "has been that if you legislate to make the masses prosperous, their prosperity will find its way up through every class which rests upon them."

Bryan and his Republican opponent, William McKinley, between them gave more than nine hundred speeches in the campaign of 1896, the Republican from his front porch in Canton, Ohio, to throngs of admiring visitors shipped in by party managers, and the "Boy Orator of the Platte" at every whistle-stop in the West where local leaders could collect a crowd. Bryan traveled some 18,000 miles in the pioneer presidential railroad campaign, the last of which would be President Harry Truman's half a century later. Behind his picket fence in Canton, McKinley sounded the old Republican refrains of the "dignity of labor" and the danger of "cheap money" while appealing to American patriotism. "In America," he told his listeners, "we scorn all class distinctions. We are all equal citizens and equal in privilege and opportunity." The candidates' speeches riveted national attention on the money question, which quickly brought into focus cultural and social disagreements between urban and rural America. When a hostile eastern press accused Bryan of a lack of dignity in playing the demagogue, he replied that he would rather have people say "that I lacked dignity than...that I lacked backbone to meet the enemies of the Government who work against its welfare in Wall Street." To the delegations of war veterans, temperance leaders, ministers, loyal editors, and local notables who made the paid-for pilgrimage to his front porch in Canton, McKinley prophesied that the coming year would be "a year of patriotism and devotion to the country":

> I am glad to know that the people in every part of the country mean to be devoted to one flag, and that the glorious Stars and Stripes (great applause); that the people of the country this year mean to maintain the financial honor of the country as sacredly as they maintain the honor of the flag.

Bryan soon expanded his economic indictment of the Money Power to a plea for a national moral revival. Republicans, capitalizing on the gradual upturn in the economy late in the summer, continued to denounce Bryan's platform as "revolutionary and anarchistic...subversive of the national honor and threatening to the very life of the Republic."

**Bryan: A Crusading Prophet**    A powerful orator and an appealing political figure, Bryan was new to the business of presidential campaigning. In casting his party adrift from its eastern financial moorings, he was forced to improvise. The professional politicians in the Democratic party withheld their support, sensitive to the sound-money opinions of their business backers and appalled by the prospect of an inflationary free silver. Bryan rejected the limited offers of the few party leaders who remained loyal to him. Sensing the need for new rules and definitions, he cast himself in the role of a crusading prophet who could purify his party and his country—by eliminating corruption, paring campaign budgets, purging the party of hacks, and preaching principles rather than praising men and cutting deals.

As the new mass leader, Bryan appeared an avenging angel of outraged American yeomanry, the people's savior stopping his campaign train for just one more sermon to his flock. He invariably apologized to his listeners, confessing that "a large portion of my voice has been left along the line of travel, where it is still calling sinners to repentance." Bryan's speeches drew on a fund of stock religious images as he mixed indictments of the Money Power, the tariff, and the gold standard with allusions to the Old Testament. His message was always the same: the people must arise in their majesty to smite the moneylenders and destroy their temple. Audiences came to know his arguments by heart and gathered to hear confirmation of their beliefs in the Protestant ethic of hard work and a just reward. When their leader assured them that "every great economic question is in reality a great moral question," they understood instinctively and they cheered. As Bryan preached the saving word of free silver, his audiences saw the stone suddenly rolled away and "the door . . . opened for a progress which would carry civilization up to higher ground."

**"Live and Let Live" with McKinley**   Republicans, following the orders of their new managers, chief among them Mark Hanna of Ohio, willingly exchanged places with their Democratic rivals. Tossing aside their moralistic reform heritage as a burden, they embarked on a pragmatic course toward a coalition of business and labor in the nation's major cities, where most of the votes lay. Their chosen candidate was the veteran Ohio politician William McKinley, who was a born compromiser and astute legislator, with no strikingly original ideas but presumably with plenty of political horse sense.

Behind McKinley in the shadows stood Ohio's Mark Hanna, a new breed of political boss—the wealthy businessman with an urge to play kingmaker. Hanna had made a fortune in the street railway business, and by 1896 was president of a large midwestern bank and a rich merchant prince whose fleet of ore boats on the Great Lakes brought coal and iron to the region's steel mills. A rival businessman once observed that "life meant war to Mark Hanna. . . . And he made war, not to bend men but to break them." Building on an interest in municipal politics to protect his franchises, Hanna turned to state politics and pioneered in forming Republican businessmen's associations in the Midwest. He was heard to say that in defining economic issues as primarily moral questions Bryan was quite wrong—"all questions of government in a democracy [are] questions of money." Money was just what he so successfully raised for his protégé McKinley. Hanna's career as Republican party manager represented a shift in the locus of power— from regional party professional to national businessman boss, and from the Northeast to the Midwest. Both these displacements were in evidence in a campaign confrontation in 1896 between Massachusetts Republican Senator Henry Cabot Lodge, the imperious "scholar in politics" and McKinley's burly,

**Campaign Styles: Old and New**
*Bryan (above) barnstormed the country in the time-honored political fashion, while Republicans advertised McKinley (left) with an icon of prosperity.*

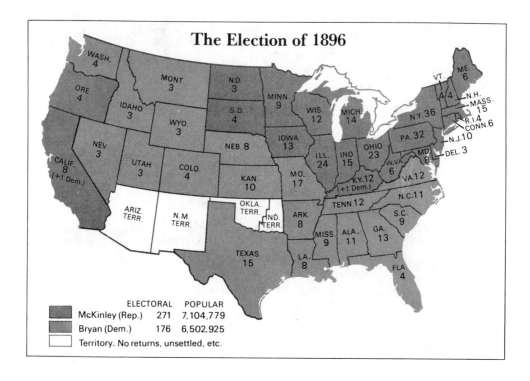

**The Election of 1896**

| | ELECTORAL | POPULAR |
|---|---|---|
| McKinley (Rep.) | 271 | 7,104,779 |
| Bryan (Dem.) | 176 | 6,502,925 |
| Territory. No returns, unsettled, etc. | | |

rough-hewn campaign manager. Lodge presented Hanna with an ultimatum: he would follow Lodge's orders and put a gold plank in the platform for eastern banking interests or "we'll rip you up the back."

> "Who in hell are you?"
> "Senator Henry Cabot Lodge, of Massachusetts."
> "Well, Henry Cabot Lodge, of Massachusetts, you can go plumb to hell! You have nothing to say about it."

McKinley's image was the clever contrivance of Hanna and his Republican managers, who recognized the liabilities of moralism and a legacy of reform in an age of secular industrial organization, and the need for full-time professional organizers, effective propaganda, and a full treasury. From his front porch McKinley dispensed sage advice in the form of nostalgia and political truisms: "What we want, no matter to what political organization we may have belonged in the past, is a return to the good times of years ago. We want good prices and good wages, and when we have them we want them to be paid in good money...in dollars worth one hundred cents each." Meanwhile Republican workers released an unprecedented flood of pamphlets, posters, printed speeches, and editorials that reached into every corner of the country. All their efforts were carefully orchestrated to new themes of cultural and ethnic toleration and were arranged to appeal to farmers and workers, small businessmen and big bankers, shippers and consumers, Catholics as well as Protestants, and a variety of ethnic groups to whom the gold standard was offered as the last best hope of democracy. McKinley himself summed up the new Republican message: "We have always practiced the Golden Rule. The best policy is to 'live and let live.'" With the blessings of their candidate, the Republicans turned their backs on their moralist past and squared to the task of engineering a broad social consensus.

The Republicans won a decisive victory in the election. With 7 million popular and 271 electoral votes, McKinley swept the entire East and Midwest, carried California and Oregon, and held on to Minnesota, North Dakota, and Iowa. Bryan, with 6.5 million popular and 176 electoral votes, won the Solid South together with the Plains and Mountain States. Beneath the regional features of the election of 1896 lay the deeper meaning of the political turnabout. With their votes a majority of Americans declared their preference for toleration and accommodation.

The meaning of the Democrats' defeat was clear. The American electorate had rejected the producerist countercrusade against corporatism, modernism, and secularism. There would undoubtedly be new reforms as the twentieth century opened, but they would be tailored to the mounting demands of economic and political consumers. From now on, political parties would have to consider and cater to the wishes of a multitude of social interests, welcoming newcomers from a wide variety of ethnic, cultural, and religious groups, meeting their needs, listening to their complaints, and serving their interests.

The election of 1896 also made it clear that the organizational revolution that was transforming business and finance had now invaded politics. Just as both houses of Congress were beginning to modernize their procedures for doing the nation's business, so the two principal political parties had learned the importance of efficient organization, continuing communications, flexible and politically sophisticated candidates, and, above all, money with which to run their political machinery.

**The Party System Realigned**

Finally, and most significant for the immediate future, the election of 1896 broke the grip of party discipline and loyalty that throughout the Gilded Age had been considered a permanent feature of American politics. The election freed the American party system for a long-term realignment of voting patterns that would reveal the average voter as considerably more independent than the professionals had once assumed.

Bryan had uncovered a latent American suspicion of machine politics, a set of misgivings that had been buried in the rubble of the Civil War. In his unsuccessful campaign he had located this skepticism in the agrarian mind, had attempted to exploit it, and had failed. But by 1896 young urban reformers were already experiencing a similar distrust of entrenched political power and were beginning to experiment with still another form of politics. The political program of these emerging reformers, while it promised to end machine politics and return power to the people, envisioned not the rule of righteousness but the triumph of middle-class professionals. The vision of social reformers organizing American cities after 1890 centered on an efficient, accountable, economically run "organic city" that was man-made rather than God-given. With the stirring of these reform hopes came a second, more potent challenge to the old Gilded Age politics—the challenge of progressivism.

## CHRONOLOGY

| | | | |
|---|---|---|---|
| **1880** | James A. Garfield elected president. | | McKinley Tariff raises duties to average 49.5 percent. |
| **1881** | Garfield assassinated; Chester A. Arthur becomes president. | **1892** | Populists organize, nominate General James B. Weaver for president. |
| **1883** | Pendleton Act establishes independent Civil Service Commission. | | Grover Cleveland elected president. Homestead Strike in Carnegie steel mills. |
| **1884** | Grover Cleveland elected president, defeating Republican James G. Blaine. | **1893** | Financial panic sends U.S. economy into four years of depression. |
| **1887** | Interstate Commerce Act attempts to control railroads. | | Congress repeals Silver Purchase Act. |
| **1888** | Benjamin Harrison narrowly defeats Cleveland and is elected president. | **1894** | Pullman Strike broken by federal troops; Eugene V. Debs jailed. "Coxey's Army" of unemployed marches on Washington. |
| **1890** | Sherman Silver Purchase Act passed, resulting in depleted gold reserves. Sherman Antitrust Act passed in attempt to regulate monopolies in restraint of trade. | **1896** | William McKinley elected president, defeating William Jennings Bryan and "free silver." |
| | | **1897** | Dingley Tariff raises duties to a new high of 57 percent. |

## SUGGESTED READINGS

The end of Reconstruction is chronicled in Eric Foner, *Reconstruction: America's Unfinished Revolution* (1988), and William Gillette, *Retreat from Reconstruction, 1869–1879* (1979). Michael Perman, *The Road to Redemption: Southern Politics 1869–1879* (1984), analyzes the return to power of the Democrats in the South after the Civil War, and Joel Williamson, *The Crucible of*

*Race: Black-White Relations in the American South Since Emancipation* (1984), traces the course of race relations in the South since the Civil War.

An invaluable introduction to American politics and society from the end of the Civil War to 1900 is Morton Keller, *Affairs of State: Public Life in Nineteenth Century America* (1977). There are several useful guides to politics in the Gilded Age. David Rothman, *Politics and Power: The United States Senate, 1869–1901* (1966), traces the emergence of the modern Senate as it is organized in the 1890s by new wealthy representatives of big business. H. Wayne Morgan, *From Hayes to McKinley: National Party Politics, 1877–1896* (1969), concentrates on the organizational problems of the two major parties. Robert D. Marcus, *Grand Old Party: Political Structure in the Gilded Age, 1880–1896* (1971), analyzes the workings of the Republican party, and Samuel Merrill, *Bourbon Democracy of the Middle West, 1865–1896,* gives a good regional account of the Democrats for the same period. Southern politics is perceptively treated in four important works: C. Vann Woodward, *The Origins of the New South, 1877–1913* (1951); Dewey Grantham, Jr., *The Democratic South* (1963); Albert D. Kirwan, *Revolt of the Rednecks: Mississippi Politics: 1876–1925* (1951); and Morgan Kousser, *The Shaping of Southern Politics: Suffrage Restriction and the Establishment of the One-Party South, 1880–1910* (1974). Lawrence Goodwyn, *Democratic Promise: The Populist Movement in America* (1976), rehabilitates the image of southern Populists. Stanley P. Hirshon, *Farewell to the Bloody Shirt: Northern Republicans and the Southern Negro, 1877–1893,* considers the race issue as it affected party politics. Mary R. Dearing, *Veterans in Politics* (1952), covers the activities of Civil War veterans, and Marc Karson, *American Labor Unions and Politics, 1900–1918* (1958), discusses unions and politics in the opening years of the twentieth century.

On agrarian political protest in the Gilded Age, see Steven Hahn, *The Roots of Southern Populism: Yeoman Farmers and the Transformation of the Georgia Upcountry, 1850–1890* (1983); Peter H. Argersinger, *Populism and Politics: William Alfred Peffer and the People's Party* (1974); and Martin Ridge, *Ignatius Donnelly: Portrait of a Politician* (1962). On African-American political participation in the New South, consult Howard N. Rabinowitz, *Race Relations in the Urban South* (1978); J. Morgan Kousser, *The Shaping of Southern Politics: Suffrage Restriction and the Establishment of the One-Party South* (1974); C. Vann Woodward, *The Strange Career of Jim Crow* (3d ed., 1966); and Louis R. Harlan, *Booker T. Washington: The Making of a Black Leader, 1865–1901* (1972).

There are a number of good studies of crucial elections in the 1880s and 1890s. Among the best are Paul W. Glad, *McKinley, Bryan, and the People* (1964); Stanley Jones, *The Presidential Election of 1896* (1964); and J. Rogers Hollingsworth, *The Whirligig of Politics: The Democracy of Cleveland and Bryan* (1963). Two challenging studies, Paul Kleppner, *The Cross of Culture: A Social Analysis of Midwestern Politics, 1840–1900* (1970), and Richard J. Jensen, *The Winning of the Midwest* (1971), explore cultural factors as determinants of voting behavior in the Midwest during the Gilded Age.

There are several excellent biographies of major political figures. Three of the best studies of Bryan are Paolo E. Coletta, *William Jennings Bryan: Political Evangelist, 1860–1908* (1964); Paul W. Glad, *The Trumpet Soundeth: William Jennings Bryan and His Democracy, 1896–1912* (1964); and Louis W. Koenig, *Bryan: A Political Biography of William Jennings Bryan* (1971). For McKinley see H. Wayne Morgan, *William McKinley and His America* (1963), and the very readable study of McKinley's life and times, Margaret Leech, *In the Days of McKinley* (1959), as well as the more recent, fuller account of the McKinley years, Lewis L. Gould, *The Presidency of William McKinley* (1980). Biographies of other major figures include Horace Samuel Merrill, *Bourbon Leader: Grover Cleveland and the Democratic Party* (1957); Kenton J. Clymer, *John Hay: The Gentleman as Diplomat* (1975); and a brilliant recent biography of Eugene V. Debs by Nick Salvatore, *Eugene V. Debs: Citizen and Socialist* (1982).

On the troubled 1890s a good overview is Harold U. Faulkner, *Politics, Reform and Expansion, 1890–1900* (1959).

# 24

# *The Progressive Impulse*

N 1915, as the progressive movement neared its peak, a young professor of government at New York University, Benjamin Parke DeWitt, published a book entitled *The Progressive Movement,* in which he catalogued the political and social reforms in the United States in the previous two decades. DeWitt, an active progressive and ardent admirer of Theodore Roosevelt, looked behind the campaigns and the elections and discovered three interlocking reform tendencies:

> *The first of these tendencies is found in the insistence by the best men in all political parties that special, minority, and corrupt influence in government—national, state, and city—be removed; the second tendency is found in the demand that the structure or machinery of government . . . be so changed and modified that it will be more difficult for the few, and easier for the many, to control; and finally, the third tendency is found in the rapidly growing conviction that the functions of government are too restricted and that they must be increased and extended to relieve social and economic distress.*

DeWitt's analysis was accurate. The progressives believed that government at all levels was both inefficient and corrupt. Because it was corrupt, it ignored the needs of the people. Therefore, the people themselves had to seize the initiative in repairing the whole system. According to progressive logic, the first job was to remove unworthy and inept politicians and to replace them with reliable public servants drawn from the popular ranks and equipped with the needed expertise. These new leaders would then see to it that government—city, state, and national—performed an expanding range of tasks efficiently and responsibly. Progressives, in short, found in the idea of scientific government the materials for building a national reform movement.

A variety of forces shaped the progressive movement. There was no single progressive type among the leaders or the rank and file; there was no typical age, status, background, religion, or education. The progressives were drawn from the mainstream of the native-born middle class that dominated American politics in the first two decades of the twentieth century. Educated, articulate, and eager to apply their ideas for reforming society and politics, they held no monopoly on political gentility and could be found in equal numbers in the reform wings of both the Republican and the Democratic parties.

The progressives had no uniform platform. They offered a wide array of reform proposals: initiative, referendum, recall, corporate regulation, child-labor laws, tariff reform, city-manager plans, zoning regulations, immigration restriction—even prohibition. Their priorities differed according to region and immediate interest. Farmers fought hard for regulation of railroad rates but ignored the problem of industrial accidents. Southern progressives pushed hard for tariff and banking reform but disfranchised the blacks. Settlement-house workers grappled with the bosses for control of their cities but neglected the problems of the small-town businessman.

With this great variety in progressivism from 1890 to 1914, it seems useful to analyze it not as a movement at all, but rather as a patchwork of the efforts of different interest groups that occasionally agreed on specific measures but were unable to combine behind a unified and coherent program. The progressives thought otherwise. They realized that the United States was entering a new era of economic and political consolidation, one that required new techniques for managing what all of them agreed was a flourishing national enterprise. Even though they admitted that there was much wrong with America, they saw little that could not be mended by using governmental authority and scientific efficiency. In the spirit of the Founders, whose nationalism they so admired, progressive reformers, despite their differences, thought of themselves as the architects of a stable social order based on many of the principles that had guided their Federalist ancestors.

With their experiments in new political techniques, the progressives were innovators, but at a deeper level they were conservatives and restorationists. They picked up the promise of American life where their eighteenth-century forebears had dropped it—with the creation of a strong national government capable of harnessing and directing the energies of all its citizens. Part of the progressives' call for the people to take power back from their corrupt rulers seemed to invoke the spirit of Jefferson. But the heart of their program was the Hamiltonian demand for a new national leadership using the power of government to set priorities and provide direction. The ghosts of Hamilton and Jefferson fought over the progressive terrain just as the two statesmen had bitterly contested each other's principles a century earlier. To the delight of his many progressive admirers, Hamilton won the victory that had been denied him during his lifetime. For in effect, if not in intent, progressivism marked the rebirth of original Federalist hopes for a managed republic in which men of talent and training guided the affairs of a prosperous people.

## Consolidation Sweeps Forward:
## The Building of Corporate America

**The Merger Movement**

As the twentieth century opened, prosperity seemingly depended on ever-greater economic concentration. By 1900 the integration of the American economy was entering a second phase of "horizontal consolidation" as a sudden surge of industrial and financial mergers demolished the old entrepreneurial order of Gilded Age capitalism and cleared the ground for new twentieth-century corporate giants. From one angle the great merger movement at century's end appeared to be a towering peak of corporate consolidations. The annual number of mergers of American industrial firms traced a sharp trajectory: 69 in 1897, 303 in 1898, and 1208 in 1899, leveling off in the next three years at between 350 and 425. In 1900 there were 73 so-called trusts, each with a total capital investment of more than $10 million. Two-thirds of them had been established in the previous three years.

Viewed negatively, the merger movement simply looked like a gigantic black hole into which some 300 businesses tumbled each year, swallowed by huge new combinations like United States Steel and General Electric. United States Steel absorbed more than 200 manufacturing and transportation companies and soon controlled almost two-thirds of the steel market. American Tobacco combined 162 independent companies and ruled all but 10 percent of the tobacco market. By 1904 the approximately 2,000 largest firms in the United States composed less than 1 percent of the total number of the nation's business firms yet produced 40 percent of the annual value of the country's industrial goods. By 1910 monopoly (entire control of an industry by a single firm) and oligopoly (control of an industry by a few large firms) had secured the commanding positions from which to dominate twentieth-century American life.

The merger movement, which climaxed a half-century's search for industrial system and economic order, was both a logical outgrowth of rapid industrial development and an unsettling departure from remembered ways. It was natural for the newly emerging generation of promoters and industrial bankers to see in combination, if not the hand of God, at least an unchanging law of nature at work ordering the business affairs of the world. Samuel C. T. Dodd, Rockefeller's counsel, warned of the futility of tinkering with the celestial machinery: "You might as well endeavor to stay the formation of the clouds, the falling of the rains, or the flowing of the streams as to attempt by any means or in any manner to prevent organization of industry, associations of persons, and the aggregation of capital to any extent that the ever-growing trade of the world may demand." And indeed, the seeming success of mergers seemed hard to deny.

By 1895 the remarkable growth and sizable profits of Standard Oil, American Sugar Refining, and American Tobacco marked what appeared to be a sure route to salvation through combination and system. The Federal Steel Corporation's president, Judge Elbert Gary, boasted that his integrated firm "takes the ore from the ground, transports it, manufactures it into pig iron, manufactures pig iron into steel, and steel into finished products, and delivers those products." Even more impressive was the formation in 1901 of United States Steel, into which went not only some 200 manufacturing plants and transportation companies, but also 1,000 miles of railroad, 112 blast furnaces, and 78 ore boats. Soon United States Steel was employing 170,000 workers as it gathered control over 60 percent of the country's steel. Its initial capital investment at $1.4 billion was three times the annual expenditure of the federal government.

Increased efficiency, elimination of waste, bigger shares of the market, anticipated but often elusive economies of scale, and, above all, mounting profits—all these convinced adventurous big businessmen of the need to pursue mergers. By 1910 mergers had spread to all the principal sectors of the economy. When the great wave of mergers receded in 1903, it left in its wake a new corporate capitalism—a system of mammoth integrated enterprises with interlocking structures, selling their increasing variety of products in shared markets at prices jointly agreed on by the dominant firms. The great merger movement declared the bankruptcy of old-fashioned small-scale competition and announced the arrival of a modern corporate society that needed new definitions and values to replace the outworn Horatio Alger pieties of pluck and luck. In place of a host of small and medium-sized businesses scrambling for a share of the market, there now stood huge unified structures. The corporate revolution was by no means over by 1914, and the nation throughout this period—known as the Progressive Era—continued to support a dual economy of big and little businesses. But the central message of the merger movement was clear to most Americans: bigger was better.

Organizing the mergers and raising the capital to launch them became the specialty of investment bankers like J. P. Morgan and Jacob Schiff. Their role was critical, and they dominated the American economy at the turn of the twentieth century as they never would again. While taking a handsome slice of stock in the new consolidations for themselves, these bankers became powerful middlemen between a public eager to invest and an expansive business community. The investment bankers arranged mergers and floated (sold) stock; they dictated terms and dominated the workings of their new creations; they even manufactured the favorable publicity needed to popularize them. Their success could be read most clearly in the achievements of the House of Morgan, which by 1912, together with the Morgan-controlled First National Bank of New York and the Rockefeller-managed National City Bank, held 341 directorships in 112 corporations worth $22.2 billion.

To the public the investment banker personified the whole merger movement, its promise as well as its awesome concentration of power. The banker was part savior of a threatened economy, part devil in disguise. As though to conceal embarrassing questions of right and wrong, an air of conspiracy or an atmosphere of inevitability characterized even the fictional portraits of the big businessmen of the day—Van Harrington in Robert Herrick's *Memoirs of an American Citizen*, S.

**J.P. Morgan Poses for Photographers**
*Next to President Theodore Roosevelt, Morgan was perhaps the most powerful man in America in the first decades of the twentieth century.*

Behrman in Frank Norris's *The Octopus,* and Frank Cowperwood in Theodore Dreiser's portrait of a Progressive Era big businessman. For their everyday heroes Americans might have preferred the homely inventor and the unassuming engineer—Thomas Edison, Alexander Graham Bell, George Westinghouse—but they also admired, feared, envied, and puzzled over the giant captains of industry and the financial wizards who mysteriously ran the country: the predatory J. P. Morgan, the cautious Jacob Schiff, and their clients and lesser breeds of big businessmen.

The builders of the new corporate America, like their many admirers, were never entirely clear about their ultimate aims. Heavy capital investment, rapid plant expansion, increased production and reduced overhead, economies of scale, and systems of mass distribution—all to what greater good? For huge profits, surely, and for rising quantities of consumer goods for more and more people. But beyond that? What did the discovery of new needs and essentials and the constant manipulation of consumer demand through mass advertising signify for individual freedom of choice? How were Americans to balance rising standards of living with loss of control over the workplace? Could big business be made to deliver on its promise of economic security for all citizens? Were huge industrial and financial combinations compatible with political democracy and social responsibility? In short, was big really better? Neither the corporate revolutionists nor their uneasy admirers could quite answer these questions, which posed a dilemma that would persist throughout the century.

**Agricultural Cooperatives**

By 1900 the Populists' prediction of social and spiritual ruin had failed to materialize and their original political hopes had flickered and died. The twentieth century opened with a sharp economic upturn, and in this rapid recovery the American farmers abandoned their demands for massive change. In return they accepted the more immediate gains furnished by rising farm incomes as domestic consumption and world demand suddenly mounted. The advantages of organization, consolidation, and integration, which were the same lessons being taught by big business, had now become too obvious for farmers to ignore. They too—whether New England dairy farmers, midwestern corn and wheat farmers, or cotton farmers in the South—could learn to read the statistics that told them what to do. The encouraging figures on production and prices that farmers began to consult were being compiled by the Division of Statistics of the Department of Agriculture, whose other busy departmental divisions—soils, chemistry, and animal husbandry—were proof of the continuing bureaucratic revolution of American agriculture.

These figures, whether for rising staple prices, declining shipping costs, or estimates of increasing production, assured farmers down to World War I that their sudden prosperity was real. Between 1900 and 1910 the price of corn shot up from 35 cents to 52 cents a bushel; wheat jumped from 62 cents to 91 cents. The wholesale farm price index rose 50 percent, and the average price of farmland doubled from $20 to $40 an acre. At last the economy seemed to be responding to farmers' needs and demands. Just as American businessmen were applying the lessons of consolidation, so American farmers were learning to follow the seemingly simple rules for finding safety in system and prosperity in new organization. The Country Life Commission itself was proof of the growth of the farmers' political influence. Appointed by President Theodore Roosevelt in 1908, the commission was charged with the task of improving rural life in the United States. After taking the pulse of rural America in all the nation's regions and listening to a recital of its ailments, the commissioners concluded that farmers needed to catch up with their city cousins, to "even up" the amenities between city and country. The recovery of the patient, according to the commissioners' diagnosis, required more agricultural credits, improved technology, a highway program, rural free delivery of mail, and better schools. By 1910 Hamlin Garland's Populist cry for justice "for the toiling poor wherever found" in rural America had become a faint echo as American farmers entered their golden age.

The most efficient of the early twentieth-century farm organizations were producers' cooperatives, adapted from the earlier experiments of the Farmers'

Alliance, which concentrated on solving the problems of pricing and marketing. Except for their official nonprofit status and their democratic voting procedures, cooperatives were really modern corporations—as streamlined and efficient as their counterparts in business. Like corporations, cooperatives came to rely on experts and specialists, trained managers and accountants, legal advisers, lobbyists, and public relations men. And like integrated industrial firms, they achieved forward integration by building their own facilities at railroad terminals and by writing ironclad contracts with their members, compelling them to hold their crops off the market until the price was right. By 1910 the antimonopoly scruples of big farmers were fast disappearing.

The new farm cooperatives advertised no grandiose social aims nor did they demand radical political change. Rather, they were content, with the return of prosperous times, to perfect the means that the organizational revolution had assigned them. Their members were essentially agricultural trade unionists who thought and behaved like cotton planters, corn-hog producers, apple-growers, and dairy farmers. Why, they asked themselves, replace an economic system capable of producing abundance that, however belatedly, was now being showered on them?

Soon the cooperative marketing movement was in full swing, and dozens of livestock unions, dairymen's leagues, grain exchanges, cotton cooperatives, and tobacco pools were being founded each year. Cooperatives in turn spawned hundreds of new pressure groups—the Farmers' Equity Union, the Farmers' Mutual Benefit Association, the Farmers' Social and Economic Union, the Farmers' Relief Association. All these groups proclaimed as their own the slogan of the American Society of Equity: "What the farmer wants to produce is not crops, but money." In 1912 cooperatives secured the blessing of the Department of Agriculture, which provided them with their own fact-finding agency, the Bureau of Markets. Eight years later the formation of the American Farm Bureau Federation announced the imminent appearance of modern agribusiness as a national force. If the arrival of progressivism signaled an attempt at discovering a national order, farmers as well as businessmen joined enthusiastically in the search.

**Workers Respond to the Challenge of Organization**

As the twentieth century opened, big business and organized labor entered a new age of wary alliance and cautious cooperation, both sides beginning to count the costs of industrial strife. But American labor won grudging recognition only slowly. The American Federation of Labor (AFL), modest in its aims, indifferent to unskilled workers, overcame the determined resistance of small and medium-sized employers only with great difficulty. Although AFL membership grew from 140,000 at its founding in 1886 to more than 2 million in 1914, less than one-third of the country's skilled workers could be found in its ranks in 1900. When World War I broke out in Europe in 1914, only 15 percent of the nonagricultural workers in the United States were members of any union.

American workers faced formidable obstacles to organization placed in their path by a stubborn small-business community abetted by a conservative Supreme Court. Two antilabor Court decisions in the first decade of the twentieth century severely limited the AFL's right to protest. In the *Danbury Hatters* case (1908) the Court upheld a lower court decision outlawing a boycott of a Connecticut hatmaker and awarding the company damages while holding the union leaders fully accountable for them. A year earlier, in the *Bucks Stove and Range Co.* case, the Court upheld an injunction against Gompers and the executive committee of the AFL while removing the jail sentences imposed on the leadership for ignoring the injunction. In 1903 the National Association of Manufacturers (founded in the 1890s to advance the interests of small businessmen) organized the ultraconservative Citizens Industrial Association to spread the gospel of the nonunion "open shop" under the name of "The American Plan," which touted businessmen as freedom-loving individualists, made heroes of strikebreakers, and damned union leaders as anarchist agitators and dangerous socialists. The success of their American Plan, reactionary businessmen promised, would spell the doom of "un-American" unions. Confronted with the "iron fist" of employer resistance, labor leaders like Gompers turned to the Democratic party and more receptive big businessmen in hopes of escaping judicial harassment and business animosity.

More enlightened big-business leaders for their part hoped to control labor through the concept of guided democracy. They stressed a paternal concern for the American worker, along with arbitration schemes and appeals to "responsible leadership" on both sides of the bargaining table: "A man who won't meet his men half-way is a God-damn fool!" Mark Hanna, one of the new business leaders, announced in deriding the obstinacy of George Pullman and similarly old-fashioned businessmen. The new corporate leaders recognized that many of labor's grievances were real and its demands for better treatment legitimate—a belated acknowledgment that American workers' needs for security and stability were not so very different from the goals of management. In 1900 progressive financiers like George E. Perkins and J. P. Morgan, together with industrialists like Mark Hanna, struck a bargain with the beleaguered Gompers and founded the National Civic Federation. The federation's basic principle was that labor, like business, must be encouraged to organize its interests responsibly and rally its forces for full participation as junior partners in the new corporate society.

Any strategy for improving industrial relations required, first of all, vastly improved working conditions. Well into the twentieth century factory work remained alarmingly dangerous. A survey of industrial accidents for the year 1913 showed that some 25,000 workers had been killed on the job and another 750,000 seriously injured. Then there were problems of incentive, alienation, and the loss of worker solidarity resulting from increased scale and the impersonality of the plant. These conditions contrasted with earlier ones within the memory of aging workers, one of whom, a veteran shoe worker, described the old routines for the Industrial Commission in 1899. "In these old shops," he told the commissioners, "one man owned the shop; and he and three, four, five or six others, neighbors, came in there and sat down and made shoes, and there was no machinery. Everybody was at liberty to talk." The present rule for survival in a large factory was a guarded silence: "Keep your mouth shut and don't tell any man, woman, or child on the face of the earth what wages you get, unless you don't get what you are worth, in which case go to the office *alone* and fix it at once. Remember that."

Could a long-vanished shop-floor comradeship be recovered or re-created? "We do not want to go back to the time when we could do without the sewing machine or the machinery for manufacturing purposes, or the large aggregations of capital," the shoemaker told the congressmen, "but we want capital controlled in such a way that it will not result in the displacement of three-fourths of the population for the increased wealth of one-fourth of the population." In grudging admissions like this and plaintive calls for equity lay the secret of big business's success.

## Cities in Revolt: The Rise of Urban Progressivism

The progressive search for order in a disordered world began in the city. Wherever urban reformers looked in the closing years of the nineteenth century, they saw disorganization and fragmentation. Wealthy neighborhoods with million-dollar mansions were set apart by parks and boulevards from teeming ghettos with dilapidated tenements and filthy streets. These conditions presented all-too-visible proof of the immense distances—social and psychological as well as economic and geographical—that separated the rich from the poor.

It was to close the distance between urban affluence and sprawling poverty that in 1889 Jane Addams, the pioneer settlement-house worker, moved into Hull House, a battered mansion on the corner of Polk and South Halstead streets in the heart of Chicago's Nineteenth Ward.

> The streets are inexpressibly dirty [she reported], the number of schools inadequate, factory legislation unenforced, the street-lighting bad, the paving miserable and altogether lacking in alleys and smaller streets, and the stables defy all laws of sanitation....Hundreds of houses are unconnected with the street sewer....Back tenements flourish; many houses have no water supply save the faucet in the back yard; there are no fire escapes; the garbage and ashes are placed in wooden boxes which are fastened to the street pavements....Our ward contains two hundred and fifty-five saloons; our own precinct boasts of eight....There are seven churches and two missions in the ward.

In listing the Nineteenth Ward's needs, Jane Addams summarized the main points in the urban progressive indictment of boss politics. Progressivism began as a spontaneous revolt of city dwellers who were convinced that they had been short-changed in their share of the American social fund.

**Mulberry Street in the Lower East Side of New York City**
*By 1910 the Lower East Side was one of the most densely populated spots on earth.*

A pragmatic assessment of urban blight was the first phase in the drive to clean up the nation's cities. Broad coalitions of voters demanded immediate solutions to a wide range of problems: they sought tax reforms, more effective health regulations, lower streetcar fares, better utility services, and efficient city governments free of corrupt bosses and greedy special interests. The depression of the 1890s, by placing new burdens on consumers, created a sense of urgency and focused public attention on the shortcomings of rule by the political machines.

The progressive attack centered on "invisible government," the alliance between municipal authorities and business interests. The connection between "corrupt government" and "corporate arrogance," which the progressives fought to destroy, was a simple one of mutual need. In attempting to modernize their cities, machine politicians had discovered that secret agreements with transit, utility, and construction interests were a handy device for providing minimal service while lining their own pockets. At the same time, the new and unstable industries that were involved with urban development were undergoing rapid reorganization and were always short of funds. These industries saw in monopoly franchises, wholesale bribery, and kickbacks a measure of certainty in an otherwise unpredictable world. By 1890 such bargains had been sealed in most of the country's major cities. The only real loser in this arrangement was the public.

Thus progressivism began as a "people's movement" aimed at eliminating corruption and inefficiency. Cutting across class lines and focusing on specific issues like dangerous railway crossings, poor sanitation, and high streetcar fares, the progressive movement in its early years developed a style that was both democratic and moralistic. The twin devils in the reformers' morality plays were the businessman and the boss. Lincoln Steffens, the dean of reform journalists, pronounced the American businessman "a self-righteous fraud": "I found him buying boodlers in St. Louis, defending grafters in Minneapolis, originating corruption in Pittsburgh, sharing with the bosses in Philadelphia, deploring reform in Chicago, and beating good government with corruption funds in New York." From the beginning the progressives developed an antibusiness rhetoric that continued to obscure the real contributions of businessmen to urban reform.

**Progressive Mayors**    The bosses offered even more enticing targets. Urban reformer Frederick C. Howe reported that Boss Cox of Cincinnati ruled his city "as a medieval baron did his serfs." The only remedy for boss rule lay in building citizens' coalitions to unite a fragmented community. "The very nature of city life," one progressive commentator pointed out, "compels manifold cooperation. The individual cannot 'go it alone'; he cannot do as he pleases; he must conform his acts in an ever increasing degree to the will and welfare of [his] community. . . . "This concept of the organic city fitted neatly with the interests and ambitions of a new group of reform mayors in the 1890s who launched individual campaigns to overhaul their cities.

The first of these progressive mayors was Hazen Pingree, mayor of Detroit from 1889 to 1896, when he was elected governor of Michigan. Pingree, a shoe manufacturer turned "reform boss," campaigned vigorously in all the wards of the city. He steered clear of controversial moral and religious questions like prohibition and parochial schools, concentrating instead on the hard economic issues that would win him the broadest support. Pingree exposed bribery in a local electric company's dealings with his predecessors and embarked on an extensive program of school and park construction. After a long battle with the transit and utility interests, he succeeded in reducing streetcar fares and gas rates while building the city's municipal lighting plant. During the depression of the 1890s, he started work-relief programs for Detroit's unemployed and extended a variety of social service programs. Pingree set a pattern for his successors by attacking Detroit's "invisible government" and replacing it with an efficient, responsive administration.

It remained for Tom Johnson, the mercurial mayor of Cleveland from 1901 to 1909, to exploit most fully a whole new range of possibilities for leadership. Johnson had made his fortune by reorganizing transit systems, and he had been converted to reform after reading Henry George's *Social Problems*. After two successful terms in Congress as a reform Democrat, he returned to Cleveland to build a political coalition to fight Republican boss Mark Hanna and the transit interests. Energetic, tough-minded, and the ultimate politician, down to the unlit cigar he waved while speaking from the nearest soapbox, Johnson borrowed the techniques of the machine politicians and improved on them. He inaugurated his reform program by arranging for a regulated system of prostitution free from police graft. Like Hazen Pingree, he threatened the transit interests with regulation; his most widely acclaimed achievement was the 3-cent fare. Johnson provided his city with free public bathhouses, recreational facilities, and effective sanitary inspection, and he continued to agitate for municipal ownership of utilities.

Progressive mayors who launched their careers from a platform of pragmatic opposition to the "interests" were frequently driven to face broader questions of social welfare. Some mayors—like Pingree, Johnson, and later Brand Whitlock in Toledo, Ohio, and Mark Fagan in Jersey City, New Jersey—were forced to adjust to shifting economic interests within their reform coalitions and to support welfare measures that went far beyond the political and structural reforms they originally had called for. The "social justice" mayors, as they have been called, also came to question the value of strict party identification. Increasingly they relied on the advice and services of new nonpartisan experts in municipal management who were concerned with finding more efficient ways of running American cities.

**Social Experimentation**

"Streetcar politics" was only the most visible sign of the urban revival in the 1890s. City churches were keenly aware of their declining membership among the working class and responded to the crisis by developing the "institutional church" in lower-class neighborhoods. By providing services like lodging houses, reading rooms, recreational halls, and day nurseries, church progressives hoped to spread the "social gospel" of Christianity. Then too, by 1890 groups of earnest young college graduates, many of them women, were moving into slums to live in settlement houses modeled on London's famed Toynbee Hall. By 1895 there were more than fifty such settlements in major cities around the country, each with a staff of idealistic college graduates and seminarians.

Settlement-house workers were invariably young (most were under thirty), religious (predominantly Congregationalists and Presbyterians), college-educated, and single, and overwhelmingly they came from middle-class families. For these young intellectuals and professionals, some of them with advanced training in the new social sciences taught in German universities, the city settlement offered an escape from gentility and from feelings of uselessness, and provided the chance to practice new skills. Settlements freed them from what Jane Addams called "the snare of preparation" for unknown careers. More important, they developed a new and deeper understanding of the complex social and cultural relations that made up the modern city. Teachers, housing reformers, charity

**How the Other Half Lived**
*Reform journalist and photographer Jacob Riis documented his exposé of life in New York City's slums with startling photographs of tenement interiors.*

organizers, child-labor opponents, health inspectors, and visiting nurses found a congenial home in the reform settlements, which seemed to them miniature models of the good society.

The reform achievements of the settlement-house workers were limited but real. Their biggest gains were won in securing public health and safety regulations for their cities, ensuring improved working conditions for urban industrial workers, and extending the reach of progressive education out from the metropolis. They enjoyed only modest and frequently ephemeral success in checking the abuses of machine politics, and—like most middle-class Americans in the progressive period—they failed to note the ravages of racial inequality or prevent the growth of ghettos. Yet if they hesitated to acknowledge the deeper structural problems generated by a maturing corporate capitalism, settlement-house people brought with them from the countryside, where most of them had been born, reassuring notions of the neighborhood and extended households that helped make the city with its collisive ethnic cultures seem not just manageable but challenging and exciting. And women, whose numbers dominated the movement in the United States from the beginning, found not simply new careers and satisfactions in their communal homes but a sudden sense of equality with men as organizers, directors, and publicists of a new message of social solidarity.

The progressive movement was not only a major effort in social engineering. It involved also a profound intellectual revolution. The reformers came to understand the complexity and the interconnectedness of modern life. They experienced firsthand the difficulty of isolating the underlying causes of the problems they dealt with, and the futility of proposing simple solutions. Whether they were lawyers, engineers, clinicians, historians, sociologists, or economists, the progressives found themselves working with a new approach to knowledge that the philosopher John Dewey, one of their teachers, called "creative intelligence," and another powerful intellectual, William James, called "pragmatism." James taught these young reformers to seek truth not in abstractions, but in action. "How will truth be realized? What, in short, is truth's cash-value in experiential terms?" Truth was not a "stagnant property" inherent in an idea, as Emerson and the Transcendentalists had believed. Truth *worked,* James insisted. *"True ideas are those we can assimilate, validate, corroborate, and verify. False ideas are those we cannot."*

John Dewey, whose interest in social reform was as strong as James's, saw the origins of this so-called instrumentalist logic in Charles Darwin's evolutionary biology and in the scientific thinking that did away with the old search for "absolutes and finalities." This new logic, Dewey told his progressive students, brought new intellectual responsibilities. Philosophy would hereafter have to deal with "the more serious of the conflicts that occur in life" and develop a method of "moral and political diagnosis and prognosis." Oliver Wendell Holmes, Jr., judge and legal instrumentalist, was even more specific. He taught the progressives that the true function of law was the expression not of abstract principles, but of "accurately measured social desires."

By 1900 the settlement house had become an indispensable laboratory of social experimentation. In devising urban programs and services, the progressives relied heavily on new methods of research and fact gathering as essential to the work of reordering urban society. One of Jane Addams's first assignments was to collect and collate the raw data on the surrounding neighborhood; in 1895 *Hull House Maps and Papers* appeared as the first detailed account of an immigrant community published in the United States. In 1903 Lawrence Veiller and Robert W. DeForest published their two-volume *Tenement House Problems,* an attempt to relate housing to the larger setting through statistics and firsthand observation. Perhaps the most ambitious project for studying the city in its entirety was the six-volume *Pittsburgh Survey* (1909–14), which treated politics, crime, prostitution, the family, housing, and working conditions as aspects of a functioning social organism.

Social surveys underscored the need for trained personnel and scientific management. The independent commission, staffed by trained professionals and given the power to revamp tax structures, regulate transit and utility rates, and provide efficient city services, quickly became an essential agency of effective urban reform. The multiplication of commissions increased the demand for trained personnel. University education in key fields spread throughout the nation, and a new range of professions, each with its own organization, arose. By 1910 economists, political scientists, sociologists, tax reformers, charity organizers, settlement-house workers, and dozens of other specialized professionals had formed national societies, each with its own publications and communications network. These national organizations both strengthened the sense of professional community among progressives and cemented an alliance with newly founded universities that provided the training and facilities for investigating urban problems. In Chicago the residents of Hull House soon established close connections with the new University of Chicago through reform-minded academics like John Dewey, sociologists Albion Small and William I. Thomas, and political scientist Charles Merriam. In New York economists and sociologists from Columbia University joined freelance writers and publicists in analyzing city problems and working out solutions. Settlement houses proved vital for young professors by providing laboratories for testing their new concepts of behavior and by drawing them into the exciting world of business and politics beyond university walls.

Businessmen and professors often disagreed, however, on the question of how to apply the new critical spirit of reform. University scholars—historians, economists, and social theorists—now had sharp analytical tools for dissecting old conservative myths and challenging entrenched institutions. Historian Charles A. Beard was the best known of the young professors who were beginning to question the narrow interpretations of American law and the Constitution as well as the ancestor worship they encouraged. Beard's own Columbia University typified the new tradition-breaking spirit. There, economist Edwin Seligman, James Harvey Robinson, an earnest advocate of the "New History" as a reform tool, and pioneer students of administrative law such as Frank Goodnow were busy probing the economic roots of political behavior. At the same time, political scientist Arthur F. Bentley, in the *The Process of Government* (1908), approached political decision making as a complex process that was subject to the shifting forces of interest groups. At the University of Washington radical historian J. Allen Smith, in a book entitled *The Spirit of American Government* (1907), dismissed the Constitution as a "reactionary document" designed to restrict the forces of democracy. After 1900 the alliance between highly critical academics and their corporate financial supporters grew increasingly strained as the professors began to question the very business civilization on which their universities had come to depend.

**Scientific Reform**     The universities also supplied a more conservative product. With the appearance of concepts of "social control" and "scientific efficiency," progressive reformers made contact with another reform tradition. This tradition was alien to the open tolerance of reform politicians and to the democratic and humanitarian hopes of social workers, and concentrated instead on efforts to impose strict efficiency and economy. For many progressives the modern corporation embodied these business values and procedures. The picture of the efficient, impersonal corporation was not drawn by businessmen alone. It was a widely accepted model of organization that appealed to intellectuals and professionals as well as to industrialists and financiers who recognized its uses in rebuilding American politics. The progressives criticized the trust largely because unscrupulous promoters had misused it, not because of its seemingly rational structure. "The trust is the educator of us all," Jane Addams announced in explaining the need for new kinds of collective action. Seen in this light, the corporation appeared as a corrective of the waste and inefficiencies of an earlier age, an actual model of social and political reform that, like the utopian communities before the Civil War, could be extended to American society as a whole.

The "scientific" urban reformers believed, however, that they could manage the city simply by tightening expenditures, consolidating power in the hands of experts, and revising the political system without particular regard to human needs. Good government, they reasoned, would be rigorously honest, determinedly efficient, unfailingly frugal, and strictly accountable. But such scientific reform restricted democratic participation. It limited the influence of "uninformed" voters—workers and immigrants—whose numbers it sought to reduce through literacy tests and tighter political registration laws. Such restrictions were comparable in spirit to the disfranchisement of blacks then under way in the South.

These scientific reformers considered the city a challenge that was not very different from the challenges met by industrialists and financiers. Efficiency and economy came to be equated with business practices of budget paring, cost cutting, tax trimming, and service chopping according to the ledger-book ethics of corporation accountants. "Municipal government is business, not politics," was the slogan of the scientific reformers. The modern corporation's shaping power in determining these reformers' outlook was reflected in their vocabulary, which developed a set of useful analogies. The mayor served as *chairman of the board* of an urban *corporation* composed of big and little *stockholders,* who were expected to vote their *proxies* at *annual meetings* and to accept their *dividends* without constantly interfering with the *managers* of the *enterprise.*

It was hardly a coincidence that the last years of the century, which saw the triumph of the corporation and the advent of scientific municipal reform, also witnessed the opening assault on the concept of a rational "public opinion," once considered the cornerstone of democratic politics. In dismissing ordinary public opinion as frivolous or perverse, scientific reformers demonstrated a distrust of democracy. The first order of reform business, insisted Frank Goodnow, an expert in administrative law and spokesman for the scientific reformers, was to recruit loyal and politically unambitious civil servants whose efficiencies would allow "the business and professional class of the community to assume care of the public business without making too great personal sacrifice." For the good-government advocates and business-dominated mayors who tried to clean up the cities after 1900, urban reform meant a chance for middle- and upper-class

Americans, armed with new technical skills, to regain control of urban politics that an earlier generation had abandoned to the bosses.

The progressive businessmen and professionals shared a new set of values that reshaped their aims into concepts of system, control, stability, and predictability. Charity organizers now realized the need for accurate data in drafting workable solutions to social disorganization. A giant lumber company like Weyerhaeuser came to appreciate the importance of planning and cooperation with the new experts in the United States Forestry Service. College professors and high school teachers recognized the need for professional solidarity to protect their rights. Public-service lawyers, among them Louis Brandeis, acknowledged the complexities of new legal relations and began to play the role of "counsel to the situation" in experimenting with new techniques of arbitration.

The social perceptions of these middle-class leaders in the bureaucratic revolution stemmed from their sense of American society as a national collectivity in need of a new set of operating procedures. To implement their bureaucratic values, progressive reformers centralized authority in a hierarchical order, concentrated decision-making power in an energetic executive, established impersonal relations in restructuring their organizations, and above all planned for maximum efficiency.

The urban reform movement was therefore split between those who sought to extend popular influences in government and those whose programs limited popular participation. Reformers faced a choice between two widely different estimates of democracy and human nature. Some of them, like sociologist Edward A. Ross, frankly rejected the idea of democratic participation in favor of open elitism. Politically, Ross argued, democracy meant not the sovereignty of the average citizen, "who is a rather narrow, shortsighted, muddleheaded creature," but the "mature public opinion" of an educated elite. The case for democracy was most forcefully explained by Brand Whitlock, novelist, social welfare reformer, and mayor of Toledo from 1905 to 1913, who defined the "city sense" as democracy and as "the spirit of goodwill in humanity." Whitlock predicted that cities would arise that would "express the ideals of the people and work wonderful ameliorations in the human soul."

The conservative bias of many progressive reformers could be clearly seen in their attacks on the boss and the machine, but their real intentions were often obscured, even to themselves, by their seemingly democratic enthusiasm. "The people are finding a way," exclaimed progressive publicist William Allen White, who pointed in astonishment to the rapid growth of "fundamental democracy" throughout the country. A whole roster of progressive proposals for open government was billed as a democratic device for ensuring popular control at the grass roots. Thus the direct primary and direct election of senators would release the bosses' stranglehold on the electoral process. Referendum would send important questions of policy to the people, over the heads of unresponsive legislators. Recall would return the power to remove officeholders to the voters, with whom it belonged.

Urban progressives were not hypocrites in advertising their reforms as democratic, but they did not always make it clear that by "the people" they meant not the huddled masses in center cities, but solid citizens with sensible views and sober habits. Below the blaring trumpets of democracy could be heard, subdued but distinct, the progressive call for the politically vanquished middle class to return to the struggle armed with new weapons.

By 1900 a dual tradition had emerged, polarized around conflicting values of social efficiency and democratic liberation. These contrasting principles, which had combined briefly in the 1890s to challenge the politics of the bosses, would continue to diverge in the twentieth century, creating tensions within progressivism that would make it a confused yet creative movement.

The nerve center for urban progressivism after 1900 consisted of municipal leagues, civic federations, citizens' lobbies, commercial clubs, and bureaus of municipal research. These civic groups provided forums for the lively exchange of ideas between academics and businessmen eager to try out new concepts of efficiency and economy. From organizations like the National Municipal League and the National Civic Federation poured a flood of proposals and plans for repairing city government: home rule and charter revision; ballot reform and literacy tests; citywide election schemes and city-manager plans, all of them aimed at the bosses' power base.

At first the reformers concentrated on improving procedures. They proposed segregated budgets for economy. They introduced time clocks, work sheets, job descriptions, and standardized salaries. They developed systematic ways of giving out contracts to replace the old patronage system. But the heart of their reform program was the commission and city-manager plans, modeled on the corporation. Combining executive and legislative functions in a single board, the commission plan spread rapidly until by 1913 more than three hundred cities in the United States had adopted it. The city-manager plan, a refinement of the original commission idea, further consolidated decision making in municipal government, and by the 1920s it too had been widely adopted.

Urban progressives never succeeded in putting the political boss out of business. Nevertheless progressivism successfully challenged boss politics by confronting it with another way of doing the business of the city. The machine's power lay in the center city, with its immigrants and working classes. Middle-class reformers generally operated from power bases along the suburban periphery. Boss politics, for all its sins, was marked by a high degree of accountability and popular participation in the wards and precincts. Progressives tried to reduce direct popular involvement at both the voting and the officeholding level. Bosses were wasteful but democratic; progressives were economical and bureaucratic.

Progressive success was limited. All too often, procedures changed but official policy did not. Still, if the boss and his clients proved adept at smashing the electoral hopes of reform candidates, they could no longer ignore the cries for more effective city government. The progressives' dream of a shiny, streamlined administrative model never materialized. Yet the modernizing of American cities proceeded with or without the politicians' approval. In their partial overhaul of the nation's cities, the progressives scored important gains for the new bureaucratic order.

## The Man with the Muckrake

Many of these contradictions could be seen in the work of the muckrakers who supplied progressivism with an agenda. The name *muckrakers* was given to a new brand of reform journalists by President Theodore Roosevelt, who complained that their relentless exposure of corruption in high places hindered rather than helped him in his work of improving American society. Roosevelt compared this group of headstrong publicists to the gloomy figure who, in the seventeenth-century English Puritan John Bunyan's *Pilgrim's Progress,* refused a celestial crown and kept a muckrake. The president denounced these muckrakers' "crude and sweeping generalizations" and their delight in pointing the finger of civic shame. For their part the muckrakers—Lincoln Steffens, Ida Tarbell, Ray Stannard Baker, David Graham Phillips, and many less famous colleagues—accepted the label and wore it defiantly as proof of their devotion to the Jeffersonian principle of a free and vigilant press.

Muckraking was the product of two forces that had combined by the end of the nineteenth century: major advances in the technology of printing, which made it possible to produce inexpensive, illustrated popular magazines; and the simultaneous arrival on the metropolitan scene of reform reporters sensitive to the new social concerns of the middle-class reader and eager to exploit them. S. S. McClure, founder of *McClure's,* was one of the pioneer explorers of the lucrative field of reform journalism, and he was quickly joined by dozens of competitors who were drawn to social criticism by their keen sense of the market and the prospect of sizable profits. From the outset muckraking proved that reform could be a paying proposition. Gathering a staff of trained, well-paid newspapermen, McClure and other editors launched an attack on the underside of American life with articles on sweatshops, tainted meat, the white slave traffic, insurance company scandals, labor racketeering, city bosses, and high finance. Muckrakers happily compiled a list of all the social wrongs that their enlightened readers would presumably set right.

Muckraking offered both a new kind of factual reporting and an old form of moral publicity. Always extravagant and frequently sensational, the muckrakers perfected the uses of contrast and contradiction in pointing to the gap between venerable American ideals and startling social facts. In an article for *Cosmopolitan* on child labor in southern cotton mills, for example, poet Edwin Markham depicted "The Hoe Man in the Making" in the faces of "ill-fed, unkempt, unwashed, half-dressed" children penned in the narrow lanes of the mills, little victims whose dreary lives mocked the "bright courtesy of the cultured classes." Social gospelist Ernest Crosby contrasted the appearance of a majestic United States Senate with the reality of a "House of Dollars," a political

# Collier's

## THE NATIONAL WEEKLY

**"U.S. $enate 'House of Dollars'"**
Collier's, *one of the leading Muckraking journals, featured this cartoon on the cover of an issue denouncing the political power of trusts and monopolies.*

monopoly modeled on an industrial trust. Samuel Hopkins Adams explained the national failure to regulate the food and drug industries as the result of "private interests in public murder" when "everybody's health is nobody's business."

Muckraking thus presented a publicity technique rather than a philosophy, a popular journalistic style rather than a searching analysis. As social critics, journalists like Lincoln Steffens and David Graham Phillips were tough-minded and factual but also romantic, moralistic, and sentimental. Like their millions of readers, they were the beneficiaries of a fundamental change in the idea of publicity, which they conceived of as an open-ended process of fact gathering that reflected the shifting nature of social reality. Read in this subdued light, their articles could be considered wholesome remedies and useful correctives. Their work, the muckrakers insisted, was never done, since an unfolding social process required constant adaptation of old theories to new facts—of accepted values to changing conditions.

Muckraking also tapped traditional morality while exploiting the time-honored role of the disinterested observer—the clear-eyed, hard-nosed investigator with a fierce desire to get all the facts and expose them to the sanitizing rays of publicity. Muckrakers liked to think of themselves as brave detectives, dashing from one hidden clue to another, looking for the fragments of information that, once collected and arranged, would tell reformers what to do next. There was a strong bias against party government in the muckrakers' view of American politics, as well as a weakness for conspiratorial interpretations. They believed that the masses of American voters, once given the facts, would demand reform. Tell the people the truth, they said, and they would correct injustice forthwith. Conscience, duty, character, virtue—these were the muckrakers' watchwords, and also a measure of their limited understanding of the problems confronting progressive America. Muckrakers identified the symptoms of disorder, but they could not isolate its causes or prescribe effective remedies. For these tasks a clearer understanding of the workings of modern industrial society was needed.

## Progressivism Invades the States

After 1900 the progressives, building on urban achievements, set out to reform state politics. Beginning in 1900 with the first administration of Wisconsin governor Robert M. La Follette, reform swept across the nation in the next decade and transformed the conduct of state politics.

Although progressivism varied widely in the different sections of the country, there were enough similarities to give political reform at the state level the appearance of a national movement. In the South progressives who had inherited a number of Populist grievances often wore the trappings of a redneck revolt against the business-minded Bourbons. By the opening years of the twentieth century, one governorship after another was falling to economy-minded agrarians from upcountry or downstate. The southern rebellion against the alliance of big business and Democratic politicians drew on popular sympathies and produced railroad and corporate regulation, antimonopoly laws, insurance company controls, and improved public education and child-labor laws—but all with mounting racist demagoguery and the continuing disfranchisement of the black population.

Progressivism in the Midwest and on the Pacific Coast also grew out of a revolt, usually within the Republican party, which was perceived to be too generous to railroads and corporations. Midwestern progressives drew more heavily from the arsenal of democratic political reforms—the initiative and referendum, for example—than did their counterparts in the East, who tended to rely more on administrative reforms. But everywhere big business's control of state legislatures made an inviting target. Corporate dominance of New Jersey state politics, for example, was all but complete by 1900. "We've got everything in the state worth having," a spokesman for corporate interests boasted. The legislature regularly elected two senators who represented the utility interests and the insurance companies; and the executive branch of the state government was staffed by former employees of the Pennsylvania Railroad.

**Massachusetts Machine Shop, 1895–96**
*Working on lathes lacking proper safety guards and powered by uncased belts was highly dangerous.*

The governors who organized the revolts against these statehouse rings headed the cast of new progressive folk heroes. The most popular of the reform governors cast themselves as western heroes, riding into office with a mandate to clean up the state, setting about their task with grim determination, and moving on to bigger things when the job was done. Typically the reform governor, denied office by state party leaders, collected his small band of rebels and tried, unsuccessfully at first, to take over the party. To help in subsequent efforts, he enlisted other mavericks and began to explore such electoral reforms as the primary system of party nomination and the direct election of senators. Fixing his sights on the "interests," he eventually defeated the party regulars.

Once elected, the progressive governor moved quickly to neutralize his opposition by absorbing some of its members into his reform coalition. He learned to wield patronage with a surprising ruthlessness, and with secure majorities in the legislature he went to work on his reform program. This generally included strict regulation of railroads and public-service corporations, a revamped tax structure, and major pieces of social legislation to improve working and living conditions in the state. After a hectic term or two in which he managed to complete at least part of this reform program, the progressive governor moved on to the United States Senate, where he was joined by other like-minded rebels from similar backgrounds who had the same hopes of imposing their reform designs on national politics. The career of one such progressive hero, Robert M. La Follette, illustrates the main features of this legend of progressive reform.

**"Battling Bob"**    La Follette, an intense, unsmiling, self-made man, was a small-town lawyer who struggled to the top of the political heap in Wisconsin. In his three terms as governor after 1900, he enacted a reform program that became the envy of progressives across the country. Young La Follette was a walking example of the Protestant ethic. Born in Primrose, Wisconsin, in meager circumstances, he put himself through the state university at Madison by teaching school, and he prepared himself for a career in politics by studying for the bar. At the University of Wisconsin he came under the reform influence of its president, John Bascom, who was just beginning to build a public-service institution, a task that La Follette himself would complete a quarter of a century later.

Short and wiry, with a shock of bristly iron-gray hair, La Follette combined a rock-hard moralism with a fanatical combativeness. He won his first office as district attorney without the endorsement of the Republican machine by barnstorming the county and haranguing rural voters on the need for integrity and independence. In 1884, again without the support of party regulars, he was elected to the first of three terms in Congress, where he was the youngest member of the House. He was defeated for reelection in the Democratic landslide of 1890 and came home to a lucrative law practice.

In Wisconsin as in a number of other states, the Republican party had been the effective instrument of the railroad and lumber companies. Faced with a lawsuit against their corrupt state treasurers, the party bosses tried to bribe La Follette to secure his influence with a judge, who happened to be his brother-in-law. La Follette promptly cried havoc and later reckoned the attempted bribe as the turning point of his career: "Nothing else ever came into my life that exerted such a powerful influence upon me as that affair." In exposing the machine's crime to the voters, he effectively isolated himself from the party leaders and spent nearly a decade trying to collect enough votes from Scandinavian farmers and industrial workers in Milwaukee to overthrow the machine. By 1900 he had succeeded.

La Follette's victory won him instant national acclaim. After destroying the power of the old machine by winning over some of its leaders to his own cause, he set out to modernize Wisconsin. The "Wisconsin Idea," as it came to be known, depended on a progressive majority in the state legislature, which the new governor secured by campaigning personally for his supporters and then holding them strictly accountable. Soon his enemies were complaining that he had made himself the boss of a ruthlessly efficient machine of his own. The substance of the

Wisconsin Idea was a set of related reforms: a direct primary law, an improved civil service, a railroad rate commission, a fair tax program, state banking controls, conservation measures, a water power franchise act, and protective labor legislation. At the center of La Follette's reform movement stood the independent regulatory commission, staffed by experts from the state university and given wide administrative latitude.

To his many admirers across the country, La Follette seemed a political anomaly, a popular leader with his feet firmly planted in the grass roots but at the same time an enthusiastic convert to scientific government. Exacting, fiercely partisan, and a powerful hater, he often viewed the world as a gigantic conspiracy against "Battling Bob." He kept ready for display at a moment's notice the image of the sea-green incorruptible who preached the virtues of direct democracy and constantly urged his followers to "go back to the people." "Selfish interests," he declared, "may resist every inch of ground, may threaten, malign and corrupt, [but] they cannot escape the final issues. That which is so plain, so simple, and so just will surely triumph."

The other half of La Follette's reform equation, however, was filled with the facts and figures that his investigatory commissions collected. His own interminable speeches came loaded with statistics and percentages provided by a corps of tax experts, labor consultants, industrial commissioners, and social workers. He hammered these facts at the voters of Wisconsin in the belief that the people, once they learned their meaning, would hardly fail him. The conflicting principles

**Senator Robert M. La Follette Discusses His Campaign Plans with His Son and Namesake**
*"Battling Bob" founded a reform tradition that he passed on to his two sons who carried it into the New Deal.*

of popular democracy and government by an expert elite hardly bothered La Follette. The expert commission, secure above the battle of parties and interests—the key agency of the Wisconsin Idea—seemingly embodied the detachment and patriotism it was designed to foster in the people. La Follette's growing national reputation, in fact, rested on the belief he inspired that direct democracy and scientific government were not simply compatible, but complementary.

**State Progressive Reform** An important feature of progressive reform programs in the states was a package of new laws, drawn up by civic groups, women's organizations, and consumer interests, that humanized working conditions. As late as 1900, more than half the states had no laws that established a minimum age for workers. By 1914 every state but one had an age limit on the employment of children. In most states new laws for the protection of women in industry paralleled the drive to abolish child labor. Illinois led the way in 1892 by limiting hours for women. New York and Massachusetts followed, and then the movement spread rapidly westward. When the Supreme Court upheld the principle of state regulation of hours for women in the celebrated case of *Muller* v. *Oregon* in 1908, barriers collapsed. By the time America entered World War I in 1917, thirty-nine states had written new laws protecting women or had significantly strengthened old laws, while eight states had gone even further by passing minimum wage laws for women. Another feature of the progressive social reform program was the campaign for employers' liability laws and industrial accident insurance, which did away with the worst abuses of the older legal rules that governed workplace safety and contributory negligence. By 1916 nearly two-thirds of the states, reacting to mounting pressures from a progressive public, had established insurance programs.

Progressivism, taking different forms in different states, marked a shift in power within the American political system. Cumbersome, interest-dominated legislatures gave way to a new public authority lodged in the executive branch and in its supporting administrative agencies that were charged with discovering and then serving the public interest. To justify their roles as custodians of the public interest, progressives unearthed a national-interest theory of politics as old as the Founders. "I would not be a dredger congressman, or a farm congressman, or a fresh-egg congressman," a typical progressive told his constituents in summoning up the spirit of Edmund Burke and virtual representation.* "I would like to be an American congressman, recognizing the union and the nation." If warring economic and class interests were chiefly responsible for the lack of direction and the low tone of American politics, progressives reasoned, then it was wise to ignore them and appeal instead to a potential public virtue in the concept of citizenship. "Progressivism," another reformer added, "believes in nationalism... opposes class government by either business, the laboring class, or any other class." This tendency to reject interest-group government (govern-

---

*For Burke and virtual representation in the eighteenth century, see volume 1, chapter 7, pp. 240–42.

ment as a bargaining process between blocs of big business, big labor, and big agriculture) drove progressives to embrace the idea of leadership from above—from those "good men" in whom idealism presumably ran deeper than self-ishness. "While the inspiration has always come from below in the advance of human rights," the California progressive William Kent insisted, the real accomplishments in improving American society must always be "the disinterested work of men who, having abundant means, have ranged themselves on the side of those most needing help." In the progressive interpretation of American politics, underdogs announced their needs, but topdogs filled them.

Draped with the mantle of disinterested benevolence, state progressivism resembled, more than anything else, a rebuilt model of Federalism, suitably modernized to fit an industrial society. Like their Federalist ancestors, progressives feared the idea of party government and class division, and they sought to take the politics out of American life in the name of scientific management. In place of eighteenth-century rule by republican notables, they substituted leadership by experts whose skills were to command the instant allegiance of all enlightened citizens. Most progressive political reforms aimed at securing stability and control. And in the same fashion, the progressive social justice programs initiated by the states were designed to strengthen corporate capitalism by empowering the government to reassign responsibilities and lessen the harshness of the American industrial environment. To carry out their policies at the national level, the progressives looked to the figure of the new statesman, and in Theodore Roosevelt they found their hero.

## Theodore Roosevelt: The Progressive as Hero

In September 1901 President William McKinley died in Buffalo of an assassin's bullet, and Theodore Roosevelt—"this crazy man," as Republican managers thought him—was catapulted from the vice-presidency into the post of national leader. Blueblood, historian, student of the classics, amateur naturalist, cow-puncher, and Rough Rider, Roosevelt at forty-two appeared to millions of admirers as the last of the universal men, but to uneasy Republican bosses like Mark Hanna as "that damned cowboy."

With an audible sigh of relief, Old Guard Republicans heard the new president announce his intentions "to continue, absolutely unbroken, the policy of President McKinley." McKinley had stood for high tariffs, the gold standard, a not-too-vigorous prosecution of the trusts, and just the right amount of imperial ambition.* The prospect of a continuing custodial presidency reassured those congressional conservatives who feared above all a rambunctious executive. Yet within the year, Roosevelt had begun to challenge congressional authority, and, by the time he retired from his second term in March 1909, he had succeeded in

---

*For American expansionism under McKinley, see chapter 26, pp. 260–70.

creating a national progressive movement, reinvigorating American foreign policy, and laying the foundations of the twentieth-century welfare state.

**A Patrician Cowboy**   Roosevelt was the product of New York society, the son of a banker-philanthropist who had dabbled in genteel reforms and organized the city's upper-class contribution to the Union cause during the Civil War. A graduate of Harvard, where he had amused his classmates with his odd earnestness and vibrancy, young Roosevelt immediately settled on a life of politics among the "kittle-kattle" of spoilsmen and mugwumps. He held the comfortable classes chiefly to blame for the moral chaos of Gilded Age politics, and with a highly developed sense of the upper class's social responsibility he entered the New York State Assembly as a representative from one of the city's wealthy Republican districts.

In the assembly, where he served a single term from 1882 to 1884, he displayed the unique mixture of social conservatism, pugnacity, and political shrewdness that was to become his distinguishing mark. In 1886 he accepted the Republican nomination in the three-way mayoralty race in New York City and ran a respectable third behind Democratic winner Abram S. Hewitt and single-taxer Henry George. The 1880s also saw the growth of a sizable body of Roosevelt's historical writing—*The Winning of the West,* a biography of Gouverneur Morris, and another of Thomas Hart Benton—in which Roosevelt proclaimed his unqualified approval of the nationalist designs of the Federalists, denounced Jefferson as a humbug and a hypocrite, and hymned the glories of westward expansion and the fulfillment of America's continental destiny.

When his first wife died in 1884, Roosevelt retired to the frontier he had described so eloquently, finding solace in Dakota ranch life filled with cowboys, frontier justice, and manly virtues. As a steadfast but unpredictable young Republican, he was appointed to the United States Civil Service Commission by President Benjamin Harrison in 1889 and served in Washington in a blaze of publicity until 1895, when he returned to New York to head the Board of Police Commissioners. Here he made another name for himself as a result of late-night prowls with his friend, journalist Jacob Riis, in futile efforts to enforce the city's blue laws. McKinley rewarded such energy by appointing him assistant secretary of the navy, despite Roosevelt's outspoken views on behalf of American military power.

The Spanish-American War in 1898 drew Roosevelt out of the shadows of appointive office and into the limelight of electoral politics. As self-appointed leader of the Rough Riders, the First Regiment of the United States Cavalry Volunteers, he caught the fancy of a jingoistic public that followed with keen interest his dramatic, if somewhat excessive, exploits in charging up San Juan Hill, pausing now and then to exult over all "those damned Spanish dead" as he rallied his own disorderly troops.

Disembarking to the tune of "There'll Be a Hot Time in the Old Town Tonight," Roosevelt was promptly elected governor of New York and just as quickly upset party bosses by taking a firm progressive stand on a state factory inspection law and on another law regulating the hours of state employees. "If there is going to be any solution of the big social problems of the day," he warned his supporters, "it will come, not through a sentimental parlor socialism, but through actually taking hold of what is to be done, working right in the mire." Republican leaders in New York responded by lifting their governor out of the mire of reform politics and into the clean and safe office of the vice-presidency. Their hopes for squelching the exuberant progressive were curtailed when McKinley's assassination put Roosevelt in the White House.

**Roosevelt as President** Americans soon learned what kind of president they had acquired, for Roosevelt had strong opinions on every conceivable subject and delighted in publishing them in pungent and readable phrases. The objects of his interest ranged from the novels of the French writer Emile Zola (which he generally disliked) to the "full baby carriage" (which he heartily endorsed); and his advice ranged from conduct becoming football players and would-be reformers ("Don't flinch, don't foul, hit the line hard!") to what one observer called an "unflagging approval of the Ten Commandments." A vigorous intellectual, interested in birds and political bosses, trusts and big game, divorce and "practical idealism," Roosevelt collected facts and ideas that he regularly assembled in print—not writing with a pen, as one reader put it, so much as charging with it.

Roosevelt's forceful and sometimes contradictory opinions revealed two distinct personalities. The first was described by a New York politician as "the most indiscreet guy I ever met," the keeper of the national conscience always ready to speak his mind. This public Roosevelt served as the confident spokesman of an aggressive American nationalism—prophet of a coming Anglo-Saxon supremacy, celebrant of military valor, unblushing advocate of power politics, and a true believer in the American mission to order the affairs of the rest of the world. The national hero, "Teddy"—a name he disliked—looked the part. With pince-nez adorning a bulbous nose, toothy grin stretched in a near grimace, a full square face with its several chins resting on heavyset shoulders, a reedy voice, and pump-handle gestures, he was a cartoonist's dream.

In the role of the mad American of his generation, as he has been called, Roosevelt could and frequently did talk great nonsense. He lashed out with equal contempt at "radical fanatics" and the "lunatic fringe" of soft-headed reformers. "Sentimental humanitarians" he denounced as "a most pernicious body, with an influence for bad hardly surpassed by that of the professional criminal classes." He stressed the importance of "good blood" flowing through the veins of well-bred, self-denying gentlemen. He predicted race suicide for any of the world's people who preferred "effeminacy of character" to the "rougher and manlier virtues." For handling mobs he recommended "taking ten or a dozen of their leaders out, standing...them against a wall, and shooting them dead." For anarchists and socialist agitators he had a similar prescription—troops supplied

**Theodore Roosevelt
Campaigning in Wyoming, 1903**
*Against a backdrop of patriotic
bunting and antler horns,
Roosevelt demonstrates his
Square Deal.*

with real bullets and "the most wholesome desire to do them harm." Americans, whether delighted or appalled by such balderdash, recognized in Roosevelt the authentic American hero, the compulsive man of action who shot from the hip and whose motto read: "Get action; do things; be sane."

The other Roosevelt, unlike the trigger-happy dispenser of justice, was a thoughtful if highly partisan student of American history with a keen appreciation of the original work of the Founders. Young progressives entering the political arena after 1900 with credentials from the new universities brought with them training in such new disciplines as economics and sociology. But for the slightly older progressive leaders, the study of history was still the primary tool for examining American society. Despite the rapid growth of the "scientific" monograph, much of the popular history written after 1880 continued to be the work of gentlemen amateurs like Roosevelt and his friends Henry Adams and retired industrialist James Ford Rhodes, who measured the achievements and noted the shortcomings of nineteenth-century American democracy. The thrust of much of this popular history was toward political nationalism and social conservatism, whether in John Fiske's admiring account of the Founders, in Henry Adams's search for the principles of scientific government in his magnificent nine-volume history of the administrations of Jefferson and Madison, or in Roosevelt's own hymns to national valor in *The Naval War of 1812* and *The Winning of the West.*

**Roosevelt's Political Philosophy**

This reflective, history-minded Roosevelt was the first president after Lincoln and the last of the moderns with an understanding of the eighteenth century. Beneath his dramatic account of America's rise to greatness lay a clear grasp of the original Federalist design and the men who fashioned it. National greatness, it seemed to Roosevelt, was based, just as it had been in the past, on the "power to attain a high degree of social efficiency." By this he meant "love of order" and the "capacity to subordinate the interests of the individual to the interests of the community." The Federalists, he believed, led by such farseeing nationalists as Hamilton and Gouverneur Morris, had tried to teach the first Americans the same lesson that his own generation had just learned—that "the sphere of the State's action may be vastly increased without in any way diminishing the happiness of either the many or the few."

Roosevelt was convinced that the American people had been given the wrong directions by a demagogic Jefferson and had drifted steadily toward the Civil War even as they had expanded and enriched their domain. From Jefferson and his Jacksonian heirs they had acquired the illusions that little government was needed and that the moral order was self-regulating. Despite their magnificent material accomplishments in filling out a continent and building an industrial empire, the American people had failed to devise the political means of managing it. Only briefly during Lincoln's wartime administration had Americans caught a glimpse of true national unity. With the onset of the Gilded Age, the original stateman's question "Will it work?" had been replaced by the huckster's demand "Does it pay?" and the national energy had been squandered in money grubbing. One fact was clear at last—Americans had to "abandon definitely the *laissez-faire* theory of political economy, and fearlessly champion a system of increased Governmental control."

The opening years of the twentieth century, Roosevelt believed, represented "an era of federation and combination" that had been foreshadowed by the age of the Founders. The president, like his Federalist teachers, deplored class politics and called for the rule of enlightened men of integrity, whom he always identified with the better half of the Republican party. But wherever found, the disinterested patriot, Roosevelt was convinced, held the key to the future. By the time Roosevelt took over the presidency in 1901, he had acquired a clear definition of his role as general manager of the United States, even though the details of his plan for its "orderly development" emerged only gradually from the recesses of his conservative mind.

## *"Wise Radicalism and Wise Conservatism": The Square Deal*

As president, Roosevelt firmly established the regulatory principle as the foundation of administrative government. What he and the country came to call the Square Deal as he campaigned for reelection in 1904 began as a loose collection of proposals for directing national economic development. Roosevelt had inherited from Gilded Age Republicanism an Old Guard of conservatives. They had built their stronghold in the Senate, where they kept firm control over the lawmaking process and saw to it that presidents followed their dictates. Roosevelt was immediately forced to bargain with their leader, Senator Nelson W. Aldrich of Rhode Island, and to agree to keep his hands off the tariff question in exchange for a limited freedom to pursue his plans for intervention elsewhere. These concerns, like those of his progressive followers, first centered on the trusts.

**Trustbusting**     When Roosevelt took office in 1901, the fortunes of the opponents of monopoly appeared to improve. The Sherman Act, besides breaking up the Northern Securities Company in 1903, was applied successfully under Roosevelt's handpicked successor, William Howard Taft, against the Standard Oil and American Tobacco companies (1911). Yet by the end of Roosevelt's second administration in 1909 it was already clear that the act, far from achieving the results its framers had intended twenty years earlier, was strengthening rather than stopping the forces behind industrial and financial mergers. By admitting that not every restraint of trade was unreasonable, and by ruling cartel behavior unacceptable but full-blown mergers legitimate, the courts, first in Roosevelt's and then in Taft's administration, simply invited big business to abandon looser forms of organization for tighter and more effective ones.

Roosevelt shared the progressives' ambivalence toward big business. "Nothing of importance is gained," he admitted, "by breaking up a huge interstate and international organization which has not offended otherwise than by its size.... Those who would seek to restore the days of unlimited and uncontrolled competition ... are attempting not only the impossible, but what, if possible, would be undesirable." He believed that the trusts' behavior, not their size, constituted the test of their utility, and he declared it the government's duty to operate "in the interest of the general public." To prevent the trusts from fixing prices and manipulating the market, he proposed a watchdog agency modeled on the Interstate Commerce Commission, a body appointed by him and staffed with "trained administrators, well known to hold the scales exactly even in all matters." After a sharp skirmish with big business and its defenders in Congress, he succeeded in 1903 in establishing the Bureau of Corporations within the new Department of Labor and Commerce to police business practices and report its findings to the public.

Publicity formed the keystone of Roosevelt's regulatory program, and he quickly perfected the art of disclosure in launching a series of actions under the Sherman Antitrust Act. He advised the beef trust of his strictly honorable intentions to "Destroy the Evils in Trusts, But Not the Prosperity," and he insisted publicly on settling "the absolutely vital question" of federal power to regulate the trusts with the Northern Securities Company, the United States Steel Company, and the American Tobacco Company. It was essential, he announced, for the president and his administrators to maintain "strict supervision" of big business and see that it did not go wrong.

To make good his promise, in 1902 Roosevelt gave the signal to the Department of Justice to move against J. P. Morgan's railroad combine, the Northern Securities Company. Morgan, he recalled with relish, "could not help regarding me as a big rival operator who intended to ruin all his interests." But it was power that interested the president, who considered the clash with Morgan a dynastic one of rival sovereignties. In upholding the government's case against the railroad merger in *Northern Securities Co.* v. *United States* in 1904, the Supreme Court gave Roosevelt his precedent. In the *E. C. Knight* case (1895), he announced with obvious satisfaction, the Court had erroneously decided that the federal government lacked the power to break up dangerous combinations: "This decision I caused to be annulled." He did not add what soon became obvious—that he had not at the same time suppressed the merger movement.

Roosevelt's views on organized labor mirrored his convictions on big business: the ultimate test for both sides was a willingness to provide order and stability of their own volition. If trusts threatened the balance of economic power with irresponsible behavior, Roosevelt reasoned, labor could prove disruptive and greedy. If there were "good" and "bad" trusts, there were also dependable labor leaders like Samuel Gompers, and dangerous visionaries like Eugene Debs. In either case it was the president who had to distinguish legitimate demands from crackpot notions. The only standard he could finally invoke was conduct: "Where in either one or the other, there develops corruption or mere brutal indifference to the rights of others, and short-sighted refusal to look beyond the moment's gain, then the offender, whether union or corporation, must be fought."

The test of Roosevelt's opinion of unions, strikes, and injunctions came early in the first administration, when the United Mine Workers struck against the anthracite coal operators. The confrontation alarmed the whole country and gave Roosevelt welcome public support. Led by the canny John Mitchell, the miners demanded a pay increase and an eight-hour day along with acknowledgment of their right to organize the coal industry. George Baer, president of the Reading Railroad, bungled the case for the coal operators from the outset. Baer proclaimed it his "religious duty" to defeat the strikers, insisting that "the rights and interests of the laboring men will be protected and cared for—not by labor agitators, but by Christian men to whom God in his infinite wisdom has given control of the property interests of the country."

Roosevelt, his hand strengthened by the operators' obstinacy, quickly called for an investigation by his labor commissioner and used the findings to try to force the coal companies to compromise. When they refused, he ordered both parties to a conference in Washington, where the operators, under a presidential threat to send in troops, finally agreed to an arbitration panel. The Anthracite Coal Strike Commission awarded a 10 percent pay increase and a reduction of hours to the miners, while refusing their demand for a closed shop. Once again, as in regulating the trusts, it was principle and procedure—the orderly disposition of grievances by disinterested men—that most concerned the president.

**New Consumer Legislation**

Roosevelt's theory of expanded executive power developed from his belief that only "a great exertion of federal authority" could meet the needs of all the people. The most vulnerable members of a largely unregulated commercial society were American consumers. In consumer legislation, as in his dealings with big business and labor, Roosevelt assumed the leadership of forces that had already begun to organize by 1900. The Pure Food and Drug Law, passed in 1906, was the result of a carefully orchestrated public outcry and shrewd presidential direction. Although limited, the law capped a strenuous campaign for effective legislation by Harvey Wiley, chief chemist of the Department of Agriculture, who twice had seen his recommendations accepted in the House only to languish in the Senate, where the food and drug interests dominated. Aided by a series of lurid exposés furnished by the muckrakers, Roosevelt finally collected the votes he needed to prohibit the manufacture and sale of misbranded or adulterated foods and drugs, a limited power that has been wielded cautiously ever since.

Support for the Meat Packing Act (1906) also came from consumers, many of whom learned of the appalling conditions in the industry from Upton Sinclair's sensational novel *The Jungle.* In attacking the packers, Sinclair traced the shipment, from prairie to slaughterhouse, of cows "that developed lumpy jaw, or fell sick, or dried up of old age," carcasses "covered with boils that were full of matter." Although Roosevelt was annoyed by Sinclair's fictionalized account, the president promised him action. An investigation verified most of Sinclair's charges in a fact-studded report that Roosevelt, in a calculated piece of blackmail, threatened to release unless the packers accepted minimum regulation. Like most of the Square Deal legislation, the final bill represented a series of compromises—increased appropriations for inspection in exchange for the removal of inconvenient requirements for enforcement. The legislation left the matter of appeal to the courts in what Roosevelt called "purposeful ambiguity." Once the industry had accepted the principle of federal regulation, the big packers welcomed those requirements that could be expected to drive out their smaller competitors. For his part the president was perfectly willing to compromise on details in order to gain the principle of federal control.

In his willingness to sacrifice specifics for the precedent, Roosevelt frequently disappointed his more determined progressive supporters, who complained that he gave in too easily on points that might have been won. His critics appear to have won their case in the tug of war over the Hepburn Act (1906), which regulated railroad rates. In 1903 the railroad senators who refused to grant the government effective control over rate making had drafted the Elkins Act, a piece of legislation supposedly prohibiting discriminatory rebates to favored shippers. But Roosevelt was determined to acquire this authority. An administration measure passed by the House was designed to strengthen the Interstate Commerce Commission by giving it genuine power to fix rates and make them stick. In the Senate, however, Roosevelt's plan met the stubborn opposition of Nelson Aldrich and the railroad senators, who had decided to teach the president a

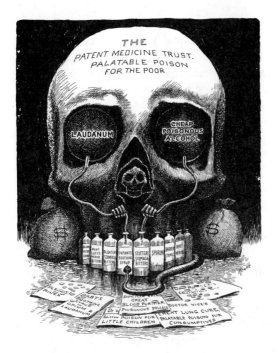

**Death-Dealing Drugs**
*Popular cartoons helped make
the case for national legislation
regulating the food and drug
industries.*

lesson. Aldrich and his conservatives quickly bottled up the bill in committee, where they conducted interminable hearings for the benefit of its enemies.

Roosevelt tried a second time with another bill, this one sponsored by Representative William P. Hepburn of Ohio. This even more moderate measure would empower the ICC to set reasonable rates after hearing complaints from shippers. Once again Aldrich stepped in, sent the bill to the Senate floor without endorsement, and looked on with detachment as one amendment after another stripped the bill of its original intent. In the end Roosevelt failed to rally a successful coalition of faithful Republicans and disgruntled Democrats, but he did manage to win over enough moderate Republicans to force Aldrich to compromise. The final version of the Hepburn bill increased the powers of the ICC but left intact the provision against enforcing new rates in cases that were under court appeal. At best, Roosevelt had won a very limited victory.

**A Formula for
Conservation**
In the case of conservation, the last main item on the Square Deal agenda, compromise again weakened principle. Although Roosevelt himself was a nature lover and preservationist by inclination, he abandoned the tradition of the naturalists Henry David Thoreau and John Muir for a developmentalist strategy designed for multiple use of the nation's natural resources. He called on citizens to look ahead to "the days of our children" and warned against the waste and destruction that would "result in undermining...the very prosperity" that ought

to be passed on to them "amplified and developed." Yet his formula for conservation remained the same as that for other national needs: expert advice from scientists committed to development rather than preservation, much publicity, and permissive governmental oversight of private interests.

These long-term limitations were obscured for the moment in the flurry of executive actions during Roosevelt's second term as he added 43 million acres to the national forests, withdrew from entry more than 2,500 water power sites and 65 million acres of coal lands, and established 16 national monuments and 53 wildlife refuges. The issue of conservation assumed a crucial symbolic significance in Roosevelt's mind as he found himself blocked by Congress from pursuing other social justice goals. He turned to the management of natural resources as "the fundamental problem which underlies almost every other problem in national life," the acid test of federal power. He flouted the congressional will with a "midnight proclamation" that set aside twenty-three new forest reserves and then threw down his challenge: "If Congress differs from me . . . it will have full opportunity in the future to take such positions as it may desire anent the discontinuance of the reserves." While Congress fumed, he moved rapidly ahead with plans for building a conservation empire consisting of bureaus and commissions filled with geologists, hydrologists, foresters, and engineers taking their orders from Gifford Pinchot, his volatile but capable chief forester. In 1908, sensing widespread public interest, Roosevelt called a National Conservation Congress, which was attended by forty-four governors and over five hundred conservation experts.

Yet despite its appearance as a popular crusade, Roosevelt's conservation program was less a grass-roots movement to save the environment than an executive scheme for national resource management imposed from above. The president envisioned a grand design in which irrigation, flood control, forestry, and reclamation would be "interdependent parts of the same problem" of regional development. He had to settle for much less. Government experts and lumber company executives shared a strong distaste for the preservationists' ideas. The new federal agencies were understaffed and underfinanced, and they soon found themselves dependent on the goodwill of the same private interests they were supposed to police. Small operators, whose reputation for gouging the landscape was well earned, were sometimes driven out, but the large companies continued their policies of exploiting national resources under a government seal of approval. From the perspective of three-quarters of a century, Roosevelt's national conservation program, like the original Federalist partnership between wealth and government, appears to have identified with the welfare of powerful private interests.

## The Limits of Neofederalism

Having retired from the presidency after two terms in office, Roosevelt embarked for Africa on a hunting trip in the spring of 1909, leaving in the White House his handpicked successor, the ponderous William Howard Taft, to "carry on the work substantially as I have carried it on." In many ways the conservation issue symbolized both the partial success and the ultimate limitations of Roosevelt's attempt to forge a new national purpose. The key to his plan was teaching the American electorate the meaning of national unity and strong government, an educational task he performed admirably for seven years.

The conservation campaign, which slowly moved to the center of the progressive consciousness, meant a fight against sectionalism, states' rights, business interests, and a Congress that gave them all voice. To halt these divisive forces and hold the allegiance of his reform followers, Roosevelt had revitalized the presidential office and buttressed it with new concepts of civic duty and loyalty. "I believe in a strong executive; I believe in power," he announced, and he proceeded to use his power in ways that no president since Lincoln had contemplated. To aid him in his work of executive renovation, he drew heavily from the ranks of progressive experts and professionals, whose cause of scientific government he championed enthusiastically. His reform program, for all its timid approach to the regulatory principle and its deference to vested interests, marked at least a step toward the orderly republic he envisioned.

If Roosevelt's utopia lay well over the horizon in 1909, it was because he intentionally set conservative limits to the application of governmental power and in the last analysis believed firmly in a guided democratic process. Although he chafed under the restraints placed on him by his party and a laggard Congress, he managed both of them with consummate skill, alternately bullying and cajoling both, but breaking with neither. In negotiating for his limited reforms, he was willing more often than not to take the shell and leave the kernel, concerned as he was with winning a principle. Yet his presidency was no mere exercise in educational politics. Roosevelt wanted results that the country would accept, and to get them he willingly used traditional and even conservative political methods. When he left office, the results were clear. He had raised the presidency to its twentieth-century position of dominance. He had laid the foundation for a governmental bureaucracy and had collected the presumably disinterested professionals to run it. And finally, he had preached with unflagging zeal the virtues of high-mindedness, integrity, and service as indispensable to the new citizenship.

Further than this neither Roosevelt nor the nationalist-minded progressives could go. Roosevelt spoke for progressives across the country in demanding the return to service of "the man of business and the man of science, the doctor of divinity and the doctor of law, the architect, the engineer, and the writer," all of whom owed a "positive duty to the community, the neglect of which they cannot excuse on any plea of their private affairs." An organized army of political hacks had long since defeated the ordinary citizen, "to whom participation in politics is a disagreeable duty." Now, Roosevelt and the progressives believed, it was time to try the extraordinary citizen wherever he could be found. Neither Roosevelt nor the progressives would have been surprised to learn that the average citizen was taking less rather than greater interest in politics. Voter turnout, which in the Gilded Age had averaged nearly 80 percent in presidential years and 60 percent in off-years, fell a full 15 percent after 1900. Possibly because they were disenchanted with the prospects of a managed republic that the progressives promised them, or perhaps simply because they were discovering more pressing concerns outside the political arena, fewer Americans were troubling themselves with the duty of taking what Roosevelt called "their full part in our life."

Here indeed lay the outermost reaches of Roosevelt's political domain. If Jefferson's political formula had long since proved hopelessly inadequate for managing an industrial republic, his original estimate of the diverse sources of American energy had not. Jefferson had counted the advantages as well as the dangers of sectional division, religious variety, ethnic diversity, and even class disagreement. With Roosevelt's retirement in 1909, these forces of social and political pluralism began to take revenge on his promise of national unity, first shaking the party structure and then disrupting the national social consensus that Roosevelt and his followers had attempted to construct. In a suddenly revived Democratic party the American people would find a different variety of progressive reform, and in Woodrow Wilson a very different kind of leader.

## CHRONOLOGY

| | | | |
|---|---|---|---|
| **1889** | Jane Addams founds Hull House; beginning of settlement-house movement. Hazen Pingree elected mayor of Detroit; first progressive mayor. | **1901** | Theodore Roosevelt becomes president after McKinley assassinated. Tom Johnson elected mayor of Cleveland. |
| **1890** | Muckraking photo-journalist Jacob Riis publishes *How the Other Half Lives,* depicting life in New York's slums. | **1902** | Roosevelt launches antitrust action against Northern Securities Company. Roosevelt settles anthracite coal strike through arbitration. |
| **1893** | First issue of *McClure's* magazine. Conference for Good City Government inaugurates urban progressive reform movement. | **1903** | Bureau of Corporations established within new Department of Labor and Commerce. |
| **1899** | John Dewey's *School and Society,* pioneer progressive education tract. | **1904** | Roosevelt elected president, defeating Democrat Alton B. Parker and Socialist Eugene V. Debs. Case of *Northern Securities Co.* v. *U.S.* upholds government's case against railroad mergers. Lincoln Steffens's *The Shame of the Cities* published. |
| **1900** | Robert La Follette elected to his first of three terms as progressive governor of Wisconsin. William McKinley reelected president, defeating William Jennings Bryan. | **1906** | Upton Sinclair's novel *The Jungle* published. |

**1906** Meat Packing Act passed.
Pure Food and Drug Act passed.
Hepburn Act passed,
strengthening powers of
Interstate Commerce
Commission.
John Spargo's *The Bitter Cry of
Children,* exposé of child labor,
published.

**1907** Financial panic; Roosevelt turns to
J. P. Morgan and the bankers for
help.
William James's *Pragmatism*
published.

**1908** Supreme Court upholds state
regulation of working hours for
women in *Muller* v. *Oregon.*
Roosevelt convenes National
Conservation Congress.
William Howard Taft elected
president, defeating Bryan and
Debs.

**1911** Frederick Winslow Taylor's
*Principles of Scientific
Management,* pioneer work in
industrial efficiency.
"Dissolution" of Standard Oil and
American Tobacco trusts.

---

## Suggested Readings

George E. Mowry, *The Era of Theodore Roosevelt, 1900–1912* (1958), and Arthur S. Link, *Woodrow Wilson and the Progressive Era, 1900–1917* (1954), provide an excellent survey of the politics of the progressive period. Recent interpretive essays include William L. O'Neill, *The Progressive Years: America Comes of Age* (1975); David M. Kennedy, ed., *Progressivism: The Critical Issues* (1971); Lewis L. Gould, *The Progressive Era* (1973); and John D. Buenker, *Urban Liberalism and Progressive Reform* (1973). Two recent overviews of progressivism are John D. Buenker, John C. Burnham, and Robert M. Crunden, *Progressivism* (1977); and Arthur S. Link and Richard L. McCormick, *Progressivism* (1983). Dewey W. Grantham, *Southern Progressivism: The Reconciliation of Progress and Tradition* (1983) provides a regional survey of the movement, and Jack Temple Kirby, *Darkness at Dawning: Race and Reform in the Progressive South* counts the cost of progressive racism.

The literature on bosses and machines in the progressive period is impressive. Among the best accounts are Lloyd Wendt and Herman Kogan, *Bosses in Lusty Chicago: The Story of Bathhouse John and Hinky Dink* (1943); Zane L. Miller, *Boss Cox's Cincinnati* (1968); Lyle Dorsett, *The Pendergast Machine* (1968); and Walton E. Bean, *Boss Ruef's San Francisco* (1952).

Two autobiographical accounts provide the best introduction to muckraking: Lincoln Steffens, *The Autobiography of Lincoln Steffens* (1931), and Ida M. Tarbell, *All in the Day's Work* (1939). Harold S. Williamson, *McClure's Magazine and the Muckrakers* (1970), is a good account of the career of the pioneer muckraking editor. Arthur Weinberg and Lila Weinberg, eds., *The Muckrakers* (1961), and Harvey Swados, ed., *Years of Conscience: The Muckrakers* (1962), offer a wide range of muckraking reporting.

Robert La Follette's career in Wisconsin and in the United States Senate is chronicled in David Thelen, *Robert La Follette and the Insurgent Spirit* (1976); Robert S. Maxwell, *La Follette and the Rise of Progressivism in Wisconsin* (1956); and Herbert Margulies, *The Decline of the Progressive Movement in Wisconsin, 1890–1920* (1968). For a portrait of another progressive political leader who was the temperamental opposite of La Follette, see Robert F. Wesser, *Charles Evans Hughes: Politics and Reform in New York State, 1905–1910* (1967).

There are many good biographies of major political figures on the national scene during the Progressive Era. John Milton Cooper, Jr., *The Warrior and the Priest: Theodore Roosevelt and Woodrow Wilson* (1983) is a deft comparison of presidential styles and philosophies. For Roosevelt they include William H. Harbaugh, *The Life and Times of Theodore Roosevelt* (1961); the brief but perceptive John Morton Blum, *The Republican Roosevelt* (1954); G. Wallace Chessman, *Theodore Roosevelt and the Politics of Power* (1969); and Edmund Morris, *The Rise of Theodore Roosevelt* (1979), a highly readable account of Roosevelt's prepresidential years. A useful study of Taft is Donald E. Anderson, *William Howard Taft* (1973). Biographies of other important progressives include Alpheus T. Mason, *Brandeis: A Free Man's Life* (1946); Melvin I. Urofsky, *Louis D. Brandeis and the Progressive Tradition* (1981); Dexter Perkins, *Charles Evans Hughes and American Democratic Statesmanship* (1956); Richard Lowitt, *George W. Norris: The Making of a Progressive* (1963); John A. Garraty, *Right-Hand Man: The Life of George W. Perkins* (1960); Richard Leopold, *Elihu Root and the Conservative Tradition* (1954); and M. Nelson McGeary, *Gifford Pinchot: Forester-Politician* (1960).

Progressive social issues have been discussed in several important works. John W. Chambers II, *The Tyranny of Change: America in the Progressive Era, 1900–1917* (1988) traces the course of progressive reformers' intervention in the economy and society at large. James H. Timberlake, *Prohibition and the Progressive Crusade* (1963), examines the connections between progressive politics and moral reform. Jack Holl, *Juvenile Reform in the Progressive Era* (1971), explores another important aspect of progressive reform. The progressive concern with eugenics and birth control is described in Donald K. Pickens, *Eugenics and the Progressive Era* (1971), and David Kennedy, *Birth Control in America: The Career of Margaret Sanger* (1970). Changing patterns of morality emerge clearly from William L. O'Neill, *Divorce in the Progressive Era* (1967), and crucial developments in progressive education from Lawrence Cremin, *The Transformation of the School: Progressivism in American Education, 1876–1956* (1961). Samuel P. Hays, *Conservation and the Gospel of Efficiency* (1959), provides a close look at the less democratic features of that reform movement. Walter I. Trattner, *Crusade for Children* (1970) is a good account of child labor reform. John F. McClymer, *War and Welfare: Social Engineering in America, 1890–1925* (1970) explains the impact of war on progressive social engineering.

The intellectual climate of progressivism has been discussed in several excellent studies. Charles Forcey, *The Crossroads of Liberalism: Croly, Weyl, Lippmann and the Progressive Era, 1900–1925* (1961), gives a lively account of three leading progressive publicists. Robert W. Schneider, *Five Novelists of the Progressive Era* (1965), traces reform ideas through popular fiction. Roy Lubov, *The Progressives and the Slums* (1962), shows the concerns of leading reformers with cleaning up the cities. The best introduction to the writing of progressive history is Richard Hofstadter, *The Progressive Historians* (1968). Samuel J. Konefsky, *The Legacy of Holmes and Brandeis* (1956), explains the legacy of the two great progressive jurists. Samuel Haber, *Efficiency and Uplift: Scientific Management in the Progressive Era, 1890–1920* (1964), shows the effect of the ideas of Frederick Winslow Taylor in shaping progressive values. For sharply etched portraits of three key intellectuals in the Progressive Era, see David Riesman, *Thorstein Veblen: A Critical Introduction* (1963); Ralph Barton Perry, *The Thought and Character of William James* (2 vols., 1935); and Sidney Hook, *John Dewey: An Intellectual Portrait* (1939).

Personal reflections—sometimes illuminating, always entertaining—on the meaning of progressivism by two active progressives are collected in William Allen White, *The Autobiography of William Allen White* (1946), and Frederic C. Howe, *The Confessions of a Reformer* (1925).

# 25

# Progressives and the
# Challenge of Pluralism

---

$\mathcal{I}$N 1910 Theodore Roosevelt, after a year's trek through Africa and the
capitals of Europe, returned home to a rebellion in his own party. Once he
learned of the widening rift between President William Howard Taft's supporters and his own leaderless progressive followers, Roosevelt moved quickly to
return the Republican party to his original vision of a unified national purpose. In
an incisive speech in 1910 dedicating a state park in Osawatomie, Kansas, where
John Brown had fought with Missouri ruffians a half-century earlier, Roosevelt
gave his program a name—the "New Nationalism." In part, Roosevelt's speech
owed its clarity to his recent reading of Herbert Croly's *The Promise of American
Life,* a progressive's indictment of American political drift with which the former
president fully agreed. But in a broader sense both Croly's lengthy analysis and
Roosevelt's call to action at Osawatomie summed up the arguments for an
organized national society that Roosevelt had formulated years earlier.

Roosevelt was not calling for "overcentralization," he assured his Kansas
audience, but for "a spirit of broad and far-reaching nationalism" to guide the
American people as a whole. His New Nationalism, which put national needs
ahead of sectional interests and private advantage, would bring an end to "the
utter confusion that results from local legislatures attempting to treat national
issues as local issues." After listing the many unfinished tasks awaiting federal
action, Roosevelt drove home his point with a comparison that he hoped would
have meaning for the few aging veterans of the Civil War in the crowd. "You
could not have won simply as a disorderly mob," the Rough Rider reminded
them. "You needed generals; you needed careful administration of the most
advanced type.... You had to have the administration in Washington good, just
as you had to have the administration in the field.... So it is in our civil life."

Unfortunately for Roosevelt, administration of the most advanced type was
not yet a fact, as the man who was to be his chief rival in the election of 1912

already sensed. Woodrow Wilson, a Southerner and a Democrat, drew on both these traditions in sounding the principal countertheme of progressivism. As a former professor of political science and president of Princeton, currently the reform governor of New Jersey, Wilson was fully Roosevelt's match as a historian and intellectual. In examining the American political and social system in 1910, he came closer to understanding the complex play of social forces at work in the country than both of his Republican rivals, Taft and Roosevelt.

Roosevelt's New Nationalism called for the reordering of American priorities and the acquiring of new habits and duties. The "New Freedom"—as Wilson came to call his vision—offered another view of progressivism as a liberation movement. Wilson pictured an open, complex society, composed of immigrants and women as well as native-born white males, Catholics and Jews as well as Protestants, reformers as well as professional politicians, and visionaries of all sorts as well as political realists. In the election year of 1912, these broader strokes of Wilson's New Freedom seemed to present a truer picture of the complexity of early-twentieth-century American life than did the views of Roosevelt and the New Nationalists. But it remained to be seen whether the Democratic party, emerging from sixteen years of enforced retirement, could succeed in turning these various energies into a political program.

## Changing the Progressive Guard

By 1910 it seemed that reform had slowed. Congress, with a bipartisan faction of conservatives in both houses, was in no mood to finish the work of building a national banking system or designing a program of business regulation. And a watchful conservative Supreme Court stood ready to stop any further advances toward the social service state.

Of all the branches of the federal government, the Supreme Court was the least responsive to the problems confronting industrial society and the most alert to the dangers of curtailing corporate privilege. Although it had agreed to Roosevelt's breaking up of the Northern Securities trust and the oil and tobacco monopolies, the Court was much less enthusiastic about the new progressive forms of administrative regulation and the use of commissions to make and enforce rulings. The struggle for administrative effectiveness after 1890 often seemed to be waged between a handful of conservative justices clinging tenaciously to the right of judicial review and a circle of frustrated congressional reformers hoping to strengthen the administrative arm of the federal government. To these reformers the Supreme Court's stubborn defense of its prerogatives seemed a usurpation—taking away from the Interstate Commerce Commission and other federal agencies the power to do their job. Progressives remembered, too, that the Supreme Court had recently declared a federal income tax unconstitutional and had set severe limits on the powers of the states to enact social legislation.

**Justice Holmes and the Court**

The spirit of progressivism invaded the Supreme Court with the appointment of Oliver Wendell Holmes, Jr. He was chosen by Roosevelt in the hope that he would reeducate his senior colleagues in the uses of judicial restraint and bring a more enlightened view of regulatory power to the Court. Holmes considered the Constitution not a yardstick for measuring the shortcomings of imperfect laws, but rather a flexible instrument for providing for the "felt necessities" of the modern age. The life of the law, he was convinced, was inherent in its utility and function. Holmes dismissed those of his colleagues on the Court who still claimed to believe in higher law as willing captives of "that naïve state of mind that accepts what has been familiar and accepted by them and their neighbors as something that must be accepted everywhere." As for himself, the outspoken newcomer admitted, "I . . . define truth as the system of my limitations and leave absolute truth for those who are better equipped."

Holmes explained his belief in the necessity of social experimentation in the famous *Lochner* case of 1905, a decision overturning a New York law that reduced the workweek for bakers to sixty hours. In a five-to-four decision the majority of the Court declared that the law was another "meddlesome interference with the rights of individuals" and thus unconstitutional. In his dissent Holmes lectured his fellow justices on the danger of intruding their laissez-faire views into the law. The Constitution, he declared, had not been intended "to embody a particular economic theory, whether of paternalism and the organic relation of the citizen to the state or of laissez-faire." Instead it was made for people who frankly differed, and "the accident of our finding certain opinions natural and familiar, or novel and even shocking, ought not to conclude our judgment upon the question whether statutes embodying them conflict with the Constitution of the United States." In a series of similar dissents during the next two decades, Holmes— together with Justice Louis Brandeis, who joined the liberal side of the Court in 1916—argued for restraint on the judicial activism of a conservative majority that was concerned with slowing the progressive drift toward a managed society.

**Political Conflicts Under Taft**

Congress was frequently divided within itself after 1909 and could make little headway against the Supreme Court's certainty of conservative purpose. Both the House and the Senate witnessed a series of sharp clashes between aggressively reform-minded Insurgents and stubborn conservatives over tariffs, conservation, and governmental reorganization. With no leadership from President Taft, who backed the majority of conservative Republican regulars, reformers lost heart.

Meanwhile Taft's political lethargy and his ineptitude made an inviting target for the barbs of Republican reformers, including La Follette. Although Roosevelt had recommended Taft as a thorough-going reformer, the new president lacked Roosevelt's concern with strengthening the federal government, as well as the former president's skill in managing his party. Taft was graceless, stubborn,

**William Howard Taft**
*Taft preferred conservative Republicans to crusading Insurgents.*

unschooled in the arts of political persuasion, and wholly lacking in Roosevelt's popular appeal—and he quickly made it clear that he was no crusader.

Taft's administration accordingly was punctuated by a series of political explosions. The first was touched off by a struggle over conservation policy. Gifford Pinchot, chief of the United States Forest Service, "Sir Galahad of the Woods," as his numerous enemies called him, accused Taft's secretary of the interior, Richard Ballinger, of neglecting his duties. More specifically, Pinchot accused Ballinger of unsavory conduct in validating the Bering River coal claims that had mysteriously come into possession of the Morgan-Guggenheim syndicate. Although a congressional investigation cleared Ballinger of any hint of fraud, and although the feisty and self-righteous Pinchot overplayed his hand by appealing to the American public at large, Ballinger felt obliged to resign. Taft, who had supported Ballinger, lost face and with it the loyalty of a sizable group of Roosevelt progressives.

Taft only increased his problems in his handling of the tariff question. After promising downward revision of the schedules, he backed away from the ensuing congressional struggle and looked on as the protectionist forces of Nelson Aldrich and the Old Guard loaded the original bill with higher schedules. Then, to the amazement of the progressive Insurgents, the president hurried to their midwestern stronghold, where he proclaimed the now unrecognizable Payne-Aldrich Act the "best tariff ever passed by the Republican party."

**Roosevelt: The Bull Moose Candidate**  Roosevelt watched Taft's mismanagement of his party with growing disdain. "A lawyer's administration," he snorted, was proving itself "totally unfit" to lead the country. For like-minded progressives who had recently formed the Progressive Republican League, there were two choices. The first was to appeal to Roosevelt to intervene in party councils in their behalf and help them replace Taft with a candidate of their choosing; the second, and more desperate, strategy was to bolt the Republican party altogether and set up an independent reform party. By 1912 Republican progressives remained sharply divided on this question.

As the election year approached, Roosevelt himself was undecided about the best course. On the one hand, he was convinced that the Taft regime had paid little attention to the "needs of the country." On the other hand, he was dubious of the success of any movement on his own behalf, and he confessed to little enthusiasm for "staggering under a load on my shoulders through no fault of my own."

Whether he knew it or not, Roosevelt had practically declared his availability with his "New Nationalism" speech at Osawatomie. The New Nationalism, composed of schemes for the improved regulation of corporations, physical evaluation of railroads, a graduated income tax, a reformed banking system, labor legislation, a direct primary, and a corrupt practices act, seemed exhilarating to his progressive followers but nothing less than revolutionary to the Old Guard Republicans. Far from closing the breach between the two wings of the Republican party, the New Nationalism speech in effect was Roosevelt's challenge to Taft and his conservatives.

When Taft refused to step out of Roosevelt's way and Senator Robert La Follette entered a rival bid for the nomination, Roosevelt, who distrusted Taft and heartily disliked La Follette, decided to run. But Taft regulars put to good use the southern Republican delegates, whom they held securely. Roosevelt's hopes at the convention rested on some 252 contested seats, at least 100 of which he needed in order to win the nomination. With the credentials committee and the whole party apparatus in the hands of the regulars, he succeeded in winning only 14 of these contested seats. After hurried consultations with his financial backers, George W. Perkins and Frank Munsey, who promised to see him through, Roosevelt agreed to bolt and call his own convention to launch an independent Progressive party.

The loyal 10,000 who gathered in the Chicago Auditorium in August 1912 to hear their leader pronounce himself as fit as a "bull moose" and to sing with them the "Battle Hymn of the Republic" constituted a motley collection of mavericks and reformers, nationalists and big businessmen, social workers and intellectuals, all determined to stand with the "Colonel" at Armageddon and to "battle for the Lord." Conspicuously absent were most of the original liberal Insurgents, who declined to make a risky investment in third-party politics. Although the vibrant spirit of the old progressivism was evident at Chicago, Roosevelt and his advisers realized that winning the election would prove difficult. As Roosevelt intoned the Eighth Commandment and called down divine judgment on his Republican betrayers, he must have known that a Democratic victory was all but inevitable.

**Wilson: The Shining Knight of Progressivism**   Yet if fortune was about to shine its face on the Democrats in the election of 1912, it gave no sign. Democrats had their own liabilities, chief among them their titular head and perennial candidate, William Jennings Bryan, who had labored sixteen years to undo the damages of his ill-fated experiment in pietistic politics. In the center ring at the 1912 Democratic convention stood "Champ" Clark, speaker of the House and veteran southern leader of the party, who had the support of the rural wing; William Randolph Hearst, the demagogic newspaper publisher and pseudo-reformer; and Woodrow Wilson, the shining knight of New Jersey progressivism. Fresh from a series of legislative encounters that had seen the passage of a direct primary law, railroad legislation, workmen's compensation, and a corrupt practices act, Wilson represented the hopes of urban progressives in the East.

The Democratic convention in Baltimore was every bit as uproarious as the Republican convention. Clark, armed with preconvention pledges, jumped out to an early lead, which he maintained until the Wilson forces finally caught up. On the forty-sixth ballot, after endless maneuvering and a final agreement between southern agrarians and northern city bosses, the deadlock was broken and Wilson received the two-thirds vote necessary for nomination. Before they adjourned, the Democrats patched up their differences in a platform that roundly condemned Republican centralization—as Democratic platforms had unfailingly done since Reconstruction—and advertised its own brand of progressivism guaranteed to lower the tariff and break up the trusts, give the banks back to the people, and destroy all special privilege.

But the heart of the Democratic promise in 1912 lay in Wilson's call for liberation from the rule of big business and big government. Taft's official Republicanism, Wilson predicted, would spell continuing business domination, while Roosevelt's plan for monitoring the trusts simply added the powers of the government to those of the monopolists. Wilson pictured Democratic deliverance as "coming out of the stifling cellar into the open," where people could "breathe again and see the free spaces of the heavens." Remove the restrictions on private enterprise, Wilson urged, so that the younger generation would never

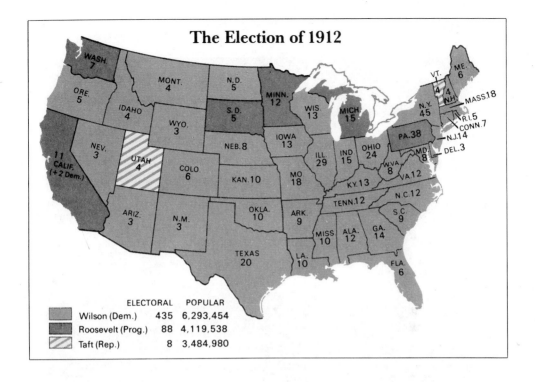

## The Election of 1912

| | ELECTORAL | POPULAR |
|---|---|---|
| Wilson (Dem.) | 435 | 6,293,454 |
| Roosevelt (Prog.) | 88 | 4,119,538 |
| Taft (Rep.) | 8 | 3,484,980 |

become "the protégé of benevolent trusts" but rather would be free to go about making of their lives whatever they wished.

Wilson won the presidency with 6,286,214 popular votes—42 percent—and 435 electoral votes. Even with the split among the Republicans, who gave Taft some 3.5 million votes and Roosevelt's Progressive party more than 4 million, Wilson's victory was impressive. It remained to be seen whether the new president represented a new kind of leadership.

**President Wilson: Schoolmaster to the Nation**

If the intellectual sources of Roosevelt's New Nationalism lay in the eighteenth-century world of the Founders, the roots of Woodrow Wilson's New Freedom were firmly planted in nineteenth-century morality. Wilson, who was born in 1856 in Staunton, Virginia, grew up in the heart of the Confederacy, briefly attended Davidson College, and graduated from Princeton in 1879. After a year spent studying the law, for which he had no particular liking, he turned to his real interests, political science and history. He studied with the great historian of institutions Herbert Baxter Adams at Johns Hopkins University and earned a doctorate there in 1886. Then came several years of climbing the academic ladder, with appointments at Bryn Mawr, Wesleyan, and Princeton, where he taught for twelve years before becoming its president in 1902. Wilson's books, polished although not sparkling works of political science and history, made a varied collection: *Congressional Government* (1885); an extended essay, *The State* (1889); a history of the Civil War years, *Division and Reunion* (1893); the

**Woodrow Wilson: Schoolmaster to the Nation**
*Wilson was a diligent campaigner and a highly effective speaker.*

five-volume *History of the American People* (1902); and *Constitutional Government in the United States* (1908).

By temperament as well as training, Wilson was an academic, an educator-scholar who felt a calling to instruct a progressive generation in the science of good government. As schoolmaster to the nation, he looked the part—with a lean, angular face, a long nose adorned by a pince-nez, full pursed lips, and eyes that seemed to look through his visitors rather than at them. Distant, formal, somewhat severe in his relations with the public, he appeared correct but cold. He recognized this deep reserve in himself and thought it a weakness. "I have a sense of power in dealing with men collectively," he once confessed, "which I do not feel always in dealing with them singly." There was little familiarity in the man and no feeling of camaraderie. As president of Princeton, governor of New Jersey, and chief executive, Wilson was a man one worked *for* but not *with*. Both as a teacher and as an administrator, he had a problem not so much in disciplining his followers, at which he excelled with a frosty politeness, as in controlling his own high-voltage temper and his tendency to bristle when challenged. When opposition to his plans mounted, as it did in a serious struggle over the graduate school at Princeton, Wilson would cling to his position, personalize the conflict, and accuse his opponents of malice while avowing the purity of his own motives.

At his best, however, Wilson was a superb leader, directing the work of his subordinates with cool precision, holding their loyalty with ideals, and winning the American public over with his moral authority. On the few occasions when his self-confidence flagged in the face of enemy attack, he could be petty and vindictive. But at all times he lived the role of the statesman as educator, standing before and slightly above the American people, to whom he sought to teach effective government.

Some of the lessons Wilson taught were curiously old-fashioned and abstract—moral precepts rather than practical proposals. For him words like *liberty, justice,* and *progress* still retained their mid-nineteenth-century clarity. In his mind these words were connected with the Christian principles of "obligation," "service," and "righteousness" that his father, a Presbyterian minister, had preached. These moral abstractions were the skeletal truths around which Wilson packed such flesh-and-blood meaning as fitted his southern Democratic heritage. His intellectual origins led him to view American politics in terms of both individual rights and pluralistic values. In his vision of America, Wilson agreed with the English liberal philosopher John Stuart Mill's definition of liberty as the absence of external restraint. On the other hand, Wilson's southern upbringing had given him a generally unenlightened view of race and a quiet respect for the South's reasoning in discriminating against blacks.

Wilson sensed clearly that American life in the opening years of the twentieth century remained too disorganized, its forms too complex to be encased in a formula like the New Nationalism. "The life of the nation has grown infinitely varied," he reminded his fellow Democrats in pointing to a flourishing cultural and ethnic diversity. In his view the most urgent American reform task was releasing the creative impulses of a free people. Nations, he argued with strict Jeffersonian logic, are renewed from the bottom up, from "the great struggling unknown masses of men" at the base of society. The nation must preserve these Jeffersonian values even as it becomes industrialized and urbanized. Ultimately, Wilson hoped to reconcile modernization with the traditional values of small-town and rural America.

> If America discourages the locality, the community, the self-contained town, she will kill the nation. A nation is as rich as her free communities. . . . The welfare, the very existence of the nation rests at last upon the spirit in which they go about their work in the several communities throughout the broad land.

What the nation needed most, Wilson firmly believed, was to listen to the counsel of the working men and women of the country—and indeed Wilson sought and received labor backing in his campaigns, although he did not always give the labor movement what it asked.

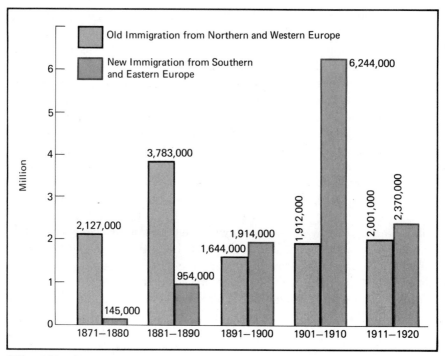

**Old and New Immigration, 1871–1920**

## Americans—New and Old

Many of the men and women who did the nation's daily work were recent arrivals from Europe. The decade after 1900 saw the climax of a century-long European exodus in the cresting of a wave of new immigrants from new sources. Until roughly 1890 the great majority of immigrants had come from northern and western Europe. Although these early newcomers were the source of fears and of problems of cultural identity for native-born Americans, these anxieties paled beside those accompanying the arrival of the so-called new immigration. In the first place, the very number of new immigrants overwhelmed the nativists, who stood for the values and interests of old-stock Americans. The nativists' worst fears were confirmed in statistics. In the quarter-century before World War I, 18 million new arrivals walked down the gangplanks, 80 percent of them from southern and eastern Europe. In the first decade of the twentieth century alone, some 5.8 million people arrived from Austria-Hungary, Spain, Italy, and Russia.

Another set of figures reinforced the nativists' fears. In the peak year, 1882, · when more than three-quarters of a million immigrants had disembarked at Atlantic ports, a third of their numbers had come from Germany, while Italy sent only 32,000 people and Russia not quite 17,000. The peak year in the progressive era, 1907, reversed this balance: Germany sent only 37,000, while Italy dispatched 285,000 citizens; the Austro-Hungarian empire, another 338,000; and Russia (including Russia's Baltic provinces), still another 250,000 people. For the entire period the Italians headed the list of European immigrants with 3 million. Next came the Jews, most of them from Russia, numbering about 2 million, followed by a million Poles by 1914. These three main groups, together with Hungarians, Greeks, Armenians, Syrians, and Turks, attested to the results of leaving the gates open.

**A Bewildering
Ethnic Variety**

Four out of five of the new arrivals settled in industrial cities in the Northeast and the Midwest in areas where jobs could be found. Their collective impact on these cities became clear to progressives when they suddenly realized that 75 percent of the populations of New York, Chicago, Cleveland, and Boston were immigrants or children of immigrants. Like it or not, progressives faced a bewildering ethnic and religious variety in the unmistakable presence of many new people eager to get ahead in their new home.

The new immigrants, like the earlier ones, were attracted by economic opportunity, which drew them off worn-out lands and out of the ghettos of European port cities into an American setting of deprivation that at first seemed all too familiar. Once arrived, they started at the bottom of the occupational

**Labor Agency on New York City's Lower West Side**
*Here recently arrived immigrants found the menial jobs allotted to them by labor contractors.*

ladder doing the nation's dirty work—construction, mining, smelting, factory work, and domestic service. They usually settled in tight ethnic communities near their work, finding security in an enforced segregation. This pattern of inner-city concentration fed old-stock American fears even as it made the "foreigners" invisible to suburbanites. Frequently, too, the newcomers elbowed their predecessors out of the neighborhoods, sending them further out along the city's extremities.

Old-stock Americans tended to assign the new arrivals a national identity that most of them did not possess. For example, nativists were inclined to stereotype these new immigrants as Poles, Italians, or Russians, but in fact the vast majority did not conform to the stereotypes. Most had come from provincial cultures whose outlook had long been restricted to the locale, the region, or the village. Although the immigrant enclaves in American cities appeared compact and uniform to outsiders, in fact they were splintered ethnic and religious clusters: each neighborhood boasted its own churches and patron saints, feast days, and civic associations.

Packed into slums, exploited by native-born employers and their own contractors alike, harassed by nativist groups and earlier arrivals, fighting among themselves for a foot on the economic ladder, millions of the new immigrants at first lived marginal lives close to the edges of defeat. The going rate for piecework in New York's garment industry was 8 cents an hour. Steelworkers in Pittsburgh sweated a sixty-hour week for $12.50. A husband-and-wife team on Tenth Street in New York's Lower East Side in 1900 could expect $3.75 for every thousand cigars they wrapped. By working fifteen hours a day, the two of them could turn out 3,000 cigars. Leisure for educational and cultural pursuits was a scarce commodity in America's Little Italys and Little Warsaws.

Slowly these immigrant communities gained a measure of stability. Neighborhoods built lively subcultures through their churches, foreign-language newspapers, service organizations like the Sons of Italy and the Pan-Hellenic Union, and a variety of social agencies and immigrant-aid societies. Edward Corsi, who later became President Herbert Hoover's commissioner of immigration and naturalization, recalled the congested tenement-house life of New York's East Harlem, with "five thousand human beings in one city street, as many as fifteen to a four-room flat; two, three, and even four hundred to a tenement intended for fifty"—twenty-seven nationalities all told, including Chinese laundrymen, Syrian shopkeepers, and gypsy phrenologists. On the East River there were Italians; along Pleasant Avenue, Poles, Austrians, and Hungarians; over in West Harlem, Jewish shopkeepers besieged by Turks and Spaniards. And driving all before them, the blacks. Old-stock Americans lived in lonely social islands in this sea of immigrants, "like refugees in exile."

Corsi's East Harlem boasted a lusty popular culture—not the imposing facades of opera houses, theaters, and hotels, but Old World pageants in cafés, rathskellers, spaghetti houses, cabarets, and dance halls. "We have Yiddish theaters and Italian marionette shows," Corsi boasted, "not to mention movie

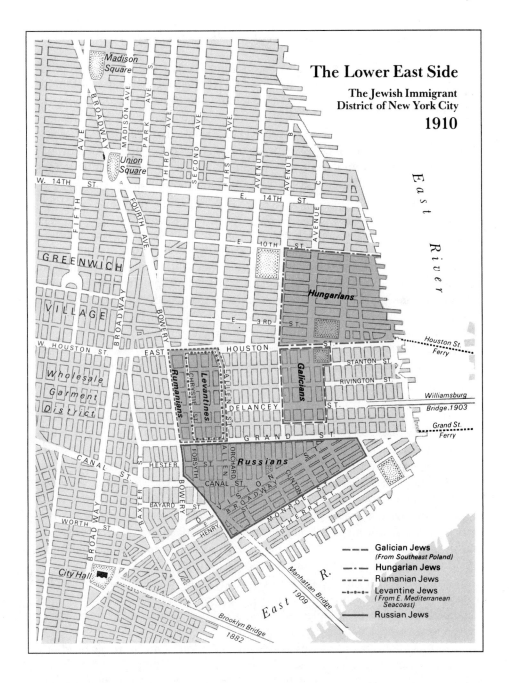

**The Lower East Side**

New York City's Jewish community in 1910 was splintered into national neighborhoods.

and vaudeville houses. Our secondhand book shops are as good as those of Paris. So are our music stores."

**The "New Immigration": Unassimilable?**

Mystified and a little frightened by the variety of immigrant life, most progressive Americans took refuge in increasingly irrelevant schemes for "Americanizing" the new arrivals. At dockside, civic-aid societies handed out pamphlets, printed in English, warning the newcomers to be "honest and honorable, clean in your person, and decent in your talk"; but these instructions scattered in the swirl of numbers like so many pious hopes. Advocates of immigration restriction agreed with Theodore Roosevelt in deploring the "tangle of squabbling nationalities" as "the one certain way of bringing the nation to ruin," yet the fact remained that hyphenated Americanism—Italian-Americanism, Greek-Americanism, Polish-Americanism—was the only avenue to full citizenship. Even the hopeful immigrant Israel Zangwill, looking ahead to the day of total assimilation, described a dream rather than a reality. The composer-hero of Zangwill's popular play *The Melting Pot* hears the melodies for his "American symphony" in the "seething crucible—God's crucible," where a new amalgam, "the coming superman," is being forged over divine fires. Yet Zangwill told progressive audiences what they wanted to hear, not what they saw around them.

A clearer view of the forces of cultural pluralism came from the more reflective immigrants themselves, who exposed the progressive idea of complete Americanization as the myth it really was. "There is no such thing as an American," a Polish priest told the genteel social worker Emily Greene Balch. Poland, he explained, was a nation, but the United States was simply a country—in the beginning an empty land open to all comers in turn. Immigrants, according to the recently arrived Mary Antin, who later published a vivid account of the immigrants' hardships, were just people who had missed the *Mayflower* and taken the next available boat.

A growing number of young progressive intellectuals responded enthusiastically to this concept of cultural diversity and ethnic pluralism. In the excitement of cultural variety they found escape from stifling middle-class gentility. Randolph Bourne, a radical young student of John Dewey at Columbia University, found a title for this diversity—"Trans-National America"—and hailed the United States as the "intellectual battleground of the world . . . a cosmopolitan federation of national colonies, of foreign cultures, from whom the sting of devastating competition has been removed."

Bourne's concept of America as a world federation in miniature ran headlong into the barrier of national fears. The concept of the "new immigrants" took on a variety of ugly shapes. Immigrants, some said, were dangerously illiterate and culturally deprived; they brought with them either an unenlightened Catholicism or private visions of the destruction of free society; they were doomed to a permanently inferior place on the Darwinian scale of races and could never master the skills that democracy demanded. Amateur and professional sociologists consulted the numbers and predicted "race suicide." Sociologist Franklin Giddings announced hopefully, if somewhat ambiguously, that the traits of Americans—who were "preeminently an energetic, practical people"—would undergo "softening" as Mediterranean instincts crept into the national character. Eventually, he claimed, old-stock Americans with their original Baltic and Alpine ethnic heritage would be transformed into "a more versatile, a more plastic people," both gentler and more poetic. But Giddings's prophecy raised the inevitable question that a progressive reformer asked in an article in the magazine *Charities:* "Are we not, most of us, fairly well satisfied with the characteristics, mental and physical, of the old American stock? Do we not love American traits as they are?"

The Dillingham Commission, a joint House-Senate investigatory panel appointed by Theodore Roosevelt in 1907, underscored these progressive anxieties by making an official distinction between the already assimilated "old immigration" and the presumably unassimilable "new immigration." The commission took four years to complete its report, which filled forty-two volumes. Although it collected much useful information on the work patterns and living conditions of immigrants, the Dillingham Commission assumed from the beginning the need to limit the flow of new arrivals—if not through a literacy test, then through a quota system. When Congress obliged by passing a literacy test bill in 1913, the outgoing president Taft vetoed it in deference to Republican employers who still sought cheap labor. But the idea of a quota system survived, and it was made into law in the 1920s. The Dillingham Report marked a reversal in American attitudes toward cultural minorities: by 1910 the hopes of the immigration restrictionists soared as the more tolerant aims of the pluralists flickered and died.

**Wholesale Discrimination Against Blacks**

In the case of black Americans, white fears produced an even harsher reaction. The progressive generation had inherited from the late nineteenth century most of the ingredients of a racist myth, and progressives improved the formula of exclusion with new "scientific" evidence of the black race's biological inferiority. Not surprisingly, the opening years of the twentieth century saw the nearly total disfranchisement of black voters in the South.

This disfranchisement was hastened by the defeat of Populism everywhere in the South. Populism had pitted the poor white farmers against the region's white establishment and had sometimes appealed to black farmers as well. Thus the rise of the Populist movement had offered blacks an opportunity to gain political leverage by supporting the side that offered them the most. In some areas blacks quickly became politically active. After Populism went down to defeat, the white political establishment decided that such a danger would not recur and set about systematically denying blacks the right to vote. The techniques varied from state to state—poll taxes, grandfather clauses, literacy tests, white primaries—but all served effectively to bar the great majority of blacks from the polls throughout

**Rural Virginian Family**
*In 1900 most African-American families, like this one, still lived in the rural South.*

the South. Politically, the Solid South was now firmly in the grip of the Democratic party, which vowed to keep the blacks "in their place." Some former Populists, among them Georgia's Tom Watson, who had once courted the black vote, turned to bitter racist appeals in order to keep their political careers alive. While deploring such crude demagoguery, southern liberals and progressives often justified discrimination against the black man with a variant of the argument that northern reformers used to exclude the immigrant—that good government required the political removal of the untrained, the inferior, and the unfit.

Most northern liberals continued to regard blacks as a uniquely southern problem, despite mounting evidence to the contrary. But it was South Carolina's racist demagogue Ben Tillman who probed the softest spot in the progressives' plan for political improvement—the lack of moral certainty. "Your slogans of the past—brotherhood of man and fatherhood of God—have gone glimmering down the ages," he chortled. A progressive age, lacking the moral absolutes that once guided the abolitionists, readily accepted the racist conclusions presumably proved by up-to-date science.

In the opening decade of the twentieth century, however, statistics obscured the long-term effects of the industrial revolution on southern blacks, most of whom were tied to the land by tenancy and sharecropping. In 1900 there were fewer than 1 million blacks north of the Mason-Dixon line, and thirty years later a full 80 percent of the black community still lived in the South. Nevertheless, the intervening years saw a net gain to northern cities of 1.4 million black migrants from the South, drawn northward by the often illusory lure of economic opportunity and personal freedom. Herded into big-city ghettos—New York's black community numbered 70,000 by the turn of the century—they encountered wholesale discrimination. As lynchings in the South slowly declined, their northern counterpart, race riots, increased—in the small Indiana town of Greensburg in 1906; in Springfield, Illinois, two years later; and in explosive racial tensions in New York, Chicago, Philadelphia, and most of the major industrial cities of the North. Blacks paid a high price for their escape from sharecropping and the Jim Crow laws.

**Booker T. Washington and W.E.B. Du Bois**
Black American leaders attempted to counter discrimination and economic exploitation with two strategies, neither of them very successful in overturning white progressive prejudices. The official black spokesman, the "office broker for the race," as admiring white officials called him, was Booker T. Washington. The son of a slave, Washington learned the gospel of self-help at Hampton Institute in Virginia and put it into practice at Tuskegee, Alabama, where he founded the Normal and Industrial Institute for Negroes. There he trained thousands of young men and women in the industrial and domestic arts. Washington explained his philosophy in a famous address at the Atlanta Exposition in 1895: he urged his black listeners to strike their roots in southern soil by "making friends in every manly way of the people of all races by whom we are surrounded." To whites he offered the same suggestion, urging them to cast down their buckets among a race "whose habits you know, whose fidelity and love you have tested." Publicly, Washington continued to disclaim the vote for southern blacks, explaining in his autobiography *Up from Slavery* (1901) that "the opportunity to freely exercise such political rights will not come in any large degree through outside or artificial forcing, but will be accorded to the Negro by the Southern white people themselves." Privately and often secretly, however, Washington supported many of those blacks calling for stronger measures.

Most white liberals took Booker T. Washington to their hearts as a "credit to his race," although not all of them approved of Theodore Roosevelt's inviting him to lunch at the White House. Washington became the symbol of the "good Negro" who knew his place and aspired only to keep it—the man of sorrows who accepted the fact of racial prejudice while rejecting all its assumptions and who labored patiently to lift his people the few notches that a dominant white society allowed. The question Washington's program did not address, however, was the one that muckraker Ray Stannard Baker asked in his pessimistic commentary on American race relations, *Following the Color Line* (1908): "Does democracy really include Negroes as well as white men?"

**W.E.B. DuBois**
*The famous black progressive
reformer is shown in this 1919
photograph.*

By 1900 the black progressive William E.B. Du Bois, together with several
northern liberals of both races, had concluded that until blacks gained full
political rights, democracy would never be theirs. The northern black leadership
in the big cities appealed to a constituency different from Booker T. Washington's, and it presented another approach to black advancement. Du Bois, a
New Englander and a graduate of Harvard, had followed the typical progressive
route to professionalism by studying in Berlin before returning to an academic
career at Atlanta University in 1897. Like his counterparts among white liberals,
he recognized the pressing need for accurate data on the actual living conditions
of blacks, particularly in urban America. To provide some of the evidence, Du
Bois pioneered with a sociological study of the Philadelphia blacks, in which he
gave a clear picture of life in the ghetto. In *The Souls of Black Folk* (1903), he
appealed to potential black solidarity by criticizing Booker T. Washington's
"gospel of work and money." Washington's doctrine, complained Du Bois, "has
tended to make the whites, North and South, shift the burden of the Negro
problem to the Negro's shoulders and stand aside as critical and rather pessimistic spectators; when in fact the burden belongs to the nation." In place of
accommodation and outmoded programs for industrial arts, Du Bois suggested
the cultivation of a black intellectual and cultural elite—the "Talented Tenth"—
and called for immediate plans to mobilize a black political vanguard. In this
early and optimistic phase of his career before World War I, Du Bois developed

an unmistakably progressive program aimed at substituting "man-training" for moneymaking, and at fostering "intelligence, broad sympathy, knowledge of the world" in a new elite.

Although Washington's accommodationist tactics and Du Bois's elitist strategies complemented each other in theory, a bitter rivalry for the limited support available developed between the Tuskegee machine and the Niagara Movement of northern radicals agitating for full political and social equality for blacks. By the time the National Association for the Advancement of Colored People was founded in 1909 through the joint efforts of white neo-abolitionists Mary Ovington and Oswald Garrison Villard and the black followers of Du Bois, neither a moderate nor a militant approach to the "race problem" had succeeded in denting the prejudices of most white Americans. Actively or passively, whites continued to support strict segregation and the fiction of "separate but equal"— a formula endorsed by the United States Supreme Court in its 1896 decision in *Plessy* v. *Ferguson,* which upheld the practice of racial segregation.

The Jeffersonian tradition of decentralization and localism worked to the distinct disadvantage of black Americans throughout the progressive period. It perpetuated sectional patterns of discrimination and fostered a national disregard for what was quickly becoming the fundamental challenge of the twentieth century. The progressive compromise with bigotry and prejudice blocked any real hopes for a federal program to give blacks their political rights or to open the door of economic opportunity. For all its liberating idealism, progressivism rested on unspoken racist assumptions and condoned discrimination that had changed little since the Civil War.

**Women's Organizations**     One of the outlets for women's growing social concerns was the Women's Club movement, which provided a useful, if somewhat limited, perspective on the problems of industrial society. In 1904 the recently elected president of the General Federation of Women's Clubs, Sarah Platt Decker, announced to her membership that "Dante is dead. He has been dead for several centuries, and I think it is time that we dropped the study of his *Inferno* and turned our attention to our own." A commanding presence and effective organizer, Mrs. Decker restructured the federation and recruited new talent like the progressive journalist Rheta Childe Dorr, whom she appointed chair of the Committee on the Industrial Conditions of Women and Children. Dorr, in turn, drew on her numerous settlement-house contacts for the statistics and information with which to lobby Congress for federal legislation on the working conditions of women and children. Although the federation avoided political partisanship, individual branches took up controversial issues like factory inspection and child labor, agitated for criminal justice reforms, and experimented with tenement-house improvements. In a variety of "study groups" its middle-class members discovered an expanding range of problems: the poor quality of municipal services, urban political graft, the need for pure food and drug laws, conservation, and, ultimately, the crucial importance of the vote for women.

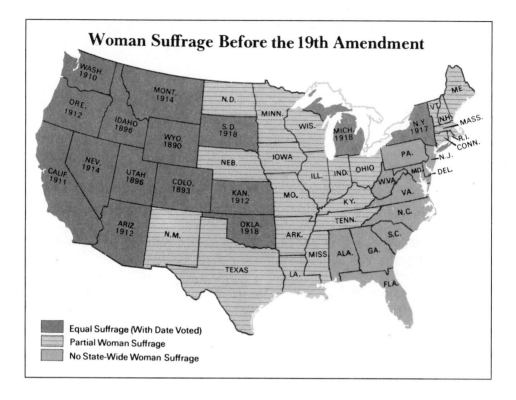

## Woman Suffrage Before the 19th Amendment

**Legend:**
- Equal Suffrage (With Date Voted)
- Partial Woman Suffrage
- No State-Wide Woman Suffrage

Women's clubs generally popularized and supported rather than initiated progressive reforms. Their most important contribution lay in their support, however cautious, for women's suffrage as the campaign for the vote gained momentum after 1910. In the meantime they succeeded in gradually shifting the interests of well-to-do women from the home to national social concerns.

A second and more sharply focused women's organization, which gave a practical point to the humanitarian concerns of the women's clubs, was the National Consumers' League (NCL). Modeled on English precedents, the NCL grew out of the early work of the upper-class charity organizer Josephine Shaw Lowell, who had taken up the cause of New York City's working girls late in her career. Out of her efforts in the 1890s came a small group of well-to-do women who decided to use their buying power to enforce an enlightened labor policy on the city's employers. As the consumer movement spread to other cities, a national league arose in 1899, headed by a remarkable administrator, Florence Kelley. An abolitionist congressman's daughter, trained at Cornell University and later in Zurich, a socialist, a superb lobbyist, and Illinois's first factory inspector, Florence Kelley brought impressive credentials and skills to her job. Under her firm guidance the National Consumers' League grew rapidly until it numbered sixty local branches in twenty states, all applying the league's White Label to approved products.

The league specialized in protective legislation for women and children, lobbying successfully for the Ten-Hour Law in Oregon and retaining Louis Brandeis to argue this law's constitutionality before the United States Supreme Court. The league also joined the campaign for establishing the Children's Bureau within the Department of Labor; and it helped its sister organization, the National Child Labor Committee, to press Congress for a child-labor law. Working together in a new spirit of professionalism, the social feminists recruited such dedicated administrators as Frances Perkins (later to be Franklin D. Roosevelt's secretary of labor) and Pauline and Josephine Goldmark, who would carry their crusade against child labor and social abuse into the 1920s. These women reformers, skilled in bureaucratic methods but free from the profit motive, were experimenting with an alternative to what Rheta Childe Dorr called the "commercial ideal" of American business.

Working-class feminism arrived with the formation in 1903 of the National Women's Trade Union League (NWTUL), modeled on its counterpart in England. At first women workers, most of them young, unskilled, and underpaid, proved difficult to organize, and the league received scant encouragement from trade unionist Samuel Gompers and his AFL. In these early years the NWTUL's chief accomplishment was winning the support of middle-class women like Mary Dreier and her sister, Margaret Dreier Robins, who provided money and leadership. Gradually, however, recruitment reached down into the ranks of the workers and included effective organizers like Pauline Newman, Leonora O'Reilly, and Rose Schneiderman, who provided a new activism. Their greatest success came among the women in the garment trades in New York City—a majority of them Jewish, many of them socialist. In major strikes in the garment industry—in New York in 1909, Chicago a year later, and Lawrence, Massachusetts, in 1912—the league provided invaluable support, publicizing the workers' grievances, raising substantial amounts of money, and distributing much-needed relief supplies. Such activities as these united working-class and middle-class women, muting class consciousness in favor of moral publicity that called the nation's attention to the horrific conditions in urban factory lofts and calculated for American consumers the human costs of exploitative business practices.

**Settlements**  The same distaste for the business world also characterized the settlement-house movement. In contrast to its British counterpart, in which young men from Oxford and Cambridge universities took the lead in founding settlements in the slums of London's East End, the American wing of the movement was dominated by women from the outset. The settlements themselves stood in the middle of sprawling slums and quickly became focal points for the public activities of their inhabitants. To the busy complex at Hull House, for example, or to New York's Henry Street Settlement or Boston's South End House came neighborhood children to nurseries and playgrounds, their mothers for classes in hygiene and domestic economy, and, in the evenings, men for lessons in English and discussions of politics.

The impulse behind settlements was religious, although not sectarian, and Christian ethics dominated the atmosphere of all of them—Graham Taylor's Chicago Commons, New York's University Settlement, Kingsley House in Pittsburgh. Inevitably the earnestness of young college women, bent on lifting the tone of immigrant neighborhoods with lectures on the English art critic John Ruskin and with displays of reproductions of pre-Raphaelite paintings, drew sneers. Economist and social critic Thorstein Veblen dismissed the settlements as "consistently directed to the incubation, by precept and example, of certain punctilios of upper-class propriety." But it was not long before the settlement-house workers learned to estimate the needs of their neighbors more accurately, and cultural uplift gave way to hard practicality.

The restless energies of residents, combined with their vagueness about political means, gave the settlement houses all the features of a full-fledged alternative to progressive bureaucracy. Turnover remained high in the settlement houses, which were often mere collecting points for members whose jobs as teachers, social workers, visiting nurses, architects, and planners kept them out in city streets. For both men and women reformers, settlements provided halfway houses between the closed intellectual communities of the college or university and the specialization of a professional career. Settlement houses made possible flexible arrangements of work and leisure based on shared commitments to solving social problems.

Education formed the core of settlement-house work. Initially settlement workers conceived of the educational process as a one-way street of instruction and learning that would lead immigrants toward citizenship. But education was quickly redefined as a mutual learning experience, one that involved genuine exchange and not simply the bestowal of education. As Jane Addams explained to an increasingly receptive public, "A settlement is a protest against a restricted view of education." The settlement-house workers' guide was the educational theory of John Dewey, which defined learning as a social experience and suggested ways of unifying settlements and the life of the community.

When women first founded their settlements, they carefully avoided clashes with the city bosses on the theory that urban politics was hopelessly corrupt. Soon, however, they came to agree with Jane Addams that "to keep aloof from it [politics] must be to lose one opportunity of sharing the life of the community." Still, they found it difficult and often impossible to work with the unsympathetic ward bosses, who distrusted them as do-gooders and rivals for the affections of their clients. Cooperation turned to confrontation over matters of garbage removal, street lighting, police protection, and the location of a neighborhood park. The boldest of the settlement-house workers opposed the bosses, but the contest was unequal, as Jane Addams learned in trying to unseat Alderman Johnny Powers in Chicago's Nineteenth Ward. She attacked Powers with every argument she could muster and capped her indictment with the charge that, although he dispensed free turkeys at Christmastime, he gave poor service on the other 364 days of the year. But turkeys continued to turn the political trick, and the likes of Johnny Powers generally succeeded in maintaining political control in their districts.

Struggling to resist the politicians' counterattacks, the settlement-house women deliberately turned their institutions into public forums where social and political opinions of every kind could be aired. Chicago Commons, for example, featured a weekly "Free Floor Discussion" billed as "self-conscious democracy," in which a labor leader, a college professor, an anarchist, and a businessman discussed the future of capitalist society. From these discussions the women themselves learned valuable political lessons as the logical thread connecting reform to the vote became too obvious to ignore: women needed the vote to make good their promise to improve American life. Without the franchise they could do little more than advance moral arguments, while their enemies—the crooked contractors and sweatshop owners—used their votes to intimidate the politicians. By 1910 mounting frustrations were beginning to lead many settlement-house women to join the drive for women's suffrage.

**The Suffragists Divided**

The two main groups in the suffrage movement after 1912 were the staid and cautious National American Woman Suffrage Association, headed by Carrie Chapman Catt, and its more militant offshoot, the National Women's Party, organized by the formidable Quaker agitator Alice Paul. Suffragists presented two basically

**Suffragist Rally**
*A suffragette addresses a middle-class crowd from the backseat of an automobile in a new version of tailgate campaigning*

different and even contradictory arguments. The first was well suited to the progressive political temper and was summed up by Mary Putnam Jacobi, a veteran suffragist and leading woman doctor:

> No matter how well born, how intelligent, how highly educated, how virtuous, how refined, the women of today constitute a political class below that of every man, no matter how base born, how stupid, how ignorant, how vicious, how poverty-stricken, how brutal.

The second suffragist argument singled out women's special interests and capabilities that were in need of recognition. According to this reasoning, women were uniquely endowed with humanizing qualities and, given the vote, could soften the rigors of industrial society and nurse the United States back to health. Such was Jane Addams's explanation for the feminine political role: "If women have in any sense been responsible for the gentler side of life which softens and blurs some of its harsher conditions, may not they have a duty to perform in our American cities?" In justifying their claim to the vote, middle-class women could take their choice between a demand for simple justice and the promises of a healing creed.

Idealistic or purely practical, the case for women's suffrage was strengthened by the more glaring absurdities of its male opponents. One of them, a worried military officer, warned against the "dilution with the qualities of the cow, of the qualities of the bull upon which the herd's safety must depend."

The suffrage movement gathered momentum at the state level. In 1910 the state of Washington gave the vote to women, and the next year California succumbed to a high-pressure campaign and also awarded women the vote. In 1912 Arizona, Kansas, and Oregon followed suit as Theodore Roosevelt's Bull Moose party, despite its leader's initial reservation, adopted a plank calling for national women's suffrage.

In the presidential election campaign of 1912, a more militant strategy emerged, which concentrated on congressional and presidential candidates— few of whom were particularly sympathetic to the suffragist cause. Alice Paul, the leader of a small band of radical suffragists working at the national level, began to take direct action. She was a grimly determined feminist who had earned a doctorate at the University of Pennsylvania and had spent five years in England studying suffragist Emmeline Pankhurst's disruptive tactics before returning home to try them out for herself. Intense, untiring, a stickler for principle, and an able tactician, Alice Paul promptly singled out Woodrow Wilson and the occasion of his inauguration for a giant protest parade, involving 5,000 women, which ended in a near riot. Then, applying the idea of the English suffragists, she organized an aggressive and highly verbal lobby, which soon became the National Women's Party, dedicated to direct action. The National American Woman Suffrage Association, stung by the success of its more militant rival, began to revive under Mrs. Catt's leadership, and a reorganized board of directors redoubled its efforts to reach women at the state and local levels.

**Charlotte Perkins Gilman**
*The well-known feminist author
and reformer.*

By 1917, as the country prepared to enter World War I, Wilson's administration faced two groups of political feminists with distinctly different views of the world conflict: a small organization of militants who bitterly protested American participation in the war and demonstrated against "Kaiser Wilson" with marches and hunger strikes; and a much larger group of moderates who supported the war in the belief that peace would bring victory to women as well as to the cause of democracy. In June 1919 Congress rewarded the moderates' patience by passing the Nineteenth Amendment, which gave the vote to all adult Americans regardless of sex. Yet the cause of democracy and reform, American women would learn, was not to be advanced by their sudden invasion of the polls. Notwithstanding their arguments to the contrary, women did not compose an interest group with special needs and talents, nor did their demands for their share of political responsibility alter the course of progressivism. Proposals for a comprehensive recasting of industrial society and for the complete reordering of American priorities were put forward only by the socialists.

## Paradise Lost: Socialism in America

American socialism in the years before World War I was a lively and varied critique of the capitalist system presented by an inventive but faction-ridden party, drifting steadily away from its nineteenth-century revolutionary moorings. Despite its official collectivist ideology, American socialism in action kept alive a Jeffersonian tradition that defied the wishes of progressive nationalists.

In its best days between 1900 and 1914, the socialist movement was a volatile combination of regional groups. Party members included industrial workers in the cities of the Northeast, members of older ethnic groups in the urban enclaves of the upper Midwest, agrarians with memories of Populism in the Plains states, hard-bitten miners and lumber stiffs from the Rocky Mountains and the Pacific Northwest, and a core of college-trained intellectuals preaching everything from Christian Socialism and gradualist doctrines derived from the British Fabians to revolution-for-the-hell-of-it. If socialists never quite lived up to their reputation as the chief American menace to law and order, they nevertheless presented a case against corporate capitalism that progressives found deeply disturbing.

Socialism as a political force dated from the turn of the twentieth century. In 1901 disgruntled members of the tiny Socialist Labor party, fed up with the dictatorial ways of their hard-lining Marxist leaders, bolted. Collecting other splinter groups, including Eugene V. Debs's Social Democratic party, they formed the Socialist Party of America. The 94,000 votes Debs won in the presidential election of 1900 marked the beginning of a shift among the majority of American socialists toward the moderate center. They also drifted toward a theory of nonviolent parliamentary socialism, a move that was not always clear to the embattled participants themselves.

**The Two Faces of Socialism**

American socialism showed two faces. To progressive outsiders it was a menace to their capitalist system. According to the socialists, capitalism was traveling a historically determined road to oblivion, destroying small-scale enterprise, saturating international markets, and establishing spheres of influence and imperialist outposts along the way. Most progressives took comfort in the conviction that class war did not in fact appear likely. Yet to most Americans the very vehemence of socialist prophesying suggested a conspiracy of chronic grumblers and political madmen. The progressives prepared to deal with the enemy in the best way they knew—by intimidation and suppression.

To socialists themselves, American development seemed a baffling exception to the doctrines of economic determinism. Their list of unanswered questions lengthened as American capitalism continued to display surprising powers of accommodation. Did the immediate goals of shorter hours and improved working conditions strengthen class solidarity, or did they simply adjust workers to a wage system in which they had no power? Could socialists accomplish more through political action—by running candidates of their own—or did such politicking amount to betraying the interests of the working class? Was the overthrow of the capitalist system imminent, or would the socialist takeover come only gradually, following the education of the workers? The socialists' failure to reach agreement on these matters was seen by most progressives as proof of the absurdity of their ideas—but also as a warning to a society willing to tolerate them.

Gradually the center of the Socialist party was occupied by solid and sensible moderates—men like Milwaukee's shrewd tactician, Victor Berger; New York's scarred veteran of innumerable ideological campaigns, Morris Hillquit; and the "Pennsylvania Dutchman," James Hudson Maurer, who hoped for an alliance with the major trade unions. This moderate center hoped to educate the country away from its capitalistic habits with the lessons of evolutionary socialism. The moderates were bitterly attacked by the diehard members of the militant Socialist Labor party, and also by their own left wing, which had come to believe in industrial unionism and direct action. In the years after 1900, the Socialist party, far from solving its theoretical and organizational problems, kept on dividing into camps of pragmatists and hard-lining idealists, opportunists and "impossibilists."

**The "Wobblies"**  Of all the dissident left-wing socialist groups, the most alarming to progressives was the Industrial Workers of the World (IWW), a faction of militant industrial unionists led by the charismatic "Big Bill" Haywood. The "Wobblies," as they were called by a derisive but apprehensive American public, rejected all forms of political action and recommended strikes and sabotage as the only way to make the world over. The IWW aroused fear and resentment far out of proportion to its membership, which was mostly made up of unskilled and migratory workers. The Wobblies saw their mission as the total destruction of capitalist exploitation and the forming of a new society "within the shell of the old." Progressives shuddered at the prospect.

**Lawrence, Massachusetts, Strike, 1912**
*Soldiers confront striking factory workers organized and led by the IWW.*

The Wobblies waged a desperate struggle for survival during their brief and stormy existence. Although they scored short-lived victories in strikes in the Pennsylvania steel town of McKees Rocks in 1907 and again in the Lawrence, Massachusetts, mills in 1912, they lacked the funds and the organization for sustained membership drives and strikes. Their myth of the "general strike" and the vision of "one big union" served chiefly to rally the spirits of marginal men who dreamed of participatory democracy among the downtrodden. At no time did the Wobblies threaten the American capitalist order.

Seen in perspective, the Wobblies represented another attempt of a nineteenth-century producerist mentality to recover an imaginary world without politics, where abundance automatically rewarded the natural cooperation of free men. "Big Bill" Haywood could have been speaking for progressives when he confessed his hopes for the elimination of politics:

> I have had a dream that I have in the morning and at night and during the day, that there will be a new society sometime in which there will be no battle between capitalist and wage-earner... there will be no political government... but... experts will come together for the purpose of discussing the means by which machinery can be made the slave of the people instead of part of the people being made the slave of machinery.

Ironically, it was a progressive majority bent on finding another way of going beyond politics with the rule of experts that clubbed the Wobblies' dream to death.

Moderate socialists were burdened with many of the same liabilities that the radicals faced—a tradition of local self-government within the movement, fierce rivalries for leadership, and a host of competing views on the meaning of history. Somehow Eugene Debs retained the leadership of this splintered party. Tall, angular, with a shambling gait and an easygoing manner, Debs served the party faithfully as a national walking-delegate, captivating hundreds of thousands with homely speeches filled with allusions to America's past. His talents were the home-grown ones of the moral agitator; his heroes were the abolitionists Wendell Phillips and William Lloyd Garrison. A spellbinder with no large fund of useful ideas, Debs was nevertheless an able conciliator and a durable campaigner. In 1904 he won some 400,000 votes for his party, and four years later he duplicated the feat with a whirlwind rail tour across the country in his "Red Special," giving as many as twenty speeches a day. The big leap in Socialist party totals, however, came in 1912, when voters gave Debs nearly a million votes in his fourth try for the presidency.

**Socialism as a Dissenting Party**　　The chief socialist contribution to the American pluralist tradition was the example it set of the open society it sought to create. The Socialist party remained a model of pluralism in action—a loosely organized, tactically divided community that was in general agreement on condemning capitalism but unable to unite on

**Socialist Party Campaign Poster, 1904**
*In 1904 the tireless Socialist Party campaigner Eugene V. Debs headed the ticket in the second of his presidential campaigns.*

the question of how to replace it. These disagreements crystallized in the lives of young academics, artists, and intellectuals who were drawn to socialism as much by its promise of cultural revolution as by its economic platform. Socialist intellectuals made it clear that they opposed both the moral pieties of progressivism and the bureaucratic collectivism of Socialist party centrists. They made their spiritual home in the Intercollegiate Socialist Society (ISS), the brainchild of the novelist Upton Sinclair, which was composed primarily of students and their teachers, artists, and intellectuals. The membership rolls of the ISS listed some of the most impressive and varied talent in the country and offered a range of criticism extending from the moderate Fabianism of John Spargo to the protocommunism of Louis Budenz; from the civil libertarianism of Roger Baldwin and Alexander Meiklejohn to the protest fiction of Ernest Poole and Zona Gale; from the progressivism of Walter Lippmann to the pacifism of A. J. Muste and Jessie Wallace Hughan. Connecting these diverse personalities were a strong distaste for the commercial spirit, an abiding fear of privilege, and not much more.

The striking variety of American socialism, its shifting assessment of ends and means, and its inventiveness in tapping the rich reserves of American dissent made it a lively, if not ultimately powerful, opponent of progressivism. Despite occasional successes at the local level, the Socialist party was never a major political force, even before World War I. Perhaps its greatest days were spent in vocal but isolated opposition to that war and to the destructive mindlessness of superpatriots.* Its most effective role, like the role of the Populist party before it, was largely educational. It taught, more by example than by design, the uses of a secular, imaginative, permissive society. In doing so it supplied useful correctives for a compulsive progressive order, from which Americans might have profited. Its disruption and decline with the coming of the war dealt a major setback to the Jeffersonian tradition that Woodrow Wilson was pledged to preserve.

## The New Freedom

Woodrow Wilson, like Theodore Roosevelt before him, believed in a strong presidency. In the course of his scholarly career, Wilson had made an extensive examination of American institutions and political leadership. His training at Johns Hopkins had come at a time when political scientists were beginning to turn away from their preoccupation with constitutional questions and definitions of sovereignty, but before they had acquired the economic and sociological skills to examine the ways institutions actually function. "My purpose," Wilson announced in one of his books, "is to show...our constitutional system as it looks in operation." Yet the workaday reality of American politics was precisely what Wilson's analysis always lacked—the linking of larger social forces with political action. Despite repeated promises to "look below the surface" of American institutions, Wilson was at his best in expounding a philosophy of politics that his rival Theodore Roosevelt would have endorsed: "All the country needs is a new and sincere body of thought in politics, coherently, distinctly, and boldly uttered by men who are sure of their ground." Like Roosevelt, Wilson believed that the key to effective democratic government rested in the hands of a powerful and energetic president who offered "the best chance for leadership and mastery."

**Wilson's Program**  Wilson, then, favored strong executive leadership yet felt a contradictory urge to dismantle federal power and liberate the energies of a free people. These seeming contradictions—strong presidential authority and the reduction of regulatory power—were linked in his mind by the figure of the national leader, such as the great nineteenth-century British prime minister William Gladstone, who could sense the aspirations of the common people and give them voice as commands to the legislature. But more would be required than sensing the "generous energies" of citizens. The federal government, in particular the presidency, had its uses, as Wilson understood. The real question was whether it could be used to eliminate business coercion, break up clusters of privilege, restore competition, and rescue the little man from the grip of impersonal economic forces. For this work Wilson needed a man with a better understanding of social and economic forces than he himself possessed.

---

*For the home-front excesses of World War I and its aftermath, see chapter 27, pp. 300–05.

The chief architect of the New Freedom was Louis Brandeis, the nation's leading progressive lawyer, who had made a career of challenging big business. In the course of this combat, Brandeis had worked out a complete alternative to Roosevelt's New Nationalism. His program rested on the conviction—reached after watching corporate capitalists play loosely with other people's money—that the country was drifting toward oligarchy. Financial power, he warned, would soon become political despotism through the same process that had made Julius Caesar master of the ancient Roman Republic. In referring to the fate of Rome, Brandeis touched a sensitive Democratic nerve in Wilson, who also feared monopoly but had not yet devised an effective method of controlling it.

Brandeis supplied the guiding concepts for Wilson's first administration. The core of Brandeis's program was a dismantling operation that would ensure the survival of regulated business competition by shoring up small businesses, breaking up new conglomerates, returning the market to free enterprise, dispersing wealth more widely, and reaching out a helping hand to the workingman.

Out of the collaborative thinking of Wilson and Brandeis came the New Freedom's attack on monopoly and a distinction between acceptable and anti-social business behavior, which recalled Roosevelt's program. Big business, Wilson agreed, was natural and thus inevitable, but trusts were artificial and wholly undesirable. "A trust is an arrangement to get rid of competition, and a big business is a business that has survived competition by conquering in the field of intelligence and economy," the president announced in explaining how it was that he could support big business yet oppose monopoly. Wilson was also sure that Roosevelt's scheme of a regulatory commission to oversee the operations of big business was impractical: "As to the monopolies, which Mr. Roosevelt proposes to legalize and welcome, I know that they are so many cars of juggernaut, and I do not look forward with pleasure to the time when juggernauts are licensed and driven by commissioners of the United States." But could the New Freedom offer a better solution? Was the destruction of monopoly really feasible?

Before Wilson tackled the trusts, he decided to make good on the perennial Democratic party promise to lower the tariff. Calling Congress into special session and breaking precedent by appearing in person, he called for immediate tariff reduction. The Underwood Tariff rode through the House quickly, but in the Senate it ran into a barrier erected by Republicans and Democrats representing the sugar and wool interests. Wielding patronage skillfully, Wilson turned aside the protectionists' attacks. The Underwood Tariff lowered duties an average of 10 percent, placed the manufactured goods of the trusts on the free list, and added a small income tax to compensate for the loss of revenue.

Tariff reform tested Wilson's skills as an "honest broker," but banking reform strained them to the limit. Most Americans were primarily interested in obtaining more credit than the eastern banking establishment was currently providing. But there were also traces of Andrew Jackson's Bank War in the struggle between big bankers in the East, with their plans for a central banking system under their direct control, and smaller regional bankers, who sought freedom from Wall Street in a decentralized system. Ranged somewhere between these contenders was a third group of progressives in both parties who wanted a genuinely national system under government management that would ensure stability.

**Federal Control of Currency**    The Federal Reserve Act (1913) was another compromise between conflicting interest groups with diametrically opposed notions of what the country needed. Establishing twelve districts, each with a Federal Reserve branch bank owned and directed by the member banks, the act provided for a certain degree of decentralization and regional control. But the creation of a new national currency—Federal Reserve notes—and a supervisory seven-member board in Washington gave the federal government an effective instrument of monetary control.

Big bankers need not have fretted, however. Much depended on the willingness of the Federal Reserve Board to interpret its powers generously. Not for another two decades would the board feel a vigorous urge to regulate the nation's financial machinery. The immediate effect of the Federal Reserve Act was to strengthen rather than weaken the control of New York banks by consolidating their partnership with the government. As a stabilizing device for corporate capitalism involving a minimum amount of government interference and direction, the Federal Reserve System worked with reasonable efficiency. As a "democratic" reform designed to parcel out financial power to the people, it was an illusion. The gain for monetary efficiency was immediate, but the democratic social goals would be postponed for a later generation to achieve.

Wilson's experience with the trusts also ended in compromise. The spirit of the original antimonopoly crusade survived down to World War I. Trustbusting seemed to gather new economic coherence from the economic analysis and social ideas of Louis Brandeis and other of Wilson's advisers who supplied the impetus for the passage in 1914 of the Clayton Antitrust Act. The confusions of a quarter-century's attempted enforcement of the Sherman Act had made clarification essential. The question was how to proceed. What degree of monopolistic control of an industry was permissible, and what degree constituted undue restraint of trade? The Clayton Act, as originally drafted in 1914, had tried to answer this question with a long list of "thou shalt nots." The bill listed unfair trade practices in tedious and confusing detail. Continuing debate, however, and anguished cries from big business made it increasingly obvious that a complete list of forbidden practices was an impossibility. Yet if it was impossible to specify each and every example of wrong conduct, the only alternative lay in vesting a regulatory commission with the discretionary power to make concrete applications of a very general rule. Here was the course Roosevelt and the New Nationalists had advised all along—regulating rather than forbidding and dismantling.

In reluctantly agreeing to the commission proposal, Wilson endorsed administrative government, which he had earlier rejected. His intentions in securing passage of the supplemental Federal Trade Commission Act in 1914 closely paralleled Roosevelt's aim of creating an objective body of experts whose judgments would rest on scientifically assembled evidence. In any case, the advantages of bigness now seemed undeniable, a fact that was attested to by the incorporation of the giant General Motors soon after the Clayton Act was passed. The counterattack against big business had failed.

As a regulatory agency with power to mediate conflicts between public needs and private economic opportunity, the Federal Trade Commission (FTC) disappointed its progressive champions. During World War I its functions in preventing business concentration were drastically curtailed, and after the war even its fact-finding powers brought down the wrath of big business and of Congress itself. Congressional conservatives demanded an investigation of its methods. In a series of adverse decisions, the courts stripped the FTC of its power to define unfair practices. Business simply defied the FTC by denying it access to company records and ignoring its rulings. Government by commission in the 1920s provided no cure for a new rash of financial consolidations.

In other areas of national life as well, Wilson's dream of liberating the energies of "the great struggling unknown masses of men" ended in perplexity and defeat. Not the "people" of his earlier progressive imaginings, but highly organized interest groups—exacting, clamorous, selfish—descended on Washington, seeking protection and advancement of their concerns. In some cases Wilson's administration proved generous: for newly organized farmers there were rural credit facilities; for labor, a federal employees' compensation act; for consumer groups, the National Child Labor Act (promptly declared unconstitutional). But there were limits to Wilson's receptivity to interest-group politics. He disapproved of women's suffrage, and he refused to lift the burden of antitrust suits from the backs of labor organizations. He also tacitly supported the secretary of the interior and the postmaster general in maintaining racial segregation in their departments and only reluctantly reversed himself when liberals objected. Not all interests, it was clear, could command the attention of a broker president.

**Wilson's Program: More, Not Less, Government**

By 1916, as Americans watched the war in Europe settle into a protracted and bloody stalemate, the Wilson administration had largely completed its progressive program. The president's initial promise of reversal and restoration had not been fulfilled. In each of his major attempts at reform—lowering the tariff, building the Federal Reserve System, controlling the trusts—the president had preferred to disperse power; but instead he had been driven in exactly the opposite direction. He had created the Tariff Commission to systematize the nation's trade policies, the Federal Reserve Board to manage the monetary affairs of the country, and the Federal Trade Commission to police big business.

The meaning of these reforms was unmistakable: *more,* not *less,* government; an increase rather than a decrease in governmental agencies; a greater rather than a lesser reliance on experts and bureaucratic procedures; and a supportive relationship rather than a supervisory one between government and the large organized interest groups it presumably sought to regulate in the name of the people. And presiding over this expanded system of government agencies and bureaus was a president who was fully as powerful as the most ambitious New Nationalist could ever have wished.

## CHRONOLOGY

**1896** Supreme Court in *Plessy* v. *Ferguson* establishes "separate but equal" doctrine, whereby separate facilities for blacks and whites are declared constitutional.

**1899** National Consumers' League founded.

**1901** Socialist Party of America organized.
Booker T. Washington's autobiography *Up from Slavery* published.

**1902** Oliver Wendell Holmes appointed to Supreme Court by Roosevelt.

**1903** W.E.B. Du Bois's *The Souls of Black Folk* published.

**1904** Theodore Roosevelt elected president.
Anna Howard Shaw becomes head of National American Woman Suffrage Association.

**1905** *Lochner* v. *New York;* Supreme Court declares unconstitutional a state law regulating work hours for bakers.
Niagara Movement formed to agitate for integration and civil rights for blacks.
Industrial Workers of the World (IWW) formed.

**1907** Dillingham Commission investigates "new" immigration problem.

**1908** William Howard Taft elected president, defeating William Jennings Bryan and Eugene Debs.

**1909** Payne-Aldrich Tariff raising rates to protect eastern manufacturers provokes opposition of South and Midwest.
National Association for the Advancement of Colored People (NAACP) founded.

**1910** Woodrow Wilson elected New Jersey governor.
Roosevelt's "New Nationalism" speech at Osawatomie, Kansas.
Women enfranchised in state of Washington.

**1911** Triangle Shirtwaist Factory fire in New York City's East Side kills 146 women; investigation and revision of state factory codes follow.

**1912** Woodrow Wilson elected president, defeating Republican regular Taft, Progressive "Bull Moose" Theodore Roosevelt, and Socialist Eugene Debs.

| | | | |
|---|---|---|---|
| **1912** | Lawrence (Massachusetts) strike against American Woolen Company led by IWW. | | Federal Trade Commission created to regulate business practices. |
| | Radical National Women's Party under Alice Paul formed. | **1916** | Louis Brandeis appointed to Supreme Court. |
| **1913** | Federal Reserve System created. Underwood Tariff lowers duties. | **1919** | Congress passes Nineteenth Amendment, giving vote to women; ratified in following year. |
| **1914** | Clayton Antitrust Act passed. World War I begins in Europe. | | |

## Suggested Readings

A good introduction to the study of immigration and assimilation is Leonard Dinnerstein and David Reimers, *Ethnic Americans: A History of Immigration and Assimilation* (1975). Oscar Handlin, *The Uprooted* (2d ed., 1973), although challenged on many points by more recent studies, is nevertheless a classic, as is John Higham, *Strangers in the Land: Patterns of American Nativism* (1955), on the hostile reactions of native Americans. Philip Taylor, *The Distant Magnet* (1971), is particularly good on the European setting. Milton Gordon, *Assimilation in American Life: The Role of Race, Religion and National Origins* (1964), corrects old American myths of the melting pot and easy assimilation. For a good survey of immigrants and the industrial process, see John Bodnar, *Immigration and Industrialization* (1977); for an account of immigrant urban life, see Alan M. Kraut, *The Huddled Masses: The Immigrant in American Society, 1860–1921* (1982).

The literature on specific minorities is extensive. Among the best collective portraits are Moses Rischin, *The Promised City: New York's Jews, 1870–1914* (1970); Irving Howe, *World of Our Fathers: The Journey of the East European Jews to America and the Life They Found and Made* (1976); Humbert Nelli, *The Italians of Chicago, 1880–1920* (1970); Stanford M. Lyman, *Chinese Americans* (1974); and Stephan Thernstrom, *The Other Bostonians: Poverty and Progress in the American Metropolis, 1880–1970* (1973).

August Meier, *Negro Thought in America, 1880–1915* (1963), is the best assessment of black aspirations and programs during these years. Jack Temple Kirby, *Darkness at the Dawning: Race and Reform in the Progressive South* (1972), gives an accurate estimate of the social price of progressive reform in the region, while the story of Harlem is well told in Gilbert Osofsky, *Harlem, The Making of a Ghetto, 1890–1930* (1966). Louis R. Harlan, *Booker T. Washington* (1972), is a definitive account of that leader, and Elliot M. Rudwick, *W.E.B. Du Bois: Propagandist of the Negro Protest* (1969), analyzes the contributions of a mercurial black progressive. Charles F. Kellogg, *NAACP: The History of the National Association for the Advancement of Colored People, 1909–1920* (1967), is a solid survey of that pioneer organization.

Two readable surveys of women's rights and social feminism are Eleanor Flexner, *Century of Struggle: The Woman's Rights Movement in the United States* (1959), and Lois Banner, *Women in Modern America* (1974). Aileen Kraditor, *The Ideas of the Women's Suffrage Movement, 1890–1900* (1965), is an account of the ideology of suffragism, and Robert Smuts, *Women and Work in America* (1959), discusses the problem of work. Entrance of women into the work force is chronicled in Alice Kessler-Harris, *Out to Work: A History of Wage-Earning Women in the*

*United States* (1982), and Elyce J. Rotella, *From Home to Office: U.S. Women and Work, 1870–1930* (1981).

On socialism Howard Quint, *The Forging of American Socialism* (1953), and David Shannon, *The Socialist Party of America: A History* (1955), present helpful overviews. For more critical treatments of the subject, see James Weinstein, *The Decline of Socialism in America* (1967), and Daniel Bell, *Marxian Socialism in the United States* (1967). An excellent survey of the rest of the radical spectrum in the early twentieth century is contained in John P. Diggins, *The American Left in the Twentieth Century* (1973). Melvyn Dubofsky, *We Shall Be All: A History of the Industrial Workers of the World* (1969), is a full account of the Wobblies, and Christopher Lasch, *The New Radicalism in America, 1889–1963* (1965), presents an indictment of cultural radicalism in the Progressive Era. The best study of the nineteenth-century legacy to American socialism is Nick Salvatore, *Eugene V. Debs* (1982).

On the intellectual and cultural transformation of American society in the opening years of the century, Henry F. May, *The End of American Innocence* (1959), is still standard. Literary histories of the new Age of Realism abound. Among the best are Alfred Kazin, *On Native Grounds* (1942), and two volumes by Maxwell Geismar: *Rebels and Ancestors: The American Novel, 1890–1915* (1953), and *The Last of the Provincials: The American Novel, 1915–1925*. Kenneth S. Lynn, *William Dean Howells: An American Life* (1970), is a sensitive portrait of a fractured artistic sensibility in a rapidly modernizing age. A useful survey of progressive political ideas is John D. Buenker, *Urban Liberalism and Progressive Reform* (1973). For changing notions of marriage and the family, see Elaine Tyler May, *Great Expectations: Marriage and Divorce in Post-Victorian America* (1980). Robert Crunden, *Ministers of Reform: The Progressives' Achievement in American Civilization* (1982) presents a series of intellectual portraits of Progressive Era figures.

Indispensable for an understanding of Woodrow Wilson and the New Freedom is the magisterial Arthur S. Link, *Wilson* (5 vols., 1947–65), although the hostile John Blum, *Woodrow Wilson and the Politics of Morality* (1956), and the skeptical John Garraty, *Woodrow Wilson* (1956), offer critical insights unavailable to the sympathetic Link. Biographies of other important figures during the New Freedom years include Dorothy Rose Blumberg, *Florence Kelley: The Making of a Social Pioneer* (1966); Charles Larsen, *The Good Fight: The Life and Times of Ben Lindsey* (1972); Julius Weinberg, *Edward Alsworth Ross and the Sociology of Progressivism* (1972); Robert C. Bannister, *Ray Stannard Baker: The Mind and Thought of a Progressive* (1966); and H. C. Bailey, *Edgar Gardner Murphy* (1968). Melvin I. Urofsky, *Louis D. Brandeis and the Progressive Tradition* (1981), defines the great liberal justice's intellectual and political legacy.

# 26

## The Path to Power

### American Foreign Policy
### 1890–1917

⁓

OR MOST of the nineteenth century, Americans managed their affairs with no general foreign policy except that of George Washington's determination to avoid entangling alliances. The defeat of Napoleon in Europe, coupled with the brilliant success of the American peace commissioners in 1815 following the near disaster of the War of 1812, brought a strong conclusion to an era of diplomatic failure for the new nation, perched so precariously on the rim of the Atlantic world and subject to the buffetings of the two major European powers, Britain and France. After 1815 geographical isolation and ideological separation gave the American people an open continent to explore and exploit without interference. By the mid-nineteenth century, George Washington's prediction of a separate American destiny had seemingly come true. Secure on its own continent, its dominance of the Western Hemisphere guaranteed by British sea power, the United States turned inward to explore its interior and develop its resources.

A favorable international climate, together with unlimited opportunity at home, fostered extravagant versions of an American "Manifest Destiny," which at one time or another pointed to the annexation of Canada, the acquisition of Cuba, and the taking of "all Mexico." Expansionists such as the naval officer and oceanographer Matthew Fontaine Maury, who plotted to colonize Mexico with ex-Confederates, dreamed of the Caribbean as an American lake, or of the Mississippi Valley as the center of a vast heartland empire reaching eastward across the Atlantic and westward to China shores. But these flickering dreams of empire, like the extravagant reckonings of farmers, businessmen, and shippers who visualized huge profits to be found in untapped foreign markets, were hopeful predictions rather than policy directives. Despite occasional American interest in the fate of republican movements in Europe, Manifest Destiny remained primarily an article for home consumption—exuberant, aggressive, but not really intended for export. The slavery problem also curbed the American expansionist appetite after the Mexican War; the debate over the future of slavery in the newly opened territories monopolized national attention and absorbed the nation's political energies.

By the last quarter of the nineteenth century, however, a chain of circumstances abroad began to draw the United States into international power politics. The most important development was the sudden imperialist scramble by the major European powers—first Britain, then France, Germany, and Russia—to carve out generous colonies for themselves in Asia and Africa. American diplomats abroad and politicians in Washington watched with growing apprehension as the European powers, following the lead of business investments, rushed for possessions and spheres of influence in the undeveloped regions of the world.

Still, in his inaugural address in 1885, President Grover Cleveland offered only the briefest word on American foreign policy. The unique nature of American democratic institutions and the real needs of the people, Cleveland explained, required a "scrupulous avoidance of any departure from that foreign policy commended by the history, the traditions, and the prosperity of our Republic." In case his audience might have forgotten that traditional policy, he restated it clearly: "It is the policy of independence, favored by our position. . . . It is the policy of peace suitable to our interests. It is the policy of neutrality, rejecting any share in foreign broils and ambitions upon other continents and repelling their intrusion here."

This traditional passivity was reflected in the dilapidated foreign-policy establishment over which the president presided. A casual and still largely amateur operation, the diplomatic service had no effective fact-gathering apparatus; although it boasted a handful of able diplomats, it was saddled with a great many nobodies and friends of influential politicians. Most of the useful information trickling back to Washington from European capitals came from cosmopolitan private citizens personally concerned with the shifting scenes of international politics. Until 1890 Europe appeared willing to take this American claim of disinterest at face value and considered the United States a second-class power. The diplomatic corps residing in Washington was not on the whole a distinguished one, and more than once a European state simply neglected to fill a vacant post in this country that had come to seem unnecessary.

Yet at the very moment when Cleveland spoke the platitudes that had passed for foreign policy throughout the nineteenth century, new forces were beginning to collect around a different set of propositions, which were drawn directly from the study of European imperialist adventures. Lord Bryce, whose perceptive analysis of American government and society, *The American Commonwealth*, appeared in 1888, noted the difference between those who shaped foreign policy in England and their counterparts in the United States. In America, Bryce explained, "there are individual men corresponding to individuals in that English set, and probably quite as numerous." There were a sizable number of journalists of real ability, a handful of literary men, and not a few politicians who understood the mechanisms of international power politics. But these Americans remained isolated and disorganized for the most part, vulnerable constantly to public pressures and mass opinions, while the "first set" in England clearly was not. "In England the profession of opinion-making and leading is the work of specialists; in America...of amateurs." By the time Bryce published this observation, however, a small group of like-minded amateurs concerned with foreign affairs was already at work in Washington, building the intellectual foundations for a foreign-policy establishment and calling for a more vigorous pursuit of world power.

## The Origins of American Expansionism

By the 1890s it began to dawn on the small number of Americans concerned with the conduct of foreign affairs that the United States was in danger of being left far behind in the race for territory and markets. Looking back on the last decade of the nineteenth century, the rabid expansionist Senator Albert J. Beveridge summed up the lessons taught the American people as trustees "under God" of world civilization: "He has made us the master organizers of the world to establish system where chaos reigns." Not all Americans in 1900 agreed with Beveridge that destiny had mapped an imperial course for the nation, but it had become clear that they could no longer view the international scene indifferently. Somehow the United States would have to catch up with its European rivals.

A second force pushing the United States into the imperialist competition— a concern with world markets—was not so easy to analyze. After 1875 American businessmen, bankers, industrialists, and shippers began to call for readier access to global markets. Their demands took on dramatic point with the erratic development of the domestic market—the repeated depressions and gluts—and growing doubts as to its capacity to absorb American manufactured and staple goods. But the American market in the undeveloped areas of the globe remained quite small as late as 1900, despite increasingly noisy demands for enlarging it. The state of overseas markets furnished a focus for popular debate around which both expansionists and antiexpansionists, interventionists and isolationists argued over the proper role for the United States. No one denied the importance of foreign markets in the American economy and their importance too in spreading the blessings of democracy. But did the search for markets necessarily mean intervention in the domestic affairs of undeveloped and politically unstable countries? Did it require outright annexation? Were markets for the investment of capital fundamentally different from markets for manufactured or staple goods? And, most troublesome of all, how could the spokesmen for new and bigger markets catch and hold the attention of an unresponsive federal government?

Conditions in the United States also helped focus attention on possibilities abroad. The 1890s saw severe economic disorder, rising class conflict, political instability, and intellectual discord. The combined effect of these tensions and struggles was a growing popular belief that the United States had reached maturity as a fully developed modern nation. Whether or not they read the historian Frederick Jackson Turner's famous warning in 1893 of the consequences of the closing of the frontier, many Americans were well aware of the passing of an era in which free land and geographical mobility had been all-important. Viewed as a fact or a symbol of America's vast, seemingly limitless possibilities, the frontier had dominated the American imagination for two centuries. The announcement of its closing reinforced a widely shared sense of irreversible change. For the generation of the 1890s, the extension of the frontier concept into territories overseas quickened the old sense of mission and enterprise, and it released pent-up feelings of humanitarianism as though the answer to a loss of certainty at home was the vigorous pursuit of democratic purpose abroad.

**Pacifism or Power?** In these shifting circumstances abroad and at home, a struggle developed for control of an emerging American foreign policy. The contestants played a variety of roles in the quarter-century before American entry into World War I. Some upheld international law or preached pacifism. Others advocated national power or defended American honor. Yet beneath the diversity lay two conflicting ideas about American power and responsibility.

The first view of the nature of power and of America's future was forcefully summarized by Captain Alfred Thayer Mahan, naval strategist and geopolitical theorist, in his *Interest of America in Sea Power, Present and Future* (1897). Mahan argued that since governments could not be expected to act on any ground except national interest, patriotism and the will to fight were indispensable human qualities.

> Not in universal harmony, nor in any fond dream of unbroken peace, rest now the best hopes of the world.... Rather in the competition of interests, in that reviving sense of nationality... in the jealous determination of each people to provide first for its own... are to be heard the assurance that decay has not touched yet the majestic fabric erected by so many centuries of courageous battling.

The second and opposing view of the American mission was most effectively expressed by William Jennings Bryan, who limited the nation's role to that of providing a moral example. Nations, Bryan insisted, redeem only by force of example: "Example may be likened to the sun, whose genial rays constantly coax the buried seed into life, and clothe the earth, first with verdure, and afterward with ripened grain; while violence is the occasional tempest, which can ruin, but cannot give life."

Until 1900 Mahan's invitation to national greatness took precedence over Bryan's warnings of its eventual costs. Mahan had spent most of his career wandering about the world observing the patterns of European imperial politics.

Now his notice to Americans was direct and unmistakable. The United States, he announced, must pursue an aggressive expansionist foreign policy based on naval supremacy and undisputed control of the world's sea lanes, a vigorous development of foreign markets, and an energetic cultivation of all the domestic spiritual resources needed to promote the national mission overseas. In a Darwinian world of warring nations, he argued, the United States must organize itself into a spiritual and military garrison ready to defend its interests with power. Mahan did not deny the existence of a universal law of conscience, but he anchored it in the concept of the national state fully aware of its duty and prepared to perform it. In his view, the "evils of war" paled before the dangers of "moral compliance with wrong." In the last analysis all depended on Americans' willingness to take up their appointed tasks as the democratic saviors of civilization: "Whether they will or no, Americans must now begin to look outward."

**Architects of Empire**     Mahan's arguments, which won him enthusiastic support in Britain and Germany, were also warmly received by a small circle of influential Americans whose own examination of the international situation in the 1890s led them to conclude that the United States should take its place among the imperialist powers. "You are head and shoulders above us all," wrote Theodore Roosevelt in promising Mahan that he would do all he could "toward pressing your ideas into effect." Other important converts to the captain's expansionist doctrines joined in: John Hay, soon to become McKinley's secretary of state; the freewheeling romantic reactionaries Brooks and Henry Adams, and their protégé, Senator Henry Cabot Lodge; young, aggressive cosmopolitans like the diplomat Richard Olney, and staid conservatives like lawyer Joseph Choate; academic popularizer John Fiske, with his own version of Manifest Destiny; and social-gospeler Josiah Strong, whose best-selling *Our Country* (1885) argued the Christian evangelist's case for spiritual renewal through expansion. The views of these would-be architects of American empire were expressed with increasing frequency in metropolitan newspapers and liberal journals, which called for a higher appraisal of American capabilities. And when the test of strength came between imperialists and anti-imperialists over a "large policy" for the United States, these spokesmen for expansion would prove to be particularly effective.

In the meantime, American diplomacy continued to heat up. A series of minor crises early in the 1890s signaled America's intention to take a firmer hand in managing foreign policy by asserting national interest and defending national honor whenever the opportunity arose. In the South Pacific a German threat to impose a protectorate over the entire group of Samoan islands brought United States naval forces steaming into the Samoan harbor of Apia—in time to be destroyed by a typhoon. In Chile a barroom brawl involving American sailors ended in an American ultimatum to that country. And in 1895 a dispute between the unstable and financially irresponsible Venezuela and Great Britain over the boundary of British Guiana called forth a declaration of American power in the

Western Hemisphere. "Today," Richard Olney, Cleveland's secretary of state, boasted to the startled British, "the United States is practically sovereign on this continent, and its fiat is law upon the subjects to which it confines its interposition . . . its infinite resources combined with its isolated position renders it master of the situation and practically invulnerable against any or all other powers." By 1896 events like these, minor irritations evoking a disproportionate American belligerence, paved the way for a popular American crusade on behalf of Cuban independence.

## President McKinley's "Wonderful Experience"

In 1895 the Cuban revolution against Spain, which had been smoldering for nearly a quarter of a century, flared up once again, and Spain sent 50,000 soldiers to extinguish it. American sympathies, a mixture of genuine outrage and "jingo" bluster, instinctively went to the underdogs, who were widely credited with wanting to establish a Yankee-style republic. The Cuban rebels responded to this encouragement by dispatching a high-powered lobby to New York City with orders to raise money and goodwill while supplying a steady stream of atrocity stories to the reporters of the sensationalist newspapers owned by William Randolph Hearst and Joseph Pulitzer. Soon the Cuban revolutionaries in New York began to receive help from unexpected quarters—from Latin American trading interests, promoters of a canal across Central America, a variety of patriotic groups, and even trade unions. Carefully orchestrated "spontaneous" rallies across the country whipped up enthusiasm for American intervention. Democrats and Populists vied with their Republican rivals in denouncing Spain and demanding a declaration in support of the Cuban rebels. It was obvious to the incoming McKinley administration that the president would have to move quickly to avoid being captured by a warlike public mood.

**Annexation or "Cuba Libre"** As late as 1896, however, the exact meaning of this public clamor over Cuba's fate was not altogether clear. To the small group advocating the "large policy," intervention on the island seemed a foregone conclusion. Roosevelt, who admitted to being "a quietly rampant 'Cuba Libre' [Free Cuba] man," told Mahan that intervention was inevitable if the United States was to retain its self-respect. Many expansionists agreed: the Cuban affair would be a heaven-sent opportunity to annex Hawaii. As for Cuba's fate, no one could predict. Even Roosevelt, although he angrily dismissed "the craven fear and brutal selfishness of the mere money-getters" who opposed American intervention, doubted the wisdom of annexing Cuba "unless the Cubans wished it." "I don't want it to seem that we are engaged merely in a land-grabbing war," he explained. Until war was actually declared, there was little support for the idea of permanent United States involvement on the island, even among the most vocal interventionists.

In the fiercely contested presidential election of 1896, the issue of Cuba had given way to domestic problems of free silver and the tariff. It took the renewed campaigns of the Cuban revolutionaries in December 1896 and the murder of their leader, Maceo, to anger the American public once more. This time the response was different. Instead of planned demonstrations and organized rallies, there were loud outbursts of protest all over the country—genuinely spontaneous meetings in which businessmen joined patriots and humanitarians in demanding an end to Spanish rule. McKinley's administration now had to contend with a powerful popular indignation.

At this point Spain added fuel to the interventionist fire when its troops on the island began brutally herding Cubans into makeshift camps, where they died by the thousands. Meanwhile a wavering government in Madrid continued to agonize over the dwindling options left to it. The decaying Spanish monarchy, torn by rival factions of liberals and conservatives, unable to pacify the island but unwilling to give it up, temporized hopelessly. Confusion was nearly as great within the McKinley administration as the president found himself in an intense crossfire between Republican expansionists crying for justice at the point of an American sword and his conservative business backers fearful of the effects of a war on business recovery from the depression of the 1890s. As popular pressure for intervention rose alarmingly, McKinley was also driven to play for time. Publicly the president demanded promises of instant reform from Madrid, while privately he reined in the most radical members of his party with promises of his own.

**War with Spain**     By 1897 the horrors of Spain's reconcentration program in Cuba had forced the president to press for even firmer Spanish concessions. Then a series of incidents brought relations between the two countries to the breaking point. First came the release of an indiscreet letter from Depuy de Lôme, the Spanish minister in Washington, to his government, in which he ungenerously—but not inaccurately—described McKinley as "weak" and "a bidder for the admiration of the crowd." Then came the explosion in Havana harbor that destroyed the American battleship *Maine.* There were rumors everywhere that Spain had engineered the explosion—this "gigantic murder" of innocent American sailors, as Senator Lodge put it. At last the expansionist jingoes had an aroused American public crying for retaliation in the name of justice and democracy.

McKinley's dilemma grew more painful as conflicting reports of Spanish intentions came flooding into Washington. On the one hand there were accounts of the Spanish government's total unwillingness to compromise; on the other there were assurances that it was ready to comply with demands for full self-government for Cuba. Given the choice between waiting and taking immediate action, McKinley finally decided to act. Two days after Spain had agreed to his demands for an immediate armistice and an end to reconcentration—while still declining to grant Cuban independence—the president sent a message to Congress requesting authority to intervene and restore peace on the island. By the time word of Spain's partial compliance reached Washington, it was too late. Intervention, McKinley knew, meant war, and Congress made the decision official

**The Cause and the Cure**
*The battleship* Maine *on the morning after the explosion.*

**The Spanish Brute**
*A magazine cover reflects the rising war fever.*

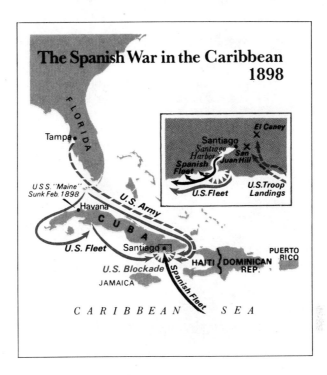

The Spanish War in the Caribbean 1898

on April 19, 1898, by declaring that a state of war existed. McKinley had lacked a clearly defined set of goals and the means of achieving them, and he had been caught in a domestic political crossfire. He accepted the prospect of what Secretary of State John Hay called "a splendid little war" for no particularly compelling reasons of national interest.

In the brief war that followed, the United States made short work of Spain's broken-down navy and demoralized army. Commodore George Dewey's Asiatic Squadron quickly demolished the monarchy's Pacific fleet in the battle of Manila Bay, and the United States' Atlantic Squadron as easily penned up Admiral Cervera's ships in Santiago, Cuba, and systematically destroyed them. Spanish troops scarcely did any better when they fought the American land forces, although the Americans were poorly trained, badly equipped, and disorganized. After endless confusion General William R. Shafter finally succeeded in assembling some 18,000 troops for an invasion of Cuba and managed to land his army, complete with press corps, foreign dignitaries, and well-wishers, near Santiago. There Colonel Roosevelt and his Rough Riders, a flamboyant cavalry regiment recruited from the cattle ranges and mining camps of the West, seized the lion's share of the glory of what the colonel called a "bully fight," the capture of San Juan Hill. The battle of Santiago capped the successes of the navy, and American soldiers settled in on the jungle heights above San Juan, where more of them died from yellow fever than in actual combat. A small expeditionary force that was dispatched to nearby Puerto Rico encountered no real resistance. In August 1898, Spain's meager military resources were entirely spent, and its morale shattered. The Spanish had no choice but to give up and sign the peace protocol.

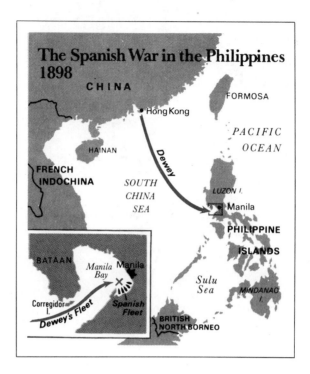

**The Philippines: "Those Darned Islands"**

The problem of disposing of the remnants of Spain's empire caught McKinley by surprise. In the case of Cuba, Congress in an unaccountable burst of self-denial had rushed through the Teller Amendment, declaring the island free and independent and disavowing any American intentions of annexing it. Not for conquest nor for empire had American soldiers fought so bravely, but, as one Republican senator put it, "for humanity's sake... to aid a people who have suffered every form of tyranny and who have made a desperate struggle to be free." But within a year these expressions of high-mindedness had been cast to the winds.

The new question of the Philippines, together with the old problem of Hawaii, added to McKinley's worries. "If old Dewey had just sailed away when he smashed the Spanish fleet, what a lot of trouble he would have saved us," the president grumbled, confessing that he "could not have told where those darned islands were within 2,000 miles." But with Spain's collapse the barriers to American empire also began to fall, both within the administration and in the nation at large, as groups once hostile to the idea of acquiring new territory began to have second thoughts. Business leaders, banking and mercantile interests, church organizations, and even social reformers joined in calling for the retention of the Philippines, if not as a permanent possession, at least as a temporary way station on the route to Asian markets.

When the Senate came to debate the question of annexation, the opponents of the new imperialism argued strenuously that "political dominion" was not commercially necessary and that, in any case, both the Constitution and the

Declaration of Independence forbade it. Under the Declaration, Senator George F. Hoar told his colleagues, "you can not govern a foreign territory, a foreign people, another people than your own . . . you can not subjugate them and govern them against their will, because you think it is for their good. . . . " But the logic of expansion worked against the anti-imperialists. Annexationists argued that if, in order to secure commercial opportunity, the United States needed political stability in Hawaii and the Philippines, then why not go the whole way and at the same time lift untutored peoples to the level of democratic self-government? McKinley spoke the public mood in presenting a narrow range of choices. It would be "cowardly and pusillanimous," he insisted, for the United States "to turn the islands back to Spain, giving them power again to misrule the natives." Equally "despicable" was the notion of handing them over to Britain or allowing Japan to take them by default. "There is only one logical course to pursue," McKinley announced:

> Spain has shown herself unfit to rule her colonies, and those [that] have come into our possession as a result of war, must be held, if we are to fulfill our destinies as a nation . . . giving them the benefits of a christian civilization which has reached its highest development under our republican institutions.

The problem of ruling the Philippines admitted of no such simple solution as McKinley proposed. Before war with the United States broke out, Spain had finally suppressed an uprising of Filipino independence fighters by bribing their leader, General Emilio Aguinaldo, to leave the islands. Following his smashing naval victory, Admiral Dewey brought Aguinaldo back to Manila to help fight the Spanish in exchange for a vague promise of eventual independence. But when it became clear that the United States had no intention of giving up control of the Philippines, Aguinaldo and his followers took up arms again, this time against their former allies. In the course of a savage four-year guerrilla war, the Filipino patriots, suffering heavy military and civilian casualties at the hands of American "pacifiers," killed more than 4,000 American soldiers before surrendering and swearing allegiance to the American flag.

As the debate over the peace terms intensified, there emerged a small vocal group of "anti-imperialists," as they called themselves, hastily assembled and ranged along a broad spectrum of opinion. The nucleus of this anti-imperialist opposition consisted of venerable mid-nineteenth-century liberals whose distinguishing mark and chief liability was their advanced age and distrust of mass democratic politics. Veteran antislavery campaigner Carl Schurz was seventy-one; free trader Edward Atkinson, seventy-three; Republican maverick George F. Hoar, seventy-four; steelmaker Andrew Carnegie, sixty-five. Most of the anti-imperialists stood on the margins of their parties and the government, respected but minor figures who held long and honorable records in the cause of dissent against the Gilded Age. As imperial ambition swept up the majority of their countrymen, they found themselves severely handicapped by their caution and

**McKinley's "Little Brown Brothers"**
*American troops pacify the Filipino followers of Aguinaldo.*

self-denial. "Who will embarrass the government by sowing seeds of dissatisfaction among the brave men who stand ready to serve and die, if need be, for their country?" McKinley demanded of a cheering crowd in Omaha in the heartland of America. "Who will darken the counsels of the republic in this hour, requiring the united wisdom of all?" The anti-imperialists could not prevail against such expansionist ardor. Unskilled in the new arts of mass propaganda, advocating a negative program, often distrustful of the democratic forces supporting the president, the anti-imperialists were quickly outmanned and outmaneuvered by the expansionists.

Some anti-imperialist arguments expressed racist doubts about the wisdom of incorporating dark-skinned, unschooled peoples. Others appealed to the Constitution and the spirit of the Founders in denying Congress the power to govern other people against their wills. With social scientist William Graham Sumner, a loyal few railed against the prostitution of statesmanship to mere party interest. But the core of the anti-imperialists' case against expansionism was the charge that in betraying the cherished principles of the Declaration of Independence, their country had abandoned the moral law. Charles Eliot Norton, professor of the arts at Harvard, spoke to this point most eloquently:

> We believe that America had something better to offer to mankind than those
> aims she is now pursuing, and we mourn her desertion of her ideals which were

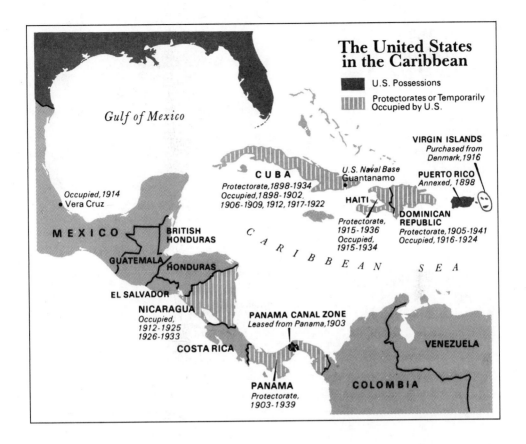

**The United States in the Caribbean**

U.S. Possessions

Protectorates or Temporarily Occupied by U.S.

*Gulf of Mexico*

VIRGIN ISLANDS
*Purchased from Denmark, 1916*

CUBA
*Protectorate, 1898-1934
Occupied, 1898-1902,
1906-1909, 1912, 1917-1922*

U.S. Naval Base
Guantanamo

PUERTO RICO
*Annexed, 1898*

Occupied, 1914
• Vera Cruz

HAITI

DOMINICAN
REPUBLIC
*Protectorate, 1905-1941
Occupied, 1916-1924*

Protectorate,
1915-1936
Occupied,
1915-1934

MEXICO

BRITISH
HONDURAS

C A R I B B E A N   S E A

GUATEMALA

HONDURAS

EL SALVADOR

NICARAGUA
*Occupied,
1912-1925
1926-1933*

PANAMA CANAL ZONE
*Leased from Panama, 1903*

VENEZUELA

COSTA RICA

PANAMA
*Protectorate,
1903-1939*

COLOMBIA

not selfish nor limited in their application, but which are of universal worth and validity. She has lost her unique position as a potential leader in the program of civilization, and has taken up her place simply as one of the grasping and selfish nations of the present day.

A few of the older anti-imperialists looked back to a less complex world of a half-century earlier, when the United States, as one traditionalist put it, was "provincial, dominated by the New England idea." These venerable men, however, were joined by younger pragmatic critics of imperialism, among them William James, who skillfully probed the false "realism" of the expansionists and dissected their flabby arguments. As the bloody and inconclusive pacification program in the Philippines dragged on and the freedom fighter Emilio Aguinaldo gave American troops a lesson in jungle warfare, James centered his own attack on the American inclination to substitute "bald and hollow abstractions" for the "intensely living and concrete situation." An unrestrained appetite for power, he scoffed, had caused the country to "puke up its ancient soul ... in five minutes without a wink of squeamishness."

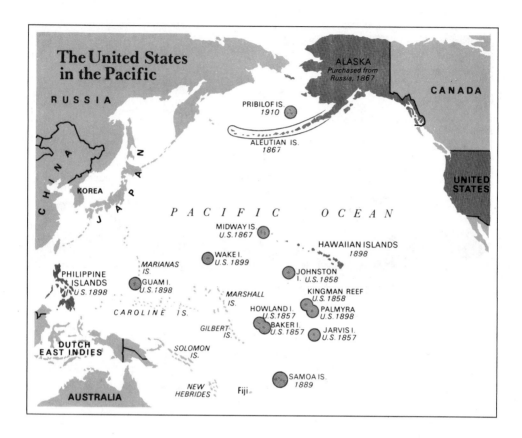

The United States in the Pacific

Could there be a more damning indictment of that whole bloated idol termed "modern civilization" than this amounts to? Civilization is, then, the big, hollow, resounding, corrupting, sophisticating, confusing torrent of mere brutal momentum and irrationality that brings forth fruits like this?

Until the Philippine uprising revealed the shallowness of American expressions of benevolence, the opponents of expansion made very little headway against the winds of imperial destiny. McKinley, after wrestling with his conscience, announced that "without any desire or design on our part," the war had brought new duties to "a great nation." Accordingly, he instructed his peace commissioners to stand firm against any and all Spanish protests over the dismantling of Spain's empire. By the terms of the peace treaty signed late in 1898, Spain agreed to dismemberment, giving up Cuba, the Philippines, Puerto Rico, and Guam. In 1898 the United States also annexed Hawaii, which was dominated by American sugar planters who five years earlier had overthrown the native queen, Liliuokalani, and established a nominal republic.

**Colonial Fruits of War**

In the Senate the treaty was taken in hand by the Republican faithfuls, including Lodge and Beveridge, who were aided in their work by Bryan's odd notion that the course of empire could be determined only in the presidential election of 1900. The majority of senators agreed with Beveridge in striking a balance between the immediate material rewards of expansion and long-term spiritual gains. "It is God's great purpose," Beveridge declared, "made manifest in the instincts of the race whose present phase is our personal profit, but whose far-off end is the redemption of the world and the Christianization of mankind." Despite the anti-imperialists' warnings that the nation was descending from the "ancient path" of republican righteousness into the "cesspool" of imperialism, the Senate voted 57 to 27 to accept the treaty. Hawaii became an incorporated territory under the Organic Act of 1900. Guam was acquired as a naval station administered by the Navy Department. And Puerto Rico, under the Foraker Act (1900), was attached as unincorporated territory with an elective legislature and a governor appointed by the president.

With the gathering of the colonial fruits of war with Spain and the arrival of Theodore Roosevelt in the White House, the initiative in formulating foreign policy fell to the activists who agreed with the new president that the aggressive pursuit of national interest provided the only sound base for a democratic foreign policy. "If we stand idly by," Roosevelt warned as the century opened, "if we seek merely swollen, slothful ease and ignoble peace, if we shrink from the hard contests where men must win at hazard of their lives and the risk of all they hold dear, then the bolder and stronger people will pass us by.... Let us therefore boldly face the life of strife." Strife marked and often marred Roosevelt's conduct of foreign policy from first to last—in Cuba and Panama and throughout Latin America, and in American dealings with China and Japan. In the Roosevelt years national interest came to mean national egotism.

In Cuba the occupation by American forces continued as the United States launched a program of administrative and public health reforms that culminated in a successful campaign against yellow fever. The Platt Amendment of 1901 drew even tighter the "ties of singular intimacy" between the United States and the island by providing for American intervention in case an unstable new government failed to protect life, liberty, and property. With the help of some heavy pressure on the Cuban leadership, this provision was written into the new republic's constitution in 1901 and was incorporated in the treaty between Cuba and the United States two years later. By 1903 the United States, despite earlier disavowals, had established a virtual protectorate on the island and reserved to itself the right to intervene in the internal affairs of its neighbor, a privilege it would regularly invoke in the next half-century.

In the Philippines the establishment of American control awaited the outcome of Aguinaldo's uprising, which dragged on until March 1901, when the Filipino leader was captured and his scattered forces surrendered. Under the terms of the Philippine Organic Act of 1902, the United States provided for a bicameral legislature and a governor with broad executive powers appointed by the president. Although there would be a gradual loosening of the governmental reins in the Philippines for the next three decades, full independence would not be achieved until 1946.

The turn of the century marked the final achievements of American expansion. Within a decade the dreams of a handful of "large policy" advocates had become a reality. The United States, without actually willing it, had acquired an imperial base for commercial and ideological expansion throughout the world.

## Open and Closed Doors: Progressive Foreign Policy Under Roosevelt and Taft

If a "splendid little war" had suddenly thrust the United States into the ranks of the world's big powers, the war's aftermath taught corrective lessons on the limits of American influence. The United States proved a slow and often stubborn pupil in the school of international power politics, and as late as 1914, when war broke out in Europe, it still had much to learn about world affairs and a democracy's proper role in managing them.

### An "Open Door" in China

American education in the limits of power began in China at the turn of the century. The dream of a rich and limitless China market was older than the nation itself; it had been a prime motive in original explorations and in the search for the fabled Northwest Passage. After the American Revolution the dream became a reality as the new nation began to open markets in the Far East to compensate for the loss of old ones. Success in these distant markets in the age of the clipper ships, the 1840s and 1850s, continued to feed American hopes for gaining untold riches in the Orient. Still, by the end of the nineteenth century, less than 2 percent of United States foreign trade involved China, and it was with expectations of increasing this slim total that commercial and banking interests, concession hunters, and investment seekers nervously watched European influence mount in the Far East. The fatal weakness of the Manchu dynasty, which ruled China, had become apparent in China's disastrous war with Japan in 1894–95. By 1900 Germany, France, Russia, and Japan had secured generous "spheres of influence" in China, together with exclusive economic "concessions" to develop these areas through long-term leases and special trading privileges. If the United States intended to establish its own foothold on the Chinese mainland, it would have to move quickly.

Once again, as in the case of the Monroe Doctrine seventy-five years earlier, American and British interests coincided on the point of equal trading rights and market opportunity for all nations. And once again the British Foreign Office proposed a joint statement, only to be told by the McKinley administration that the United States preferred to make its own unilateral pronouncement. The result of this decision was a series of notes dispatched to the European capitals and Tokyo by Secretary of State John Hay, announcing America's Open Door policy. This policy embodied three principles. Nations with spheres of influence in China (1) would promise to respect the "vested interests" of other nations within their own spheres; (2) would agree to allow Chinese customs officials to continue to collect duties in every sphere of interest "no matter to what nationality it may belong"; and (3) would pledge not to discriminate against competitor nations in levying port duties and railroad rates within their respective spheres of interest. At best Secretary Hay received ambiguous replies from all the governments to which he had sent the notes setting forth American policy. Nevertheless, he boldly announced the "final and definitive" acceptance of the principles of the Open Door.

Hay's optimism was soon severely tested by the Boxer Rebellion, a series of militant antiforeign riots in China that cut off the international community in Peking from the outside world. The European powers, Japan, and the United States retaliated by sending a rescue expedition (including 2,500 American soldiers fresh from the Philippines) to lift the siege and punish the Chinese nationalists. Once again the road lay open to further Chinese concessions that might lead to the dismantlement of the Chinese empire. Now Hay was forced to write a second note to the other powers, this one announcing simply that the United States intended to maintain the territorial integrity of the empire. Here was a sharp departure in American diplomacy—not simply a commitment to preserving equal economic opportunity on the mainland, but a pledge to uphold the sovereignty of China.

The Open Door, it was clear, would control imperialistic ambitions exactly to the extent that Britain and the United States wanted it to. Events soon disillusioned American policymakers. The Chinese empire lay in shambles, its days numbered before revolution toppled the dynasty in 1911. In the decade between the Boxer Rebellion and the outbreak of the Chinese Revolution, Britain accepted the inevitable by hastening to make overtures to Japan, acknowledging that country's predominant interests on the Chinese mainland. Meanwhile the rivalry between Russia and Japan over mining and railroad concessions in Manchuria led to the outbreak of war in 1904. In a series of smashing victories over the Russians, Japan played to perfection the part of "underdog" so appealing to Americans, and forced Russia to accept the mediation of President Roosevelt, who suddenly appeared in the unfamiliar role of peacemaker.

**The Portsmouth Treaty**

The Portsmouth (New Hampshire) Treaty of 1905, which Roosevelt forced on an unhappy but thoroughly beaten Russia, established Japan as the dominant power in the Far East. But the treaty did not advance the principles of the Open Door. In a secret agreement in 1907, Russia and Japan agreed to divide Manchuria, Mongolia, and Korea into spheres of influence with "special interests." Roosevelt reluctantly recognized Japan's special interests in Manchuria in the Root-Takahira Agreement (1908), thus presiding over the ceremonial closing of the Open

Door. Although the president admitted that the Open Door principle was "an excellent thing" so far as it could be upheld by general diplomatic agreement, he nevertheless confessed that the policy simply disappeared once a nation like Japan chose to disregard it. In this sense the Open Door ended in failure.

**Intervention in North Africa**

In the Moroccan crisis of 1905–06, Roosevelt managed to salvage at least some aspects of an Open Door policy while improving on his record as a peacemaker. The crisis grew out of conflicting French and German interests in North Africa, and a clash resulted in which the United States, according to Roosevelt's secretary of state, Elihu Root, was not justified in taking "a leading part." Nevertheless Roosevelt broke a tradition of nonintervention by actively directing the Algeciras Conference (1906). As he intended, the settlement halted German penetration of North Africa momentarily, united France and Great Britain in solid opposition to Kaiser Wilhelm II, and reaffirmed for the United States the principles of the Open Door. Roosevelt, who already distrusted German military power, boasted of having stood the Kaiser on his head "with great decision." Yet imperial Germany soon righted itself, and it was clear that Roosevelt's departure from a century-long tradition of nonentanglement in European affairs would not soon be repeated.

**Intervention in the Caribbean**

No such doubts about the American role of policeman inhibited progressive foreign policy in the Caribbean. Here economic interests and dominant American power combined in a shortsighted policy of constant intervention that would leave a legacy of ill will and distrust. American interference in the internal affairs of unstable Latin American governments quickly became a pattern. Behind this pattern lay rapidly expanding American economic interests—not just in trade, but in banking, investments, and the development of natural resources, all of which seemingly required a favorable political climate and the willingness of Caribbean governments to grant generous concessions to the United States.

Trouble began in that "infernal little Cuban republic," as Roosevelt called it, in admitting to a recurrent urge to "wipe its people off the face of the earth." Four years after the removal of American forces in 1902, the troops were back again for another attempt at restoring order. A policeman's lot, the president agreed, was not a happy one. "All that we wanted from them was that they would behave themselves and be prosperous and happy so that we would not have to interfere." Instead, the Cubans persisted in playing at revolution and "may get things into such a snarl that we have no alternative save to intervene—which will at once convince the suspicious idiots in South America that we do wish to interfere after all, and perhaps have some land hunger." The president neglected to add that it was not land hunger but the drive to establish economic dominance in Latin America that dictated his interventionist strategy.

A habit of constantly intervening in the domestic affairs of neighbors to the south required an explanation, and Roosevelt provided this in the famous "corollary" to the Monroe Doctrine in his annual message to Congress in 1905. Once again, as in Cleveland's administration ten years earlier, the occasion was a fiscal crisis in Venezuela, where a chronically unstable and corrupt dictatorship refused to honor its debts. In 1903 Germany tried to nudge the Venezuelan government toward a more conciliatory stance by bombarding Fort San Carlos, and only prompt American condemnation of the "outrage" dissuaded the Germans from taking further measures. To forestall similar European moves to protect their investments, Roosevelt offered his corollary. "Chronic wrongdoing," he admitted, would inevitably invite retaliation from the "civilized" nations determined to protect their investments in Latin America. Since the Monroe Doctrine effectively prevented the European powers from intervening directly, the United States, "however reluctantly," might be forced to step in "in flagrant cases of such wrongdoing or impotence." In short, Latin America properly belonged within the sphere of influence of the United States, which would undertake the work of an "international police power."

The meaning of the Roosevelt Corollary became clear in the Dominican Republic in 1905 when, after considerable urging from the United States, the Dominican government agreed to request American assistance in straightening out its finances. Despite congressional reservations, President Roosevelt was more than happy to provide such advice. With the control of the Dominican customhouse firmly in American hands, the United States succeeded in preventing German intervention once again, but at the cost of a policy that would continue to breed hemispheric ill will throughout the twentieth century.

**The Panama Canal Affair**

The problem of Panama and of securing American rights to a canal across the Central American isthmus offered the clearest example of a foreign policy based on narrow and shortsighted national interest. High-powered lobbying by the new Panama Canal Company, the successor of a defunct French company that had tried and failed to build a Panamanian canal, caused the American government to abandon the Nicaraguan route, which had intrigued Americans for more than a century. A combination of French adventurers and American entrepreneurs succeeded in convincing Roosevelt, Mark Hanna, and other Republican leaders of the distinct advantages of the route through Panama, which was then a province of Colombia. With the help of a few carefully placed investments in the future of their party, they managed to win congressional support for their lucrative deal. By 1902 all that remained was to convince the inept Colombian government of the benefits that civilization was about to confer.

For a while negotiations proceeded smoothly. The Hay-Herran Treaty of 1903 gave the United States rights to a canal zone six miles wide for the price of $10 million plus an annual rental of $250,000. Then suddenly Colombian patriots,

274

**"Teddy" Defends Civilization**
*Anti-imperialist cartoon lampoons Roosevelt's Latin American policy.*

**Digging the Panama Canal**
*Roosevelt poses at the controls of a giant steam shovel in Panama.*

preparing to overthrow a corrupt dictator and realizing that they were being swindled, forced the Colombian senate to withdraw the treaty.

Roosevelt duly denounced his new opponents as "inefficient bandits" and "contemptible little creatures" who were willfully blocking the march of progress across the hemisphere. With his initial scheme now frustrated, the president agreed to an alternative plan for a pocket revolution in Panama, engineered by canal promoters and by a handful of native *insurrectos,* who proceeded to establish Panamanian independence from Colombia with the blessing of the United States and the help of its navy. After hasty recognition by the United States, the new state of Panama obliged its benefactor by granting the terms for the canal that Colombia had just refused. Roosevelt had his canal project, the Panamanian patriots had their revolution, and the promoters had their profits. Roosevelt never ceased defending his part in the affair: "If I had followed traditional conservative methods, I would have submitted a dignified state paper of probably two hundred pages to Congress and the debates on it would have been going on yet; but I took the Canal Zone and let Congress debate; and while the debate goes on the Canal does also."

**Roosevelt's Style of Diplomacy**

With this bald assertion of presidential and national power, Roosevelt drew together the strands of his diplomacy. In the first place, his diplomatic style was a highly personal one that assumed that most of the issues in foreign affairs were best handled, as he said, "by one man alone." Although on occasion he made effective use of his secretaries of state, John Hay and Elihu Root, just as often he bypassed them completely, and he seldom gave them credit for decisions that he rightly or wrongly considered his own. Roosevelt was determined to play the lone hand, and he fumed at the Senate's constant interference and its tampering with what he considered an executive prerogative. Deliberative bodies, he insisted, were virtually useless when there was "any efficient work" to be done. It was for the president alone to take charge of foreign policy in the same way that he took the lead in formulating domestic priorities of reform and reorganization. His aim in intervening in Latin American affairs, he later wrote, was to wake up the American people "so that they would back a reasonable and intelligent foreign policy which would have put a stop to the crying disorders at our very doors."

"Crying disorders"—here was the link between domestic progressive reform and foreign policy. Order and stability in Asia, Roosevelt was to learn, lay beyond the reach of American policy. In Europe, where his leverage was greater, he could mix balance-of-power diplomacy with hopes for a perpetual Anglo-American supremacy throughout the world. But it was in the Western Hemisphere that the benefits of order and system seemed to him the greatest, and he did not hesitate to seek these benefits for American business.

Although Roosevelt presided over the transformation of territorial imperialism into a policy of economic penetration, his language revealed his ignorance of his historical role. He spoke constantly of "honor, territorial integrity and vital interests" as the only basis for an American foreign policy. There were higher things in life, he kept insisting, than the enjoyment of material comforts or the pursuit of wealth: "It is through strife, or the readiness for strife, that a nation must win greatness." And greatness for Roosevelt was primarily spiritual. His speeches rang with the clichés of "righteousness" and "duty" as he combined moralism and nationalism in a blend of power politics that glossed over the hard economic motives he never clearly acknowledged.

The central theme running through Roosevelt's foreign policy pronouncements was the danger that American preoccupation with domestic prosperity would turn right-minded citizens into a mere "assemblage of well-to-do hucksters" who cared for nothing beyond their own borders. But to argue the case for an aggressive foreign policy purely in terms of high-mindedness was to ignore the economic forces that increasingly controlled the making of American foreign policy. These forces included investment opportunities, concessions, corporate resource development, and other forms of economic penetration—all requiring political and economic stability, which was essential to the effective exploitation of colonial economies. Roosevelt's rhetoric concealed the fact that as president he became, if not the captive, at least the ally of exactly the economic forces he presumably distrusted.

**Taft's "Dollar Diplomacy"** The Taft administration substituted dollars for bullets and displayed no such squeamishness in acknowledging the reality of economic imperialism. Taft's choice of secretary of state, corporation lawyer Philander C. Knox, was itself proof of the growing intimacy between the Wall Street investment community and the State Department. Knox, who was given a much freer hand in formulating policy than Roosevelt had allowed his secretaries of state, was the chief architect of Taft's program of "dollar diplomacy." Dollar diplomacy, a form of democratic state capitalism, used American export capital, together with dominant political and military power, to give force, as Taft himself put it, "alike to idealistic humanitarian sentiments, to the dictates of sound policy and strategy, and to legitimate commercial aims."

Dollar diplomacy extended the principles of domestic progressivism to the conduct of foreign policy. Investment capitalists were encouraged to proceed with the economic penetration of undeveloped areas under conditions of stability and profitability provided by the government. "In China," Taft told Congress in citing his favorite example, "the policy of encouraging financial investment to enable that country to help itself has had the result of giving new life and practical application to the open-door policy." Taft's administration was committed to encouraging the use of American capital in China to promote "those essential reforms" that China had pledged to the United States and to the other major powers. Taft offered for congressional approval a "new diplomacy," practiced by a foreign service "alert and equipped to cooperate with the businessmen of America" and dedicated to "improved governmental methods of protecting and stimulating it."

Taft's open avowal of the economic motive did not alter the pattern of American success and failure—conspicuous success in attracting investment to nearby Latin America, where the bankers were more than willing to go, and nearly total failure in the Far East, where the bankers were not willing to go. In attempting to open China once more to American capital, Taft met the determined resistance of British, French, and German bankers, who excluded the Americans from an international business group to finance and build the Hukuang Railway in China, an ill-considered project that was never completed. By placing heavy diplomatic pressure on the Chinese emperor, Knox succeeded in gaining admission to the railway consortium. But he needlessly made trouble for himself by another poorly conceived experiment in state capitalism in Manchuria. Like Hay's original plan, the Taft administration's attempt to pry open the door for American capital ended in failure.

No such difficulties were encountered in Latin America, where American capital continued to pour in. Here a combination of supersalesmanship and regular government intervention to protect American investments—in Nicaragua, Guatemala, Honduras, and Haiti—kept the gates open.

Taft's foreign policy concentrated on Latin America and the Far East and virtually neglected Europe. In warning against an exclusive concern with the Far East, progressive writer Herbert Croly (who had also presumed to advise Roosevelt in *The Promise of American Life*) predicted the early arrival of an international confrontation of major powers that might force the United States to interfere "in what may at first appear to be a purely European complication." When that time came, Croly hastened to add, American policymakers ought to meet it with "a sound, well-informed, and positive conception of American national interest rather than a negative and ignorant conception." Taft, however, preferred to keep his distance. The legal framework for dollar diplomacy was provided by a deep faith in arbitration: with arbitration Taft hoped to defuse international crises in much the same way that boards of mediators in domestic affairs depoliticized economic conflict. Twenty-five arbitration treaties had been signed in the last days of the outgoing Roosevelt administration, and Taft sought to apply the same principle to all "justiciable" issues. The Senate, however, eliminated the procedures for discussion and consultation in every case in which the United States might be presumed to have an interest. Nevertheless, the arbitration scheme lived on as a progressive panacea, drawing the attention of Woodrow Wilson and his secretary of state, the "Prince of Peace," William Jennings Bryan. There would be continuities as well as new departures in Wilson's missionary diplomacy.

## *"The Organized Force of Mankind": Wilsonian Diplomacy and World War*

At first Woodrow Wilson appeared to represent a new constituency in American foreign policy. The years after 1900 saw peace groups, proponents of arbitration, and other idealists combine in a broad coalition behind the principles of missionary diplomacy, moral publicity, and open rather than secret international agreements. In rejecting both Roosevelt's role of big brother to the oppressed and Taft's dollar diplomacy, Wilson entered office with an appeal to national high-mindedness that warmed the hearts of moralists everywhere. "My dream is that as the years go on and the world knows more and more of America," the president told a Fourth of July audience in 1914, "it . . . will turn to America for those moral inspirations which lie at the basis of all freedoms . . . and that America will come into the full light of day when all shall know that she puts human rights above all other rights and that her flag is the flag not only of America but of humanity." Yet three months earlier Wilson had ordered the occupation of the Mexican port of Vera Cruz to vindicate American honor.

One of the ironies of American foreign relations in the early twentieth century was that both of the widely divergent formulations of policy—national egotism and national high-mindedness—led to similar involvements of the United States throughout the world and almost constantly to forcible intervention in the affairs of neighboring countries. Both the demands of national interest and the less precise requirements of moral mission ended in the application of raw power. By 1917 the United States had clearly arrived as a world power, but it remained to be seen how American power would be used in reordering a world at war. Americans entered World War I still seeking an answer to this question.

Like most Americans before 1914, Woodrow Wilson had given little serious attention to the specifics of American foreign policy. Diplomatic questions had not figured prominently in the campaign of 1912, and to solve such questions Wilson could offer only the conventional wisdom of an active peace movement in the United States concerning the exportability of the American democratic way. During his two terms Wilson often served as the mouthpiece of this movement and adopted many of its principles, fashioning them into an alternative to balance-of-power politics.

By 1914 there was a well-established faith among progressive intellectuals in the imminent arrival of an age of international harmony. Progressive reformers and professionals believed that improved worldwide communications, international technology, and arbitration would soon create a new moral order. The peace movement in the United States was made up of a variety of groups and interests: church-affiliated peace societies and new secular foundations (including Andrew Carnegie's Endowment for International Peace); students of international law intent on constructing new legal frameworks; preachers of disarmament; and prophets of a vast people-to-people crusade. Many of these peace advocates shared a uniquely American set of assumptions that defined peace as an adjunct to domestic progressive reform.

**Arbitration: The Key to World Order**    The first of these assumptions was the belief that the path to world order had been discovered by the United States as it progressed from a loose federation of sovereign states to a genuine union of all the people. From similar beginnings, the promoters of peace reasoned, one world of harmony and democratic striving might take shape. A second assumption that was associated with this golden vision of an Americanized world order was a stubborn faith in arbitration itself. Arbitration, many assumed, was a key mechanism for resolving tensions and potential conflicts. This mechanism could take various forms: the International Court at the Hague, the Netherlands, which had been created by international agreement in 1899; a body of international law; or bilateral "cooling off" treaties.

These progressive beliefs led Wilson to accept the views of the peace advocates. His language, like Roosevelt's, was consistently abstract. But whereas Roosevelt, a self-declared "realist," spoke of national duty, honor, and integrity, Wilson translated these terms into the language of idealism. He denounced narrowly understood national interest as "selfishness" and the rule of unbridled materialism. "Balance of power" to him meant unstable coalitions of aggressive interests. The outlook of "average" people the world over, on the other hand, was becoming "more and more unclouded" as national purposes fell more and more into the background and the "common purpose of enlightened mankind" took their place. Wilson spoke of the time, not far distant, when these "counsels of plain men" would come to replace the "counsels of sophisticated men of affairs" as the best means of securing world peace. Then the statesmen of the world would be forced to heed the "common clarified thought," or they would be broken.

These views constituted a preliminary version of Wilson's plan for an alternative system of world politics, which had begun to take shape in his mind even before war broke out in Europe. Wilson's schoolmasterish language was equal to his vision as he took on what his critics called his "papal role" in dispensing a humanitarian theology. "I do not know that there will ever be a declaration of independence or grievances for mankind," he told an audience at Independence Hall in Philadelphia in 1914, scarcely a week before the outbreak of war, "but I believe that if any such document is ever drawn it will be drawn in the spirit of the American Declaration of Independence, and that America has lifted high the light which will shine unto all generations and guide the feet of mankind to the goal of justice and liberty and peace." The president, noted the acid-tongued editors of *The New Republic* magazine, uttered nothing that might sound trivial at the Last Judgment.

The first fruits of this Wilsonian "missionary" spirit were bitter ones for the promoters of dollar diplomacy. Wilson quickly dashed the hopes of the outgoing Taft administration for continued investment in China by rejecting a scheme for railroad financing as a violation of Chinese sovereignty. In the delicate negotiations over the Panama Canal tolls, he argued that American exemption from payment showed a "dishonorable attitude," and at the risk of dividing his own party he secured a repeal. Then in October 1913, in an address in Mobile, Alabama, that became famous, he completed the reversal of dollar diplomacy by promising to emancipate Latin America from its "subordination" to "foreign enterprise."

**Intervention in Mexico**

Yet in Latin America, where United States business interests were real and compelling, Wilson found it impossible to reverse his predecessors' policy of intervention. His formal disavowal of American interference ended in bitter irony. In fact, under Wilson the United States intervened in the affairs of its neighbors more often than ever before. There was a military occupation of Haiti in 1915; financial supervision in the Dominican Republic in 1916; renewed controls in Cuba in 1917; and minor meddling in behalf of American investors throughout the Caribbean. Moralistic though he frequently was, Wilson was not blind to the operation of economic motives nor deaf to the appeals of American entrepreneurs. His difficulties in Latin America resulted in large part from his tendency to identify the beneficent workings of American capital with the welfare of "the submerged eighty-five per cent" of native populations, to whom he wanted to bring the blessings of parliamentary democracy.

Wilson's theories of moral diplomacy were tested by events in Mexico and were found inadequate. In 1911, following a long period of oppressive rule, Mexican dictator Porfirio Díaz was overthrown by moderate constitutionalists led by Francisco Madero. The new government received prompt recognition from the Taft administration. Then, less than two years later, Madero himself fell victim to a counterrevolutionary coup directed by one of his lieutenants, Victoriano Huerta, who murdered his former chief and seized the presidency. This was the situation confronting Wilson as he took office.

Outraged by Huerta's brutality, Wilson lost no time in denouncing him as a thug and a butcher, and refused to recognize his government. Wilson's refusal to grant recognition rested partly on genuine moral revulsion but also on the knowledge that Britain had recognized Huerta's dictatorship in the hope of gaining further economic concessions. Wilson meant to put an end to Britain's pretensions by toppling Huerta. Although economic and strategic concerns usually appeared on the fringes of Wilson's moral vision, they were never quite out of sight. He continued to insist that the United States must never abandon morality for expediency. But in Mexico, profits for American investors and parliamentary democracy for the Mexican people seemed to him wholly compatible.

Wilson was determined to replace Huerta with the moderate rule of Venustiano Carranza, another constitutionalist who had succeeded in rallying popular opposition to the dictator. Wilson seized the occasion for overthrowing Huerta when a boatload of American sailors was arrested and unlawfully detained in Tampico. The president demanded an immediate apology. When Huerta predictably refused to concede to a government that had refused to recognize him, Wilson ordered the occupation of Vera Cruz, an exercise that cost the lives of nineteen Americans and a great many more Mexicans. Under heavy pressure from the United States, and besieged by the forces of Carranza's constitutionalists, Huerta resigned and fled to Spain in 1914. Yet Carranza's liberal regime was no more willing to tolerate American intervention than the deposed dictator

**Mexican-American Relations, 1916–17**

*Pancho Villa's (left) raid on a New Mexico town and his murder of American citizens called for a U.S. punitive expedition led by General John J. Pershing (below).*

had been. Only a timely offer by the so-called ABC Powers (Argentina, Brazil, and Chile) to mediate the dispute allowed Wilson to withdraw American forces and save face.

The second act of the Mexican crisis opened with the attempt of Pancho Villa, a bandit leader and an unsavory associate of Carranza, to overthrow his chief and take power for himself by provoking war with the United States. Wilson very nearly obliged him. On January 10, 1916, Villa and his band stopped a train at Santa Ysabel in the northern provinces, took seventeen Americans off, and shot sixteen of them. Then in March, Villa raided the tiny New Mexico town of Columbus, burned it to the ground, and killed nineteen more American citizens. Wilson responded, as Villa had hoped he would, by dispatching General John J. Pershing and his troops on a punitive expedition. Pershing chased the bandit chief some three hundred miles back into Mexico without managing to catch him. Carranza demanded the immediate withdrawal of Pershing's expeditionary force. Faced with the near certainty of war with Germany, Wilson could only comply. In 1917, as Villa roamed the Mexican countryside and an unstable Carranza government lurched toward still another constitutional crisis, Wilson had nothing to show for his five-year labors. Now, however, his attention was fixed on Europe.

**War in Europe**   In the summer of 1914 World War I broke out in Europe. When Serbian nationalists assassinated the heir of the multinational Austro-Hungarian empire in June 1914, Austria-Hungary decided to crush its troublesome small neighbor, Serbia. Russia, as Serbia's protector, warned Austria-Hungary not to attack and began to mobilize its vast armies. Germany, which regarded Austria-Hungary as its sole dependable ally, demanded that Russia halt its mobilization; when the Russian tsar refused, Germany declared war on August 1. Germany then demanded that Russia's ally, France, give assurances that it would not come to Russia's aid; and when these assurances were not offered, Germany declared war on France on August 3. Germany promptly set its military plan in motion by striking a heavy blow in the west to knock out France before the slow-moving Russian armies could do serious harm in the east. The German plan involved an invasion of France through neutral Belgium. On August 4, when Germany attacked Belgium, Britain declared war on Germany. The German armies in the west drove deeply into northern France, but Paris was saved, and by the late fall of 1914 the war had settled down to a bloody stalemate on the Western Front. After a Russian offensive against Germany and Austria-Hungary failed, a similar stalemate developed in eastern Europe. Meanwhile Japan entered the war in order to seize Germany's Pacific islands and holdings in China. By 1915 Italy had joined the anti-German coalition, and Bulgaria and Turkey had taken Germany's side.

The outbreak of war caught the Wilson administration and the entire United States by surprise. At first the news that Austria was threatening tiny Serbia evoked little more than the traditional American sympathy for the underdog.

Because neither European nor American diplomats yet realized the scope of the coming catastrophe, it was not difficult for Wilson to declare American neutrality and to call on all citizens to remain "impartial in thought as well as in action." Behind the proclamation of neutrality lay the president's conviction that the war would be a short one that would end in a settlement that the United States, from its Olympian station above the battle, could help arrange. And behind this unwarranted assumption lay still another belief—that America could play an effective role in creating a new moral order.

As the war dragged into its second year, all of Wilson's hopes for remodeling the world of power politics came to hinge on a doctrine of neutrality that itself rested on two misconceptions. First, developments quickly showed that the United States was not and could not be unconcerned with the outcome of the war. As shrewd observers had noted before the war broke out, Britain had directly contributed to American growth and well-being by upholding the European balance of power throughout the entire nineteenth century. And Germany, at least since 1890, had consistently threatened American security with a belligerent new diplomacy, an arms buildup, and a frightening doctrine of militarism. An Anglo-German conflict was thus bound to affect the United States in crucial ways.

The first year of the war drove this lesson home. Britain increasingly monopolized direct access to information about the war and supplied the American press with a constant stream of accounts (most of them greatly exaggerated) of German "atrocities." Except for many German Americans and Irish Americans, ordinary people in the United States came to view the war in pro-Allied, anti-German terms, even if they did not favor actual American entry. The British skillfully manipulated their propaganda advantage until the president and his advisers came to argue, as one of them put it, that "Germany must not be permitted to win this war." By 1915 the administration began, not always consciously, to act on that assumption. The American economy was placed at the disposal of the Allies, who, despite the embarrassing presence on their side of Imperial Russia, were presumed to be fighting autocracy and militarism in the name of democracy and freedom. The government proclaimed trade with the Allies "legal and welcome." When Allied credit soon evaporated, American bankers rushed to the rescue with credits and loans that totaled $2.5 billion by the time the United States entered the war in 1917. On the other hand, there were virtually no American wartime investments in Germany. Wilson continued to press both Britain and Germany for a settlement of the war, but when neither side agreed he tended to excuse the former and blame the latter for the disastrous military stalemate.

**The *Lusitania* Incident**
The second misconception underlying Wilson's doctrine of neutrality stemmed from his failure to understand the logic of total war or to acknowledge the effect of modern technology. The submarine had made the traditional rights of neutrals obsolete. As they grappled for an economic stranglehold on each other, both

**"He Kept Us Out of War"**
*Wilson campaigns for re-election
in 1916.*

combatants had to resort to novel practices that were clear violations of the established rules of war. Britain extended the right of naval search to new lengths and established a blockade that virtually extinguished the rights of neutrals. Yet American diplomatic exchange with Britain settled into a predictable pattern of violation, protest, discussion, and eventual resumption of the objectionable practice.

With Germany, on the other hand, the exchange grew brittle, and Wilson's language became increasingly blunt. The Germans' use of submarines, which struck without warning and made no provision for the safety of passengers and crew, touched a raw nerve in the American people. When in May 1915 a German U-boat torpedoed without warning the British liner *Lusitania* with the loss of 128 American lives, Wilson initiated an angry dialogue that grew more and more strident in the next year and a half. Germany quite correctly pointed out that the ship was carrying munitions, but that fact hardly weakened Wilson's determination to apply the old rules. For the president, the sinking of the *Lusitania* was proof of the practical impossibility of using submarines "without disregarding those rules of fairness, reason, justice, and humanity, which all modern opinion regards as imperative." In deciding to hold Germany "strictly accountable," Wilson put the United States on a collision course. Secretary of State Bryan, realizing that Wilson's policy was no longer truly neutral, resigned in protest.

In the meantime, following the *Lusitania* incident, Germany said it would comply with Wilson's terms. Then in 1916 the German attack on the unarmed French passenger ship *Sussex* in the English Channel resulted in injury to American citizens, and the meaning of "strict accountability" suddenly became clear to the president. Submarine warfare, he informed Germany, "of necessity, because of the very character of the vessels employed," was "incompatible" with the "sacred immunities of noncombatants." Unless the Kaiser's government agreed to abandon its methods forthwith, the United States would have no choice but to sever relations. Germany agreed to discontinue the practice, but only if the United States could force Britain to lift the blockade. Until then the German government reserved the right to take back its pledge. The president's options were dwindling fast.

Wilson's growing indignation reflected another, more personal, anxiety. For three years he had continued to pile a heavy load of moral principles onto the conventional concept of neutral rights. Now he was forced to admit that the United States might not be able to impose its will on warring Europe without joining the Allies. A nation that, as he had said, had been "too proud to fight" and that had reelected him on the slogan "He kept us out of war" now faced the prospect of securing a "peace without victory" only by becoming a participant. As he became aware of this, Wilson began to redefine America's mission as nothing less than the building of a system of collective security to replace the collapsed system of balance of power. If compelled to fight, the United States would fight for utopia.

**A New World Order**    In January 1917, a week before Germany announced its decision to resume unrestricted submarine warfare, Wilson described his vision of a new world order to the Senate. The United States, prepared by "the very principles and purposes" of its humanitarian policy, must rebuild the machinery of diplomacy. Its terms for peace must "win the approval of mankind" and not merely "serve the several interests and immediate aims of the nations engaged." As an integral part of the peace settlement, Wilson proposed the establishment of a perpetual league of peaceful nations. This league should be a collective instrument that would be "so much greater than the force of any nation now engaged or any alliance hitherto projected" that governments and their leaders would instinctively bend to its dictates. The future of the world would thus come to depend not on a balance of power, but on a community of opinion; not on "organized rivalries," but on "organized peace." Wilson proposed, in short, to concentrate the moral force of peoples themselves who, with open covenants openly arrived at, would enforce their collective will for national self-determination, democratic government, and lasting peace. To skeptical senators, particularly those in the Republican ranks, Wilson explained that his were at once "American principles" and "the principles of all mankind."

A week later the German imperial government renewed its submarine attacks in a desperate gamble to win the war before the United States could enter. In March, German submarines without warning sank four unarmed American merchantmen, and on April 2, 1917, Wilson appeared before a joint session of Congress to request that it accept the war that had been "thrust" upon the United States. By a vote of 82 to 6 in the Senate and 373 to 50 in the House, Congress agreed to the presidential request.

United States citizens would learn from a year and a half of war and another year of peacemaking that their country had arrived at a position of world power that very few of them could have envisioned thirty years earlier. The nation had gone to war with Spain on the flimsiest of pretexts and had built an empire on its victory. But in the intervening years most Americans, far from embracing imperial responsibilities, had neglected the chores of maintaining an empire. Except in their own hemisphere, they had forgotten their regenerative mission. Now, as their president called on them to fight another and infinitely greater war, they turned to him for a sense of direction and for a definition of their moral commitment.

For his part the president, having determined that war was the only option left open to him, made a prophecy to the nation and a private confession in considering his course. "We are at the beginning of an age," he told the country, "in which it will be insisted that the same standards of conduct and responsibility for wrong done shall be observed among nations and their governments that are observed among individual citizens of civilized states." But privately, in the solitude of the White House on the eve of his appearance before Congress, he admitted to fears about the unintended and uncontrollable effects of going to war. "Once lead this people into war," he told Frank Cobb, the editor of the *New York World,* " and they'll forget there ever was such a thing as tolerance. To fight you must be brutal and ruthless, and the spirit of ruthless brutality will enter into the very fibre of our national life, infecting Congress, the courts, the policeman on the beat, the man in the streets." The meaning of Wilson's prophecy of a new international morality awaited the outcome of the war, but his prediction of the domestic dangers involved in fighting it soon proved all too accurate.

## CHRONOLOGY

**1895** United States intervenes in boundary dispute between Britain and Venezuela as Secretary of State Richard Olney declares nation "practically sovereign on this continent."
Spain sends troops to quell Cuban revolution.

**1896** Cuban rebel leader Maceo murdered, resulting in American popular support for Cuba.
William McKinley elected president.

**1897** A letter from Spanish minister

Depuy de Lôme, in which he calls McKinley "weak" and "a would-be politician," is intercepted, worsening American and Spanish relations.
U.S. battleship *Maine* explodes in Havana harbor.

**1898** Spanish-American War; United States acquires Philippines, Puerto Rico, and Guam, and annexes Hawaii.

**1899** Hay's "Open Door" notes to world powers, calling for "equal and impartial trade" in China

and preservation of "Chinese territorial and administrative" integrity.
Senate ratifies peace treaty with Spain.
United States, Germany, and Great Britain partition Samoa.

**1900** Foraker Act establishes civil government in Puerto Rico.
Organic Act incorporates Hawaii as a territory of the United States.
McKinley reelected president, defeating Bryan once again.
Boxer Rebellion in China.

**1901** Platt Amendment authorizes U.S. intervention in Cuba.
Theodore Roosevelt becomes president after McKinley assassinated.
Hay-Pauncefote Treaty with Great Britain gives United States sole right to build, control, and maintain neutrality of an isthmian canal in Central America.
Philippine Organic Act passed, making Philippine islands an unorganized territory of the United States.

**1902** United States returns civil government to Republic of Cuba.

**1903** Hay-Herran Treaty with Republic of Colombia, giving United States ninety-nine-year lease on Canal Zone, is rejected by Colombia.
Roosevelt aids revolt in Panama.
Hay-Bunau-Varilla Treaty gives United States full sovereignty in Canal Zone.
United States–Cuba reciprocity treaty forms close economic ties between both countries.

**1904** Roosevelt Corollary to Monroe Doctrine.

Roosevelt elected, defeating Democrat Alton B. Parker and Socialist Eugene V. Debs.

**1905** Roosevelt mediates in Russo-Japanese War.

**1906** American troops intervene in Cuba to restore order.
Algeciras Conference with Roosevelt's help settles French-German conflict in Morocco.

**1908** William Howard Taft elected president, defeating Bryan and Debs.
Root-Takahira Agreement; United States recognizes Japan's interests in Manchuria.

**1909** Taft inaugurates "Dollar Diplomacy" in China and Latin America.
United States intervenes in Haitian and Nicaraguan finances.

**1911** Marines sent to Nicaragua.

**1912** Woodrow Wilson elected president, defeating Republican regular William Howard Taft, progressive "Bull Moose" Theodore Roosevelt, and Socialist Eugene V. Debs.

**1914** World War I begins; Wilson declares American neutrality.
Wilson orders occupation of Vera Cruz, Mexico.
Panama Canal opened.

**1915** United States troops occupy Haiti.
United States recognizes Carranza government in Mexico.
Germans declare unrestricted submarine warfare and sink *Lusitania* with loss of American lives.
Preparedness movement.

| | |
|---|---|
| **1916**　Wilson reelected, narrowly defeating Charles Evans Hughes. House-Grey Memorandum on United States' efforts for negotiated peace. American troops occupy Dominican Republic. | General John J. Pershing's expedition into Mexico. |
| | **1917**　Germans resume unrestricted submarine warfare and United States enters war. Purchase of Danish Virgin Islands. |

## Suggested Readings

The boundaries of post-1890 American foreign policy are established in two critical surveys. George F. Kennan, *American Diplomacy, 1900–1950* (1951), points to consistently unprofessional and uninformed leaders as the chief difficulty, while William Appleman Williams, *The Tragedy of American Diplomacy* (1959), cites economic expansion as the source of a peculiar kind of American imperialism. Robert E. Osgood, *Ideals and Self-Interest in America's Foreign Relations* (1953), evaluates the positions of both parties to the great debate over ends and means in the conduct of American diplomacy. Richard W. Leopold, *The Growth of American Foreign Policy* (1962), provides an excellent survey of the development of American interests in the rest of the world, as does Foster R. Dulles, *America's Rise to World Power, 1898–1954* (1955). For an extended review of American anti-imperialism before World War I, see E. Berkeley Tompkins, *Anti-Imperialism in the United States: The Great Debate, 1890–1920* (1970). For an analysis of expansionist fervor from the 1890s through World War II, consult Emily S. Rosenberg, *Spreading the American Dream: American Economic and Cultural Expansion, 1890–1945* (1982). Robert Seager II, *Alfred Thayer Mahan* (1977), is a good introduction to the most determined and articulate of American expansionists.

The origins of American expansionism are critically but carefully examined in Walter LaFeber, *The New Empire: An Interpretation of American Expansion, 1860–1898* (1963). The best account of the diplomatic crisis leading to the Spanish-American War is Ernest R. May, *Imperial Democracy: The Emergence of America as a Great Power* (1961). Robert L. Beisner, *The Anti-Imperialists, 1898–1900* (1968), assesses the arguments and the futile activities of the opponents of expansionism. Leon Wolff, *Little Brown Brother* (1961), gives an outraged account of the Philippine insurrection and the American pacification program. For a fuller and more balanced account of pacification and American colonial policy in the Philippines, see Stuart Creighton Miller, *"Benevolent Assimilation": The American Conquest of the Philippines, 1899–1903* (1982). Richard E. Welch, *Response to Imperialism: The United States and the Philippine-American War* (1979), concentrates on war in the islands, while David R. Trask, *The War with Spain in 1898* (1981), surveys the entire contest.

Areas of growing American interest and control in international affairs have been covered in a number of excellent monographs: Merze Tate, *The United States and the Hawaiian Kingdom* (1965); Charles Vevier, *The United States and China, 1906–1913* (1955); Paul A. Varg, *The Making of a Myth: The United States and China, 1899–1912;* Warren Cohen, *America's Response to China* (1971); Michael Hunt, *The Making of a Special Relationship: The United States and China to 1914* (1983); Charles E. Neu, *The Troubled Encounter: The United States and Japan* (1975); Howard F. Cline, *The United States and Mexico* (1953); Samuel F. Bemis, *The Latin American Policy of the United States* (1967).

On Theodore Roosevelt's foreign policy, see Howard K. Beale, *Theodore Roosevelt and the Rise of America to World Power* (1956), and the more recent Raymond A. Esthus, *Theodore Roosevelt and the International Rivalries* (1970). Dwight C. Miner, *Fight for the Panama Route* (1966), tells a complicated story well, and Robert A. Hart, *The Great White Fleet: Its Voyage Around the World* (1965), is a highly readable account of Roosevelt's colorful gesture. Walter V. Scholes and Marie V. Scholes, *The Foreign Policies of the Taft Administration* (1970), analyzes the workings of dollar diplomacy, and Dana G. Munroe, *Intervention and Dollar Diplomacy in the Caribbean, 1900–1921* (1964), examines its consequences in Latin America.

The fullest discussion of Woodrow Wilson's diplomacy from a presidential point of view is to be found in the volumes of Link's *Wilson*. P. Edward Haley, *Revolution and Intervention: The Diplomacy of Taft and Wilson with Mexico, 1910–1917* (1970), is an even-handed assessment of Mexican policy, as is Robert Freeman Smith, *The U.S. and Revolutionary Nationalism in Mexico* (1972), for the later period. Robert E. Quirk, *An Affair of Honor: Woodrow Wilson and the Occupation of Veracruz* (1962), criticizes the president for his misguided actions in that unfortunate affair. John M. Cooper, Jr., *The Warrior and the Priest* (1983), presents contrasting portraits of Roosevelt and Wilson with their differing views of the conduct of both domestic politics and foreign policy.

Neutrality and American intervention in World War I fascinated a depression generation reluctantly preparing for another war and produced a number of highly critical accounts of American intervention, the best of which is Walter Millis, *The Road to War* (1935). Among the best of more recent accounts are Ernest R. May, *The World War and American Isolation, 1914–1917* (1959); John M. Cooper, Jr., *The Vanity of Power: American Isolation and the First World War, 1914–1917* (1969); Ross Gregory, *The Origins of American Intervention in the First World War* (1971); and Daniel M. Smith, *The Great Departure: The United States in World War I, 1914–1920* (1965).

# 27

# *Progressivism and the Great War*

✒

BY THE time the United States entered the war in April 1917, the European powers were rapidly approaching exhaustion. After three years of stalemate, Germany was suffering from starvation as a result of Britain's naval blockade, as well as a collapse of civilian morale. Austria-Hungary managed to continue the war only by imposing martial law. Russia was crippled by astronomical losses that had led to the overthrow of the tsarist regime in March 1917, and now it stood on the brink of a second revolution that would bring Lenin's Bolsheviks to power by the end of the year. France, its national will shattered, faced widespread mutiny in its armies. Britain, having sacrificed an entire generation of young men to German machine guns since 1914, was beset with severe manpower shortages both at home and in the field.

## Slaughter on the Western Front

The original prediction of both sides—Germany's hopes for a six-week war and the Allies' plans for rolling back the enemy on the vast Western and Eastern fronts—had long since been buried under mounds of casualties. Shared strategic obsessions with artillery barrages and with massed infantry assaults on entrenched positions had created a war of appalling senselessness and butchery. Two million casualties on the Western Front in 1916 had failed to move the line of advance for either side, and the war had descended once again into the trenches, which stretched in an unbroken line from the sea to the mountains. A week after President Wilson asked for a declaration of war in April 1917, the British launched still another frontal assault in Belgium on the Ypres sector of the front; in five days they gained only 7,000 yards, at the terrible cost of 160,000 dead and wounded.

**"Over There"**
*American aviators prepare to take off in a French-built Caudron in France, 1918.*

**Saying Good-Bye...**
*War Department photograph, 1917.*

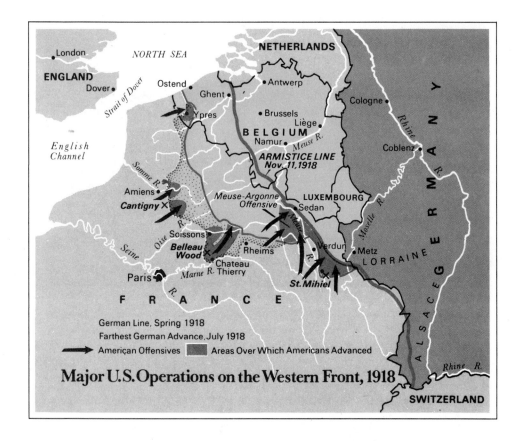

Major U.S. Operations on the Western Front, 1918

Although the United States entered the war late and suffered proportionately fewer losses, the meaning of the slaughter lingered in the American imagination for a generation. In a scene in F. Scott Fitzgerald's *Tender Is the Night,* one of the characters leads a party of sightseers across the Somme Valley after the war. "See that little stream," he says. "We could walk to it in two minutes. It took the British a whole month to walk to it—a whole empire walking very slowly, dying in front and pushing forward behind. And another empire walked very slowly backward a few inches a day, leaving the dead like a million bloody rugs." American soldiers in the last year of the war followed the footsteps of their British and French predecessors. In joining the Allies the United States committed its forces to a war in which the ultimate loser was the side that won the most battles. Woodrow Wilson's hopes for a just peace died along with more than 100,000 American soldiers on the Western Front.

It took eight months for American troops to join the fighting on the Western Front in effective numbers, and it was nearly a year before they were decisively engaged in helping to turn back the final German offensive. In the meantime the Allied cause hung in the balance. In November 1917 Lenin and the Bolsheviks overthrew the provisional revolutionary government of Russia, established a party dictatorship, and took Russia out of the war. Russia's withdrawal released badly needed German divisions for a last offensive on the Western Front. In the spring drive along the Somme beginning in March 1918, the Germans routed the British and penned up the French, but without making a decisive breakthrough.

In May and June the American Second Division was dispatched to the Marne River, where it bolstered sagging French defenses. In the first big American engagements of the war, United States forces halted a German advance at Chateau-Thierry and slowly drove the enemy out of Belleau Wood. These American actions were only preliminaries to the great Allied counteroffensive, which in late summer began to push the German army relentlessly back toward its frontier. By September the American commander, General John J. Pershing, who had stubbornly held out for an independent command, had over half a million men at his disposal, a number that would double by the end of the war two months later. In October, Pershing, in conjunction with British and French offensives elsewhere along the line, opened a massive American drive out of the Argonne Forest aimed at the railhead at Sedan—the last sustained American action of the war.

On November 3 Austria-Hungary collapsed, and on the same day the German navy mutinied at its main base, Kiel, raising the specter of another communist revolution. Six days later a general strike in Germany, led by the Independent Socialists, forced the Kaiser to abdicate, and a coalition of socialists and liberals proclaimed a republic. Forty-eight hours later the new German republic accepted as the basis for an armistice the peace proposals that Wilson had put forward in January 1918, the Fourteen Points.* The Great War was over.

It was immediately clear that the American entry had brought desperately needed troops and supplies to the Allies at a critical moment. American troops provided the decisive advantage of power needed to win the war. Equally important was the role of the United States in replenishing stockpiles of food and materiel with its "bridge of ships," replacing the merchantmen sunk by German submarines, and experimenting successfully with the convoy system of protecting Allied shipping, which in the last analysis saved the Allies. The American contribution was essential, and it came at a crucial time. Yet despite the provisional German acceptance of the Fourteen Points as the agenda for peacemaking, the American war effort had not wiped out national fears and hatreds embodied in wartime secret agreements and arrangements among the Allies, nor had it established the moral climate, either at home or in Europe, that Wilson knew was essential to lasting peace.

With the American entrance, a conflict that had already grown fiercely ideological became a crusade for democracy and national rebirth. All the powers had secured control over the actions and opinions of their civilian populations as they accepted the logic of total war. But the United States entry completed an

---

*For the Fourteen Points, see pp. 315–17.

**American Soldiers in France**
*Elderly French couple welcomes American doughboys.*

ideological shift for the Allies by defining the war in moral as well as political terms, as a struggle of the forces of peace and democracy against the dark powers of militarism. In announcing his Fourteen Points, and by explaining American war aims as "the right of those who submit to authority to have a voice in their own government" and "a universal dominion of right by . . . a concert of free peoples," Wilson unconsciously hardened the resolve of his allies to seek an unconditional surrender and a punishing peace. Perhaps the greatest irony of World War I lay in the president's determination to inject into it a democratic ideology that in the end would make his own role as the evenhanded peacemaker impossible.

Total war also imposed an organizational logic on the participants, all of whom were forced to adjust to the national need for centralization and control. Early in the war Germany recruited civilian administrators for its War Raw Materials Department, which established efficient mechanisms for allocating manpower, arms, and equipment. Britain organized its dwindling resources under the Defense of the Realm Act, which provided for full mobilization of all available manpower. France, which had lost its northern industrial provinces for

**The Kaiser and His Victims**
*The American entrance into the war brought a surge of anti-German propaganda.*

the duration, used the powers of government to relocate factories and regulate food production. Once in the war the United States followed the same pattern in building a war machine, enlisting civilians in the war effort, and improvising the bureaucratic controls demanded by the emergency. By the time the war ended in November 1918, Wilson's administration had completed an organizational revolution and had brought the power of government into nearly every phase of American life.

## War and the Health of the State

For some progressives the coming of the war seemed a heaven-sent opportunity to realize the American promise. The war, they confidently predicted, would bring genuine national unity and an end to class and ethnic division. It would discredit dangerous radicalism by giving the nation's citizens a new spirit of patriotism. The demands of war would also destroy all selfish materialism and preoccupation with profits and replace both with the higher goals of service and sacrifice. National preparedness and mobilization, central features of the New Nationalism, would foster moral virtue and civic purity in soldiers and civilians alike. Those progressives who continued to define their basic purpose as creating a new American morality and citizenship saw in the impending war effort the outlines of what one of them called a "true national collectivism" based on efficiency, social control, high-mindedness, and revived moral purpose.

On a more practical plane many more progressives responded enthusiastically to the organizational and reform challenges that were furnished by the war. Those reformers who saw their work as a form of moral cleansing—of vice, alcoholism, and prostitution—viewed the war as a chance to purify democracy at home while saving it abroad.

World War I drew to the political surface darker currents of coercion and repression that had been part of progressive reform from the beginning— programs for checking unacceptable behavior and encouraging healthy attitudes in American citizens. Old progressives like Theodore Roosevelt who had been born during or soon after the Civil War carried into the twentieth century Victorian notions of propriety and righteousness, which they continued to define as "natural" and "normal." They were concerned with preserving "manliness" and fostering the "strenuous life," and they worried openly about the "feminization" of American life. Moral progressives had long targeted the saloon and the house of prostitution, and they sought remedies in a national prohibition campaign and federal laws like the Mann Act (1910). Some progressive believers in Americanization proposed strict limits on immigration and stringent literacy tests to exclude recently arrived immigrants and African Americans from the political process. Other reformers discovered in the science of eugenics and programs for sterilization a method for controlling breeding patterns of Americans and presumably eliminating the "unfit," however defined. A few progressives capitulated to the illogic of popularizers of racism like Madison Grant, whose *The Passing of the Great Race* (1916) predicted the decline of civilization as a result of the loss of "Nordic" purity. Many progressives also worried about the enervating effects of movies, vaudeville, amusement parks, and dance halls in seemingly weakening the fiber and sapping the vitality of the lower orders. All these prescriptions and programs stemmed from a progressive conviction of the need for more effective devices for securing what sociologists now began to call "social control." The coming of war simply opened the doors to such fears of cultural pluralism and political permissiveness, and strengthened the urge in moral progressives to direct their fellow citizens into the paths of civic righteousness.

The war advanced the progressives' hopes in a number of important ways. The preparedness campaign furthered the ideal of universal military service as a school for citizenship. Americanization programs aimed at controlling the immigrant took on new life. Prohibitionist hopes soared, and women's suffrage suddenly seemed possible. City planners, social-justice workers, child-labor reformers, and other progressive humanitarians warmed to the prospects of a domestic reformation in the midst of a foreign war.

The war seemed to hold the greatest promise for progressives in administration and public service—those reformers who sought to join Roosevelt's New Nationalist emphasis on efficiency, administrative centralization, and executive power with Wilson's New Freedom faith in fact finding, voluntary cooperation, and democratic participation. "We must speak, act, and serve together," Wilson reminded the nation. Efficiency quickly became the watchword for a new managerial elite that descended on Washington with proposals for a planned war effort. Wesley C. Mitchell, a professor-turned-bureaucrat who joined the Division of Planning and Statistics of the War Industries Board, explained why government service appealed to professionals and businessmen, many of whom signed up for the duration. "Indeed I am in a mood to demand excitement and make it up when it doesn't offer of itself. I am ready to concoct a new plan for running the universe at any minute." Efficiency as the dominant progressive ideal fixed itself to the image of the war machine turning out men and materiel automatically without the interference of politics and partisanship.

**Regulations and Controls**

American performance fell far short of the progressive ideal. The most urgent task for Wilson's war state was mobilizing industry. Even before war was declared, Congress established the Council of National Defense, an advisory body composed of cabinet members and industrial and labor leaders, which was charged with taking an inventory of national resources. Out of the council's preliminary survey came the War Industries Board, which attempted—at first unsuccessfully—to control production, arrange purchases, allocate scarce resources, and regulate labor relations. The War Industries Board failed to function effectively until Congress overhauled it, conferring near-dictatorial powers on the president. In turn Wilson brought Wall Street banker Bernard Baruch to Washington early in 1918 to head the agency and gave him sweeping powers to establish priorities and increase production. Baruch's agency, however, was hampered in its work by inadequate information. By the end of the war, the War Industries Board was just beginning to unsnarl the problems of production.

In addition to regulating industry, Wilson moved quickly to bring food, fuel, and transportation under control. To head the Food Administration he appointed Herbert Hoover, who used his powers under the Lever Act to extend government control over staples. Poor harvests complicated Hoover's problems, and he was forced to experiment with price fixing and a massive consumer-education campaign to limit consumption. His strategy succeeded, first doubling and then tripling the amount of food that could be exported to starving Europe. Hoover's efficient management of food production represented the chief accomplishment of wartime progressivism. The Fuel Administration, headed by progressive Harry A. Garfield, followed Hoover's lead in the Food Administration by seeking to increase coal production with price supports fixed to guarantee profits, and, less successfully, with schemes for systematizing production and distribution on a national scale.

Managing the nation's railroads proved even more difficult than increasing food production. At first Wilson experimented unsuccessfully with a voluntary system under the Railroads War Board. Attempts to increase the number of

**Women on the Home Front**
*Women contributed significantly to the war effort with various kinds of work.*

railroad cars and to equalize traffic broke down completely in December 1917. Congress demanded an investigation, out of which came a revised United States Railroad Administration with effective power. Gradually the Railroad Administration extricated itself from confusion, and by the end of the war it too, like the War Industries Board, was beginning to function effectively. Shipping presented Wilson's administration with its most severe problem. Here the challenge was deceptively simple—to build or commandeer ships faster than the German U-boats could sink them. The solution, the Emergency Fleet Corporation—originally an offshoot of the United States Shipping Board—failed. Divided leadership impeded effective planning, and the heads of the competing agencies spent half the war quarreling over priorities and programs. Wilson finally removed them and put the competing interests under a single director. By September 1918 the Emergency Fleet Corporation had built only 500,000 tons of new shipping, less than German submarines had sunk in an average month early in 1917.

The Wilson administration's labor policy was aimed at including the workingman in the wartime partnership with business and government—as a junior partner, but one entitled to a fair share of war prosperity. Yet here too success came slowly. Not until April 1918 did Wilson move to establish the National War Labor Board, with power to hear and settle disputes between labor and management. Under the direction of former President Taft and progressive lawyer Frank P. Walsh, the National War Labor Board heard over a thousand cases during the war involving three-quarters of a million workers. In general, Wilson's labor policy was a generous one that was designed to tolerate, if not encourage, unions; to establish an eight-hour workday; to avert strikes through the use of arbitration; and to sanction limited increases in wages.

Overall, the wartime effort in planning was hardly an unqualified success. Lacking an effectual bureaucracy at the outset, Wilson's administration necessarily fumbled and improvised, dispersing rather than centralizing power through a host of overlapping and competing agencies. Not surprisingly, confusion and inefficiency resulted as bureaucrats painfully groped their way toward centralization, learning slowly from their many mistakes. When the armistice came, the American war machine was just beginning to produce at a level approaching full capacity.

The most important consequence of the national war effort was the completion of the alliance between big business and the government. This collaboration was inevitable, because it was only from within the consolidated national industries that the government could recruit needed managerial talent. To Washington, accordingly, came the leaders of business and industry, primed with patriotism but also determined to advance the interests of their sector—which they quickly identified with the national good. Wilson's appointment of Bernard Baruch was only the most visible symbol of this new alliance. From the ranks of railroad management and from big steel, the machine tool industry, finance, and banking came the self-appointed leaders of national mobilization. Along with expertise all of them brought demands for stability and predictability in their industries, which could be furnished only by the government.

**Corporate War Profits**

Big business profited from the war directly and indirectly—directly, in the form of arrangements like the cost-plus contract, which guaranteed high levels of profit; indirectly, in the education that business leaders received in the uses of government power. Labor fared less well. The cost of living, soaring on the crest of wartime inflation, more than doubled between 1913 and 1920 and cut deeply into wage increases. Farmers benefited from a substantial rise in real income during the war, a gain that would quickly disappear with the return of peace. But corporate profits skyrocketed in the years between 1914 and 1919, increasing threefold by the time the United States entered the war and leveling off in the following years at an annual increase of 30 percent. Gains in the steel industry ranged from 30 percent to 300 percent. In the lumber industry they averaged 17 percent; in oil, 21 percent; in copper, 34 percent. Even with the moderate excess-profits tax and steeper levies on higher incomes, the war made an estimated 42,000 millionaires. If the progressive programs of Theodore Roosevelt and Woodrow Wilson had sought, at least in part, a fairer distribution of American wealth, the war tended to reverse the effects of their efforts by piling up profits in the upper reaches of the economy.

The progressive plans for constructing an effective system of bureaucratic management also came to little. American governmental bureaucracy in 1917 was still in its infancy. The handful of federal agencies at the policymaking level—the Federal Reserve Board, the Federal Trade Commission, and other fledgling agencies—had not yet fully asserted their powers. Inevitably, the wartime administrative apparatus creaked and strained under the pressures of mobilization. Ambitious reorganizational schemes were never carried out. Programs broke down. Authority almost always overlapped, and agencies collided over matters of precedence and priority. By a method marked by more trial and error than most progressives expected, the United States moved hesitantly from administrative chaos to at least some bureaucratic order at war's end.

**Repression and Hysteria**

If the gains for the federal bureaucracy brought by the war proved partial and in some cases temporary, the same was not true of the wartime campaign for loyalty and uniformity. Here the original progressive dream of an aroused and patriotic citizenry turned into a chauvinist nightmare, and the country experienced a crisis of civil liberties.

The American people responded to war with a spontaneous burst of nationalist fervor, which triggered a chain reaction of repression and hysteria. In the first few months of the war, hundreds of thousands of self-styled patriots banded together in vigilantelike groups bearing impressive titles—the American Defense Society, the National Security League, the American Anti-Anarchy

JOIN THE NAVY
America's new prestige
in world affairs will
mean a greater Navy
BE A PART OF IT

AMERICA ADVANCES

Apply at Navy Recruiting Station:

U. S. NAVY RECRUITING S
LAW BUILDING
9TH & MARKET ST
WILMINGTON. · DE

U. S. NAVY RECRUITING STATION:
LAW BUILDING

**World War I Recruitment Poster**

Association, even the Boy Spies of America—and dedicated to rooting out heresy wherever they found it. The directors of these grassroots purges were usually leaders in local communities—businessmen, professionals, and merchants—who combined more useful service for the Red Cross and YMCA with the witch-hunting escapades common to superpatriots in any age. Wilson's administration, unable or unwilling to stop these popular excesses, joined in purging dissent. The result was a fevered public uprising against nonconformity of all kinds, and the ruthless suppression of American liberties.

The war hysteria fed a progressive appetite for national unity that had not been offset by a tradition of civil liberties. The central weakness of the progressive program had been the absence of a libertarian concern with protecting basic freedoms, and this absence made a domestic war on liberalism wholly predictable. Patriots and vigilantes, equipped with ropes, whips, and tar and feathers, enjoyed a ritualistic field day complete with flag-kissing ceremonies and forced declarations of loyalty. German Americans, including some prominent persons, were often the targets of this reign of terror. But the victims were mainly marginal people, uneducated or alienated, isolated and without power. In Bisbee, Arizona, the "best" people rounded up some 1,200 striking miners led by the Industrial Workers of the World ("Wobblies"), piled them into freight cars, and hauled them across the state line into the desert, where they were left stranded. In Montana a mob dragged the IWW organizer Frank Little out of his boardinghouse and hanged him from a railroad trestle. Soon the federal government itself joined in the campaign to crush radical dissent: in September 1917 Justice Department agents rounded up 113 officers and organizers of the IWW and impounded five tons of books and pamphlets with which to arraign and convict them.

Out of these acts of suppression came loose national organizations and federations, perversions of the original progressive consumer and reform leagues, dedicated to rooting out subversion and punishing disloyalty. With support from local and state law enforcement agencies, the National Security League and the Council of Defense fixed on new targets—the Non-Partisan League in North Dakota, which aimed at nothing more seditious than interest-group politics, and the People's Council of America for Peace and Democracy, a group of pacifists widely condemned as "traitors and fools." Within six months of Wilson's declaration of war, a rigid censorship, combined with political repression, had reached into the American press, schools and universities, the churches, and even the new movie industry.

**A Pyramid of Repression**

This mass popular reaction formed the base of a pyramid of repression supporting a middle range of official and semiofficial bodies, from citizens' councils to state administrative agencies such as the Minnesota Commission on Public Safety, which became a model for the rest of the country. Other states passed criminal syndicalism laws that were aimed primarily at left-wing dissenters but were also designed as dragnets for a variety of nonconformists. Soon the traditional American distinction between public and private had dissolved in a welter of competing patriotic agencies.

The federal government itself completed the apex of this national system of extralegalism through a number of agencies and activities. The chief agency was the Committee on Public Information, headed by progressive journalist George Creel and charged with mobilizing public opinion behind the war. Creel perfected the progressive technique of moral publicity and encouraged a voluntary censorship program. And he turned to the new public relations industry for a national core of opinion shapers, who launched a propaganda campaign of frightening proportions.

Another weapon in the government's domestic arsenal was an administrative technique inherited from prewar progressivism—deportation of undesirable aliens and radicals. The deportation procedure was a simple administrative process. Not courts but magistrates made the decision to deport undesirable aliens. As a result, maximum freedom was provided for administrators and minimum safeguards for the rights of the accused. This original procedure for the

**The New York Stock Exchange at the Turn of the Century**
*"Wall Street" became the hated symbol of those leftwing opponents of the war and war profiteers.*

swift removal of undesirables had been created by the Immigration Act of 1903, and the war simply gave widened scope for these summary actions.

The federal government's main contributions to the repression of basic liberties were the Espionage Act of 1917 and the Sedition Act of 1918. Like the Federalists' Alien and Sedition Acts of the 1790s,* these laws were twin declarations of bankruptcy by a society that had reached the limits of toleration. The Espionage Act dictated fines of up to $10,000 and twenty years in prison for anyone convicted of causing insubordination, mutiny, or disloyalty in the armed forces by "false reports or false statements." The law also empowered the postmaster general to withhold mailing privileges to newspapers and periodicals that were considered subversive. Wilson's postmaster general, Albert S. Burleson, turned this authority into a formidable weapon against dissent. With Wilson's knowledge, if not always with his approval, Burleson wielded discretionary power with a vengeance in banning socialist periodicals such as *The Masses* and Victor Berger's *Milwaukee Leader;* he even banned a single-tax journal for suggesting that more revenue be raised through taxation.

---

*For the Alien and Sedition Acts, see chapter 10, pp. 329–30.

The Sedition Act of 1918 was designed to close the few loopholes in the Espionage Act through which thousands of "spies" and "traitors" were presumed to have escaped. The new law provided punishment for anyone who should "utter, print, write or publish any disloyal, profane, scurrilous, or abusive language about the form of government in the United States, or the uniform of the Army or Navy" or any sentiments intended to bring the government or the military "into contempt, scorn, contumely, or disrepute."

More than 1,500 Americans were tried and more than 1,000 convicted under these laws. Senator Hiram Johnson pointed out that the government was simply warning, "You shall not criticize anything or anybody in the Government any longer or you shall go to jail." For example, Eugene Debs was convicted and sentenced to ten years in prison under the Sedition Act for telling a socialist audience that the master class causes wars while the subject class fights them. But most of the victims of this heresy hunting were ordinary people guilty of nothing worse than saying that John D. Rockefeller was a son of a bitch who helped start a capitalist war.

**Administrative Agencies**

In part, the war hysteria of the years 1917–19 was simply a deviation, a brief departure from good sense, and a betrayal of progressive ideals. But at a deeper level the excesses were growths—malignant, to be sure—of progressivism itself. Discretionary power vested in administrative agencies—a progressive innovation—provided flexibility and promptness but at the expense of more deliberate regular processes amenable to judicial oversight. The progressive device of administrative government, whose aim was to free policymakers and administrators from constant interference by the legislature, had its merits. But when it was applied to citizens' ideas and opinions rather than to administrative procedures, the new process revealed the evils of government action cut adrift from accountability and control.

At times the war crisis lowered the principle of administrative autonomy to the level of license. In the case of Postmaster General Burleson, for example, even the president was unable to limit misguided enthusiasm and the personal conviction that no American should ever be allowed "to say that this Government got into the war wrong. . . . It is a false statement," Burleson fumed, "a lie, and it will not be permitted." Such arbitrary power lodged either in the federal bureaucracy or in the lower levels of state and local administrations inevitably fostered an alarming national irresponsibility by subjecting opinion and expression to the whims and caprices of petty officials who were freed entirely, as one of them boasted, from "exaggerated sentimentalism [or] a misapplied reverence for legal axioms."

It would have been difficult in any case for Wilson's administration to have curbed the patriotic passions of an American generation preoccupied with rescuing national unity from a vigorous cultural pluralism. But the wartime policy of the federal government amounted to issuing hunting licenses to superpatriots to track down and destroy dissent—in pacifists, liberal reformers, socialists, anarchists, and also in many cultural as well as political radicals opposed to war. These dissenters were not simply outside the mainstream of the war effort. They were part of a more general movement, growing quickly after 1900, of what might be called cultural radicalism—a movement running counter to progressivism with deep roots in America's prewar experience. By 1917 a major shift in the artistic and intellectual life of the country had long been evident in a series of clashes, some symbolic and others real, between an inherited system of truth and the powerful, diverse forces of cultural modernism.

## The Little Rebellion: Progressivism and the Challenge of Culture

On February 17, 1913, the International Exhibition of Modern Painting opened in the cavernous Sixty-ninth Regiment Armory in New York City. To the music of a military band, beneath rafters festooned with huge banners and pine boughs, visitors strolled through a maze of 1,600 paintings, drawings, prints, and pieces of sculpture. The Armory Show, two years in the planning, took for its motto "The New Spirit," which was emblazoned on a mammoth replica of the Revolutionary-era Massachusetts Pine Tree flag—a message that many American viewers translated as "the harbinger of universal anarchy."

The exhibition had originally been conceived as a strictly American affair, and it was actually dominated numerically by American work, which made up three-quarters of the show. The initial plans, however, had been scrapped for the more ambitious idea of a vast international retrospective tracing the rise of modernism from its nineteenth-century sources in Goya, Ingres, and Delacroix, through the French realist Courbet, to impressionism and the bewildering canvases of post-impressionists, expressionists, and cubists. It was not the dark, looming shapes of the American painter Albert Pinkham Ryder that outraged patrons, or the realistic cityscapes of the "New York Eight," with their conventional images and brushwork, but rather what one critic called "the imported ideology" of the new European artists—Picasso, Matisse, Brancusi, Picabia, Léger, Rouault, Kandinsky, Duchamp, and Lehmbruck. Their collective impact carried the force of revolution. Staid art critic Kenyon Cox admitted to spending "an appalling morning" at the show, where he had witnessed the "total destruction of the art of painting.... To have looked at it is to have passed through a pathological museum where the layman has no right to go. One feels that one has seen not an exhibition, but an exposure."

The Armory Show collected into a single public image the disparate meaning of European modernism. In the bold thin colors of Matisse's *The Red Studio* or the splashes of one of Kandinsky's *Improvisations* or the frozen motion of Duchamp's *Nude Descending a Staircase,* Americans viewed the results of a perceptual revolution that had transformed the European intellectual and artistic world and had now arrived in the United States. Here were the visible effects of a general revolt—embodied in the work of such controversial European cultural

**Henri Matisse, *The Red Studio*, 1911**
*This painting, first shown in the United States at the Armory Show, outraged viewers who were used to scenes of social realism.*

figures as Nietzsche, Bergson, Sorel, Freud, Ibsen, and Strindberg—against nineteenth-century positivism, with its faith in scientific objectivity. The new art was the all-too-apparent result of recent explorations into the unseen, the unknown, the irrational, and the relative, yielding new definitions of time, space, energy, force, and will. For those progressives who chose to examine the work of the modernists, the Armory Show took on the dimensions of a social crisis.

**An Artistic Revolution**

The crisis rose directly out of the challenge to the comfortable realism and moralism of the average educated American, who firmly believed in the solidity of the objective social world and in the power of "good art," whether in print or on canvas, to represent that world. Socially useful art, most progressives believed, was the art of representation. Progressivism was nourished by a strong sense of social reality—the belief that the world, after all, consisted of commonplace and everyday occurrences strung in orderly and predictable sequences. Progressivism had been born in the country and had moved to the city, and it relied on the moral code of an earlier rural society to make otherwise bewildering problems manageable. There was also a lingering idealism in the progressive outlook—Theodore Roosevelt called it "practical idealism"—that combined easily with newly discovered techniques of social analysis. These two halves of the progressive outlook were held together by the belief that science and the scientific method, baffling as they might seem to the layman, would ultimately establish the unity of truth and the fact of progress.

These social opinions supported a set of aesthetic preferences. The progressives' favorite novelist was the reliable William Dean Howells, who once (like so many progressives) had been a young man from the provinces who had come to the metropolis to make his way. Howells built a career and a considerable fortune as a novelist and an editor with his cautious, sensitive probings of modern issues: divorce and the disintegration of the family; economic inequality and the insecurities of a commercial existence; the decline of an older business ethic in a new world of bigness. Howells weighed all these complexities in terms of the loss of certainty among small-town Americans and the hope that it might somehow be restored. In his portraits of the puzzled editor Basil March in *A Hazard of New Fortunes* and of the confused businessman in *The Rise of Silas Lapham,* Howells offered recognizable modern types, and progressive readers could find their own problems stated and finally solved in his fiction. And when realism paled, there was always fantasy and that favorite fictional hero, Owen Wister's "Virginian," the unassuming yet self-assured cowboy untainted by corrupting commercialism.

Tolerance of the excessive, the outsized, and the grotesque was strictly limited by a psychology that insisted on the rational, the measurable, the predictable. Whatever lay beyond these borders was ignored or rejected as unhealthy or unclean—Frank Norris's examination of regression and bestialism in *McTeague,* Henry James's subtle studies of corruption, Mark Twain's experiment in determinism in *The Mysterious Stranger,* Theodore Dreiser's frank exploration of sexuality in *Sister Carrie.*

In the visual arts informed opinion had reluctantly come to terms with the so-called Ashcan School of New York painters, among them John Sloan, George Luks, and George Bellows, whose realistic paintings of street scenes and city types drew from the same sources as those of progressive reformers and writers. The New York Eight, as members of this group were also called, sought to encompass the whole city scene with their illustrators' techniques and documentary style. Most progressives understood and accepted the social realism of the Eight, for it was directly involved with the pictorial aspects of twentieth-century urban life. "The tramp sits on the edge of the curb," the Eight's spokesman, Robert Henri, explained. "He is huddled up. His body is thick. His underlip hangs. His eyes look fierce. . . . He is not beautiful, but he could well be the motive for a great and beautiful work of art." Progressives who were engaged in similar explorations of city life agreed with Henri, for they shared his insistence on "fundamental law" and those axioms "controlling all existence." By 1910 realism had broken the Genteel Tradition's grip on the American imagination without, however, dissolving its view of objective reality.

It was just this sense of the manageability of their world that gave progressives the confidence to reform and improve it. Experimenting with the new tools of social analysis helped sharpen the progressive method, but it also strengthened the belief that the world was plastic after all and could be molded into a controlled environment. The recent knowledge explosion in American universities had shaken but not destroyed the progressive idea that the great facts in life were simple.

This conviction that art and politics amounted to the same thing made the Armory Show a troubling spectacle for most American viewers. It threatened not simply their aesthetic preferences, but also their belief in the possibilities of planning and social control. The "detestable things" created by Picasso, Matisse, and Duchamp—"degraded, indecent, and insane," they were called—disclosed the lurking presence of the unpredictable and the ungovernable, of flux and formlessness. A Matisse painting reminded humorist Gelett Burgess of the havoc a "sanguinary" girl of eight, "half-crazed with gin," might wreak on a blank wall with a box of crayons. In choosing a revolutionary theme for their exhibition, the organizers of the Armory Show were only following the path their European counterparts had taken for more than a century. But American viewers took the show's political challenge literally. As one hostile critic announced: "The exploitation of a theory of discords, puzzles, ugliness, and clinical details is to art what anarchy is to society and the practitioners need not so much a critic as an alienist [psychiatrist]." Artistic madness would certainly lead to barbarism.

Criticism flowed naturally from aesthetic into political channels. "The United States is invaded by aliens," warned the archconservative critic Royal Cortissoz, "thousands of whom constitute so many acute perils to the health of the body politic. Modernism is of precisely the same heterogeneous alien origin and is imperiling the republic of art in the same way." The Armory Show, Cortissoz warned, was dominated "by types not yet fitted for their first papers in aesthetic naturalization—the makers of true Ellis Island art."

**Proletarian Art: The Paterson Pageant**   Modernism in the Armory Show presented most viewers with a symbolic dilemma: how to ensure the improvement of American society without underwriting revolution. Once again, as in all other matters concerning America, Theodore Roosevelt had the last word. "It is vitally necessary," the retired president reminded his followers, "to move forward to shake off the dead hand of the reactionaries; and yet we have to face the fact that there is apt to be a lunatic fringe among votaries of any forward movement." Still, the problem remained—how to give support to the sane and deny it to the dangerous. The political evidence was obvious. In New York City on a June evening in 1913, less than four months after the Armory Show, 1,000 silk workers from Paterson, New Jersey, stepped off the ferry and marched in a solid phalanx up Broadway and into Madison Square Garden. There, before a crowd of 15,000, they proceeded to reenact the events of their prolonged strike against mill owners. Spectators witnessed a new form of proletarian art—social drama as participatory ritual.

**The Paterson Pageant**
*Workers, many of them women, march up Broadway to Madison Square Garden to participate in John Reed's pageant.*

The Paterson Pageant was the brainchild of young radical journalist John Reed and a handful of socialist intellectuals and artists who dreamed of fashioning a new mass art out of working-class grievances and the formal protest of the intellectuals. The Paterson strike had been triggered by the mill owners' decision to increase the work load for unskilled silk weavers and dyers already living on the edge of destitution. Most of the workers in the Paterson dye houses and mills, some 25,000 in all, were new immigrants from Italy, Russia, and eastern Europe, a large number of them young girls earning an average wage of $6 or $7 a week. The IWW entered the town in the winter of 1913 to help organize this unpromising material around the immediate issues of shorter hours and higher wages. "Big Bill" Haywood, fresh from his triumph in the Lawrence, Massachusetts, textile workers' strike, joined the young Wobbly agitator Elizabeth Gurley Flynn and the romantic syndicalist Carlo Tresca in teaching the Paterson workers that it was "far better to starve fighting than to starve working." By February 1913 they had succeeded in uniting the unskilled workers and shutting down the town.

In trying to break the strike with its skilled workers, the AFL fed the progressive tendency to identify the immigrant with radicalism. Yet throughout the spring the strikers' ranks held firm. The mill owners fought back, stirring up hatred of "outside agitators" and enlisting the police in their efforts to break the strike. "There's a war in Paterson," John Reed told his fellow artists and intellectuals in Greenwich Village. "But it's a curious kind of war. All the violence is the work of one side—the Mill Owners."

Reed had reason to know. Like many of the Village socialists and radicals, he had made the Sunday excursion to Paterson to see for himself the clash between the workers and the bosses. He had been jailed, and he later returned to New York to compose his indictment of the owners for Max Eastman's *The Masses*. A cultural radical as yet without any clear sense of ideological direction, Reed dreamed of rallying artists and intellectuals to the strikers' side as the beginning of a permanent alliance for the radical reconstruction of American life. This was the idea he brought back to socialite Mabel Dodge's salon, the gathering place of New York's radical writers and intellectuals. Out of the sessions at Dodge's came the plans for a gigantic pageant to raise money for the strike fund and to educate liberals on working-class solidarity. Reed threw himself headlong into the project, spending eighteen hours a day on the script, drilling a thousand amateur performers into a theatrical company, designing the massive sets with the artist John Sloan and stage designer Robert Edmond Jones. By June he was ready, Sloan's huge factory scenes and red curtains were in place, and the cast was primed for performance.

The pageant caught the spirit of solidarity that Reed had sensed in Paterson. As it opened, throngs of workers moved down the center aisle to linger in front of the huge gray mills before entering to the sound of whirring machinery. Suddenly the chant began—"Strike! Strike!"—growing louder and more insistent until the workers came pouring out of the factory doors, and life moved outside the empty, dark mills. In front of these dead industrial husks, the workers reenacted the scenes of the strike—mass picketing, police harassment, the clash between strikers and the scabs in which a worker was killed, and finally the climactic funeral procession.

The audience, many of them workers admitted at 25 cents a seat, joined in booing the police, chanting strike slogans, and lustily singing the socialist anthem, the "Internationale." For a brief moment it seemed that Reed and the radical cultural critics had succeeded in forging new weapons for social justice out of the materials of mass art.

But life did not imitate art, and the pageant brought a cresting of radical hopes that quickly receded. The spectacle had originally been intended to replenish the strike fund, but actually it yielded a check for only $150. The 24,000 strikers who had not participated began to question the dubious honors bestowed on them by the intellectuals. "Bread was the need of the hour," Elizabeth Gurley Flynn complained, "and bread was not forthcoming." The gulf between art and politics could not be bridged by mere ceremony. The skilled

**"Loop the Loop," Coney Island**
*Commercialized leisure provided escape from the workaday world.*

workers broke ranks during the summer and returned to the mills. Then the mill owners, in a series of shop-by-shop settlements that conceded nothing to the unskilled workers, shattered their morale and routed the IWW leadership. By summer's end the Paterson workers were back on the job on their employers' terms. John Reed's script for the oppressed laborers of America acting out "the wretchedness of their lives and the glory of their revolt" had failed to close the distance between the intellectual radicals and the workers.

Instead, the gap between industrial workers and their bosses in the Progressive Era was being bridged by a new mass consumer culture. This rising popular culture, while it did not erase organized labor's list of grievances, softened workers' convictions of being exploited. By 1917, when the United States entered the war, a culture of commercialized leisure was already at work ministering to a mass American public's hunger for all kinds of fantasy—for toylands and dream worlds, remembered play and recovered childhoods—made possible by what the novelist Henry James called "a willing suspension of disbelief." The new counterculture of longing and fulfillment offered a full-blown alternative to the workaday progressive world of efficiency, routine, and time clocks with seductive promises of never-ending amusement. At Coney Island's Luna Park, in New York City's huge Hippodrome (the largest commercial theater in the world), and hundreds of music halls and vaudeville houses across the country, in baseball parks and football stadiums, along the gaudy midways ringing a succession of world's fairs and international expositions, in 25-cent movie palaces—an adversary world of carnival for the masses flourished. Here for a paying public stood a gigantic playground complete with dazzling lights and exotic colors, fake oriental architecture and circus barkers, outsized dolls and marionettes, sports celebrities, cartoon characters, and matinee idols, all providing temporary escape from the world of the ten-hour day. This new consumer culture counseled self-indulgence rather than self-denial, urged spending rather than saving, and promised mounting abundance. Twentieth-century consumer culture, aided by technology, mass marketing, and the sales pitch, continued to adjust—though it never succeeded in completely reconciling—American workers to their lot in a corporate economy. Genuine abundance still eluded the great majority of American workers in 1917, but the prophecy together with its supportive cultural fantasies continued to stimulate the appetites of millions of consumers in all classes of society.

## Artists and Scientists: Critics of Progressivism

Other critics of progressivism before World War I perceived different divisions in American society and suggested other ways of closing them. In 1914 Walter Lippmann published his *Drift and Mastery,* and a year later Van Wyck Brooks brought out his bitter essay *America's Coming of Age.* Both authors demanded a reassessment of progressives' aims and aspirations. Lippmann and Brooks represented a new intellectual type, the liberal publicist directing criticism toward the progressive elite. They were neither journalists in a traditional sense nor philosophers, but rather saw themselves as cultural and social commentators whose task it was to direct the flow of American life through channels of publicity and informed criticism toward new national goals. They sought to lift their roles as critics to the realm of public power through their analysis of American society.

**Brooks's Critique**        Van Wyck Brooks, a recent graduate of Harvard, where he had studied under philosophers William James and George Santayana, was the chief spokesman for the "little renaissance" in American art and culture that swept across the country after 1912. By the time Brooks issued his challenge to progressivism, the signs of cultural rebellion were everywhere. Brooks joined the expanding circle of artists and intellectuals in Greenwich Village after a brief teaching career at Stanford University and at the Worker's Educational Association in Cambridge, England. In the Village he met Walter Lippmann, who urged him to contribute to the literary renaissance by closely examining the "noble dream" of American democratic culture in the light of the "actual limitations of experience." Brooks promptly obliged with what he called an address to his own "homeless generation" of intellectuals and would-be critics.

Brooks perceived a basic American duality in the cultural split between "highbrow" and "lowbrow"—a fatal division, he said, that had paralyzed the creative will of the nation for more than a century. He argued that the American impasse stemmed from the conflict between high-flown theory and the "catchpenny realities" of a business civilization. Between these poles lay a cultural wasteland in which no true community could thrive. Brooks traced the roots of this American schizophrenia to the original sin of Puritanism, "the all-influential fact in the history of the American mind." He attributed to Puritanism both the "fastidious refinement" of current tastes and the "opportunism" of American moneymakers.

Like the progressive historian Vernon L. Parrington, who was already at work compiling the materials for his *Main Currents of American Thought* that would document this view, Brooks presented his authors in sets of paired opposites: Jonathan Edwards and Benjamin Franklin; Henry Wadsworth Longfellow and Mark Twain; James Russell Lowell and Walt Whitman—figures on opposite sides of a chasm between literate and illiterate America. Brooks argued that throughout the nineteenth century the divorce of the real from the ideal had resulted in an "orgy of lofty examples, moralized poems, national anthems and baccalaureate sermons" until the average citizen was now "charged with all manner of ideal purities, ideal honorabilities, ideal femininities, flagwavings and skyscrapings of every sort." In the meantime the American landscape had become a stamping ground for every greedy commercial impulse of every last businessman who held that "society is fair prey for what he can get out of it."

Brooks pointed to the shortcomings of the progressive approach to reform. Progressivism, for all its moral certainties and good-government ideals, had failed to solve the fundamental problem of modern industrial society—the "invisible government" of business and the profit motive. So far, well-meaning progressive reformers' efforts to change American priorities had added up to nothing. Progressivism simply consolidated the rule of "commercialized men." Of what use was it, Brooks demanded, to tinker with political mechanisms or "do any of the other easy popular contemporary things" unless the quality of American life could also be improved?

Here Brooks reached the core of his critique. Meaningful betterment of American society would require more than rationalizing a business system, more than the cheerful cooperation of business and government, whether in the name of the New Nationalism or the New Freedom. All that would suffice now would be the massive shift of American energies from business and politics to psychology and art. Otherwise progressivism would fail in its mission to give America new life. When World War I broke out, Brooks still hoped for the cultural rebellion for which he spoke. Three years later, American entrance into the war broke these hopes on the rocks of the war state.

**Lippmann's Analysis**  Walter Lippmann also saw a split in twentieth-century American life that progressivism had failed to repair. But his definition centered on the conflict between Victorian silences—what he called the "sterile tyranny of taboo"—inherited from the nineteenth century, and his own generation's desire "to be awake during their own lifetime." "Drift" was the result of the rule of old bogeys. "Mastery" meant applying the scientific method to politics. Like Brooks, although for different reasons, Lippmann faulted the progressives for their lack of rigorous thought. Although the New Nationalism had examined some of the worst abuses of industrialism, it still spoke the language of the old moralists. The New Freedom continued to make false promises of a return to free competition. "You would think that competitive commercialism was really a generous, chivalrous, high-minded stage of human culture," Lippmann scoffed, instead of "an antiquated, feeble, mean, and unimaginative way of dealing with the possibilities of modern industry." Lippmann agreed with Brooks on the need for relocating American energies outside politics, but he differed dramatically on the means. Unlike Brooks and the cultural radicals, he championed the cause of business consolidation and the rule of industrial statesmen who would go beyond politics by lifting decision making out of the marketplace to the level of scientific management. Whereas the cultural radicals hoped to destroy the rule of big business, Lippmann sought to rationalize and reform it. His aim was to create a truly cooperative society, neither strictly capitalistic nor wholly collectivist, but a new commonwealth composed of managers, workers, and consumers, each applying the instruments of measurement and control provided by modern science.

**The Seven Arts and**
**The New Republic**
American entry into World War I threatened Van Wyck Brooks's plans for reconstructing American culture. But it brought a welcome test for Lippmann's pragmatic liberalism and his design for a businessmen's government. Brooks deplored the war as a betrayal of his dreams; Lippmann embraced it as a challenge. By 1917 these two critiques of progressivism had been institutionalized in two very different magazines: *The Seven Arts,* which Brooks and his cultural radical friends Randolph Bourne and James Oppenheim founded in 1916 and nursed through a year of shaky existence; and *The New Republic,* which Lippmann together with liberal nationalists Herbert Croly and Walter Weyl had launched in 1914. The war records of these two magazines testified to the divergent fates of cultural radicalism and liberal nationalism under emergency conditions.

*The Seven Arts* lasted just a year before the fervor of the patriots killed it. Brooks's mantle fell on the diminutive frame of Randolph Bourne, who more clearly than any of the other opponents of the war saw the coming defeat of "that America of youth and aspiration" standing below the battle. In "War and the Intellectuals," the most scathing of his attacks on Lippmann and the prowar liberals, Bourne ridiculed the "war technique" of liberal reform that had led the intellectuals to the illusion that they had willed the war "through sheer force of ideas." Bourne charged that in welcoming the war *The New Republic* editors had allied themselves with the least democratic forces in American society, those primitive interests that still were trumpeting notions of the national state and the doctrines of economic privilege. The war, Bourne concluded, provided an escape for progressives who had become prisoners of their own fantasies of the ordered society. The collapse of *The Seven Arts* after a year of lonely opposition to the war, along with Bourne's untimely death, marked the end of the cultural radical attempt to reconstruct progressivism by supplying it with higher values.

Lippmann and the other editors of *The New Republic* continued to cling to the belief that they could help direct a democratic war and write a liberal peace. The American entrance, Lippmann explained soon after Wilson's declaration of war, would prove "decisive in the history of the world": the United States could now proceed to "crystallize and make real the whole league of peace propaganda." Nor did he fear the effects of a war psychology on the prospects of liberalism. In October 1917 he offered his services to the administration and was appointed secretary of The Inquiry, Wilson's handpicked body of experts charged with preparing the American agenda for the peace table. Herbert Croly, who remained in his editorial post at *The New Republic,* quickly grew disillusioned as he realized the nature of the liberal impasse both at home and abroad. Lippmann's hopes for a liberal peace remained high. But eighteen months later, discouraged by the president's failure at the Paris Peace Conference and dubious now about the uses of war as a means of social reconstruction, Lippmann joined those "tired radicals" seeking to defeat the treaty.

## The Ordeal of Woodrow Wilson

In his address to Congress on January 8, 1918—at the low point in the American war effort—Woodrow Wilson outlined the steps the United States and the Allies would have to take to ensure a postwar world "made fit to live in." Wilson presented his Fourteen Points as a blueprint for peacemaking drawn to his own progressive specifications. The central element in his thinking was the principle of "open covenants openly arrived at"—the extension of the New Freedom idea of moral publicity to international politics. A counterweight to this first point in Wilson's moral scales was the fourteenth, calling for "a general association of nations . . . formed under specific covenants for the purpose of affording mutual guarantees of political independence and territorial integrity to great and small states alike." The main substantive points in Wilson's utopian scheme included a general disarmament, complete freedom of the seas, fair adjustment of colonial claims in the interests of the peoples involved, and a series of specific provisions for drawing national boundaries in Europe on the basis of the language spoken in each region ("linguistic nationalism"). These were the lofty terms that Wilson, in the face of mounting opposition from his war partners, intended to impose at the peace table.

**Problems with the Fourteen Points**
In attempting to achieve his aims, Wilson was driven by circumstance, as well as by his own intensely moral nature, to make several costly miscalculations. Part of his trouble lay in the Fourteen Points themselves. What, for example, did his principle of national self-determination mean, and by what general formula could

it be applied? What adjustments might be needed when linguistic nationalism failed to coincide with economic viability or military aims? Then, how could the new Soviet regime with an exportable totalitarian ideology, which had been established two months before, be given "an unhampered and unembarrassed opportunity" for political development? How, in short, could Wilson, as the representative of the only impartial power at the peace table, establish in each and every instance his claim to be the enlightened conscience of mankind?

A related set of problems concerned Wilson's political position at home. Who but himself—the president—he asked, could convert the Allies to his program and ensure the triumph of collective security? Determined to play the dominant role at the Paris conference, he insisted on making his peace program a partisan issue in the fall elections of 1918 by warning that a Republican victory would be a rejection of his leadership and vision. Republicans, who had already grown restive under the nonpartisan war policy, now retaliated by accusing Wilson himself of partisan dealings. In 1918 the Republicans regained control of both houses of Congress. If their victory did not quite mean a vote of no confidence, it did serve to warn Wilson that the spirit of party politics had been revived and would be decisive in settling the fate of his peace program.

Even more serious was Wilson's refusal to include Republican leaders among his advisers at the peace conference. Former President Taft, the 1916 Republican presidential nominee Charles Evans Hughes, and a number of other leading Republicans had expressed cautious interest in the idea of a League of Nations. But Wilson's calculated exclusion of these men from the American delegation to Paris isolated him from the moderate Republican internationalism he so desperately needed. On the eve of his departure for Europe in December 1918, there were already ominous signs of a growing presidential detachment from the realities of domestic politics, as Wilson began to retreat into the recesses of his moralistic nature. "Tell me what is right," he urged his advisers as he prepared for the conference, "and I'll fight for it." Wilson fought tenaciously, even heroically, for his Fourteen Points against overwhelming odds. But in forgetting the first rule of politics and ignoring the domestic disarray he had left behind, he fatally compromised his position.

**Problems in Paris**     In Paris the president confronted other national leaders who, as he came to realize with chagrin, spoke for their countrymen as he could not: David Lloyd George of Great Britain, Georges Clemenceau of France, and Vittorio Orlando of Italy. The Allies had suffered grievously during the war, and their leaders could count on unwavering support at home for a peace that would punish Germany—one that would assign all the war guilt to Germany, completely strip it of its colonial possessions, extract enormous reparations, and provide all the necessary safeguards against future aggression. To counter these narrow nationalistic aims, Wilson brought with him to Paris only the Fourteen Points and his vision of a new concert of power. Despite his initial popularity with the peoples of Europe, his lone voice became

**The Council of Four**
*From left to right: Vittorio Orlando of Italy, David Lloyd George of England, Georges Clemenceau of France, Woodrow Wilson.*

lost in the clamor of competing nationalisms. The American story of the peace deliberations was one of mounting frustration and a forced retreat from idealism.

The first of the Fourteen Points to be abandoned was the utopian concept of "open covenants." Soon after the conference began, the plenary sessions (open meetings of all delegations) gave way first to a Council of Ten, dominated by the heads of state and their foreign ministers, and then to a Council of Four, composed of Wilson, Lloyd George, Clemenceau, and Orlando, meeting behind closed doors. The press was barred from working sessions and became almost wholly dependent on news releases that were handed out after each plenary session. Wilson added to his problems of communication by withdrawing coldly from his colleagues on the council and ignoring most of his advisers, who complained of his aloofness. Removed from presidential oversight, the American staff floundered in confusion. Wilson announced that he had no desire "to have lawyers drafting the treaty of peace" and played a lone hand at Paris. He quickly exhausted his reserves of moral capital.

On a few of the specific issues of the peace settlement, Wilson was partially successful in moderating the extortionate demands of his partners. After an epic battle of wills with the cynical Clemenceau, who likened his adversary to Jesus

Christ and Moses bearing the Ten Commandments, Wilson forced France to agree to a multinational defense pact. But he gained this victory at the cost of the immediate return to France of Alsace-Lorraine,* French occupation of Germany's Rhineland, and huge reparations to be paid by Germany. On the question of the former German colonies, he abandoned the principle of "impartial adjustment" but salvaged his plan for a mandate system under League auspices. For Poland he secured a corridor to the sea at the expense of linguistic nationalism.† In constructing a new Austria out of the Austro-Hungarian empire, which had disintegrated at the end of the war, he presided over the transfer of some 200,000 German-speaking people to Italy in order to assure the latter of a militarily defensible frontier. When he refused to agree to a similar transfer to Italy of a strip of the Dalmatian coast—territory inhabited overwhelmingly by Yugoslavs—he brought on a major crisis by appealing for self-restraint directly to the Italian people over the heads of their representatives. This blunder only hardened Italian resolves and further discredited Wilson with his colleagues at the peace table. Self-determination of peoples speaking the same language—a legacy of nineteenth-century romantic nationalism—was violated at Paris as often as it was successfully applied.

But the president suffered his sharpest defeat on the question of reparations. France originally suggested the preposterous figure of $200 billion, and Britain seemed unwilling to settle for much less. Clemenceau and Lloyd George, bowing to heavy pressure from their respective publics, overrode Wilson's objections to their crippling demands and forced him to accept the inclusion of civilian damages and military pensions in the final assessment on Germany. The president, pushed beyond the limits of endurance, had become ill and confused. He agreed to the principle of massive repayments and allowed the fixing of specific amounts to be postponed. The Council of Four provided for a reparations commission, which in 1921 set the indemnity at $56 billion without regard for Germany's ability to pay or for the political consequences for the struggling new German republic.

**The League of Nations** Throughout the agony of daily defeat, Wilson was sustained by his hopes for the League of Nations and the work of drafting the League Covenant. The League, he told himself, would correct the mistakes and make good the deficiencies of the peace settlement, to which it must be firmly tied. By tying the League closely to

---

*Alsace-Lorraine was a largely German-speaking region in eastern France that Germany had annexed in 1871, against the wishes of most of its inhabitants. The recovery of Alsace-Lorraine had been a primary French aim in World War I. Wilson would have preferred settling the issue by a plebiscite.

†The so-called Polish Corridor, a strip of territory assuring Poland access to the Baltic Sea, contained a large German minority unwilling to come under Polish rule. The corridor also cut the province of East Prussia off from the rest of Germany. The German-speaking port of Danzig (now Gdansk) was transformed into a free city under League of Nations auspices. In 1939 Hitler's demand for the return of Danzig and the Polish Corridor led to the outbreak of World War II.

the treaty,* the president hoped to get around his congressional opponents by presenting them with a complete package that they would have to accept or reject as a whole. He never seriously considered that they might succeed in destroying his great work.

Article X of the League Covenant became the great symbolic issue that eventually wrecked his dream. Article X provided that

> the members of the League undertake to respect and preserve as against external aggression the territorial integrity and existing political independence of all the Members of the League. In case of any such aggression or in case of any threat or danger of such aggression the Council shall advise upon the means by which this obligation shall be fulfilled.

For Wilson, Article X represented the triumph of moral force. The details of applying sanctions against future aggressors concerned him less than did the simple recognition by the nations of the world of his principle of collective security. This principle, at least, he had managed to rescue from the ruins of the treaty, and he meant to defend it at all costs.

The League of Nations, on which Wilson ultimately pinned all his hopes, in part represented the progressive idea of commission government applied to international politics. Like a federal commission designed to free policymaking from the whims of politicians, the League, together with its various branches and agencies, would provide the means of defusing international crises and resolving conflicts through arbitration. But in another and more profound sense, Wilson's League was simply the application of inherited nineteenth-century liberal principles and a doctrine of progress.

In the president's mind the League embodied old truths and moral principles. The most important of these was the belief that as American institutions and ideas reformed the rest of the world, and as the beneficent workings of trade and commerce gathered peoples together in harmony and abundance, the old selfish national interests would die out. Ultimately a worldwide legal community would arise in place of the discredited system of balance of power. Wilson had witnessed four years of international slaughter and had seen embittered nationalists at Versailles impose a savage, punishing peace on Germany, and he was convinced that the time had finally come for building such an international moral order. Although he was willing to concede much—and in fact had conspicuously failed to control the peace conference—he was not prepared to compromise on the League of Nations or on the role his country would have to play in its creation.

Wilson's utopian commitment led him to overlook two fundamental problems. The first resulted from attaching the League to the peace treaty. A second problem was that of intent. Was the League intended simply to enforce a victor's

---

*Actually, not one peace treaty was drawn up, but five. The Treaty of Versailles, which included the League Covenant, applied only to Germany; separate treaties were imposed on each of Germany's allies: Austria, Hungary, Bulgaria, and Turkey.

**"When Johnny Comes Marching Home"**
*Fifteenth New York Regiment marching up Fifth Avenue, 1919.*

peace, or would it work to adjust shifting balances of national power, incorporate new members including the defeated nations, and underwrite orderly change and development? No amount of Wilsonian rhetoric about "the general moral judgment of mankind" could obscure the basic uncertainty of purpose in the president's attempt to replace power relations with moral force.

**The Red Scare**　　　Wilson returned to the United States in the summer of 1919 and found a nation already in the throes of reaction. The shadow of the Russian Revolution, which had fallen over the peace table, now lengthened across the Atlantic. The threat of revolution strengthened the forces of reaction everywhere in Europe as conservatives rushed to defend their states from the Bolshevik menace. The Soviet challenge seemed particularly frightening to Americans because it threatened their own revolutionary tradition. Russia was undergoing no mere political rebellion and rearrangement, sensibly completed and solicitous of property rights and personal liberties, but instead a vast social upheaval with a collectivist ideology that was the antithesis of Western capitalist democracy.

**Red Scare, 1919**
*Political cartoon shows a dangerous "Red" creeping into the country under the American flag*

The American response to the new Soviet regime was twofold. First, the Wilson administration undertook an abortive attempt to strengthen the counter-revolutionary forces in Russia by landing American troops (soon withdrawn) at Murmansk in North Russia and Vladivostok in the Far East. These operations were undertaken in conjunction with larger (but equally unsuccessful) British, French, and Japanese interventions. Second, there was a tendency at home to see "Reds" everywhere. By the summer of 1919, the so-called Red Scare had taken full possession of the national imagination as a wartime fear of subversion was suddenly turned into a dread of imminent revolution. In fact, two rival American Communist parties were established in September 1919. (They united only in 1921 under pressure from Lenin.) One was led by left-wing defectors from the Socialist party and the other by John Reed, recently returned from witnessing the Russian Revolution, which he described dramatically in his book *Ten Days That Shook the World*. Neither group attracted an important following, and Reed soon returned to Russia, where he died in an epidemic and was buried in Red Square. Much more significant was the widespread fear of radicalism. This fear branded as subversive not only the tiny communist and IWW movements and the larger, moderate Socialist party, but also liberal ideas in general, whether in art or politics. All were met with strident protests against nonconformity and demands for unconditional loyalty.

**Republicans Oppose Wilson**

Wilson also felt the force of a congressional reaction that had been building since the armistice. Mobilization for war had concentrated power in the executive branch of the government, thus completing the political cycle that had begun with Theodore Roosevelt's presidency. But now, with reconversion and demobilization, the political pendulum began to swing the other way, as Congress moved firmly to reassert its control over foreign affairs as well as domestic policy.

Congressional resurgence had already become a highly partisan matter with the revival in the 1918 elections of the Republican party, which with forty-nine seats in the Senate now enjoyed a two-vote margin over the Democrats. Republicans could scarcely resist an opportunity to limit Wilson's power by modifying the terms of American participation in the new League of Nations. Republican leaders were also prepared to roll back wartime controls and curb the regulatory power of federal agencies, whose activities they now tended to equate with socialism. The League was only the most obvious issue with which the Republican party aimed to establish itself in the majority once again.

Yet the Republican members of the Senate remained divided on the question of accepting Wilson's treaty and American participation in the League. On the right of the party stood some dozen or fifteen "irreconcilables"—isolationists opposed to nearly any continued international involvement. At the other end of the spectrum were the "mild reservationists," who supported the League in principle but were concerned with the extent of Wilson's commitment to collective security and were anxious to limit it. Ranged between these two ideological poles were the "strong reservationists," making up the majority faction and led by Senator Henry Cabot Lodge. Lodge combined a cordial hatred of the president with a narrow nationalism that had not changed since the Spanish-American War. The "strong reservationists" were willing to consider United States participation in the League only on their own terms, and they were fully prepared to force on Wilson significant reservations limiting American commitments and making Congress rather than the president the final judge of their applicability.

Within his own party Wilson could count on solid internationalist support, but it was clear at the outset of the struggle that he would have to win a sizable majority of moderates away from Lodge in order to gain acceptance of his League of Nations. By July 1919 Wilson faced a formidable but not an impossible task, one that would require great patience and even greater flexibility.

For his part Lodge followed a clever strategy contrived to exploit every advantage over his opponent. He packed the Senate Foreign Relations Committee with his followers; he conducted lengthy hearings that gave voice to every conceivable opponent of the League; he courted right-wing businessmen like Henry Clay Frick and Andrew Mellon; and he loaded the treaty down with amendments. By fall his original forty-five amendments had been reduced to fourteen reservations—one for each of Wilson's initial Fourteen Points. The first reserved to the United States the sole right to decide whether it had fulfilled its obligations under the covenant, and it gave Congress the power to withdraw the United States from the League. The second, directed at the controversial Article X, was also aimed at Wilson's greatest weakness. It provided that the United States would accept no obligation to enforce the collective-security provisions of the covenant without the consent of Congress in each and every case. Other reservations rejected any mandates assignable to the United States, reserved the right to determine which questions involving American interests might be submitted to the League, and stipulated that the Monroe Doctrine was not to be subjected to international debate. Taken together, Lodge's reservations were significant but not crippling modifications, as the subsequent history of the League would show.

Yet, as Lodge hoped, Wilson believed otherwise. He consistently refused to make a realistic assessment of the situation. He was unwilling to discuss the specific circumstances under which the United States might be called on to apply sanctions—either economic or military—against other nations because he was convinced that full discussion in the forum of the League would make sanctions unnecessary. For him the real questions were simple: Was the United States prepared to make the significant moral gesture toward peace and international security? Would the American people see to it that the Senate carried out its obligation? Although the actual fight in the Senate grew complicated with proposals and counterproposals, amendments, reservations, and interpretations, the president's position remained essentially the one he had taken in presenting the treaty to the Senate: "The stage is set, the destiny disclosed. . . . We cannot turn back. We can only go forward, with lifted eyes and freshened spirit, to follow the vision."

Wilson's own vision led him away from Washington on an 8,000-mile tour of the nation, during which he gave forty speeches explaining to the American people the League's importance to their future security and welfare. In taking his case to the country, Wilson was violating one of his own rules. "The Senate," he once wrote, "is not . . . immediately sensitive to [public] opinion and is apt to grow, if anything, more stiff if pressure of that kind is brought to bear upon it." Now President Wilson ignored Professor Wilson's advice. His tour of the nation carried him farther and farther away from political reality and the problem of securing the Senate's consent. Although he referred frequently to specific issues and explained the limited nature of the American commitment, he returned to the theme of moral principle:

> You have no choice, my fellow citizens. . . . You cannot give a false gift. . . . Men are not going to stand it. There is nothing for any nation to lose whose purposes are right and whose cause is just. . . . The whole freedom of the world not only, but the whole peace of mind of the world, depends upon the choice of America. . . . I can testify to that. . . . The world will be absolutely in despair if America deserts it.

Worn out and distraught, collapsing under the weight of his moral mission, Wilson suffered a stroke in Pueblo, Colorado, on September 26, 1919, and was rushed back to Washington. A week later a second stroke left him paralyzed. Wilson in effect had spoken his last word on the treaty. Desperately ill, physically isolated from his followers and advisers, he was locked in a private moral world. Loyal Democrats received their presidential orders: vote to reject the treaty with the Lodge reservations. On November 19, 1919, by a vote of 39 for and 55 against, the Senate rejected the Treaty of Versailles with the reservations; the Democrats had dutifully joined with the irreconcilables to defeat it. Wilson still hoped to make the presidential election of 1920 the occasion of a giant referendum on the League. But his advisers, along with more objective observers, knew the fight was over. The president's dream was dead.

Domestic discord in the year 1919 mirrored the collapse of Wilson's moral world. A calendar of violence marked the decline of original progressive hopes:

In January shipyard workers in Seattle struck for higher wages, organized a general strike, and paralyzed the city. At the mayor's request the federal government sent in the Marines.

In May four hundred soldiers and sailors sacked the offices of a socialist newspaper, the New York *Call,* and beat up the staff.

In the summer race riots erupted in twenty-five cities across the country; the most serious outbreak was in Chicago, where thirty-eight were killed and more than five hundred injured.

In September the Boston police force struck for the right to unionize, and the city experienced a wave of looting and theft until leading businessmen and Harvard students restored order.

In September 350,000 steelworkers struck for the right to unionize and for an eight-hour day.

In November a mob in Centralia, Washington, dragged IWW agitator Wesley Everett from jail and castrated him before hanging him.

In December agents of the Labor Department rounded up 249 Russian-born American communists and deported them to Finland.

There were Americans in 1919 who recalled Wilson's definition of the progressive task six years earlier as "the high enterprise of the new day. . . . Our duty is to cleanse, to reconsider, to correct the evil without impairing the good, to purify and humanize every process of our common life without weakening or sentimentalizing it." For those who remembered, there could be little doubt that the new day had ended.

# CHRONOLOGY

| | | | |
|---|---|---|---|
| **1913** | Armory Show in New York City. Paterson strike. | **1918** | Wilson's Fourteen Points, outlining administration's peace aims. United States troops at Belleau Wood. Saint Mihiel salient, first United States offensive. Meuse-Argonne offensive. Sedition Act, providing severe penalties for expressing "disloyal" opinions. Armistice; Germany defeated. |
| **1914** | World War I begins; Wilson declares American neutrality. "Ludlow Massacre"; National Guard attacks tent colony of strikers in Ludlow, Colorado, killing eleven women and two children. | | |
| **1915** | Germans declare unrestricted submarine warfare and sink *Lusitania* with loss of American lives. | **1919** | *Schenck* v. *U.S.,* upholding Espionage Act and government curtailment of free speech during wartime. *Abrams* v. *U.S.,* upholding Sedition Act. Eighteenth Amendment (Volstead Act), prohibiting sale or manufacture of alcoholic beverages. Steel strike. Race riots in Chicago, East St. Louis, and Washington. |
| **1916** | Wilson reelected, narrowly defeating Charles Evans Hughes. House-Grey Memorandum on United States efforts for negotiated peace. | | |
| **1917** | Germans resume unrestricted submarine warfare and United States enters war. Russian Revolution; "February Revolution," establishing provisional government; "October Revolution," engineered by Bolsheviks. Draft Act. Espionage Act. Purchase of Danish Virgin Islands. Creation of War Industries Board. First Pulitzer prizes awarded. | **1920** | Great Red Scare. Defeat of Versailles Treaty by Senate. Nineteenth Amendment gives vote to women. Warren G. Harding elected president, defeating James M. Cox and Eugene Debs. |

## SUGGESTED READINGS

There are two good surveys of American military conduct of the war: Edward M. Coffman, *The War to End Wars: The American Military Experience in World War I* (1968), and Russell F. Weigley, *The American Way of War* (1973). Ellis W. Hawley, *The Great War and the Search for a Modern Order: A History of the American People and Their Institutions, 1917–1933* (1979) traces the effects of the war on American social policy. Robert D. Cuff, *The War Industries Board* (1973) recounts the activities of a major administrative agency, and Maurine W. Greenwald, *Women, War and Work* (1980) surveys working women's war participation.

The years since World War II have seen a growing number of studies of American civil liberties during and after World War I. Beginning with Zechariah Chafee, *Free Speech in the*

*United States* (1941), the list includes Harry N. Scheiber, *The Wilson Administration and Civil Liberties, 1917–1921* (1960); Donald M. Johnson, *The Challenge to American Freedoms* (1963); H. C. Peterson and Gilbert Fite, *Opponents of the War, 1917–1918* (1957); William Preston, Jr., *Aliens and Dissenters: Federal Suppression of Radicals, 1903–1933* (1963); and Paul L. Murphy, *Red Scare: A Study of National Hysteria, 1919–1920* (1955). For accounts of wartime management of public opinion see Alfred E. Cornebise, *War as Advertised: The Four Minute Men and America's Crusade, 1917–1918* (1984); Carol S. Gruber, *Mars and Minerva: World War I and the Uses of Higher Learning in America* (1975); Stephen Vaughn, *Holding Fast the Inner Lines: Democracy, Nationalism, and the Committee on Public Information* (1980). David M. Kennedy, *Over Here: The First World War and American Society* (1980) is a highly readable account of the domestic war effort.

The immediate shock of war as experienced by artists and intellectuals is described in Stanley Cooperman, *World War I and the American Novel* (1967), and its lingering effects in Malcolm Cowley, *Exiles Return: A Literary Odyssey of the 1920's* (1951). Sam Hunter, *American Painting and Sculpture* (1959), and Barbara Rose, *American Art Since 1900: A Critical History* (1967), are good accounts of American art in the early twentieth century. For the Armory Show see Milton Brown, *The Story of the Armory Show* (1963); the best brief discussion of its revolutionary impact is Meyer Schapiro, "Rebellion in Art," in Daniel Aaron, ed., *America in Crisis* (1952).

The best approach to the intellectual history of the progressive years is through the writers themselves. Major works of social and political analysis, now considered classics, include Jane Addams, *Twenty Years at Hull House* (1910); Randolph Bourne, *Youth and Life* (1913), and a collection of Bourne's war pieces, *War and the Intellectuals* (1964), edited by Carl Resek; Louis Brandeis, *Other People's Money* (1914); Van Wyck Brooks, *America's Coming of Age* (1915); Charles H. Cooley, *Human Nature and the Social Order* (1922); Herbert Croly, *The Promise of American Life* (1909); John Dewey, *School and Society* (1899); W.E.B. Du Bois, *Souls of the Black Folk* (1903); Charlotte Perkins Gilman, *Women and Economics* (1898); Walter Lippmann, *Drift and Mastery* (1914); John Reed, *Insurgent Mexico* (1914), and *Ten Days That Shook the World* (1919); and Walter Weyl, *The New Democracy* (1912).

On the diplomacy of war and peacemaking, Arno J. Mayer, *Political Origins of the New Diplomacy, 1917–1918* (1959), and *Politics and Diplomacy of Peacemaking: Containment and Counterrevolution at Versailles, 1918–1919* (1967), are both ponderous and provocative. N. Gordon Levin, *Woodrow Wilson and World Politics: America's Response to War and Revolution* (1968), focuses on the presidential strategies, as does Warren Kuehl, *Seeking World Order: The United States and World Organization to 1920* (1969). Two older works by Thomas A. Bailey, *Woodrow Wilson and the Lost Peace* (1944) and *Woodrow Wilson and the Great Betrayal* (1945), detail Wilson's tragic postwar course. On the opposition to the League of Nations, Ralph A. Stone, *The Irreconcilables: The Fight Against the League of Nations* (1970), is admirable. John Garraty, *Henry Cabot Lodge* (1953), offers a sympathetic but not uncritical appraisal of Wilson's archenemy. Two recent accounts of Wilson and his chief adversary are Robert H. Ferrell, *Woodrow Wilson and World War I, 1917–1921* (1985) and William C. Widenor, *Henry Cabot Lodge and the Search for an American Foreign Policy* (1980). On Soviet-American relations, see George F. Kennan, *Russia Leaves the War* (1956), and *The Decision to Intervene: Prelude to Allied Intervention in the Bolshevik Revolution* (1958). Peter G. Filene, *Americans and the Soviet Experiment* (1967), and Christopher Lasch, *The American Liberals and the Russian Revolution* (1962), consider the varied American reactions to the Revolution. Betty M. Unterberger, *America's Siberian Expedition* (1956), explains the failure of that misguided action. Lawrence E. Gelfand, *The Inquiry: American Preparations for Peace, 1917–1919* (1963), is an account of the role of the president's advisers at Versailles. Paul Birdsall, *Versailles: Twenty Years After* (1973), assesses the peacemaking from the perspective of a later crisis.

# PART SIX

# Modernizing the Republic

### 1920 to the Present

Robert Dallek

$\mathcal{I}$N THE generation before 1920 the United States experienced far-reaching economic and social alterations, and these changes accelerated greatly in the next seven decades. This transformation encompassed a vast movement of peoples to and within the country; an enormous expansion of industrial and agricultural production and the rise of a consumer and service economy; a substantial growth of federal power at the expense of the localities; a concentration of authority in the White House; sweeping changes in relations between races, between ethnic and religious groups, and between men and women; and a shift in America's world role from reluctant power broker to dominant superpower.

Yet all was not change. An enduring affinity for free enterprise, individualism, federalism, and the separation of national powers, majority control, and limits on governmental intrusion into private affairs and on overseas involvements has given Americans a sense of continuity and stability throughout the last seven decades.

Traditional thinking was little more than a restraining force on modernism. The interaction of the American political and economic systems (that is, the nation's political economy) offers a good case in point. Beginning with the late-nineteenth-century industrial consolidations, the main subdivisions of the economy—production and distribution, finance, skilled labor, and commercial agriculture—had become increasingly organized, committed to nationwide cooperation, and alert to the usefulness of the government in Washington. World War I had accelerated these trends. By the mid-1920s, the national government had adopted a consistent policy of support for these organized groups, and the components of the nation's modern political economy fell into place. Although the operations of the political economy grew vastly more complex during the next seven decades, its essential character did not change. But alternate spells of prosperity, depression, and recession, of inflation and stagflation, raised fundamental questions about the modern political economy and gave old laissez-faire ideas a continuing resonance.

American politics since 1920 has also undergone a major transformation. Authority has largely shifted from local centers of power—cities, counties, and states—to the federal government. In response to the Great Depression, World War II, the Cold War, and chronic economic and social injustices, Washington acquired unprecedented powers to manage the economy, reduce poverty and inequality, and defend national security. But abuses by federal officials have troubled many Americans. They have come to feel increasingly ambivalent about a powerful central government that has conferred desirable benefits on numerous citizens and defended the national interest overseas, but has also created a federal establishment that seems to intrude excessively in people's daily lives and mismanages some of its responsibilities. One of the century's more disturbing political trends, indeed, has been the steady decline in voter participation, an erosion of citizens' sense of personal responsibility for the public good that began in the Progressive Era and has continued erratically down to the present.

Twentieth-century Americans have fretted as well over what values should govern the individual in society. The growth of large business organizations employing the majority of Americans, as well as the rise of a consumer culture encouraging leisure and self-indulgence, has contradicted traditional assumptions about rugged individualism and hard work. If Americans have found much to attract them to the new cultural values and social-reform impulses of the post-1920 period, they have also worried about the loss of old habits, and they continue to give at least rhetorical allegiance to traditional ideas. Tension between liberalism and conservatism—to use the modern terms applied to these competing values—thus has been a mainstay of twentieth-century American life. These political alignments originated in the Progressive Era, and they sharpened (and to some extent were redefined) during the period of New Deal reforms in the 1930s. Liberalism reached its political highwater mark in the Kennedy and Johnson administrations of the 1960s, but since then liberals have often found themselves on the defensive. By 1990, although firmly committed to an organized, decentralized society, and devoted more to consumption and personal absorption than to frugality and public concerns, the American people have also clung to the conventional, locally oriented mores enunciated by Ronald Reagan, one of the most popular presidents of the twentieth century. The liberal-conservative dichotomy, in short, offers an illuminating insight into the national experience—cultural and social as well as political—over the past ninety years.

In its foreign relations as well, the American republic has swung between two poles. In the 1920s and 1930s the United States tried to limit its political involvement in world affairs as much as possible, relying principally on moral injunctions against aggression and war. To protect itself against the Axis challenge in the 1940s, however, the nation first prepared itself for battle and then plunged into World War II after being attacked at Pearl Harbor. When the United States emerged from the war as the premier world power and confronted a perceived threat from international communism, it abandoned old-style isolationism and developed a long-range, systematic pattern of foreign commitments that projected American power around the globe. But the unsuccessful war in Vietnam eroded popular support for the global containment of communism and revived the habit of national soul-searching about what America's proper role in world affairs should be. By 1991, the resurgence of Western European and Japanese power, the collapse of communism in Eastern Europe and perhaps even in the Soviet Union itself, the apparent end of the cold war, and a war with Iraq in the Persian Gulf had raised additional questions about America's new world role.

Unsettling domestic and international changes since 1920 have encouraged an attraction not only to a usable past but also to an authoritative national figure who can speak for all Americans, define and carry out public policy, and embody the symbols that remain unifying forces in the republic. Beginning with Theodore Roosevelt in the first years of the century, the president has consistently served as the most important figure in the country's public life. No chief executive has avoided criticism during his term, and several have been repudiated by the voters after losing their hold on the popular imagination. Yet even unsuccessful presidents tell us much about the state of national affairs. In short, the presidential administrations of the post-1920 era make an excellent organizing framework for studying the affairs of a diverse and dynamic nation.

# 28

# *The Emergence of the Modern Republic*

## *The Twenties*

*P*RINCIPAL features of the Roaring Twenties were a new technology, a new prosperity, a new emphasis on personal self-indulgence, and a new faith in the future. But for all its forward-looking characteristics, the decade was also notable as a cramped, mean-spirited time of repression and conformity at home and of backward-looking isolationism abroad. These contrasts added up to a clash between modernizing and traditional forces. Generalizing broadly, urban America, where the majority of Americans now lived, led the way into the future; rural, small-town folks spoke for old values. The clash of ideas and standards expressed itself in struggles over Prohibition, immigration restriction, and the teaching of evolution in the schools. The presidents of the era—Harding, Coolidge, and Hoover—also reflected the divisions in the country. On one hand, the three Republicans appealed to conventional pieties and opposed government activism; on the other, they stood in the forefront of those forces that encouraged modernization through industrial and agricultural consolidation.

Above all, it was in the twenties that the foundations of the modern nation were laid. The economic structure, government responsibilities, social divisions, and overseas commitments that evolved during these years marked the emergence of modern America and shaped its development in later decades.

### *Politics in the 1920s: The Struggle for Traditional Values*

Political events at the threshold of the twenties gave no indication of the major changes about to grip the nation. Reacting against the crusading fervor and the growth of presidential power during the eight preceding years of the Wilson administration, both major parties nominated for president conventional mediocrities who reflected the public's nostalgia for an earlier way of life. For the

Democrats, Governor James M. Cox of Ohio offered the best alternative to the stricken but still-ambitious President Wilson. Adding a dash of color to Cox's rather dull candidacy, the Democrats nominated as his running mate jaunty young Franklin D. Roosevelt, the assistant secretary of the navy. The Republicans broke a convention deadlock by selecting weak, affable Senator Warren G. Harding, also from Ohio, and for vice-president the conservative, probusiness governor of Massachusetts, Calvin Coolidge. Cox defended Wilson's foreign policy and the League; Harding opposed both. As the candidates traded platitudes, the tide that had been flowing against the Democrats since 1918 swept the Republicans to power. Soured by the disruptions of the war and the disillusionment of the peace, 61 percent of the American voters, a larger popular majority than any previously given to a presidential candidate, chose the amiable Harding. It was the first national election in which, as a consequence of the Nineteenth Amendment (1920), women throughout the United States voted. Considering all the passions that had been stirred up by the suffragist movement before the war, the results in 1920 were anticlimactic. The women's vote divided about the same as the men's. Like men, women voted overwhelmingly for traditional values. With Harding's election, conservative Republicans not only reestablished their control over the White House but also sustained the majorities they had won in both houses of Congress in 1918—and would maintain until 1930.

**Antiradicalism and Bigotry**
Harding, a decent man, came to office with vague impulses toward creating a quiet national harmony. "America's present need," he had declared during the campaign, "is not heroics, but healing; not nostrums, but normalcy." Many Americans, however, believed there could be no healing without major surgery first. Movements against disruptive radicals, labor unions, and immigrants, which had originated early in the century and swelled during the war, were cresting. Neither Harding nor his successor, Coolidge, had the will or the strength to check this repressive nativism.

Fears of Bolshevik revolution, touched off by the Russian upheaval of 1917, had stirred up the so-called Red Scare of 1919–20 in the United States. During these years a host of private vigilantes and public officials moved with devastating effect against organized radicalism. They completed the destruction of the Industrial Workers of the World (IWW),* ransacked offices of the Socialist party, and even stopped legally elected Socialists from taking their seats in the House of Representatives and the New York State Assembly. Wilson's attorney general, A. Mitchell Palmer, twice ordered extensive raids on the nation's fledgling Communist party and came very close to annihilating it. Eventually the absence of real revolutionaries overcame the public's nightmares of a Bolshevik under every bed. When Palmer predicted that there would be massive bombings on May Day of

---

*For background on the IWW, see chapter 25, pp. 245–46.

1920 and nothing happened, the scare rapidly fizzled out, and with it ended one phase of antiradicalism.

Nevertheless, a more general antiradicalism remained pervasive during the early twenties. Such groups as the American Legion imposed provincial, patriotic textbooks on the public schools and forced the firing of liberal teachers. Officials in the Navy Department campaigned against an imaginary "spider web" of women's organizations said to be subverting the nation's fighting spirit. "America," evangelist Billy Sunday declared, "is not a country for a dissenter to live in." One victim of this antiradical attitude was the Non-Partisan League, an alliance of respectable farmers, lawyers, and merchants in the Northwest that won control of the North Dakota government and tried to use state funds to aid local farmers. In 1921 and 1922 a group of bankers boycotted the league and succeeded in undermining its "socialist" program.

Antiradicalism also merged with a drive against organized labor. Immediately after the war, businessmen and their allies created "open shop" committees throughout the nation to smash unions. Although Samuel Gompers, the president of the American Federation of Labor, and most other labor leaders were vigorous antiradicals, they still could not protect their own unions from being labeled socialist and un-American. In 1919 the steel companies crushed an ambitious drive to organize workers in their industry. Two years later the biggest meatpackers cleared the unions from their plants. Conservative judges prohibited a variety of strikes, including ones by the coal miners in 1919 and the railway shopmen in 1922. Under these blows union membership fell from a peak of more than 5 million in 1920 to about 3.6 million in 1923, and union morale suffered even more than statistics could reveal.

The famous Sacco-Vanzetti case epitomized the antiradicalism of the time. In 1921 two Italian immigrant anarchists, Nicola Sacco and Bartolomeo Vanzetti, were tried, convicted, and sentenced to death for the murder of a paymaster in South Braintree, Massachusetts. For years legal appeals delayed their execution. The bias of the trial, and the dignity and eloquence of the prisoners during their long ordeal, attracted a wide range of sympathizers, who fought fervently for their pardon. Despite complaints that the evidence against the men was circumstantial and that their real "crime" was being foreign-born radicals, they both died in the electric chair in August 1927. (Recent evidence indicates that Sacco, but not Vanzetti, may have been guilty.) Large crowds in America and abroad mourned in public. Nevertheless, the executions marked a shift in national mood that put conservatives on the defensive. Prominent citizens who had once screamed "Bolshevik!" at every dissenter in sight remained remarkably quiet while an embarrassing legacy from the recent past ran its course.

The early twenties was generally an oppressive time for immigrants, who faced not only social and economic problems, but also widespread charges that their alien influences were permanently corrupting American society. Even before the war a growing number of "native Americans"—white Protestants with northern and western European ancestors—became convinced that they needed special protection against a deluge of Catholics and Jews from southern and eastern Europe. Some accused the immigrants of flooding the labor market and lowering the American standard of living. Others, citing the newcomers' support of political bosses, declared them unfit to vote. Advocates of Prohibition condemned their saloons, and urban reformers deplored their living habits. By 1920 innumerable Americans were justifying these prejudices with racial theories that categorized the "dirty little dark people" of southern and eastern Europe as a genetically inferior breed, mongrelizing the American population. Unrestricted immigration, the popular writer Kenneth Roberts warned, would create "a hybrid race of people as worthless and futile as the good-for-nothing mongrels of Central America and southeastern Europe."

Economic considerations also shaped the early twenties' debate on immigrants. In 1920–21 the country experienced a sharp economic downturn after the wartime boom, with farm income plunging over 60 percent and unemployment spurting up from 2 percent to 12 percent of the work force. Although the economy largely righted itself in 1922, unemployment, spurred by industrial automation, never dipped below 5 percent during the rest of the decade. Moreover, the average industrial wage of $1,300 in the twenties was well below the $2,500 a year needed by a family of four for a minimum standard of living. Not surprisingly, organized labor, which was concentrated in cities, saw unrestricted immigration as a cause of depressed wages and increased joblessness, and it advocated legislative limits on migration to the United States.

Despite the efforts of a minority of Americans who defended the immigrants and the American tradition of open gates, public debate in the early twenties focused on the best techniques for restricting the immigrant influx. The fact that rigid regulatory measures ran counter to popular laissez-faire or free-market ideas by no means checked Americans' eagerness to restrict the free flow of immigrants to the United States. The government's first attempt, the Literacy Test of 1917, had failed because, contrary to common prejudice, most immigrants could read and write. So opponents of immigration shifted to a more effective device: the setting of annual immigration quotas by nationality. In 1921 Congress set each European country's quota at 3 percent of the number of foreign-born persons from that country in the 1910 census. Then in the comprehensive National Origins Act of 1924, Congress substituted even lower quotas as an interim measure until experts could prepare the long-range solution—an annual limit of 150,000 immigrants, divided according to the presumed percentage of each European nation's historical contribution to the white population in the United States.*

The justification of these laws was explicitly racial and defensive. They were passed at a time when a considerable amount of anti–Semitism pervaded Amer-

---

*The complicated calculations on national origins were not completed until 1929. The system then went into effect and remained the fundamental law on immigration until 1965, when Congress in a new law made "family reunification" and the nation's need for skills the basis for deciding who should be admitted.

ican society. At each stage in the legislative sequence, Congress discriminated more harshly against southern and eastern Europe, where by far the largest number of potential immigrants lived. The act of 1924 not only placed a ceiling on immigration that was less than one-fifth of the normal prewar flow, but assigned the English, Germans, and Scandinavians higher quotas than they were able to fill and almost closed the door on the Italians, Poles, and other Slavs. A decade later these quotas would bar many Jewish fugitives from Hitler's Third Reich. In a direct slap at the Japanese, the law totally excluded Asians. Africans and Hispanics, who represented only a tiny percentage of the recent migrations to the United States, also lost the chance to come to the country. The point of the law was to maintain roughly the same ethnic composition as in the pre–Civil War era. Seldom had Congress managed to embitter so many people at home and abroad with a single law.

The Ku Klux Klan came to embody all the bigotry of the early twenties. In 1920 two talented promoters, Edward Clarke and Elizabeth Tyler, took charge of a small southern organization with a name made notorious in the days of Reconstruction.* Capitalizing on the attractions of its fraternal secrecy, white-hooded ritual, and elaborate titles, they built the Ku Klux Klan into a nationwide organization of about 4 million members by 1924. The Klan viewed blacks, aliens (which translated into Catholics and Jews), and "moral degenerates" as its primary enemies, and in fighting them it often resorted to intimidation and violence. The fiery cross and the midnight whipping became its symbols of justice.

The Klan was a collection of local organizations that fought particular enemies in each community but shared an aversion to the rapid social changes of the twenties. Disturbed by manifestations of modernism—rapid growth of cities populated by alien peoples and liberal thinkers who championed relaxed social mores—Klansmen attacked anything that seemed at odds with traditional American values—even (in Denver, for example) labor unions and welfare programs. In the Oklahoma oil fields a local "klavern" boasted of transforming "'no counts' of men and females . . . almost [into] a 'Sunday-School class.'" Its counterpart in Calypso, North Carolina, announced, "All the Catholic gold in the universe can't buy our manhood and our liberty."

Aided by the glorification of the earlier Klan in the 1915 film classic (and racist vehicle) *Birth of a Nation,* the Klan extended its influence into state and national politics. Early in the 1920s its leaders seized political control of states as varied as Oklahoma, Oregon, and Indiana. The Klan's national spokesmen supported every campaign against radicals and immigrants, and Klansmen proudly paraded through the nation's capital. At the Democratic convention of 1924, a resolution condemning the Klan, narrowly lost; debate over it almost tore the party apart.

The Klan remained a formidable presence in American politics until 1925, representing only an exaggerated, somewhat disreputable, version of a common

---

*For the nineteenth-century origins of the Ku Klux Klan, see chapter 20, pp. 35–37.

**The KKK Marching in Washington, D. C., 1926**
*Though it wrapped itself in the flag and declared itself the defender of American values, the Klan embodied all the bigotry of the early twenties.*

American impulse. Principally living in small towns and rural areas, Klansmen longed openly for a mythical America of hardworking, churchgoing, small-town citizens, all white, Anglo-Saxon, and Protestant. This same quest for a lost virtue and a lost unity dominated all twenties movements against radicals, unions, and immigrants. Klansmen, like other Americans in all walks of life, expected public policy to reflect their cultural and moral visions, and to a striking degree these expectations were fulfilled by 1924.

Yet these grim assaults dwindled rapidly at mid-decade. The battle against radicals, unions, and immigrants had largely been won. In 1924 the national government abandoned the cause of antiradicalism, and by 1928 thirty-four states allowed the feeble Communist party a place on their ballots. Pressure on the public schools lifted. At the annual meeting of the American Legion in 1925, one officer complained that "Americans have become apathetic to the monotonous appeal of the patriotic exhorter." Vigilante activities also declined dramatically. Between 1922 and 1926, the American Civil Liberties Union reported, the number of disrupted public meetings dropped from 225 to 21. By 1925 the Klan was demoralized by exposés of corruption and by the conviction of Indiana's leading Klansman, David Stephenson, in the sex murder of his secretary, and its membership plummeted from 4 million in 1924 to 200,000 in 1928. By the mid-twenties traditional consensus politics and economic issues once again occupied the center of American life.

## Traditional Politics, 1923–1929

If antiradicalism and nativism were central features of the twenties, so were conventional politics. The presidential candidates of both parties, the cabinet officers, and congressional leaders were generally familiar political figures. They were also representatives of the business interests and political machines that had become mainstays of the nation. The chief executives during the decade— Warren G. Harding, Calvin Coolidge, and Herbert Hoover—stood for the traditional values of rugged individualism, free enterprise, and limited government powers. Despite these presidents' significant support for the economic innovations under way in the 1920s, their old-fashioned pronouncements provided a strong sense of continuity with the past.

**Scandals**
Twenties' bigotry and repression played out against a backdrop of ineffective national political leadership. Harding, essentially a small-town American, floundered beyond his depth as president. "I knew that this job would be too much for me," he confided to one White House visitor. As president, Harding supported some worthwhile agricultural and budgetary reforms, found the compassion Woodrow Wilson lacked to pardon Eugene V. Debs, and persuaded the steel industry to abandon a seven-day week for workers. He also made some excellent appointments, including Secretary of State Charles Evans Hughes, Secretary of Treasury Andrew Mellon, Secretary of Commerce Herbert Hoover, and Secretary of Agriculture Henry C. Wallace. Generally, however, he made little use of federal power to deal with national problems and surrounded himself with old friends who embarrassed and undermined his administration.

Harding's system has been described as "government by crony." Attorney General Harry Daugherty, Harding's close friend, was caught accepting bribes to protect former clients from federal prosecution. Then Charles Forbes, a chance acquaintance whom Harding had appointed director of the Veterans' Bureau, and Thomas Miller, the alien property custodian, were indicted and jailed for extensive frauds. Most sensational of all was the revelation, during long congressional inquiry in 1923 and 1924, of a crude string of bribes and backroom deals behind the leasing to private concerns of government oil lands on Teapot Dome in Wyoming and Elk Hills in California. Two oilmen, Harry Sinclair and Edward Doheny, had bought the leases from Secretary of Interior Albert Fall for almost half a million dollars in cash, bonds, and cattle. As a consequence of the "Teapot Dome Scandal," Fall (who looked for all the world like a Hollywood sheriff) was convicted of bribery and became the first cabinet officer in history to serve a prison sentence. Harding's close associate Daugherty barely escaped being the second.

The ineffectual Harding had sensed disaster. "My God, this is a hell of job," he told a journalist. "I have no trouble with my enemies..., but my Goddamn friends...they're the ones that keep me walking the floor nights!" In June 1923, as he began a tour of Alaska and the western United States, Harding asked

**Calvin Coolidge**
*A thoroughly conventional
American, Coolidge symbolized
traditional values in an
unsettling era.*

Herbert Hoover: "If you knew of a great scandal in our administration, would you for the good of the country and the party expose it publicly or would you bury it?" Hoover counseled publicizing it. Shortly after, still on his trip, a despondent Harding died of a heart attack.

Vice-President Calvin Coolidge inherited the mess. A taciturn, morose New Englander with a constricted view of government—he impressed Theodore Roosevelt's daughter as having been weaned on a pickle—Coolidge nevertheless appealed to the country as a symbol of venerable old American virtues: frugality, honesty, hard work, and religious faith. Coolidge turned this image to his advantage in the 1924 election. His identification with old Puritan virtues seemed the perfect antidote to the corruption of the Harding administration. It also gave the Republicans a satisfactory answer to a collection of dissident farm spokesmen, union officials, socialists, and Republican reformers who had revived the Progressive party under the leadership of Robert La Follette.* Too divided among themselves to form a workable coalition, the progressives carried only Wisconsin. Nor could a splintered Democratic party effectively challenge Coolidge. Torn between an eastern urban bloc and a southern and western rural bloc, the Democratic convention had gone through 103 ballots before nominating John W. Davis, a drab Wall Street lawyer. In November "Silent Cal" swamped Davis by 382 electoral votes to 136.

---

*For the earlier political career of Robert La Follette, see chapters 24 and 25.

Coolidge's triumph coincided with a new calm in national affairs. Indeed, few presidents have encountered as meek a Congress as Coolidge faced after 1924. Liberal opponents such as Senator William Borah of Idaho and Senator George Norris of Nebraska won occasional skirmishes but no important campaigns. The president's Bureau of the Budget, relying on the advice of the United States Chamber of Commerce, set the level of government spending, and congressional appropriations were an almost perfect carbon of the bureau's recommendations. In 1926 even the controversial tax program of Secretary of the Treasury Andrew Mellon was enacted. To release more money for private investment, Congress lowered the rate of income tax for the very wealthy from 46 percent to 26 percent and cut inheritance taxes in half. As Coolidge sagely averred, "The business of America is business."

The only significant signs of a congressional rebellion came over farm policy. Commodity prices, which had fallen sharply in 1921, revived sluggishly during the rest of the twenties. In 1929 net farm income was still $3 billion lower than it had been in 1919. During the early twenties the farm lobby had won an array of laws from Congress, including higher tariffs, tighter regulation of the grain exchanges and the stockyards, and easier credit for commercial farmers. When none of these helped very much, sentiment shifted toward the proposals of the persistent George Peek, a manufacturer of agricultural equipment who crusaded for agricultural reforms throughout the twenties. Seal off the domestic market with high tariffs, Peek told the farmers, and sell what you can in this protected market. Then have the government buy the surplus, dump it abroad at the best price, and tax the farmers a small amount to cover any losses.

In Washington, Peek's plan became the McNary-Haugen bill. First in the West and then in the South, Peek gathered enough support to push the McNary-Haugen bill through Congress twice, in 1927 and again in 1928. Coolidge vetoed it both times. Yet by 1928 the actual difference between the farm lobby and the Coolidge administration was not very great. The administration's solution, which was enacted into law in 1929, also sought to regulate the marketing of agricultural products. When prices fell, commodity cooperatives would receive temporary government payments while they stored their products. As prices improved, the cooperatives would gradually sell their surplus and repay the government. In fact, the second McNary-Haugen bill included this scheme. Therefore, considerable optimism prevailed in 1929 when Congress created the Federal Farm Board with an unprecedented $500 million in government credit to help the cooperatives market their products at the best prices.

**Traditional Versus Modern Politics**
In the twenties Americans felt close attachments to neighborhood and community. They cared very much about jobs and income, but they tried to manage these problems locally. Their networks were personal, woven through families, friends, and local business contacts, and consciousness of a shared culture strengthened these connections. Outside the cities this usually meant pride in being white,

Anglo-Saxon, and Protestant. In the cities many groups were trying to preserve their ethnic differences. Black, brown, yellow, or white skin; Italian, Polish, German, or Irish ancestors; Catholic, Protestant, or Jewish religion—all drew critical social lines.

In the cities, small towns, and countryside alike, these tight local attachments made it extremely difficult to create any kind of broad political organization. Local politics remained the one natural center for the mixture of economic, cultural, and moral concerns. Traditional local politics dominated innumerable county organizations in which friendship and family ties, not efficiency and expertise, determined who would receive most of the jobs and favors. In the big-city political wards, similar private bargains tied individuals, families, and cultural groups into little political alliances. These many personal arrangements were linked together to form the political machines that thrived during the twenties. Although the machines were known by the names of their bosses—Tom Pendergast in Kansas City, Big Bill Thompson in Chicago, Ed Crump in Memphis, Frank Hague in Jersey City, and James Michael Curley in Boston— these political organizations were decentralized and popular.

During the twenties it took an exceptionally powerful force to excite national interest. The strongest magnet was the Eighteenth, or "Prohibition," Amendment, which banned the production and sale of liquor. Long-standing beliefs that drink reduced efficiency in the workplace and that it particularly injured women who were victimized by alcoholic husbands—and of course alcohol's association in the minds of traditional rural and small-town Americans with urban aliens— gave special force to the antiliquor movement. Put into effect in January 1920 and enforced by the strict Volstead Act, the Eighteenth Amendment began its career in an atmosphere of high optimism. Drinking, declared William Jennings Bryan, was as dead an issue as slavery.

But countless Americans decided otherwise. Continuing demand in the big cities and a considerable market elsewhere in the nation created a massive business out of illicit production and distribution. As one investigating commission ruefully noted, "Few things are more easily made than alcohol." A little machinery and a bathtub transformed any thirsty citizen into a distiller. Moreover, the long boundary of the United States provided many unpatrolled areas where illegal importers could smuggle liquor into the country. Rumrunners trucked it in from Canada and Mexico, and ferried it in small boats to isolated coves along both coasts. To police these many violations, the Treasury Department employed about 2,000 officials. Herbert Hoover later estimated that effective enforcement would have required at least 250,000. Indeed, Prohibition's most serious long-term consequence was to encourage a general disrespect for law and expand and strengthen the organized crime syndicates (such as Al Capone's in Chicago) that quickly established control over the illegal liquor traffic.

In 1920 most prominent citizens dutifully endorsed the Eighteenth Amendment. But in the course of the decade, although Prohibition brought a decline in alcoholism and especially in deaths from cirrhosis of the liver, successful Americans increasingly turned against it. Millions of citizens came to consider Prohibition an insufferable violation of their rights. Prohibition, they said, artificially created a new class of criminals—those who drank and those who supplied the liquor—and then increased taxes to pay for the enforcement of the law. Those who favored repeal assumed that the use of alcohol did not matter very much: drinking should be a question of individual choice.

The "wets" not only made a joke of the law in their neighborhoods and communities; they increasingly demanded action from national and state governments. Americans of immigrant Catholic extraction protested a policy they knew to be directed in considerable measure against them and their neighborhood saloons. In 1923 New York repealed the state law that enforced Prohibition; by 1930 six other states had followed New York's lead. But with equal fervor millions of locally oriented "drys" regarded Prohibition as the keystone of American morality or, more modestly, as a reasonable response to the enormous private and social devastation that drinking wrought. Beyond pressing for Prohibition in their localities, they sponsored stern laws to uphold what Herbert Hoover and many liberal Democrats called "an experiment noble in motive and far-reaching in purpose." In Michigan a fourth offense under the Prohibition law meant life imprisonment. The battle over Prohibition was a powerful expression of the tension between modernism and traditionalism; the struggle was not simply between those who favored and opposed drink but between people fighting for what they saw as irreconcilable truths.

From these same sources came the emotions that made Alfred E. Smith the most controversial politician of the 1920s. A capable governor of New York who very much wanted to be president, Al Smith touched the nerve centers of traditional, local politics. He was a Catholic, an antiprohibitionist, and a self-taught politician who wore Tammany Hall's traditional brown derby askew and spoke in the nasal twang of Manhattan's East Side streets. The thought of Al Smith in the White House roused feelings of wonder and horror across the nation. Self-conscious ethnic groups in the northern cities who were Catholic and wet gave him their fanatical devotion. White Protestant Democrats in the rural South who were dry looked on Smith as the Antichrist. At the Democratic convention of 1924, Smith's friends and enemies had fought over his nomination to the point of exhaustion before turning to John W. Davis. But in 1928, in the absence of a serious competitor, southern delegates finally allowed Smith's nomination for president, although with profound misgivings.

The election of 1928 provided a unique meeting ground for the conflicting spirits of modern and traditional politics. To oppose Smith, the Republicans chose Herbert Hoover, by all odds the outstanding leader of the modern political economy, but, like Coolidge, also a symbol of old America. After an impressive early success in business as a mining engineer, Hoover had won renown during World War I as an administrator, first of international relief, then of agriculture. There was talk of Hoover as president in 1920. Instead he had served in the

**Al Smith Campaigning**
*Al Smith, the 1928 Democratic
candidate, symbolized the
growing influence of urban,
ethnic America in the twenties.*

cabinets of Harding and Coolidge and made himself the unofficial center of the executive branch: "Secretary of Commerce and assistant secretary of everything else." He was serious and shy, extremely proud and highly ambitious. Too formidable for Coolidge, who disliked him, and too independent for many professional politicians, who preferred a weaker man, Hoover went after the nomination with absolute confidence in his ability to be president. Successful Americans overwhelmingly supported him. Of those listed in *Who's Who,* for example, 87 percent endorsed his candidacy.

Al Smith sought to pitch his campaign to all Americans. An essentially conservative man, the Democratic candidate thought of himself as an eminently qualified leader for the American system, not only as a product of New York City's Lower East Side, but as a classic example of a self-made man. To oversee his campaign, Smith selected a prominent General Motors executive, John J. Raskob, rather than a professional politician. The partisans of traditional politics on both sides, however, would not let Smith rise above his origins. In November 1928 Smith's name on the ballot drew large, jubilant majorities in the industrial cities, where working-class people of immigrant ancestry clustered, but it also sent millions of Protestant townspeople to the polls with a religious commitment to Hoover and put seven formerly Democratic southern states in the Republican column. Hoover, the symbol of both modern prosperity and old American values, swept to victory with 444 electoral votes against Smith's 87. Smith's Catholicism had something to do with his defeat, but in 1928 even a more

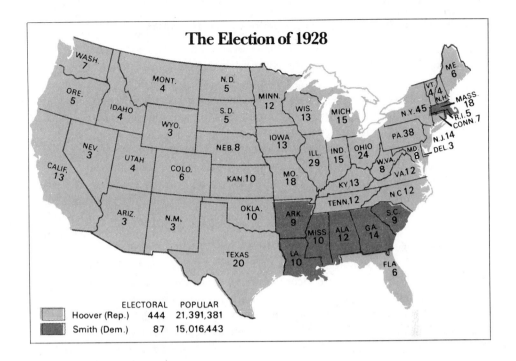

**The Election of 1928**

| | ELECTORAL | POPULAR |
|---|---|---|
| Hoover (Rep.) | 444 | 21,391,381 |
| Smith (Dem.) | 87 | 15,016,443 |

traditional Protestant Democrat would have found it nearly impossible to beat Hoover and Republican prosperity.

## America's Response to the World, 1920–1930

At the close of World War I, the great majority of Americans longed to insulate themselves from further contact with the outside world. Disillusioned by postwar turmoil in Europe, fearful of Bolshevism, and antagonistic toward immigrants bringing alien habits to the nation's shores, the country rejected participation in the League of Nations in 1920. It cut its army and navy in 1921 to fewer than 250,000 men, raised barriers to trade in the Fordney-McCumber Tariff Act of 1922, and throughout the decade refused to recognize the Soviet Union. Americans, it seemed, wanted walls to protect themselves against everything foreign— people, goods, ideas, and responsibilities.

Yet disengagement after the war was not a simple process. American soldiers who had invaded Siberia in a muddled attempt to counter the Bolsheviks lingered there until 1920 in an equally muddled attempt to counter Japanese influence. Until 1923 the United States also kept a token force in Germany's occupied Rhineland provinces, more to temper French belligerence than to punish Germany. Despite outrage from former allies, the United States insisted on the repayment of large loans that had been made during the war. Because the European debtors tried to link their payments to the United States to the amount of reparations they were collecting from Germany, Americans once more found themselves entangled in the issues that had defeated Wilson at Versailles.

Perhaps most important in the country's continuing involvement in world affairs after 1920 were its enduring sense of responsibility for international peace and its extensive ties to the world economy. Eager to support political and economic stability abroad without commitments that could force it into another war, Washington settled on a policy of what has been called "moral cooperation": paper agreements to control arms, and unofficial backing for private financial arrangements designed to prevent international economic collapse.

The first step in this process was the Washington Conference of 1921–22. This international meeting occurred in response to postwar demands for disarmament and for economy in government, and to fears of Japan's imperial ambitions on the mainland of Asia and toward colonies in the Pacific controlled by Western nations, especially the Philippine Islands. With the Far East in mind, Secretary of State Charles Evans Hughes, an astute diplomat, used as justification for calling the conference the growing concern over a worldwide naval armaments race. During the winter of 1921–22, representatives from industrial nations with interests in East Asia (except Soviet Russia) met in Washington. To everyone's surprise, Hughes insisted that the delegates act as well as talk. Consequently, the Washington Conference produced three important agreements, each seeking in some way to freeze the existing balance of power and privileges in East Asia. The critical Four-Power Treaty of nonaggression among the United States, Japan, Great Britain, and France superseded the prewar Anglo-Japanese alliance and committed the signatories to respect each other's rights in the Pacific. The Five-Power Treaty added Italy to the Big Four and established tonnage limitations on major warships according to a ratio approximating the current strength of these nations. The Nine-Power Treaty committed all imperial nations to the principle of equal opportunity inside an independent China—the American doctrine of the "Open Door."

These treaties reflected America's inward-turning, defensive impulses. They pulled the United States away from a naval confrontation with Japan, and they included no provisions for enforcement. Yet they acknowledged a crucial inter-connection among the world's industrial nations, a mutual dependence that required negotiation, coordination, and a broad structure of rules.

In the same spirit of coordination and stabilization, Americans responded to the European crisis of 1923–24. When Germany defaulted on its reparations and French troops occupied the industrial nerve center of the Ruhr, runaway inflation convulsed the German economy. Dependent on German reparations, the French economy also staggered. Through the Dawes Plan of 1924, the United States unofficially took the lead in negotiating large private loans to revive Germany. Simultaneously, J. P. Morgan and Company arranged a loan to France on the understanding that it would not disrupt the fragile German recovery. As Germany resumed paying reparations, the former Allied Powers made some payments on their war debts, and the United States did not press them very hard for more. Without a formal government commitment, the United States presided over a complex process of international stabilization.

These initial efforts to create international order remained basic to American policy. The Young Plan of 1929 reformulated the Dawes Plan in hopes of managing war debts and reparations far into the future. A year later the London Naval Conference expanded the scope of the Washington Conference naval agreement to cover a full range of warships. In addition the United States diverted France's proposal in 1927 for a bilateral treaty into a general, multilateral declaration against war. More than sixty nations eventually ratified the Kellogg-Briand Peace Pact of 1928, which took its name from the principal negotiators, Coolidge's Secretary of State Frank B. Kellogg and France's Foreign Minister Aristide Briand. "An international kiss," snorted Missouri's flinty Senator James Reed. Other critics complained that the treaty—a pledge by its signatories not to go to war with each other—wasn't worth a postage stamp and amounted to no more than a New Year's resolution or a letter to Santa Claus. Nevertheless, a popular isolationism would allow no greater American involvement in global enforcement. When the Coolidge administration recommended that the United States join the World Court, the weak judicial arm of the League of Nations, the Senate attached so many special conditions to America's participation that the other members of the World Court refused the terms.

An aversion to aggressive action extended to Latin America as well. During the twenties the three Republican administrations gradually rejected the "Roosevelt Corollary" to the Monroe Doctrine, which had made the United States a policeman over Latin America's unstable, defaulting governments. The best evidence of a change was from the long, difficult negotiations with revolutionary Mexico over the rights of oil corporations. President Coolidge dispatched the adroit banker Dwight Morrow as ambassador and won a settlement of the oil controversy in 1928.*

In all, American foreign policy in the twenties endorsed an international rule of law for the peaceful settlement of differences among countries. From the perspective of World War II and the cold war, the international system that the United States helped to construct in the twenties looks particularly naive. But the peace-loving, isolationist temper of the time would not allow policymakers to do more. Not until the Great Depression and the rise of aggressive regimes in Germany and Japan did Americans become persuaded that international affairs required more than paper promises to ensure economic and political stability around the globe. Only then would more "realistic" assumptions about the world shape Washington's handling of overseas affairs.

## The Modern Political Economy, 1920–1929

In contrast to the reactionary political trends of the early twenties, fundamental changes in social and economic organization spread through the nation. These transformations fueled the antagonisms between those who clung to traditional

---

*In 1937, however, the Mexican government nationalized all foreign-owned oil companies.

ways and those willing to accept change. None of the changes individually made the headlines; in combination they completed an organizational revolution that had been under way for more than a generation and had been accelerated by World War I. Since the turn of the century, national groups in business, labor, agriculture, finance, and the professions had been coalescing—associations of lumber companies, retail druggists, railroad workers, investment bankers, civil engineers, and the like. Each group organized itself according to the special economic function it performed, and each wanted to stabilize its own sphere with its own rules. Each expected long-range planning to increase its efficiency and its income. Each recognized the importance of linking its activities with the activities of other groups around it. Taken together, they created a new national system of specialized organizations that were integrated by a common ability to think nationally rather than locally, by a common concern for the vigor of the whole economy, and by a common belief in the value of cooperation and coordination.

**Business in the Twenties**

The most successful means of business stabilization was oligopoly, the domination of an industry by a few large firms. A trend toward oligopolistic organization of the national economy had been under way since the 1870s.* By 1920 oligopolies controlled almost every basic industry that needed a heavy investment of capital. In railroading, for example, a handful of corporations, approximately equal in strength, divided the nation's territory among themselves. In the automobile industry, Ford and General Motors set the standard for an expanding market. In steel one huge firm, United States Steel, rose above the other corporations—collectively called Little Steel—to become the industry's leader. Oligopoly simplified the problems of industrial coordination by limiting the number of companies that had to agree on a common business policy. Buccaneers of business like Jay Gould no longer ran these industrial giants. Now management teams, working through elaborate corporate structures, coordinated the nation's big business.

In such industries as clothing manufacture, building construction, and most branches of retailing, where capital demands were less and many small firms competed, trade associations offered an alternative way of minimizing competition. About 2,000 trade associations already existed in 1920, and they continued to multiply. With their activities ranging from secret price-fixing pacts to occasional lunch meetings, the trade associations shared a belief that pooling information would stabilize their industries and increase their profits. Although they seldom coordinated business affairs as effectively as did the oligopolies, the trade associations too were moving toward cooperation and planning.

Most businessmen expected wage earners to play their part in these coordinating programs. Unlike the captains of industry of the late nineteenth century,

---

*See chapter 24, p. 182.

who had usually treated wage earners much as they did hunks of ore or gears in the machinery, modern business managers considered laborers as individuals whose efficiency would increase as their morale and incentive improved. Specialists in personnel policy organized company recreational programs, prepared chatty company bulletins, and invited workers to suggest improvements in the firms' procedures. Large corporations in particular sponsored shop committees, company unions, and employee representation plans—"the world's greatest democracy," boasted the president of Standard Oil of Indiana. An increasing number of the unions in the AFL and the Railroad Brotherhoods adapted to such company policies. Under an accommodating new president, William Green, the AFL in 1925 listed the improvement of industrial productivity among its primary objectives. "[The] new, suave, discreet unionism," one commentator noted late in the 1920s, "talks the language of the efficiency engineer and busies itself about ways and means of increasing output."

Despite their leaders' willingness to cooperate with business, workers shared only part of the economic benefits of the period. In the best years of the twenties, the annual income of about two-thirds of the nation's families fell below the $2,500 that experts considered minimally adequate for a decent standard of living. These families had only an indirect stake in the economic system that was forming on the national level. When economic downturn replaced expansion at the end of the twenties, working-class Americans lacked the purchasing power to fuel a fresh burst of buying and economic growth.

For good reason, and continuing a trend that had begun about 1900, successful commercial farmers regarded themselves as businessmen. As chemical fertilizers and the gasoline engine were revolutionizing agriculture, only the wealthy investor, using the latest improvements on a large scale, could expect to profit from modern farming. These "agribusinessmen," as they were beginning to be called, like their industrial counterparts, wanted to coordinate their affairs, and they too organized. Local farm bureaus distributed information about scientific farming techniques, and lobbied for favorable government policies through the national organization, the American Farm Bureau Federation. Dairy farmers formed cooperative marketing associations. Groups of commercial farmers behaved so much like conventional business organizations that the same men who had staffed Bernard Baruch's War Industries Board in 1918 became the most prominent agricultural advisers of the twenties.

Bankers acted as auxiliaries to these various business groups. The wizards of Wall Street no longer dominated American business as they had twenty years earlier. Not only did the regional structure of the new Federal Reserve System encourage financial decentralization, but an increasing number of important corporations also gained control over their own banking. During the 1920s, companies as diverse as Eastman Kodak, Aluminum Corporation of America, Ford, and Sears, Roebuck routinely financed business expansion from their own vast profits. Banks too, as agencies of service, organized themselves in subdivisions that matched the needs of their business clients. The professions formed a second band of auxiliaries to business. Legal specialties in such fields as contracts, taxation, and labor policy grew up alongside modern industry. A variety of engineers, economists, statisticians, psychologists, sociologists, educators, and, above all, scientists also became willing helpers to the nation's business. Where an important profession, such as research chemistry, was not adequately developed, powerful industries encouraged its growth. Business increasingly needed an educated work force with a twelfth-grade education. High schools sprung up all over the country to meet the need.

Most wage earners during the 1920s were not union members, and most farmers never joined the agricultural organizations. Everywhere, very small businesses remained outside the economic leagues and trade associations; the United States Chamber of Commerce discouraged membership in towns under 5,000, and businessmen in these small communities kept largely to themselves. But although many millions of Americans did not belong to them, the emerging national economic organizations were the principal force in shaping the nation's economic life and had as great an impact on America's small towns as on its large cities.

**The New National and International Economy**

Because the new network of economic groups was national in scope and outlook, only the government in Washington could meet its needs. In the broadest sense the national government was expected to facilitate the work of private groups, to promote cooperation among them, and to surround them with a favorable legal framework. During the early twenties one after another of the government's offices shaped its policies to serve the new national economy. By 1925 expansion in the activities of the federal government had raised the federal budget to 250 percent of its sum in 1915.

Herbert Hoover, as secretary of commerce (1921–29) the most important cabinet official of the decade, led his department in its efforts to help manufacturers standardize production, to distribute business statistics for the trade associations, to enable the major broadcasting companies to stabilize the new radio industry, and to publicize the virtues of business cooperation at every opportunity. Hoover's actions were part of a concerted effort to stabilize the business cycle and promote the nation's first peacetime system of national economic planning. Other departments expanded their services. Commercial farmers, hydroelectric power companies, and private industries in food, mining, and lumber all benefited. Each of the independent regulatory commissions, so vital to progressive reform, found a way to assist business coordination. Through the Transportation Act of 1920 the Interstate Commerce Commission secured extensive authority over almost all areas of the railroad industry, and it used these broad powers to encourage oligopoly and cooperative agreements. By 1925 the Federal Trade Commission specialized in sponsoring conferences for trade associations. Because the Federal Reserve Board in Washington proved to be ineffective, the New York Regional Federal Reserve Bank coordinated national banking policy.

The Supreme Court endorsed all these developments. First, it sanctioned oligopolies. In *United States* v. *United States Steel Co.* (1920), the Court allowed the nation's largest corporation to dominate its industry as long as some competitors survived. Then, after considerable hesitation, the Court in the *Maple Flooring Manufacturers' Association* case of 1925 declared that trade associations, like oligopolies, were legal if they did not eliminate competition in their areas of business. The Justice Department advised the trade associations on how best to stay inside the law. Meanwhile the Court limited the constraints that the labor unions might impose on business. Led by its new chief justice, former president William Howard Taft, whom Harding had appointed in 1921, the Court sharply restricted organized labor's right to picket and boycott, and it watched approvingly as the lower courts expanded the use of injunctions against striking workers. In addition, the Supreme Court overturned a national child-labor law in *Bailey* v. *Drexel Furniture Co.* (1922) and a state minimum wage law in *Adkins* v. *Children's Hospital* (1923).

The national economic system could not function without the government's assistance. At the center of the national system were production and distribution, with agriculture connected at the side and labor linked below, and bankers and professionals contributing specialized services; the government's part was to wrap the system in protective rules, expert counsel, and helpful mediation. Herbert Hoover, the leading proponent of this national political economy, envisaged the system as a "third alternative" to laissez-faire capitalism and state socialism—a voluntary, cooperative commonwealth that followed the scientific principles of coordination and efficiency.

American policymakers also saw an intimate connection between international stability and economic expansion. Each, they thought, could be made to serve the other. At home or abroad, of course, the modern political economy was a profit system. Herbert Hoover's Department of Commerce gathered and distributed to American business extensive data on foreign markets, and the Congress passed laws freeing from antitrust regulations companies set up for export trading and permitting American banks to establish foreign branches. When American diplomats failed to break the European petroleum monopoly in the Middle East, the government allowed American oil companies to conduct their own diplomacy. At the same time, the government facilitated American companies' efforts to break the near-monopoly of British, French, and German businessmen over raw materials and utilities in Argentina, Brazil, Chile, and Uruguay. Yet foreign trade remained only about 5 percent of the national income during the twenties, and foreign investments never reached 3 percent of the nation's total assets. It was difficult to argue that the health of the American economy required drastic diplomatic measures abroad. Hence, in its efforts to assimilate business expansion into a healthy international order, Washington kept as much as possible to a voluntary cooperative system.

*The New Ford Convertible Cabriolet*

## Features of the Ford car

**The 1929 Ford**

*In the twenties the automobile, which came within the reach of most American families, helped to promote a national economic boom and to give Americans a greater sense of freedom.*

Sturdy body construction  ⋅⋅  Ease of control  ⋅⋅  Four Houdaille hydraulic double-acting shock absorbers  ⋅⋅  Triplex shatter-proof glass windshield  ⋅⋅  Fully enclosed, silent six-brake system  ⋅⋅  Quick acceleration  ⋅⋅  55 to 65 miles an hour  ⋅⋅  Smoothness and security at all speeds  ⋅⋅  Vibration-absorbing engine support  ⋅⋅  Choice of colors  ⋅⋅  Tilting beam headlamps  ⋅⋅  Theft-proof ignition lock  ⋅⋅  Reliability  ⋅⋅  Economy  ⋅⋅  Long life

*Ford*

**A Consumer Paradise**

By the mid-twenties the new national system was in place and performing miracles. After the sharp recession in 1921–22, the gross national product climbed 5 percent a year, and during the decade manufacturing output rose 64 percent. The automobile and construction industries led the boom. Both the number of automobile sales and the value of construction more than tripled between 1915 and 1925, and these economic leaders created benefits widely for such related industries as steel, petroleum, rubber, and cement. By the end of the twenties, the number of registered cars almost equaled the number of families. America's passionate love affair with the automobile had begun.

Cars, roads, and houses were nationally visible benefits. So was a second category of consumer products that relied on the spread of electricity. Midwestern utilities magnate Samuel Insull pioneered in selling metered electrical service to households, and other companies soon recognized the genius of his scheme. Before World War I, one out of five households had electricity; by the end of the twenties two out of three did. Into their new electrical outlets Americans plugged lamps, refrigerators, washing machines, vacuum cleaners, irons, and toasters, each a marvel in the twenties that freed women from much of their traditional household drudgery. Above all, electricity brought the radio. In November 1920 the crackling sounds of America's first radio station, KDKA of

## PRACTICAL GIFTS
### That will delight any woman

ELECTRICAL devices for the home—things that make the duties lighter and the home brighter—these are the gifts most welcome. And they exemplify the true Christmas spirit—the spirit of doing good to others in the most practical manner.

Why not surprise your wife or mother with a Western Electric vacuum cleaner—a washing machine—a dish washer—an electric iron or an Inter-phone between bedroom and kitchen? All of these save much hard work and many steps. Or, why not give her the soothing comfort of a Western Electric warming pad, or the convenience of the toaster, or the beauty of the table lamp? These, and many more needfuls, comprise the list of

## Western Electric
### Household Helps

They exemplify the high quality of all Western Electric merchandise, and are guaranteed by the world's largest distributors of electrical supplies. The Bell Telephone, which you use so often, is made by this company, and is an evidence of Western Electric worth.

This is the "Push-a-Button Age," in which the well-equipped housewife has electricity's power at her beck and call. Electricity is a willing helper, and the cost of current to operate any of these household helps is surprisingly low.

Electrical dealers all over the country sell our goods. Write to any of our houses in the cities listed below, and we will send you our booklet, "An Electrical Christmas," and tell you where in your vicinity our goods may be purchased. Ask for Booklet No. 61-T.

### WESTERN ELECTRIC COMPANY
Manufacturers of the 8,000,000 "Bell" Telephones

| | | | | |
|---|---|---|---|---|
| New York | Chicago | Kansas City | San Francisco | Montreal |
| Buffalo | Milwaukee | St. Louis | Salt Lake City | Portland |
| Philadelphia | Pittsburgh | Oklahoma City | Oakland | Toronto |
| Boston | Cleveland | Minneapolis | Los Angeles | Winnipeg |
| Richmond | Detroit | St. Paul | Dallas | Calgary |
| Atlanta | Cincinnati | Denver | Houston | Vancouver |
| Savannah | Indianapolis | Omaha | Seattle | Edmonton |
| New Orleans | EQUIPMENT FOR EVERY ELECTRICAL NEED | | | |

*Electric Table Lamp $4.50*

*The Vacuum Cleaner not built like a broom.*

*No. 11 Vacuum Cleaner $32.50*

*Electric Warming Pad $6.50 The successor to the hot-water bag.*

*Electric Toaster $4.00*

*American Beauty Electric Iron $5.00*

*Two Inter-phones Complete with Material for Installing $15.00*

*Electric Dish Washer*

*Electric Washing Machine*

**The New Electrical Appliances of the 1920s**
*The availability of electrical appliances in the twenties freed women from much of their traditional household drudgery.*

East Pittsburgh, opened a modern era of mass communication. By 1923 over five hundred broadcasting stations with much-improved equipment were in operation. Electrical technology also created a new lord of the entertainment world, motion pictures, which grew from a scattering of nickelodeon shows and occasional full-length features to a systematized $2 billion industry with a steady flow of films. By the end of the twenties, more than 80 million people were going to the movies each week. Radio and movies opened vistas that semiliterate Americans had never glimpsed before, making them conscious of the world beyond their small towns and urban ghettos.

For countless white, middle-class citizens, America became a consumer paradise. The availability of so many material goods that improved people's standard of living worked a revolution in the traditional attitude toward debt. Abandoning the time-honored rules to buy cautiously, fear debt, and save each small surplus, Americans turned consumer credit into a national necessity, and soon made it available through a great variety of convenient outlets. How the economy worked impressed some people even more than how much it produced. A broad range of manufacturing plants, following the lead of Henry Ford, introduced the moving assembly line, a revolution in factory procedure. Through electricity in industry and the gasoline engine in agriculture, the amount of horsepower per worker rose well over 50 percent during the twenties. As a consequence of these changes, output per working hour increased an astonishing 35 percent, almost twice the gains of the previous decade. America, it seemed, had answered all the riddles of economic growth. Throughout the twenties a stream of delegations came from abroad in hopes of discovering the secret of American productivity.

Contemporaries hailed the dawn of a "new era." "The first responsibility of an American to his country," announced one newspaper, "is no longer that of a citizen, but of a consumer." Former critics of American society now became its ardent champions. Socialism was "reactionary," said John Spargo, once a leader of the Socialist party, and American capitalism offered "the greatest hope for mankind." As the number of strikes declined drastically, praise resounded for the nationwide spirit of cooperation. "I can find no historic parallel, outside of the great religious revivals, with which [the present] has much in common," marveled a veteran of the social gospel. "Thru business...," another publicist promised even more grandly, "the human race is to be redeemed." From the vantage point of the Great Depression, the grandiose claims would be easy to ridicule: poverty on the verge of extinction, a chicken in every pot and two cars in every garage, anyone with self-discipline and common sense a millionaire. Yet during the late twenties, as later in the fifties and eighties, innumerable Americans and millions abroad believed in the American dream. And when the economic bubble would burst in the thirties, many who had spent so freely against future earnings would find themselves unable to pay their debts.

## Modern Culture

The new technology and participation in the consumer economy revolutionized the personal experiences of a great many Americans in the 1920s and created a stronger sense of national identity. This was true of people in both large cities and the countryside. Whether or not they fully accepted its implications, most Americans now found themselves enmeshed in broad new networks created by automobiles, telephones, radios, and motion pictures. The average middle-class person and many workers could now afford an automobile, so that people who had never traveled fifty miles from their hometowns discovered a wider world and came home with different points of view. Through extended and improved telephone services, they wove wider networks of family, friendship, and community ties. Radio and motion pictures brought still another dimension to their lives. National and international news broadcasts and musical entertainment (especially jazz) opened up a vast world for people trapped in parochial settings. The voices from the radio and the faces on the movie screen constituted a new, synthetic world of familiarity and trust in which no personal participation was necessary, or even possible. In a distinctively modern way, millions now felt more intimately involved with people they would never meet than with the people next door.

Rapid standardization in production in the automobile, radio broadcasting, and film industries created an illusion of American homogeneity that had not existed before World War I. By 1930 three automobile manufacturers—General Motors, Ford, and Chrysler—were making 83 percent of the nation's automobiles. Soon they would be synchronizing industrywide changes in car styles. The formation of the National Broadcasting Company in 1926 and of the Columbia Broadcasting System in 1927 superimposed national network programming over the previously decentralized radio industry, and after 1927 the total number of stations declined. In the fall of 1931, one-third of the population listened weekly to the comedy "Amos 'n' Andy" (in which white actors satirized black foibles). A flourishing advertising industry had Americans everywhere humming the jingles for Campbell's soup and Rinso soap. Hollywood films issued from a handful of gigantic studios, among them Warner Brothers and Metro-Goldwyn-Mayer. Standardization was a hallmark of the decade. At the same time, however, local newspapers, especially in the cities, where black, German, Spanish, and Yiddish dailies and weeklies flourished and radios carrying programs tailored to special audiences helped sustain diversity.

**Modern Values**     Among the messages coming from the modern centers of communication was a new model of the good life. A public vocabulary of frugality, work, and economic gain now gave way to an emphasis on leisure and play, conformity, and personal charm. Scientists, businessmen, and statesmen—the "idols of production"—had been the most prominent Americans at the turn of the century. Now the most admired public figures were the professional athletes and entertainers—the "idols of consumption." The newspapers of the era began to describe American life less as a political and economic struggle and more as "a hilarious merry-go-round of sport, crime, and sex."

In the twenties numerous Americans reveled in an exhilarating sense of freedom to enter the consumer market and simply enjoy themselves. Clothes worn during leisure hours became a matter of personal taste rather than an expression of solid character. The styles of the twenties stated the modern freedom: new colors and patterns for men's clothing, the departure of corsets and hobbling long skirts for women. Both men and women now smoked casually in public, and cigarette sales climbed 250 percent during the decade. The symbol of the exciting new freedom was the "flapper." Hair bobbed, face painted, and cigarette in hand, she waved an airy good-bye to yesterday's rules. Her flattened breasts, loose-fitting clothes, and short skirt gave her the appearance of a modern Peter Pan, seizing the pleasure of the moment in the spirit of eternal youth.

As the areas of private discretion expanded, leisure activities no longer had to be justified as morally beneficial but were simply considered good ways for people to release their tensions and return refreshed to their jobs. Between 1919 and 1929, as more people worked a fixed number of weekly hours and the work week itself contracted, American expenditures on recreation more than doubled. The best expression of the new meaning of leisure was the annual vacation, a period of time set aside specifically for relaxation. Once the prerogative of a very small, prosperous minority, the annual vacation became widely accepted during

**American Youth in the Twenties**
*The flapper, smoking in public, face-painted, and dressed in loose-fitting clothes, was a symbol of modern America.*

the twenties. Early in the decade, according to a study by the sociologists Robert and Helen Lynd, most white-collar employees in Muncie, Indiana, assumed for the first time in their lives that they had a right to an annual vacation, and many received one with pay. Increasing numbers flocked to the parks maintained by the expanding National Park Service for those vacations. Parks were recognized as a valuable public facility where the nation's city dwellers could turn once a year for their recreation.

At the same time, however, the country's traditional work ethic became more diversified. While some workers labored thirty-five to forty hours a week, enjoying coffee breaks and the annual two-week vacation, others, including lawyers, journalists, salespeople, and university teachers, expanded their workweek to sixty-five or seventy hours. Yet others became part of a permanent class of unemployed or nonworkers who gave up the search for productive employment. The traditional standard of hard work had not disappeared; but fewer people practiced it in a country where leisure and self-indulgence no longer seemed sinful.

**Changing Morals**   A higher premium on personal freedom meant a lower premium on traditional morals. Although church membership increased a striking 31 percent between 1916 and 1926, so did the emphasis in white-collar congregations on a soothing, largely undemanding religion that stressed good human relations rather than sin and salvation. But even some liberal Protestants winced at Bruce Barton's best selling *The Man Nobody Knows* (1925), which transformed Jesus into a vigorous executive who had taken "twelve men from the bottom ranks of business and forged them into an organization that conquered the world." Nevertheless, few liberal Protestants during the twenties expressed much concern of any kind for theological details or even denominational distinctions. To many of them, Catholicism now seemed less an evil religion than an odd but purely private choice. The anti-Catholic furor surrounding Al Smith's presidential campaign in 1928 simply made no sense from the new, liberal Protestant perspective.

Nor did the long-standing association between sex and sin. During the twenties a variety of psychologists, including the American disciples of Sigmund Freud, told Americans to consider sex a human need to satisfy; the more complete the satisfaction, the healthier the individual. Repression and guilt only warped the personality. Public displays of affection did not, as in the past, imply loose morals. Even premarital sex became a legitimate subject for discussion. America's pioneer advocate of birth control, Margaret Sanger, once scorned in respected circles, now won the approval and even the financial support of many well-to-do Americans. Although too much "petting" remained a parental worry and any hint of "free love" met sharp condemnation, sex emerged in the twenties as a subject for rational examination instead of moral taboo.

**The New Urban Standard**

The new values concerning recreation, religion, and sex found their strongest support in metropolitan areas, where for the first time in the country's history a majority of Americans now lived. During the 1920s some 6 million people moved from farms to cities. Urban centers of 100,000 or over grew more than twice as fast as the population as a whole. White-collar workers, whose numbers increased at about the same rate, congregated in and around these cities and reinforced one another's values. An urban way of life became the ideal, and city people used it to judge the rest of the nation. Instead of praising the education given at the little red schoolhouses in the countryside, urban educators recommended that these schools be consolidated to lower costs and modernize instruction. Sociologists at the University of Chicago declared the urban family emotionally healthier than the rural family. The farther that life was removed from the styles of the big city, the less attractive it appeared. Urban readers, some of them fugitives from the backcountry, joined even hinterland Americans in assenting to descriptions of the constricting sides of small-town life in Sherwood Anderson's *Winesburg, Ohio* (1919) and Sinclair Lewis's *Main Street* (1920).

The new urban standard was particularly hard in its judgment of the South, the region seen as the most stubbornly resistant to the twentieth century. In 1925 H. L. Mencken, critic, essayist, and high priest of the new urban culture, visited Dayton, Tennessee, to report on the trial of high-school biology instructor John Scopes, who had broken a state law by teaching Darwin's theory of evolution. Pitting the famous criminal lawyer Clarence Darrow, speaking for modern values, against William Jennings Bryan, the aging champion of traditional evangelical Protestantism, the trial became a national spectacle.

An urban audience, unable to comprehend why anyone would legislate against science, treated the Scopes trial like a carnival of freaks. Not long after

**Dorothy Thompson and Sinclair Lewis**
*These two writers were literary heroes of urban sophisticates.*

**H. L. Mencken, American Critic**
*High priest of the new urban culture, H. L. Mencken savaged traditional Americans and their values.*

Mencken jeered at the "anthropoid rabble" of Tennesseans for protecting them-selves "from whatever knowledge violated their superstitions," the modern caricature of the South had taken shape. Sharecropping, soil leaching, and unmechanized farming retarded southern agriculture. A crude racism dominated its society, and a narrow Protestant theology tyrannized its spirit. Support for Prohibition and opposition to Al Smith thrived there. When Erskine Caldwell's *Tobacco Road* appeared in 1932, many Americans were already prepared to accept this account of a stunted life on Georgia's barren soil as a picture of the true South.

**Black Americans in the Cities**

Between 1910 and 1930, close to a million blacks (about 13 percent of African Americans in the region) left the South in search of jobs in northern cities. The northern urban experience altered black attitudes. During the same years that whites argued over what percentage of which race should be allowed to immigrate, urban blacks were also showing a stronger racial consciousness. Claude McKay, a Jamaican immigrant, launched a literary and artistic movement known as the Harlem Renaissance with writings about black folk culture and poems protesting white oppression of blacks. Countee Cullen, Langston Hughes, Zora Neal Hurston, James Weldon Johnson, and Jean Toomer wrote eloquently about the black spirit. They drew on the African American experience in the rural South and urban ghettos for material. Toomer's novel *Cane,* for example, depicted life in rural Georgia and urban Washington, D.C., while Johnson's *Black Manhattan* graphically described Harlem. Although partly a protest against the plight of blacks in white America, their work went beyond mere protest and portrayed black culture as inherently rich and vital.

Early in the twenties some blacks found inspiration in the African nationalism of Marcus Garvey, an immigrant from Jamaica whose Universal Negro Improvement Association (UNIA) promised racial glory in the Empire of Africa. Speaking for racial pride, education, and economic independence from whites, Garvey attracted a mass following of over 500,000 supporters. When he was convicted of mail fraud in connection with the promotion of his Black Star shipping line, a steamship company set up to take blacks back to Africa, he served two years in a federal penitentiary and was then deported to Jamaica. During this time his movement fell apart, and nothing comparable arose to take its place. His memory, however, became an inspiration to later black nationalists in the 1960s.

The northern urban experience in the twenties stimulated another kind of national movement for black rights. Its primary organization was the National Association for the Advancement of Colored People (NAACP), which allied itself with an elite corps of black lawyers at the Howard Law School in Washington, D.C. The primary spokesman for the NAACP was Walter White, a talented writer and persistent lobbyist who in 1931 began his twenty-four-year tenure as the association's national secretary. When it became clear that only the national government could significantly improve the position of blacks, the NAACP

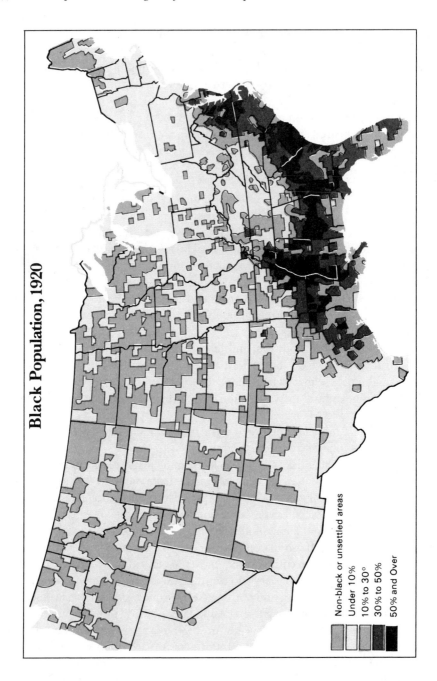

**Black Population, 1920**

Non-black or unsettled areas
Under 10%
10% to 30°
30% to 50%
50% and Over

pressed two kinds of arguments on the government's leaders. Appealing to conscience, the organization demanded racial equality; appealing to political interests, it offered to trade black votes for black rights. Unlike the southern cotton fields, the northern cities lay in competitive, two-party states with large

**Marcus Garvey**
*Marcus Garvey (second from right) captured the imagination of black Americans in the twenties by advocating racial pride, education, and economic independence.*

electoral votes. The NAACP tried to convince the Democratic party in particular that an effective effort to attract traditional black Republican voters to its side could tip the electoral balance in these states.

NAACP activism for black rights in the twenties netted some gains. The organization helped elect the first black congressman since 1901, Oscar DePriest from Chicago. It also lobbied for passage of a federal antilynching bill. Although it was successful in the House, a southern filibuster blocked action in the Senate. Nevertheless, public agitation against lynchings embarrassed southerners and reduced the number of incidents in the twenties from the previous decade by two-thirds. In 1930 the NAACP, in conjunction with organized labor, Senate progressives, and southern Democrats opposed to a southern Republican, blocked the confirmation of Judge John J. Parker, a North Carolina racist, to the Supreme Court.

**Modern Families and Careers: The "New" Woman**

Modern values also reshaped the role of the family in American life. In the white-collar world around the cities, occupations were the primary source of men's prestige; their reputations were created in their offices. Extramarital sex, especially in the large cities, became increasingly acceptable. So in Sinclair Lewis's *Babbitt* (1922), the hero could have a brief affair without damaging his career, even in the fictional city of Zenith. Wives were expected to restrain their husbands' drift away from the family. Advertisements promised that housewives who served better dinners and maintained cleaner houses would keep husbands close to home. Newspaper advice columns revealed how to soothe a tense, weary man at the end of the workday. A thriving cosmetics industry encouraged wives to enhance their physical charms as a means of holding husbands within the home.

Unlike the nineteenth-century wife who had been solemnly charged with preserving society's morals, her modern counterpart found herself bound by no such lofty responsibilities. In a system of values that honored expertise, her talents as a homemaker could never compete with the claims of business and the professions despite the national promotion of a "science" of home economics. As women's traditional sphere shrank, however, other opportunities beckoned. "Bedroom towns"—the residential areas from which men commuted daily to their downtown offices—became uniquely female domains where women moved and talked and acted much as they chose during the daytime hours. Under radically less surveillance than their grandmothers had experienced, they purchased most of the food and clothing for their families, and consequently their preferences had a powerful influence on the local consumer market.

Few of these women, however, had their own occupations. Work opportunities for women had expanded dramatically during World War I, but most of these jobs disappeared after 1918. While the actual number of female workers increased by over 2 million during the twenties, the proportion of females in the work force remained largely where it had been before 1917, at about 25 percent. Many of these women, moreover, continued to labor at what was traditionally considered women's work, as schoolteachers and nurses or in southern textile mills (especially in North Carolina), or in the New York needle trades. But more middle-class women became wage earners, and the kinds of work women did changed. Ten times as many women worked as typists, bookkeepers, and clerks in the twenties as before the war; thousands became manicurists, cosmeticians, and hairdressers in the 40,000 beauty parlors that opened across the country. The great majority of white married women did not work outside the home. In 1920 only some 6.5 percent of these women were in the work force, and by 1940 this number had grown only to about 12 percent. In 1930 nearly 60 percent of working women were either black or foreign-born, most of them toiling as domestics, waitresses, or in the garment industry.

Neither did women make significant political gains during the twenties. Prior to 1920 the principal assumption of suffragists and antisuffragists alike had been that women would vote as a bloc to end war, crime, vice, and injustice. During the twenties, however, women voted in smaller proportions than men and essentially the same way as they did. The women's movement in the twenties splintered into the League of Women Voters (LWV), which worked for informed voting, and the National Woman's Party, which urged an Equal Rights Amendment (ERA) to the Constitution. The LWV called the amendment a "slogan of the insane," and argued that the ERA would take away protections women enjoyed as mothers and nonunionized workers. The league saw passage of the ERA as leading to the abandonment of the protective legislation feminists had won in the Progressive Era for mothers and children and for women in the workplace. In keeping with the general fate of feminism in the twenties, the ERA stalled in the Congress.

Most women in the twenties fixed their attention on their families and their children, whom they reared to enter a world oriented to occupations. The home, it was assumed, could provide very little of the knowledge that children would later need to make their way in twentieth-century society. Because parents had a relatively small part in equipping their children for successful adult careers, they had to prepare their sons and daughters to accept directions from outside the home. Experts on child rearing warned parents of the dangers of an excessive emotional attachment or a domineering authority over them. Mothers heard about the perils of the Oedipus complex, as Freudian psychologists termed what they believed to be young sons' subconscious drive to compete with their fathers for maternal affections. Manuals on child care gave specific instructions on cuddling and comforting that would prevent psychological "invalidism." Further, a well-developed and widely publicized youth culture provided adolescents with the means of rebelling against their parents and declaring themselves ready for the occupational world. Modern parents not only subsidized the youth culture; they were told to worry if their children did not fully participate.

**Schools and Behaviorism**

The erosion of the family coincided with greater and greater influence for the schools. During the twenties and thirties the public school system underwent considerable expansion and adaptation. The elementary grades, which changed the least, increasingly served simply as feeders into the high schools. Enrollment in high schools doubled during the 1920s and then rose another 50 percent during the 1930s. In 1920 one-sixth of America's adult population had high school diplomas; in 1940 one-half held them. Secondary education had become so significant to white-collar families that some of them chose places to live on the basis of the local high school's reputation. The Winnetka System under Carleton Washburne, for example, made that Illinois community nationally famous.

Modern families wanted a school system that at once instructed their young in basic skills and shaped them to adapt to modern society. The prevailing trends in "progressive" education favored precisely this combination. The modern high school tried to prepare young minds, as one committee of educational experts stated in 1929, "to be suited to the changing situations" of modern society. The more progressive high schools, therefore, taught general methods of thinking and a general open-mindedness rather than a specific body of information and moral absolutes.

If young people could make a successful adjustment in high school, the assumption ran, they would be prepared for a happy, rewarding life. Aptitude tests and counseling centers, both suddenly prominent in the high schools of the 1920s, guided students into the proper occupations or, for increasing numbers, to college for further specialization. Those college graduates who entered the best white-collar occupations were supposed to have superior mental powers. According to a variety of publicists during the twenties, individuals who mastered a specialty in business or the professions developed a general capacity for rational thought that placed them in a select minority. By implication, the majority of Americans, in Mencken's blunt but revealing term, were "boobs," a highly suggestive public subject to manipulation by an intellectually superior few.

Along with this belief came the well-known school of psychology called behaviorism, which offered a simple, persuasive formula for mass manipulation. As behaviorist John B. Watson explained the human personality, a clear stimulus produced a predictable response in the individual. Regular repetition of the stimulus would establish a habit. Occasional reinforcement would make this reaction automatic. During the 1920s behaviorism became an article of faith among many Americans and gave them extraordinary confidence in their powers of social control. By using the right techniques, an expert in mass communication boasted, the rational minority could "regiment the masses according to our will without their knowing it."

A number of otherwise routine white-collar jobs, particularly selling, now took on a new significance. The insights into mass manipulation even offered a fresh view of history. "Galileo failed because he was an investigator and not a salesman," one psychologist revealed in 1925. "Consequently, he could not get his goods marketed. . . . His competitors, Aristotle, Moses, and the church fathers, had monopolized the market, and their stockholders would not let him do business." Advertising developed into an especially honored field. A new group of experts in personnel management promised employers that techniques of mass manipulation would guarantee employers a loyal and productive work force.

Americans of many different persuasions accepted this assumption of a two-tiered society: a minority of manipulators and a mass to be manipulated. Neither liberal nor conservative, the notion simply came with America's modern values. What Republican businessmen in the 1920s applied to the sale of their goods, New Dealers in the 1930s applied to the sale of their reforms. By World War II these habits of modern leadership were so ingrained that businessmen and reformers alike automatically went about the tasks of "selling" the war, "conditioning" the public for bad news from the battlefront, and experimenting with better ways to improve American morale.

**Intellectuals' Fears for the Individual**    The alterations of the twenties jeopardized the freedom of the individual. Signs of a new concern for the individual were already appearing before 1920. The American Civil Liberties Union, which had originated as an emergency committee to defend dissenters from the repression the government imposed during World

War I, remained after 1918 as a permanent center to protect the individual's freedom of speech, religion, assembly, and press under the First Amendment. Even before the war, two of America's most creative poets, Ezra Pound and T. S. Eliot, had moved to Europe, starting an exodus of young writers and artists who felt stifled by American culture. Although bigotry and snobbery also partly explain Pound's and Eliot's departures, a sense that they would be freer to express their views abroad largely influenced them to leave the United States. "A Lost Generation"—so the expatriate Gertrude Stein described America's intellectual exiles. In 1920 the nation's greatest playwright, Eugene O'Neill, won the first of four Pulitzer prizes for *Beyond the Horizon,* launching his long, agonizing exploration into the power of irrational forces over the individual's fate. From such scattered beginnings developed a broader and broader survey of the perils confronting the individual in modern society.

The first danger to receive serious attention was the dehumanization wrought by modern institutions. During the 1920s the best of the antiwar novels—John Dos Passos's *The Three Soldiers* (1921), e. e. cummings's *The Enormous Room* (1922), and Ernest Hemingway's *A Farewell to Arms* (1929)—said relatively little about war itself. Instead they used the war as a means of portraying the individual's jeopardy inside an impersonally mobilized society. In 1923 theater critics gave a warm reception to the American version of Czech playwright Karel Capek's *R.U.R.,* introducing robots as modern society's citizens, and to *The Adding Machine,* Elmer Rice's biting comedy on the effects of dull, repetitive work.

Among all the routine tasks of their time, intellectuals singled out work on the assembly line as the most threatening to the individual. It was, in fact, less wearing than harvesting fruit, less demanding than working in a sweatshop, and less dangerous than mining coal. But factory labor combined monotony and mechanization in a way that seemed to embody the depersonalization of the century. Henry Ford's plant produced cars at the price of humanity, the young pastor Reinhold Niebuhr recorded in his journal, and a company spokesman validated Niebuhr's fears: "[Ford] prefers machine-tool operators who...will simply do what they are told to do, over and over again from bell-time to bell-time. The Ford help need not even be able bodied." One of the most acclaimed scenes in an American movie was Charlie Chaplin's rebellion in *Modern Times* (1936) against the intolerable discipline of the assembly line, and his glorious escape through a maze of giant gears and monstrous machinery. The nation's great challenge, the cultural critic Lewis Mumford wrote in 1934, was to make "the machine...our servant, not our tyrant." By the 1930s it had become commonplace for intellectuals to condemn everything about the factory as ugly and alien.

Critics were also disturbed by the all-consuming passion for goods and money. The modern era, one observer acidly concluded, was testing the proposition "that human beings can live a generally satisfactory life...so long as they are kept powerfully under the spell of a great number of mechanical devices."

**Charlie Chaplin in "The Gold Rush"**
*In his silent films, Charlie Chaplin created the character of the little tramp, celebrating the virtues of individuality or freedom from conformity.*

During the 1920s old progressives as dissimilar as the moralistic westerner George Norris and the patrician easterner Gifford Pinchot warned of the corrosive influence that the pursuit of money was having on American values. John Dos Passos made this corrupting passion a central theme in his powerful, rambling trilogy *USA* (1930–36).

No part of the nation's heritage suffered more severely at the hands of American writers than the success ethic, which such important novels as F. Scott Fitzgerald's *The Great Gatsby* (1925) and Theodore Dreiser's *An American Tragedy* (1925) attacked for its destructive effects on the individual. In *I'll Take My Stand* (1930) twelve southern intellectual writers, attacking the worship of money along with "the tempo of industrial life" and the cult of machinery, declared that their region's agrarian tradition offered the sole "defense of the individual" in modern times. To the surprise of both authors and publisher, the book won an enthusiastic national following.

Urgent as many of these critics sounded, they were rarely desperate or radical. They located danger spots in America's industrial order. They usually cautioned the individual to keep a safe distance from modern society's most threatening centers. The individual's protection, then, was a calculated detachment. Such was the detachment of Lieutenant Frederic Henry in Hemingway's *A*

*Farewell to Arms.* Henry, an American volunteer for the Italian ambulance corps early in World War I, watched the impersonal forces of the war devour more and more people around him. When they threatened to swallow him too, he deserted—a sane and courageous act, as Hemingway described it. Escaping to Switzerland, he found fulfillment briefly in a love affair with a nurse, Catherine Barkley. When her death left Frederic Henry absolutely alone, his core of inner strength enabled him to survive in an indifferent universe.

One threat to the individual, the emptiness of old age, required a separate set of solutions. For two reasons, the problem of the aged was growing more severe in modern times. As the average life expectancy for an American rose from forty-seven years in 1900 to fifty-eight years in 1950, the proportion of old people increased steeply. Meanwhile the sources of self-respect for the aged were shrinking. Wherever modern values prevailed, old people felt useless. Knowledge in a specialized society was supposed to be advancing too rapidly for an older generation to master. Only the young could keep pace with America's highly technical and increasingly complex progress. As adults reached middle age, therefore, they had reason to believe that their best years were behind them and that the future, which belonged to the young, opened a huge void before them.

**Traditional Local Values in a Modern Society**

A great many Americans responded to these modern trends with mixed feelings. Most people's jobs—in shops, on farms, in factories—did not belong in the specialized upper ranks of the economy and therefore brought very little national prestige. Mass communication, moreover, made it impossible to ignore the disparity between their own lives and the lives of the most successful Americans. Millions of Americans with unskilled or routine jobs hoped that they, or their children, would eventually move upward in occupation. Yet almost all of them found the modern values unacceptable to some degree. They lived by local values. In rural communities and city neighborhoods, people judged one another by family reputations, church preferences, work habits, and a variety of other personal characteristics—standards that applied specifically to their own localities.

During the twenties and thirties the churches, particularly in the countryside, condemned the new license in dressing, drinking, dancing, smoking, and sex. A large majority of Protestant church members belonged to conservative evangelical denominations. Smaller bodies of Lutherans and Seventh-Day Adventists were even stricter than the stern Baptist and Methodist congregations in their denunciations of dancing and smoking.

As the modern system subdivided knowledge into a bewildering array of specialties, the churches continued to guide tradition-minded Americans in understanding the basics of life. Evangelical Protestantism had produced the political pressure behind Tennessee's antievolutionary law of 1925, which led to the Scopes trial. In other southern states as well, officials cooperated in keeping evolution out of the classroom. In the northern cities, the Catholic church often set its considerable weight against the new values, especially those on sex. Like the public schools in areas where evangelical Protestantism predominated, the Catholic parochial system carefully instructed its pupils in religious morality. According to nationwide studies in the twenties and thirties, a majority of American schoolchildren were still receiving this kind of traditional, moral education.

Some of the mass media also catered to traditional values. In magazines and newspapers, countless stories told of how the time-honored virtues of honesty, thrift, and perseverance had enabled ordinary people to weather and overcome their troubles. To vast daytime audiences, such radio soap operas as "Ma Perkins' Family" and "Just Plain Bill" recounted the tribulations of ordinary, small-town people who preserved their simple goodness under the most extraordinary hardships. Norman Rockwell's famous covers for the *Saturday Evening Post,* depicting the comforts of life in the family and the small town, ennobled many of the same traditional values. The success ethic also remained intact. In the late thirties the black ghettos would revere the black heavyweight boxing champion Joe Louis for his rise from poverty to fame. He would also capture the imagination of middle-class whites who followed his bouts and meteoric rise with equal interest and enthusiasm.

Only a minority of Americans in a few localities totally rejected the new ways. A compromise between new and traditional values was much more common. Almost all Americans wanted some share in the new culture, and a great many of them hoped to participate without feeling that it would corrupt them. At the beginning of the twenties, for example, motion pictures exploited sex so boldly that most state legislatures threatened to censor them. In 1922 the movie industry responded by creating the Hays Office, a self-censorship agency that designated what parts of the female anatomy had to be covered, decided what language was taboo, and determined what values must triumph in the end. These moral formulas created just the right aura of respectability. Without basically altering the movies, they appeased the critics and assured a mass audience.

**The American Dream**   Perhaps the most important need of the mass of Americans was some evidence that they could still succeed without abandoning their values. During the twenties an abundance of publicity assured them that the avenue upward was not only broad but especially well traveled by people of solid character and good habits. Salesmanship offered a particularly enticing route because it held out the prospect of success without a highly specialized training. Throughout the twenties, manuals, lectures, and correspondence courses fed a popular passion for the salesman's skills, promising to reveal to any ambitious American the secret of the selling art. The example of especially successful businessmen encouraged hopes of an even more spectacular rise to riches. If immigrants such as utilities magnate Samuel Insull, banking king A. P. Giannini, and movie mogul Samuel Goldwyn could make it to the top,

American society must still be rewarding the traditional virtues of hard work and high ambition.

No one's reputation swelled more grandly from such notions than Henry Ford's. Here was a country boy who had turned mechanical genius and dogged persistence into a fabulous fortune and international fame. He had mastered the modern economy so thoroughly that everyone came to him to learn the best techniques of mass production and distribution. Yet he gave the appearance of a man who never capitulated to the slick ways around him. He attacked the evils of Wall Street, publicly ranted about "the international Jew," belittled the significance of higher education, and demanded strict moral standards from his workers. He could even give new values the sound of old truths: "One day some one brought to us a slogan which read: 'Buy a Ford and Save the Difference.' I crossed out the 'save' and inserted 'spend'—'Buy a Ford and Spend the Difference.' It is the wiser thing to do. Society lives by circulation and not by congestion."

American society in the twenties gave birth to a new kind of hero for the traditional Horatio Alger, rags-to-riches tale—a hero endowed with an all-conquering power. In the nineteenth-century form of this tale, the hero had won the rich man's daughter through his sterling character, her father's approval, many lucky breaks, and aid from mentors. In the modern variation, physical attraction and personal charm, the qualities valued most in a consumer society, catapulted the hero to the top. The rich man's daughter, finding the poor but virile and charming man irresistible, convinced an angry father that she could not live without him. In the mirror image of this tale, a sexually charged Cinderella story, the poor but beautiful and vivacious woman finally fell into the arms of a rich, adoring husband.

The star system that came to dominate the entertainment industry during the twenties reflected a growing popular demand for heroes possessed of an all-conquering power. The stars themselves seemed superhuman: the irresistible lover Rudolph Valentino, thrilling millions of moviegoers; the "Galloping Ghost," Red Grange, scoring five touchdowns in one game; the courageous young Gertrude Ederle, swimming the English Channel; even the widely publicized flagpole sitters who, perched high in the air, stayed awake for days on end.

Whether accentuating the personal qualities of success or endowing modern heroes with traditional attributes of initiative and individualism, Americans preferred the idiosyncratic star who ignored many of the usual rules of the game. Fans demonstrated more enthusiasm for the erratic fighter Jack Dempsey than for the steadier "boxing machine" Gene Tunney, and more feeling for the high-living, casual "Sultan of Swat," Babe Ruth, than for the intense, consistent batting champion Ty Cobb—or for the black pitcher Satchel Paige, the best of them all, although segregation barred him from the major leagues for decades. In a crowded arena of eager competitors, success depended on a star's ability to attract public attention through a carefully staged "event." J. Edgar Hoover, the popular director of the Justice Department's Federal Bureau of Investigation,

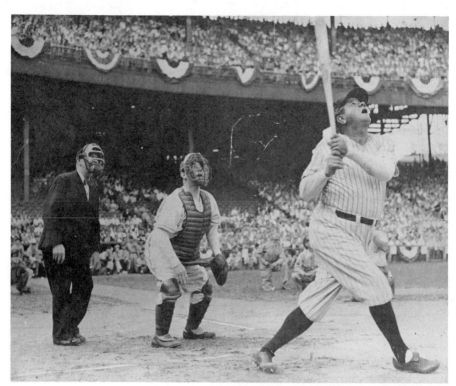

**Babe Ruth, the "Sultan of Swat"**
*In the twenties, Babe Ruth symbolized traditional values to millions of Americans.*

**Charles Lindbergh, American Hero**
*Charles Lindbergh was America's symbol of the individual's triumph over the machine and Nature.*

mastered the technique in a series of orchestrated manhunts for criminals, each of whom he spotlighted as "Public Enemy Number One." An enthralled audience followed the real-life Hoover crime show, chapter by chapter.

Charles Lindbergh, the star of stars, rose to fame in the most dramatic event of the twenties. In May 1927, as liberally financed and elaborately organized competitors remained stalled on the ground, this unknown pilot became the first person to complete a solo airplane flight from New York to Paris. Americans instantly made the quiet, handsome midwesterner a national idol. Lindbergh's triumph, as millions interpreted it, was the accomplishment of an indomitable individual who demonstrated complete mastery over *the machine*—his plane, the "Spirit of St. Louis"—and over Nature, embodied in the vast Atlantic. Literally and figuratively, the "Lone Eagle" had soared beyond the ordinary individual's limitations to purely personal success. Moreover, Lindbergh's sudden fame did not appear to affect his traditional virtues of modesty, simplicity, and self-reliance. Of all the stars, Lindbergh had the greatest popularity.*

But however strong the impulse to preserve traditional individualism in the twenties, and however great the desire to cling to familiar American customs and truths, the attraction to old, local ways was not powerful enough to hold back the economic and social trends that began the modern period of American life.

## CHRONOLOGY

| | | |
|---|---|---|
| **1920** | Warren G. Harding elected president. Transportation Act gives ICC extensive authority over railroads and other means of transportation. | National Origins Act further limits immigration by quotas. Teapot Dome and other Harding administration scandals exposed. Coolidge elected president. |
| **1921** | First bill passed restricting immigration by national quotas. | |
| | | **1927** Sacco and Vanzetti executed. |
| **1922** | Fordney-McCumber Act reestablishes high tariff. Washington Conference treaty limits naval tonnage among major powers. | **1928** Kellogg-Briand Pact outlaws war. Second McNary-Haugen bill to regulate the marketing of agricultural products passed but vetoed. Herbert Hoover elected president. |
| **1923** | President Harding dies; Calvin Coolidge becomes president. | **1929** Congress creates Federal Farm Board. |
| **1924** | Dawes Plan negotiates loans to revive Germany. | Young Plan reformulates Dawes Plan to manage war debts. |

*The tragic kidnaping and death of Lindbergh's son produced a new surge of public interest in 1932. But Lindbergh's laudatory reception in Nazi Germany, his insinuation that American Jews were pushing the nation into the war, and his advocacy in 1941 of a negotiated settlement with Hitler sharply diminished his popularity.

## SUGGESTED READINGS

Geoffrey Perrett, *America in the Twenties* (1982), and John D. Hicks, *Republican Ascendancy, 1921–1933* (1960), are good general guides to the decade. Robert K. Murray, *The Harding Era* (1969), and Donald R. McCoy, *Calvin Coolidge* (1967), generously assess these presidents and their policies, and Burl Noggle, *Teapot Dome* (1962), covers the major scandal of their administrations. David Burner's perceptive study, *The Politics of Provincialism* (1967), recounts the pulling and hauling in the Democratic party during the twenties. An interesting picture of the politics of natural resources emerges from Donald C. Swain, *Federal Conservation Policy, 1921–1933* (1963), and from Norris Hundley, Jr., *Water and the West* (1975). Gilbert C. Fite's *George W. Peek and the Fight for Farm Parity* (1954) analyzes the politics of commercial agriculture. Paula Elder, *Governor Alfred E. Smith: The Politician as Reformer* (1983), and David Burner, *Herbert Hoover* (1979), are fine studies of the two men and their politics.

For the limitations of liberal reform, see LeRoy Ashby, *The Spearless Leader: Senator Borah and the Progressive Movement in the 1920s* (1972); Richard Lowitt, *George W. Norris: The Persistence of a Progressive, 1913–1933* (1971); and Arthur Mann, *LaGuardia: A Fighter Against His Times, 1882–1933* (1959). In *Seedtime of Reform* (1963), on the other hand, Clarke A. Chambers discovers a maturing process during the twenties. For Supreme Court decisions, see Paul L. Murphy, *The Constitution in Crisis Times, 1918–1969* (1972). George B. Tindall's *The Emergence of the New South, 1913–1945* (1967) sets that region in a national context.

The most provocative interpretation of the age of corporate capitalism appears in William Appleman Williams, *The Contours of American History* (1961), which may be supplemented with James Gilbert, *Designing the Industrial State* (1972). Thomas C. Cochran, *American Business in the Twentieth Century* (1972), gives a clear overview of its subject. The final section in Alfred D. Chandler, *The Visible Hand* (1977), analyzes the managerial structure of the giant corporations, while Louis Galambos, *Competition and Cooperation: The Emergence of a National Trade Association* (1966), traces the pattern of organization among the scattered firms in cotton textiles. William J. Barber, *From New Era to New Deal: Herbert Hoover, the Economists, and American Economic Policy, 1921–1933* (1985), is a fine recent study of economic thinking in the twenties. Allan Nevins and Frank Ernest Hill, *Ford: Expansion and Challenge, 1915–1933* (1957), covers the peak years of the flivver king's career. On labor, the best study is Irving L. Bernstein's *A History of the American Worker, 1920–1933: The Lean Years* (1960). Also see David Brody, *Workers in Industrial America* (1980). Grant McConnell's *The Decline of Agrarian Democracy* (1953) centers on the American Farm Bureau Federation.

The best introduction to the ethnic and cultural issues of the twenties is John Higham's excellent *Strangers in the Land* (1955), which deals with American nativism to 1925. Paul A. Carter, *Another Part of the Twenties* (1977), also comments generally on these issues. William Graebner, *The Engineering of Consent: Democracy and Authority in Twentieth-Century America* (1987), is a fine recent study of American culture. David M. Chalmers, *Hooded Americanism* (1965), is a lively history of the Ku Klux Klan, and Kenneth T. Jackson, *The Ku Klux Klan in the City, 1915–1930* (1967), is an important supplement to the story. G. Louis Joughlin and Edmund M. Morgan, *The Legacy of Sacco and Vanzetti* (1948), remains the richest account of events surrounding the trial of these men. But for recent new evidence on the case, see William Young and David E. Kaiser, *Postmortem: New Evidence in the Case of Sacco and Vanzetti* (1985), and Francis Russell, *Sacco and Vanzetti: The Case Resolved* (1986). The rise and fall of the "noble experiment" is traced skeptically in Andrew Sinclair, *Prohibition: The Era of Excess* (1962), and sympathetically in Norman H. Clark, *Deliver Us from Evil* (1976). Joseph R. Gusfield, *Symbolic Crusade* (1963), explores the emotional force behind Prohibition, and Norman F. Furniss, *The Fundamentalist Controversy, 1918–1931* (1954), reviews the antimodernist legislative campaigns. How cultural issues have translated into politics is described generally in Oscar Handlin, *Al Smith and His America* (1958), and more specifically in J. Joseph Huthmacher, *Massachusetts*

*People and Politics, 1919–1933* (1959). See in addition Humbert S. Nelli, *The Business of Crime* (1976).

There is a growing literature on the impact of blacks during the twenties. Nathan Irvin Huggins, *Harlem Renaissance* (1971), minimizes the cultural significance of its subject. Important recent books on the black experience in the twenties include David Lewis, *When Harlem Was in Vogue* (1981); Jacqueline Jones, *Labor of Love, Labor of Sorrow: Black Women, Work, and the Family from Slavery to the Present* (1986); Arnold Ramperstand, *Langston Hughes* (1986–88); Wilson Moses, *The Golden Age of Black Nationalism, 1850–1925* (1988); James R. Grossman, *Land of Hope: Chicago, Black Southerners, and the Great Migration* (1989); and Neil R. McMillen, *Dark Journey: Black Mississippians in the Age of Jim Crow* (1989). On Marcus Garvey and his followers, see E. David Cronon, *Black Moses* (1955); Thomas G. Vincent, *Black Power and the Garvey Movement* (1971); and Judith Stein, *The World of Marcus Garvey* (1986). St. Clair Drake and Horace R. Cayton, *Black Metropolis* (2 vols., rev. ed., 1962), remains a valuable study of the Chicago ghetto, as is Alan Spear, *Black Chicago* (1967). For New York's Harlem, see Gilbert Osofsky, *Harlem: The Making of a Ghetto* (1965). The most important organizations serving blacks are discussed in Langston Hughes, *Fight for Freedom: The Story of the NAACP* (1962), and Nancy J. Weiss, *The National Urban League, 1910–1940* (1974). Also see Walter White's autobiography, *A Man Called White* (1948). Manning Marable, *W.E.B. Du Bois: Black Radical Democrat* (1986), and Martin Duberman, *Paul Robeson* (1989), are valuable biographies.

L. Ethan Ellis, *Republican Foreign Policy, 1921–1933* (1968), provides a sound introduction to the postwar years. So does Warren I. Cohen, *Empire Without Tears: America's Foreign Relations, 1921–1933* (1987). The most influential work on America's international affairs is William Appleman Williams, *The Tragedy of American Diplomacy* (rev. ed., 1962), an essay on the dominance of economic expansion in the nation's foreign policy. Two excellent books, Joan Hoff Wilson's *American Business and Foreign Policy, 1920–1933* (1971), and Michael J. Hogan's *Informal Entente: The Private Structure of Cooperation in Anglo-American Economic Diplomacy, 1918–1928* (1977), further explore the process of economic expansion; so, in a particular case, does Gerald D. Nash, *United States Oil Policy 1890–1964* (1968). Stephen A. Schuker, *The End of French Predominance in Europe* (1976), is a complicated but rewarding account of the issues surrounding the Dawes Plan. Melvyn Leffler, *The Elusive Quest: America's Pursuit of French Security and European Stability, 1919–1933* (1979), is first-rate. So is Frank Costigliola, *Awkward Dominion: American Political, Economic, and Cultural Relations with Europe, 1919–1933* (1984).

A clear, reliable survey of United States policy in East Asia is presented in Warren I. Cohen, *America's Response to China* (1971). Akira Iriye's *After Imperialism: The Search for a New Order in the Far East, 1921–1933* (1965) locates American policy in an international setting. The postwar treaties on Asia and arms limitation are studied in Roger Dingman, *Power in the Pacific: The Origins of Naval Arms Limitation* (1976), and in Raymond G. O'Connor, *Perilous Equilibrium: The United States and the London Naval Conference of 1930* (1962). Keith L. Nelson, *Victors Divided: America and the Allies in Germany, 1918–1923* (1975), is a careful study. Peter G. Filene's *Americans and the Soviet Experience, 1917–1933* (1967) traces responses from the Bolshevik Revolution to America's recognition of the Soviet Union. In *Herbert Hoover's Latin American Policy* (1951), Alexander DeConde finds a liberalizing trend.

Modern culture is explored broadly in Daniel J. Boorstin, *The Americans: The Democratic Experience* (1973). William E. Leuchtenburg, *The Perils of Prosperity, 1914–32* (1958), has particularly revealing chapters on the consumer culture of the twenties and the changes in values accompanying it, subjects that are also covered in Frederick Lewis Allen's *Only Yesterday* (1931). Isabel Leighton, ed., *The Aspirin Age* (1949), contains a lively set of essays on the twenties. There are perceptive analyses of the new sexual morality in Christopher Lasch's *The New Radicalism in America 1889–1963* (1965) and in Paul Robinson's *The Modernization of*

*Sex* (1976). Robert H. Elias, *Entangling Alliances with None* (1973), probes the meaning of individualism in the twenties. The city's dominance in twentieth-century society is discussed generally in Zane L. Miller, *The Urbanization of Modern America* (1973), and more interpretively in Sam Bass Warner, Jr., *The Urban Wilderness* (1972). Some effects of urbanization of suburban values appear in Peter J. Schmitt, *Back to Nature* (1969), and Kenneth Jackson, *Crabgrass Frontier* (1985). Carl Bode, *Mencken* (1969), assesses the leading spokesman for the new urban culture. An intriguing section in Gilman M. Ostrander, *American Civilization in the First Machine Age: 1890–1940* (1970), defines the place of youth in modern society, as does Paula Fass, *The Damned and Beautiful: American Youth in the 1920s* (1977). For studies of the aged, see W. Andrew Achenbaum, *Shades of Gray: Old Age, American Values, and Federal Policies Since 1920* (1983), and Howard P. Chudacoff, *How Old Are You? Age in American Culture* (1989). John R. Seeley et al., *Crestwood Heights* (1956), examines the importance of the schools in modern suburban life.

Books that evaluate women's part in the new culture include Nancy Woloch, *Women and the American Experience* (1984), an excellent survey of women's history; William L. O'Neill, *Everyone Was Brave: The Rise and Fall of Feminism in America* (1969); and William Henry Chafe, *The American Woman* (1972), tracing the decline of earlier trends toward emancipation. J. Stanley Lemons, *The Woman Citizen: Social Feminism in the 1920s* (1973), concentrates on women's continuing action after World War I, while Susan Strasser, *Never Done: A History of American Housework* (1982), and Ruth Schwartz Cowan, *More Work for Mother* (1983), look at housewives' experiences. Winifred Wandersee, *Women's Work and Family Values, 1920–1940* (1981), is a useful study. In *Birth Control in America* (1970), David M. Kennedy adds a critical analysis of Margaret Sanger's career.

Several books illuminate the values of important institutions and occupations. James W. Prothro, *Dollar Decade* (1954), summarizes the attitudes of businessmen during the twenties. Otis Pease, *The Responsibilities of American Advertising* (1958), and Swart Ewen, *Captains of Consciousness* (1976), provide contrasting interpretations of a particularly thriving field. These should be supplemented by Daniel Pope, *The Making of Modern Advertising* (1983); Stephen Fox, *The Mirror Makers: A History of American Advertising and Its Creators* (1984); and Roland Marchand, *Advertising the American Dream: Making Way for Modernity, 1920–1940* (1985). Radio is studied in Susan J. Douglas, *Inventing American Broadcasting, 1899–1922,* and Erik Bernouw, *A Tower in Babel: A History of Broadcasting in the United States to 1933* (1966). The engineer's dedication to business values is the subject of Edwin T. Layton, Jr., *The Revolt of the Engineers* (1971), and the social scientists' dedication to the same values is the subject of Loren Baritz, *The Servants of Power* (1960). Roy Lubove, *Professional Altruists* (1965), describes the businesslike efficiency of social workers. The section on the United States in Reinhard Bendix's *Work and Authority in Industry* (1956) investigates the strategy of the new specialists in personnel management. Also see Milton Derber, *The American Idea of Industrial Democracy, 1865–1965* (1970). The effects of the new culture on education are analyzed in Patricia Albjerg Graham, *Progressive Education from Arcady to Academe: A History of the Progressive Education Association, 1919–1955* (1967); August Hollingshead, *Elmtown's Youth* (1949); and Solon Kimball and James E. McClellan, Jr., *Education and the New America* (1962). Christopher Jencks and David Riesman, *The Academic Revolution* (1968), explores the modern university. Barry D. Karl, *Charles E. Merriam and the Study of Politics* (1974), and Fred H. Matthews, *Quest for an American Sociology: Robert E. Park and the Chicago School* (1977), discuss a new breed of academic entrepreneurs.

Traditional values in modern America have attracted less scholarly attention. Two interesting books analyze these values under challenge: Ray Ginger's *Six Days or Forever? Tennessee v. John Thomas Scopes* (1958) and Don S. Kirschner's *City and Country: Rural Responses to Urbanization in the 1920s* (1970). *Middletown* (1929) and *Middletown in Transition* (1937), classic studies of Muncie, Indiana, by Robert S. and Helen Merrell Lynd, reveal a mixture of traditional and modern values. Donald B. Meyer, *The Positive Thinkers* (1965), examines modern variations on the traditional doctrine of self-help. Other books cast light on traditional values through the study of popular heroes. In *The Hero* (1959), Kenneth S. Davis discusses the fame of Charles Lindbergh. Reynold M. Wik, *Henry Ford and Grass-Roots America* (1972), explains the automobile magnate's powerful appeal, and Keith T. Sward, *The Legend of Henry Ford* (1948), contrasts the public image with the actual record. Robert Sklar, *Movie-Made America* (1975), and Larry May, *Screening Out the Past* (1980), interpret the development of a new mass medium, and John G. Cawelti, *Adventure, Mystery, and Romance* (1976), anatomizes the most popular forms of fiction.

The best account of modern relativism is Morton G. White, *Social Thought in America: The Revolt Against Formalism* (rev. ed., 1957). Three excellent books discuss early discontents with relativism and various quests for certainty: Donald B. Meyer, *The Protestant Search for Political Realism, 1919–1941* (1960); Edward A. Purcell, Jr., *The Crisis of Democratic Theory: Scientific Naturalism and the Problem of Values* (1973); and David A. Hollinger, *Morris R. Cohen and the Scientific Ideal* (1975).

Other studies trace ideas in creative writing. Alfred Kazin, *On Native Grounds: An Interpretation of Modern American Prose Literature* (1942), is a stimulating essay. Frederick J. Hoffman, *The Twenties* (rev. ed., 1966), discusses American fiction in an artistically critical decade. The strains of modern society are revealed in Maxwell Geismar's *Writers in Crisis: The American Novel 1925–1940* (1942). Thomas R. West, *Flesh of Steel* (1967), deals with the effects of the machine on the literary imagination. Of course, the creative writers themselves remain our indispensable sources.

# 29

# *The Modern Republic in Crisis*

## *1929–1941*

*T*HE SOARING hopes of the 1920s suddenly vanished in the great stock-market crash of October 1929. The depression that followed was not the first great downturn in American economic history; there had been depressions in 1837, 1857, 1893, and 1920, as well as other less drastic contractions in the economy. But 1929 marked the onset of America's worst economic collapse. The modern American economy that had evolved since the Civil War had become a nationwide, interdependent system encompassing greater numbers of Americans than ever before. When it cracked and collapsed, countless lives were blighted in the crisis.

One consequence of the Great Depression was the defeat in 1932 of Herbert Hoover, the symbol of the 1920s business ethos and a man with impeccable old progressive credentials. Franklin D. Roosevelt, the governor of New York and a man of generally progressive impulses, was elected president and charged with leading the nation out of chaos. Forced to improvise in desperate circumstances, the Roosevelt administration evolved a new governmental agenda for action to meet the crisis and prevent its recurrence. FDR's promise of a "new deal" for Americans quickly gave his presidency its name.

Not surprisingly, the New Deal responded unevenly to the crisis. Roosevelt and his advisers drew freely on elements of old free-market nostrums and progressive social engineering, but they rejected the socialist solution of nationalization and central planning, as well as probusiness policies for strict nonintervention. Instead the New Deal took a more pragmatic approach, combining expanded government intervention in the economy with continued freedom for markets to recover on their own. Consequently, the right complained that the New Deal was taking a long step toward socialism, while the left dismissed it as a conservative defender of capitalism, too cautious to relieve the nation's economic ills. Although the New Deal introduced significant economic and social reforms, it fell well short of lifting the nation out of its economic crisis. Only the coming of World War II ended the Great Depression.

But the New Deal holds a pivotal place in twentieth-century American history because it largely set the agenda and ideology of modern liberalism: a commitment to state action to regulate the capitalist economy, ensure stability, and combat social problems like poverty and injustice. Modern liberalism as created by the New Deal differed from nineteenth-century liberalism in its willingness to accept the expansive state as an ally in social engineering; generally liberals tended to welcome social and cultural modernization. Modern liberalism, like the older progressivism, saw itself as combating social evils; the White House and government generally, to borrow Theodore Roosevelt's phrase, had been a "bully pulpit" for fighting the good fight. Yet modern liberalism has differed from older progressivism in its greater willingness to appeal to class distinctions and to rely on ethnic Americans and the country's minorities for political support. Opponents of the New Deal, who objected to its reliance on the state or centralizing intrusion into local affairs and its willingness to court class conflict and seek minority backing, joined forces with probusiness advocates of laissez-faire economics, and thereby created modern conservatism. Although the conservatives constituted a distinct minority in the four decades after the New Deal came to power, they returned to power in the 1970s and 1980s, throwing liberals on the defensive and leaving them struggling to find new ways to recapture the public imagination.

Internationally, the 1930s was the last decade of traditional American isolationism. The country and the world paid a high price for American reluctance to abandon outdated ideas. By failing to join forces with the democracies of western Europe in working for economic recovery and resisting the rising tide of totalitarianism—specifically as embodied in Nazi Germany and Fascist Italy—the United States contributed to the onset of another world war in 1939. The Japanese attack on Pearl Harbor in December 1941 ended a debate on what America's role in the conflict should be. Just as important, the United States' entry into World War II compelled the American republic to take on military and political burdens abroad that continue to this day.

## *Depression, 1929–1932*

By 1929 countless Americans had convinced themselves that they were riding on an escalator of unlimited progress, and along with Herbert Hoover they anticipated "the day when poverty will be banished from this nation." A wealthy minority expressed this happy faith by investing in the stock market. Excited by stories about a millionaire who multiplied his fortune thirtyfold in eight months and a peddler who turned $4,000 into $250,000, investors pushed up prices on the New York Stock Exchange by 40 percent in 1927, then another 35 percent in 1928. Such stock prices bore no relation to the actual growth of the nation's production. Yet the Great Bull Market charged heedlessly onward. With scarcely

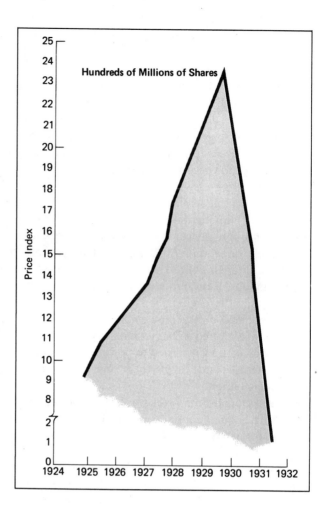

**Index of Common Stock
Prices, 1924–1932**

a pause, stock prices continued to climb week after week until by September 1929 they stood at a dizzying 400 percent above their level of only five years earlier.

Spasms of doubt shook the stock market in September and early October. Then on October 24, 1929—"Black Tuesday"—confidence died. For almost a week the stock exchange was a mad scene of frantic sellers, elusive buyers, and exhausted clerks struggling to sort out the wreckage. By October 29 all the paper profits of 1929 had vanished into thin air. Early in November the gains of 1928 disappeared, and during the summer of 1930 those of 1927 dissolved. The stock market finally hit bottom on June 8, 1932, 50 percent below its modest level at the time of Coolidge's inauguration.

The market's crash was more symptomatic of the country's economic problems than its cause. No one, then or even now, can fully explain the economic collapse of the 1930s. At the time many economists explained the depression as caused by a loss of business confidence. But this was a circular argument that, like the stock-market crash, does not go very far in helping us understand an extremely complex event.

**The Great Depression**

Although it did not cause the Great Depression, the collapse of the Great Bull Market did trigger it. Consumption dropped. Business retrenched. Marginal enterprises in farming, banking, and business went bankrupt. During the first three years after the crash, the economy, like a tin can in a vise, was relentlessly squeezed to half its size. Some indicators—such as labor income, salaries, and national income—fell somewhat less than 50 percent; others, such as industrial production, manufacturing wages, dividends, and farm income, dropped somewhat more. For people living through these years, there seemed to be no bottom at all.

The human costs were incalculable. Dramatic headlines told about the fall of the mighty—among them, the utilities king Samuel Insull and the New York banking baron Charles Mitchell—whose empires of speculation crumbled. Later studies argued that the most severe anxieties struck white-collar males, whose sense of personal worth depended almost entirely on their jobs and earnings. But the most crushing burdens of depression fell on the poor. Millions already living on the edge of poverty could afford no decline in farm income, no shorter hours of work. And the unemployed, about one-third of the labor force by early 1933, soon had nothing. "Folks that ain't never been poor," said one struggling

**Help Unwanted**
*The depression forced as many as 13 million Americans onto the unemployment rolls. In 1939 there were still 9 million Americans who could not find work.*

housewife, "don't know nothin' at all about doing on nothing." The chicken that Herbert Hoover had once promised for every pot had gone into charity's soup kettle, and each year longer lines of hungry, bewildered people formed in front of it with their empty bowls.

Why the depression was so deep and the fall so prolonged defies easy understanding. But an inventory of economic weaknesses in 1929 provides a part of the answer. By that year a maldistribution of income, with workers and farmers sharing substantially less in the prosperity of the 1920s than did industry, reduced consumer purchasing power and the demand for manufactured goods. Major industries like construction and automaking were forced to reduce production; that reduction in turn caused cutbacks in other industries and led to a general downturn in the economy. All these factors combined with monetary, tariff, and federal tax policies favoring special business interests over consumers or middle- and working-class Americans, a faulty banking system, and excesses in consumer credit to send the economy into a tailspin. More specifically, the Federal Reserve, applying outdated economic ideas, tightened rather than loosened credit, making it even more difficult for people to borrow and spend. In addition, the high-tariff barriers put into place by the Fordney-McCumber Act (1922) and the Hawley-Smoot Tariff (1930) reduced imports to the United States and undercut American efforts to sell goods abroad.

Yet by 1931 the economy was improving, and the crisis looked similar to many other sharp downturns. Because farm prices had fallen much farther than wages, most urban consumers were actually able to buy foodstuffs more cheaply than before. An intelligent person with money to invest in business or the stock market could find a variety of attractive prospects at home and abroad. Yet the consumers and the investors refused to spend. By summer the Great Depression, following a number of banking collapses, was sweeping Europe, and the American economy was sliding toward new depths. Hoover sensed the profound importance of this paralyzing irrationality. How else could one explain a drop of 95 percent in private investment while most indicators were declining about 50 percent?

President Hoover's initial responses to the depression were clear and firm. If the cooperative principles behind the modern economy were correct, as everyone seemed to believe, Americans should use them to recover prosperity. "Progress is born of cooperation," the president reminded the nation. "The Government should assist and encourage these movements of collective self-help by itself cooperating with them." For business, Hoover sponsored White House meetings to establish common industrial policies. For labor, he won a promise from business leaders to spread the work in their firms rather than simply fire some percentage of their employees. For agriculture, the new Federal Farm Board dispensed large amounts of credit so that the commodity cooperatives could keep their products off the market and halt the decline in farm prices. For hard-pressed Americans everywhere, Hoover established various presidential committees to coordinate private relief. Between 1929 and 1932 donations for relief

**An Old-Fashioned Individualist**
*Herbert Hoover lacked the
flexibility to use government
programs to meet the challenge
of the depression.*

increased about eightfold, a remarkable accomplishment by any previous standard. Viewing the economy as a national system, Hoover used the prestige of his office and some of his executive power to become the first president in history to attack a depression systematically.

In spite of his efforts, the economy continued to spiral downward, and in 1931 his political influence waned. As Hoover's sense of control over affairs began to slip, he grew more rigid, more persecuted by the specter of vast, oppressive forces. The White House became a funeral parlor. The president, never a charmer, looked (one visitor remarked) as if a rose would wilt at his touch. In that mood Hoover called together the villains of Wall Street who, in the president's view, had fed the Great Bull Market instead of facilitating legitimate business. When he demanded that they make massive new investments, they stalled. Finally Hoover accepted the necessity of an emergency government credit agency, the Reconstruction Finance Corporation, which in 1932 invested $1.5 billion in private enterprise. Meanwhile, to ease the pressures on international finances and avert a default on war debts owed to the United States by its former allies against Germany, he negotiated a one-year moratorium with the European powers on intergovernmental debts.

By 1932 the president's policies lay in shambles. Employers discarded their programs for spreading the work, and unemployment shot above 12 million, nearly 25 percent of the work force. Local relief funds, both public and private, evaporated. Abhorring the thought of federal relief, Hoover fought with Congress, which the Democrats now controlled, and eventually approved an inadequate law that authorized some new public works and modest loans to the states for relief.

As commodity prices continued to fall, the Federal Farm Board simply ran out of credit. Farmers burned their corn and left their cotton unpicked because it no longer paid them to market the crop. In some midwestern county seats, silent men with hunting rifles closed the courts so that their mortgages could not be foreclosed. When thousands of jobless veterans marched to Washington asking for early payment of bonuses that had been promised for their services in World War I, President Hoover thought he heard revolution in their cries for a little cash, and in July 1932 he ordered the army to drive them away, which it did, killing one child with tear gas. By the end of the year 20 percent of the banks that had been operating in 1929 were closed and depositors, whose accounts were uninsured, lost their funds. As tremors shook the entire banking system, Hoover hardened the conviction he had held in October 1929: "We have been fighting for four years to preserve the system of production and distribution from . . . [the] failure of the financial and credit system."

Hoover's words were cold comfort to suffering Americans. Millions of unemployed were ill-fed, ill-clad, and ill-housed. "Many lived in the primitive conditions of a preindustrial society," to quote one description of their plight. Families took shelter in unheated tents or makeshift shacks and sheds on vacant lots, along river banks, and in city dumps that became known as Hoovervilles. Without money to buy food or access to public food kitchens, which ran out of funds to feed the starving, men fought over garbage set outside of restaurants, scoured city dumps for half-rotted vegetables, or ate wild greens and weeds consumed by cows. A lack of shoes and clothing kept many children from attending school.

**Hoover Repudiated** During the years 1921–29 relatively little was expected of the president as an individual. The modern political economy was, after all, a complex impersonal system, not the product of a particular administration, and it appeared to operate on its own momentum. But when the thoroughly national system broke down, only the national government had the scope and authority to repair it. Because the executive branch dominated the national government, people naturally looked there for help. Atop the executive branch stood the president, and the longer the depression lasted, the more he alone seemed the one person who could lead the nation out of the wilderness. Hoover was judged by new, demanding standards, and the popular verdict condemned him. By 1932 millions who had no other place to turn were blaming Hoover in a bitter, personal way for their troubles. A humane man with great administrative talents, Hoover lacked the flexibility, political instincts, and inspirational leadership required by the crisis. He conveyed an image of aloofness, and consequently seemed callous to most Americans. "I have no Wilsonian qualities," he freely admitted to friends. Millions of Americans wanted

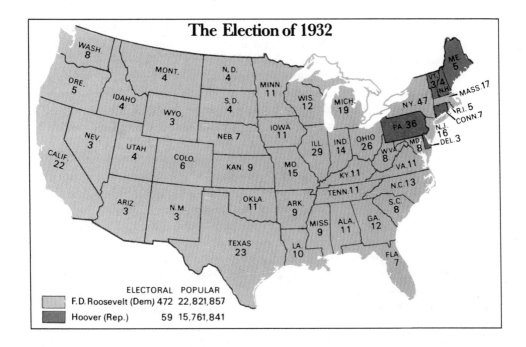

The Election of 1932

| | ELECTORAL | POPULAR |
|---|---|---|
| F.D.Roosevelt (Dem) | 472 | 22,821,857 |
| Hoover (Rep.) | 59 | 15,761,841 |

desperately to believe that a brave new leader with a magic touch might still transform the toad of depression into a dazzling prince of prosperity.

Hopes for a dynamic, masterly executive focused on Franklin D. Roosevelt, whose name associated him with his distant cousin Theodore, a strong leader and exceptional president. FDR had been assistant secretary of the navy (TR's old job) in the Wilson administration, then the vice-presidential candidate in the futile Cox campaign of 1920. A year later polio paralyzed him from the waist down. But with dedicated assistance from his wife, Eleanor, and his aide Louis Howe, Roosevelt returned to politics, overcame the Republican tide in 1928 to become governor of New York, and began gathering delegates for the 1932 national convention. A bargain with House Speaker John Nance Garner of Texas, which made "Cactus Jack" his running mate, sealed Roosevelt's nomination. Demonstrating the dramatic flair that marked his entire career, Roosevelt flew to the convention, stood erect at the podium, the weight of his crippled body supported by his powerful arms, and thrilled the hall with a ringing acceptance speech that promised a "new deal for the American people."

The Democrats ran a highly successful campaign. They promised not only to overcome the depression but also to end Prohibition. In 1932 many Americans thought the ban on drinking was almost as important as the depression. An end to Prohibition appealed to voters on two counts: liquor production would generate jobs and would signify the triumph of modern impulses over repressive parochial ones. It was, however, Hoover's failure to overcome the depression and Roosevelt's implied promises to do so that determined the election's outcome.

Roosevelt received 472 electoral votes to the hapless Hoover's 59. FDR defeated Hoover by a 17 percent margin in popular votes, 57 percent to 40 percent, duplicating the advantage Hoover had gained over Smith in 1928; it represented the greatest party reversal in presidential history. Roosevelt's victory rested on a coalition of traditional white southern Democrats, patrons of northern urban machines, modern-minded critics of Prohibition, progressives blaming business for the economic debacle, and millions of poor or newly impoverished people whose lives had been devastated by the depression.

**The New Deal Arrives, 1933–1934**   At the start of Roosevelt's term there were justified suspicions that he would not be very bold in meeting the economic crisis. During the campaign he had accused Hoover of extravagance and promised to balance the budget. But the problems he faced in reviving the economy quickly overcame his impulse to clamp down on government spending and follow familiar remedies. Surrounded by advisers offering a variety of answers to the crisis, Roosevelt saw a need for flexibility and experimentation in trying to overcome the depression. In a famous exchange with reporters he compared himself to a quarterback in a football game who tries different plays to make needed gains.

As he improvised, Roosevelt enjoyed the advantage of a striking presidential personality. The reversal in presidential character from Hoover to FDR was startling. Hoover, one associate remarked, "didn't like the human element." Roosevelt reveled in it. Not only did he mix easily with all kinds of people, but he also made them feel that intuitively he sympathized with them. Hoover, taking no one's counsel, thought he knew what the nation wanted. Unlike Hoover, Roosevelt welcomed the challenge of selling his programs to a demoralized nation. A master of popular phrasing and simple analogies, Roosevelt had a strong, warm voice that reached into millions of American homes through radio "fireside chats" that were bits of genius in the use of a mass medium. Where Hoover cast somber eyes downward, the tilt of Roosevelt's chin and the cocky angle of his cigarette holder invariably gave the sense of a man looking upward. Always he radiated confidence. Roosevelt's personality would prove to be one of his greatest assets in dealing with the domestic and international crises that confronted his presidency in the 1930s and 1940s. It gave him a hold on public confidence that calmed the nation and emotionally fortified it in some of the darkest years in its history.

Urging "bold experimentation" for a devastated land, Roosevelt attracted a swarm of newcomers to Washington, a curiously mixed but effective group of advisers. For secretary of the treasury, Roosevelt selected his close friend and neighbor from Hyde Park, New York: Henry Morgenthau, Jr., whose conscientiousness and loyalty made him indispensable to the president. For secretary of agriculture, Roosevelt appointed Henry A. Wallace, the son of Harding's secretary of agriculture, whose broad liberal vision compensated for his occasional inattention to practical matters. Another liberal Republican, Harold Ickes,

**FDR Taking Reporters to See
His Trees, Hyde Park, 1937**
*FDR was a master of symbolic
politics who helped restore
national confidence in the midst
of the worst depression in
American history.*

became secretary of the interior and watched over his domain, which included public works projects, with a fierce jealousy and a scrupulous honesty. From his New York administration, Roosevelt brought both the first woman to hold a cabinet post, Frances Perkins, to become secretary of labor, and the tough, dedicated administrator of relief, Harry Hopkins. All of them served, some of them in a variety of positions, to the end of Roosevelt's presidency.

The new administration also drew in people who had never before influenced government policy: an obscure Montana professor named M. L. Wilson with a proposal for limiting agricultural production; Raymond Moley, Rexford Tugwell, and Adolf Berle of Columbia University, the "brains trust" of Roosevelt's 1932 campaign, with ambitious plans to improve the economy's organization; social workers with plans to aid the unemployed, the disabled, and the aged; and progressive social engineers from a variety of backgrounds but sharing a faith in the ability of government to fashion enduring solutions to economic and social problems. Together this patchwork of people composed the "New Dealers." During Roosevelt's long tenure this term became part of America's everyday language—used with affection by some and with hatred by others to express their strong feelings about Roosevelt and his administration.

Beneath Roosevelt's easy public style and gracious private manner lay a keen, calculating mind that always sought to direct people and events. The din of demands around his powerful office never ruffled him. Moreover, Roosevelt brought to office a firm faith in the basic principles of the new national system. He wanted business to organize, industry by industry; and agriculture, commodity by commodity. He believed that an efficient labor force and private financial institutions working with industry and agriculture could restore prosperity. The government had only to assist them in regaining their strength and finding their proper places in the system. Roosevelt would experiment—but within these boundaries. Not surprisingly, the new president selected equally orthodox men, deep-dyed fiscal conservatives, for the crucial administrative posts of the early New Deal: Hugh Johnson and Donald Richberg in business affairs, George Peek and Chester Davis in agriculture, Jesse Jones for the Reconstruction Finance Corporation, (RFC), and Lewis Douglas for the Bureau of the Budget. In fact, these appointments gave a slightly conservative cast to Roosevelt's initial list of lieutenants, but they were more than balanced by the imaginative, liberal appointees, among them attorneys Ben Cohen and Tom Corcoran, who set the long-term tone and direction of the New Deal.

**The "Hundred Days"**   Roosevelt's very first problem—the collapse of the banking structure—fell on him as he entered the White House. He responded with a fine sense of style and an instinctive moderation. During the worst winter of depression, 1932–33, accumulating panic spread from banks in the agrarian regions toward America's financial centers. State after state closed its banks until on March 4, 1933—inauguration day itself—the pressure finally overwhelmed the citadels of national finance, New York and Chicago. As those doors closed, the entire system stopped. Borrowing an adman's phrase, Roosevelt immediately declared a nationwide "bank holiday," dispatched expert teams to classify all banks as strong, wavering, or hopeless, and started a transfusion of over $1 billion from the RFC into the banking system. In the first of his "fireside chats," the president spoke soothing words to the nation, assuring jittery citizens that it was safe to return savings to banks. In less than two weeks 90 percent of the frozen deposits were again available to customers, and all over the country money came out of the mattresses to fill the banks. It was an exemplary performance in the service of the capitalist financial system, and Wall Street joined Main Street in cheering the president. "In one week," the journalist Walter Lippmann marveled, "the nation, which had lost confidence in everything and everybody, has regained confidence in the government and itself."

Roosevelt's treatment for the banking emergency revealed the broad strategy of the New Deal's first months. Among the many popular prescriptions for halting an apparently endless economic decline, none appealed more to the Roosevelt spirit than a nationwide surge of activity that headed upward instead of downward. Mobilize confidence, synchronize energy, and prosperity would return because throughout the land people would suddenly behave as if it were returning. To a president who in his inaugural address had told Americans "that the only thing we have to fear is fear itself," that kind of grandiose bootstraps operation made perfect sense.

As Roosevelt took office, he called Congress into special session, plied it with proposals, and during a whirlwind "Hundred Days" guided through fifteen major laws, the greatest outburst of far-reaching legislative activity in American history. They seemed to cover everything: unemployment relief through grants to the states, public works, and a Civilian Conservation Corps; a cheaper or inflated currency brought about by taking the dollar off the international gold standard; agricultural aid through the Agricultural Adjustment Act; mortgage supports through the Farm Credit Administration and the Home Owners' Loan Corporation; industrial cooperation through the National Industrial Recovery Act; banking reforms, including the creation of the Federal Deposit Insurance Corporation (FDIC); conservation of natural resources through establishment of the Tennessee Valley Authority; a securities law that regulated the issuance of new stocks; and more.

**The NRA and the AAA**

Amid this array of legislation, two measures formed the heart of the early New Deal. One was the National Industrial Recovery Act (NIRA) of June 1933, which represented a continuation of 1920s government-sponsored business cooperation. The NIRA's most important provisions authorized each specialized segment of business to prepare a code of self-governance and established the National Recovery Administration (NRA) to supervise the process. To serve as NRA chief, the president chose General Hugh Johnson, a brash, noisy veteran in public affairs, who immediately launched a circus of a campaign to rally all Americans behind his program. Through parades, speeches, and assorted hoopla, Johnson made the Blue Eagle, the NRA's emblem of cooperation, almost synonymous with the New Deal itself, and he counted on public opinion to make it almost synonymous with Americanism.

In the NRA's first four months, business groups wrote more than seven hundred constitutions to govern their affairs. Where one or more large firms dominated an industry, the NRA relied on them to prepare the codes; where no firm dominated an industry, the NRA turned to a trade association. Although the codes varied from industry to industry, they usually included some agreement on prices, wages, and the acceptable limits of competition. The only integration among them was a common commitment to stabilization, a common freedom from antitrust prosecution, and a common dependence on the industrial groups themselves to regulate their own members. Johnson exalted the spirit of cooperation and swore at the "slackers," but never coerced the businessmen. In some respects the whole thing was a throwback to Gilded Age solutions to falling profits—the cartels, pools and trusts that in the late nineteenth century had been designed to limit competition and hold up prices. Now, however, the government, in an unprecedented intervention in the economy, was doing much the same thing.

Section 7a of the National Industrial Recovery Act authorized workers to organize and bargain in their own behalf, and some labor leaders, notably John L. Lewis of the United Mine Workers, acted as though the government was now their sponsor: "THE PRESIDENT WANTS YOU TO JOIN THE UNION!" Although the NRA did not actually encourage an independent labor movement, it provided labor with other important benefits: it fostered a national pattern of maximum hours and minimum wages, and it eliminated child labor and the sweatshop.

Critics rightly complained that the NRA did not bring sustained recovery; nevertheless it achieved significant accomplishments. It helped stop the downward economic spiral, gave jobs to nearly 2 million workers, and reduced some of the cutthroat business competition that hurt the economy.

The second basic law of the early New Deal was the Agricultural Adjustment Act of May 1933. A grab bag of traditional nostrums, it included provisions for almost every farm program that had been proposed in this century: marketing agreements, commodity loans, export subsidies, government purchases, and (reminiscent of William Jennings Bryan) even currency inflation. To these familiar devices the government added a favorite in New Deal circles, production restrictions, aimed at reducing agricultural surpluses at their source. During its first months the Agricultural Adjustment Administration (AAA) used production cutbacks as a way of getting emergency cash relief to the countryside. In midseason farmers were paid to plow under their crops and slaughter their livestock, a bitter expedient with so much hunger in the nation. After 1933 the AAA expected each farmer growing a particular crop to reduce production by a nationally fixed percentage.

The goal of the new law was to increase farm income to a level of "parity," or equality, with the farmers' purchasing power just before World War I. Although the AAA gave farmers, especially tenant farmers, little immediate relief from the depression, it had a solid impact in the longer run. By the close of FDR's first term, gross farm income had risen 50 percent and rural debt had dropped sharply. The rise in farm prices and improved conditions for farmers in part has to be attributed to a drought lasting from 1932 to 1936; but the AAA, by curtailing production and subsidizing farmers, also did its share.

**Financial Regulation**  Roosevelt and many of his advisers laid particularly heavy blame on financial institutions for causing the depression. "The money changers have fled from their high seats in the temple of our civilization," the president bitingly said of the bankers in his inaugural address. While congressional investigations were revealing how bankers had speculated with bank deposits, new laws sought to hold finance within proper bounds. Through the Glass-Steagall Act of 1933, Congress required banks to separate their investments in securities from normal commercial banking. The next year it placed the stock exchange under the regulation of the Securities and Exchange Commission (SEC). FDR appointed Joseph P. Kennedy, an adroit stock manipulator in the 1920s who knew all the tricks, to head the commission. In 1935 Congress outlawed holding companies that had been formed in the 1920s for no other purpose than the sale of stock, and it gave the SEC authority to dissolve other questionable holding companies.

Between 1933 and 1935 the federal government also acted to ensure the future stability of the banking industry and to protect the savings, farms, and homes of the mass of Americans. The RFC, which had been established under Hoover in 1932 to rescue banks, railroads, and other institutions, pumped loans into the nation's solvent banks. In 1933 Congress created the Federal Deposit Insurance Corporation so that ordinary citizens would no longer lose their savings if a bank failed. New executive agencies, especially the Farm Credit Administration and the Home Owners Loan Corporation, underwrote farm and housing mortgages. By 1935, when Congress consolidated the regulatory powers of the Federal Reserve System in a centralized board of governors, the government had completed the construction of a national framework of supports around American finance that protected the country from the kind of financial instability that had plagued it in 1932–33. The effect of these laws was to make the federal government the watchdog and the guarantor of America's banks and stock exchanges. The network of laws fulfilled the ambitions of some nineteenth- and early-twentieth-century reformers for government guarantees against market forces in an industrial economy that worked havoc with people's lives.

**The Tennessee Valley Authority**

The most daring government venture of the early New Deal was the Tennessee Valley Authority (TVA). Its origins lay in a long, inconclusive debate during the 1920s over the disposition of a dam at Muscle Shoals, Alabama, that the government had started to build in wartime but never completed. When Henry Ford, widely regarded in the 1920s as a great public benefactor, offered to lease and develop it, the tenacious old progressive Republican senator George Norris of Nebraska skillfully blocked the proposal. In time Norris convinced a majority of his colleagues that the government itself should develop the dam. During the 1920s, however, no one anticipated the vast undertaking ahead. Beginning in 1933, Muscle Shoals became merely the point of departure for a new concept in regional rehabilitation, which soon gained international fame. The Tennessee Valley Authority, armed with sweeping administrative powers over a domain that wound through seven southern states, embarked on two decades of activity that created a network of dams and canals, rejuvenated the soil and protected it against floods, and harnessed electric resources to service millions of homes and thousands of new businesses.

From the outset the TVA challenged the customary rights of private enterprise by selling the electric power it generated. Conservatives probably hated it as much as any New Deal program. Nevertheless the TVA had not completely abandoned the traditional principle of local control. The regional concept itself was a way of avoiding distant direction from Washington. At every step the TVA's directors worked through the existing organized groups in their region. Chambers of commerce, leagues of bankers, commercial farming associations, and the farmers' local associates from the Department of Agriculture and the state agricultural colleges channeled the TVA's information, chose its demonstration farms, and distributed many of its political benefits. The same local groups were the TVA's primary allies in the long legal battle with the private utility companies over the issue of publicly controlled electric power, a battle that the TVA did not

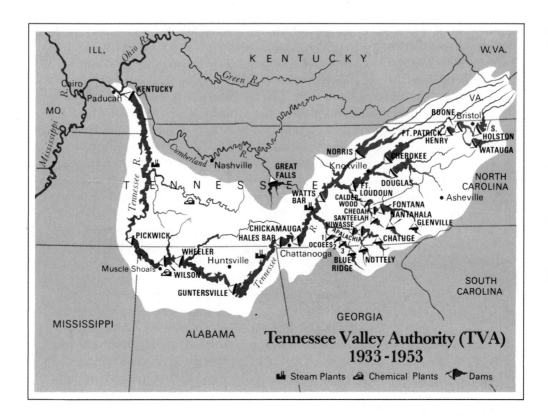

Tennessee Valley Authority (TVA)
1933-1953

⏹ Steam Plants  ⚗ Chemical Plants  ◀ Dams

fully win until 1939. None of this, however, held back the TVA from bold actions that significantly altered the life of the region it served.

**Public Relief**     The New Deal responded to the problem of unemployment and relief with an innovative use of government power. The collapse of state, local, and private relief efforts created a sense of urgency about having the federal government take over the job. To generate work for the unemployed, Congress appropriated $3.3 billion for the Public Works Administration (PWA) as part of the National Industrial Recovery Act of 1933. Secretary Harold Ickes, the PWA's director, vowed that no corruption would tarnish his bureau and spent the funds with a miser's caution. The Civilian Conservation Corps, one of the most popular measures of the "Hundred Days," functioned like an army summer camp for unemployed young men. The 2.5 million Americans employed by the corps during its existence labored on flood control and soil conservation projects and helped restore America's forests. Their planting of new growth exceeded all that had previously been done in the nation's history. They also improved and added to the country's parks and recreational areas.

Although Roosevelt opposed a permanent use of federal funds for relief, he understood how essential it was for the government to come to the aid of the destitute. To meet this challenge, the New Deal established the Federal Emergency Relief Administration (FERA) in 1933. When an initial appropriation of $500 million for FERA proved inadequate, Roosevelt drew an additional $400 million from Ickes's PWA for a hastily devised program, the Civil Works Administration. In February 1934 Congress finally authorized more funds for FERA. Harry Hopkins, Roosevelt's administrator of relief, employing a small staff, relied on local governments to distribute most of the money. "Nothing in the new federal act was meant to change that local responsibility, nor did the federal administration have any intention of doing so," an expert on public relief concluded. To the starving, all that mattered was that an administration was providing desperately needed help.

Since the Civil War, suffering was never so widespread in the country as during the depression. Things had been so bad in 1932 that numerous journalists and labor leaders predicted revolution. Kansas newspaper editor William Allen White said that only relief would keep down the barricades in the streets. AFL President William Green believed that unless people found a way to earn a living, "desperation and blind revolt [would] follow." The desperate situation of many Americans is captured in some of the letters they sent to the White House. An Oregon man wrote: "We do not dare to use even a little soap when it will pay for an extra egg or a few more carrots for our children." An Oklahoma woman described how former middle-class folks began to *feel* old and *look* and *act* poor in the depression: "The unemployed have been so long with out food-clothes-shoes-medical care-dental care etc—we look pretty bad—so when we ask for a job we don't get it. And we look and feel a little worse each day—when we ask for food they call us bums—it isent [*sic*] our fault . . . no we are not bums." But "with shabby suits, frayed collars, worn shoes and perhaps a couple of front teeth gone," men *looked* like bums. A West Virginia man wrote his senator: "My children have not got no shoes and clothing to go to school with, and we havent got enough bed clothes to keep us warm." A Pennsylvania man asked a government relief worker for advice on how to dispose of himself and his family: " . . . This is about the only thing I see left to do. No home, no work, no money. We cannot go along this way. They have shut the water supply from us. No means of sanitation. We can not keep the children clean and tidy as they should be."

At the start of Roosevelt's term as many as 15 million people had lost their jobs and could not find work. Between 1 million and 2 million of them wandered the country in a fruitless search for employment. Fifty percent of blacks were unemployed. Many Americans lucky enough to find jobs labored at miserably low wages. Industrial workers received 7.5 cents an hour and less. In Tennessee mills women earned $2.39 for a fifty-hour week; Connecticut sweatshops paid young girls 1 to 2 cents an hour, between 60 cents and $1.10 for a fifty-five-hour week. Some American families forced onto relief rolls received less than $2.50 a week.

## The New Deal at the Crossroads, 1935–1936

In 1934, shortly before Raymond Moley left the New Deal to become its conservative critic, he commented, "This administration is as far from socialism or communism as any group ever assembled in a national government." The sheer quantity of government activities during 1933 and 1934 had misled some people into believing that the country was abandoning its free-enterprise system for a state-controlled economy. But they were wrong. Economic and political caution were watchwords of Roosevelt's administration. The president's second major action during the Hundred Days, for example, was an economy bill that slashed $500 million from the federal budget for veterans' benefits and government employees. Despite the broadened range of government services and innovations that made America a more humane society, the nation's leaders had no radical intentions. With fresh faces and tactics, through experiments and expedients, the New Deal fought to preserve a particular political economy that had formed during the 1920s—but also to alter it so that such an awful depression could not occur again.

The New Deal had, in fact, brought only limited recovery. By late 1934 the NRA was faltering, the victim of the businessmen's self-serving codes, widespread violations of these same rules, and criticism from almost every segment of American society. Now it was the National Run Around. The administration's own review board condemned the NRA, and Roosevelt himself lost interest in the grand experiment. The depression refused to lift. Although unemployment declined from the darkest months of early 1933, it was about as bad as it had been the day Roosevelt was elected. Net farm income was a dismal 50 percent of its level in 1929, and food shortages—caused by a cruel drought and by a generation of unwise farming practices that turned the Great Plains into the infamous Dust Bowl, choking farmers in vast clouds of topsoil that swirled from Texas to the Dakotas—accounted for most of the price increases since 1933. Only corporate profits were making strong gains in 1934.

The manifest failure of the first phase of the New Deal to bring back prosperity caused Roosevelt and most of his advisers to shift ground. In 1935, modern welfare-state liberalism took shape in a new burst of legislative reform. In response, conservatives, warning of threats to traditional institutions and habits—free enterprise, freedom from centralized government control, excessive power in executive hands—began to attack the New Deal as the advance wave of communism or, at the very least, welfare-state socialism that would destroy individual initiative and traditional freedoms. And as liberal and conservative politicians maneuvered, a persistent drumbeat of radical cries for more drastic action grew louder.

**Radical Critics**  Waning confidence in the New Deal drew millions of angry, suffering Americans to new leaders and new causes. From Louisiana came the shrewd, flamboyant Huey Long, promising to make "every man a king." By appealing to the forgotten poor whites of his state,

**A Dispossessed Arkansas Family**
*Few groups in America suffered more than small farmers during the depression.*

**FDR's New Deal Remedies**
*The New Deal experimented with a variety of measures to overcome the depression and permanently improve living conditions for the mass of Americans.*

**The "Kingfish"**
*Huey Long was one of a trio of demagogues driving Roosevelt's New Deal to the left in 1935.*

Long became governor in 1929 and quickly established an almost dictatorial control of Louisiana, ruling through an extensive, ruthless political machine. After his election to the Senate in 1930, the Louisiana "Kingfish" used his heightened prestige and national visibility to spread the gospel of Share Our Wealth, a simple, sweeping program that would expropriate the wealth of the very rich in order to provide all families with a $5,000 homestead and an annual income of about $2,500—a glorious vision at depression prices.

From a Detroit suburb came the rich radio voice of a Catholic priest, Father Charles Coughlin, who blasted Wall Street, warned darkly of Jewish plots, called for the nationalization of the banks, and demanded an immediate, massive monetary inflation. From Long Beach, California, came the mellow appeals of Dr. Francis E. Townsend, an elderly dentist who envisioned prosperity for everybody through monthly government payments of $200 for each retired person over sixty years of age. By requiring the pensioners to spend their $200 within the month, the Townsend Plan promised to revitalize the entire economy. All three campaigns accelerated rapidly in late 1934 and early 1935.

No one ever knew how many Americans accepted these formulas for prosperity, which recalled the spirit of 1890s Populism. Although Long, Coughlin, and Townsend each claimed millions of adherents, none formed an effective organization. The imposing facades of Long's Share Our Wealth clubs, Coughlin's

National Union for Social Justice, and Townsend's Old Age Revolving Pensions club covered a thoroughly scattered, locally oriented following that defied a head count. Nor could the New Dealers calculate the number of workers who had given up on the system and were ready for a revolution. During 1934 blue-collar workers, seizing upon provision 7a of the NIRA authorizing collective bargaining by employees, launched a series of tumultuous strikes. They involved more than 7 percent of the labor force and shook many in the nation, who saw them as portents of revolution. Longshoremen in San Francisco, teamsters in Minneapolis, and textile workers along the East Coast were embroiled in particularly bloody conflicts with radical overtones.

**Changing the New Deal's Direction**
Partly because no one could estimate the strength of these rumbling movements, they sent tremors of anxiety through the Roosevelt administration. With the New Deal also stalled late in 1934 and a more progressive Congress sent to Washington by the 1934 elections, the president felt compelled to head off critics on the left by pushing a new package of recovery and reform legislation in 1935. Wasting no time, in January he called for a huge work relief program and a comprehensive social security measure.

Three months later Congress established the Works Progress Administration (WPA). The very size of the appropriation indicated how central the New Deal considered relief. With almost $5 billion—the greatest single appropriation by any nation in history to date, and ten times the amount originally given to FERA—the WPA absorbed close to half the government's total expenditures. Like its predecessors, the act claimed to be a temporary measure.* By 1935, however, very few people thought that local or private contributions could ever again carry the burdens of relief in a depression. Harry Hopkins, who administered the WPA, now emerged as Roosevelt's most powerful lieutenant. Through Hopkins's large staff the WPA supervised an extraordinary variety of projects, ranging from theatrical productions to road repairs, and on the average employed more than 2 million people who would otherwise have been jobless. The WPA was testimony to the administration's determination to create, in Roosevelt's words, "a government that lives in a spirit of charity rather than one frozen in the ice of its own indifference."

The Social Security Act of August 1935, more cautious in approach, was an equally striking innovation with a more lasting influence. It established a national system of old-age insurance funded by a tax on workers' wages and an equivalent tax on their employers. The act also taxed employers to finance state programs for unemployment compensation, and it offered the states matching grants to aid dependent mothers and children and the disabled. If the Social Security Act was

---

*The original relief agency, the PWA, had been established under the NIRA in 1933 simply to give work to unemployed Americans. By contrast, the WPA had broader objectives of enriching the nation's social and cultural life while also giving emergency employment.

a conservative version of the schemes for social insurance that had been discussed since the early 1900s, and if the act did not equal the generosity of the Townsend Plan, it nevertheless coped with the same ills. Originally excluding millions of workers—farmers and agricultural laborers, domestic servants, and the self-employed among them—Social Security was an expandable formula. Later Congresses gradually extended its range until by the 1980s it covered almost all employees and many more of life's hazards, including escalating medical costs to the aged.

Liberal congressmen produced the third basic law, which the president after months of hesitation finally endorsed. Passage of the National Labor Relations Act—the Wagner Act—in July 1935 marked another startling shift in New Deal policy. Before 1935 the government had considered labor primarily as a dependent part of industry. With the Wagner Act, however, the New Deal committed itself unequivocally to supporting unions that were independent of management. The Wagner Act outlawed company unions and any form of company discrimination that might inhibit workers from joining an independent union. The National Labor Relations Board, which was created to administer the law, could conduct an election among a company's employees to ensure their free choice of a bargaining agent, and it could compel employers to comply with the new rules.

**The Liberal-Conservative Polarization**
The first important consequence of these three unprecedented acts was a powerful release of emotions. During 1935 and 1936 the New Deal, and above all Roosevelt himself, generated both hope and hatred that would run like a high-voltage charge through the next generation of American politics. If the New Deal neither cured the depression nor saved the nation from suffering, it communicated a humane concern when no one else seemed to care. "I do think that Roosevelt is the biggest-hearted man we ever had in the White House," declared one typical citizen. The legislation of 1935, which offered millions of hard-pressed Americans a bit of help, simultaneously held out the promise of much more to come. Moreover, it offered a promise of dignity. The WPA gave people real jobs, not charity. Social Security raised miraculous visions of a decent life in old age. The Wagner Act told countless wage earners that through their own organization they could command respect as full-fledged citizens. In one worker's words, "Roosevelt is the only president we ever had that thought the Constitution belonged to the poor man too."

What gave hope at the bottom of society spread horror at the top. Among many people with a strong stake in the existing system—bankers, lawyers, corporation executives, and doctors—the new laws conjured up images of a chaotic society in which government pitted the masses against everyone else's privileges. Year after year conservatives' inability to explain what had gone wrong with the economy or predict what the government would do next had deepened their frustration. Conservative doubts about the New Deal in 1933 turned into charges of incompetence in 1934, then outright hatred in 1935. Much more powerful than the millions who loved Roosevelt, the wealthy foes of the New Deal had the means of making their feelings heard. They spoke from chambers of commerce and from bar, medical, and banking associations. They formed new organizations such as the American Liberty League, which spent millions to discredit the New Deal. Through newspapers, radio, and venomous little rumors ("Polio? Syphilis!"), they mounted a furious assault on "that man in the White House" even more than on his administration.

When the New Deal changed course in 1935, it abandoned the vision of the economy that had dominated public policy since World War I. During the 1920s and early 1930s, policymakers had sought harmony among the nation's big economic units: business, labor, agriculture, and finance. It was assumed that business, with encouragement from Washington, would lead the other units in a coordinated march to prosperity. When the administration abandoned this conception of the economy in 1935 and focused instead on winning economic and social gains for the country's middle and working classes, it touched off the modern conflict between liberalism and conservatism. Prominent Democrats like Raymond Moley and Al Smith, who now saw excessive statism and the promotion of class conflict in administration actions, broke with Roosevelt and joined the conservative opposition, which to that point had been little more than a limited, although influential, fringe group. By abandoning its original conservative economic assumptions and accommodating itself to left-wing critics with new relief, old age, and labor programs, Roosevelt's New Deal turned itself into a vehicle for modern liberal ideas. But it also gave life to a broader conservative coalition determined to fend off a reputed assault on traditional American opposition to big government and the country's long-standing taste for rugged individualism.

New Deal liberalism as well as 1930s conservatism were not early full-blown versions of what Americans took to be liberal and conservative in the thirty years between 1960 and 1990. Conservatives in the 1930s would not have been comfortable with the government activism or intrusion into people's daily lives that by the 1980s even most Reaganites would generally accept as irreversible institutional changes. Similarly, the New Deal was hardly the forebear of the civil rights and feminist movements that later loomed so large in liberal concerns. Although Roosevelt had selected the first woman to hold a cabinet post, neither Frances Perkins nor Roosevelt's active wife, Eleanor, nor anyone else in the New Deal had wanted to revive and remold the pre–World War I movement for women's rights. Nor was anyone in the Roosevelt administration urging an all-out battle for minority rights, particularly for blacks to vote and share fully in the economic and social gains the administration aimed to give the urban white working class.

The New Deal's brand of liberalism appealed nevertheless to women, even though the New Deal had no specifically feminist goal. The fact that it appointed a number of women to prominent government positions and pursued a variety of progressive policies was enough for most liberal-minded women. In addition to Eleanor and Secretary of Labor Perkins, for example, women served for the first time as ambassadors and on the Federal Court of Appeals. They also held appointments as Assistant Secretary of the Treasury, Director of the Mint, heads of the Women's and Children's bureaus in the Labor Department, administrators of relief, and board members of the NRA and the Social Security Administration. By 1935, under repeated prodding by Molly Dewson, head of the Democratic party's Women's Division, fifty women had been appointed to high-level posts in the New Deal. Also serving in leadership roles in the Democratic party, women played an unprecedented part in helping Roosevelt and the Democrats win the election of 1936. "The change from women's status in government before Roosevelt is unbelievable," Molly Dewson said.

Yet this translated into only limited economic gains for women. The depression created new barriers to women seeking jobs. Over 80 percent of Americans, including 75 percent of the women who were asked, believed that wives of working men should stay home. Many large businesses and school systems refused to hire married women, and the federal government denied employment to more than one family member. Despite these restrictions, the number of women workers rose 25 percent during the 1930s. Because "women's jobs" in sales and services and as clerks were less hard hit by the depression than "men's work" in heavy industries, and because sectors employing women recovered most rapidly, women found more job opportunities than men. Yet women's pay was substantially lower than men's. On WPA projects, for example, women received only 60 percent of what men earned. Although New Deal minimum-wage and maximum-hour regulations improved the living standards of many women, federal policies excluded domestic workers, who were mostly women, from the protections of the Social Security and Fair Labor Standards acts, allocated far more relief jobs to men than women, and barred women from working in the Civilian Conservation Corps.

On matters of ethnicity and religion, the New Dealers were in many ways impressively liberal. As the battles over Al Smith had already demonstrated, the Democrats had been attracting a mixture of ethnic groups during the 1920s. The elections of 1932 and 1934 had added even more urban cultural segments to the party's new majority. Prominent members of the administration were closely identified with the nation's ethnic and religious minorities. Eleanor Roosevelt, having overcome her strong prejudices of girlhood and early marriage, spoke eloquently for religious equality. The president himself appointed a Jew as secretary of the treasury, an ironic reply to the anti–Semitic hallucinations of Coughlin, Ford, and others about a Jewish plot to control world finance. Catholics were also prominent in a government that reached out to America's minorities more than had any administration in the past.

Perhaps most impressive of all, the New Deal tried to reverse the long, cruel trend of native American impoverishment and tribal disintegration. In the late 1920s government reports began to reveal the rampant white greed and injustice that under the terms of the old Dawes Act of 1887 had transformed tribal lands into the private property of individual members. In 1934, spurred on by John

Collier, the New Deal's director of Indian affairs, Congress passed the Indian Reorganization Act, which enabled nations of native Americans to re-create communal control over their lands, and offered some assistance toward tribal self-sufficiency. Throughout the 1930s, the zealous Collier scrambled for money to implement this program.

If Roosevelt and other New Deal leaders were demonstrably broad-minded on religious and ethnic matters, they also knew that their liberality was good politics. The New Deal primarily worked through local Democratic leaders and machines that were spokesmen for minorities who had begun to vote in great numbers in the 1920s and 1930s. These Democratic "bosses" and machines had little genuine interest in racial justice or equality, but they recognized that their power rested on their ability to speak effectively to the concerns of local minorities. National Democratic leaders gave local politicians the financial means to attend to such needs by allowing them to distribute public funds in their own areas by their own standards. In the large cities government funds passed through urban politicians to the interested families and cultural groups. In only five of the forty-eight states did the WPA bypass the established local powers. In such cities as Pittsburgh and Kansas City, the New Deal's relief laws shored up the existing political machines, and in Chicago, WPA funds actually saved the budding Democratic organization of Mayor Edward Kelley. These beneficiaries ranked among the Roosevelt administration's most dedicated supporters. Across the country organized labor declared Roosevelt its champion.

**Blacks and the New Deal** Of all the country's minority groups, black Americans fared least well under the New Deal. No group in America was harder hit by the depression than blacks. Normally the most impoverished members of American society, they experienced a worsening of their economic plight in the 1930s. Yet the NRA and the AAA provided blacks with few economic benefits; in fact, AAA policies forced many black tenant farmers and sharecroppers off the land. Moreover, the New Deal did little to reduce racial discrimination against blacks. The Federal Housing Authority refused to guarantee mortgages for blacks trying to buy homes in white neighborhoods and made no effort to support racial integration in low-cost federal housing projects. Federal relief programs like the Civilian Conservation Corps and the National Youth Administration (NYA) were strictly segregated in the South. When Congress rejected an amendment to the Wagner Act that would have required racial equality on the job, the New Deal left the issue of bias in the unions to the labor leaders themselves. By 1935 the NAACP complained "that the powers-that-be in the Roosevelt administration have [done] nothing for" the black American. Moreover, later black leaders pointed out that not a single civil rights law was passed during FDR's twelve years in office. He refused to support abolition of the poll tax, which systematically denied the franchise to southern blacks and poor whites. Nor did he ever support legislation aimed against

**Eleanor Roosevelt Greeting Educator Mary McLeod Bethune**

*Although blacks were not a favored minority in the New Deal years, the Roosevelt administration was impressively liberal on matters of race and religion and extended enough of a helping hand to blacks to break their traditional affiliation with the Republican party.*

lynchings in the South; no antilynching law was passed during his term. Viewing southern whites as a mainstay of his New Deal coalition, Roosevelt refused to do anything for blacks that might alienate white southern support.

Yet African Americans were increasingly drawn to the New Deal coalition. The Roosevelt administration appointed more blacks to high government jobs than ever before in the country's history, although the appointments never equaled in rank and prestige what blacks received in the Reconstruction era. Still, the New Deal positions represented an advance on what had occurred since the end of Reconstruction in the 1870s. More important than the jobs given to blacks in the federal government was the fact that New Deal agencies like the WPA and the NYA provided blacks with a measure of economic relief. Moreover, in matters of personal discrimination, some of the men and women around FDR responded with sensitivity and imagination. Secretary of the Interior Harold Ickes was a veteran member of the National Association for the Advancement of Colored People (NAACP). Eleanor Roosevelt spoke eloquently for racial equality, and Henry Wallace, vice-president from 1941 to 1945, became one of the most prominent champions of black rights. In 1939, moreover, when the world-famous black contralto Marian Anderson was denied the use of Constitution Hall in Washington, Harold Ickes arranged for a dramatic concert on the steps of the

Lincoln Memorial. Although blacks were last in line under the New Deal, they did receive enough to break their identification with the Republican party and to make them solid backers of Roosevelt and the Democrats.

**The Election of 1936** The primary political test of the New Deal's methods came in the elections of 1936. Roosevelt's Republican opponent was the honest, uninspired governor of Kansas, Alfred Landon. The Union party, formed by Coughlin, Townsend, and the remnants of Huey Long's supporters (left in disarray by Long's assassination in 1935), nominated Representative William Lemke of North Dakota for president. Although Coughlin personally promised 9 million votes for Lemke and the popular magazine *Literary Digest* predicted Landon's victory, most people expected Roosevelt to win. The margin of victory, however, would serve as the critical index to the New Deal's success. And Roosevelt won by a tremendous landslide, carrying every state except Vermont and Maine. Along with huge Democratic majorities in Congress—75 out of 96 senators and 333 out of 435 representatives—the election gave Roosevelt a breathtaking 523 electoral votes to a mere 8 for Landon. The Socialist and Communist parties did very poorly. The woebegone Union party did not even collect a million popular votes, and Coughlin announced his retirement from politics, although it was not long before he returned to the political wars.

The Democratic conquest of 1936 ratified the New Deal's policies in two crucial and interrelated areas. First, it placed responsibility for the national economy squarely in the lap of the government. After 1936 Washington became the guarantor of the nation's economic welfare, and the populist economics and ethnic prejudices of people like Long, Coughlin, and Townsend never again won a mass following. The business leadership of the 1920s was trounced. Wealthy Roosevelt-haters had to bide their time and fight another day. Second, the landslide of 1936 solidified the core of a new and enduring Democratic majority. To the solid South (where the Democrats' control was unchallenged as long as the national party accepted local white supremacy) were now joined the nation's industrial centers. Here the party's greatest strength came from the relatively poor, Catholics, Jews, and blacks. Other voters would slip away from the Democrats after 1936, but the heart of their support would hold firm for decades.

## The New Deal Fades and Liberalism Consolidates, 1937–1939

Although Roosevelt swept into his second term on a high tide of popularity, his next four years produced far less domestic change than his first. Although Roosevelt had established modern liberalism in the last two years of his first term, he was not ready to launch additional bold initiatives in his second four years. Having introduced far-reaching reforms in his first administration, FDR was reluctant to press forward too quickly with actions that might antagonize middle-class Americans and drive some of them into the conservative camp. By being so cautious, Roosevelt lost his chance to end the depression and found himself in a weakened position common to most second-term presidents.

Roosevelt's second-term difficulties began with a battle in 1937 to reform the Supreme Court. In the tense climate of 1935 and 1936, as the New Deal was expanding its scope, the Court grew increasingly rigid. A bare majority of five justices attacked the national government's primary source of power over the economy—the regulation of interstate commerce. Mining and farming, in the Court's view, were local, not interstate, activities. By implication these interpretations jeopardized a full range of the New Deal's policies in industry and agriculture. Moreover, a narrow construction of interstate commerce automatically cast doubts on the government's authority to regulate labor-management relations through the Wagner Act, and to tax employers and employees through the Social Security Act.

**FDR Versus the Supreme Court**
The most publicized of the Court's many decisions during 1935 and 1936 were the Schechter case (1935), which struck down the National Recovery Administration (NRA), and *United States* v. *Butler* (1936), which invalidated the tax on food processing in the Agricultural Adjustment Act. Neither decision crippled the New Deal. The NRA, a loosely worded delegation of powers to the executive that all nine justices condemned, was practically dead by 1935; the Court's judgment in the *Schechter* case merely gave it a decent burial. Following the *Butler* decision Congress continued the New Deal's farm program of restricted production under the guise of soil conservation. But the Court's willingness in 1935 and 1936 to strike down two such important laws, along with so many other threatening precedents aimed at inhibiting the expanded federal intrusion into economic and social affairs, forced a confrontation between the Roosevelt administration and the Supreme Court. As the president complained, the New Deal could not function with a "horse and buggy" conception of interstate commerce.

Reading his victory in 1936 as a mandate to alter the Court's composition and perspective, Roosevelt submitted a judiciary reorganization bill to Congress in February 1937. The president requested the right to enlarge the Court from nine to a maximum of fifteen members if those justices over seventy years old did not voluntarily resign. If, as Chief Justice Charles Evans Hughes stated, the Constitution was what the Court made it, Roosevelt would remake the Court. But the president pretended that the issue was judicial efficiency rather than judicial interpretation. The existing Court, he claimed, could not manage its heavy load of work, a charge that Hughes easily refuted. In this political battle Roosevelt showed himself uncharacteristically inept. When Congress rebelled at his plan, Roosevelt hesitated to negotiate. Although liberal congressmen were prepared to impose extensive restrictions on the Court through constitutional amendment, the president, knowing that three-fourths of the state legislatures would not approve, held to his own scheme. Meanwhile the Court defused the central issue through an abrupt change in constitutional law. By a vote of 5 to 4, the Court in *NLRB* v. *Jones and Laughlin Steel* (1937) upheld the Wagner Act with a broad interpretation of interstate commerce. Then, by a larger margin, the Court validated the Social Security Act. "A switch in time saved nine," the wags chortled. The president's campaign looked more and more like a personal war against the Court, and a reach for unprecedented power. Defensively, he gave the public "solemn assurance" that he did not seek "the destruction of any branch of government or any part of our heritage of freedom." It did no good. After 168 days of exhausting, bitter battle, Roosevelt's bill was defeated.

In the end the conservatives did lose their judicial stronghold. A rapid sequence of retirements and deaths between 1937 and 1941 enabled the president to select seven associate justices and a chief justice. By the time of *United States* v. *Darby* (1941), the New Deal Court had authorized sweeping federal powers over interstate commerce and approved all the principal legislation that still mattered. But the price of victory was high. Roosevelt's attempt to pack the Court with pro–New Dealers tarnished his reputation as a leader. Instead of pitting the New Deal against the Court, his course set Congress against the White House. In the future even Democratic congressmen would feel much freer to vote against the president.

**Labor Strife and Agrarian Troubles**

Nevertheless the court battle was only one part of a complex process leading to the New Deal's decline. At least as much strain in the New Deal coalition came from the labor movement. As the Wagner Act passed in 1935, the labor movement split into warring camps. John L. Lewis, president of the powerful United Mine Workers, led a group of dissident unions out of the craft-oriented AFL in order to organize the semiskilled and unskilled workers in the major mass-production industries. The rebels eventually formed the Congress of Industrial Organizations (CIO), while the skilled trades remained in the AFL. Looking at the leaders of the two organizations, one saw little contest. Lewis's dramatic flair and imaginative leadership made him a national attraction in the mid-1930s, second only to Roosevelt, and the baggy, bushy-browed giant of the CIO appeared capable of demolishing the AFL's mild little William Green with words alone. "Explore the mind of Bill Green," the advocates of labor compromise had suggested to Lewis. "I have done a lot of exploring in Bill's mind," Lewis retorted, "and I give you my word there is nothing there." But the AFL proved to be a resourceful enemy that mobilized local opposition to the CIO, collaborated with employers who were fighting the new unions, and helped antiunion congressmen brand the CIO a communist organization.

In addition, the CIO faced a formidable challenge from the unorganized industries themselves. From the docks of San Francisco to the textile mills of North Carolina, employers murdered, gassed, beat, and intimidated their workers in order to demoralize them and to block the CIO's unionizing efforts. The first crisis in this rough, uncertain struggle began in December 1936 when workers at a number of General Motors affiliates sat inside the company plants to gain recognition for their new organization, the United Auto Workers (UAW). Ignoring court orders to evacuate the buildings, receiving supplies from their friends outside, and turning back the police in "The Battle of the Running Bulls," the autoworkers, with the help of cooperative state and national politicians, includ-

**United Mine Workers Union Head**
*John L. Lewis was a driving force in the creation of the Congress of Industrial Organizations (CIO).*

ing Roosevelt, achieved the CIO's first great victory. In February 1937 General Motors and the UAW signed a peace pact. Illegal sit-down strikes quickly spread nationwide.

Meanwhile a CIO drive in the steel industry won a second stunning success. In March 1937 the very symbol of antiunionism in America's mass-production industries, United States Steel, ended a bitter strike by recognizing the steelworkers' union. Almost all the corporations in "Little Steel," however, adamantly refused to follow suit, and bloody counterattacks stalled the organizing campaign there. In the "Memorial Day Massacre" outside Republic Steel's plant in Chicago, for example, police shot into a fleeing crowd, killing or wounding dozens of strike sympathizers. In fact, there was an epidemic of industrial violence in 1937.

The turmoil of sit-down strikes and local warfare broke an uneasy truce over labor policy within the Democratic party. While an exasperated Roosevelt condemned management and labor alike by wishing "a plague on both your houses," Democratic factions in Congress angrily debated the sins of employers and unions. Fortunately for the CIO, a partisan National Labor Relations Board continued to fight vigorously in behalf of the new unions. By 1941, with almost 10 million members divided between the AFL and the CIO, the union movement had safely passed the first round of crisis. In the process, however, it had made a host of enemies, Democrats as well as Republicans.

**Principal New Deal Measures, 1935–1938**

| | |
|---|---|
| Works Progress Administration (WPA) | May 1935 |
| Wagner Act, creating the National Labor Relations Board (NLRB) | July 1935 |
| Social Security Act | August 1935 |
| Bankhead-Jones Farm Tenancy Act, creating the Farm Security Administration (FSA) | July 1937 |
| Fair Labor Standards Act | June 1938 |

Growing hostility to the labor movement decreased the likelihood that the government would assist other Americans to organize in their own behalf. Tenant farmers, for example, stood in particular need of the government's help. Always the poor relations in an era of commercial agriculture, they had suffered cruelly from depression and drought in the 1930s. In 1935, when some of them formed the Southern Tenant Farmers' Union, landlords and sheriffs crushed their organization. When reformers in the Department of Agriculture argued the tenants' cause, they were fired.

The first serious attempt to reverse this tide was the Bankhead-Jones Farm Tenancy Act of 1937. Through a new agency, the Farm Security Administration (FSA), the law provided credit with which tenants could purchase the farms they were working. In addition the FSA explored ways to develop a diversified, cooperative community life for small farmers and to protect the interests of the forgotten farm laborers. The FSA was one logical extension of the New Deal's innovations in 1935, a rural counterpart of the program for organized labor. But in 1937 the opposition of the established agricultural organizations and the flagging reform spirit in Congress kept the FSA budget small and the agency's future precarious. However much a token advance, it was another expression of the New Deal's turn in the direction of modern welfare-state liberalism.

The most substantial expansion of New Deal liberalism in FDR's second term was the Fair Labor Standards Act of 1938. After much wrangling, Congress established a minimum wage level and an official rate of time-and-a-half for overtime work, and it abolished child labor. With wholesale exemptions in agriculture, special dispensations for southern employers, and meager minimum wage scales, this law represented only a first step toward fair labor practices. Yet in combination with Social Security and the WPA, the Fair Labor Standards Act reinforced a fundamental new liberal assumption: the national government should protect the economic welfare of its poorer citizens.

**The New Deal Legacy**

By 1938 the New Deal was drifting. Its limited accomplishments in the two years after 1936 reflected the decline in Roosevelt's authority. On Capitol Hill an informal coalition of Republicans and conservative, largely southern Democrats moved into the vacuum of leadership. A defensive league, it concentrated primarily on opposing "socialist" measures that would enlarge the national government's responsibilities or "giveaway" programs that would expand its services. In the spirit of the 1920s, many of the opposition still equated prosperity with a self-regulating economy. In 1938, when the president proposed a bill for executive reorganization to manage the government's broadening obligations, the conservative coalition—with cries of dictatorship—defeated the measure. And when Roosevelt tried to "purge" a few prominent opponents in his own Democratic party by campaigning against them during the off-year elections of 1938, his failure only emphasized before the public the president's diminishing power.

More important, however, in the last two years of Roosevelt's first term the New Deal established modern liberalism. In 1935 it abandoned the idea that laissez-faire capitalism or big interdependent economic blocs, with encouragement from Washington, would lead the country back into prosperity. Instead it opted for a broadly defined liberalism—for policies serving the needs of the oppressed or disadvantaged and small economic units encouraged to ask the government for programs serving their needs.

There were no more NRAs for all of American business. Instead Congress in 1935 created "little NRAs" for coal, for trucking, and, through an interstate oil compact, for petroleum. Two new laws strengthened the rights of small businessmen. The Robinson-Patman Act of 1936 sought to protect independent retailers against such huge chains as A & P and Woolworth, and the Miller-Tydings Act of 1937 legalized "fair trade" agreements (that is, fixed retail pricing) in behalf of similar small firms. Between 1934 and 1937 special legislation responded to particular agricultural interests such as cattle grazers, cotton and tobacco growers, and dairy farmers. The labor movement not only sharpened the distinction between the unorganized and the organized, but also highlighted the very different grievances separating carpenters from steelworkers from longshoremen from hatmakers—a decentralization of interests far greater than just a division between the AFL and the CIO.

Only the hub in Washington connected these many spokes of special interest. Economic policy was now government policy. But no one in the New Deal had a fully developed strategy for integrating these economic fragments. Since the beginning of the New Deal, some voices had advocated national planning. Yet their statements were studies in vagueness. Reach "a reasonable meeting of minds," the historian Charles Beard proposed; "coordinate private industry" with public enterprises like the TVA, the philosopher John Dewey suggested. The president had authorized the Justice Department to bring more antitrust suits against big business. Yet Roosevelt never longed for the old days of small-unit competition, and the administration's new antitrust policy did little to destroy giant corporations. Nor did Roosevelt follow some of his advisers' advice of striking a closer alliance between the New Deal and the unions. The president was reluctant to entangle himself in organized labor's raw battles, and he distrusted John L. Lewis, its strongest leader.

FDR rejected the only economic theory of the decade that, had he acted on it, might have overcome the depression. Marriner Eccles, the chairman of the Federal Reserve Board, wanted to regain prosperity through government spending. But Roosevelt retained a traditional faith in balanced budgets. When a new economic crisis occurred in 1937—a sharp downturn in the fall of that year, wiping out all the gains made since 1935—Roosevelt worsened matters by sharply reducing the government budget. Instead he should have instituted a radical increase in government spending. But in any event the budgets of the 1930s were simply too small a fraction of the economy's total activities, and the New Deal was attempting to move a boulder with a stick. In 1935 the British economist John Maynard Keynes published *The General Theory of Employment, Interest, and Money,* a book that in later decades would have a revolutionary impact on capitalist countries' policies by arguing for deficit spending in times of depression and reduced private investment. But Roosevelt gave little heed to Keynes's "rigmarole of figures." Although Roosevelt was profoundly disturbed by the vision of "one-third of a nation ill-nourished, ill-clad, ill-housed," he could not understand and would not accept Keynes's prescription for defeating the depression. Indeed, it would take the large deficits caused by the defense spending of 1939–40 and after to decisively break the hold of the depression on the economy.

Still, the New Deal accomplished more in five years than had any other administration in American history. Taking office in 1933, Roosevelt set out to save a crumbling American system, and he succeeded. If there was ever a crisis in United States capitalism that might have provided the opportunity for the country to choose a socialist alternative, it was in the 1930s. Instead socialism (and communism) dwindled to marginal sectarianism. Through new departures during 1933–38, the New Deal generated popular hopes where despair had prevailed, and it set the political economy in a fresh, more promising direction. Most important, through a series of bold reforms, it sought to make America a more humane industrial society by committing itself to welfare-state liberalism.

Yet if events between the onset of the Great Depression and America's entry into World War II worked fundamental changes in American life, they by no means cut the country off from its old habits. Although the Roosevelt presidency did much to bring the country more fully into the modern era, in part building on what had occurred in the 1920s, it maintained an attachment to traditional ways, refusing to be too innovative; and by so doing it left many questions unanswered. By 1941 prosperity had returned, but the government had no new programs planned to sustain and expand it; war had come, but the Roosevelt administration had no goal beyond winning it. It would not be until after World War II that the United States established a more coherent long-term foreign policy. And not until the 1960s would the federal government commit itself to a systematic Keynesian policy for assuring lasting prosperity and, building on New Deal programs, adopt new means to protect the economic security of the middle class and bring the impoverished one-quarter of the nation into the mainstream of economic life.

## The Republic in Crisis and the American Dream

The Great Depression irreparably damaged the American dream of the poor man rising to wealth and power, which in the 1920s Henry Ford had symbolized. After 1929 Ford's popularity declined drastically, and no businessman ever quite replaced him. Not even the prosperous 1940s revived the vision of a simple man's rise from humble origins to the pinnacle of the corporate system. The avenues to fame and fortune grew increasingly obscure. Dale Carnegie's phenomenally popular *How to Win Friends and Influence People* (1936), the counterpart for the 1930s of the salesman's manuals of the 1920s, promised wonders for its readers if only they would master an elementary set of rules for tapping their inner resources. Yet unlike the literature of salesmanship, Carnegie's book was vague about where in modern society the ambitious but poor person should look for success. A critical element of hope was dwindling in the lives of millions of Americans.

The Roosevelts were the idols of the depression years—not only because New Deal policies rekindled hope, but also because both Franklin and Eleanor Roosevelt possessed warm, friendly personalities that they communicated to a traditionalist public. The fact that they led quite separate lives, signaling marital estrangement, did not seem to bother many people. The Roosevelts' larger public roles overshadowed and muted their personal differences. The president's battle with polio, his hobbies, and his anecdotes all gave indispensably human qualities to the nation's leader. "I remember when he was at the Chicago Stadium [in 1936] and all of us ran from school to get there," a teacher recalled. "He came in on his son's arm. We didn't realize that he was really and truly crippled until we saw the braces. He got up there and the place just absolutely went up in smoke. What was tremendous about him was—with all the adoration—his sense of humor. He acted as though he didn't take himself seriously." Far more than had any other president's wife, Eleanor Roosevelt traveled throughout America to express her personal concern for the needs of its citizens. Her syndicated newspaper column, "My Day," significantly lessened the distance between the nation's First Lady and a large, attentive body of readers. "And Eleanor. Eleanor," the teacher went on: "I think she's the greatest thing that ever happened to anybody. I think of the way they talked about her, about her looks, about her voice. I used to get so rabid. Why I didn't have high blood pressure, I don't know."

**Responses to Depression**
In the short run, the Great Depression contributed to the most powerful general force in behalf of traditional values. Immediately after the crash of 1929, Americans rejected the 1920s as frivolous, wasteful, and amoral. It was widely believed that the economy could be revived through a reassertion of solid, old-fashioned common sense in everyday life. Skirt lengths dropped well below the knees, and women heard lectures on their primary obligations inside the home. Public tolerance for innovative architecture, design, and music declined, and a simple realism in painting and sculpture became the vogue. After a burst of creativity in

literature during the 1920s, the experimental novels of a major writer such as William Faulkner were largely ignored in the 1930s; Margaret Mitchell's nostalgic (and historically inaccurate) *Gone with the Wind* of 1936 was the hit of the decade.

As Americans rejected the recent past, they looked back to earlier traditions that they could reaffirm. Thomas Jefferson and Walt Whitman, generally interpreted as simple, homespun democrats, enjoyed a surge of popularity. In *The Flowering of New England* (1936), Van Wyck Brooks glorified the same antebellum literary heritage that he had disdained twenty years before.* A deepening sense of democracy at bay in a totalitarian world strengthened the conservative cast of this search for cultural roots. Shattering Wilsonian dreams of democracy's global expansion, the nightmare of the 1930s pictured America fighting firmly to preserve its traditions against the swelling currents of fascism and communism sweeping Europe. Now was a time for bedrock values, not for trivial novelties. Then, as World War II revived the economy, the temporary constraints on cultural innovation disappeared, and traditionalists once again found themselves living in an atmosphere resonant with modern values.

Many New Deal supporters were more comfortable with traditional than with modern cultural values. They preferred rugged individualism and old-style convictions about hard work, savings, and morality—all conservative verities— to the liberal credo of collectivism, consumerism, and experimentation. Later, in the 1960s, when middle-class anxieties about the economy had abated and liberalism focused more on helping the impoverished, the unspoken tensions many middle Americans felt toward the cultural modernism of liberals would surface and make the middle class more receptive to conservative political appeals.

**The Yearning for Unity**

During the 1920s and 1930s the individual had received a good deal of general advice and a variety of palliatives. But a clear statement of the individual's situation and future prospects in modern society failed to appear. A new round in search of an answer to this problem began rather vaguely in the depression, when a number of prominent figures conceived of the individual as part of a broad social enterprise. New Deal enthusiasts attacked the evils of "rugged individualism" and foresaw a new age of social responsibility. The reputation of philosopher John Dewey, America's leading advocate of a social ethic, rose impressively during the 1930s. Moreover, as depression crippled America, one group of intellectuals looked abroad to the Soviet Union as a model of the healthy society; a few took the logical next step and applied Karl Marx's theories of class conflict to American society. But in most cases the affair between American intellectuals and the Soviet Union was a brief infatuation rather than a passionate romance. (In the 1950s, some would pay dearly for their youthful attraction to communism.) Never willing to

---

*For Brooks as a radical cultural critic of the World War I era, see chapter 27, pp. 312–14.

**Migrant Field Worker, Imperial Valley, California, 1937**
*Migrant farmers, depicted movingly in John Steinbeck's* The Grapes of Wrath, *were some of the depression's worst victims.*

relinquish human rights in favor of an abstract ideology, most American leftists were revolted by the bloody Soviet purge of the late 1930s. Increasingly such intellectuals became convinced that Americans should develop their own kind of social consciousness.

At best, the search in the 1930s offered a hope for the future, but not a solution for the times. John Steinbeck, who had once been attracted to Marxism and who continued to feel a strong social conscience, captured this hope for the future at the end of his finest novel, *The Grapes of Wrath* (1939). Steinbeck told the grim but highly sentimental story of an impoverished Oklahoma farm family, the Joads, tracing them from their uprooting early in the depression through their futile quest for a fresh start in California. Then on the last page of his otherwise tragic novel, Steinbeck suddenly shifted moods and in a few sentences sketched a vision of a new fellow feeling just beginning to surface in America.

For a great many Americans, that spirit of a collective endeavor finally arrived with World War II. In 1940 Hemingway's hero from the 1920s reappeared in *For Whom the Bell Tolls* as Robert Jordan, who no longer stood alone because he had found a social commitment. This time Hemingway's hero was fighting in the Spanish Civil War. Instead of deserting, as Frederic Henry had done in *A Farewell to Arms,* Jordan chose to die for human values in the battle against fascism. A year later the former pacifist Robert E. Sherwood, winner of four Pulitzer prizes, announced his conversion to the same crusade in his play *There Shall Be No Night.* World War II found Americans, intellectuals and ordinary people alike, even more genuinely united in a sense of common, uplifting purpose than had World War I—and far more united than they would be in America's subsequent wars in Korea and Vietnam.

## International Disintegration, 1931–1939

The system of moral cooperation sponsored by the United States in the 1920s fell apart in the 1930s. By 1931 the pall of depression had spread worldwide. The German economy was virtually bankrupt, the British credit system was tottering, and the foundation beneath every other industrial nation was badly shaken. Economic nationalism thrived, as government after government (Washington included) moved to protect its weakened domestic economy from outside competition. Some powers—notably Japan, Germany, and Italy—also tried to renew their economic strength through military imperialism. Where they conquered, they assimilated, absorbing governments and integrating dependent economies into their own.

The first of the military imperialists to strike was Japan. When depression pinched its lifelines of commerce, Japan looked more avidly than ever to its most natural area for economic expansion, the Asian mainland. But Japan could expect little profit in a China plagued by civil wars and carved into many spheres of foreign influence. In September 1931 Japan's Kwantung Army, stationed in Manchuria, took the initiative by seizing all of this rich province in northern China. Twelve months later, Manchuria became the Japanese puppet state of Manchukuo.

Only a year before the Manchurian assault, President Hoover's secretary of state, Henry L. Stimson, had thought of Japan as a stabilizing force in East Asia, a "buffer state" between the United States and a chaotic China. Outraged, Stimson now hastened to find some way of thwarting Japan through collective international action. As an outsider, however, the United States could not collaborate effectively with the League of Nations. And the Nine-Power Treaty on the Open Door in China, a vague document at best, contained no sanctions against a violator.* Wanting at least to threaten Japan with a stronger American policy, Stimson was blocked by Hoover, who publicly renounced either economic or military sanctions against Japan. What emerged was a purely American statement of principle. The Hoover-Stimson Doctrine of 1932, relying on the Kellogg-Briand Peace Pact's repudiation of war, declared that the United States would refuse to recognize any treaty that impaired the sovereignty of China or infringed on the Open Door policy.

An even more formidable imperialism emerged in Germany. Against a background of economic collapse, the National Socialist party legally wormed its way to the top of the German government early in 1933; its leader, Adolf Hitler, became dictator and proceeded to stamp out all opposition. For a time, outsiders

---

*For the Nine-Power Treaty, see chapter 28, p. 344.

refused to take seriously the Nazis' militaristic pomp, crude racism, and ranting speeches. But the new government proved ingenious in attracting German loyalties and mobilizing the country's resources. As the Nazis consolidated power at home, they also asserted it abroad. Hitler, repudiating the Versailles Treaty as an unfair settlement needlessly accepted by Germany's democratic politicians, left the league in 1933 and two years later unilaterally announced that Germany would rearm. Italy also joined the new imperialists. Benito Mussolini, a fascist who had risen as Italy's dictator in 1922, longed to dominate the Mediterranean but lacked the power. In October 1935, hoping to distract Italians from their economic woes at home, the opportunistic Mussolini settled for an invasion of the independent African state of Ethiopia.

**America's Mixed Response**  Franklin Roosevelt entered office eager to sustain the commitments to peace and arms control reached in the 1920s and to expand America's role in world affairs. During his first two years in office, he supported international economic agreements, additional arms limitations, and a continuing role for the League of Nations in keeping the peace. More substantively, he recognized the Soviet Union in November 1933, signed a reciprocal trade bill in June 1934, and proposed American participation in the World Court in January 1935.

Yet FDR quickly found himself hamstrung by disillusionment about American participation in World War I and economic and political conditions at home and abroad. Recognizing that national economic recovery had to take precedence over international agreements, which in any case world tensions had put beyond reach, Roosevelt felt compelled to make overseas cooperation a secondary goal. Consequently, at the London Economic Conference in 1933, the last faint hope for a collective approach to the world's financial crisis, the president disrupted proceedings by rejecting European proposals contrary to American interests. At the same time he took the United States off the gold standard, tinkered for a while with the international value of the dollar, and generally let it be known that America would solve its depression alone.

Unable to do much about European or Asian affairs, Roosevelt concentrated on the Western Hemisphere. The administration's policy toward Latin America completed a process that had begun in the 1920s: the United States formally abandoned any authority to intervene in a Latin American state. With his uncanny talent for the right phrase and gesture, Roosevelt proclaimed a "Good Neighbor Policy" and in 1936 made an unprecedented, highly successful tour of Latin America. Beneath the new surface, however, the old substance held quite firm. The United States still sought to consolidate its hemispheric hegemony. In 1933, when a revolutionary government arose in Cuba, for example, the Roosevelt administration undermined it through nonrecognition, then supported the corrupt and repressive military regime of Fulgencio Batista.* The Cuban economy fell even further under American control, and the State Department pursued

---

*Batista would remain in power until 1959, when he was ousted by Fidel Castro.

reciprocal trade agreements with special zeal in Latin America. Still, the administration demonstrated genuine regard for the autonomy of the Latin republics and, as a consequence, greatly improved its relations with America's southern neighbors.

**Military Actions**    In 1936 the pace of military imperialism abroad quickened. In May, Italy annexed Ethiopia and made it a colony. Two months later civil war in Spain offered Mussolini another chance to extend Italy's influence in the Mediterranean. That same year the Italian and German dictatorships forged an alliance, the Rome-Berlin Axis. Between 1936 and 1938 Italian military intervention on behalf of General Francisco Franco's army in Spain contributed critically to the eventual fascist victory, more than matching French and Soviet assistance to the Spanish Republicans. By early 1939 Franco ruled Spain. Meanwhile German troops in 1936 occupied the Rhineland provinces, which the Versailles Treaty had demilitarized. Then in March 1938, demanding the political unification of all German-speaking people, Hitler annexed Austria. Across the Pacific, in 1936 Japan discarded the international agreements that limited the size of its navy and signed an alliance with Nazi Germany, the Anti-Comintern Pact. A year later, after a vain attempt to make a vassal of China's most successful warlord, the nationalist leader Chiang Kai-shek, Tokyo released its impatient army to conquer all of China. By October 1938 Japan occupied China's most important cities.

In response to these waves of violence, each threatened nation set its own course. The League of Nations' futile attempt to impose economic sanctions against Italy for attacking Ethiopia merely exposed the League's helplessness. No European power had the energy to confront Japan. Britain and France, although fretful about their own imperial interests in Asia, neither condoned nor seriously challenged Japan's conquests. The Soviet Union and France were particularly vehement in condemning Hitler's advances, yet neither trusted the other sufficiently to take an effective joint stand. Moreover, both Hitler and Mussolini, by keeping the hopes for compromise alive with hints of moderation, discouraged a collective retaliation. It was British Prime Minister Neville Chamberlain who most earnestly explored these prospects of a peaceful settlement. When Hitler demanded Czechoslovakia's German-speaking borderland, the Sudetenland, Chamberlain carried the primary burden of diplomacy that culminated in the Munich Conference of September 1938. At Munich, England and France averted war by agreeing that Germany and its central European allies could divide about one-third of Czechoslovakia among themselves. Chamberlain returned to London promising "peace in our time."

**American Isolationism**    America reacted to deteriorating conditions abroad by withdrawing more than ever from world affairs. The more violent the world became, the more intensely most Americans felt a chasm between their lives and the bloody struggles overseas. "Europe's quarrels are not ours," one isolationist declared. "To hell with Europe and the rest of those nations!" exclaimed Minnesota's Senator Thomas D. Schall. Reinforcing the urge toward separation, a committed band of liberals branded war the "enemy of democracy," and that viewpoint found a wide audience through the investigations of Senator Gerald Nye's subcommittee, which blamed bankers and munition makers for America's entry into World War I. Where ethnic loyalties did give some Americans attachments abroad, they usually strengthened the case against a confrontation with fascism and for isolationism. Catholics could identify much more readily with Franco than with his anticlerical Republican enemies asking help from the United States. Italian Americans rarely demanded war with Mussolini, and Irish Americans rarely sided with the British against any opponent. By contrast, Jewish Americans, watching Nazi laws strip German Jews of virtually all rights and foreseeing yet greater depredations by Hitler against other European Jews, favored some American action to answer Germany's aggressive moves.

During the 1930s, Congress translated isolationist sentiments into law. The Tydings-McDuffie Act of 1934, which set a schedule for attaining independence for America's Philippine colony, promised to remove a particularly dangerous outpost of responsibility. The Johnson Debt-Default Act of 1934, establishing the narrowest possible definition of America's friends and enemies abroad, denied credit to any foreign government that had not honored its war debt. Then between 1935 and 1937 Congress enacted major neutrality laws to prevent a repetition of action that had led into the previous war. It embargoed arms and munitions to belligerents, banned the use of American vessels to ship them, prohibited the arming of American merchant ships, and proscribed the extension of credit to belligerents. Later the neutrality laws would be ridiculed as a scheme to "Keep America Out of the First World War." But Americans, determined not to repeat the experience of 1914–18, praised these laws as their protection against the madness of a world in arms. A final step in this sequence barely failed. In 1938, when Congress debated the "Ludlow amendment" that would require a national referendum to declare war, only heavy pressure from the White House kept it from coming to the floor of the House for a vote.

Most Americans concentrated their feelings of horror on Japan and Germany. The full-scale Japanese invasion of China in 1937 gave Americans their first appalling revelations of what a modern air force could do to an urban population. On the eve of World War II, Nazi-Fascist bombings of Spanish cities and Japan's air war against helpless Chinese civilians produced the same kind of humanitarian outcry in America that talk of bayoneted babies had roused during World War I. Kristallnacht, a nationwide attack by the Nazis in November 1938 on German Jews and their property, horrified Americans. FDR recalled his ambassador from Berlin, but resistance in America to relaxing immigration quotas barred most German Jews from escaping to the United States. At the same time the British closed off Palestine to additional Jewish migrants. Although most Americans would not realize until 1942–43 how literally the Nazis sought to exterminate the Jews, news about mass arrests and concentration camps increasingly identified Hitler's anti–Semitism as a threat to all civilized values. Japan and Germany, a majority of Americans concluded, were the centers of an insane barbarism.

Between 1933 and 1939 Roosevelt moved with the dominant currents of opinion. Although in private he despised the Axis dictators, Hitler and Mussolini, and wished to block their aggressive moves, he seldom said anything in public on foreign affairs. Convinced that any sustained attempt to reverse the country's isolationist course would undermine his ability to ensure the success of the New Deal at home, Roosevelt accepted the neutrality laws without significant opposition. He also congratulated the British and French leaders for their efforts at the Munich Conference to keep the peace.

Yet at the same time Roosevelt made subtle gestures toward stopping the fascist advance. In 1936 and 1938 he sponsored agreements among all the American republics declaring that an external threat to one of them would be the common concern of all. Moreover, in October 1937 he warned Americans of international dangers by publicly calling for a "quarantine" of aggressors. Speaking in Chicago, the heartland of isolationist sentiment, the president directly challenged the opponents of a more active foreign policy. When isolationists warned that a "quarantine" would mean America's political and military involvement abroad, however, Roosevelt denied having any such aim in mind.

## *World War, 1939–1941*

In March 1939 Hitler devoured the rest of Czechoslovakia and hungrily eyed the former German territories placed under Polish rule after World War I.* As Chamberlain's illusion of peace dissolved, Britain and France committed themselves to Poland's defense and frantically prepared for war. Then in August 1939 Germany and the Soviet Union, hitherto relentless foes, shocked the world by signing a nonaggression pact. With the Nazi army prepared to strike at Poland, all eyes fixed on Berlin.

Hitler invaded Poland on September 1, 1939, and Britain and France immediately declared war on Germany. After the quick conquest and division of Poland by Berlin and Moscow, the fighting slowed until the spring of 1940. Then in April Germany began a lightning sweep through western Europe, taking Norway, Denmark, the Netherlands, and Belgium. By June, France itself had fallen. Only Britain remained. German bombers devastated London and other British cities, and German submarines squeezed the United Kingdom's lifeline of supplies, apparently in preparation for an invasion of the British Isles.

While Germany swallowed Europe, Japan extended its rule southward into French Indochina—ostensibly to tighten the blockade of China but actually to

---

*For the transfer of German-speaking populations to Poland under the Treaty of Versailles, see chapter 27, p. 318.

**The Führer and Il Duce**
*Exploiting the weakness of the democracies, Hitler and Mussolini conquered Europe in the late thirties and early forties.*

control a new area rich in natural resources. Beyond lay Southeast Asia's precious oil and rubber. In September 1940, Japan joined the Axis powers in a defensive pact. It was a tentative connection: many Japanese leaders never trusted Hitler. Yet from the outside Tokyo's link with Berlin and Rome verified the impression of a unified fascist force rolling toward global domination.

At the outbreak of war, America had hugged its shore. In 1939 the United States had induced the Latin American nations to join it in declaring a huge neutrality zone between Europe and the Western Hemisphere. A revision of the neutrality law had allowed Britain and France to purchase war materials in the United States, but the terms had been "cash and carry": Americans could provide neither credit nor shipping for a belligerent. They had hoped that the arms reaching Hitler's democratic opponents would be enough to defeat him and keep the United States out of the fighting.

But with Germany astride western Europe and threatening Britain with invasion, Americans no longer felt so distant or safe. In the summer and fall of 1940, the number of Americans who believed that the country could close itself off from the war began to shrink. A majority held tight to their desire for peace, but a growing minority believed that the United States should support Britain's resistance. The rough guideline became "all aid short of war."

**Roosevelt's Unprecedented Third Term**

As the war raged, the nuances in Roosevelt's thinking grew ever more critical, for in an emergency the president had immense power over foreign policy. Early in his career Roosevelt came to believe that a great power such as the United States should play an important role in world affairs. His background and training equated Anglo-American culture with civilization, and his instincts told him that Germany was the nation's enemy. Unlike many of his contemporaries, Roosevelt had never questioned either the wisdom or the justice of America's entry into World War I. But Wilson's political difficulties over the League of Nations convinced FDR that effective action abroad required a stable foreign policy consensus at home, and he was determined to ensure that his handling of the current crisis would rest on majority support. These attitudes were central to all Roosevelt did in the period between 1939 and 1941, including his decision to run for an unprecedented third term.

If Roosevelt had doubts about running for reelection, world crisis resolved them. By 1939 the nation's parlor game was guessing whom the president might designate as his successor. But by keeping a serene silence, Roosevelt held the spotlight on himself and at the last minute allowed the Democratic convention of 1940 to nominate him. That event stirred the latent emotions about Roosevelt the aspiring dictator and Roosevelt the indispensable man. As the president knew very well, he himself would be the issue of the 1940 campaign.

This time the Republicans selected a candidate able to challenge Roosevelt. Wendell Willkie, a former utilities executive who had once led the fight against the TVA, was an inspired amateur in national politics. Liberal enough to attract independent voters yet conservative enough to satisfy most opponents of the New Deal, Willkie eagerly took on "the Champ" in a vigorous presidential campaign. With flailing arms and sparkling eyes he became the first Republican candidate in twenty years to elicit a warm popular response. Moreover, some of the president's former allies, including John L. Lewis and Vice-President Garner, deserted him, while many conservative Democrats talked as if they might bolt the party when Roosevelt selected the liberal Henry Wallace to replace Garner as his running mate.

Nevertheless the New Deal's coalition of diverse ethnic and regional groups continued to be a powerful political force, especially as defense spending buoyed up the economy. Willkie's chances lay in foreign affairs. Here, however, the Republican's enthusiasm for resisting fascism at least matched the president's. When fierce debates surrounded a bill to create America's first peacetime draft, Willkie supported it. In September 1940, when the president announced an exchange of fifty old American destroyers for the lease of British bases in the Western Hemisphere, Willkie also approved this clear commitment to the British cause. Then at the last moment Roosevelt gave the guarantee most Americans wanted desperately to believe: "Your president says this country is not going to war." By 449 electoral votes to Willkie's 82, "the Champ" won four more years.

**United States Aid to Britain**
After the election the politician who had promised peace became the president who, in defense of the national interest, prepared for war. By the winter of 1940–41 Britain's dwindling assets in the United States could not begin to pay for the war materials it needed. Describing the United States as the "arsenal of democracy," Roosevelt proposed that Britain have almost unlimited access to American production and credit. An "America First" movement, which had opposed his reelection, fought frantically against lend-lease legislation. Lend-lease, its enemies cried, was a Grim Reaper's AAA that would "plow under every fourth American boy." Publicly, Roosevelt tried to calm these fears of war. But in private he knew that passage of lend-lease legislation would wipe out the last traces of American neutrality and bring the country closer to war. In March 1941 Congress, despite these dangers, passed the open-ended Lend-Lease Act.

By the summer of 1941 Roosevelt and other administration leaders realized that the United States would eventually have to join the fighting. Although the Royal Air Force had won the Battle of Britain, the danger did not diminish. Hitler turned eastward, and the Nazis, with feeble assistance from their Italian ally, conquered the Balkans. Then in June 1941 Hitler launched the fateful thrust of the war, an attack on Russia. The Nazi-Soviet Pact of 1939 had been a calculated expedient between enemies, enabling Hitler to dominate the heart of Europe and Stalin to seize a portion of Poland, the Baltic states of Latvia, Lithuania, and Estonia, and a slice of Finland. Now the Nazis were ready to smash their last great opponent on the Continent, and the German war machine rumbled across a broad eastern front against the Soviet Union's primary cities, initially duplicating its successful advances in 1940. Before the onset of winter stopped their drive, Nazi armies had surrounded Leningrad and had almost reached Moscow. In their wake came SS units devoted to the extermination of all Europe's Jews. And although news of the "Final Solution" reached the British and American governments and was published in the press, neither Britain nor the United States attempted to give refuge to those who still might have been rescued from the Nazis.

Determined as ever to supply their British ally, American convoys carried their lend-lease cargoes closer and closer to the British Isles. In April 1941 the United States extended its patrols to the mid-Atlantic. Then in July, following Germany's invasion of Russia, American convoys moved a big step closer to the British ports by escorting the supplies as far as Iceland, and FDR committed himself to sending Moscow material support. A month later Roosevelt astonished the nation by meeting with British Prime Minister Winston Churchill on an American cruiser off Newfoundland, where the two leaders announced the Atlantic Charter of postwar principles. Meanwhile the American navy expanded its protection to cover British merchant ships as well as American, and along the Atlantic sea-lanes the two nations collaborated in locating and attacking German submarines. In September one German submarine, as it fled from the USS *Greer,* fired at the American destroyer. Roosevelt, pretending that the submarine had been the aggressor and likening German power to a "rattlesnake" that was coiled to strike at the Western Hemisphere, authorized American ships to "shoot on sight." By October Congress allowed convoys to land in Britain. "All aid" to Britain could not stop "short of war."

**Pearl Harbor**   During these crucial months of 1940 and 1941, Asian affairs appeared to be far less important. Most Americans agreed that Japanese imperialism in China and Indochina during the previous decade had posed some kind of threat, but few could define it. Fewer still in 1940 believed that Japan would dare to fight the United States. Roosevelt largely left the negotiations with Japan to his crusty secretary of state, Cordell Hull, who in turn relied on the rigid, moralistic Stanley Hornbeck, a State Department expert on Asian matters. Hull demanded that Japan honor the Nine-Power Treaty on the Open Door, which, in effect, required a withdrawal from the mainland of Asia. As leverage, the United States imposed an increasingly tight embargo on trade with Japan. During most of 1941, conciliatory forces in the Japanese government under Prince Fuminaro Konoye, the prime minister, sought some way to mollify the United States short of capitulation. Although Konoye would not reopen the question of Manchuria, he proposed a Japanese military withdrawal elsewhere on the Asian mainland in exchange for a friendly Chinese government and American economic cooperation. But Hull was unrelenting. Before serious negotiations could begin, he insisted, Japan must accept the Open Door throughout the area of Japanese expansion. In the midst of American efforts to counter Nazi aggression, it was inconceivable to Hull and most Americans that they should recognize Tokyo's conquest of Manchuria or any other foreign territory.

By the summer of 1941 the two nations were drifting toward a war that most Americans and many Japanese did not want. In July, Japan completed its occupation of French Indochina, and Roosevelt retaliated by freezing Japanese assets in the United States. Washington was now in the curious position of opposing Japanese imperialism to defend European imperialism in Southeast Asia. Appraising their limited resources, Japan's leaders realized that if they had to fight the United States for their empire, the time had come. Although Prince Konoye continued to explore various formulas of compromise, his authority at home was waning. In October 1941 the militant Hideki Tojo replaced him as prime minister, and Japan prepared for war. Washington, beginning to sense much deeper trouble than it had expected, finally gave hints of flexibility. It was too late.

Because American intelligence had broken Japan's secret code, Washington knew that a Japanese attack of some kind was pending. Roosevelt's inner circle guessed that Japan would strike in Southeast Asia. For two reasons no one seriously considered Hawaii. First, American policymakers to the very end

**Pearl Harbor**

underrated Japan as a second-class power with more bluff than nerve. Second, American intelligence intercepted so many clues leading in so many directions that it made no sense from any of them as to where Japan would strike. At dawn on December 7, as waves of Japanese planes from aircraft carriers roared across the naval base at Pearl Harbor, Hawaii, and crippled America's Pacific force, no one was ready. A stunned nation found itself at war.

Although the American military commanders in Hawaii were dismissed for having failed to prepare more effectively for the attack, the Roosevelt administration conceded that the surprise at Japan's audacity in attacking Pearl Harbor extended to all high government officials. Some administration critics believed that FDR and his closest political and military advisers anticipated and welcomed the attack as a backdoor to the European war. But this conspiracy theory never explained why Roosevelt would have been willing to sacrifice so much United States naval power in the Pacific to get the country into the war. He could have had the same result by sending the bulk of the fleet to sea and leaving just a few ships in Pearl Harbor. Why leave the United States so vulnerable by allowing Tokyo to establish a substantial edge in naval power with its attack? In fact, the Japanese assault on Pearl Harbor was a genuine surprise that cost the United States dearly and set back the day when it could overcome Japan's might.

The attack on Pearl Harbor clarified issues around the world. Congress declared war on Japan after Roosevelt, in a memorable speech, called December 7 "a date that will live in infamy." Britain immediately joined the United States against Japan. The unpredictable Hitler had no obligation to act, but he decided to declare war on the United States, and Italy followed suit. Hence a surprise attack precipitating an unwanted war became the event that dissolved America's doubts and propelled it into global conflict. The vast long-range consequences of the plunge—the destruction of isolationism as a controlling policy—would take years to unfold.

## CHRONOLOGY

**1929** Stock-market crash begins the Great Depression.

**1930** Hawley-Smoot Tariff raises protective barriers.

**1931** Japan occupies Manchuria.

**1932** Hoover-Stimson Doctrine refuses recognition of Japanese conquests.
Franklin D. Roosevelt elected president.
Reconstruction Finance Corporation invests $1.5 billion in private enterprise.

**1933** Nationwide "Bank Holiday."
Federal Deposit Insurance Corporation guarantees depositors' savings.
Agricultural Adjustment Act passed.
Civilian Conservation Corps formed.
National Industrial Recovery Act creates National Recovery Administration and Public Works Administration.
Tennessee Valley Authority established.
Prohibition repealed.

**1934** Reciprocal Trade Agreement Act passed.

**1935** Supreme Court broadens attacks on New Deal legislation.
Social Security establishes old-age, other social insurance programs.
Wagner Act affirms collective bargaining rights, sets up National Labor Relations Board.
Works Progress Administration increases funds for relief of unemployed.
Hitler announces Germany's intent to rearm.
Italy invades Ethiopia.

**1936** Roosevelt reelected president.
Spanish Civil War erupts.
Wave of sit-down strikes begins.

**1937** U.S. Steel recognizes CIO.
Law to reorganize Supreme Court fails.
Japan invades China.

**1938** Fair Employment Practices Act establishes a minimum wage and outlaws child labor.
Munich Conference attempts to appease Hitler by surrendering Czechoslovakia.

**1939** Germany invades Poland, starting World War II.

**1940** Germany conquers western Europe.
Japan joins Axis powers.
First peacetime draft passed.
U.S. swaps 50 overage destroyers for leases on British Caribbean bases.
Roosevelt elected to a third term.

**1941** Congress approves Lend-Lease, American supplies to Allies.
Japan attacks Pearl Harbor; United States enters war.

SUGGESTED READINGS

John Kenneth Galbraith's *The Great Crash, 1929* (5th ed., 1979) is an interesting essay, but Lester V. Chandler, *America's Greatest Depression* (1970), and Peter Temin, *Did Monetary Forces Cause the Great Depression?* (1976), are more authoritative, as is John Garraty, *The Great Depression: An Inquiry into the Causes, Course, and Consequences of the Worldwide Depression of the Nineteen Thirties as Seen by Contemporaries and in the Light of History* (1987). Arthur M. Schlesinger, Jr., *The Crisis of the Old Order* (1957), the first volume of his *The Age of Roosevelt,* evokes the desperate confusion of depression. More on its human meaning can be found in Federal Writers' Project, *These Are Our Lives* (1939); Studs Terkel, *Hard Times: An Oral History of the Great Depression* (1970); Ann Banks, ed., *First Person America* (1980); and Robert S. McElvaine, ed., *Down and Out in the Great Depression: Letters from the Forgotten Man* (1983). David Burner, *Herbert Hoover: A Public Life* (1979), is the standard account of his career to 1933. Another evaluation is Martin L. Fausold, *The Presidency of Herbert C. Hoover* (1985); Joan Hoff Wilson's *Herbert Hoover: Forgotten Progressive* (1975) is also well worth reading. J. Joseph Huthmacher and Warren I. Susman, eds., *Herbert Hoover and the Crisis of American Capitalism* (1973), adds the spice of debate. Fuller accounts of government policy during Hoover's administration appear in Albert U. Romasco, *The Poverty of Abundance* (1965); Jordan A. Schwarz, *The Interregnum of Despair* (1970); William J. Barber, *From New Era to New Deal: Herbert Hoover, the Economists, and American Economic Policy, 1921–1933* (1985); and James S. Olson, *Herbert Hoover and the Reconstruction Finance Corporation, 1931–1933* (1977).

William E. Leuchtenburg, *Franklin D. Roosevelt and the New Deal, 1932–1940* (1963), is an outstanding survey. For a more critical appraisal, see Paul K. Conkin, *The New Deal* (rev. ed., 1975). Volumes 2 and 3 of Arthur M. Schlesinger, Jr., *The Age of Roosevelt—The Coming of the New Deal* (1958) and *The Politics of Upheaval* (1960)—provide a thorough and readable account of Roosevelt's first administration. Other overall treatments are Albert U. Romasco, *The Politics of Recovery: Roosevelt's New Deal* (1983); Katie Louchheim, ed., *The Making of the New Deal: The Insiders Speak* (1983); Robert S. McElvaine, *The Great Depression: America, 1929–1941* (1984); and Harvard Sitkoff, ed., *Fifty Years Later: The New Deal Evaluated* (1985).

There is a vast literature on a variety of New Deal subjects. The initial problem that FDR encountered is considered in detail in Susan Estabrook Kennedy's *The Banking Crisis of 1933* (1973). Robert F. Himmelberg, *The Origins of the National Recovery Administration* (1976), analyzes the complex background to the NRA. For the history of the NRA and its aftermath, the most valuable work is Ellis W. Hawley's *The New Deal and the Problem of Monopoly* (1966). Van L. Perkins, *Crisis in Agriculture* (1969), covers the beginning of the Agricultural Adjustment Administration. On the most innovative New Deal policy, C. Herman Pritchett, *The Tennessee Valley Authority* (1943), supplies basic information; Phillip Selznick, *TVA and the Grass Roots* (1949), discusses the authority's social orientation; and Thomas K. McCraw, *TVA and the Power Fight, 1933–1939* (1971), traces the principal challenge to its program. The CWA and the RFC are covered in Bonnie Schwartz, *The Civil Works Administration, 1933–1934* (1984), and James Olson, *Saving Capitalism: The RFC and the New Deal, 1933–1940* (1988). Grace Abbott, *From Relief to Social Security* (1966), records the story of public assistance, as do Richard Lowitt and Maurine Beasley, eds., *One Third of a Nation: Lorena Hickok Reports on the Great Depression* (1981), and James T. Patterson, *America's Struggle Against Poverty* (1981). Roy Lubove, *The Struggle for Social Security, 1900–1935* (1968), explains the origins of the Social Security Act. Michael E. Parrish, *Securities Regulation and the New Deal* (1970), is an illuminating monograph on that area of public policy; and Kenneth R. Philp, *John Collier's Crusade for Indian Reform, 1920–1954* (1977), is the basic study of another area.

The battle over the Supreme Court that opened Roosevelt's second administration is reported in Joseph Alsop and Turner Catledge, *The 168 Days* (1938). Also see William E.

Leuchtenburg, "The Origins of Franklin D. Roosevelt's 'Court Packing' Plan," in Philip Kurland, ed., *The Supreme Court Review* (1966). On the struggles of organized labor, the best survey is Irving Bernstein's *A History of the American Worker, 1933–1941: Turbulent Years* (1970). Sidney Fine, *Sit-Down* (1969), captures the drama of a crucial strike in the automobile industry; and Jerold S. Auerbach, *Labor and Liberty: The La Follette Committee and the New Deal* (1966), examines one form of government assistance to the new unions. Other more recent books on labor in the New Deal period are David Milton, *The Politics of U.S. Labor: From the Great Depression to the New Deal* (1980); Irving Bernstein, *A Caring Society: The New Deal, the Worker, and the Great Depression* (1985); and John Barnard, *Walter Reuther and the Rise of the Auto Workers* (1983). For the curious story of labor's outstanding leader, see Melvyn Dubofsky and Warren Van Tine, *John L. Lewis* (1977).

Raymond Wolters, *Negroes and the Great Depression: The Problem of Economic Recovery* (1970), tells a grim story of the early 1930s, and Dan T. Carter's smoothly written *Scottsboro* (1969) recounts the most notorious abuse of justice in the South during that decade. Other essential books on African Americans in the 1930s are Harvard Sitkoff, *A New Deal for Blacks* (1978); John B. Kirby, *Black Americans in the Roosevelt Era: Liberalism and Race* (1980); Robert L. Zangrando, *The NAACP Crusade Against Lynching, 1909–1950* (1980); and Nancy J. Weiss, *Farewell to the Party of Lincoln: Black Politics in the Age of FDR* (1983). Mexican Americans are studied in Mark Reisler, *By the Sweat of Their Brow: Mexican Immigrant Labor in the United States, 1900–1940* (1976); Rodolfo Acuña, *Occupied America* (1981); and Mario T. Garcia, *Mexican Americans: Leadership, Ideology & Identity, 1930–1960* (1989).

Women in the New Deal years are covered in Lois Scharf, *To Work and to Wed: Female Employment, Feminism, and the Great Depression* (1980); Susan Ware, *Holding Their Own: American Women in the 1930s* (1980) and *Beyond Suffrage: Women in the New Deal* (1982); Winifred Wandersee, *Women's Work and Family Values* (1981); Alice Kessler-Harris, *Out to Work: A History of Wage-Earning Women in the United States* (1982); and Nancy F. Cott, *The Grounding of Modern Feminism* (1987).

The bottom of the rural economy is explored in David E. Conrad, *The Forgotten Farmers: The Story of Sharecroppers in the New Deal* (1965), in Pete Daniel, *The Shadow of Slavery: Peonage in the South, 1901–1969* (1972), in Paul Mertz, *The New Deal and Southern Rural Poverty* (1978), in Donald Worster, *Dust Bowl: The Southern Plains in the 1930s* (1979), in Theodore M. Saloutos, *The American Farmer and the New Deal* (1982), and most feelingly in James Agee and Walker Evans, *Let Us Now Praise Famous Men* (1941). Sidney Baldwin's *FSA* (1968) is an appealing history of the New Deal's major effort to help the rural poor. Several interesting studies—Paul Conkin, *Tomorrow a New World: The New Deal Community Program* (1959); Jane DeHart Mathews, *The Federal Theater, 1935–1939* (1967); Jerre Mangione, *The Dream and the Deal: The Federal Writers' Project, 1935–1943* (1972); Richard McKinzie, *The New Deal for Artists* (1973); and Marlene Park and Gerald Markowitz, *Democratic Vistas: Post Offices and Public Art in the New Deal* (1984)—suggest the breadth of interests affected by the New Deal. Barry Dean Karl, *Executive Reorganization and Reform in the New Deal* (1963), and Richard Polenberg, *Reorganizing Roosevelt's Government: The Controversy over Executive Reorganization, 1936–1939* (1966), discuss an important political contest in the late 1930s. These studies, along with two other fine books—Richard S. Kirkendall's *Social Scientists and Farm Politics in the Age of Roosevelt* (1966) and James T. Patterson's *Congressional Conservatism and the New Deal* (1967)—help explain the decline of reform.

On Roosevelt himself, the best study for the New Deal years is James MacGregor Burns, *Roosevelt: The Lion and the Fox* (1956). Frank Freidel's massive biography, *Franklin D. Roosevelt* (4 vols. to date, 1952–73), has carried FDR through his first critical months in the White House. Freidel's one-volume study summarizes his findings on FDR's whole career: *Franklin D. Roosevelt: A Rendezvous with Destiny* (1990). Other recent biographies are Ted Morgan, *FDR:*

*A Biography* (1985); Kenneth S. Davis, *FDR: The New Deal Years, 1933–1937* (1986); and Geoffrey Ward's two volumes on FDR's prepresidential years (1985, 1989). Additional insights into the Roosevelt household appear in Alfred B. Rollins, Jr., *Roosevelt and Howe* (1962), and Joseph P. Lash, *Eleanor and Franklin* (1971). The best recent book on Eleanor is Lois Scharf, *Eleanor Roosevelt: First Lady of American Liberalism* (1987). Among the many published journals and memoirs by participants in the New Deal, Raymond Moley's critical *After Seven Years* (1939) and Rexford G. Tugwell's appreciative *The Democratic Roosevelt* (1957) are especially useful. Also see Joseph Lash, *Dealers and Dreamers: A New Look at the New Deal* (1988). Complimentary accounts of other important officials include J. Joseph Huthmacher, *Senator Robert F. Wagner and the Rise of Urban Liberalism* (1968); Paul A. Kurzman, *Harry Hopkins and the New Deal* (1974); George McJimsey, *Harry Hopkins: Ally of the Poor and Defender of Democracy* (1987); and George Martin, *Madam Secretary: Frances Perkins* (1976). Otis L. Graham, Jr., *An Encore for Reform* (1967), explores the generally unfavorable responses of the old progressives to the New Deal, and George Wolfskill, *The Revolt of the Conservatives* (1962), describes the outrage of the American Liberty League. Dissent is also studied in Alan Brinkley, *Voices of Protest: Huey Long, Father Coughlin, and the Great Depression* (1982); Leo Rebuffo, *The Old Christian Right: The Protestant Far Right from the Great Depression to the Cold War* (1983); and Harvey Klehr, *The Heyday of American Communism: The Depression Decade* (1983).

Local politics is an elusive subject. James Patterson, *The New Deal and the States* (1969), analyzes one source of resistance to national power. John M. Allswang's *A House for All People: Ethnic Politics in Chicago, 1890–1936* (1971) sketches an interesting picture for one big city, and Arthur Mann's *La Guardia Comes to Power: 1933* (1965) explores the roots of an important election in New York City. For LaGuardia's career as mayor, see Thomas Kessner, *Fiorello LaGuardia and the Making of Modern New York* (1989). The relation between the New Deal and the local bosses is considered in Bruce M. Stave, *The New Deal and the Last Hurrah: Pittsburgh Machine Politics* (1970); Lyle W. Dorsett, *The Pendergast Machine* (1968); and Charles H. Trout, *Boston, the Great Depression, and the New Deal* (1977). Charles J. Tull, *Father Coughlin and the New Deal* (1965), and T. Harry Williams, *Huey Long* (1969), examine the New Deal's leading competitors in local politics. The cultural values of the New Dealers themselves are summarized in E. Digby Baltzell, *The Protestant Establishment* (1964), and Warren Sussman, *Culture as History: The Transformation of American Society in the Twentieth Century* (1984).

America's reaction to the early imperialist crisis in Asia is explored in Robert H. Ferrell, *American Diplomacy in the Great Depression: Hoover-Stimson Foreign Policy, 1929–1933* (1957), and Christopher Thorne, *The Limits of Foreign Policy: The West, the League, and the Far Eastern Crisis of 1931–1933* (1973). Dorothy Borg's *The United States and the Far Eastern Crisis of 1933–1938* (1964) continues the story into the full-scale Sino-Japanese War. The best discussion of the London Economic Conference appears in Frank Freidel's *Franklin D. Roosevelt: Launching the New Deal* (1973). The title of Arnold A. Offner's *American Appeasement: United States Foreign Policy and Germany, 1933–1938* (1969) indicates the author's approach to the years when Hitler was consolidating power. Alton Frye, *Nazi Germany and the American Hemisphere, 1933–1941* (1967), minimizes Hitler's transatlantic ambitions. Lloyd C. Gardner's *Economic Aspects of New Deal Diplomacy* (1964) emphasizes an insatiable urge for profits. The American response to Hitler's persecution of the Jews in the 1930s is discussed in David S. Wyman, *Paper Walls: America and the Refugee Crisis, 1938–1941* (1968), and Henry L. Feingold, *The Politics of Rescue: The Roosevelt Administration and the Holocaust, 1938–1945* (1970). David H. Culbert, *News for Everyman: Radio and Foreign Affairs in Thirties America* (1976), brings a new perspective to the decade's developments. Relations with Latin America are covered in Irwin Gellman, *Good Neighbor Diplomacy* (1979); Walter LaFeber, *Inevitable Revolutions: The United States in Central America* (1983); and John Findling, *Close Neighbors, Distant Friends: United States–*

*Central American Relations* (1987). On the Spanish Civil War, see Douglas Little, *Malevolent Neutrality: The United States, Great Britain, and the Origins of the Spanish Civil War* (1985).

The most thorough account of diplomatic events leading to World War II is the two-volume study by William L. Langer and S. Everett Gleason, *The Challenge to Isolation, 1937–1940* (1952) and *The Undeclared War, 1940–1941* (1953), a detailed justification of American policy. Robert A. Divine's two volumes *The Illusion of Neutrality* (1962) and *The Reluctant Belligerent* (1966) are only slightly more critical. On the other hand, Charles A. Beard's *President Roosevelt and the Coming of the War, 1941* (1948) indicts FDR for maneuvering the nation into war, and Bruce M. Russett's thin but thoughtful essay *No Clear and Present Danger* (1972) dismisses the claims of a fascist threat to the United States. The best recent account of American involvement in the war is Waldo H. Heinrichs, Jr., *Threshold of War* (1988). Manfred Jonas, *Isolation in America, 1935–1941* (1966), presents the basic facts about the domestic opposition to the government's policies. Richard Steele, *Propaganda in an Open Society: The Roosevelt Administration and the Media, 1933–1941* (1985), is the best book on the subject. Garry Clifford and Samuel R. Spencer, Jr., *The First Peacetime Draft* (1986), studies the introduction of selective service. Warren F. Kimball, *The Most Unsordid Act: Lend-Lease, 1939–1941* (1969), discusses the issue that aroused the fiercest resistance. James R. Leutze, *Bargaining for Supremacy: Anglo-American Naval Collaboration, 1937–1941* (1977), traces secret adjustments of power preceding the war. Relations with Britain are effectively reconstructed in David Reynolds, *The Creation of the Anglo-American Alliance, 1937–1941* (1982). The narrow American vision is revealed in Paul W. Schroeder's *The Axis Alliance and Japanese-American Relations, 1941* (1958) and Charles E. Neu's *The Troubled Encounter: The United States and Japan* (1975). The official in Tokyo who tried to broaden Washington's view is the subject of Waldo H. Heinrichs, Jr., *American Ambassador: Joseph C. Grew and the Development of the United States Diplomatic Tradition* (1966). A recent account of how we got into war with Japan is Jonathan Utley, *Going to War with Japan* (1985). Roberta Wohlstetter, *Pearl Harbor: Warning and Decision* (1962), analyzes the controversy surrounding the Japanese strike at Hawaii. The debate is continued in Gordon W. Prange, *At Dawn We Slept: The Untold Story of Pearl Harbor* (1981), and John Toland, *Infamy: Pearl Harbor and Its Aftermath* (1982). All these issues in the Roosevelt foreign policy are reviewed in Robert Dallek, *Franklin D. Roosevelt and American Foreign Policy, 1932–1945* (1979).

# 30

# *The Modern Republic Becomes a Superpower*

≈

ORLD War II produced lasting changes in American life, changes at least as great as those wrought by the Great Depression and the New Deal. In the short run, involvement in the fighting led to an expansion of the economy that ended the depression, and it pushed the United States into a military and political alliance with Britain, China, and Russia that did not outlive the war. But there were also more enduring effects. The war permanently expanded the power of the national government at home, and it raised the country's responsibilities abroad to unprecedented levels. Because the president is the principal official making foreign policy and because overseas affairs became more important than domestic ones after 1941, the chief executive gained a position of greater importance in American political life than at any time in the country's history. Indeed, the postwar era saw the rise of an imperial presidency that posed a threat to traditional republican values. Secret government operations, undeclared wars, and abuses of constitutional rights became regular occurrences in post-1945 America. A heightened emphasis on foreign (as opposed to domestic) affairs, and on the necessity of preserving the nation from the communist threat and aiding other countries in the same effort, also gave conservatives a political advantage over liberals. Exploiting a traditional conservative reverence for patriotic symbolism, Republicans would win seven of the eleven presidential elections after 1945.

The conflict had obvious domestic consequences as well. Technologies developed to wage war, ranging from small electronic gadgets to nuclear energy, would find myriad applications in postwar life; so would the sulfa drugs, first introduced to fight battle wounds and tropical diseases. Within the nation's borders, military service and wartime demands for factory labor uprooted hundreds of thousands of rural and small-town people, many of them blacks and Appalachian whites, and few of them drifted back from the cities to the country when peace returned in 1945. Other domestic changes would manifest themselves only in the long run, as postwar society evolved. Many women, for example, acquired a liking for paid work and only reluctantly returned to domestic routines after 1945. Racism flared up on the home front during the war, but minorities' self-confidence and unwillingness to accept discrimination also emerged strengthened by wartime experiences. Exposure to the horrifying consequences of Nazi racial hatreds, moreover, led many Americans to begin rethinking their own prejudices, and the federal government took its first halting steps against Jim Crow. Much of the sweeping change that would transform postwar American society, culture, institutions, and world power would have roots in the republic's wartime experience.

## World War II, 1941–1945

Between December 1941 and May 1945 the United States, unlike its allies, was continuously engaged in two very different wars. In the Pacific theater of war, where victory hinged on control of the seas, the United States fought almost alone. In the European theater, where victory could be won only on the Continent, America contributed to a complex collective effort and suffered only a small fraction of the casualties inflicted on the U.S.S.R., Germany, Poland, and Britain.

**Initial Defeats**    During the early months of the war, the same dismal picture of retreat and jeopardy dominated both theaters. Japanese units swept away the last resistance in Southeast Asia, occupying the Netherlands East Indies (Indonesia), capturing the British base at Singapore, and driving to the frontiers of India. Japan's naval victory in the Java Sea assured its control of the western Pacific. In May 1942 the remnants of America's small, isolated force in the Philippines surrendered to the Japanese. Across a vast expanse from the tip of Alaska's Aleutian Islands through the central Pacific to the mountain passes of Burma, imperial Japan dominated. From beleaguered China, General "Vinegar Joe" Stillwell, America's adviser to Chiang Kai-shek (the head of the nationalist government), summarized the first round of the Asian war: "We got a hell of a beating." The only bright spot was General Douglas MacArthur's escape from the Philippines to Australia, where he rallied Allied spirits by declaring, "I came through, and I shall return."

In Europe, Germany's successes were even more ominous. Its fleet of submarines, which had been held in check before December 1941, unleashed a devastating attack on the Allies' Atlantic supply lines. In the early months of the war, they roamed all along the American coast and into the Caribbean, for the United States had not yet developed an effective counterattack to the elusive submarine. Nor could American shipyards yet replace the tonnage lost at sea. Meanwhile Nazi mechanized divisions under General Erwin von Rommel drove across North Africa into Egypt, threatening the Suez Canal. Above all, a renewed offensive in Russia spread German troops from the outskirts of Leningrad in the North to the strategic industrial city of Stalingrad in the South. Into the late fall of 1942 the greatest potential disaster, a Soviet collapse, loomed as a strong possibility.

**Establishing War Strategy**

How could the United States best use its massive resources to alter the balance of the war? In broad strategic matters, the answers came quickly and clearly. The European theater had priority over the Pacific. Anglo-American leaders agreed that the defeat of Germany before Japan offered the most direct path to total victory. The first objective, therefore, was to ensure Soviet survival by continuing the flow of lend-lease goods, the food and war materiel that had been going to Russia since the summer of 1941. Despite the menace of the German submarines, which took a terrible toll along the icy routes in the North Sea, the quantity of these supplies slowly increased. Finally, to relieve the pressure on the Soviet army, American and British forces had to launch a "second front" as soon as possible in the West.

The men who ultimately made these decisions were President Roosevelt and Prime Minister Winston Churchill, Britain's brilliant, calculating war leader. Their personal collaboration had begun with the destroyer-for-bases deal in September 1940 and widened at the Atlantic Conference of August 1941, where the United States and Great Britain had declared to the world that they stood together against the Axis. From December 1941 to January 1943, through a series of private meetings, the two men grew even closer. Although Russia's fate also hung on the decisions that Roosevelt and Churchill made, the Soviet Union remained a distant ally, declaring its needs and awaiting a response from the Western powers.

The initial American impulse was to open at least a token second front in Western Europe during 1942. Hoping to boost Soviet morale in the spring of 1942, when Moscow's ability to hold out against Hitler's armies remained in doubt, FDR promised to open a second front in Europe before the end of the year. But no one had anticipated the complexities of global warfare. The Nazis more than held their own during 1942 in the battle for the Atlantic sea-lanes. Without guaranteed supplies, the Allies would never breach the coast of France. And such crucial items as landing craft remained very scarce. Moreover, the Pacific war also demanded attention and resources, especially because the attack on Pearl Harbor gave it a special importance to the many Americans who favored a Pacific-first strategy.

By mid-1942 the United States began to stabilize its position against the weaker but more remote foe in Asia. Because Congress had authorized a program of naval construction well before Pearl Harbor, the American fleet was able to return in strength to the Pacific less than a year after Japan's devastating attack. In May 1942, even as Japan was overrunning the Philippines, a successful American assault on a Japanese fleet in the battle of the Coral Sea secured Australia. A

**FDR, Churchill,
and Military Chiefs**
*Roosevelt and Churchill
established a close partnership
that helped defeat the Axis
powers.*

month later, the United States Navy repulsed a Japanese naval force in the battle of Midway, blocking a potential enemy attack on Hawaii. Then in November 1942 the American navy won a three-day encounter off the Solomon Islands near Australia. With these three battles, the balance of sea power in the Pacific shifted back to the United States. Meanwhile, eyeing morale back home, American forces in August launched small, difficult counteroffensives at Guadalcanal in the Solomon Islands and on the far larger contested island of New Guinea.

Sobered by the complications of a global war, Roosevelt and his advisers, despite complaints from Moscow, abandoned plans for a quick attack on France and accepted Churchill's alternative of a North African campaign. In November 1942 Operation Torch under General Dwight D. Eisenhower invaded French Morocco and Algeria. British General Bernard Montgomery halted Rommel's Afrika Korps in its drive toward Suez and pushed the Germans westward; Eisenhower's troops swept eastward. By May 1943 Montgomery and Eisenhower had forced Axis power out of North Africa.

The North African campaign was only part of a worldwide turn in the tide of battle: the Soviet Union had already won the pivotal engagement of the European war. Hitler, trying to crack Russia's resistance before another winter froze his

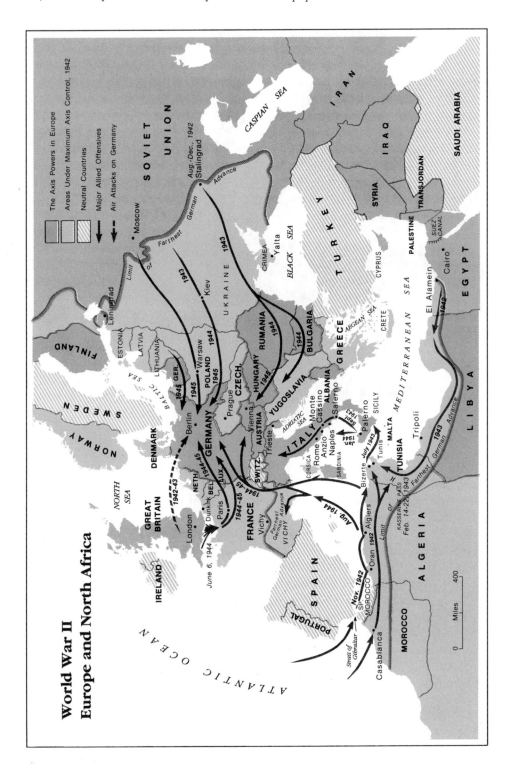

**World War II**
**Europe and North Africa**

army in place, gambled recklessly on an assault against Stalingrad. During the winter's war of 1942–43, a relentless Soviet counterattack not only saved Stalingrad but actually cost Germany half a million troops. The following summer the Soviet army took the initiative against its weakened, overextended German foe and began the westward drive toward the heart of the Reich. In the Southwest Pacific, American forces cut the first wedge through the enemy perimeter north of Australia, forcing the Japanese on the defensive, and charted the winding trail of island conquests that led to Japan itself. In the summer of 1943, radar, long-range air patrols, and Ultra—Britain's ability to read coded German messages—finally tipped the balance against the German submarines in the battle of the Atlantic.

**Victory in Europe**    When the United States and Great Britain bypassed France for North Africa in 1942, Soviet leader J. V. Stalin was again promised a second front in Europe for the following year. But in 1943 Churchill once more persuaded Roosevelt to postpone an attack on France. Believing the buildup of men and supplies, especially landing craft, had not yet reached sufficient levels to mount a successful cross-Channel attack, Roosevelt and Churchill agreed to postpone the invasion until 1944. Instead they decided to strike at the weakest Axis power, Italy. In July 1943, in the most dubious strategic

**Ike with American Troops**
*Eisenhower was a popular general who enjoyed great rapport with his subordinates.*

**The Infantryman's War**
*Behind every move on the generals' maps lay a terrible price in human suffering. This soldier, wounded by shrapnel, receives a transfusion of blood plasma as a Sicilian family looks on.*

decision by Anglo-American commanders of the war, an Allied force landed in Sicily; in September it crossed into Italy. Nothing in the campaign went well. Although Italy almost immediately surrendered, German troops filled the vacuum from the north, fortified the critical mountains and passes, and stalled the large Allied army. Stalin, whose soldiers continued to bear the primary burden of the ground war against Germany, strongly complained about his allies' timidity.

Not until June 6, 1944, did the United States and Britain finally establish a successful second front in France. After feints to the northern coast of France had confused Germany's waiting army, Operation Overlord struck the beaches of Normandy in the greatest amphibious assault in history, commanded by General Eisenhower. After six weeks of struggle, the Allies broke through Germany's coastal defenses. In August another force invaded southern France, and that same month Paris fell. By then Rome had also fallen, and the Soviet army had reached

**Life on a Crowded Troop Transport**
*The Allied invasion of Europe required an unprecedented buildup of U.S. forces abroad.*

the outskirts of Warsaw (halting there while the Nazis crushed a massive uprising in the Polish capital). The systematic bombing of Germany, after accomplishing relatively little in 1943, was now devastating its cities. The Allies controlled the air, and American supplies flowed freely across the Atlantic.

Hitler's most effective response to the Allied assault came a week after Overlord, when the first rocket-launched bombs whined across the English Channel. In September the silent and more deadly V-2 rockets, replacing the V-1 "buzz bombs," hit London. They brought terror to England but no success for the Nazis. That same month British and American troops for the first time reached German territory. The Russian army smashed through the Balkans and resumed its offensive in Poland. The Nazis made a desperate counterattack at the German-Belgian border—the "Battle of the Bulge," in December 1944, which cost heavy American casualties. Thereafter, Germany's army collapsed inside the Allied vise. By the end of April, Russian troops were fighting in the streets of Berlin. Hitler, ill and deranged, committed suicide in an underground bunker in Berlin, and on May 7, 1945, German officers formally capitulated to the Allied command.

Russian lives and American productivity had been the basic determinants of victory in Europe. About 20 million Soviet citizens died in the conflict with Germany. By contrast, British losses were about 500,000, and American losses in both theaters of war were about 300,000. The United States served as the arsenal of the Allied cause. By 1942 America's war production equaled the combined output of the Axis powers; by 1944 it doubled the enemy's total. When Germany could no longer slow the delivery of American goods, the Nazis were doomed to fall beneath the crushing weight of war matériel.

After Germany's surrender, the numbing facts about the Nazis' anti-Jewish policy were more fully disclosed. Systematically, the German government had applied the most effective techniques of modern organization to destroy 6 million European Jews. Although the Roosevelt administration had had substantial knowledge during the war of what was happening, it had rejected any special effort to rescue the victims of the Holocaust: it had made no request to Congress to relax immigration restrictions barring persecuted Jews from America, and had even left existing quotas unfilled. It also rejected plans to bomb the transportation lines into the death camps and the huge gas chambers, even though United States planes attacked targets within a few miles of Auschwitz. Arguing that "rescue through victory" was the best policy for saving people from the Holocaust, the Roosevelt administration resisted suggestions for anything that might divert resources from the war effort and retard Nazi defeat, even though hundreds of thousands of Jews from Rumania, Hungary, and especially Italy could have been saved. If the policy seemed politically wise at the time—a way for the Roosevelt administration to avoid antisemitic charges of fighting the war to save the Jews—in retrospect it has impressed people as callous insensitivity to a problem that could not wait. Had FDR appealed for public support, he would surely have stirred traditional humane impulses in the United States and won political backing for a rescue effort.

**Bloody Advances in the Pacific**     While American troops slogged through the Italian mud in 1943, the pace of the Pacific war had remained slow. That November, on the assumption that only an occupation of Tokyo itself could end the war, naval forces under Admiral Chester Nimitz, along with a combination of American, Australian, and New Zealand ground forces under General Douglas MacArthur, began a grim, two-pronged assault toward the Japanese mainland. Nimitz's command had to regain control over the myriad islands in the central Pacific. Bloody links lay in the chain ahead: Tarawa in the Gilbert Islands, Saipan in the Marianas, Iwo Jima, and then Okinawa, just south of Japan's home islands. From the south MacArthur's command had to hack its way through the jungles of New Guinea and converge with Nimitz's forces on the Philippines.

Early in 1944, as America's production expanded to serve both the European and Pacific wars, the drive on Japan gained momentum. By summer the United States controlled the central Pacific. Then in October, with General MacArthur

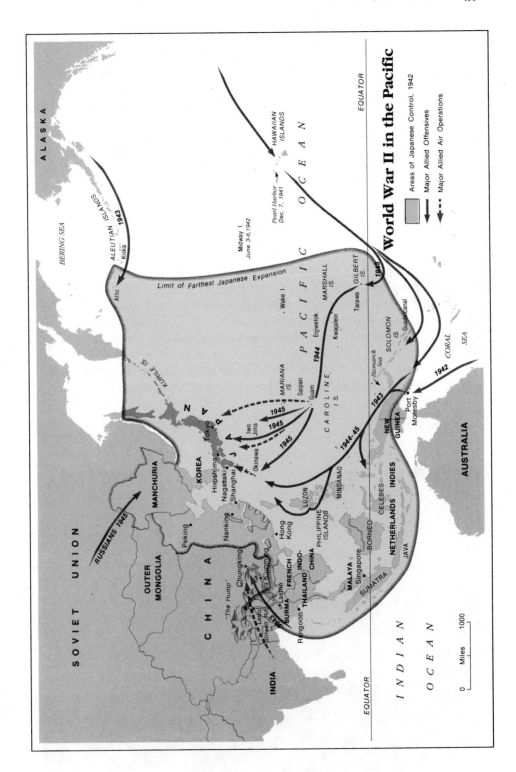

## World War II in the Pacific

Areas of Japanese Control, 1942

Major Allied Offensives

Major Allied Air Operations

dramatically leading his troops to the site of a humiliating defeat early in the war, American forces invaded the Philippines. Also in October, in the battle of Leyte Gulf, Japanese naval power was destroyed. Fierce Japanese resistance continued to keep casualties high. As late as March 1945, a month's fight for the tiny, desolate island of Iwo Jima left 20,000 Americans dead and wounded. But Japan now lay open to systematic bombing. Napalm raids burned its compact cities one by one. In March 1945 a single attack on Tokyo killed more than 80,000 inhabitants. When Germany surrendered in May 1945, an utterly exposed Japan was already tottering, but not defeated. The battle for Okinawa in May and June cost America heavy casualties.

**The Atomic Bomb**    The climactic blow of the Asian war had been in preparation even before Pearl Harbor and had been originally aimed at Germany, not Japan. In 1939 refugee physicists from Europe, knowing that German scientists were trying to split an atom, began urging the American government to explore the possibility of producing an atomic bomb before the Nazis could develop it. Within a year, in cooperation with Britain, the awesome project was under way. In utmost secrecy, which aimed to hide developments from the Soviets as well as from America's enemies, groups of scientists at separate laboratories struggled against time to master the secrets of the atom. They learned to control a chain reaction of atomic fission so that it would generate enormous power; this they then converted into a technically practical

**Hiroshima, 1945**
*Was modern society on the brink of suicide? The awful power of the atomic bomb raised fundamental questions about the meaning of science, progress, and civilization.*

military device. In July 1945 the task was finally completed when a test bomb was exploded in the New Mexico desert under the direction of physicist J. Robert Oppenheimer. By then, however, Germany had fallen. A new, inexperienced president, Harry S Truman, sat in the White House. An array of military and civilian advisers counseled the president to use the new weapon against Japan, explaining that it might eliminate the need for an invasion of the Japanese home islands, which everyone expected to produce heavy American casualties. Although the terrifying dimensions of atomic and nuclear weaponry became crystal clear only after World War II, at the time the weapon impressed many American military and government leaders as essentially a more efficient way of using air power to terrorize the enemy. It was also assumed that FDR would have used the weapon and that, so much tax money having been spent in developing the bomb, Congress and the public would expect the expenditures to be justified by dropping it. Finally, some American military and political leaders felt using the bomb would serve postwar peace by intimidating the Soviets. On August 6 a single bomb demolished the city of Hiroshima, immediately killing about 80,000 people and maiming and poisoning thousands more. Three days later, just as the Soviet Union declared war on Japan, a second bomb razed Nagasaki. On August 14, Japan surrendered.

## The Home Front

World War II ended the depression in the United States. Before the war was over, net farm income almost doubled, and corporate profits after taxes climbed 70 percent. From a total of more than 8 million unemployed in 1940, the curve dropped below a million in 1944. Moreover, an abundance of jobs and an industrial wage scale that rose 24 percent drew into the labor market an additional 7 million workers, half of whom were women. There had been no comparable economic boom in American history.

**The Wartime Boom**   Economic organization for a worldwide conflict required an extraordinary expansion of governmental power. Washington suddenly teemed with hundreds of thousands of new arrivals, jammed into cubbyhole offices with a bewildering array of alphabet labels. The main divisions of the government bureaucracy matched the major functions of the modern economy. The War Production Board, the Office of Price Administration, the War Manpower Commission, the Office of Defense Transportation, and the War Food Administration each had broad authority to manage its subdivision of the economy. Beginning in October 1942 the skillful South Carolina politician James Byrnes ruled these agencies through the Office of Economic Stabilization, and subsequently through the Office of War Mobilization.

Allocating scarce resources and controlling inflation were the problems that most bedeviled the wartime agencies. Blessed with an abundance of natural resources, the United States had enough raw materials for most wartime programs. When a shortage of rubber created a crisis, the rapid development of

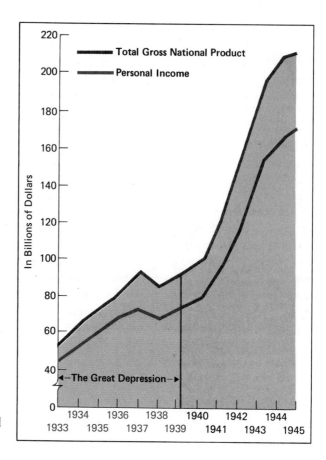

220

- - - - - **Total Gross National Product**

——— **Personal Income**

200

180

160

140

120

100

80

60

40

←—The Great Depression—→

0

In Billions of Dollars

1933　1934　1935　1936　1937　1938　1939　1940　1941　1942　1943　1944　1945

**Recovery of the National Economy**

synthetic rubber eventually resolved it. The shortage of skilled labor, however, defied solution. Not only did the armed services absorb over 15 million men and women, but civilians could not resist hopping from job to job in search of better wages. "Stabilization," or job-freeze, orders from Washington had little effect on labor turnover, and Roosevelt's 1944 proposal to draft workers into an industrial army collapsed in the face of united opposition from employers and unions alike.

The demand for a larger body of laborers at home to provide materiel to troops at the front significantly expanded the role of women in the work force. During the war years some 6.5 million women took jobs, a 57 percent increase in the number of working women; more than half of them had previously been unpaid housewives. By the summer of 1944 over 35 percent of all employed persons in the United States were women, an unprecedented proportion of American laborers. Women became an indispensable part of the national war effort. Equally striking, the percentage of married working women jumped from 36 percent in 1940 to 50 percent in 1945. Sixty percent of new women workers were former housewives over thirty-five; one-third of them had children under the age of fourteen. More women in the work force, however, did not mean equality in pay with men. In 1945, women in manufacturing received only 65 percent of what men earned. Moreover, most Americans did not favor postwar

**On the Home Front**
*Wartime labor shortages brought women into the work force in great numbers. By 1945 they made up 57 percent of all employed persons in the United States.*

work for women at wartime levels. Eighty-six percent of Americans said they wished to see women resume their traditional roles as mothers and housewives and leave the jobs to returning GIs. Although in the long run the entrance of women into new parts of the work force during World War II would have a transforming effect, in the short run traditional attitudes toward working women remained unchanged.

Scarce labor and scarce goods drove up prices during the early months of the war. The Office of Price Administration (OPA), under the able economist Leon Henderson, lacked the power to control inflation because Congress refused to hold down the rise of agricultural prices. Only late in 1942, when Byrnes took charge of the entire mobilization program, did a semblance of order begin to emerge. By mid-1943 a broad legal ceiling over prices, wages, and rents finally stopped the upward spiral. Although the cost of living increased about 33 percent during the war, relatively little of that increase occurred after the summer of 1943.

Finance posed another basic wartime problem, the solution to which permanently expanded governmental presence in everyday life. Although more than half the costs of war accumulated as national debt, massive new funds still had to be raised. The answer came in the revolutionary Revenue Act of 1942, which established America's modern structure of taxation. The heart of the measure was a steeply graduated income tax that for the first time covered most middle-income and lower-income groups. Thirteen million Americans had paid federal income taxes in 1941; the 1942 law increased the number to 50 million. By 1945 revenues from the income tax were an astronomical twenty times above their level in 1940. To ease the pain yet increase the flow, in 1943 the government withheld most of these taxes directly from workers' paychecks rather than demand them in a lump sum once a year.

Inside the intricate framework of wartime rules, extreme decentralization prevailed. The tax laws contained numerous loopholes for the wealthy. Thousands of local draft boards decided who should fill the quotas for military service. To get the planes and tanks and beef and wheat it needed, the government simply offered to pay a lot of money. It signed lucrative contracts with individual companies guaranteeing costs, profits, and large tax write-offs. Companies negotiated these contracts through the various bureaus of the wartime government, then fought with one another for the labor and raw materials all of them needed. After the government allowed farm prices to skyrocket for a year, it continued to subsidize many farmers at a level above the market price for their products. Even the unpopular OPA, which rationed out to grumbling consumers such scarce commodities as gasoline, meat, shoes, and sugar, exercised little control over the widespread violation of its rules. The government's chief administrators intervened only when the many small decisions below them had created a hopeless mess.

In the wartime scramble for advantage, the strong reaped the greatest benefits. In 1940 the one hundred leading companies manufactured 30 percent of the nation's output. By 1943 the one hundred leaders produced 70 percent. The conservative coalition in Congress grew larger and bolder. As the unemployed came back to work, Congress in 1942 terminated the WPA. Calling the Farm Security Administration a "communist" center, its congressional opponents abolished the agency's social programs for the rural poor. Despite President Roosevelt's efforts, Congress lightened the tax burden on the rich in 1943. Overall, the war increased the concentration of wealth at the top of America's socioeconomic pyramid.

The one child of the 1930s to thrive during the war was the union movement. In 1941 two more citadels of the open shop—Ford and the corporations in "Little Steel"—surrendered. During the war, union membership rose 40 percent. Even more important, many employers, in an effort to hold their workers and maintain production, actually bargained with the unions for the first time. Yet here also the conservatives had their say. Although the number of strikes remained quite low between 1941 and 1945, important ones in the coal and railroad industries during 1943 triggered an angry public reaction, and Congress responded with the Smith-Connally Act, which authorized the president to postpone a strike for thirty days and seize a plant that had been struck. Strikers could be fined and imprisoned.

Fearing a drift toward "socialism," conservatives fought every executive agency that tried to make economic plans for the postwar years. Not one of these proposals survived the congressional budget cuts. As the war drew to a close, the only significant preparation for peace was the Servicemen's Readjustment Act of 1944, popularly known as the GI Bill, which provided unemployment compensation, medical care, mortgage funds, and educational subsidies for returning troops. The bill had far-reaching consequences for veterans, whose economic prospects improved greatly. Equally important, the measure assured that millions would get training for future employment that would serve the national economic well-being.

The ailing Roosevelt remained an inspiring public figure in spite of the little he did to arrest the domestic confusion. Investing most of his energies in world problems—"Dr. Win-the-War" had replaced "Dr. New Deal," he said—the president left the home front to his subordinates. Except in military affairs, Roosevelt had lost almost all influence in Congress by late 1943. At the beginning of 1944, when in the most radical speech of his career he announced an economic bill of rights for the postwar era, Congress responded with hostility. FDR's sensitivity to this conservatism was evident in the 1944 campaign: he replaced Henry Wallace, whose desire to expand the New Deal and usher in the "century of the common man" tagged him as ultraliberal, with the more moderate Missouri Senator Harry S Truman as his vice-presidential running mate. Further, Roosevelt campaigned listlessly against Thomas E. Dewey, the smooth and capable but aloof Republican governor of New York. Although Roosevelt's percentage of the popular vote declined, he still won handily, 439 to 99 electoral votes. Perhaps the nasty Democratic comment that no one wanted "little Tom Dewey sitting on two Washington telephone books" at the peace conference captured the essence of Roosevelt's strength. At a grand juncture in world affairs, the president had an appropriately grand international prestige. But domestically, America had no strong leadership entering 1945.

**Racial Crosscurrents**   While the Roosevelt administration struggled to win the war and ensure postwar peace and prosperity, racial conflicts raised basic questions about the republic's traditional commitments to equality and freedom. Assertions that World War II was a crusade for democracy stumbled over the fact that white Americans' subjection of Japanese, Mexican, and African Americans to racial prejudice deprived them of basic rights.

The most shocking instance of arbitrary government power occurred immediately after the Japanese attack on Pearl Harbor. A large majority of West Coast whites had long nursed hostility toward Asians. After the surprise attack on American territory, they readily believed rumors of a seditious Japanese "fifth column" in the United States that was planning extensive sabotage and communicating with enemy submarines off America's shores. The government, they cried, must destroy the danger from within. These popular, bipartisan emotions found a willing servant in Lieutenant General John DeWitt, who headed the army's Western Defense Command. Responding to DeWitt's request, Washington gave the general broad powers in February 1942 to solve the Japanese problem as he chose.

**Prisoners**
*With pride as their only defense,
these Japanese Americans await
shipment to one of the wartime
concentration camps.*

At the outset DeWitt planned to use stronger measures against the 40,000 alien Japanese (immigrants who by law were denied the right to become American citizens) than against the 70,000 who were American citizens by birth. But that distinction quickly disappeared. Early in 1942, saying "the Japanese race is an enemy race," DeWitt ordered all Japanese Americans along the coasts of Washington, Oregon, and California and in southern Arizona to abandon their homes. From temporary stockades, they were transported to ten inland centers in Arizona, California, Utah, and Wyoming, where the Army Relocation Authority guarded them for the duration. The camps themselves were nightmarish, isolated in arid, desolate spots and surrounded by barbed wire; families shared a single room in wooden barracks, with communal toilet, dining, and bathing facilities. Along with their liberty, Japanese Americans lost about $500 million in property and income. In *Korematsu* v. *United States* (1944), the Supreme Court upheld the "relocation" on grounds of national security.

Concentration camps for 110,000 Japanese Americans were an embarrassment to the Roosevelt administration, which officially described them as "relocation centers." After the initial wave of panic passed, government officials discussed ways of releasing the prisoners. But public opinion opposed this policy change. The administration learned that no communities would accept the Japanese Americans. As a compromise, the army during 1943 and 1944 issued individual leaves to 35,000 imprisoned Japanese Americans, most of whom served in the United States armed forces. Only in January 1945 did the prison gates open to everyone. A generation later, in 1983, a federal judge declared the internment a gross miscarriage of justice, and in 1988 the United States government finally apologized to the 60,000 surviving victims and promised to pay $20,000 to each of them.

Meanwhile, in response to the desperate wartime need for unskilled labor, the United States in 1942 negotiated an agreement with Mexico for the importation of *braceros,* or temporary workers. Los Angeles, booming with war contracts and bursting with new arrivals, was a favorite destination for both legal and illegal immigrants from Mexico. City officials did nothing to ease the newcomers' transition. Ethnic tensions simmered in the overflowing metropolis until the local hostility toward Chicanos erupted in the "zoot suit"* riots, which in most cases meant the beating of young Mexican Americans by United States sailors and marines.

Even sharper racial tensions polarized black and white Americans thrown together in northern cities. During the depression, when the unemployed crowded the large cities, 400,000 blacks had left the South and gone north. Then, during the early 1940s alone, another million responded to the wartime jobs that beckoned from Los Angeles to Boston. By 1950 approximately one-third of America's black population lived outside the South.

The small economic gains made by blacks under the New Deal had provoked black leaders to press for more. In 1941 A. Philip Randolph, the shrewd president of the Brotherhood of Sleeping Car Porters, introduced a new tactic in the fight for black rights. As the economy was mobilizing for war, Randolph rallied blacks throughout the nation for a mass march on Washington that would publicize America's racial discrimination around the world and possibly disrupt the early stages of war production. Randolph's price for canceling the march was President Roosevelt's intervention in behalf of black workers. Despite his irritation at Randolph's threat, Roosevelt on June 25, 1941, issued a precedent-setting executive order that banned discriminatory hiring "because of race, creed, color, or national origin" both within the national government and throughout its expanding network of war-related contracts. The executive order also established the Fair Employment Practices Committee (FEPC) to oversee these rules. Yet the Roosevelt administration did nothing to desegregate the armed forces or oppose the widespread residential segregation that existed in all American cities. In Europe, American troops occasionally beat up and even shot black soldiers, who were not only segregated but given the most menial jobs to perform.

It was the need for labor, not the weak FEPC, that broadened economic opportunities for blacks during the war. Both in the war industries and in the armed services, Jim Crow rules weakened only slightly under the pressure of an increasingly severe manpower shortage. Racial tensions were mounting, however, especially over access to housing and public facilities in the swollen industrial areas of the large cities. During the summer of 1943 these emotions exploded from coast to coast in a series of violent racial encounters in forty-seven cities.

The worst of the riots occurred in Detroit, a primary center of war production, into which 500,000 newcomers, including 60,000 blacks, had squeezed since

---

*"Zoot suits" were baggy suits popular especially among poor and lower-middle-class youths in the 1940s.

1940. On a hot Sunday in June 1943 a fight between teenage whites and blacks ignited two days of guerrilla warfare and widespread looting. Twenty-five blacks and nine whites were killed, hundreds were wounded, and millions of dollars in property was lost. A terrible riot also occurred in Harlem in 1943. By then some Democrats were openly worrying about "the Negro vote." Yet every national election between 1936 and 1944 seemed to verify the political wisdom of Democratic policies. If blacks were really discontented, why did they vote as heavily Democratic as any other urban group? Wait until after the depression, the Roosevelt administration (primarily concerned with winning unqualified southern support) had told its black critics in the 1930s. Wait until after the war, it told them in the early 1940s. Refusing to rely on the goodwill of the Roosevelt administration, the Democratic party, or white America generally, blacks joined civil rights organizations in unprecedented numbers. Between 1940 and 1946 the NAACP increased from 50,000 members to 450,000, and in 1942 black civil rights activists established the Congress of Racial Equality (CORE).

Thus racism continued to scar American life. But minorities' resistance to injustice had stiffened, many blacks had left the rural isolation where they were most vulnerable, and many whites' acceptance of racial discrimination had been undermined by the spectacle of Nazi racism. In race relations the clock could never quite be turned back in the years after World War II.

## Postwar International Planning for Peace

Even as the United States fought the war, President Roosevelt had been planning the peace. As in domestic affairs, the president was an eloquent spokesman of hope, not only for Americans, but also for yearning peoples throughout the world. Even before Pearl Harbor, Roosevelt and Churchill had met at sea to sign the Atlantic Charter, which proclaimed their vision of the postwar world. These ideals recalled the Wilsonian principles of political self-determination, free economic exchange, and international cooperation, and the Atlantic Charter's "Four Freedoms"—freedom from want and from fear, freedom of speech and of religion—became international bywords.

**International Organizations** During the war the president emphasized his hope for postwar international cooperation among Britain, China, the Soviet Union, and the United States, and he envisioned all peace-loving nations joining in a new world league. To achieve these goals, the Roosevelt administration moved decisively to create new international organizations. At a conference in Bretton Woods, New Hampshire, in 1944, the United States took the initiative in developing a program for international monetary stabilization. The American dollar became the basis for most international monetary transactions. To facilitate global finance, the conference planned two new agencies—the World Bank, which would help to regularize transactions among the industrial powers, and the International Monetary Fund, which would issue loans to the poorest nations.

At the same time the Roosevelt administration led the movement for another attempt at worldwide collective security. Secretary of State Cordell Hull, a devoted Wilsonian, deserved the primary credit for negotiating the establishment of the United Nations. Recalling Wilson's failure to win approval of the Versailles Treaty and the League of Nations, the secretary successfully wooed the Senate. He included prominent Republicans in the planning of a new league, and he persuaded isolationist senators like Arthur Vandenberg of Michigan to accept the need for participation in it. At every opportunity, Hull also pressed America's wartime allies for firm commitments to an international organization. When the secretary retired in 1944, the hardest work had been done. Despite Britain's fears for its empire and Russia's fears for its security, their representatives came to San Francisco in 1945 to join delegates from forty-six other nations in founding a world organization. Overcoming final Soviet resistance, the delegates signed the charter of the United Nations in June. In July the United States Senate overwhelmingly approved America's participation.

**Soviet-American Relations: Alliance and Mistrust**

Between the Bolshevik Revolution of 1917 and the German invasion of Russia in 1941, Soviet-American relations had been an almost unrelieved story of mutual hostility. Until 1933 the United States had not even recognized the Soviet Union. Americans had responded with disgust to the Nazi-Soviet Pact of 1939 and the Russian invasion of Finland that winter,* both of which seemed to show the Soviets' true colors. Even after the United States and the Soviet Union had become wartime allies, their early exchanges were sometimes sharp, especially over delays in opening a second front in western Europe. To assure the Soviets that they had no intention of abandoning Russia partway through the war—and to prevent a possible separate Nazi-Soviet peace—FDR and Churchill in January 1943 announced their commitment to "unconditional surrender."

In November 1943, at the depths of Russia's wartime doubts, Roosevelt opened a dialogue with the Soviets when he, Stalin, and Churchill held their first joint meeting in Tehran, Iran. Their conversations ranged over the second front in Europe, Russia's future entry into the Asian war, and punishment for Germany. Roosevelt responded to Stalin's proposals in encouraging tones. During a second meeting, at the Black Sea port of Yalta in February 1945, Roosevelt renewed his conciliatory efforts, offering only token resistance to Soviet domination of Eastern Europe and accepting a central role for the USSR in both postwar Europe and Asia. At the very end of the European war, when Churchill argued for troop movements that would place the Western powers, not the Soviet Union, in Berlin and the Balkans, Roosevelt refused to play military chess with Stalin. It was not a

---

*In 1939–40 Stalin waged war on neighboring Finland, which had refused Soviet demands for territorial concessions. After a heroic resistance, Finland finally succumbed. But when Hitler attacked the USSR in 1941, Finland joined the Axis in the hope of regaining lost territory.

**The Big Three**
*Wartime meetings among Churchill, Roosevelt, and Stalin sustained the military alliance but failed to create a stable postwar structure of peace.*

case of a politically minded Churchill and a militarily minded Roosevelt; the president simply had different political objectives.

Roosevelt's goals were twofold. First and foremost, he wished to ensure that the United States would emerge from the war ready to shed its isolationist past. He hoped that wartime cooperation with the Allies would lead to postwar collective security arrangements that would make the Wilsonian vision of a world at peace a reality. To succeed, however, he believed that he must guarantee Soviet security through concessions to Stalin in Europe and Asia. Roosevelt hoped that postwar Soviet domination of Eastern Europe, which he saw as inevitable for the short term, would be eased by Soviet recognition that no one intended to invade them again. Roosevelt believed that once Moscow felt more secure it would continue to insist on Eastern European sensitivity to Soviet national-security concerns but leave the Eastern European peoples free to shape their own domestic affairs. Not until 1989, however, would Roosevelt's expectation become a reality.

The president knew that he had only narrowed, not closed, the gap between the United States and the Soviet Union. Roosevelt's second postwar aim, therefore, was to maintain the modern American tradition of a tacit Anglo-American alliance. Although Roosevelt twitted Churchill about the British Empire, he used none of his wartime leverage to alter Britain's colonial policies. Churchill—but not Stalin—was kept informed about the atomic bomb as it was being developed. If Soviet-American relations deteriorated because Moscow refused to trust Western professions of peace and wanted to press for a world of communist-controlled states, American diplomats expected the United States to rely on this Anglo-American basis for a broad structure of international cooperation.

Roosevelt spoke of "four policemen"—Great Britain, the Soviet Union, the United States, and China—maintaining the postwar peace. But FDR also expected each policeman to patrol his natural region of influence, a division that might draw the United States back to its old role as the great power of the Western Hemisphere. Even during the war, the presence of American troops abroad had seemed unnatural. Almost everyone expected the soliders to come home and stay home after the war; Roosevelt himself voiced this assumption to Stalin at Tehran. For emotional as well as logistical reasons, therefore, Americans increasingly favored a powerful air force to provide a maximum of protection with a minimum of involvement. As the fighting came to an end, Chief of Staff General George C. Marshall was planning the nation's postwar defense in these terms. But no one had a clear picture of what the United States would be defending, or against whom. Although the emergence of the Soviet Union to fill the adversary's role was hardly a big surprise to many Americans, it was not inevitable that the United States and the USSR had to get at cross purposes.

## The Truman Presidency Begins, 1945–1949

On April 12, 1945, only a few weeks after his fourth inauguration, Franklin Roosevelt died. As millions mourned in public, they worried about the future under the new president, Harry S Truman. The new chief executive was an able Missouri judge who had entered the Senate in 1935 and built a reputation for hard work, party loyalty, and stubborn determination. During the war he had gained prominence by heading a Senate committee investigating government waste and corruption, and in 1944 had eased conservative-liberal tensions in the Democratic party by becoming the vice-presidential nominee. (One wit called him the "second Missouri compromise.") Yet no one—including Truman himself—had thought of the little man from Missouri as a possible president. Republican Senator Robert Taft of Ohio once said, in rejecting the office, that the vice-president had nothing to do except "inquire about the president's health." Truman had not even done that. During his short time as vice-president, he had little contact with FDR; he had not been briefed on the atomic bomb, and he had gleaned no definite idea of what Roosevelt intended to do in his fourth term.

Perhaps Roosevelt himself had had no clear plan. Washington had become a bewildering place in which to try to shape any kind of policy. The last years of the New Deal and the war years had seen innumerable special interests fighting with one another in Washington for the government's favor. The stakes were high, the rules loose, and the results chaotic. By the end of the war the big economic associations of bankers, manufacturers, and farmers were shattered. Even the oligopolies were less integrated, for the latest wave of corporate consolidation was tending to produce purely financial combinations of distinct and often very different kinds of business firms.

A permanent professional bureaucracy, moreover, was taking shape in Washington to deal with each specialized subdivision of the economy. During the war the government bureaucracy had swelled to four times its 1939 size; and once created, the bureaucracy tended to perpetuate itself. Although, for example, rapid demobilization and reduced defense spending would follow the peace, the huge defense establishment built up during the war and including many civilian employees did not disappear after the fighting. A job in Washington now became what it had rarely been before—a career. Administrators grew accustomed to protecting their domains from outside intrusion and to developing intricate links with private groups and friendly congressmen. Any president who sought to regain control over the bureaucracy and to create a broad public policy faced an immense task.

**The Transition to Peace**

Without a blueprint of where FDR was headed, Truman had to devise his own plans for mastering the chaos in Washington and guiding the nation's transition from war to peace. Even the most experienced leader would have had difficulty guiding America's economy out of the war. Lost in a maze of complex problems, "quick and brittle" in his decisions, Truman simply foundered. Even before Japan surrendered in August 1945, he could not withstand the popular pressures for a rapid demobilization of the armed forces and a rapid dismantling of most wartime regulations. Industries now made their own decisions in their own behalf, and during the first postwar year corporate profits shot up 20 percent.

Labor discontent spread across the nation. By January 1946, 3 percent of the labor force, including auto, steel, electrical, and packinghouse workers, were simultaneously on strike. When a new round of strikes occurred that spring, a furious president went before Congress to threaten the railroad workers with an army draft, even though the railroad brotherhoods had already canceled the strike. Of the wartime controls, only those governing prices remained, and a feud between the president and Congress needlessly allowed these to end all at once in June 1946, producing the highest rate of inflation in the nation's history. Farm prices rose almost 14 percent in a month and nearly 30 percent before the end of the year. As the saying went, "To err is Truman." "Had enough?" asked the Republican campaign slogan.

Apparently many Americans had, for the off-year elections of 1946 cost the Democrats eleven seats in the Senate and fifty-four in the House. When the Eightieth Congress convened in 1947, the Republicans were the majority party for the first time since Hoover's administration. With the cooperation of conservative Democrats, they could even override the president's veto. Yet the Eightieth Congress had little to offer as an alternative to Truman's erratic policies. Its primary contribution was the Taft-Hartley Act of 1947, a culmination of the congressional antagonism toward unions that had been growing for a decade. A complicated law, Taft-Hartley required financial reports from the unions, restricted their political activities, and prohibited a list of "unfair" labor practices. It also empowered the president to postpone a major strike for an eighty-day "cooling-off" period and allowed state governments to pass antiunion "right-to-work" laws that reduced the pressure on workers to join unions, slowing their postwar growth and influence. But despite these new rules and the howls they brought from the unions, labor-management relations proceeded much the same after Taft-Hartley as before.

**The Beginnings of the Cold War**

At the same time the Truman administration wrestled with domestic problems, it had to confront a crisis overseas. Within two years after Truman took office, the United States and the Soviet Union were locked in a "Cold War" along a line approximating the location of their victorious armies in the summer of 1945. Although no experienced observer had expected a smooth transition from war to peace, relatively few people anticipated the bitter animosity that in fact developed. The United States and the Soviet Union both seemed to desire some accommodation, but the two nations found it impossible to compromise on a set of basic problems. The underlying causes of the rift were extremely complex, and for decades reasonable people would differ sharply over their meaning. The immediate source of conflict, however, was obvious to everyone. Now that the war had been won, what should be done about conquered Germany and Soviet-occupied Eastern Europe?

At the Yalta Conference in February 1945, Roosevelt, Churchill, and Stalin had taken a first step toward resolving this complex package of problems. Stalin stated the Soviet position in detail: for Germany, which had invaded Russia twice in thirty years, he demanded a harsh settlement. He insisted that Germany be stripped of war-making potential and that it send massive reparations in machinery and labor to the Soviet Union. In Eastern Europe, which had been Germany's avenue for invasion, Stalin wanted friendly governments from Poland in the North to the boundary of Greece in the South. Where Stalin was rigid and determined, Roosevelt, who was by then gravely ill, seemed vague and agreeable. The president apparently accepted Stalin's argument that these measures were essential to Russian security. Churchill, not Roosevelt, futilely resisted $20 billion as an estimate for German reparations. And it was Churchill more than Roosevelt who forced the insertion of the words *free and unfettered elections* into the Yalta agreement on the postwar Polish government. Neither Churchill nor Roosevelt challenged a general Soviet sphere of influence covering Hungary, Rumania, Bulgaria, and Yugoslavia.

All parties regarded the agreements at Yalta as no more than the outline for a later settlement. But instead of proceeding toward a full-scale peace treaty, the Soviet Union and the United States each began reshaping the Yalta decisions to suit its own ends. Stalin made it clear that his candidates would have to be elected in Poland. Truman not only attacked Russia's coercion of Poland, but also challenged the entire concept of a Soviet sphere in Eastern Europe. Meanwhile the United States reconsidered the plans for a harsh peace in Germany. As a temporary measure, Germany had been divided into American, British, French, and Russian zones of military occupation. By treating these zones as self-contained administrative units, the United States was able to shield the Western industrial portions of Germany from most Soviet demands for reparations.

By summer, Soviet-American tensions had risen so high that any meeting between Stalin and Truman was in doubt. In July 1945, however, the two did confer at Potsdam, outside Berlin. Although they issued bland statements of unity and Stalin renewed a promise to declare war on Japan, it was an unhappy conference for both leaders. The crucial exchanges concerned Germany. Unable to find a common ground, the great powers accepted the separate position that each one already held. The Soviet Union could set its own policy in the Eastern zone of Germany; the United States, Great Britain, and France would determine policy in their Western zones. The divisive issue of German reparations was cast vaguely into the future. After Potsdam, neither Truman nor Stalin sought another summit meeting.

**The Iron Curtain Falls**

There were many other sources of Soviet-American friction in 1945 and 1946. Soviet annexation of Latvia, Lithuania, and Estonia in 1940 continued to trouble American opinion. Soviet actions turning Poland and Rumania into satellites and threatening to do the same to Hungary, Bulgaria, and Yugoslavia strengthened anti-Soviet feeling in the United States. At the San Francisco conference to found the United Nations, the Soviet delegates had come close to disrupting the proceedings. Stalin continued to view the United Nations as a league of potential enemies and often obstructed its work. Moreover, to contest American and British influence in the Middle East, Russia kept its troops in Iran and withdrew them early in 1946 only after strong protests and indications that the United States would send troops there. For its part, the United States abruptly ended economic aid to the Soviet Union immediately after Germany's defeat, despite Russia's desperate need for assistance. Bluntly, Truman made any future assistance dependent on a Soviet acceptance of American policies. In addition the United States excluded the Soviet Union from the occupation government of Japan, as it already had from the occupation government of Italy.

Yet each of these problems by itself was either negotiable or tolerable. Only the issues of Germany and Eastern Europe defied any accommodation. In what Soviet officials viewed as an assault on their vital interests, the Truman administration pursued a policy of reconciliation with Germany and demanded independent governments throughout Eastern Europe. The German zones rapidly became permanent Eastern and Western spheres; the Soviet Union tightened its authority over the Balkans. "From Stettin in the Baltic to Trieste in the Adriatic," Churchill somberly intoned in a speech of March 1946 at Fulton, Missouri, "an iron curtain has descended across the Continent." More and more stories of Soviet mass killings, deportations, and labor camps filtered through that curtain. Although there were moments of hope for a year after the Potsdam Conference, the main trend in Soviet relations ran strongly toward suspicion and anger. By the end of 1946, even the occasional hopes disappeared.

**American Rationale for Confronting the Soviets**

What led the United States to confront the Soviet Union in Europe? The answer, which politicians and (more recently) historians have argued about continually, has four parts. The most elusive element, but perhaps the most important, was a powerful tradition of mutual distrust. There was a natural inclination in both the United States and the Soviet Union to regard the other nation as the "communist" or the "capitalist" enemy. During the war people had become accustomed to thinking of the world as composed of two diametrically opposed philosophies—fascism and democracy. Now, by substituting "communism" for "fascism," many Americans assumed a simple response to a bewildering snarl of global problems. At the founding of the United Nations, the influential Republican Senator Arthur Vandenberg noted in his diary, "The basic trouble is that we are trying to unite two incompatible ideologies." Americans favored universalist or Wilsonian measures to inhibit postwar aggression, while the Soviets trusted only traditional power arrangements—alliances and spheres of influence. Moreover, because both Soviet and American leaders viewed their counterparts as inherently expansionist, feelings of distrust easily turned into fears of aggression. Understandably, there was little distinction in American minds between Hitler and Stalin as mass murderers. But in 1945 Stalin, ruling a decimated land, had little capacity to expand beyond Eastern Europe. It was the United States that filled the great vacuums of power in the Pacific, the Middle East, and Western Europe. Nevertheless, as power met power in the middle of Europe, each nation assumed the worst of the other, and Americans realistically assumed that Stalin was eager to subvert pro-Western regimes everywhere and replace them with pro-Soviet governments.

The second reason why the United States confronted the Soviets concerned American expectations following a victory. The United States, never before in a position of world supremacy, assumed that it would control the terms of a postwar settlement. An "American century" was dawning, declared *Time* magazine publisher Henry Luce. Policymakers could hardly resist acting as lords of the domain. After the war the United States made its own decisions on distributing American food abroad instead of relying on a neutral international relief agency (UNRRA), and Washington treated both the World Bank and the International Monetary Fund as instruments of American policy. Under the Baruch Plan of 1946, the United States offered to internationalize the control of atomic power only if America retained an indefinite monopoly and was assured that no other nation was developing its own atomic weapons. The Soviet Union hotly rejected the plan as no bargain at all. In this climate of national self-confidence, most Americans assumed that an able president could manage any international problem. Such a high level of popular expectations and low level of popular patience contributed to a hard line in foreign affairs in 1945 and 1946.

The third element in America's postwar policy was Truman's personal inclination toward a hard line. By temperament he was a fighter. In a characteristically Trumanesque way, the president wrote his secretary of state in January 1946, "I'm tired of babying the Soviets." Moreover, Truman took pride in his ability to reach a decision promptly, then hold to it firmly. After a meeting with J. Robert Oppenheimer over the moral implications of the atomic bomb, the president snapped: "Don't ever bring the damn fool in here again. He didn't set that bomb off. I did. This kind of snivelling makes me sick." With the unyielding, intensely suspicious, and aggressive Russians on one side and the pugnacious Truman on the other, the possibilities of a compromise were always slender.

Truman's advisers made the fourth contribution to America's postwar foreign policy. In his first months as president, Truman turned everywhere for advice on foreign affairs. The group of counselors whom he inherited from Roosevelt could not look at Truman without seeing the giant shadow of FDR behind him. Understandably, the new president allowed them to drop away one by one. Harry Hopkins, Roosevelt's most intimate aide, and Henry Wallace, now secretary of commerce, felt particularly unhappy about Truman's hard line with Stalin. By the fall of 1945 Hopkins lamented that "we are doing almost everything we can to break with Russia, which seems so unnecessary to me." After a long period of strain Wallace finally cut ties with the Truman administration in a major speech of September 1946: "'Getting tough' never brought anything real and lasting— whether for schoolyard bullies or businessmen or world powers. The tougher we get, the tougher the Russians will get."

Truman found more support among his former political associates from Congress. One of these, the conservative southern Democrat James F. Byrnes, became secretary of state in July 1945. Following an impressive career in Congress, on the Supreme Court, and as "assistant president" in charge of America's wartime mobilization, Byrnes took his new office with the attitude that he himself, not Truman, really should have been Roosevelt's successor. Although Byrnes was a firm anticommunist, he was also a bargainer, and he kept an element of flexibility in America's relations with the Soviet Union.

Discreetly at hand stood a third group of advisers, whose base of operations was the State Department. As America's world affairs increasingly demanded a wider range of diplomatic services, the State Department emerged as a significant center of government power, with extensive connections in those business, military, and publishing circles that affected its work. The expanding department attracted an able and strong-minded set of leaders, including W. Averell Harriman, the son of a railroad magnate and ambassador to the Soviet Union; George F. Kennan, a career diplomat with uncommon knowledge of the Soviet Union and special talents as a writer and planner; and Dean Acheson, a wellborn lawyer who had found his true calling in the State Department. Through such men as Harriman, Kennan, and Acheson, the department offered Truman something that his other advisers failed to provide: the outlines for a systematic world policy.

As the leaders in the State Department interpreted Soviet behavior, the Russians were following a long-term plan to destroy all capitalist societies. Communist ideology made them committed revolutionaries. Because of their terrible wartime losses and fears of future attacks, Soviet officials kept a large army mobilized after Germany's surrender. State Department leaders thought that if weakness in a neighboring country gave the Russians the opportunity, they would seize it. The Soviet army had already attempted such a probe in Iran. From its base in central Europe, the Soviet Union could strike the devastated, chaotic nations of Western Europe at any time. To counter this broad threat, the United States, too, needed a long-term plan. American power had to meet Soviet power on a global scale. Otherwise, as Harriman warned, the Russians would pursue their goal of world domination by continuing to build "tiers [of satellites], layer on layer," until they crushed the forces of freedom. Only firmness, or a policy of what Kennan in 1947 called "containment," could stop them. As the history of fascism proved, appeasement merely whetted a dictator's appetite. Kennan's moderate, restrained approach to the Soviets won high praise from most Americans eager for a sensible way of dealing with Moscow.

To meet the Soviet challenge, government officials saw the need for both a unified defense establishment to coordinate the armed services and an intelligence organization to deal with worldwide Soviet subversion. Consequently, in 1947 Congress passed the National Security Act creating the Department of Defense, headed by a secretary and subordinate secretaries of the army, navy, and air force. It also set up the National Security Council to advise the president on national security matters, and the Central Intelligence Agency, a successor to the wartime Office of Strategic Services, responsible for all spy activities. At the time these agencies seemed essential to defend the national interest, but few reckoned with the possibility that they would become a government within the government that saw little need to account for its actions to elected officials or function by traditional constitutional principles.

**From the Truman Doctrine to the Berlin Blockade**

With the United States hesitating at an important crossroads in its foreign policy, Truman stood ready to follow the State Department's guidance. In January 1947 Byrnes was replaced as secretary of state by General George Marshall, a man of flawless integrity, whose inexperience in foreign affairs made him rely heavily on the judgment of Assistant Secretary Dean Acheson. In February one of Roosevelt's four policemen, Great Britain, greatly weakened by its war effort, informed Washington that it was retiring from the force. American, not British, aid would have to save the conservative government in Greece, racked with civil war between communists and right-wing anticommunists. President Truman, addressing Congress in March on aid to both Greece and Turkey, dramatically announced the new "Truman Doctrine." "At the present moment in world history nearly every nation must choose between alternative ways of life," Truman declared. One way of life was freedom and democracy. Communism, Truman warned, was the alternative:

> The second way of life is based upon the will of a minority forcibly imposed upon the majority. It relies upon terror and oppression, a controlled press and radio, fixed elections, and the suppression of personal freedoms. I believe that it must be the policy of the United States to support free people who are resisting attempted subjugation by armed minorities or by outside pressure.

Truman gave special emphasis to the moral struggle between East and West, saying little about the fact that this was a major test case of containment. The objective was not to roll back communism but to hold the line against a soviet advance in Greece and Turkey which could jeopardize United States and Western European interests in an area of strategic importance.

Meanwhile the State Department was preparing strategy for a general European defense "against totalitarian pressures." Through the Marshall Plan, which took shape in the summer of 1947, America eventually sent more than $12 billion in aid to its European allies and enabled their shattered economies to achieve a minor miracle of recovery. Like the Truman Doctrine, the Marshall Plan aimed to prevent communist advances in Western Europe, where economic rehabilitation was needed to counter communist subversion. The Marshall Plan brought the United States an extraordinary amount of goodwill in Western Europe. Moreover, in July 1947 Washington made a formal commitment to rehabilitate West Germany as part of a "free Europe." Although the communist nations of Europe were officially invited to participate in the Marshall Plan, participation would require Russia to break its security system for Eastern Europe, something it was not willing to risk for another forty-two years. As American leaders expected, the Russians refused and demanded that their European allies refuse as well. Hungary in May, and then Rumania in December, fell totally under Soviet control. American trade with the Soviet Union, which had flourished in 1946, dwindled to a trickle.

In Czechoslovakia—the very symbol of liberated Europe—the Communist party precipitated political turmoil in February 1948 and took power in a virtual coup d'état. Communications across the Iron Curtain virtually ceased. That spring, rumors raced through Washington that a real war was imminent. Instead, between April and June 1948, the Soviet Union cut the transportation lines to Berlin, which lay deep within the Russian sector of Germany. Berlin, like Germany as a whole, was administered through zones. Now the American, British, and French zones within Berlin were under siege. The United States responded with an impressively organized airlift that brought essential supplies to the citizens in these isolated zones. In May 1949 the Russians finally abandoned the blockade. More than any other event, the Berlin blockade seemed to verify the Truman administration's warnings about Soviet aggression. Although some commentators saw Soviet actions in Czechoslovakia and Berlin as defensive reactions to the resurgence of German power, a substantial majority believed them to be a test of Western resolve to resist Soviet expansion. Consequently, American opposition to the Cold War collapsed, and anti-Soviet sentiments spread in Western Europe, where communists were ejected from the governments of France and Italy.

Another challenge to administration foreign policy came in the Middle East, where Jewish settlers struggled to establish a homeland in Palestine. State Department advisers, who during the war had steadfastly resisted all measures to aid Jews or even publish news reports about the Holocaust, counseled Truman against antagonizing oil-rich Arab states by recognizing a state of Israel. But the president gave prompt recognition in May 1948. A moral conviction that Jews deserved a homeland after the suffering of the Holocaust, that Zionism was an idealistic movement that would create a democratic Israel and a staunch American ally in a strategic area, and that Jewish votes might swing some states to the Democrats in the 1948 election influenced Truman's decision.

**The Election of 1948**    Troubles at home and abroad made Truman a poor bet for election in 1948, and most Democratic leaders prayed that he would not run for president. With little choice, less enthusiasm, and no hope, the national convention dutifully nominated him. Immediately after, two rival parties formed to attract the votes of dissident Democrats. The Progressive party, like earlier American parties of the same name, depended on the reputation of one man, Henry Wallace, who symbolized the New Deal liberalism at home and accommodation with the Soviet Union abroad. In Birmingham, Alabama, a new States' Rights Democratic party—the Dixiecrats— attracted southern leaders who feared an assault on southern race relations by the Truman administration. In 1946 the president had set up a highly distinguished Committee on Civil Rights, which issued a report in 1947 urging the enactment of federal antilynching, anti–poll tax and antisegregation laws. The Dixiecrats nominated Governor J. Strom Thurmond of South Carolina and dreamed of carrying the entire South.

The Roosevelt coalition, it seemed, was crumbling. Some of the warmest advocates of old New Deal ideas and Soviet-American cooperation attached themselves to Wallace's Progressive party, while the South, which had been a mainstay of FDR's coalition, seemed ready to abandon the Democrats for a conservative, sectional party. Above all, Truman faced a formidable Republican opponent in Governor Dewey of New York, who had done better against the indomitable Roosevelt in 1944 than any of the three Republican candidates who had preceded him. The only argument among the experts was the margin of Dewey's victory.

Truman made fools of the experts in 1948 because he responded so shrewdly to the prevailing disorganization in political and economic affairs. As important, he used the 1948 election to breathe new life into modern liberalism, identifying it with civil rights and a body of legislation—the Fair Deal—that represented an

**Truman on the National Ltd.**
*Truman's 1948 whistle-stop campaign, in which supporters urged him to "give 'em hell," led to his startling upset of Thomas Dewey.*

advance on FDR's reforms. In a nation of innumerable scattered interest groups and little vision of how to provide effective leadership, Truman filled the vacuum. Using a carefully devised strategy, the president shifted the blame for weak leadership to the Republican majority in the Eightieth Congress, which he scorned as the "Do-Nothing Congress." After the nominating conventions, he called Congress into special session and challenged the Republicans to enact their program. When little happened, the paralysis in public policy appeared to be specifically a Republican malady.

To attract voters, Truman compiled a long list of favors and promises. He reminded the unions that he had vetoed the Taft-Hartley Act of 1947 and that Republican votes had overridden him. He reminded business groups of tax benefits and government contracts. He promised subsidies for everything a farmer could produce. He recommended enlarging the TVA, increasing public housing, and broadening Social Security. He favored government aid to education. At the national convention in 1948, with Mayor Hubert H. Humphrey of Minneapolis leading the drive, the Democrats committed themselves to federal laws against job discrimination, lynching, and poll taxes. Truman not only endorsed this platform, but took the cause to Harlem, where no presidential candidate had ever campaigned. Even more striking, the president embarked in 1948 on the long, difficult course of desegregating the armed forces. In 1947, when Jackie Robinson joined the Brooklyn Dodgers, becoming the first black to play in the major leagues, it signaled the changing climate of opinion on racial discrimination in the country, which Truman both encouraged and reflected.

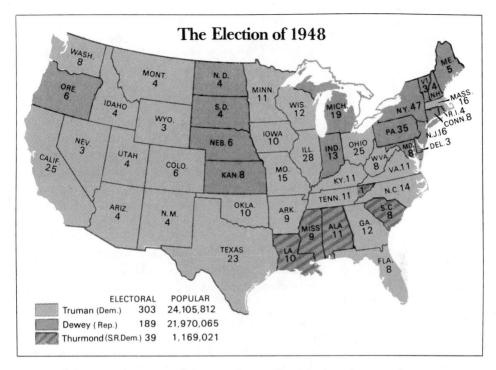

### The Election of 1948

| | ELECTORAL | POPULAR |
|---|---|---|
| Truman (Dem.) | 303 | 24,105,812 |
| Dewey (Rep.) | 189 | 21,970,065 |
| Thurmond (S.R.Dem.) | 39 | 1,169,021 |

Dewey took the high road, blandly promising a sound, sane administration. Voters judged him dull and pompous; they thought he looked like "the little man on the wedding cake" who could "strut sitting down." Truman, the Missouri bantam rooster, fought an arduous cross-country campaign, whistle-stopping his way across the country by speaking from the rear platform of a train and running for president like a country politician. His challenge to one audience summarized his message: "Vote your own interests." In 1948 Truman's old-fashioned provincial style proved highly effective. Meanwhile the deepening cold war with the Soviet Union eroded the Progressives' appeal and made Wallace appear to be the candidate of the Communist party. Truman's foreign policy was an important selling point with voters. On election day, only a stubborn handful voted the Progressive ticket. Thurmond kept only the four southern states that he had controlled in July. Truman, with 303 electoral votes to Dewey's 189, scored the most stunning upset in modern politics and instantly joined America's folk heroes in the grand old tradition of the underdog triumphant. Truman's victory meant that modern liberalism would live to fight another day with an expanded agenda for enactment in both the near- and long-term.

### Truman's Second Term, 1949–1953

Memories of FDR cast less of a shadow over Truman after he had been elected in his own right in 1948, freeing him to develop his own brand of liberalism—one that included civil rights reform, federal aid to education, and medical care for the aged. The hallmarks of his second administration, he decided, would be the Fair Deal—as he called his program—at home and the containment of communism abroad. Although Congress passed some of his domestic programs, the president fell well short of achieving the reforms he proposed, including the civil rights, education, and medical care measures. Despite these defeats, liberals, encouraged by Truman's ability to win the presidency without a solid South, were confident that they would eventually put across the whole Fair Deal program. Conservatives, by contrast, saw signs of waning interest in government activism and an affinity for old-fashioned verities as evidence that they would soon regain full control of the national government. One reason for Truman's relative lack of success in the four years after 1948, and for conservative hopes of resurgent power, was the turmoil that erupted over exaggerated fears of a domestic communist threat; another reason was the limited war in Korea that frustrated Americans, intensified their nationalism, and undermined Truman's popularity. Although Truman has subsequently been judged by many historians and the general public as a near-great president, he was vilified in his own day. He left office as one of the least popular chief executives in American history.

**The Fair Deal**     In 1946, amid the confusion of wartime demobilization and the jostling of interest groups, Truman had demanded that Congress make the maintenance of "full employment" a matter of urgent national priority. Public opinion had strongly backed the president, and thus Congress had responded with the Full Employment Act. But Congress had carefully avoided specifying how full employment was to be maintained. Nor had it undertaken any social reforms. The sprawling, government-oriented economy had been changing too rapidly, and neither the Democrats nor the Republicans had found a satisfactory technique for managing it.

Now, elected president in his own right, Truman announced a comprehensive domestic reform policy. It offered, he said, a "fair deal" for "every segment of our population and every individual." And Congress responded by passing the most progressive group of bills since 1938. It extended such New Deal measures as Social Security and the minimum wage, and it remedied substandard housing with the Housing Act of 1949.

But Congress also rejected much of Truman's program, turning aside all reform proposals that broke new ground. Federal aid to education, national health insurance, a Fair Employment Practices Commission (FEPC), a new system of crop subsidies, and the creation of TVA-style controls in the Columbia and Missouri river valleys—all went down to defeat. Not until the 1960s would other Democratic administrations finally fulfill the liberal agenda of the 1940s by enacting some of these measures.

Despite this resistance to expanding the federal government's role in managing domestic affairs, nothing could relieve the government of the responsibility it had assumed under FDR for general economic maintenance. No one could fail to recognize the intimate connection between government policy and the nation's phenomenal economic growth during the war. The gross national product (GNP) had risen a breathtaking 67 percent between 1941 and 1945. Government expenditures on domestic and defense programs accounted for an equally astonishing 40 percent of the GNP. The term *the government* became an everyday expression to designate this huge center of money and power. When the Congress enacted the Employment Act of 1946, it declared it the "responsibility of the Federal Government to use all practicable means...to promote maximum employment, production, and purchasing power." The act established a Council of Economic Advisers—experts charged with studying economic trends and proposing policies to the president to counter downturns in the business cycle. Although national expenditures dropped with the end of the war, they still remained six or seven times greater than in the 1930s and double the percentage of the GNP under the New Deal. The tax laws now bound almost all Americans into the government's financial network. By 1946 the national debt had also risen sevenfold above the level of 1939, and funding this giant debt automatically made the government the dominant force in the nation's credit system. Moreover, the Federal Reserve's board of governors in Washington now exercised far-reaching general control over the nation's monetary affairs.

The most promising means for managing the economy seemed to be through fiscal and monetary policy—the manipulation of tax and interest rates. If the economy faltered, the government could ease credit, lower taxes, and increase its deficit. If an economic boom threatened inflation, the government could tighten credit, raise taxes, and shrink the deficit. Fiscal policy at least minimized government interference with private groups or individuals, distributing its hardships and benefits impartially. The government's actions reflected the economic ideas Keynes had enunciated in the 1930s, but hardly anyone except some professional economists understood the new theory. Keynesianism did not even begin to reach a larger American audience until Paul Samuelson published the first edition of his famous undergraduate economics textbook in 1947.

Like most of his contemporaries in government, Truman did not understand Keynes and was not disposed to shape the government's fiscal powers into an acceptable public policy. He shared most Americans' general aversion to budget deficits and periodically led stern attacks on government spending. His secretary of the treasury regarded the national debt as simply an unfortunate government burden. Fiscal policy would not be used effectively until the 1960s.

Black rights was another issue on which the federal government could not avoid acting. Although Truman did not lead a general campaign for black rights during his second term, he did (partly propelled by the Korean War) end segregation in the armed forces and appoint the first black to the federal bench. More important, the NAACP joined with northern whites in an increasingly vigorous fight for equal rights. This alliance produced a string of FEPC laws in New York, New Jersey, Massachusetts, Connecticut, and other states, and an attack on racism through the courts. In *Smith* v. *Allwright* (1944) the Supreme Court had outlawed all-white primary elections in the South. In *Shelley* v. *Kramer*

(1948) it held that a racially restrictive covenant—an agreement between white homeowners not to sell to blacks—ran counter to the equal protection clause of the Fourteenth Amendment. Then in *Sweatt* v. *Painter* and *McLaurin* v. *Oklahoma State Regents* (1950) the Court voided state higher-education laws creating separate but equal facilities. The NAACP, behind its chief counsel, Thurgood Marshall, quietly prepared a legal assault on all segregated facilities.

**Anticommunism**     The issue that most strained the American social fabric at midcentury was not black rights, but anticommunism. A new wave of antiradicalism began to build after 1935, when enemies of the New Deal accused New Dealers of adopting communist ideas, and patriotic groups attacked the public schools for teaching radical doctrines. The House Committee on Un-American Activities (HUAC), established in 1938, gave lurid publicity to the charge that communists dominated the new industrial unions. Congress captured the spirit of this vague antiradicalism in the Smith Act of 1940, which set criminal penalties for teaching or advocating violent revolution, or for belonging to an organization that did either. Despite America's wartime alliance with the Soviet Union, anticommunist rhetoric remained fairly common during the early 1940s, and immediately after the war HUAC and numerous state antisubversive committees moved into action against an ever-widening range of expected dangers. The film industry became a particular focus of anticommunist concern. Convinced that communists were trying to control moviemaking as a means of brainwashing Americans, congressional anticommunists launched an attack on Hollywood writers and stars believed to be sympathetic to communism. The popular movie actor Ronald Reagan, then shifting his political allegiance from New Deal liberalism to postwar conservatism, supported a blacklist of Hollywood "subversives." For the next decade clouds of uncertainty enveloped thousands of Americans who had once advocated a reform and left a record or who had made an enemy. As one historian noted, "A perverse kind of democracy was practiced: all accusations, no matter from whom, were taken equally seriously." Reputations, friendships, and careers popped like bubbles at the prick of the charge "Communist!"

In 1947 the Truman administration declared international communism the enemy of the United States. Prominent Americans of both parties echoed the alarm. Throughout the nation—in government, in the labor unions, in the communications industries, in public and private education—a variety of oaths and reviews screened those suspected of communist sympathies. Using both the Smith Act and the new Internal Security Act of 1950, the Justice Department prosecuted some members of the Communist party and forced the rest to disband. After a dramatic series of public hearings, Alger Hiss, once a respected official in the State Department, was convicted of perjury in January 1950 for denying that he had passed government information to a Soviet agent. In June came the shock of the Korean War, precipitated by North Korea's invasion of South Korea, followed by arrests that eventually led to the execution of Julius and

Ethel Rosenberg as Soviet spies. America seemed to be a bulwark of anticommunism.

But within this apparent consensus lay two profoundly different kinds of anticommunism. One, which appeared in strength around 1947, sought to defend the United States against an international challenge: the Soviet Union, the league of communist countries it headed, and the espionage system it directed. Abroad this anticommunism tried to contain the power of the Soviet Union. At home it concentrated above all on communists in government, because the enemy's agent at a crucial spot in the government could seriously damage the nation's defense. Revelations about Alger Hiss greatly aggravated these worries.

The other anticommunism expressed the fears and frustrations of numerous ordinary Americans. To them "communism" meant a pervasive web of dangers that might appear in the guise of atheism, sexual freedoms, strange accents, civil rights, or whatever most threatened a particular group's sense of security. Although this anticommunism was also concerned with national defense and international conflict, it equated these issues with threats to traditional institutions and moral standards. The actual sources of danger might well be some of the leaders in national politics. Splintered, diffuse, and eruptive, this was the truly popular anticommunism. But however irrational, and however powerful its grip on the public, it would not have gained so much credibility without encouragement from public leaders. Some of these men and women genuinely shared the anxieties of the mass of Americans; some, however, saw an opportunity to advance their personal ambitions or public policies by associating anticommunism with fears of national change.

These two anticommunisms, one emphasizing power and the other emphasizing disturbing social innovations, were distinctly different. From a national vantage point, the many state and local committees that in the name of anticommunism attacked textbooks and library catalogues and civil libertarians were part of an aimless witch hunt. What possible relevance could these matters have to an international contest with Soviet communism? As one lawyer summarized the work of the Broyles Commission in Illinois, it "almost completely skirted... the operations of the Communist party in Illinois," and it failed totally "to cover evidence of actual subversion within the state." But such committees in Illinois, California, New York, Maryland, and elsewhere were not looking for that kind of communism. As the Broyles Commission stated, "Liberalism" was its enemy, and the educational system, the commission's primary target, was an excellent place to begin the battle. Sophisticated "Eastern internationalists" in the State Department were an equally logical target, especially after the Soviets exploded an A-bomb and China was "lost" to communism in 1949. Both developments were largely blamed on United States officials, particularly those responsible for making foreign policy.

In February 1950, a month after the conviction of Alger Hiss, an undistinguished first-term Republican senator from Wisconsin, Joseph McCarthy, elbowed forward to make anticommunism his personal crusade. For more

**Joseph McCarthy and Roy Cohn**
*Senator McCarthy enflamed and exploited anticommunist fears in the early 1950s.*

than four years this canny politician frightened government officials with charges of communist infiltration in their departments, staged melodramatic investigations of suspected enemy agents, exercised a powerful influence over government appointments, and won a nationwide following. McCarthy was the first politician to make effective use of national television, both in interviews and in broadcasts of his investigations. According to a poll early in 1954, three out of five Americans with an opinion about McCarthy favored his activities.

McCarthy opened his campaign by claiming that he had a list of authentic communists who were still employed by the State Department. Some thought he said 205. The senator later settled on 57. During Truman's administration McCarthy continued a scattergun attack on the State Department and helped to make "communism" a noisy issue in the elections of 1952. After Eisenhower's inauguration, McCarthy broadened his anticommunist fire until finally he hit the army itself early in 1954. Few politicians cared to risk an encounter with the Wisconsin slugger, because McCarthy quickly acquired an undeserved reputation for defeating his political enemies at the polls. Eisenhower also refused to engage him, saying privately, "I will not get into the gutter with that guy."

The key to McCarthy's success was his ability to raise fears over communists in government and fears over domestic subversion. McCarthy repeatedly claimed that the sole purpose of his investigations was the exposure of communist agents in high places, and after the Hiss conviction no one in Washington could lightly dismiss that possibility. As cool a head as Senator Taft endorsed McCarthy's freewheeling search for spies. When McCarthy failed to find any Soviet agents, however, he shifted his attack to the books that his suspects had written, the reforms that they had supported, and the people who had associated with them. McCarthy invariably spoke of communism as "godless" and usually discovered its American disciples among the well born, well educated, and well placed. Despite the special attention that McCarthy attracted, others used even more extreme language. "I charge that this country today is in the hands of a secret inner coterie which is directed by agents of the Soviet Union," declared Senator William Jenner of Indiana in 1952. Democrats, including Truman, contributed to the harsh anticommunist climate—in part to head off charges by such rabid extremists as Jenner and McCarthy that they themselves were part of the "communist conspiracy."

Still, McCarthy was the central figure in this unreasoning anticommunist outburst. Violating the customary procedures of the Senate, McCarthy called into question the personal integrity of his critics and branded them "gutless." The State Department, instead of selecting officials for their knowledge and skills, had to listen when it was told to "get rid of the alien-minded radicals and moral perverts." Years of such confusion in the standards of government eventually became intolerable. When McCarthy attacked the upper echelons of the army in 1954, his growing opposition in Washington began to organize. The turning point came when the senator and his aides disgraced themselves in the nationally televised Army-McCarthy hearings. In August 1954 the Senate created a select committee to review charges of senatorial misconduct against McCarthy, and that December, by a vote of 67 to 22, his colleagues condemned him for abuse of the Senate's rules. Without authority in the Senate, McCarthy faded into obscurity and died a few years later of chronic alcoholism.

**Containment**

As much as anything, McCarthy had used the continuing struggle with international communism in the years 1949–52 to exert his influence. The contest with Soviet power had grown even more intense in this period. To meet the threat, the Truman administration had completed negotiations for the North Atlantic Treaty, a pact for mutual assistance among twelve nations that was signed in April 1949.* Although the wording of the treaty was general, almost everyone interpreted it as the guarantee of American military support in case of a Soviet attack in Europe. In January 1949 Dean Acheson, the primary architect of Truman's European program, became secretary of state and received proper credit for this sweeping commitment of American power. Meanwhile the Federal Republic of Germany evolved from the Western zones of occupation and was set on its way to independence. To each of these steps, the Soviet Union responded with a countermeasure: first the German Democratic Republic in its Eastern zone, then the Warsaw Pact, a military league of Russia's European satellites.

---

*The eleven other nations were Belgium, Canada, Denmark, France, Great Britain, Iceland, Italy, Luxembourg, the Netherlands, Norway, and Portugal. By 1955, Greece, Turkey, and West Germany joined. Spain entered much later, after the Franco dictatorship ended.

With breathtaking speed, the United States had fundamentally changed its role as a peacetime world power. During the rise of fascism in the 1930s, the United States had withdrawn more and more tightly into the Western Hemisphere. Now, through the Truman Doctrine, the United States made an open-ended offer of assistance to nations everywhere in the world. Instead of demanding payment of its war debts, as the United States had done after World War I, the government devised the Marshall Plan to underwrite the economies of Western Europe. In 1940 even the fall of continental Europe had not brought the United States into World War II; in 1948 danger to the single city of Berlin threatened to trigger World War III. In 1927 Americans had shied away from a simple bilateral treaty with France renouncing war; in 1949 the North Atlantic Treaty placed eleven other nations under the shelter of American power. As the United States' first military alliance since the treaty of friendship with France in 1778, the agreement represented a decisive break with America's isolationist past.

Despite these profound changes, however, the United States still did not have a clear and detailed foreign policy. What areas of the world did the Truman Doctrine cover? Under Acheson's guidance the Truman administration concentrated on Europe and left the rest of the world in limbo. How did the United States plan to defend the nations that fell under its protection? No one expected American troops to be stationed throughout the world. Some people, including the influential columnist Walter Lippmann, hoped that American economic aid would enable groups of nations to organize their own regional leagues of defense. In his inaugural address of 1949, President Truman encouraged this kind of vision. "Point Four" of that address raised the possibility of exporting more technological skills and fewer weapons to the world's needy nations.

**Communist Gains**  Two critical events of 1949 underlined the importance of these unresolved problems. One occurred in Asia; the other, in the Soviet Union.

In Asia, Mao Zedong's communists swept through China, driving Chiang Kai-shek's tattered remnants to the island of Formosa (Taiwan). That civil war had been brewing during the years of the Chinese resistance to Japan. At times Chiang, America's East Asian ally in the Pacific war, seemed more concerned about his domestic enemy than his foreign foe. Even before the end of World War II, American officials had begun their futile attempts to mediate between Chiang's nationalists and Mao's communists. Special American missions, including a highly publicized one in 1945–46 under General Marshall, had warned Chiang about the corruption in his government, dangled the prospect of economic assistance before the two camps, and struggled to arrange a truce between their armies. Unwilling to force concessions from Chiang, yet unable to intervene effectively in his behalf, the United States had invested some military aid and much larger amounts of hope in his cause. By 1949 the Truman administration could take comfort only in the fact that nobody had guessed right on the matter of China. Stalin, like Truman, had bet that Chiang would win, and Moscow had provided Mao's forces with only limited aid. Publicly, the Soviets hailed the communist victory in China, but behind the scenes relations between the two Marxist regimes were tense from the start.

As the world's preeminent power, many argued, America could have saved China from communism—and according to the Truman Doctrine, they said, we should have. But we did not. With no basis in fact, these critics irrationally attributed the communization of China to American irresolution, possibly even to betrayal in high places. The air filled with bitter complaints about a vast territory and a huge population "lost" to the enemy. Adding China to the Soviet sphere in Eastern Europe indeed produced an appalling total effect. Simple maps traced the recent losses, and simple arithmetic summarized the human costs. In 1949, when Congressman Richard Nixon of California—already a prominent spokesman for Republican anticommunism—totaled the peoples inside and outside the communist domain, he concluded ominously that "in 1944...the odds were 9 to 1 in our favor. Today...the odds are 5 to 3 against us."

Before the communist victory in China, Americans had been comforted by the belief that people elsewhere, whenever free to choose, would select a political system similar to American democracy. The struggle against communism had continued, but many Americans had taken consolation in reassurances such as that by a sturdy liberal senator, Robert Wagner of New York, who had insisted that "history is on our side." In the administration's most cogent justification for the Truman Doctrine, George Kennan of the State Department had outlined with great foresight what would eventually happen if the United States were to apply steady, patient pressure along the perimeter of the communist sphere: in time the communist domain would erode from its own weakness, and gradually more and more people would select freedom. But the world would have to wait forty years for communism to fall apart. Meanwhile the communist revolution in China struck at the heart of this faith. For a quarter-century the United States refused to recognize the communist government of China, and many Americans clung to the belief that the Chinese, given a choice, would still follow the old warlord Chiang.

The second critical event of 1949 was the detonation of an atomic bomb by the Soviet Union. Since 1945 the American monopoly of atomic weapons had enabled the United States to expand its international commitments without spreading its military forces abroad. The Truman Doctrine seemed to say that American aid alone would protect its allies: American possession of the bomb would deter a large-scale Soviet intervention. A few months before the Soviets' atomic test, Secretary Acheson told the Senate Foreign Relations Committee that the North Atlantic Treaty Organization would require no more than token American soldiers in Europe. Truman gave this claim the ring of truth in 1949 by insisting on a reduced military budget. Before the Soviet acquisition of atomic weapons, no American leader seriously contemplated using the bomb; just having the bomb was enough.

How thoroughly the United States had relied on its monopoly of atomic weapons became clear after that monopoly was broken. Suddenly the United

States seemed terribly vulnerable. America's new security program for Europe no longer had teeth. In the scramble for alternatives, some government officials actually suggested a preemptive atomic strike at the Soviet Union. Moreover, if Soviet society was inherently inferior, as Americans had been repeatedly told, how had it manufactured its own bomb so soon? Spies must have stolen American secrets. The Federal Bureau of Investigation proceeded to uncover the communists Julius and Ethel Rosenberg, who were charged with passing information about the bomb to the Soviet Union. They were found guilty and executed. Judge Irving Kaufman, who sentenced the Rosenbergs to death in 1951, expressed the anger of a nation that had been stripped of its primary protection:

> Your conduct in putting into the hands of the Russians the A-bomb...has already caused, in my opinion, the Communist aggression in Korea, with the resultant [American] casualties exceeding fifty thousand and who knows but that millions more of innocent people may pay the price of your treason. Indeed, by your betrayal you undoubtedly have altered the course of history.

Responding to the heightened Soviet threat, in 1950 President Truman ordered the production of the hydrogen bomb, or the "super," as the new weapon was called. The administration also committed itself to the conclusions in NSC-68, the recommendations of the National Security Council that the government should mobilize congressional and public opinion behind greater defense spending.

**The Korean War**   The Korean War, which began in June 1950, completed America's global policy of "containment" and marked a revolution in American–East Asian relations. Before 1945 the United States was friendly toward China, at war with Japan, and uninterested in Korea. By 1950 it saw China as an enemy, Japan as an ally, and Korea as a testing ground for the survival of freedom from communist aggression.

In 1945, during the Soviet Union's brief war against Japan, Russian troops had moved across Manchuria into the Korean peninsula before American troops could land from the sea. The two armies had hastily agreed to occupy northern and southern halves of the peninsula, divided at the thirty-eighth parallel, until their governments could settle the fate of this Japanese colony. As in many other cases after the war, delays, Soviet-American tensions, and then the Cold War had transformed a momentary convenience into a permanent solution. Under the auspices of the United Nations, which had assumed responsibility for a Korean settlement, the United States had backed one government in South Korea. The Soviet Union had sponsored a rival government in North Korea. Each Korean government had claimed the whole of the peninsula, and each was itching to fight for it. Because Korea had little significance in the complex contest between the Soviet Union and the United States, neither power had closely supervised its dependent government before 1950.

After the United States made clear that South Korea did not hold a significant priority in its defense plans for Asia, superior North Korean forces invaded South

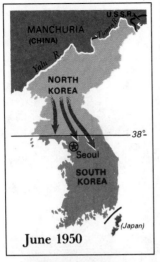

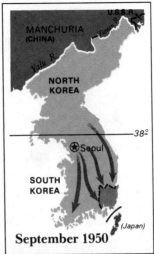

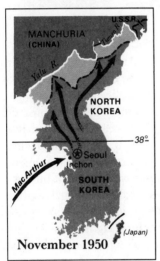

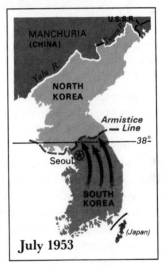

**The Shifting Front in Korea**

Korea in June 1950. Although the Truman administration had not prepared for a crisis in Korea, it fought back, asserting that failure to meet aggression in Korea might lead to World War III. Initially, the administration sent the South Koreans light reinforcements from Japan, which were driven to the southern tip of Korea and almost into the sea. But reinforcement of United States forces and a surprise attack in September behind North Korean lines at Inchon in South Korea broke the North Korean offensive and drove them back above the thirty-eighth parallel. The United States was now locked in a substantial land war, but Truman declared the fighting a police action and asked no declaration of war from Congress. His description of America's role in the fighting had been served by a United Nations Security Council resolution, passed in June after Russia had walked out of the

**New York-Herald Tribune
Reporter Marguerite Higgins
Interviews General Douglas
MacArthur**
*MacArthur's military leadership
initially turned the tide of battle
in Korea, but his insistence on
crossing the 38th parallel and
public demands for a wider war
led to battlefield reversals and
his dismissal.*

Council, endorsing intervention and putting America's cause under the authority of the United Nations. Officially, therefore, the United States did not fight a war in Korea; it cooperated in a United Nations police action.

The original purpose of American intervention had been protection of South Korea's territory. But once North Korean forces had been driven above the parallel, the administration, under pressure from MacArthur, decided to liberate North Korea and unify the entire Korean peninsula. Despite numerous warnings from Beijing that the invasion of North Korea would mean Chinese intervention, United States and South Korean forces pushed forward to the Yalu River bordering China. In response, large Chinese reinforcements surprised the American forces and drove them back below the thirty-eighth parallel. By early 1951 the war settled into a grudging, bloody struggle along the original boundary. Shortly after the inauguration of President Dwight Eisenhower in 1953, an armistice between the opposing armies more or less reestablished the division roughly along the thirty-eighth parallel. A formal peace never came. Over a million Koreans and Chinese and about 23,000 Americans had died in the conflict.

Although this limited war aroused widespread resentment in the United States, the range of opposition was quite narrow. Critics bandied about might-have-beens and should-have-beens that censured Truman and Acheson as shortsighted, fumbling leaders. But unlike the later Vietnam conflict, the Korean War almost never led to questioning of the appropriateness of American military intervention. Nor did the administration's critics rally much support for a big war against either China or Russia. The center of such ambitions was the imperious General MacArthur, whose bellicose and insubordinate behavior after China's entry into the war forced Truman to recall him from Korea in April 1951 and relieve him of his command. As the hero of two wars and the successful director of America's occupation government in postwar Japan, MacArthur received an adoring welcome home after his recall. As the advocate of Asian conquest, however, MacArthur won no important endorsements. Growing frustration over a limited war that dragged on with considerable loss of life undermined Truman's popularity, but, unlike Vietnam, the majority of Americans consistently ratified the president's policy in fighting it.

**The Election of 1952**  Truman's second term had run into a buzzsaw of difficulties. Unable to master a Congress that was dominated by rural conservatives who held strategic committee chairmanships, the president had to be content with limited legislative gains. Second, the Korean War, producing thousands of military casualties and sharp domestic inflation, created frustrations that undermined Truman's public support and ability to lead. Finally, in 1951–52, when evidence of corruption among Truman's associates and in the Justice Department sullied the administration's reputation, fewer than one in four Americans expressed approval of Truman's presidency.

Given the administration's unpopularity, Republicans looked toward the 1952 elections with high hopes for victories in both the presidential and the congressional contests. The two outstanding candidates for the Republican nomination were the brusque, efficient Robert Taft, son of former President William Howard Taft and leader of his party in the Senate, and Dwight D. Eisenhower, hero of World War II and favorite of the party's moderates. Taft had established a long record of opposition to Washington bureaucracies and government interference with business. As a practical politician, however, he had accepted the primary results of the New Deal and had acknowledged a government responsibility to protect the economy. Eisenhower, on the other hand, had established his record in the army, demonstrating an impressive talent for diplomacy as well as command. These qualities mattered very much at a tense, critical time in world affairs, and they contrasted with Taft's tendency to favor blunt, unilateral actions abroad. In a bitter contest Eisenhower defeated Taft for the Republican nomination. Despite Taft's impressive strength among party regulars, the Republicans could not resist an immensely popular war hero. As his running mate, Eisenhower chose Senator Richard M. Nixon of California, a highly partisan Republican with a reputation as a tough anticommunist who had led the effort to convict Alger Hiss.

The Democrats had more difficulty finding a candidate. A folksy campaign by the liberal Tennessee senator Estes Kefauver gave him an early lead in a crowded field, but Truman withheld his blessing. Instead the Democrats finally drafted the prudent, witty, and extremely eloquent governor of Illinois, Adlai E. Stevenson.

That fall Eisenhower overwhelmed Stevenson, whom many ordinary voters rejected as an "egghead" intellectual. Emphasizing the administration's failings in Korea, where he promised personally to go to end the fighting, and at home, where corruption and communist subversion struck responsive chords in the electorate, "Ike" transformed his radiant smile, unaffected manner, and heroic reputation into a landslide victory. He captured over 55 percent of the popular vote, and thirty-nine states to Stevenson's nine. In Congress, however, the Republicans managed to win only a slim margin in the House and a tie in the Senate. The victory was more a personal triumph for Eisenhower than an expression of faith in the Republican party.

## The American Spirit at Midcentury

With the outbreak of war in Europe in 1939, many Americans had sensed the coming of a new spirit of collective commitment to democratic values. After the attack on Pearl Harbor, the sense of a shared enterprise had spread throughout America. In ways that no government propaganda could have achieved, people linked all kinds of activities to a common cause: welding for the war effort, waking an hour early for the car pool, keeping tin cans for the scrap-metal drive, saving war stamps for a war bond. Factories were now pictured as vibrant centers of cooperation rather than as dreary mills of oppression. Intellectuals wrote confidently about "the public interest" as if everyone understood its meaning. For a brief period the individual seemed to require no special reinforcements.

Then, as soon as the war ended, the spirit of a common cause dissolved. The news told only of selfish strikers, business profiteers, and greedy farmers. The government seemed no more than an arena for squabbling interests. Where were the truly national goals? According to *The Best Years of Our Lives,* one of Hollywood's most acclaimed movies of the 1940s, the returning soldiers had to fight still another battle at home to preserve their dignity in an ungrateful society. In fact, what had the war meant? In its aftermath, total war raised questions about the threat of a technological barbarism that could no longer be attributed simply to the evils of fascism.

In these sobering postwar years, the question of the place of the individual in modern American society could be answered in four separate ways. Although each of the four was different, all dealt in some way with the clash between modern and traditional values, and all responded in some fashion to the problems and hopes of the vulnerable individual. Taken together these four answers outlined the central issues in modern American culture.

**The Achieving Individual**　　One answer was for the individual to learn the rules of the modern occupational system, abide by them, and succeed. The wartime economy had intensified the demand for greater numbers of specialists with higher levels of skill, and immediately after the war Americans turned to the schools to fulfill this demand. Bands of citizens campaigned to improve instruction in the basic skills. Funds flowed freely into the entire educational system. Between 1945 and 1950, expenditures in the public schools more than doubled; even more impressive, enrollment in higher education doubled. Just as the importance of the high school had dominated in the 1920s and 1930s, so the importance of higher education dominated the years after World War II. Now only colleges and graduate schools could satisfy a complex economy's need for specialized training. The greatest single impetus to college enrollment came from the GI Bill of 1944, which eventually subsidized the education of about 8 million former service people. Along with the sheer numbers it funded, the GI Bill helped to democratize opportunities in higher education—and hence eventually in the upper ranks of business and the professions as well.

In *Death of a Salesman* (1949), the young playwright Arthur Miller created a brilliant morality tale about using these broadening opportunities. Immediately acclaimed as one of America's greatest plays, Miller's drama provided a painful lesson on how to fail in modern America. The play's hero, Willy Loman, lived by a weakened, vulgarized version of the traditional American dream of success. Having chosen the career of salesmanship, which in the 1920s had seemed the right avenue to wealth and importance, Willy found himself trapped in humiliating failures and endless debts. Hoping that his sons might still succeed, he taught them the only values he knew—a personal style, a winning appearance, and an eye for the main chance. But this only left them athletic, shallow, and morally stunted. In contrast, Willy's neighbor had simply relinquished his son to America's system of specialized occupations, enabling the young man to become a successful lawyer with a warm, easy relationship with his father. The young man's success explained Willy's failure and ultimate suicide. Modern America's avenue upward had been there all the while, but Willy's dream had hidden the only legitimate path to success.

**The Humanistic Individual**

The second answer acknowledged that the individual would have to find an anchor of values outside science. Like the earlier critics of America's machine culture, a variety of intellectuals, educators, and publicists now warned that science and technology by themselves were amoral. Each person, they said, must find the fundamental principles in civilized life, and only the humanists—the philosophers and poets and theologians—could lead that search.

Questing for basic values became a nationwide preoccupation in the late 1940s. Some scholars explored the American past to discover its essentially American qualities, giving special attention to such brooding spirits as Thoreau, Melville, and the Puritans. Others examined the far richer resources of the Western tradition. Adults enrolled in well-attended classes on the "Great Books" of Western civilization. In colleges throughout the country, new and often required courses tried to distill wisdom not only from a long span of time, but also from a breadth of subjects such as an interdisciplinary examination of American culture or a humanistic understanding of science.

The fascination with fundamentals produced a strong reaction against the pragmatist's faith in an experimental, evolving truth. John Dewey, who more than any other intellectual leader was identified with a scientific method of ethics, became a particular target of attack in the late 1940s. Dewey's critics wanted certainties in place of his open-ended pursuit of truth. In foreign policy, for example, they sought to define a single unwavering "national interest" to guide America's international affairs. In civil liberties, they assigned to the freedoms of the First Amendment an absolute, timeless meaning that no judiciary (they asserted) should ever alter.

Critics of Dewey's scientific relativism accused its adherents of arrogance as well as fuzziness. The human mind, they claimed, was incapable of solving all the world's problems through a scientific method. This line of opposition found its most effective spokesman in the theologian Reinhold Niebuhr, who believed that all actions reflected an inevitable human fallibility and all choices involved moral risks. Nevertheless individuals had a moral responsibility to choose among alternatives and to act on their choices. The necessity of choosing from an inherently imperfect knowledge defined the human predicament. Niebuhr, supporting the containment of international communism, lectured Americans that "it is not easy . . . for an adolescent nation, with illusions of childlike innocency, to come to terms with the responsibilities and hazards of global politics." Yet meet them it must. Americans had to abandon their simple faith in man-made progress, face each situation as it arose, and, without arrogance, commit themselves to a course that might best fulfill their moral obligations.

**The Heroic Individual**

The third postwar answer defiantly championed the sovereign individual. Setting the individual at odds with modern society, it told him to overcome the dangers around him through his interior powers. In a few instances this answer was addressed to the specialist. Ayn Rand's best-selling novel *The Fountainhead* (1943), for example, glorified the right of the creative professional to discard society's ordinary rules in order to realize his genius, and in the postwar years Rand cults mushroomed on college campuses. Usually, however, the hero had no special training and no resources except his hard inner core. During the 1940s a mass audience learned about this kind of hero through a host of movies, particularly those starring Humphrey Bogart and Gary Cooper, and through a flood of inexpensive paperbacks that suddenly deluged drugstores and newsstands.

Soon after the publication of his first book in 1947, Mickey Spillane became undisputed king of the new paperback market. In less than a decade, 30 million copies of his novels had sold, a record that far surpassed any competitor's. His hero was a tough, resourceful private detective named Mike Hammer, who radiated an irresistible power. Although Spillane drew on a full tradition of fantasies about the all-conquering individual, he more than any of his predecessors gave them a contemporary urban setting pervaded by corrupt, ominous forces. Breaking free from this threatening urban jungle required an exceptional courage. Those who succeeded, however, became true individuals and survived. The number of Spillane's imitators, even more than the sale of his books, indicated that his, of all the postwar answers, found the widest audience.

**The Desperate Individual**

The fourth postwar answer was the acceptance of despair that threatened to destroy the individual. In the late 1940s Americans were listening for the first time to those Europeans who had already peered inside a soulless society and found no individuals there. Suddenly relevant were the prewar Czech writer Franz Kafka's nightmares of man as a nameless subject wandering through a fathomless system to a death he came to welcome, and the disturbing accounts of a devouring social organization in Aldous Huxley's *Brave New World* (1932), Arthur Koestler's *Darkness at Noon* (1941), and George Orwell's *1984* (1949). Because Koestler and Orwell were describing communist totalitarianism, Americans had a choice of reading their books as justifications for a free Western society. Instead many Americans used them as a frame of reference for discussing the dangers in their own lives.

World War II, as writers viewed it in retrospect, contributed significantly to this new spirit of despair. The best of the American war novels—Norman Mailer's *The Naked and the Dead* (1948), Irwin Shaw's *Young Lions* (1948), and James Jones's *From Here to Eternity* (1951)—did not simply surround their characters with danger, as the war novels of the 1920s had done. Now individuals were sucked into the very center of destruction, and all characters were equally exposed to the stray bullet. No personal choice or inner strength affected these human specks that were being tossed by the fates.

Above all, the Holocaust and "The Bomb" posed the most profoundly disturbing problems of the postwar years. Had the Germans, in systematically destroying 6 million human beings, discovered an essential truth about the impersonal mobilization of power in modern society? And what of the American atomic bombs that had demolished Hiroshima and Nagasaki? Through the development and use of the bomb, scientific genius and human annihilation were juxtaposed so sharply, the concept of civilization was so directly challenged, and the terrors of nuclear death were so vividly imprinted on the minds of Americans that even the most resolute Americans were unable to express its import.

The uniquely American way of expressing despair about the individual's lot appeared in a new image, "the Southern." In 1949 the southerner William Faulkner, with his finest writing already behind him, received the Nobel prize for literature, and a favorite intellectual game of the late 1940s was unraveling the family histories in Faulkner's "Yoknapatawpha County," the fictional Mississippi setting for his greatest works. A year earlier the young Tennessee Williams had won a Pulitzer prize for *A Streetcar Named Desire,* which with another dramatic success in the 1940s established him as a leading playwright. These two, along with other gifted southern writers such as Carson McCullers and Flannery O'Connor, created a shockingly new American image.

Understanding the Southern depended on an appreciation of the Western, for intentionally or not, the Southern was a systematic attack on America's oldest myth of individual strength. In the Western, one man entered an open plain where he confronted a direct challenge, and by a clear moral choice he overcame it. He was the pure individual: a man alone, a man of simple, sovereign convictions, a man of action whose problem, once met, dissolved in a cleansing rite of violence. Not only had the movies, the radio, comics, and pulp fiction expanded the audience for this myth since the 1920s; such thoughtful writers as Hemingway had borrowed from it. The Western hero continued to stand tall in postwar America.

Like the Western, the Southern also used a regional stereotype to communicate a national message. Just as countless Americans associated the West with a new, formless land, many regarded the South as a decaying, backward region. This popular caricature helped southern writers reach a national audience. In contrast to the Western's openness, the world of the Southern was a suffocating prison—a town or household or room in which the inmates were held by invisible shackles they could never break. This world was filled with human vulnerability: children caught in a whirl of adult terror and adults locked in a desperate battle for sanity. These struggles, unlike the gunfights of the Western, showed women managing more effectively than men. Maleness and impotence were common companions in the Southern.

Where the Western hero acted, the characters in the Southern talked. They stabbed one another with words, searched in vain for the meaning of their lives through words, and covered their own anguish with words. Occasionally someone's hopelessness or passion would explode in violence, but violence only complicated the problems that no one would ever resolve. In *A Streetcar Named Desire,* Tennessee Williams let loose a caricature of the Western hero, the physical-sexual-nonverbal Stanley Kowalski, and he wrecked the fragile human defenses around him. Perhaps only a small minority listened carefully to the agonizing message of the Southern. Nevertheless an exceptionally talented cluster of American writers was finally probing fundamental questions about the individual's chances for survival.

No one caught the special despair of black Americans in the postwar years better than the brilliant novelist Ralph Ellison. In his novel *Invisible Man* (1952), Ellison cried out against the dehumanization and loss of individuality suffered by blacks in white America. Ellison's hero struggles against an impersonal world that refuses to let him establish his own identity. "I was looking for myself and asking everyone except myself questions which I, and only I, could answer," the central character of the novel declares. The Invisible Man's odyssey was a commentary on everyone's loss of control over individual destiny. Urged by a black college president to lie to and grovel before white benefactors, pressed by communists to subject himself to party discipline, urged by the hospital he enters to cure his "abnormality" to accept a frontal lobotomy, Ellison's hero faces institutional forces, programmed responses to all his strivings for a separate self. His life is a form of imprisonment in which his only solace is an inner being that balks against his and everyone else's conformity to external controls.

At midcentury one phase in the creation of modern culture was ending. An elaborate framework of modern values relating to occupational specialization, personal freedom, and mass manipulation lay across the top of American society. Beneath it a complex pattern of traditional values simultaneously resisted and assimilated these modern ways. The long-overlapping frontier between the two spheres did not alter their basically antagonistic orientations. Hence the range of answers to a problem common to both—the fate of the individual—revealed a wide diversity of standards, aspirations, and doubts. A distant viewer might well wonder if Arthur Miller's Achieving Man, Reinhold Niebuhr's Moral Man, Mickey Spillane's Tough Man, and Ralph Ellison's Invisible Man all belonged to the same human race. To maintain the uneasy coexistence among these conflicting beliefs required a good deal of mutual tolerance—or mutual indifference. Whether an increasingly nationalized American society would contain such leeway became a crucial question in the next quarter-century.

## CHRONOLOGY

| | |
|---|---|
| **1941** Roosevelt bans racial discrimination in government and defense hiring.<br>FDR and Churchill meet in Atlantic Conference to prepare Anglo-American alliance.<br>Japanese forces attack Pearl Harbor, bringing America into World War II. | Bretton Woods Conference on international monetary stabilization.<br>Roosevelt reelected president for an unprecedented fourth term. |
| **1942** Japanese Americans moved to "relocation centers."<br>Revenue Act expands graduated income tax.<br>Government wage, price, and rent controls established.<br>Operation Torch, Allied invasion of North Africa.<br>American troops driven from Philippines.<br>United States inflicts first major defeat on Japan at battle of Midway. | **1945** Yalta Conference.<br>Roosevelt dies; Harry S Truman becomes president.<br>U.N. charter signed by forty-seven nations.<br>Germany surrenders.<br>Potsdam Conference.<br>United States drops atomic bombs on Hiroshima and Nagasaki in Japan.<br>Japan surrenders. |
| **1943** Allied invasion of Italy.<br>FDR, Churchill, and Stalin meet at Teheran. | **1946** Republicans win control of Congress. |
| **1944** Operation Overlord, Allied invasion of France. | **1947** Truman Doctrine calls for containment of communism.<br>Marshall Plan sends massive aid to Europe.<br>Department of Defense and Central Intelligence Agency established by National Security Act.<br>Taft-Hartley Act restricts actions of labor unions. |

| | | | |
|---|---|---|---|
| **1948** | Berlin blockaded by Soviets; United States organizes airlift. Truman elected president. | | Senator Joseph McCarthy launches anticommunist crusade. Korean War begins. |
| **1949** | NATO established. Soviet Union detonates atomic bomb. Communist government controls China. | **1951** | Twenty-second Amendment limits presidents to two terms. |
| | | **1952** | Dwight D. Eisenhower elected · president. |
| **1950** | Alger Hiss convicted of perjury in relation to espionage charges. | **1953** | Rosenbergs executed as spies. Armistice in Korea. |

## Suggested Readings

Gordon Wright, *The Ordeal of Total War, 1939–1945* (1968), gives an overview of the European theater in World War II. Ronald Spector, *Eagle Against the Sun: The American War with Japan* (1985), is the best one-volume study of America's Pacific war. A. Russell Buchanan, *The United States in World War II* (2 vols., 1964), details America's military activities in both the European and the Pacific theaters; and Martha Byrd Hoyle, *A World in Flames* (1970), covers them more briefly. A famous naval historian, Samuel Eliot Morison, tells of the conflict at sea in *The Two-Ocean War* (1963). Morison's *Strategy and Compromise* (1958) and Kent Roberts Greenfield's *American Strategy in World War II: A Reconsideration* (1963) evaluate broad questions of military policy. Forrest C. Pogue, *George C. Marshall* (4 vols., 1963–87), is the most authoritative biography. Ed Cray, *General of the Army: George C. Marshall: Soldier and Statesman* (1990), is the best one-volume life. Stephen E. Ambrose, *The Supreme Commander: The War Years of General Dwight D. Eisenhower* (1970), contains valuable insights. On MacArthur, see William Manchester, *American Caesar: Douglas MacArthur, 1880–1964* (1978), and the more critical book by Michael Schaller, *Douglas MacArthur: The Far Eastern General* (1989). On foreign relations, Gaddis Smith's *Diplomacy during the Second World War, 1941–1945* (1965) is a convenient introduction. Herbert Feis, *Churchill, Roosevelt, and Stalin* (1957), and Robert Beitzell, *The Uneasy Alliance: America, Britain, and Russia, 1941–1943* (1972), examine the critical issues besetting the grand alliance.

Three fine books—Diane Shaver Clemens, *Yalta* (1970); Robert A. Divine, *Second Chance: The Triumph of Internationalism in America during World War II* (1967); and Michael Sherry, *Preparing for the Next War: American Plans for Postwar Defense, 1941–45* (1977)—chart paths into the postwar years. William Roger Louis, *Imperialism at Bay: The United States and the Decolonization of the British Empire* (1978), and Christopher Thorne, *Allies of a Kind: The United States, Britain, and the War Against Japan, 1941–1945* (1978), are also useful. For the development of the atomic bomb, see Richard G. Hewlett and Oscar E. Anderson, *The New World* (1962). Martin J. Sherwin, *A World Destroyed* (1975), Barton J. Bernstein, ed., *The Atom Bomb* (1976), and Gregg Herken, *The Winning Weapon: The Atomic Bomb in the Cold War, 1945–1950* (1980), explore its international implications. Paul Boyer, *By the Bomb's Early Light* (1986), studies the effect of the bomb on American culture.

Specifically on the president's leadership, the concluding volume of James MacGregor Burns's biography, *Roosevelt: The Soldier of Freedom* (1970), and Robert Dallek, *Franklin D. Roosevelt and American Foreign Policy, 1932–1945* (1979), are basic. Robert Divine's *Roosevelt and World War II* (1969) is a keen and generally favorable appraisal. David Wyman provides a critical appraisal of FDR's response to the Holocaust in *The Abandonment of the Jews: America and the Holocaust, 1941–1945* (1984). An analysis of the press and the Holocaust is in Deborah E. Lipstadt, *Beyond Belief: The American Press and the Coming of the Holocaust, 1933–1945* (1986). Valuable material on two of Roosevelt's advisers appears in Robert E. Sherwood, *Roosevelt and Hopkins* (rev. ed., 1950), and John Morton Blum, ed., *From the Morgenthau Diaries: Years of War, 1941–1945* (1967). Lloyd C. Gardner, *Architects of Illusion: Men and Ideas in American Foreign Policy, 1941–1949* (1970), is a perceptive essay on the men who won control of America's foreign policy; and Thomas G. Patterson, ed., *Cold War Critics: Alternatives to American Foreign Policy in the Truman Years* (1971), is a collection of essays on the men who lost. Additional information on the shapers of American policy appears in George Curry, "James F. Byrnes," in volume 14 of *American Secretaries of State and Their Diplomacy* (1965); Robert H. Ferrell, *George C. Marshall* (1966), which is volume 15 of the same series; Gaddis Smith, *Dean Acheson* (1972), which is volume 16; and Arnold A. Rogow, *James Forrestal* (1964), a study of the first secretary of defense. The writings of participants themselves include these particularly useful books: Harry S. Truman, *Memoirs* (2 vols., 1955–56); Dean Acheson, *Present at the Creation* (1969); Lucius Clay, *Decision in Germany* (1950); George F. Kennan, *Memoirs, 1925–1950* (1967); and Arthur H. Vandenberg, Jr., ed., *The Private Papers of Senator Vandenberg* (1952).

The history of the Cold War is a caldron of controversy. Judicious guides are John Lewis Gaddis, *The United States and the Origins of the Cold War, 1941–1947* (1972), *Strategies of Containment* (1982), *The Long Peace: Inquiries into the History of the Cold War* (1987), and *Russia, the Soviet Union and the United States: An Intrepretive History* (2d ed., 1990); and Hugh Thomas, *Armed Truce: The Beginnings of the Cold War, 1945–1946* (1987). Walter LaFeber, *America, Russia, and the Cold War, 1945–1984*, 5th ed. (1985), is critical of American policy. For a pungent taste of the battle, however, read on the one hand Herbert Feis, *From Trust to Terror: The Onset of the Cold War, 1945–1950* (1970), the last in his series of volumes explaining modern American diplomacy; and on the other hand Gabriel Kolko, *The Politics of War: The World and United States Foreign Policy, 1943–1945* (1968), and Joyce and Gabriel Kolko, *The Limits of Power: The World and United States Foreign Policy, 1945–1954* (1972), a thorough condemnation of Washington's policies. Louis J. Halle, *The Cold War as History* (1967), and Adam B. Ulam, *The Rivals: America and Russia Since World War II* (1971), are balanced accounts.

Several careful studies add substantially to our knowledge of the crucial issues dividing the United States and the Soviet Union: Lynn Etheridge Davis, *The Cold War Begins: Soviet-American Conflict over Eastern Europe* (1974); George C. Herring, Jr., *Aid to Russia, 1941–1946* (1973); Bruce Kuklick, *American Policy and the Division of Germany* (1972); and especially Thomas G. Paterson, *Soviet-American Confrontation* (1973). On problems that hardened the pattern of the cold war, see Joseph I. Lieberman, *The Scorpion and the Tarantula: The Struggle to Control Atomic Weapons, 1945–1949* (1970); W. Phillips Davison, *The Berlin Blockade* (1958); Robert E. Osgood, *NATO* (1962); Bruce R. Kuniholm, *The Origins of the Cold War in the Near East* (1980); Michael B. Stoff, *Oil, War, and American Security* (1980); Lawrence Wittner, *American Intervention in Greece, 1943–1949* (1982); Laurence S. Kaplan, *The United States and NATO* (1984); Deborah Larson, *Origins of Containment* (1985); Francis Harbutt, *The Iron Curtain* (1986); and Michael Hogan, *The Marshall Plan* (1987). On the United States and Israel, see Cheryl Rubenberg, *Israel and the American National Interest* (1986).

The origins and the course of America's postwar policy in East Asia are discussed in Michael Schaller, *The American Occupation of Japan* (1985); William Head, *America's China Sojourn* (1983); Russell Buhite, *Soviet-American Relations in Asia, 1945–1954* (1982); William W. Stueck, Jr., *The Road to Confrontation: American Policy Toward China and Korea, 1947–1950* (1981); Akira Iriye, *The Cold War in Asia* (1974); Kenneth E. Shewmaker, *Americans and Chinese Communists, 1927–1945* (1971); and Tang Tsou, *America's Failure in China, 1941–1950* (1963). For background on the Korean War, see Leland M. Goodrich, *Korea: A Study of U.S. Policy in the United Nations* (1956); Glenn D. Paige, *The Korean Decision* (1968); and Bruce Cummings,

*The Origins of the Korean War* (1980), and ed., *Child of Conflict: The Korean-American Relationship, 1943–1953* (1983). For the fighting, see Burton Kaufman, *The Korean War* (1986). The policy struggles accompanying the war are discussed in John W. Spanier, *The Truman-MacArthur Controversy and the Korean War* (1959), and Trumbull Higgins, *Korea and the Fall of MacArthur* (1960). Several of the books mentioned above, including the ones on MacArthur, also discuss his conflict with Truman. The indefatigable journalist I. F. Stone raises some intriguing questions in *Hidden History of the Korean War* (1952).

The domestic side of World War II has received much less attention from historians. Richard Polenberg, *War and Society: The United States, 1941–1945* (1972), provides a useful overview, which should be supplemented by his *One Nation Divisible: Class, Race, and Ethnicity in the United States Since 1938* (1980); and John Morton Blum, *V Was for Victory: Politics and American Culture During World War II* (1976), offers penetrating insights. Other overviews are Richard Lingeman, *Don't You Know There's a War On? The American Home Front, 1941–1945* (1970); Mark Harris et al., *The Homefront* (1984); and Studs Terkel, *"The Good War": An Oral History of World War II* (1984). Two fine specialized studies are Harold Vatter, *The American Economy in World War II* (1985), and Clayton Koppes and Gregory Black, *Hollywood Goes to War* (1987). Joel Seidman, *American Labor from Defense to Reconversion* (1953), deals primarily with government policy. William Henry Chafe, *The American Woman: Her Changing Social, Economic, and Political Roles, 1920–1970* (1972), includes a valuable discussion of women in the wartime economy, as do Karen T. Anderson, *Wartime Women: Sex Roles, Family Relations, and the Status of Women during World War II* (1981), and Ruth Milkman, *Gender at Work: The Dynamics of Job Discrimination by Sex During World War II* (1987). Leila Rupp and Verta Taylor, *Survival in the Doldrums: The American Women's Rights Movement, 1945 to the 1960s* (1987), and Elaine Tyler May, *Homeward Bound: American Families in the Cold War Era* (1988), are valuable studies. Roland A. Young, *Congressional Politics in the Second World War* (1956), reviews the legislative record. Davis R. B. Ross, *Preparing for Ulysses* (1969), explains the GI Bill, and Stephen K. Bailey, *Congress Makes a Law* (1957), analyzes the Full Employment Act.

A growing literature examines the place of racial minorities in modern America. Two surveys—John Hope Franklin, *From Slavery to Freedom* (3d ed., 1969), and August Meier and Elliott M. Rudwick, *From Plantation to Ghetto* (rev. ed., 1970)—ably cover the years after 1920. Neil A. Wynn, *The Afro-American and the Second World War* (1976), and A. Russell Buchanan, *Black Americans in World War II* (1977), are the best monographs on the subject. Phillip McGuire, ed., *Taps for a Jim Crow Army: Letters from Black Soldiers in World War II* (1982), and Richard M. Dalfiume, *Desegregation of the United States Armed Forces* (1969), trace the history of blacks in the military during and immediately after World War II and the most striking public gain for blacks during the Truman years. In *Black Bourgeoisie* (1957), E. Franklin Frazier offers a sharp analysis of relatively well-to-do blacks. Wartime racial strife in the United States is analyzed in Dominic Capeci, Jr., *The Harlem Race Riot of 1943* (1977), and *Race Relations in Wartime Detroit* (1984). On Mexican Americans, see Mauricio Mazon, *The Zoot-Suit Riots* (1984). Roger Daniels, *Concentration Camps, USA* (1971), is a brief study of the persecution of Japanese Americans during World War II; Jacobus ten Broek et al., *Prejudice, War and the Constitution* (1954), provides many of the details; and Michi Weglyn, *Years of Infamy* (1976), expresses the feelings of the prisoners.

For Truman's administration, see Cabell Phillips, *The Truman Presidency* (1966), a reasonable introduction; Robert J. Donovan, *The Presidency of Harry S Truman* (2 vols., 1977, 1982); Robert Ferrell, *Harry S Truman and the Modern American Presidency* (1983); and Donald R. McCoy, *The Presidency of Harry S Truman* (1984). Merle Miller, *Plain Speaking: An Oral Biography of Harry S. Truman* (1974), helps to reveal the president's quality of mind. A considerably more sophisticated study, Alonzo L. Hamby's *Beyond the New Deal: Harry S.*

*Truman and American Liberalism* (1973), analyzes the place of the administration in a modern democratic tradition. A good place to begin exploring the election of 1948 is Samuel Lubell, *The Future of American Politics* (1952). Susan M. Hartmann, *Truman and the 80th Congress* (1971), covers important background in Washington. The meaning of Henry A. Wallace's third-party candidacy is evaluated in Norman D. Markowitz, *The Rise and Fall of the People's Century* (1973). V. O. Key, Jr., *Southern Politics in State and Nation* (1949), is a mine of information on its subject, and Robert A. Garson, *The Democratic Party and the Politics of Sectionalism, 1941–1948* (1974), is a useful supplement. Careful studies on particular areas of public policy include Jack Ballard, *The Shock of Peace: Military and Economic Demobilization after World War II* (1983); William C. Berman, *The Politics of Civil Rights in the Truman Administration* (1970); and Richard O. Davies, *Housing Reform During the Truman Administration* (1966). Allen J. Matusow's *Farm Policies and Politics in the Truman Years* (1967) makes a thorough assessment in its field. More critical appraisals of the president appear in Barton J. Bernstein, ed., *Politics and Policies of the Truman Administration* (1970), especially the essays by Bernstein himself.

No domestic subject since the New Deal has attracted such scholarly attention as the anticommunist issue after World War II. Robert Griffith and Athan Theoharis, eds., *The Specter: Original Essays on the Cold War and the Origins of McCarthyism* (1974), Earl Latham, *The Communist Controversy in Washington* (1966), and Walter Gellhorn, ed., *The States and Subversion* (1952), suggest the wide range of topics and interests that were involved. Thomas Reeves, *The Life and Times of Joe McCarthy* (1982), Michael Oshinsky, *A Conspiracy So Immense: The World of Joe McCarthy* (1983), and Peter Steinberg, *The Great "Red Menace": United States Prosecution of American Communists, 1947–1952* (1984), are recent important studies. Athan Theoharis, *Seeds of Repression* (1971), and Richard M. Freeland, *The Truman Doctrine and the Origins of McCarthyism* (1972), place a heavy responsibility for the rise of popular anticommunism on the Truman administration, and Alan D. Harper, *The Politics of Loyalty: The White House and the Communist Issue, 1946–1952* (1969), significantly tempers that judgment. Robert Griffith, *The Politics of Fear* (1970), analyzes McCarthy's sources of power in the Senate. In *The Intellectuals and McCarthy* (1967), Michael Paul Rogin blames conservative academicians for inflating the record of McCarthy's popular appeal, and Mary Sperling McAuliffe, *Crisis on the Left: Cold War Politics and American Liberals, 1947–1954* (1978), traces the capitulation of her subjects. On the most sensational espionage cases, see Walter and Miriam Schneir, *Invitation to an Inquest* (1965), and Ronald Radosh and Joyce Milton, *The Rosenberg File* (1983), which explore the Rosenberg case; as well as Allen Weinstein, *Perjury! The Hiss-Chambers Conflict* (1978). Fine additions to the literature on McCarthyism, Hoover, and anticommunism in general are Stanley I. Kutler, *The American Inquisition: Justice and Injustice in the Cold War* (1982); Nancy Lynn Schwartz, *The Hollywood Writers' War* (1982); Larry Ceplair and Steven Englund, *The Inquisition in Hollywood* (1983); Ellen W. Schrecker, *No Ivory Tower: McCarthyism in the Universities* (1986); Richard G. Powers, *Secrecy and Power: The Life of J. Edgar Hoover* (1987); and Athan Theoharis and John Stuart Cox, *The Boss: J. Edgar Hoover and the Great American Inquisition* (1988).

# 31

# Conformity and Conflict

## The Modern Republic Under Eisenhower

⌒

$\mathcal{T}$HE 1950s stand out in recent American history as a more conservative, less tumultuous period than the two decades that preceded it and the one that followed. The rapid economic growth and worldwide economic dominance that the United States achieved produced widespread national affluence. Weary of the public concerns that had plagued their lives for twenty years, most Americans preferred private absorptions. Emphasizing similarities rather than differences, they tended to insist on conformity as the national style. *Togetherness* and *belongingness* became popular catchwords. A 1950s best-seller, William H. Whyte's *The Organization Man,* deplored the eclipse of traditional individualism by a dreary "organization ethic."

The Eisenhower presidency was a perfect reflection of this mood. An affable, benign, seemingly apolitical figure, Dwight D. Eisenhower intended to take the country along "that straight road down the middle." His presidency, contemporary critics said, was a case study in "the bland leading the bland" and "mastery in the service of drift." Some recent historians have asserted that Eisenhower was a more dynamic and thoughtful political leader than his liberal detractors believed. Yet even when allowance is made for the new evidence about his leadership, Eisenhower's presidency seems like more an exercise in maintaining accepted standards and retarding change than a striking out in new directions to meet long-range national problems.

For all its reluctance to address major public issues head on in the 1950s, America did not escape upheavals at home and abroad. To be sure, the Eisenhower administration adroitly managed domestic and foreign crises, largely warding off violence in the United States and escaping war overseas. But unresolved internal conflicts fostered a sense of national unease. Indeed, for all the complacency, for which the decade is notable, people across the country lived with disquiet about race relations, uncertainty as to the proper mix of conservative and liberal solutions to social ills, and dread of nuclear war. Within the United States, challenges to segregation, especially in the schools, pitted blacks against whites, federal authority against state and local control, and personal prejudice against the public good. In foreign affairs the nation staunchly opposed communist advances in Asia, Europe, Latin America, and the Middle East. The Eisenhower administration struggled to contain and, if possible, to roll back communist power. The Cold War seemed to become a permanent fixture in American life, and for the first time in American history, foreign affairs seemed likely to be the nation's dominant concern for the long-term future.

## Affluence, Unity, and Disquiet

The 1950s, like the 1920s, were years of fulfillment. As the angry strikes and harsh rhetoric of the late 1940s subsided, so did most worries about a selfish, fragmented society. Despite two recessions during the decade, the gross national product rose by 50 percent to half a trillion dollars, and the economy spread out a feast of goods and services. Echoing the claims of the 1920s, publicist Peter Drucker told Americans that their society had passed "beyond Capitalism and Socialism." Once again millions believed that they not only had solved the major problems of the past, but had learned how to manage the problems of the future. Nevertheless, however muted, the country's problems—racial tensions, stubborn poverty among some one-quarter of the population, and the threat of thermonuclear conflict—cast a shadow over the decade.

**The Economics of Peace**

During the depression the birthrate had fallen to an all-time low of about 18 to 19 per thousand; the 1940s and 1950s witnessed twentieth-century America's great baby boom. By 1952 the rate stood at almost 25 births per thousand. The principal cause of this increase lay not so much in the number of children within families—here the average rose from about two children to three—but rather in the number and the timing of marriages. Americans in the 1940s and 1950s married at twice the rate they had married in the 1930s, and at a much younger age. As a consequence, the country's population swelled between 1940 and 1960 by some 48 million people, an increase of about 37 percent.

During the 1950s a combination of government expenditures, private investment, consumer borrowing, and population growth allowed the United States, which had only 6 percent of the world's people, to produce and consume approximately 33 percent of the world's economic output. Although more than 20 percent of the nation's population continued to live in poverty during the decade, numerous Americans improved their standard of living and entered the middle class.

Much of the secret of this economic upsurge can be found in the productivity of American agriculture and industry. Agricultural output began to increase substantially. During the quarter-century after World War II, the yield of wheat and cotton per acre doubled; and the yield of corn tripled; food in America became abundant and cheap. While the number of farm laborers decreased by approximately 30 percent during the 1950s, total farm production went up by a like amount. Relying on mechanical innovations that revolutionized the cultivation of crops, agribusiness made the nation's farms the most productive in the world.

At the same time, American industry produced an unprecedented flood of goods by investing some $10 billion a year in new capital equipment, by introducing more efficient methods of automation, and by relying heavily on electrical energy, the internal combustion engine, and such applied sciences as chemistry and electronics. Such light, relatively inexpensive materials as plastic and aluminum became widely used. These changes marked the beginnings of the "postindustrial" world—an economy in which the old smokestack factories, which had been the mainstays of American industrial life since the 1860s, began giving way to new light industries based on sophisticated technologies like electronics. The new industries also gave rise to a new breed of corporate managers whose skills were imitated and even improved on abroad, particularly in Japan. Not only did these new materials, industries, and management style expand the range of inexpensive goods; they created a mass market for cheap imitations of goods that had once been luxury items. Most American women could now afford to wear nylon stockings, whereas once only a few could afford silk ones. During the 1950s America's largest corporations averaged $500 million a year in sales—ten times the volume of the 1920s.

But a booming consumer sector did not entirely account for American prosperity. Military expenditures now dominated the national budget. Defense spending rose from $13 billion in 1949 to $22 billion in 1951, and went over the $50 billion mark in 1953. The size of these expenditures alone, fluctuating at about 60 percent of the government's total expenditures, made them crucial to maintaining a healthy economy. Directly or indirectly, the military program financed the research behind America's most important technological innovations. Moreover, such giant corporations as General Electric, General Motors, and Douglas Aircraft subcontracted portions of their military work to smaller companies. Were the government to terminate a big defense contract, shock waves would reverberate through a large section of the economy and undo Washington's efforts to sustain prosperity.

Multinational corporations also served to strengthen the connection between the domestic economy and world affairs. Before World War II, almost all the subdivisions that American corporations established abroad had remained small, dependent outposts of the parent companies. After the war, corporate expansion entered a new phase. American industrialists, from soft-drink makers to automobile and electronics manufacturers, gravitated to the capital-poor nations where production costs were low, governments encouraging, and ready markets inviting. Even more important than the sheer quantity of foreign subsidiaries was the fact that an increasing proportion of them duplicated the parent company's full corporate structure and rooted themselves in the societies in which they were planted. By the 1950s these corporate offshoots thrived on every continent. Still tied to their parent companies in the United States, yet assimilated into the lives of foreign nations, they gave a new transnational cast to the American economy.

But multinational corporations were only the most striking part of a massive business expansion after World War II. In 1946 America's private investments abroad approximated their level in 1929. During the next decade foreign investments tripled. By the end of the 1960s they would stand almost ten times higher than in 1946. Much of this money was spent in search of minerals that the United States either lacked or used up at a faster rate than it produced. Oil alone accounted for more than a third of these investments. Overall, American prosperity was becoming increasingly dependent on foreign resources and markets and on government policies in countries around the world. American economic involvements abroad had a significant impact on the nation's foreign policy. Traditionally the United States government had defined its vital interests principally in the Western Hemisphere. Now Washington came to view destabilizing events in Asia, the Middle East, and Africa as jeopardizing national economic and security interests, and it defended them by diplomacy or, if that proved insufficient, military might. Such were the fruits of the United States' postwar emergence as an economic and political superpower.

The principal beneficiaries of America's agricultural and industrial boom were the country's consumers, who took full advantage of easy credit to borrow and buy at a dizzying pace. Between 1945 and 1957, consumer credit rose by a breathtaking 800 percent; and as credit swelled, Americans eagerly signed up for revolving charge accounts, easy payment plans, and credit cards. Yet this economic expansion—miracles of growth—occurred with only 1 percent to 2 percent inflation. Indeed, inflation was so minor a matter in the economic thinking of the decade, that the 1950s editions of Samuelson's famous economics textbook gave it only passing attention.

During the decade American consumers purchased not only household appliances that eased life's burdens, but also television sets, electric toothbrushes, sports equipment, and swimming pools—luxury goods that indulged their tastes and filled their leisure time. Entertainment became a major American industry. Expenditures on leisure activities jumped from 7 to 15 percent of the GNP in the ten years after 1950. By 1960 it cost approximately $85 billion a year to satisfy the American demand for pleasures. Working fewer hours at higher wages than ever before, Americans spent twice as much on vacations, travel, liquor, movies, and sports, taken together, as they did on rent. While working- and lower-middle-class people still devoted a larger portion of their household budgets to rent than to luxuries, the numbers of Americans who owned rather than rented their homes greatly expanded; increasingly poverty became marginalized, concentrated among minorities and the elderly.

Above all the 1950s was the decade of television. Beginning in 1949 a quarter of a million sets a month were installed in American homes. By 1953 two-thirds of America's families owned a TV. By the late 1950s, nearly five hundred television

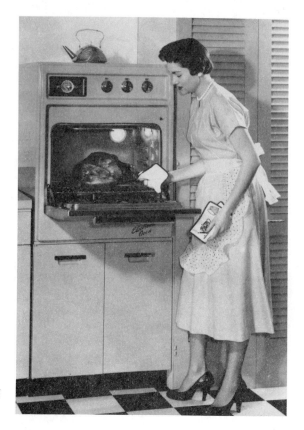

**1950s Consumerism**
*A new electronic oven could cook a 10-pound turkey in 25 minutes. Standard ovens required 4 to 5 hours.*

stations were broadcasting to 40 million TVs in homes all over the country. Ten years later 95 percent of American homes boasted at least one set, and many had several. Nothing escaped the camera's eye. Rapidly transforming itself from simply an entertainment medium emphasizing sports, dramas, and mass-consumption vaudeville, television regularly brought current events into American living rooms—the army-McCarthy hearings, political conventions and campaign debates, space launchings, American military action abroad, and domestic strife. And American advertising, understanding how the new medium could allow businesses to reach mass audiences, created fresh, imaginative means for selling the products of the consumer society.

The nationwide rush to the suburbs gave further evidence of an affluent, mobile society. During the depression and the war years, the number of new dwellings had averaged about 300,000 a year. In the 1950s, the annual average soared almost four times higher, and the demand for suburban housing seemed insatiable. By 1960 more than one in three Americans lived in suburbs—as many as lived in the cities. Instead of relying on the services of the inner city, as had the "bedroom towns" of the 1920s, the suburbs of the 1950s provided an increasingly self-contained life. Business firms, following the rush to the suburbs, hawked the national abundance along miles of neon-lit commercial avenues and inside countless suburban department stores. By the 1960s the farmer behind the plow, or the small-town dweller, or even the busy urbanite, seemed a less representative

**1950s Housing Development**
*The suburbs, like this one near Los Angeles, grew at a rapid pace in the 1950s.*

American figure than the suburbanite with all the accoutrements of the consumer culture: house, car, commuter schedule, and golf clubs.

The suburbs provided a more comfortable lifestyle for the millions of white Americans who moved there, but they also deprived the cities of resources that were desperately needed to serve the millions of blacks and Hispanics who replaced whites in the inner cities. The flight to the suburbs by middle-class whites deprived the cities of jobs and taxes. Reduced revenues meant declining school systems, diminished social services, and an aging infrastructure.

**The Other America**    For all the nation's wealth, there still remained an "invisible poor," poignantly described by the social critic Michael Harrington in his book *The Other America* (1962). Harrington described a culture of poverty whose "inhabitants did not suffer the extreme privation of the peasants of Asia or the tribesmen of Africa, yet the mechanism of the misery is similar. They are beyond history, beyond progress, sunk in a paralyzing, maiming routine." These black, Hispanic, poor white, and elderly Americans, perhaps as many as 40 or even 50 million, lived "on the outskirts of hope."

Over half of all native Americans, as well as nearly half of America's black population (over two-thirds of whom now lived in urban ghettos), made up a significant part of the country's impoverished. One large component was the some 2.5 million itinerant farm workers with an annual income of under $1,000.

**1950s Poverty**
*In Chicago this modern building made a sharp contrast with the slum dwelling of the foreground.*

Other elements were the men and women working at menial labor and earning less than $1 an hour, and the unemployed Americans scraping by on meager welfare doles. There were also as many as 8 million elderly persons who, with a mere $70-a-month Social Security payment, could not afford decent housing, proper nutrition, or adequate medical care. The Appalachian hill country, extending from western Pennsylvania to northern Alabama, was a breeding ground for mass poverty; in some counties there, a quarter of the population subsisted on a diet of flour and dried milk supplied by the federal government. A large number of the poor were women. Commonly earning only 60 percent of what men received, holding jobs not covered by minimum wage laws or Social Security, single mothers were a particularly large part of this group. In all, between 20 percent and 25 percent of the population earned less than $4,000 a year. The lowest fifth of American families earned 4.7 percent of total personal income; the highest fifth had 45.5 percent. The poor lived in misery and despair in urban ghettos, on tiny farms, or in rural shantytowns. Generally ignored in the midst of power and plenty, these Americans continued to suffer from powerlessness and want.

One great problem for America's least affluent was the resistance of the rest of the country to doing anything significant about their plight. Because American poverty, unlike that of Third World countries, was not so deadly, well-off Americans saw little need to make a substantial effort to end it. As Harrington put it, "At precisely that moment in history where for the first time a people have the material ability to end poverty, they lack the will to do so. They cannot see; they cannot act. The consciences of the well-off are the victims of affluence. . . . "

**National Harmony**  A national style of conformity emerged in the 1950s as Americans self-consciously strove for similarity and shunned difference. Consumerism contributed to this striving, and so did religion. A fanatical handful of Americans went so far as to burn "controversial books." Many more sought conformity by participating in a religious revival marked by an unthinking faith in shared assumptions; Congress captured the spirit of this revival by adding the words "under God" to the Pledge of Allegiance and the phrase "In God We Trust" to all United States currency. In 1953, "Vaya con Dios" and "I Believe" were in the top ten on America's song charts. TV ads announced: "The family that prays together stays together." These and many other instances of conformity-seeking made the United States seem to one writer a "'Packaged Society,' for we are all items in a national supermarket—categorized, processed, labeled, priced, and readied for merchandising."

Affluence and consumerism drew Americans closer together, literally and figuratively. A postwar transportation revolution shrank the nation's great distances. Between 1946 and 1956, state governments tripled their investment in road construction, and the Federal Highway Act of 1956, a major element in Eisenhower's legislative program, committed the national government to subsidizing over 40,000 miles of superhighways that would connect America's major cities. In their high-powered postwar cars, Americans greatly expanded their range of travel. The airplane shrank distances even more dramatically. Between 1947 and 1957, as passenger service grew fourfold, the airlines became a normal, accepted means of travel.

The postwar advent of television greatly added to the sense of a shared culture and a common national experience. Filling 20 percent of airtime with commercials for cigarettes, deodorants, toothpaste, automobiles, beer, and other luxuries of the affluent society, TV broadcasters gave viewers a sense of sharing in the consumer culture and enhanced the feeling of national well-being.

Moreover, Americans appeared to unite just by acting as consumers. Common cars and clothes, common houses and vacations, common foods and recreations, gave the impression of a single national commitment to the same good life. In 1933 the Roosevelt administration had issued a 3-cent postage stamp symbolizing unity in a society of large economic blocs: a farmer, a businessman, a laborer, and a housewife, each in distinctive dress, marched shoulder to shoulder "in common determination." In the consumer society of the 1950s, a comparable image of unity would have shown an assortment of shoppers, all dressed alike, filling their carts with the same standardized products. Consumerism and the American way of life had become almost synonymous.

Another sign of the times was a widespread new faith in the unique powers of science and massed expertise. Scientists reached a new peak of prestige following the awesome discoveries in atomic physics, the mass distribution of "wonder drug" antibiotics, and the conquest of polio, a disease that had afflicted thousands of children with paralysis and often shortened their lives. An increasing number of Americans looked on the experts as the keepers of a vast national pool of skills that could be used in various combinations to suit particular problems. Scientifically coordinated teams, rather than just scientifically trained individuals, held the key to the future. It required a team of specialists to harness the atom, to operate on the human heart, to measure public opinion, or to run a giant corporation. Moreover, these teams now had a marvelous new technological aid, the computer. Although the impact and popularity of the computer were still in the future, these small groups of scientists were already reaping the benefit of this new technology. The principal message of the 1950s, however, was that no lone genius could match the scientific range of computerized team research.

**Voice of Discontent**     Yet all was not togetherness during the 1950s. Conformity bred a lurking sense of disquiet. Joe McCarthy and his radical-right supporters remained a troubling expression of discontent with national affairs until the Senate repudiated him in 1954, and McCarthyite groups like the John Birch Society continued to fulminate on the fringe of society until well into the 1960s. Liberal and leftist intellectuals protested against the mindlessness of the consumer culture. One writer complained that "people no longer have any opinions; they have refrigerators. Instead of illusions we have television. Instead of tradition, the Volkswagen. The only way to catch the spirit of the times is to write a handbook on home appliances." Theologians fretted over the shallowness of the religious revival and worried that the leap in church attendance rested on no substantive understanding of Christian or Jewish traditions—in fact, seemed no more than a passing fad.

There was also considerable handwringing over the fate of the individual. The more systematized American society became in the 1950s, the less significant, or even distinguishable, was any one person within it. Perhaps, as the most critical voices of the late 1940s had implied, there really were no individuals in a modern bureaucratic society, only salespeople marketing themselves. Sociologists C. Wright Mills and David Riesman voiced these concerns in their widely read books *White Collar* (1951) and *The Lonely Crowd* (1950). Mills depicted white-collar workers as selling not only their time and training but also their personalities. Riesman described "other directed" parents discouraging children from developing "inner standards" that might play havoc with their ability to meet the expectations of others or gain popularity or sell themselves in "the personality market."

What had become of the individuals? Such popular 1950s novels and movies as *On the Beach,* which portrayed life in a thermonuclear age, touched deep fears that life on Earth would perish in the ultimate holocaust. The audience for a dehumanizing science fiction expanded. In 1950 the popular science and science-fiction writer Isaac Asimov published *I Robot,* a collection of stories, in which robots were a synonym for modern technology that human beings could not control. Many of the science-fiction and horror films of the decade, like *The Day the Earth Stood Still* (1951) and *Them* (1954), depicted the terrifying consequences of radioactive fallout from a nuclear war. The most intriguing new American writer of the 1950s, J. D. Salinger, and the most talented new American dramatist of the 1960s, Edward Albee, both emphasized the individual's agonizing, inescapable vulnerability in modern society. Many young writers accentuated the individual's isolation by using ordinary conversation as a way of hiding rather than communicating their characters' feelings. Only when the characters talked to themselves in lonely interior monologues did they honestly express their emotions. Such novelists as Saul Bellow and Joseph Heller relieved the individual's preposterous fate in modern society with an ironic laughter.

As more and more jobs became mechanized and routinized, the individual laborer developed a new attitude toward work. During the 1950s employers noted that white-collar employees were inquiring more often about fringe benefits like vacations, company cars, and retirement plans than about the challenges of their jobs. By the 1960s many corporations were discovering a new problem of morale among those executives who ran the companies' daily affairs. Rising rates of absenteeism and declining rates of efficiency expressed the refusal of "middle managers" to devote themselves to jobs that were no longer rewarding. Indeed, white-collar efficiency had become a pervasive problem. On the average, white-collar employees actually worked only about 50 percent of the time they spent in the office. Somewhere outside of the job lay an elusive something called "fulfillment," and more and more Americans set out to find it.

In 1957 Jack Kerouac published *On the Road,* a rambling celebration of the "beat" generation—the disaffected down-and-outers, drifters on the road alienated from a middle-class America that paid homage to the state, strove for material success, and practiced organized religion. In their self-absorption and detachment from larger social concerns, the beats mirrored middle America in the 1950s. More important, though, the beats were the advance guard of the counterculture that rebelled against American conventions in the 1960s. Rock 'n' roll music represented another reaction against the norms of the 1950s. Bursting suddenly on the scene in the mid-1950s, rock enjoyed great popularity among the country's rebellious-minded youth. "Rock Around the Clock," the hit tune from the 1954 film *The Blackboard Jungle,* a story of high-school juvenile delinquency—violence, sexual rebellion, and alienation—stirred teenagers to dance in movie theater aisles, to fight, riot, and vandalize. Elvis Presley, a young white truck driver from Tupelo, Mississippi, drawing on a variety of musical traditions—black rhythm and blues, country and western, gospel—exploited the rebelliousness and sexuality associated with rock music to become a consumer-culture hero. By the late 1950s he took to wearing gold lamé suits, driving pastel Cadillacs, shunning tobacco and alcohol, and even voicing respect for the older

**Beatniks**
*In the 1950s the "beat" generation expressed antagonism toward conformity as well as the national affinity for self-indulgence.*

generation. Although rock initially offended conventional Americans, who deplored it as noisy, low-class, even black, they had to admire the way Presley helped convert it into a multimillion-dollar industry.

Most Americans, of course, never indulged their rebelliousness as the beats or juvenile delinquents did. Nevertheless, more subtle means existed for rebelling against 1950s pressures to conform. Some cultivated their avocations instead of their vocations: more and more well-to-do Americans sought their primary satisfaction in boating or bridge, travel or tennis. Leisure became something much more basic in life than simply time to recuperate. Beginning with the modest "do-it-yourself" kits of the 1950s, handicrafts grew increasingly important in the lives of white-collar Americans concerned about the taste and quality of mass-produced goods. And a cult of the wilderness arose, which condemned the artificiality of modern society and advocated living close to nature. Part of this glorification of nature represented a reaction against the biological devastation that indiscriminate spraying of insecticides was causing throughout America, eloquently publicized later in Rachel Carson's chilling best-seller *Silent Spring* (1962).

The most general expression of the individual's modern quest was a nation-wide fascination with personal power, which began in the 1950s. Books coached Americans on games of "one-upmanship" in their everyday relations with friends and acquaintances. Commentators and historians praised the "strong" presidents, from George Washington to Harry Truman (thus pointedly excluding Eisenhower). The preoccupation with personal power was a mass phenomenon, and it found a variety of popular outlets. The crunching game of professional football began to compete with baseball as America's most popular spectator sport. Baseball eventually fought back with shortened fences, livelier balls, and the designated hitter, while the "big game" in tennis, the "dunk" in basketball, and the "power play" in hockey started coming into vogue. High-speed auto racing attracted more and more fans. By the 1960s everybody's car could be a personal vehicle of power: Cougar, Wildcat, Thunderbird, Stingray, Mustang. Promises of personal power suffused the advertising of everything from perfumes to breakfast foods. The theme of personal power saturated the movies and television, depicting a variety of superheroes not only in adult films but also in children's cartoons. Yet no one knew how to restore a genuine sense of autonomy in a mass society dominated by huge, impersonal organizations.

Women in the 1950s faced in new directions at the same time. The predominant view of women in the decade was as homemakers. "The suburban housewife was the dream image of the young American woman," Betty Friedan wrote in her 1963 book *The Feminine Mystique.* "She was healthy, beautiful, educated, concerned only about her husband, her children, her home. She had found feminine fulfillment." In 1956, *Life* magazine devoted a special issue to "The American Woman," picturing her as a thirty-two-year-old suburban housewife ("home manager") and mother of four who attended club or charity meetings, drove her children to school, did the weekly grocery shopping, made ceramics, and planned to learn French. The fifteen years after World War II was a period of early marriages and young families. In 1951 one-third of nineteen-year-old women were married, and the baby boom, which would hit its peak with a birthrate of 25.3 per thousand people in 1957, was in full swing. Feminism during the decade seemed "foolish or deviant."

Yet the 1950s were also notable for a dramatic increase in the number of working women, particularly working wives. In 1940 only 25 percent of women over the age of sixteen worked; by 1960 the number had swelled to 40 percent. A majority of these women entering the work force in the 1950s were married, middle-class, and middle-aged. The expansion of the economy during the decade opened numerous jobs to women in sales, service, and office work. In 1960 one in three employed women worked as clerks, and many became elementary-school teachers, entering the classrooms filled with baby-boom children. Most women workers entered sex-typed occupations and received traditionally low pay rates; in 1955 the median income of full-time female workers was 63.9 percent that of men. Because most of these women did not challenge traditional gender roles or unequal pay scales, their presence in the work force went largely unremarked.

## *"Modern Republicanism"*

During his eight years as president, Dwight Eisenhower liked to describe his philosophy as "modern Republicanism," his followers as "progressive moderates," and his program as one of "dynamic conservatism." He would be "conservative when it comes to money, liberal when it comes to human beings," the new president averred. His administration would most of all try to find "things it can stop doing rather than new things for it to do." Presenting himself as more in the Coolidge-Hoover than the Roosevelt-Truman domestic tradition, Eisenhower prized individualism and visualized its operation through private groups— political, industrial, church, school, labor.

"It has been a group effort, freely undertaken, that has produced the things of which we are so proud," Eisenhower announced, and he expected his administration to serve this "American way of life." Phrases like *free enterprise, private initiative,* and the dangers of *regimentation* peppered his conversations. He spoke of the TVA as "creeping socialism." On election night, 1952, when Eisenhower finally broke loose from the happy mob of his supporters, his first telephone call was to Herbert Hoover.

**The Washington Bureaucracy**

But between Hoover's time and Eisenhower's, Washington had changed dramatically. During the New Deal and World War II, the federal bureaucracy had ballooned enormously. By the early 1950s, physicists, chemists, biologists, engineers, hospital administrators, and a host of other scientific experts had become part of the Washington establishment, and government expenditures for scientific research and development skyrocketed from $74 million in 1940 to $7.3 billion in 1960. Other professionals, ranging from archivists and advertising specialists to specialists in race relations and traffic management, found places in the government bureaucracy.

No one appeared to coordinate Washington's vast apparatus of government. On paper it looked as though the White House was the center of control. In 1950 Congress added to the executive's powers by giving the president the right to appoint his own chairman to the independent regulatory commissions. Now each new administration could have an immediate influence on the policies of the "Big Six": the Civil Aeronautics Board, the Federal Communications Commission, the Federal Power Commission, the Federal Trade Commission, the Interstate Commerce Commission, and the Securities and Exchange Commission. Then in 1953 the new Department of Health, Education, and Welfare (HEW) combined a great variety of services and programs under one executive chief.

Nevertheless, the larger the executive branch grew, the more its authority seemed to be scattered among innumerable offices and subdivisions. As powerful a politician as Eisenhower's principal domestic aide, Sherman Adams, could do no more than respond to the issues of government one at a time as they came to him. Fortunately for the president, the tests of good management required only a strong economy and a satisfied constituency of private interest groups. By these standards the government functioned very well during the 1950s. Although Americans grumbled about incompetent bureaucrats, they generally approved the results of bureaucratic government. From the president down, few people in the country were ready to dismantle Social Security; end unemployment insurance; deny needy citizens welfare; jettison the regulation of banks, prescription medicines, or air traffic; or otherwise cancel a host of other government programs affecting all Americans' social and economic lives.

Eisenhower in fact managed the bureaucracy skillfully. Eager to limit the size of government and promote public perceptions of the chief executive as a more passive political figure, the president cultivated an above-the-battle image, seemingly staying uninvolved in day-to-day governmental management. In actuality he paid close attention to who headed government agencies, understanding that through them he could exert significant control over federal actions. He took care to appoint officials who, like him, understood that 1950s America could not simply dismantle agencies created by liberal Democratic administrations; but he also wanted administrators who would not follow in the Democrats' footsteps by expanding or aggrandizing those bureaucracies.

**Eisenhower's Conservatism**

Eisenhower also put himself forward as primarily a mediator rather than a party leader or chief legislator. Wishing to discourage a continuing expansion of executive assertiveness and yet eager to use his powers to advance domestic prosperity, the national security, and the popularity of the Republican party, he outwardly deferred to Congress, introducing fewer legislative proposals than his immediate predecessors. Yet at the same time, he repeatedly presented legislative measures that continued and, in limited ways, built upon earlier New Deal–Fair Deal programs.

His skillful management of Senator Joseph McCarthy's demise was a good example of Eisenhower's dealings with Congress. Refusing to challenge McCarthy head-on in 1952–53, when the freewheeling demogogue commanded widespread popularity and intimidated most of his congressional colleagues, the president waited until McCarthy overreached himself. But in 1954, after McCarthy had attacked the Protestant clergy and the army and had antagonized a number of conservative senators of both parties, Eisenhower actively encouraged the Senate to censure him. Led by Republican Majority Leader William Knowland, Democratic Minority Leader Lyndon B. Johnson, and a handpicked committee of three conservative Republicans and three conservative Democrats, the Senate by a lopsided vote condemned his behavior as bringing disrepute on the Upper House—exactly the result Eisenhower had wanted.

Eisenhower's fundamental impulses were conservative. From the outset he made it clear that his was to be a probusiness administration dominated by a concern for "free enterprise." He gathered so many wealthy opponents of the New Deal into his cabinet that it was popularly described as "nine millionaires and a plumber"—and the plumber, Secretary of Labor Martin Durkin, soon resigned. Because three of the president's appointees were General Motors executives, Adlai Stevenson could rightly quip that the New Dealers had "all left Washington to make way for the car dealers."

In its first months the new administration seemed bent on reducing federal controls over business and on generally reversing the flow of the past twenty years in domestic affairs. Secretary of Defense Charles E. Wilson, a former president of General Motors, declared that "what was good for our country was good for General Motors, and vice versa." Secretary of Commerce Sinclair Weeks fired the chief of the Bureau of Standards for reporting that a commercial battery additive, AD-2X, was useless; Secretary Weeks thought it should be allowed a "test of the marketplace." On other fronts, HEW Secretary Oveta Culp Hobby opposed federal legislation providing free distribution of the Salk vaccine to prevent polio; it would, she said, be a major step toward "socialized medicine." In cooperation with Treasury Secretary George Humphrey, the president encouraged the belief that he would slash the national budget and minimize the government's influence in economic matters. During three recessions, when deficit spending seemed needed to revive the economy, the administration resisted unbalanced budgets and intervention in the private sector. Eisenhower opposed "going too far with trying to fool with our economy," and he objected to creating "huge federal bureaucracies of the PWA or WPA type."

The administration's conservative leanings received substantive expression in the Submerged Lands Act of 1953 and the Atomic Energy Act of 1954. The first bill shifted title to some $40 billion worth of disputed offshore oil lands from the federal government to seaboard states. The second act allowed the administration to oppose federal power projects ("creeping socialism") and to support government-financed atomic research by such private corporations as General Electric. Subsequently, when the Atomic Energy Commission requested a new steam-power plant for an AEC facility in Kentucky, the administration refused to let the TVA build it. Instead the contract went to a private utility syndicate, Dixon-Yates. But when cries of protest forced a disclosure of the contract, a conflict of interest was revealed. The administration had to cancel the agreement as "contrary to the public interest" and to accept a proposal from the city of Memphis to build a plant that could supply the steam power.

The Eisenhower administration's opposition to government controls led it to dismantle the Reconstruction Finance Corporation, established by Hoover during the Great Depression. It also rejected significant federal support for education, public housing, and medical care for the aged—all of which Truman had proposed and for which the Democrats would keep pressing until the 1960s.

**The Politics of Moderation**
Yet New Deal programs generally remained intact. For all its conservative rhetoric, the administration never gave full expression to its stated intentions. Indeed, Eisenhower's talk of reviving the past quickly went by the boards. Private groups welcomed favors, but almost none of them wanted responsibilities. Bipartisan

**1956 Campaign Pennant**
*Despite shortcomings as an effective leader, Eisenhower had a warmth and fairness that made him a most popular president.*

leagues of businessmen, union leaders, and professionals demanded more, not less, money and assistance from Washington. For example, the farm associations were horrified when Eisenhower recommended reducing their subsidies. Under pressure, the administration revealed that its devotion to free enterprise was more talk than action, and farm groups soon learned that in fact their subsidies would not disappear or shrink significantly. By 1956 the administration had introduced an additional form of federal support: the soil bank, a government program that paid farmers to remove land from cultivation. Scientifically advanced farmers who could grow more crops on less acreage found the soil bank a bonanza. By the close of Eisenhower's presidency, Republicans had ceased to charge that the New Deal had made farmers dependent on government handouts.

In other areas as well, the administration made little effort to fulfill its original stated intentions. The president's apparent determination to balance the federal budget and resist interference in the economy was eclipsed by his pragmatic response to three recessions. Only three times in his eight-year term did Eisenhower avoid budget deficits, and he ended his term with an annual budget nearly double what Truman's had been in 1950, before the Korean War. When Eisenhower responded to the recession of 1953–54 with a firm assurance of no more New Deals and a willingness to wait for prosperity's return, a fearful nationwide outcry arose. A political and economic realist, Ike quickly shifted ground and used the government's authority to counter the economic slowdown. When the recession had passed, the president gave due credit to the "workings of the fiscal system."

A stamp of approval from impeccably conservative Republicans largely ended debate over the government's new approach to economic maintenance. By 1954 substantial majorities in Congress stood ready to support the economy by "fine-tuning" taxes and federal spending. The Treasury Department and the Federal Reserve both agreed that they should handle the national debt and regulate interest rates so that credit would expand in a weak economy and contract during inflation. In fact, the secretary of the treasury now ranked with the secretaries of state and defense as a primary government leader. Many people accepted these fiscal techniques because they seemed so neutral. They did not inhibit the stream of favor seeking and favor dispensing that flowed through Washington's busy offices. Liberals could still plan to expand government services, and conservatives could still hope to preserve the government's detachment. For the Invisible Hand that had guided Hoover's cooperative commonwealth in the 1920s, the national government of the 1950s substituted the Barely Visible Hand of fiscal manipulation.

Eisenhower also saw fit eventually to accept other progressive measures that, on entering the White House, he had spurned. Thus he approved the extension of Social Security benefits to 10 million more Americans; he backed the creation of the Department of Health, Education, and Welfare,* with its massive bureaucracy; he agreed to an increase in the minimum wage; and he supported federal funds for school and hospital construction. After the Soviet Union surprised the world by successfully launching the space satellite Sputnik in 1957, Eisenhower came out in favor of creating the civilian-controlled National Aeronautics and Space Administration (NASA) and of passing the National Defense Education Act, which financed student loans and the teaching of science, mathematics, and foreign languages.

At the end of his administration Eisenhower signed bills admitting Alaska and Hawaii to the Union. Alaska statehood stirred much less controversy than did the admission of Hawaii. A racially integrated society, Hawaii troubled southern segregationists, for whom admission of the islands looked like a challenge to Jim Crow laws everywhere. Encouraged by his attorney general, Herbert Brownell, Eisenhower had favored the passage of the Civil Rights Act of 1957 that affirmed the constitutional right of black southerners to vote. With the help of Democratic Majority Leader Lyndon Johnson of Texas, who believed an end to southern segregation was inevitable and would serve the South by bringing it more into the mainstream of American economic and political life, Congress passed the act in 1957; it was the first such statute in eighty-two years. The law was more a symbol of congressional readiness to act on civil rights questions than a substantive advance for blacks. Eisenhower supported both the Civil Rights Act and Hawaii's admission as ways to blunt communist propaganda attacks on America as a racist society.

In practice, then, Eisenhower showed himself to be more a politically moderate than a rigidly conservative president. Consequently, he entered the 1956 campaign for reelection against Adlai Stevenson with the backing of the broad middle of the American electorate. Stevenson himself was actually less liberal than his progressive supporters believed. In both the 1952 and 1956 campaigns he took moderate southern senators as his running mates, and he established a rapport with moderate and conservative southerners in the Demo-

---

*In 1979, HEW was divided into the Department of Health and Human Services and the Department of Education.

**Ike and Mamie**
*Eisenhower was one of the most popular presidents in American history.*

cratic party that surely would have restrained him in dealing with Congress had he become president. Yet whatever Stevenson's politics, he was no match for the highly popular Ike. Running on a platform of "Peace, Progress, and Prosperity," Eisenhower improved on his large popular majority of 1952, now receiving 58 percent of the vote and winning forty-one of the forty-eight states. Congress, however, was another matter. Led by two Texans, Speaker of the House Sam Rayburn and Majority Leader Johnson, who skillfully won public approval with a policy of bipartisanship (cooperation with a popular president), the Democrats retained the control they had won in 1954 over both the House and the Senate; and, for the first time since the election of 1848, a winning presidential candidate lost Congress to the opposing party.

Although Eisenhower maintained most of his popularity throughout his second term, by 1958 some began to criticize him as a weak leader and to complain of a lost sense of national purpose. In 1958 Sherman Adams found himself entangled in a scandal, and the economy went into recession. All this helped the Democrats to increase their margins of control over both houses of Congress. In substantive terms, however, this Democratic dominance made little difference: the congressional session of 1959–60 produced almost no important legislation.

## Civil Rights

The affluence and unity of the 1950s could not mask underlying strains in American society over inequality and injustice suffered by the country's black citizens. Throughout the nation—but particularly in the South, where a web of state and local statutes gave legal sanction to the practice—de facto segregation denied blacks admission to white schools and equal access to other public places. In restaurants, movie theaters, rest rooms, swimming pools, buses, and trains across the southern United States, blacks had to use separate and almost always inferior facilities.

Opposition to segregation by blacks and northern white liberals had been mounting throughout the 1930s and 1940s, led principally by the NAACP. In 1944 the Swedish sociologist Gunnar Myrdal pricked the nation's conscience in *An American Dilemma*. The book described the country's antiblack prejudice as the one great contradiction to the "American creed," a nationally accepted set of beliefs in equality, opportunity, and justice for everybody. Few successful Americans, including many in the South, could deny that segregation was inherently wrong. Among upper-middle-class professionals and managers, distinctions based on skin color had no logical justification, and a rigid structure of Jim Crow drinking fountains and bus seats seemed absurd as well as insulting. In the postwar years, segregation had become an obvious affront to America's modern values. At home it clashed with the ideal of an open society, in which citizens were

**The Jim Crow System of Southern Segregation**
*This "colored" entrance to a Deep South movie theater was one element in the rigidly enforced southern system of racial segregation practiced at midcentury.*

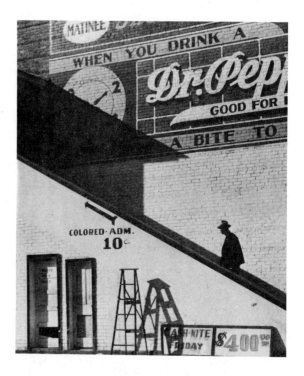

free to acquire all the skills they could learn and buy all the goods they could earn. Abroad it jeopardized America's chances of bringing people with brown or black or yellow skin into a worldwide anticommunist alliance—a consideration that troubled foreign-policy makers and made some southerners more receptive to easing segregation laws. Prominent southern liberals, who had generally ignored the race problem before the late 1940s and early 1950s, now gave increasing support to the critics of segregation. By the 1950s, educated and nationally minded Americans regarded Jim Crow as an anachronism that a modern society could no longer tolerate. Still, despite the turn against racism by the American elite, many ordinary citizens—north and south—continued to harbor unexamined racist attitudes.

**Legal Remedies**
One of the president's earliest appointments was a new chief justice of the United States Supreme Court. He chose the affable California Republican Earl Warren, who had been an extremely popular governor and the party's vice-presidential candidate in 1948. Warren, a "liberal Republican," was a skilled mediator with no record of interest in social experimentation. He had even participated in the drive to intern Japanese Americans during World War II. His appointment seemed to augur a safe, middle-of-the-road Court.

When Warren became chief justice in 1953, the most significant issue pending before the Supreme Court was racial segregation in the public schools. Precedents that challenged the Court's 1896 doctrine of "separate but equal" educational facilities had been accumulating for more than a decade, but the Court had not reversed itself on this defense of segregation.* Few observers expected the moderate new chief justice to launch a fresh departure. But in a unanimous decision in *Brown* v. *Board of Education* (1954), the Court boldly declared separate educational facilities inherently unequal and unconstitutional. At a stroke the Court had undercut the entire structure of the Jim Crow laws.

Some Americans considered education an excellent place to begin racial desegregation. Because successful Americans based their own careers on specialized skills, they immediately recognized the serious consequences of an inferior education. Moreover, they believed that completely dismantling the caste system would require slow, careful adjustments over many years. If children in integrated schools grew up free of prejudice, these new generations would eventually eliminate the last traces of racial hate. Time and the power of education lay on the side of progress. In this spirit of optimistic caution, the Supreme Court declared in the second *Brown* decision (1955) that school desegregation should proceed "with all deliberate speed."

During the next decade southern whites threw all manner of legal obstacles in the path of integration, ranging from the groundless constitutional doctrine

---

*For the 1896 *Plessy* v. *Ferguson* decision establishing the "separate-but-equal" doctrine, see chapter 25, p. 237.

(recalling Jacksonian-era nullification) of "state interposition" between the national government and citizens, to the substitution of private segregated schools for the public system. With increasing firmness the federal courts removed each impediment. But in 1957, almost three years after the Supreme Court's initial desegregation decision, there were still no integrated classrooms in the Deep South. That fall, a federal court finally ordered the schools in Little Rock, Arkansas, to begin integrating classes. When the city's Central High School accepted nine black students, Governor Orval Faubus called out the National Guard—ostensibly to prevent violence, but actually to halt integration. A federal judge compelled the withdrawal of the troops, but white mobs kept black students from reaching the school. A reluctant President Eisenhower, who had shown no sympathy for the Court's desegregation ruling and had denounced "extremists on both sides," felt compelled to call in federal troops to enforce the rule of law. Although this action allowed the black students to attend the high school, their attendance was only temporary. In 1958 and 1959 Faubus further defied the courts by closing Little Rock's high schools, and only another court order, in the fall of 1959, finally produced limited integration. In 1960, five years after the Supreme Court had ordered "all deliberate speed" in desegregating the nation's schools, only about 10 percent of southern school districts had complied. In northern school systems as well, where de facto segregation resulted from residence patterns, integration was more the exception than the rule.

Prospects were also bleak for southern blacks who wished to exercise the fundamental democratic right to vote. Arbitrary literacy tests and an atmosphere of intimidation kept most of them from the polls. The 1957 Civil Rights Act did little to change this condition. Weakening an administration bill to avoid a southern filibuster, Congress authorized federal court action to permit blacks to vote; it also established the Civil Rights Commission to monitor progress. In 1960 Congress went further, empowering the courts to appoint federal referees to protect voting rights, and making it a federal offense to threaten violent resistance to a court order. These measures, however, included provisions that largely made them unworkable. Despite the 1957 and 1960 laws, three-fourths of eligible southern black voters remained unregistered in 1960.

**Nonviolent Resistance**

As the courts and Congress were promoting the cause of black rights in the 1950s, blacks themselves mounted a highly effective campaign in their own behalf. Their movement quickly became identified with the intense, eloquent style of a young minister from Montgomery, Alabama—Martin Luther King, Jr. Not yet twenty-seven years old, he emerged in 1955 as the nationally publicized leader of a local boycott against Montgomery's segregated buses that began when Rosa Parks, a black woman, refused to give up her seat to a white man, as required by law. Through word and example, King provided blacks with a creative combination of the Christian love that their churches taught, the strategy of peaceful mass resistance that Mahatma Gandhi had formulated in India, and the self-discipline that relatively well-to-do blacks had long used to defend their rights in America's

**Martin Luther King, Jr.**
*King's passive resistance to segregation fostered the collapse of the South's Jim Crow system in the 1950s.*

own caste system. While King was inspiring his fellow blacks with appeals for nonviolent direct action through his Southern Christian Leadership Conference (SCLC), he was also attracting wide support among whites who were committed to orderly behavior and peaceful change, and who increasingly heralded King as an American statesman.

In 1960 the Student Non-Violent Coordinating Committee (SNCC), throughout the cities of the South, applied King's tactics in a dramatic wave of "sit-ins" that desegregated numerous restaurants, then a variety of other public accommodations. The following year the Congress on Racial Equality (CORE), another organization of peaceful resistance, sponsored black and white "freedom riders" on a harrowing bus trip into the South that publicized the illegal segregation in interstate travel. This pillar of Jim Crow also toppled. As in the case of Little Rock, the violent responses to these protests strengthened the bond between white liberals and black moderates. In 1963, when King led a movement against segregation in Birmingham, Alabama, national television vividly recorded the cattle prods, fire hoses, and snarling dogs that local police used to intimidate blacks. Murderers of civil rights activists that year in Birmingham and the next summer in Mississippi could not be prosecuted in the southern courts. King's SCLC and the SNCC seemed the embodiment of rationality in contrast to the revived Ku Klux Klan, the raucous rhetoric of local southern politicians, and the partiality of southern white courts.

**The 1963 March on Washington**
*A coalition of civil rights groups dramatized the need for civil rights legislation in the 1960s, leading the federal government to pass the most important civil rights laws since Reconstruction.*

White sympathy for King's inspired moderation continued to rise until, in the summer of 1963, a quarter of a million Americans (including a significant minority of whites) dramatized the plight of the blacks by marching peacefully through Washington and gathering at the Lincoln Memorial. There they heard King's moving message of hope: "I have a dream that one day...the sons of former slaves and the sons of former slave-owners will be able to sit together at the table of brotherhood." He foresaw the day when "this nation will rise up and live out the true meaning of its creed: '...that all men are created equal.'" Only then would blacks have the redemption promised in a slave song: "Free at last, free at last, thank God Almighty I'm free at last."

## The Eisenhower Foreign Policy: Cold War Orthodoxy

In foreign policy, as in domestic affairs, the United States presented a new face of national unity and common purpose during the 1950s. After the Korean War no significant group of Americans challenged the basic outlines of the nation's containment policy. Both Republicans and Democrats—conservatives as well as the liberal members of Americans for Democratic Action—defined international communism as a worldwide conspiracy directed from Moscow. The United States, the nation incessantly heard, must gird for a long, taxing struggle against the enemy. "Forces of good and evil are massed and armed and opposed as rarely before in history," President Eisenhower declared starkly in January 1953. "Freedom is pitted against slavery, lightness against dark." To Secretary of State John Foster Dulles, the struggle between the United States and the Soviet Union

**Anti-Communist Poster**
*In the 1950s Americans feared a worldwide communist takeover.*

was "an irreconcilable conflict." Dulles, the administration's dominant voice on foreign policy, was a rock-ribbed anticommunist possessed of an evangelical commitment to rescuing peoples everywhere from "godless terrorism."

**The Free World**   At the start of its first term, the Eisenhower administration tried to answer the two most perplexing questions in America's international affairs. What was the scope of America's anticommunist policy, and what were the best means of implementing it? After several years of hesitation, the government interpreted literally the words in the Truman Doctrine: any nation willing to cooperate with America's worldwide anticommunist policy became a member of the "free world." Some of these nations, such as Great Britain and Canada, were old and trusted democratic friends. Others were recent enemies: West Germany entered NATO in 1955; and Japan, with which the United States (over vehement Soviet protests) in 1951 had signed a formal peace, was incorporated into America's expanding scheme of defensive alliances, along with Australia, New Zealand, and the Philippines. But some other members of the free world, such as Franco's Spain and South Korea, were authoritarian states that ruthlessly repressed opponents. For Dulles, however, the dictatorial government of South Korea was part of "the great design of human freedom." In contrast democratic India, whose leaders desired to remain neutral in the Cold War, heard itself denounced as indifferent to "human freedom."

Officially, every member of the free world was equally important in America's global policy. The government vowed never to repeat the Truman administration's mistake of announcing that South Korea lay outside the primary American line of defense, thus inviting North Korea's invasion. Viewing the communist camp as one interrelated whole and the free world as another, American policymakers interpreted a weakness in either bloc as the sign of greater changes to come. Free nations were likened to rows of dominoes: if one tipped into communism, the rest would follow. From these concerns came the cardinal rule that would dominate the next two decades of American foreign policy: the free world must not relinquish a single additional piece of territory. No more Munichs; no more Chinas. This view of the world, however, did not originate with Eisenhower and Dulles; it had become accepted wisdom in the last two years of Truman's presidency.

During the 1950s the Eisenhower administration's rhetoric went beyond the basic containment policy and urged the "rollback" of communist power and the "liberation" of "captive nations" from communist control. Containment, a "negative, futile and immoral policy," was now to be replaced by the "contagious, liberating influences which are inherent in freedom." The administration coupled this pronouncement with a "New Look" in America's military program, described as "massive retaliation"—a primary reliance on nuclear weapons rather than conventional forces to meet a possible Soviet attack. Politically, the New Look appealed to the economy-minded, who were promised (in Secretary of Defense Charles Wilson's blunt phrase) "more bang for the buck." Militarily, however, the New Look represented only a slight change of emphasis from ground and naval forces to air and missile power.

The administration did not commit itself to military action to bring about liberation and did little to implement a rollback policy. Instead it depended on a more elaborate version of the containment idea: it believed that the mere expression of hope for liberation would alter the mood of captive peoples and lead to the desired result. Yugoslavia's refusal to accept Soviet dictation after 1948, for example, kindled hopes for the liberation of all Eastern Europe, despite the fact that internally Marshall Tito's Yugoslavia was as repressive as any Stalinist East European regime. Not surprisingly, no liberation came.

**The Middle East**    The Eisenhower administration's central goals in the Middle East were to ensure the survival of Israel, which had been formed in 1948, and to prevent the spread of communist power, especially in Iran. In 1951 the Iranian government, led by its intensely nationalistic prime minister, Dr. Muhammad Mossadegh, had nationalized the country's British-controlled oil industry. Fearful that Mossadegh might turn his country into a communist satellite, Eisenhower in 1953 approved a CIA plan to replace the prime minister with a more reliable ruler. In a cloak-and-dagger operation that the president later described as "more like a dime novel than an historical fact," the United States government secretly supported a successful coup against Mossadegh by the Iranian shah, Muhammad Reza Pahlevi. Unable to distinguish between Marxism-Leninism and militant nationalism in a country emerging from Western domination, the administration prided itself on having "saved Iran from communism." The long-term consequences would be disastrous. Uncritical

American support of the shah piled up a sullen anti-Americanism in Iran that exploded after a successful Islamic revolution against the monarchy in 1979.

A similar misinterpretation influenced the president's policies toward Egypt and Lebanon. In 1955, after President Gamal Abdel Nasser of Egypt arranged to buy arms from Moscow, the United States offered to help Nasser finance the building of the Aswan Dam, Egypt's highest economic priority at the time. Then, on reconsideration, the administration canceled the deal in 1956. "Do nations which play both sides get better treatment than nations which are stalwart and work with us?" Dulles asked.

The cancellation led directly to the Suez crisis in the fall of 1956. After Washington withdrew its offer of aid, Nasser nationalized the canal, on which Western countries depended for an uninterrupted flow of oil. Britain and France then joined Israel in an attack on Egypt. Eisenhower, who had not been informed of the attack in advance, feared that it would drive Egypt and other Arab states into the communist camp, and he pressed his allies into withdrawing from Egypt. Reluctantly, they obeyed. At the same time, however, the president worried that withdrawal would leave a vacuum for the Soviets to fill. As a preventive measure he enunciated the Eisenhower Doctrine in January 1957: warning that Russia, under tsars and Bolsheviks alike, had "long sought to dominate the Middle East," he asked Congress to approve economic and military assistance to Middle Eastern nations struggling to protect their independence. The president also requested permission to use American military power to defend those countries against "overt armed aggression from any nation controlled by International communism."

Eisenhower gave substance to his doctrine in the following year, when a coup toppled the pro-Western government in Iraq, and another pro-Western regime in Lebanon seemed vulnerable. Sending American forces into Lebanon in the summer of 1958, Eisenhower compared the situation to earlier East-West confrontations in Greece, Czechoslovakia, China, and South Korea. The next year the United States fostered a Middle Eastern anti-Soviet alliance, CENTO. But not a single Arab state joined it.* Although critics of the president's policy maintained that Arab nationalism, not Soviet communism, was the major problem, Congress followed his lead and supported the landing of troops in Lebanon. "America has either one voice or none," the Democratic speaker of the House announced, "and that voice is the voice of the President—whether everybody agrees with him or not."

**Brinkmanship in Asia**

Although the Eisenhower administration warned of stronger action in response to the Asian crises it faced, the net result was much the same as in the Middle East. The United States government attempted no massive retaliation when a communist takeover loomed in northern Vietnam and a Chinese communist offensive

---

*The members of CENTO were Great Britain, Iran, Pakistan, and Turkey.

menaced the Chinese offshore islands of Quemoy and Matsu. Instead the administration limited itself to actions that were calculated to narrow rather than broaden these conflicts.

In 1954, when French forces trying to maintain colonial rule in Vietnam faced a decisive defeat in an eight-year-old war against the Vietminh (the communist-dominated Vietnamese league for national independence), the American government confronted a difficult choice. Should it take military action? If so, should it strike with a tactical (that is, a small) nuclear bomb? Or should it avoid intervention and risk the loss of all Southeast Asia to communism? Although Eisenhower feared that a communist victory in Vietnam would set off a chain reaction toppling one Southeast Asian country after another, he decided against intervention. It would, he believed, be a poor military gamble, and it might split America and its allies. Instead the administration threw its support behind a pro-Western South Vietnamese government headed by Ngo Dinh Diem, a Catholic with strong American ties. At the same time, Dulles negotiated still another alliance—the South East Asia Treaty Organization (SEATO), uniting France, Great Britain, the United States, Australia, New Zealand, Pakistan, the Philippines, and Thailand. But SEATO was more shadow than substance. Lacking automatic provisions for collective military resistance to aggression, the treaty created little more than a symbolic coalition of "free world" states. In backing the Diem government and engineering the treaty, the administration acted in a style more reminiscent of Truman's containment policy than of anything aiming at "liberation."

The same was true of the Eisenhower administration's dealings with the two Chinas. Eisenhower had begun his term by reversing Truman's policy; no longer would the United States hold Chiang Kai-shek back from an offensive against the mainland and from answering communist artillery attacks on Nationalist-controlled offshore islands. But the president soon backed away from this policy, and Chiang was never "unleashed." In 1958, when another crisis erupted over the tiny offshore islands of Quemoy and Matsu, the administration about-faced. Initially declaring themselves ready to meet any attack on the islands, Eisenhower and Dulles quickly moved to rein in Chiang and denied any intention of using "even tactical atomic weapons in a limited operation."

A confused American public took little comfort in Dulles's description of what journalists began to call "brinkmanship." "You have to take chances for peace," Dulles lectured. " . . . Some say that we were brought to the verge of war. The ability to get to the verge of war without getting into the war is the necessary art. If you cannot master it, you inevitably get into wars. . . . If you are scared to go to the brink, you are lost." The administration's rhetoric and behavior in response to Asian problems demonstrated a combination of bluster and good sense. Further, all the talk of "liberation" and "massive retaliation" told more about the American mood in the 1950s than about what the Eisenhower administration intended to do abroad. Believing itself locked in an apocalyptic struggle against communism, the nation saw no room for dissent at home, and it called for an anticommunist crusade abroad. But when America confronted the reality that such action would risk a nuclear exchange, it reverted to the more judicious containment policy initiated in the Truman years.

**Holding the Line in Latin America**
In Central America, where geographical proximity allowed the United States to assert itself more forcefully, the Eisenhower administration gave freer expression to its anticommunist stance, particularly in the case of Guatemala. A democratically elected reform government under Jacobo Arbenz Guzman ruled the country in 1953. But because Arbenz had accepted some communists into his government and had expropriated idle lands owned by the American-controlled United Fruit Company, he came under attack from the Eisenhower administration as a tool of the worldwide Soviet communist conspiracy. Arbenz, Eisenhower believed, "was merely a puppet manipulated by communists."

Convinced that the Arbenz regime was a radical government that represented a threat to American security, President Eisenhower authorized the CIA to help oust Arbenz. Using the fact that Guatemala had accepted arms from Czechoslovakia, a Soviet satellite, and that the Guatemalan government had suspended civil liberties to prevent the CIA-planned coup, the Eisenhower administration in June 1954 aided an exiled Guatemalan army officer, who was operating from Honduras, to overturn the Arbenz government. Eisenhower and Dulles were convinced that the change of governments had "averted a Soviet beach-head in our hemisphere" and had little compunction about denying the American role in the coup. But, as columnist Harrison E. Salisbury subsequently wrote, the coup "was conceived by men who did not understand what was happening in Guatemala, who did not understand the nature of Latin America and its problems and who had no understanding of the consequences of the events they set in motion."

The Guatemalan coup, coupled with the administration's overt support of right-wing dictators in other Latin countries, aroused intense antagonism to the United States throughout the hemisphere. During a 1958 trip to eight Latin American countries, Vice-President Richard Nixon encountered a fierce outpouring of anti-Americanism, including a mob attack on his car in Caracas, Venezuela, that threatened his life. Instead of recognizing this hostility as a reaction to their indiscriminate support of anticommunist dictators, Eisenhower and Nixon believed that it confirmed the existence of an international communist conspiracy. The president described the hemispherewide anti-Americanism as part of "a pattern around the world—in Burma, in Jakarta, in South America, other places—that looks like there is some kind of concerted idea and plan. . . ." "The clear truth," Eisenhower said, was that "the threat of communism in Latin America is greater than ever before."

Nothing tended to confirm this belief more for the administration than events in Cuba, where a guerrilla struggle against the dictator Fulgencio Batista

**Nixon in Latin America**
*Nixon's 1958 Latin American trip touched off an outburst of anti–United States feeling that shocked most Americans.*

had been simmering for several years. At the beginning of 1959 Fidel Castro led the rebels to victory and began cutting Cuban dependence on the United States. Relying on American investments and markets for its economic survival, Cuba had essentially been an economic extension of the United States. American influence on the island had been so great, the United States representative to the country observed in 1960, that "the American ambassador was the second most influential man in Cuba; sometimes even more important than the president." Although Castro had made some gestures toward accommodation with the United States, his determined efforts in 1959–60 to break America's economic stranglehold and to tie himself to Moscow by increasing trade with the Soviet bloc fortyfold showed him to be a committed Marxist-Leninist. The Eisenhower administration now viewed Castro as part of the Soviet-communist drive for world power, and ordered the CIA to plot the overthrow of Castro's regime. This design was not acted on until Eisenhower's successor, John F. Kennedy, took office in 1961.

**Groping Toward Coexistence**　　Despite Eisenhower's and Dulles's conviction that Soviet-American differences caused an irreconcilable conflict—one in which the United States must defeat the communist drive for world power—the realities of international affairs forced them into seeking an accommodation with the USSR. Above all they found themselves compelled to respond to Soviet proposals for negotiations.

Stalin died in March 1953. Almost at once, the USSR's new leaders declared their desire for "peaceful coexistence" and their conviction that all unresolved questions between the two superpowers could be "settled peacefully by mutual agreement of the interested countries...." Eager to head off the rearming of West Germany, the Soviets asked for direct talks between Moscow and Washington. Moreover, when Eisenhower called for Soviet demonstrations of good intentions as a prelude to meeting, Moscow responded by agreeing in 1955 to a peace treaty with Austria, making that nation a neutral buffer zone in the Cold War. The Soviet government also advanced a substantive proposal for arms limitations. The fact that the Soviets had followed America's lead in developing the H-bomb had convinced Eisenhower that "there is just no real alternative to peace" and that a summit meeting would have to be tried.

The two sides did meet in a summit conference at Geneva, Switzerland, in July 1955; but they could not reach agreement on the two most important issues of the time, Germany and arms control. Germany was the key to any Soviet-American settlement. At Geneva the United States proposed German unification "under conditions which will neither 'neutralize' nor 'demilitarize' united Germany, nor subtract it from NATO"; the Soviet Union rejected unification for Germany unless that nation was detached from "the military groupings of the Western powers." This Soviet position on Germany would long remain the bedrock of the Kremlin's foreign policy; its abandonment would signal the end of the Cold War in 1989–90.

As to arms control, the Soviets wanted no part of an Eisenhower proposal called "open skies." An exchange of military plans and frequent aerial inspections by both sides to prevent surprise nuclear attacks, Eisenhower believed, "would undoubtedly benefit us more than the Russians," because the United States knew less about Soviet installations than vice-versa. Soviet Premier Nikita Khrushchev denounced "open skies" as "a very transparent espionage device," and the proposal came to nothing. But although the meeting in Switzerland produced no specific agreements, it did create what commentators called the "spirit of Geneva"—less fear and greater willingness to talk on both sides.

Still, tensions between the two superpowers remained high. In 1956, after Khrushchev denounced some of Stalin's crimes at the Twentieth Congress of the Communist party and called for greater diversity in the communist bloc, the Poles and Hungarians rebelled against Moscow. A more independent-minded communist leader, Władysław Gomułka, came to power in Warsaw and with considerable difficulty managed to placate his intensely anti-Russian people while staving off Soviet intervention. More rashly, a new Hungarian government declared its intention of withdrawing from the Warsaw Pact, the alliance of Eastern European nations with Moscow created in 1954. To prevent the collapse of their hold on Hungary—and perhaps on Eastern Europe generally— the Soviets sent tanks and troops into that nation. Although the Eisenhower administration refused to intervene, it condemned this fresh demonstration of Soviet contempt for freedom and national sovereignty and reiterated the difficulty of reaching accommodation with the USSR.

**Eisenhower and Khrushchev**
*Ike's meetings with Khrushchev helped ease Cold War tensions.*

A successful Soviet test of an intercontinental ballistic missile (ICBM) and the series of Sputnik launches beginning in 1957 dealt heavy blows to American self-confidence—and to conservative complacency about the nation's superiority in military power and space technology. Demands multiplied for upgrading American education. These concerns, coupled with the onset of a recession in 1958 and with Khrushchev's boasts about the rapidly growing Soviet economy "overtaking" and "burying" its capitalist rival, led many serious Americans to worry about the prospect of succumbing to superior Soviet power.

For Eisenhower, the need to avoid war with the Soviet Union remained so high a priority that he agreed to further face-to-face discussions with Khrushchev in 1959 and 1960. In September 1959 the folksy Soviet premier barnstormed across the United States on an official visit, and his candid private talk with Eisenhower about Soviet-American differences at the president's Maryland retreat created what Khrushchev called "the spirit of Camp David." One consequence of this improved mood was an agreement to hold a summit meeting in Paris in May 1960. But two weeks before the conference was to begin, an American U-2 spy plane was shot down 1,200 miles inside the Soviet Union. Eisenhower at first lied to the public, but when the Soviets produced the captive pilot in Moscow, the president acknowledged that he had approved the mission—and said that he felt it better to drop the "false cloak of camaraderie" and confront the sharp differences between the two sides. The Russians denounced him; the conference aborted; and Khrushchev declared that he would no longer deal with Eisenhower but instead await his successor.

**The Election of 1960** As long as the widely popular Eisenhower remained in the White House, for many Americans no one else seemed important as a national leader. Had Eisenhower been able to run for a third term, he probably would have won. But he was barred from running by the Twenty-second Amendment, adopted in 1951; and Vice-President Nixon, who seemed the president's logical successor, became the Republican candidate. Sensing the need for a new figure to replace Adlai Stevenson, who had twice failed to win the White House, the Democrats chose the youthful-looking forty-three-year-old Senator John F. Kennedy from Massachusetts. A well-organized and liberally financed primary campaign had given him a considerable edge over his competitors. Kennedy balanced the ticket by selecting Texas Senator and Majority Leader Lyndon B. Johnson as his running mate.

Both Nixon and Kennedy came to the 1960 presidential campaign with handicaps. Nixon's history of red-baiting and his reputation for insincerity burdened him with a negative public impression that he felt compelled to refute. But his attempt during the campaign to appear as the experienced, judicious leader who had abandoned old habits and was ready for higher office partly

**Kennedy for President**
*This broadside for Kennedy in the 1960 presidential campaign emphasizes the need for stronger leadership in the contest with communism. Making a campaign issue of the lost sense of purpose under Eisenhower, Kennedy also promised to get "the country moving again."*

**Kennedy-Nixon Debate**
*John F. Kennedy's effectiveness in his debates with Nixon helped elect him to the presidency.*

backfired. Critics complained about the manipulation of his image and wondered "whether there is anything that might be called the 'real' Nixon, new or old."

Kennedy also had problems convincing the public that he was well suited for the White House. Numerous Protestant voters distrusted him as a Roman Catholic, and his political cautiousness during his senatorial career (including a refusal to criticize McCarthy) had caused many to doubt his capacity for independent judgment. Lyndon Johnson, his own running mate and former rival for the nomination, had privately wondered how the country could entrust the White House to so inexperienced a young man. During the campaign, however, Kennedy generally overcame these earlier impressions by forthrightly supporting the separation of church and state and by boldly appealing for a renewed sense of national purpose, for "getting the country moving again" after Sputnik and the 1958 recession. Moreover, his impressive performance in four televised debates with Nixon added to the picture of a self-confident, dynamic candidate worthy of the highest office. Although it was pure demagogy, Kennedy and the Democrats insisted on the existence of a "missile gap" that frightened Americans and went far to convince voters that Kennedy and his party would be as tough as Nixon and the Republicans in dealing with the Soviets. Kennedy won the election by the narrowest popular margin—two-tenths of 1 percent—of any winning candidate since James A. Garfield in 1880. Although the Democrats maintained control of Congress, they held only a twenty-two-seat margin in the House and a two-seat advantage in the Senate. The liberalism that had been so central to the FDR and

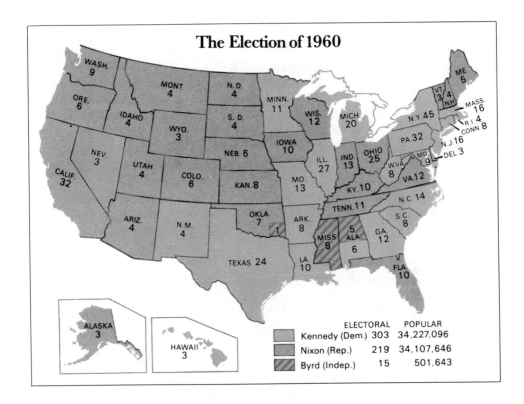

## The Election of 1960

| | ELECTORAL | POPULAR |
|---|---|---|
| Kennedy (Dem.) | 303 | 34,227,096 |
| Nixon (Rep.) | 219 | 34,107,646 |
| Byrd (Indep.) | 15 | 501,643 |

Truman presidencies seemed unlikely to make a major comeback under Kennedy. Little in his career suggested an affinity for domestic reform; he seemed more concerned with fighting the Cold War than with combating economic disparities and poverty in the United States.

## Eisenhower and the Modern Presidency

During Eisenhower's eight years in the White House, the meaning of the presidency had changed in two important respects. First, the office was separated from the normal patterns of electoral politics. Beginning with Eisenhower's triumph in 1952, the vote for president no longer followed the same curve as the nationwide vote for other Democratic and Republican candidates. Franklin Roosevelt's rising and falling majorities had roughly paralleled the majorities of the Democratic party. Even Harry Truman's surprising victory in 1948 had coincided with a similar Democratic revival. After 1952, however, the presidential vote set a course of its own. In 1954 the Democrats had recaptured both houses of Congress and continued to hold them, usually by substantial majorities. By contrast to this steady, partisan line, the presidential returns from election to election swung in big loops that expressed the public's specific choices between candidates.

The presidential vote also showed the limits of national interest in politics and public affairs. Where nearly 80 percent of eligible voters had gone to the polls in the presidential election of 1896, no more than 63 percent of the electorate had voted since 1912. In 1920 and 1924 less than 50 percent of voters had cast ballots. While the turnout varied between 50 percent and 63 percent after that, no presidential contest in the subsequent sixty-four years drew the kind of interest that White House races had generated in the nineteenth century. Part of this statistical shift may have had to do with the fact that the percentage of Americans effectively eligible to vote—women beginning in 1920 and blacks beginning in the 1960s—grew enormously. But there were other causes as well.

As Americans detached their president from normal party politics, they were developing a new relation with him that had relatively little to do with the electoral process. (Eisenhower, for example, gained from having no clear political identity until he ran in 1952.) Its crucial components were television and national opinion polls. The president spoke directly to all the people through television; they responded directly to him through opinion polls. Increasingly, voters tended to choose their candidates chiefly on the basis of empathy rather than issues—provided, of course, that candidates stayed within a broadly defined national consensus. Television image-making and intellectual blandness therefore dominated national elections from the 1950s onward.

Under these new political conditions, a presidential election was merely the most formal and dramatic moment in a continuous dialogue. Between elections a string of opinion polls charted results that were widely interpreted as substitute elections, measuring the success of the nation's leader. Any overwhelming endorsement of the president, such as Eisenhower's runaway victories in the 1952 and 1956 elections, became a sign of national strength. By the same token, a sharp drop in Truman's ratings during 1951 and 1952 signaled a severe national problem. Americans, in other words, made their month-by-month judgments of the president into a bedside graph of America's health.

The second significant change in the presidency involved the requirements for effective national leadership. The complex nature of the president's tasks forced him to act as a mobilizing leader for the whole nation and, at the same time, as a cautious manager of America's intricate foreign and domestic affairs. As early as the 1930s, Roosevelt had understood the need to be both inspiring and moderate. FDR, however, served during a bitterly partisan period when no one could hope to transcend parties and represent all the people. Moreover, his leadership was identified not with steady management, but with great emergencies: first depression, then war. Partisanship, as evidenced by Truman, Kennedy, Johnson, Nixon, and Reagan, remained a significant element in presidential politics. At the same time, however, these presidents also understood the need to transcend party identification and appeal to all the people. Moreover, presidents Eisenhower, Ford, Carter, and Bush could attribute much of their political success to their less partisan political styles.

Eisenhower was the first to meet the modern demands on the president. The general's background allowed him to appear a man above the clamor of special interests. Each landmark in his military career—wartime commander of the Allied armies of Europe, chief of staff, and commander of NATO's forces—suggested the highest level of nonpartisanship. Even as president, Eisenhower liked to think of himself as a nonpartisan leader. He projected an instinctive fairness that promised to reunite the nation after the harsh years of Truman and McCarthy. Although in private his temper and tongue could match Truman's, Eisenhower was more restrained in public. Eisenhower never mastered the art of a formal television speech, but he was irresistibly attractive in casual shots. His incomparable smile, strong stride, and easy yet authoritative manner made him everybody's Ike. In a special sense, Eisenhower seemed able to speak to all Americans at home and speak for them abroad.

Eisenhower strengthened his position as national leader by delegating much of the controversial work of his administration. While his secretary of state used the militant language of the Cold War, the president spoke in a moderate, conciliatory tone. The world identified Dulles with "brinkmanship." It identified Eisenhower with "Atoms for Peace," a program to share America's scientific knowledge that the president first proposed in 1953 and then elaborated in 1955. In election years Eisenhower relied almost always on broad, bland pronouncements. Vice-President Richard Nixon was the administration's partisan voice, and every two years he flayed the Democrats with rawhide campaign rhetoric.

Much of this was by design. Although Eisenhower had a reputation as being above politics, he was, in fact, a more adept politician than his contemporaries understood. Many of his press conferences, for example, which sneering critics said demonstrated his limited capacity to grasp and communicate issues to the public, were masterful performances by a man intent on obscuring rather than confronting controversial questions. He had an instinctive feel for how to reassure people rather than inflame them.

There is no better demonstration of Eisenhower's nonpartisan leadership—and of his ability to speak unequivocally when he chose—than his last presidential address, warning the country against "the acquisition of unwarranted influence, whether sought or unsought, by the military-industrial complex." Coming a few days before Kennedy's inauguration, the speech seemed to drop on the public out of nowhere. Nothing in the record would have led Americans to expect this solemn warning from their old-soldier president. But it was an issue about which Eisenhower had been thinking and worrying for several years. As an old-fashioned American who, despite his long military career, felt uncomfortable with a large defense budget, commitments abroad involving secret operations, and federal expenditures on a huge defense industry, Eisenhower saw dangers to traditional democratic habits of individual rights and limited government. In the spirit of George Washington's Farewell Address, Ike wished to give the country a final statement that cautioned against dangers to cherished American values.

Yet if Eisenhower re-created a sense of national unity and contributed enormously to the emergence of the late-twentieth-century presidency, he also left a legacy of unsolved problems that troubled all his successors. In presiding over a consumer society devoted to indulging personal desires, he did little to address chronic public needs. America's "private opulence," Adlai Stevenson had said, was matched by its "public squalor"; Ike never publicly recognized the contrast. Largely ignoring the suffering of poor Americans, urban blight, and unfulfilled promises of equal rights for all citizens, Eisenhower did little to advance the causes of economic and social justice and of civil rights. Likewise, although he refrained from direct challenges to the Soviets or from other actions in the developing world that might have precipitated war, he clung to a Cold-War orthodoxy that sustained, and at times intensified, Soviet-American differences and military preparations. To be sure, by 1960 the United States was reaching its apogee as a military and economic superpower. But its annual spending of approximately $25 billion to $30 billion on defense, between 5 percent and 6 percent of the country's GNP, which was the product of a fear—later proved unwarranted—that the Soviet Union was catching up to the United States militarily and economically, drove the country into wasteful arms building that eventually contributed to the relative decline of America's world economic leadership. The economic troubles that were besetting the United States by 1990 had some of their origins in the attitudes and policies developed in the fifteen years after 1945.

## CHRONOLOGY

**1953** Department of Health, Education, and Welfare formed.
Submerged Lands Act.
CIA-backed coup in Iran restores shah to full power.

**1954** Atomic Energy Act subsidizes private development of nuclear energy.
*Brown* v. *Board of Education* decision outlaws school segregation.
Coup ousts unfriendly regime in Guatemala.

**1955** Formosa Resolution authorizes president to protect Taiwan.
South East Asia Treaty

Organization (SEATO) formed.
Summit meeting at Geneva among leaders of the United States, Soviet Union, and Great Britain.
Merger of AFL and CIO, with George Meany as president.
Montgomery bus boycott initiates black struggle for civil rights.

**1956** Federal Highway Act authorizes building of superhighways.
Suez crisis.
Hungarian uprising.
Eisenhower reelected president.

**1957** Eisenhower Doctrine for the Middle East.
Federal troops enforce school

desegregation in Little Rock, Arkansas.
First civil rights law since 1875.
Soviet Union launches Sputnik.

**1958**  National Defense Education Act.
American intervention in Lebanon.
National Aeronautics and Space Administration (NASA) is created.

Recession in U.S. economy causes substantial unemployment.

**1959**  United States encourages formation of CENTO by Middle Eastern allies.
Castro comes to power in Cuba.

**1960**  U-2 incident.
John F. Kennedy elected president.

---

## Suggested Readings

William E. Leuchtenburg, *A Troubled Feast: American Society Since 1945* (rev. ed., 1979), is a lively introduction to the postwar years. Other recent studies of the decade can be found in Martin Jezer, *The Dark Ages: Life in the United States, 1945–1960* (1982); Paul A. Carter, *Another Part of the Fifties* (1983); Ronald Oakley, *God's Country: America in the 1950s* (1986); William O'Neill, *American High* (1986); and John Diggins, *The Proud Decades: 1941–1960* (1989). The confidence of the 1950s glows from *U.S.A., the Permanent Revolution* (1951), by the editors of *Fortune,* and from *The Big Change* (1952), by Frederick Lewis Allen. From a more critical perspective, the following help in assessing the political economy: E. L. Dale, *Conservatives in Power* (1960), and Harold G. Vatter, *The U.S. Economy in the 1950s* (1963). C. Wright Mills, *The Power Elite* (1956), explores what later came to be called the military-industrial complex. Grant McConnell, *Private Power and American Democracy* (1966), and Theodore J. Lowi, *The End of Liberalism* (1969), analyze the dangers to the public interest from pressure-group politics. John Kenneth Galbraith, *The New Industrial State* (1967), examines the influence of corporate managers in national economic policy, and Harry Braverman, *Labor and Monopoly Capital* (1974), surveys the influence of the corporate system on the working lives of its employees. John Kendrick's *Productivity Trends in the United States* (1961) and *United States Fiscal Policy, 1945–1959* (1961), as well as Herbert Stein's *The Fiscal Revolution in America* (1969), are useful specialized works. Michael Harrington, *The Other America* (1962), a classic 1960s study, discusses poverty in the United States. More recent discussions of poverty in the 1950s are Dorothy K. Newman et al., *Politics and Prosperity: Black Americans and White Institutions, 1940–1975* (1978), and James T. Patterson, *America's Struggle Against Poverty, 1900–1985* (1986). Women are covered in Betty Friedan, *The Feminine Mystique* (1963), another 1960s classic, as well as in Carl Degler, *At Odds: Women and the Family in America from the Revolution to the Present* (1980); Eugenia Kaledin, *Mothers and More: American Women in the 1950s* (1984); Leila J. Rupp and Verta Taylor, *Survival in the Doldrums: The American Women Rights Movement, 1945 to the 1960s* (1987); and Elaine Tyler May, *Homeward Bound: American Families in the Cold War Era* (1988). The ferment in values after World War II has yet to find a historian. Something of the concern for the individual is communicated in two important sociological studies: David Riesman et al., *The Lonely Crowd: A Study of the Changing American Character* (1950), and C. Wright Mills, *White Collar: The American Middle Class* (1951). Also see William H. Whyte, *The Organization Man* (1956). Alexander Meiklejohn, *Free Speech and Its Relation to Self-Government* (1948), and Hans J. Morgenthau, *In Defense of the National Interest* (1951), illustrate the demand for fixed values. Also see Carl L. Becker, *Freedom and Responsibility in the American Way of Life* (1945). Robert M. Hutchins, *The Conflict in Education in a Democratic Society* (1953), and Arthur E. Bestor, Jr., *Educational Wastelands: The Retreat from Learning in Our Public Schools* (1953), discuss the place of fundamentals in education. The new tough-minded approach to social values is revealed in Arthur M. Schlesinger, Jr., *The Vital Center* (1949); Max Ascoli, *The Power of Freedom* (1949); and Reinhold Niebuhr, *The Irony of American History* (1952). For mass culture in the 1950s, see Bernard Rosenberg and D. M. White, eds., *Mass Culture* (1957), and Eric Larrabee and Rolf Meyersohn, eds., *Mass Leisure* (1958). Intellectual crosscurrents are discussed in George Nash, *The Conservative Intellectual Movement in America* (1976), and Richard Pells, *The Liberal Mind in a Conservative Age* (1985). For America's changing population, see David Marc, *Demographic Vistas* (1984). The changes in popular music are discussed in Charlie Gilbert, *The Sound of the City: The Rise of Rock and Roll* (1970), and Ed Ward et al., *Rock of Ages: The Rolling Stone History of Rock and Roll* (1986).

The history of politics during the confident years focuses largely on the presidency. Herbert S. Parmet, *Eisenhower and the American Crusades* (1972), is a good general account of the Eisenhower presidency. Charles C. Alexander, *Holding the Line: The Eisenhower Era, 1952–1961* (1975), and Peter Lyon, *Eisenhower* (1974), cover the general's two terms. Marquis W. Childs, *Eisenhower: Captive Hero* (1958), gives valuable background. See also Sherman Adams, *Firsthand Report* (1961), the memoir by Eisenhower's primary domestic aide, and Emmet John Hughes, *The Ordeal of Power: A Political Memoir of the Eisenhower Years* (1963). Recent books on Eisenhower emphasizing his effective leadership include William Bragg Ewald, Jr., *Eisenhower the President: Crucial Days: 1951–1960* (1981), and Fred I. Greenstein, *The Hidden-Hand Presidency: Eisenhower as Leader* (1982). A balanced biographical treatment of Eisenhower is Stephen Ambrose, *Eisenhower: The Soldier and Candidate, 1890–1952* (1983), and *Eisenhower: The President* (1984). Ambrose also provides a judicious portrait of Nixon in *Nixon: The Education of a Politician, 1913–1962* (1987). The most thorough study of Nixon's life up to 1952 is Roger Morris, *Richard Milhous Nixon: The Rise of an American Politician* (1989). *The Life of Adlai E. Stevenson* (1976–77), a two-volume biography by John Bartlow Martin, sympathetically examines the hero of the liberals who twice lost to Eisenhower. Theodore H. White's classic *The Making of the President, 1960* (1961), includes shrewd observations on Nixon's losing campaign. In a deceptively entitled study, *The Revolt of the Moderates* (1956), Samuel Lubell explains moderate voting behavior that affected presidential politics.

Donald R. Matthews, *U.S. Senators and Their World* (1960), and William S. White, *Citadel: The Story of the U.S. Senate* (1957), contain interesting material on another center of political power. The most influential senator of the 1950s is studied in Robert Dallek, *Lone Star Rising: Lyndon Johnson and His Times, 1908–1960* (1991). John D. Weaver, *Warren* (1967), and Leo Katcher, *Earl Warren* (1967), praise the controversial chief justice; Milton R. Konvitz, *Expanding Liberties* (1966), and Bernard Schwartz, *Inside the Warren Court* (1983), evaluate some of the Warren Court's important decisions. How the national government has affected modern urban affairs is analyzed in Mark I. Gelfand, *A Nation of Cities* (1975). The suburbs are studied in Kenneth T. Jackson, *Crabgrass Frontier: The Suburbanization of the United States* (1985), and Robert Fishman, *Bourgeois Utopias* (1987). A crucial new political bloc is examined in Robert Gilpin and Christopher Wright, eds., *Scientists and National Policy-Making* (1964), and Don K. Price, *The Scientific Estate* (1965).

The hopes and concerns of the civil rights movement are revealed in Martin Luther King, Jr., *Why We Can't Wait* (1964); Tylor Branch, *Parting the Waters: America in the King Years, 1954–1963* (1988); Juan Williams, *Eyes on the Prize: America's Civil Rights Years, 1954–1965* (1987); David J. Garrow, *Bearing the Cross* (1986); Stephen B. Oates, *Let the Trumpet Sound: The Life of Martin Luther King* (1982); Clayborne Carson, *In Struggle: SNCC and the Black Awakening of the 1960s* (1981); and two studies in public opinion by William Brink and Louis Harris—*The Negro Revolution in America* (1964) and *Black and White* (1967). Carl M. Brauer,

*John F. Kennedy and the Second Reconstruction* (1977), analyzes a critical juncture in the movement. For background, see the first volume of Harvard Sitkoff's *A New Deal for Blacks: The Emergence of Civil Rights as a National Issue* (1978), and Charles F. Kellogg's *NAACP* (1967). The *Brown* decision is covered in Richard Kluger, *Simple Justice* (1975). For the beginnings of passive resistance, see William H. Chafe, *Civilities and Civil Rights* (1980). The sources of black militancy emerge from *The Autobiography of Malcolm X* (1965); Charles V. Hamilton and Stokely Carmichael, *Black Power* (1967); Eldridge Cleaver, *Soul on Ice* (1968); and James Forman, *The Making of Black Revolutionaries* (1972). Claude Brown's *Manchild in the Promised Land* (1965) is an eloquent statement on life and survival in the ghetto. On the travail of civil rights leaders, see David L. Lewis, *King: A Critical Biography* (1970), and August Meier and Elliott Rudwick, *CORE* (1973), the account of an organization transformed by the sweep of events. *Report of the National Advisory Commission on Civil Disorders* (1968) and Robert M. Fogelson, *Violence as Protest* (1971), reflect the complexity that came to surround the issue of black rights. The response of the Eisenhower administration is the subject of Robert F. Burk, *The Eisenhower Administration and Black Civil Rights* (1984), and James Duram, *Moderate Among Extremists: Dwight D. Eisenhower and the School Desegregation Crisis* (1981). Another useful monograph is Elizabeth Huckaby, *Crisis at Central High School, Little Rock, 1957–1958* (1980). The great black migration from the South to northern urban ghettos in the years between the early 1940s and the late 1960s is described in Nicholas Lemann, *The Promised Land* (1991).

John W. Spanier, *American Foreign Policy Since World War II* (rev. ed., 1980), is a clear, largely favorable summary. For a more critical account focusing on domestic forces, see Robert Dallek, *The American Style of Foreign Policy: Cultural Politics and Foreign Affairs* (1983). Richard Melanson and David Mayers, eds., *Reevaluating Eisenhower: American Foreign Policy in the 1950s* (1987), provides a variety of opinions. A positive picture of Eisenhower's leadership is presented in Robert A. Divine, *Eisenhower and the Cold War* (1981). Blanche W. Cook, *The Declassified Eisenhower* (1981), is another important recent study. On the internationalization of American business, see Raymond Vernon, *Sovereignty at Bay: The Multinational Spread of U.S. Enterprise* (1971), and Mira Wilkins, *The Maturing of Multinational Enterprise: American Business Abroad from 1914 to 1970* (1974). In *The Politics of Oil* (1967), Robert Engler examines some effects of internationalization. Paul Y. Hammond, *Organizing for Defense* (1961), discusses the place of the military in twentieth-century America. Maxwell D. Taylor, *The Uncertain Trumpet* (1960), is a prominent general's critical appraisal of the Eisenhower years that influenced the Kennedy administration; Richard A. Aliano, *American Defense Policy from Eisenhower to Kennedy* (1975), sides with Eisenhower. The sources and consequences of America's military foreign policy are explored in Richard J. Barnet, *Roots of War* (1972), and Alexander L. George and Richard Smoke, *Deterrence in American Foreign Policy* (1974).

Michael A. Guhin, *John Foster Dulles* (1972), praises one architect of American foreign policy for his flexibility, and Herman Finer, *Dulles over Suez* (1964), gives a detailed account of the international furor that the secretary of state raised in 1956 and 1957. For a critical appraisal of Dulles's leadership, see Townsend Hoopes, *The Devil and John Foster Dulles* (1973). A dangerous issue that spanned the Eisenhower and Kennedy administrations is examined in Jack M. Schick, *The Berlin Crisis, 1958–1962* (1971). Other books focusing on regional issues or American relations with specific countries are Barry Rubin, *Paved with Good Intentions: The American Experience and Iran* (1980); Burton I. Kaufman, *Trade and Aid: Eisenhower's Foreign Economic Policy* (1982); George McTurnan Kahin and John W. Lewis, *The United States in Vietnam* (rev. ed., 1969); Alexander Kendrick, *The World Within: America in the Vietnam Years, 1945–1974* (1974); George C. Herring, *America's Longest War: The United States and Vietnam, 1950–1975* (1979); Richard Immerman, *The CIA in Guatemala* (1982); and Stephen Schlesinger and Stephen Kinzer, *Bitter Fruit: The Untold Story of the American Coup in Guatemala* (1982).

# 32

# The Modern Republic in Turmoil

## The Sixties

~

*I*N 1960 the United States stood at the pinnacle of its power and influence in the world. Europeans worried about "the American challenge" to their economic independence, and Japan was still a relatively minor factor in the world economy. To be sure, Soviet achievements in space exploration and rocketry alarmed Americans, but the groundlessness of Western concerns about Soviet economic competition became apparent as the decade unfolded. Although the Soviet Union's military power made it a genuine threat to the United States, Americans still had reason to expect that "the American century" of world primacy remained a reality.

The sixties proved to be years of dramatic (and not always welcome) change for Americans. The Cold War threatened to turn hot over Berlin in 1961 and Cuba in 1962, but thereafter Soviet-American relations grew less confrontational. Economically, the United States enjoyed a decade of great prosperity as it recovered from the 1958 recession. An economic surge and increasing worker productivity made it possible to finance large-scale social reform while cutting taxes and holding inflation down to 2 or 3 percent annually until 1969. Along with impressive gains in the gross national product, a generation of baby boomers reached adolescence and young adulthood, increasing demand for everything from automobiles to a college education. Increasingly, advertisers and politicians saw money to be made and votes to be won by appealing to youth.

Most Americans of the era had strong faith in scientific and technical expertise and in the powers of national government management; many came to believe that every problem had a rational, managerial solution. The two Democratic presidents of the sixties, John F. Kennedy and Lyndon B. Johnson, embodied such expectations by seeking an enlargement of the federal government's responsibilities. During their administrations much of the Democratic party's program of liberal social reform finally became law. They also presided over the decade's greatest example of successful national management—the space program. Bedeviled by humiliating setbacks in the 1950s, NASA won spectacular triumphs in the 1960s, culminating in the landing of two Americans on the moon in July 1969. The decade's heroes, the astronauts, seemed to merge into a composite of the healthy, balanced American male.

John F. Kennedy became another of the decade's heroes. Although during his presidential campaign he had summoned the nation to seek a "New Frontier," the narrowness of his victory and continued conservative strength in Congress left JFK little room to maneuver. He spent most of his time in office sparring with entrenched congressional opponents over domestic issues. But before he was assassinated in November 1963, he had lifted the nation's spirits with his stirring rhetoric and dynamic style, and he had broken down some obstacles that blocked major domestic reforms.

Few considered Lyndon Johnson, Kennedy's successor, a hero. Nevertheless he brought to fruition JFK's reform proposals and much more, sponsoring the greatest burst of innovative legislation since the New Deal. And in an ironic turn of events, Johnson, a Texan with close ties to many southern conservatives, put across the boldest advances in civil rights since Reconstruction.

Yet for all the decade's bright promise, the second half of the sixties brought rancourous turmoil and a disturbing sense of national disunity. Inflation began to erode everyone's living standards, and American technology encountered formidable foreign challengers. A widening, but limited and consequently unwinnable, war in Vietnam blighted America's reputation at home and abroad and provoked passionate domestic opposition to the government in Washington. The civil rights movement turned into a bitter confrontation between rebellious young blacks and frightened middle- and working-class whites. A counterculture of angry young people rejected social norms of hard work and deference. The Republic's very ability to maintain domestic stability and traditional democratic customs seemed open to question. American world leadership and dominance began unraveling: the Vietnam War demonstrated that United States military power was not invincible and that America could not engineer "nation building" in the Third World. Liberal public policy found itself increasingly on the defensive. The nation's political leaders—especially the president and his closest advisers—could not alter course to reestablish their public credibility. By 1968 it was not clear that the country's leaders could surmount the crisis.

## Kennedy's New Frontier

From his first day in office, Kennedy encouraged a fresh sense of hope in the nation. By the end of the Eisenhower years, many Americans had mourned a loss of national purpose and energy, symbolized by the sluggish economy and by embarrassment over the Soviets' Sputnik achievement and the U-2 episode. As the youngest elected president in American history, Kennedy at forty-three

**John F. Kennedy**
*JFK's physical attractiveness and
personal charm—aided by the
Kennedy family's adroit skill at
exploiting the mass media—
endeared him to thousands of
journalists and millions of
Americans.*

radiated vigor. His inaugural address was a trumpet-blast summons to action and bold deeds:

> Let the word go forth from this time and place, to friend and foe alike, that the torch has been passed to a new generation of Americans . . . unwilling to witness or permit the slow undoing of those human rights to which this Nation has always been committed.

Calling for "a struggle against the common enemies of man: tyranny, poverty, disease, and war," he urged his "fellow Americans" in a memorable phrase to "ask not what your country can do for you—ask what you can do for your country." The "New Frontier," the name he had given to his program, described "not what I intend to offer the American people, but what I intend to ask of them."

By sponsoring a wide assortment of studies and reports, the new president imaginatively associated his office with broad national goals. Challenged by the Soviets in space, Kennedy promised to place a man on the moon before 1970, an objective that Americans of all kinds and ages would regard as a truly national enterprise. The organization of the Peace Corps in 1961, through which American volunteers took their skills to the world's poor nations, had a comparable appeal. Appropriate to his administration's image of youthful adventure, Kennedy appointed an extraordinary group of young men to high office, including his thirty-five-year-old brother Robert as attorney general.

The trim, handsome Kennedy made a striking appearance on television, as he had already demonstrated in his televised debates with Nixon during the 1960 campaign. As president, Kennedy continued to excel in both formal and informal uses of the medium. At home and abroad he cultivated a reputation as a leader as comfortable with poetry as with power, and sensitive to the nuances of style. "In a single short speech at the University of Wisconsin in 1959," one commentator on the president's style notes, "Kennedy had quoted Goethe, Emerson, Swift, Faulkner, Tennyson, Woodrow Wilson, Lord Asquith, Artemus Ward, Finley Peter Dunne, and Queen Victoria...." Kennedy's style became an object of international discussion, and "some even fancied that they saw in the White House circle the Arthurian idyll of Camelot." At times his private affairs seemed to loom larger across the nation than his public actions. Through the eager cooperation of the news industry, the president and his stunningly attractive, photogenic family entered everybody's lives: Jack and his wife, Jackie; their children, Caroline and John, Jr.; the president's brother Bobby; and the rest of the vibrant Kennedy clan whose affinity for sailing and touch football created an impression of physical vigor and a vogue for action.

There was more style than substance to Kennedy's leadership. During his presidency his rhetorical boldness often masked a striking degree of timidity in fighting for domestic change and in resisting some unwise actions overseas. Moreover, much of the hype about his photogenic family covered up compulsive philandering that did not become well known until long after his death.

**Limits of the New Frontier: The Domestic Record**

The record of Kennedy's presidency in domestic affairs is mixed. His fervent advocacy of a New Frontier and his exhortations to get the country moving again did not translate into sustained bold actions. Initially, the president spoke forcefully and persuasively about social programs that would ease the plight of the poor and the disadvantaged. But little came of the administration's plans for Medicare, civil rights, tax reform, and federal aid to education and the cities through creation of a department of urban affairs. A conservative coalition of southern Democrats and Republicans repeatedly blocked passage of Kennedy's liberal reform proposals. And Kennedy, whose liberal pronouncements seemed calculated only to conciliate the left wing of his party, initially made little effort to overcome congressional opposition. Kennedy thought it pointless to put "the office of the President on the line...and then be...defeated." To disgruntled liberals, Kennedy was continuing the same old "moderation" that they had seen under Eisenhower. Americans for Democratic Action, representing the most liberal wing of the Democratic party, concluded that Kennedy's actions "varied little from the formula developed when the Republican party controlled the White House. It is a formula of accommodation and compromise with the same coalition of Southerners and Republicans."

Yet despite a conservative Congress and Kennedy's cautiousness, his administration ultimately managed to lead the legislature into passing some significant reforms. The president realized that domestic change was necessary for the well-being of the country and he needed more enthusiastic liberal backing for his reelection campaign. As a result he fought successfully to break the conservative hold on the House Rules Committee, which had used its considerable power to block liberal reforms. This opened the way to the liberal-sponsored Trade Expansion Act of 1962, which, through the reduction of tariffs on goods exchanged between the United States and its major European trading partners, led to increased commerce and greater prosperity for both sides. The administration also persuaded Congress to raise the minimum wage, approve a controversial day-care bill to aid working mothers, expand Social Security benefits, and increase public-works spending in impoverished areas like Appalachia.

Kennedy's greatest domestic achievements came in his management of the economy. To overcome a small recession and a 7 percent unemployment rate inherited from the Eisenhower administration, he signed a number of congressional bills that would promote economic expansion. These measures provided for investment tax credits, greater depreciation allowances, and increased government spending. He also fought to hold down price increases, issuing wage-price guidelines to which business and labor generally adhered; when United States Steel raised prices in April 1962 after its workers had agreed to a noninflationary contract, for example, Kennedy pressured the company into a turnabout. His economic policies produced an average annual GNP growth rate of 5.6 percent, a 1.3 percent inflation rate, and a reduction of unemployment from 7 percent to 5 percent. This was largely the result of a general tax reduction. A multibillion-dollar tax cut, he argued, would lead to greater consumer spending and business investment—and, in turn, to greater productivity, noninflationary economic expansion, more jobs, and greater prosperity for all. After its enactment in 1964, the tax cut helped produce just these results, sustaining and expanding an economic recovery already under way. Like FDR and Truman, who had feared unbalanced budgets and deficit spending, Kennedy initially shied away from adopting Keynesian policy for stimulating the economy. But Walter Heller, the head of JFK's Council of Economic Advisers, convinced him to act boldly and initiate the first deliberate use of fiscal policy to spark and sustain an economic expansion. And the experiment worked: when combined with government spending on the Great Society and Vietnam, the tax cut fueled an economic boom for the rest of the sixties, providing the foundation for the wide range of reform legislation enacted under Kennedy's successor.

**Further Limits: Kennedy and the Civil Rights Revolution**

Kennedy also compiled a mixed record on civil rights. Despite the Democratic platform's strongest civil rights pledges in history, civil rights activists accused Kennedy of being "supercautious" about implementing them. During his first two years he refused to support major civil rights legislation, believing that doing so would alienate the conservative southern bloc in Congress—and hence would jeopardize the rest of his reform program and "divide the American people at a time when the international scene required maximum unity." He also believed that an assertive civil rights policy would alienate white southern voters from the Democratic party and jeopardize its hold on the region. Eisenhower had already made inroads in the South in the presidential elections of 1952 and 1956; JFK feared the Republicans might expand their Southern base in 1964 and after. But his efforts to win over southern Democrats failed: White House favors and flattery did not break southern legislators' resistance to Kennedy's larger reform plans. Internationally, moreover, his inaction cost him more than he gained, for his failure to move openly and vigorously to secure the civil rights of black Americans offended the leaders of the new, formerly colonial, nations then emerging around the globe.

Although a conservative Congress held back the administration, it had considerable leeway to support civil rights through executive action. But here the president was also very cautious. Kennedy had made campaign promises to end discrimination in federally assisted private housing covered by FHA mortgages "with a stroke of the pen," but he took no such action until a flood of pens arrived in the White House mails in 1961–62; and even then his executive order of November 1962 covered only future housing. Under Robert Kennedy the Justice Department did make greater efforts in behalf of black rights than had the Eisenhower administration. Nevertheless the Kennedy administration offered only "limited assistance" to southern blacks and to civil rights activists attacked by white racists. Yet the nonviolent protest stimulated in the South by the leadership of Martin Luther King, Jr., by the SCLC, SNCC, and CORE, and by the courageous actions of ordinary blacks like Rosa Parks assured that the issue would not go away.

A major crisis over an attempt by a black student, James H. Meredith, to register at the University of Mississippi in 1962, however, persuaded the White House to make a more concerted effort to defend a black man's rights with federal policing agencies. And this was after King complained that while southern blacks had "marshaled extraordinary courage to employ nonviolent direct action, they had been left—by the most powerful federal government in the world—almost solely to their own resources."

Other administration actions hampered the civil rights cause. For example, Kennedy appointed a number of bitter-end segregationists as southern judges. He hoped to appease Mississippi's Senator James Eastland, who as chairman of the Judiciary Committee had the power to clear other, more liberal nominees whom Kennedy had proposed. But in meeting Eastland's wishes the White House made judicial appointments that perpetuated racism in the South under the cover of law. Further, the administration in 1963 agreed to FBI wiretaps on Martin Luther King, Jr. Intimidated by nonsensical charges that King was under communist control and that the civil rights movement was a communist conspiracy, the president and the attorney general thus allowed J. Edgar Hoover to violate King's constitutional rights and to attempt to destroy his reputation and public influence.

These blemishes on the president's record, however, do not fully measure the history of civil rights in the Kennedy years. If JFK initially held back from pushing civil rights legislation, he left little doubt that, unlike Eisenhower, he personally sympathized with the Supreme Court decisions in behalf of racial justice. If he moved slowly in issuing a directive against discrimination in federally assisted housing, it was in the hope of persuading Congress to establish a new department of urban affairs, which he wished to put under the direction of economist Robert C. Weaver, who would become the first black cabinet member. If he appointed federal judges recommended by Senator Eastland, it was part of a strategy to win the approval of Eastland's Judiciary Committee for the appointment to the federal circuit court of Thurgood Marshall, the black general counsel of the NAACP, who had been active in securing the *Brown* decision. If his Justice Department did not use federal power at every turn to protect black rights, it went well beyond other administrations in the twentieth century—bringing lawsuits to defend voting rights, using federal marshals (with imperfect results) to protect "freedom riders" who challenged segregation on interstate buses and trains and in terminals, and pressing the Interstate Commerce Commission into compelling desegregation by interstate carriers in the South. If the Kennedys acceded to Hoover's wiretaps on King, they also told the civil rights leader that he was under surveillance and that they expected the allegations against him to be refuted.

Most important, events by 1963—especially the acts of black civil disobedience reproduced on television screens—had driven the administration into a historic effort to end discrimination and segregation through federal legislation. The effort in May 1961 of thirteen black and white "freedom riders" on a bus trip from Washington, D.C., to New Orleans to desegregate interstate transportation, the violence against SNCC workers trying to register black voters in 1961–62, and the confrontation over James Meredith in 1962 forced the civil rights issue before the American public more dramatically than ever before. In April 1963 public sympathy for black rights increased sharply when a massive civil rights demonstration in Birmingham, Alabama, the strongest bastion of Deep South segregation, received international attention. The city's police commissioner, Eugene "Bull" Connor, provoked worldwide indignation when he ordered attacks on the marchers by police dogs, electric cattle prods, and water hoses under such high pressure that they tore the bark off trees.

Birmingham was a turning point for President Kennedy. He believed that if other Birminghams occurred it could lead to nationwide disorders and a race war that could radicalize blacks and destabilize the country. Kennedy saw dire consequences for American foreign policy in such developments. In June, therefore, after federalized National Guardsmen had forced the integration of the University of Alabama over the opposition of Alabama Governor George C. Wallace, JFK threw the full force of his office behind the most comprehensive civil rights bill in history. Speaking to the nation on television, the president condemned the legacy of racial injustice and asked: "Who among us would . . . be content with the counsels of patience and delay? One hundred years of delay have passed since President Lincoln freed the slaves, yet their heirs, their grandsons, are not fully free. They are not yet freed from the bonds of injustice; they are not yet freed from social and economic oppression. And this nation, for all its hopes and all its boasts, will not be fully free until all its citizens are free." Asking Congress "to make a commitment it has not fully made in this century to the proposition that race has no place in American life or law," Kennedy described passage of the law as necessary "not merely for reasons of economic efficiency, world diplomacy and domestic tranquility—but above all, because it is right." Although Kennedy did not live to see the bill enacted, his action marked the first time in American history that a president had openly advocated the end of segregation.

## The Kennedy Foreign Policy

By the time Kennedy had come to office in 1961, the idea of the Cold War as a worldwide contest between monolithic communist totalitarianism and American democracy had begun to erode. Mounting evidence of a split between the two most powerful communist nations—the Soviet Union and China—undermined frightening theories of a worldwide communist conspiracy. In the early fifties, after the Cold War had stabilized, few other nations gave anticommunism the same overriding importance that the United States assigned to it. With the delineation of clear spheres of control, diminished fears of Soviet aggression, and reviving prosperity, America's allies felt freer to follow their own inclinations in world affairs. France led the resistance. By refusing to join the European Defense Community in 1954, France destroyed America's plans for a thoroughly integrated continental military force. After 1958 the Fifth French Republic, under its imperious president Charles de Gaulle, became the center for continuing European criticism of American policy. More subtly, Japan also maneuvered for greater independence from the United States. No sooner had the American occupation ended in 1951 than Japan sought full control over its own territory and policies. Here, as in Western Europe, desire to trade with communist nations contributed to the tension, for the United States opposed almost all economic relations between the communist and noncommunist blocs.

Although the world's agrarian nations enjoyed only a meager share in the prosperity of the fifties, many of them, too, were marking out their own separate paths. The electric names in Africa and Asia were those of fervent nationalists: Nasser, Kwame Nkrumah of Ghana, Jawaharlal Nehru of India, and Sukarno of Indonesia. In a variety of ways these leaders struggled to develop their nations without sacrificing their independence to either side in the Cold War. Extremely sensitive to pressures from the great powers, they retaliated in anger when the United States or the Soviet Union appeared to dangle economic aid as an incentive to enter their camps. Because the United States was allied with their former imperial masters in Europe, the recently emancipated colonies especially

**Adlai Stevenson at the United Nations**

*Stevenson's supporters hoped that Kennedy would appoint him secretary of state, but the President had no intention of doing so. Being named U.S. ambassador to the United Nations seemed to Stevenson almost an exile from the centers of power in Washington. Occasionally, he was able to employ his eloquence to good effect, but—especially as the Vietnam War got under way— Stevenson found himself defending policies that he personally opposed.*

set themselves against American domination. By the early sixties these new states were describing themselves as the Third World—nations equally independent of both superpowers.

With Kennedy's inauguration, Washington officials began exploring ways of responding to the diverse ambitions of many nations. The new president, who expected to build his reputation in foreign affairs, encouraged fresh ideas about America's policies. He promised to accept the new nations of Africa and Asia on their own terms and to negotiate with the established nations as equals. In 1961 Kennedy announced the "Alliance for Progress" with Latin America that would use economic aid from the United States to improve living standards in the Western Hemisphere. Insisting on steps toward greater economic and social justice as the only conditions for help, the administration said it wanted to "transform the American continent into a vast crucible of revolutionary ideas and efforts...." The Peace Corps, which sent American volunteers to under-developed countries to help improve their educational systems and give their citizens needed technical skills, also placed individual human needs above international military policy.

Nevertheless, in the day-to-day conduct of foreign affairs, Kennedy, his primary foreign policy adviser McGeorge Bundy, and Secretary of State Dean Rusk gave priority to the containment of international communism. In fact, the administration, reflecting the views of most Americans, saw the world in terms of a continuing, dangerous struggle between communism and freedom. During the 1960 campaign Kennedy had claimed that Soviet technological advances had outstripped those of the United States, creating a "missile gap." Although no one ever found the gap, the new president launched the largest and fastest peacetime military buildup in American history: in the seven years between 1960 and 1967 the number of American ICBMs quintupled; the Kennedy administration committed itself to having three times as many ICBMS and four times as many long-range bombers as the Soviets. To make credible America's willingness to fight a nuclear war, the administration offered federal dollars and technical assistance to localities to build fallout shelters, which supposedly would save 97 percent of the population from nuclear destruction. It was an unrealizable fantasy. Through flexible military power, Kennedy envisioned a new American mastery in the global battle against communism. In Latin America, United States policy aimed not to implement the Alliance for Progress, which came to little, but to isolate Castro's Cuba and to insulate other countries against similar revolutions. The United States aided Latin American nations in proportion to their commitment to anticommunism.

**The Bay of Pigs**     The administration's focus on containing and defeating communism found direct expression in its dealings with Castro's Cuba. The Kennedy government carried forward plans made during Eisenhower's term to topple Castro's regime, either through his assassination or by an invasion of Cuban exiles. Kennedy himself apparently was never informed of the assassination plot, despite the fact that the CIA continued to pursue the idea throughout his years in office. (Indeed, on the same day in November 1963 that Kennedy was killed, the CIA was supplying weapons to a Cuban defector planning to murder Castro.)

The invasion of Cuba by Cuban exiles in April 1961 was another matter. Kennedy had learned of the plan five months before its execution and had had ample opportunity to call it off. But he saw a compelling logic in its favor: an invasion might well bring down Castro and forestall other anti-American revolutions in the hemisphere. If it failed, the invaders could still escape into the Escambray Mountains (or so the planners believed), where they could undermine Castro's power with guerrilla operations. As important, if the United States called off the invasion, the Cuban exiles would denounce Washington's loss of nerve, which the White House feared would encourage pro-Castro revolutions all over the Caribbean and open the administration to domestic political attack by conservatives. Consequently, Kennedy allowed the CIA to complete preparations for a small army of the exiles to launch an attack. Ignoring the advice of Senator J. William Fulbright, chairman of the Foreign Relations Committee, who saw the operation as "wildly out of proportion to the threat," Kennedy approved what turned out to be a disastrous landing at the Bay of Pigs on the southern coast of the island. Attacking without sufficient air or land forces to defeat Castro's army and banking on an uprising against the Havana government that never occurred, the invaders were quickly defeated. The United States was widely denounced for its indifference to international law and for its hypocrisy in avowing a commitment to self-determination for nations everywhere. The defeat seriously injured the administration's prestige and self-confidence and emboldened the Soviet Union to commit acts of aggression that brought the two superpowers to the edge of war.

**Soviet-American Relations: From Confrontation to Détente**
Even before Kennedy had come to office, the Soviets had signaled their intention to press vigorously for their interests against the young, inexperienced president-elect, whom they hoped to intimidate. At the beginning of January 1961, Khrushchev publicly predicted the ultimate triumph of socialism through national wars of liberation. In June, two months after the defeat at the Bay of Pigs had thrown his administration on the defensive, Kennedy met Khrushchev at Vienna. The Soviet premier tried to bully the president, forecasting the victory of communism over capitalism and insisting that the West sign a German peace treaty making West Berlin a "free city" or risk being ousted by Soviet arms. American diplomats accompanying the president called Khrushchev's behavior "par for the course." That may have been true of Soviet behavior toward lower-level representatives, but Khrushchev had spoken with greater restraint in his dealings with Eisenhower. Viewing Khrushchev's threat as a first step toward the neutralization of Western Europe, and as part of a larger design on Southeast Asia and the Western Hemisphere, Kennedy responded with a call-up of reserve forces and plans for a huge military buildup, including nuclear submarines, conventional army units for fighting limited wars, and special counterinsurgency forces to combat national wars of liberation. The Soviets answered by constructing the Berlin Wall in August 1961 to halt the migration of skilled East German workers to the West, as well as by resuming nuclear testing in the atmosphere, which produced radiation fallout. Detonating some fifty nuclear bombs during the next two months, the Soviets concluded the tests with the explosion of a fifty-seven-megaton weapon, the largest ever assembled. An attempt to intimidate the United States, the testing program only added to Soviet-American tensions by persuading Washington also to resume testing in April 1962.

The Kennedy-Khrushchev clash of wills culminated in the Cuban missile crisis, the most dangerous superpower confrontation in the Cold-War era. In the fall of 1962 the Soviets began placing medium-range nuclear missiles in Cuba that could reach a large part of the United States. Despite American convictions to the contrary, the Soviets had few missiles that could reach the United States from the Soviet Union. Putting medium-range missiles in Cuba could give Moscow greater genuine military parity with Washington. Khrushchev seems to have intended using the missiles to force Kennedy into accepting a German peace treaty and an arms-control agreement that would deter Communist China from building a nuclear arsenal. Apparently Khrushchev planned to appear before the United

**"Cuban Missile Showdown"**
*The most dangerous
confrontation between the two
superpowers since 1945 occurred
in October 1962 over the
introduction of Soviet missiles
into Cuba. The successful
resolution of this crisis opened
the way to the Test Ban Treaty
in the following year.*

Nations, disclose the presence of the missiles, and offer to remove them in return for an agreement on Germany and on "atom-free" zones in central Europe and the Pacific. "If our two countries united their efforts . . ." Soviet Foreign Minister Andrei Gromyko had asked rhetorically in 1961, "who would dare and who would be in a position to threaten peace?" In other words, the Chinese, with whom Moscow was coming into sharper and more open conflict, would be deterred from building weapons that could threaten the USSR.

Before Khrushchev could act, however, New York Republican Senator Kenneth Keating in October revealed the existence of the Soviet missiles in Cuba. Kennedy went on television to confirm the ominous news. To prevent the Soviets from completing the installation of the weapons, the president announced a naval blockade of military shipments to the island. Although Kennedy thought that the missiles would not have substantially altered the strategic balance between the two sides, he believed that it "would have politically changed the balance of power" and would have further thrown his administration on the defensive at home and abroad. Hence he not only introduced the blockade, but also warned the Soviets that any use of the missiles would result in a full-scale attack on the Soviet Union. At the same time, however, he refused to launch a preemptive air strike against the missile sites that would have intensified the crisis. Days of excruciating tension marked the confrontation: the world seemed on the verge of war. We stood "eyeball to eyeball," one official later said. Both American and Soviet decision makers remembered the crisis as an agonizing moment when a misstep could have triggered the greatest catastrophe in human history. Acting responsibly, Kennedy and Khrushchev reached agreement. The Soviet leader promised to remove the missiles in return for a public pledge not to invade Cuba and a private one to dismantle American Jupiter missiles in Turkey.

The resolution of the Cuban missile crisis represented a turning point in world affairs generally and in Soviet-American relations in particular. Ironically, the confrontation had a positive consequence: it deepened the two superpowers' understanding of the dangers of nuclear weapons. To be sure, the Soviets partly responded to the crisis by starting their own huge military and naval buildup, which could secure them against another such humiliating political defeat. But at the same time, the missile crisis opened the way to a significant improvement in Soviet-American relations that came about principally through Kennedy's efforts. Recognizing more clearly than ever that "mankind must put an end to war or war will put an end to mankind," the president used his diplomatic victory not to humiliate the Soviets, but to advance the cause of peace. He forbade members of his administration to gloat over America's triumph and warned them against assuming that the Soviet pullback was a sign of weakness. Had Soviet national security been directly threatened in the confrontation, he said, they would have acted differently. Fortunately, this threat had not been present, and relations with the Soviet Union, he now concluded, "could be contained within the framework of mutual awareness of the impossibility of achieving any gains through war."

Kennedy eloquently expressed these views in a major address at American University in June 1963. In what Khrushchev called "the greatest speech by an American president since Roosevelt," Kennedy proposed a turn toward détente—a policy of lowering tensions between the Eastern and Western blocs. "What kind of peace do we seek?" he asked. "Not a pax Americana enforced on the world by American weapons of war.... Not merely peace for Americans but peace for all men and women—not merely peace in our time but peace for all time." He urged Americans and Russians alike to "re-examine our attitude toward the Cold War, remembering that we are not engaged in a debate.... We must deal with the world as it is." We are, he added, "caught in a vicious and dangerous cycle in which suspicion on one side breeds suspicion on the other, and new weapons beget counter weapons."

In the summer of 1963 Kennedy followed up his appeal for détente by successfully negotiating with the Soviet Union a ban on atmospheric and underwater nuclear explosions. Supported (according to one opinion poll) by 80 percent of the American public, he overrode the objections of a minority who were predicting the loss of America's future security and guided the treaty through the Senate. Had Kennedy lived to serve another term, perhaps—as one historian has suggested—he "might have taken the world a good deal farther along the road to disarmament and peace."

The resolution of the Cuban missile crisis and the test-ban agreement were major steps on the road to détente and ultimately the end of the Cold War. Although it would take another twenty-eight years fully to realize these goals, the Cold War never again reached the flashpoint that almost came in 1962. How far Kennedy would have advanced the détente process had he lived is open to question. The most we can know is that his Vietnam policy suggests little conviction on his part that an end to the Cold War was within reach.

Vietnam and Southeast Asia

**Kennedy and Vietnam**

Kennedy's actions in Vietnam call into question his historical reputation as a peacemaker. The difficulties he confronted in Southeast Asia were already well advanced when he entered the White House. An international conference in Geneva in 1954 had created three independent states from the former French territory in Indochina: Laos, Cambodia, and Vietnam. "Temporarily," Vietnam had been divided between a communist north and a noncommunist south, pending national elections and unification. But with American support, between 1954 and 1956 the Diem government in southern Vietnam had rejected the

Geneva plan for national elections and had established a permanent state. As Kennedy took office, the anticommunist governments in both South Vietnam and neighboring Laos were in jeopardy. Eisenhower told the new president that Laos was the key to all Southeast Asia and urged unilateral intervention, if necessary, to keep it out of communist hands.

Although Kennedy had doubts about Eisenhower's "domino" theory—the notion that the "loss" of any country in Southeast Asia would inevitably bring communist control throughout the area—he acted as if it were a sound idea. In his first State of the Union message, Kennedy warned that "the relentless pressures of the Chinese communists menace the security of the entire area—from the borders of India and South Vietnam to the jungles of Laos, struggling to protect its newly won independence." Kennedy believed the freedom and independence of the Laotian people to be at stake in the conflict, and he promised that "this Nation shall persevere in our pursuit of these objectives."

The United States negotiated the neutralization of Laos with the Soviets, but South Vietnam was a bigger problem. The Vietcong, South Vietnamese guerrillas backed by North Vietnam and China, refused to negotiate; and Kennedy and his advisers were provoked into seeing the Vietnamese struggle as part of a worldwide communist drive for power. The battle of "freedom versus tyranny," Kennedy told Congress in May 1961, was being fought in Vietnam. Vice-President Johnson warned that "we must decide whether to help these countries [in Southeast Asia] to the best of our ability or throw in the towel in the area and pull back our defenses to San Francisco and a 'Fortress America' concept." Kennedy's military advisers also urged a strong American effort, including a force of possibly 10,000 men. " . . . As I knew from experience with my French friends," George Ball, Kennedy's under secretary of state, later said, "there was something about Vietnam that seduced the toughest military minds into fantasy."

Kennedy was convinced that the Vietnamese struggle was primarily a fight to halt the advance of communism in Asia, and he expected that by defeating the communists with a successful American-sponsored "democratic revolution" the United States would send the world a powerful signal of its progressive intentions. Thus he committed American men, materiel, and prestige to the defense of South Vietnam. In a sense he saw the increased American effort in Vietnam as a militarized version of the Peace Corps. American military power would support a social revolution in Vietnam that would demonstrate the American commitment not to Western imperial control or repressive anticommunist regimes, but to the fostering of economic and political democracy around the globe. To Kennedy's satisfaction, moreover, the policy seemed to work. In 1962 Secretary of Defense Robert McNamara reported that "every quantitative measurement we have shows we're winning this war." Others in the American government echoed this belief, and by the beginning of 1963 Kennedy was telling the nation that "the spearpoint of aggression has been blunted in South Vietnam." At the same time, Secretary of State Dean Rusk saw Diem's regime making "steady movement toward a constitutional system resting upon popular consent."

These appraisals were far too optimistic. By the fall of 1963 the Saigon government had made little progress toward winning (in a phrase popular at the time) "the hearts and minds" of the South Vietnamese people. Unbiased reporters concluded that Diem was losing the war. When public demonstrations by South Vietnamese groups led by the Buddhist clergy (who felt oppressed by the Catholic Diem) made this point clear, the Kennedy administration acquiesced in a military coup, in the course of which Diem died. The American government at once recognized the new regime and renewed its commitment to keep South Vietnam free. Having already put 16,000 American military advisers in the country by November 1963, it seems likely that Kennedy, had he lived, would have expanded United States involvement to prevent defeat. But some evidence suggests otherwise. Two months earlier he had said that it was up to the people of South Vietnam to win or lose the war, and he made plans to withdraw all American military advisers from the country in 1965. He had confided these hopes to at least two American senators, contending that he felt compelled to wait until after the 1964 election, when he could be less concerned about Republican assertions that he might be "losing" South Vietnam. Still, his militant anticommunism and his determination to be "tough" in foreign affairs, especially after the Bay of Pigs and his unnerving experience with Khrushchev in Vienna, make it doubtful that he would have withdrawn United States forces from Vietnam.

On November 22, 1963, questions about what Kennedy would do in his second term suddenly became unanswerable. Kennedy was struck down in Dallas, Texas, by Lee Harvey Oswald, a drifting malcontent; and Oswald in turn was murdered in the Dallas city jail by the nightclub operator Jack Ruby. It was the most unexpected and devastating single event in the nation's history since Lincoln's assassination almost a century earlier. And television made Kennedy's death all the more dramatic; indeed, no event had ever been so thoroughly national and yet so intensely personal. During a long weekend of mourning, the nation immersed itself in every detail of the tragedy and its aftermath. Through television Americans traced the president's motorcade through Dallas, saw Kennedy jarred by an explosion of shots, shared the vigil outside the hospital, witnessed Oswald's incredible murder, and then followed the somber state funeral through the gray streets of Washington. Almost two decades later, with important questions about the assassination still unanswered, millions could recreate those "six seconds in Dallas" as if their lives too had hung in the balance.

In memory, Kennedy's popularity soared. But as time passed his record came under scrutiny and stirred controversy, and his standing—at least among historians, if not the general public—fell. Kennedy's thirty-four months in office suggest that he was a man of considerable intelligence and political astuteness who effectively responded to changing events. His more aggressive stand on civil rights and the foreign policy successes during his last year speak well of his political realism. But his initial caution on domestic affairs and escalation of American involvement in Vietnam reveal sides of him that might have put sharp limits on additional achievements in the White House. On balance John Kennedy's brief presidency brought some major national gains and some lost opportunities. Above all he will be remembered for his youth and gallant style that gave the country a sense of hope and renewed conviction that it could meet major challenges.

## Domestic Affairs Under Johnson

Lyndon Baines Johnson, Kennedy's vice-president, took the presidential oath on the airplane that carried Kennedy's body back to Washington. It was soon obvious that Johnson could not command the public affection that Kennedy had won. The tall, overbearing Texan, best known as a political wheeler-dealer who in 1948 had won a United States Senate seat by 87 tainted votes, entered the White House with little fixed national support. Many doubted that he would be able to overcome his regional and personal limitations to become an effective national leader. But he quickly removed these doubts.

Although a rough-and-ready figure who could not match Kennedy's high style, Johnson was a man of boundless drive, keen intelligence, and great compassion for the disadvantaged. He had grown up in the Texas Hill Country, where as a boy he had known personal privation, and he had taught in a south Texas elementary school, where he tried to relieve Mexican American youngsters' deprivation. During two years as head of FDR's National Youth Administration in Texas and twelve years as a congressman beginning in 1937, Johnson gained a reputation as the country's best youth administrator and a devoted New Dealer. From 1949 to 1961 Johnson served as a United States senator, becoming the most effective majority leader in American history. Although he thought of himself as a southwesterner, he understood that the nation viewed him as a southerner committed to racial segregation. Ambitious to become president and raise living standards in the South, the country's poorest region, Johnson supported federal programs that expanded the southern economy. He also helped pass the 1957 civil rights bill, the first attack on southern racial discrimination by Congress since 1875. Johnson came to the White House better prepared to lead the nation in domestic affairs than almost any other president in United States history.

Johnson's five years in the White House are among the most important in this century. Eclipsing every American president except Franklin Roosevelt in driving Congress to pass major domestic reform legislation, Johnson fought a war on poverty that he aimed to win through the creation of what he called the Great Society. Johnson described his program as leading "not only toward the rich society and the powerful society but upward to the Great Society," which "rests on abundance and liberty for all. It demands an end to poverty and racial injustice, to which we are totally committed in our time." Further, the Great Society was to be an America in which "men are more concerned with the quality of their goals than with the quantity of their goods."

**LBJ for the USA**
*Johnson's 1964 presidential campaign emphasized his qualities as a national figure who spoke for all Americans. Running against Senator Barry Goldwater, who impressed most as a radical of the right, LBJ won a landslide victory.*

**The Election of 1964**    From the moment he assumed the presidency, Johnson set about winning the office in his own right and going down in history as a great leader. With the election of 1964 less than a year away, he moved quickly to appeal to Democratic constituencies outside the South. His primary goal was the passage of the Kennedy civil rights bill, which had become a rallying point for liberal and moderate Americans across the land. On November 27, 1963, Johnson told Congress that "no memorial oration or eulogy could more eloquently honor President Kennedy's memory than the earliest possible passage of the civil rights bill. . . . We have talked long enough in this country about equal rights. . . . It is time now to write the next chapter, and to write it in the books of law." The following July, after defeating a fifty-seven-day southern filibuster in the Senate, Johnson signed the 1964 Civil Rights Act into law. It prohibited discrimination in places of public accommodation such as hotels and restaurants, required equal treatment for all in public facilities like parks and swimming pools, forbade the use of federal funds in specific hospitals, universities, and the like that practiced discrimination, and provided some—but not full—protection against loss of black voting rights.

Johnson won a number of other victories that raised his standing with liberals and partly satisfied his drive for economic and social justice in the United States. Under his prodding, Congress greatly expanded federal aid to education and approved an urban mass-transit subsidy, a food stamp program, and the $11.5 billion tax cut proposed by JFK to fuel economic expansion and greater prosperity for all. He also persuaded Congress to pass the Economic Opportunity Act of 1964, which created the Office of Economic Opportunity (OEO) to advance the "War on Poverty" that he had declared in January 1964.

Having identified himself so strongly with the liberal side of the Democratic party, Johnson worried that the Republicans might seize the middle ground from him in the campaign of 1964 by nominating New York's moderate governor, Nelson Rockefeller. But the Republicans obliged Johnson by choosing Senator Barry Goldwater of Arizona, an uncompromising conservative who candidly advocated a return to the pre–New Deal era by repealing social welfare and civil rights laws and by freeing the United States from the burdens of the Cold War through the decisive defeat of the Soviet communist threat. By telling the Republican convention that "extremism in the defense of liberty is no vice," Goldwater identified himself all the more with radical-right fringe groups nursing McCarthyite anticommunist obsessions, which were anathema to the majority of voters. Goldwater bumper stickers declared: "In your heart you know he's right"; the Democrats played on fears of nuclear war by countering: "In your heart you know he might."

Despite his obvious advantage in running against so impolitic a candidate, Johnson worried that Goldwater would arouse patriotic support by attacking the administration's "no win" actions in Vietnam. Johnson announced that he would not escalate the war: "We are not about to send American boys nine or ten thousand miles away from home to do what Asian boys ought to be doing for themselves." During the campaign, however, he ordered United States forces to bomb North Vietnam after that country's gunboats allegedly made an unprovoked attack on American destroyers in the Gulf of Tonkin. In fact, United States naval vessels there were aiding South Vietnamese raids on the North, and the evidence supporting Johnson's claim of enemy attack was questionable. In addition Johnson extracted from Congress the Tonkin Gulf Resolution, authorizing the president "to repel any armed attack against the forces of the United States and to prevent future aggression." "Like grandma's nightshirt," Johnson said of the resolution, "it covered everything." While campaigning as a "peace" candidate, Johnson also made sure that Goldwater could not attack him as too weak a defender of American interests. Johnson's appeal was reminiscent of Wilson's slogan in 1916, "he kept us out of war," and of FDR's promise in 1940 not to go to war. Like theirs, LBJ's pacific avowals were doomed to disappoint many voters who believed them.

In 1964, however, Johnson's strategy could not have been more effective. He handed Goldwater the worst defeat ever suffered by a major party's presidential candidate up to that time. Winning 61.1 percent of the popular vote—43 million

**LBJ on the Campaign Trail**
*Johnson reached a high point of popularity with the country in the 1964 campaign. By the end of his presidency, however, he could appear in public only at military bases.*

votes—as against Goldwater's 38.5 percent (27 million), Johnson held the largest popular vote, the greatest margin of victory, and the highest percentage of the vote in history. With advantages of 295 to 140 in the House and 68 to 32 in the Senate, the Democrats at last were in a position to fulfill the president's program—to carry out the agenda of liberal social reform dating back to Truman's presidency.

Yet Goldwater's decisive defeat obscured conservative impulses in the country that would dominate national politics in the seventies and particularly in the eighties. Uncomfortable with social permisiveness, with insistent minority demands for federal programs costing billions of dollars, and with crime in the streets, Americans found more appeal in Goldwater's conservative agenda than the results of the 1964 election might suggest. To be sure, Goldwater went beyond what the majority of Americans wanted in domestic and foreign affairs, but he spoke to bedrock attitudes. Just sixteen years later, Ronald Reagan, a more skillful politician than Barry Goldwater, would begin converting conservative impulses into massive electoral victories.

**The Great Society Enacts the Liberal Agenda**

Under Lyndon Johnson's direction in 1965–66, the Eighty-ninth Congress became, in the words of the House Speaker, "the Congress of accomplished hopes . . . of realized dreams." In a whirlwind of activity that astonished even the most optimistic reformers, Congress passed a series of laws that made fundamental changes in American life. Medicare provided medical and hospital insurance for the elderly under Social Security, and Medicaid meant that the indigent could also receive health care. Newly created cabinet-level departments oversaw new federal programs in transportation and in housing and urban development. A new immigration statute ended the system of national-origin quotas established in the 1920s, making family reunification and vocational skills the bases for admission to the United States. Education bills provided aid to elementary, secondary, and higher institutions of learning. A housing act created federal rent supplements for the poor, and the Model Cities program encouraged the redevelopment of decaying urban communities. Highway, traffic safety, and clean air and rivers acts were passed, and there was even a highway beautification law. To wage the War on Poverty, Johnson pushed through the Appalachian Regional Development Program, a domestic peace corps called VISTA (Volunteers in Service to America), the Head Start program for disadvantaged preschool children, the Neighborhood Youth Corps to help unemployed teenagers, the Job Corps for school dropouts, the Upward Bound drive for sending more underprivileged young people to college, and the Community Action Program, promoting direct participation by poor people in easing their plight.

The combination of the 1964 tax cut and the wide-ranging attack on poverty produced dramatic results. The gross national product, also spurred by massive military spending for the war in Vietnam, nearly doubled during the sixties, and the economy added 10 million new jobs. Like the GNP, median family income nearly doubled, while the number of Americans living below the poverty line fell by approximately 50 percent, to 11 percent of the total population.

Yet Johnson's program was never as revolutionary as some feared and others hoped it would be. The package of reforms Johnson drove through the Congress represented a high-water mark in twentieth-century American liberalism. Ideas that had been enunciated since the thirties, and in some cases as far back as the Progressive Era, now became law. Liberals, who had been arguing for years that federal programs could remedy suffering and bring the poor more into the mainstream of national economic life, saw the Johnson reforms as a realization of sorts. Many liberals complained, however, that Johnson did not follow through on what he had done. The annual budget for the War on Poverty never went much above $2 billion—less than one-quarter of 1 percent of GNP. The program did little to redistribute income and nothing to guarantee jobs. "For a mere $11 billion," the economist Robert Lekachman complained, "we could raise every poor American above the poverty line." But the administration had no intention of making the War on Poverty a "handout program" and instead relied on traditional American assumptions about ambition, education, opportunity, and success. Still, the Great Society went well beyond what had been done earlier: in announcing his program, Johnson committed his administration to a vigorous national management of matters that the localities had once controlled. Justifiable comments were heard that the Great Society gave the government more control than ever before over American economic and social life, and one critic wrote that the country had "moved...nearer to state collectivism at the federal level than in any previous period."

Whether it was limited funding or a limitation in government programs to perform up to expectations, the Johnson reforms had a number of misses. Though Medicare guaranteed health care for the elderly, its costs to the government diverted funds from other badly needed programs, including support for impoverished youngsters, and burdened all Americans with increased federal deficits. Medicaid proved an increasingly heavy financial burden on the states as well as on the federal government and entangled doctors and hospitals in endless red tape. Federal aid to education did not produce a renaissance in American schools. On the contrary, twenty-five years later, educators across the country lamented the state of the nation's schools, and numerous Americans bewailed the gap in math and science skills between American and Japanese students. Although the War on Poverty sharply reduced economic privation in the country, it had no significant impact on black urban ghettos, where conditions during the next twenty-five years worsened.

The conservative surge in the seventies and eighties partly grew out of frustration with intrusive government domestic programs that delivered only part of what they promised. Twenty-five years after LBJ declared war on poverty, liberals had become identified with government activism that troubled a majority of voters—or those who bothered to vote. The "L word" (as it became known in the 1988 election) had turned into a shibboleth with which Republicans could club Democrats. By 1990 few citizens were ready to give up the liberal programs enacted in the sixties, but neither were many prepared for additional reform efforts that might improve existing programs or attack persistent social problems.

**Civil Rights**     Behind the civil rights movement lay a faith that the American creed of equality under the law and individualism—the right of the individual to reach his or her full potential regardless of race—would inevitably triumph over its antiblack contradictions. The Warren Court depended on the creed to give social authority to its legal rulings against segregation. Martin Luther King, Jr., depended on the creed as a national white conscience that his strategy of civil disobedience could stir. The Johnson administration depended on the creed to rally the people who were still resisting a national program to eliminate racial inequalities from American life. Because of their common faith in the creed, a disciplined black minority and a well-to-do white minority had been able to work together for black rights. As a climax to the biracial civil rights movement, whites had enthusiastically applauded in 1964 when King rose in Oslo to receive the Nobel Prize for Peace.

In the summer of 1964, black and white civil rights workers launched the Mississippi Summer Project, a campaign to register black voters in the state and enroll black children in "freedom schools," where they were to be taught about their rights and turned into activists in behalf of black rights. In response, white vigilantes bombed and destroyed two dozen black churches across the state and murdered three civil rights workers—James Chaney, Andrew Goodman, and Michael Schwerner—in Philadelphia, Mississippi.

These outrages helped fuel a renewed drive in 1965 for black voting rights. Early in the year, civil rights activists under King's leadership attacked southern restraints on the freedom of blacks to vote. Throughout the South blacks, intimidated by threats of physical violence and unpassable literacy tests, remained largely barred from the polls. To dramatize the issue King led a series of demonstrations in Selma, Alabama, where blacks had been systematically excluded from the franchise. Recognizing that the way to get federal legislation was to bear the burden of white violence, King and his supporters exposed themselves to white abuses. Television carried graphic scenes of blacks being brutalized and thus helped sharpen national outrage. After several violent clashes provoked by local authorities, and the killing of a white Unitarian minister from Boston, Johnson asked Congress for a voting rights law that would "establish a simple, uniform standard which cannot be used, however ingenious the effort, to flout the Constitution." In a moving address praising the courage of black Americans fighting for freedom, as America's rebels had at Lexington in 1775, Johnson pledged to wipe out the prejudice that blighted the lives of all Americans. Quoting the anthem of the civil rights movement, Johnson said: "It is all of us who must overcome the crippling legacy of bigotry and injustice, and we shall overcome."

After a widely publicized march by civil rights activists from Selma to Montgomery in March 1965, which Johnson agreed to protect with federalized National Guardsmen, Congress passed a voting rights statute in the summer of 1965. The law authorized federal agents to register qualified voters in counties where 50 percent or more of voting-age citizens were unregistered. The law had immediate and substantial consequences: in the three years following passage, voter registration among southern blacks increased by almost 50 percent. Black registration in Mississippi, for example, increased from 6 percent to 44 percent of eligible voters. Within a decade the whole texture of southern politics would begin changing as white candidates started courting black voters. Political participation by blacks increased not only in the South, but in other parts of the country as well. In every region of the nation black Americans made some political gains, winning election to high city, state, and federal offices.

Along with legislative acts and judicial rulings securing civil rights for blacks, the mid-sixties also saw a series of Supreme Court decisions that significantly extended the rights of social outcasts, such as persons accused of spreading obscenity, rejecting majority opinion, or breaking the criminal law. The Court widened the legal definition of obscenity when it ruled that unless a book, magazine, or film was "utterly without redeeming social value," it could not be banned. The Court acted to protect religious minorities by barring required prayers and Bible readings in public schools. The Court voided federal requirements that members of subversive organizations had to register with the government. In *New York Times Co.* v. *Sullivan* (1964), it broadened First Amendment protection by making it almost impossible for public figures to win libel suits. The Court declared a state law against the use of contraceptives by married persons an unconstitutional invasion of "a marital right of privacy," and it voided a Virginia statute outlawing racial intermarriages. In *Gideon* v. *Wainwright* (1963), the Court ruled that everyone accused of a felony, regardless of economic circumstance, had a right to an attorney. *Escobedo* v. *Illinois* (1964) gave alleged lawbreakers the right to counsel during interrogation and the right to remain silent. *Miranda* v. *Arizona* (1966) required police to inform criminal suspects of their rights, including the right to an attorney and to remain silent, and to the information that anything they said might be used against them.

Led by Chief Justice Earl Warren, the majority of Supreme Court justices viewed these decisions as part of a broad pattern of "incorporating" the Bill of Rights into state law and the everyday procedures of local courts and police forces. This was the same rationale that the Supreme Court used in broadening the civil rights of racial minorities. The Warren Court outraged conservatives who saw its decisions as protecting criminals rather than victims and subverting the American way of life. "They've put the Negroes in the schools," an Alabama congressman declared, "and now they've driven God out." "Impeach Earl Warren" became a rallying cry of Court opponents who saw Warren and the Court as emblematic of everything that had gone wrong in the United States.

**Black Power**  The Johnson administration's belief that it was easing the plight of black Americans received a rude jolt in the summer of 1965. On August 11, five days after the Voting Rights Act became law, the black neighborhood of Watts in Los Angeles exploded in some of the worst racial rioting in American history. Although disturbances had erupted in northern cities in the past, including several in the summer of 1964, none of them was quite like the Los Angeles upheaval. Unlike the black slum areas of New York, Chicago, Philadelphia, and other major cities, Watts was a comparatively well-off area with numerous private homes and little evidence of substandard dwellings and littered streets. But an adult unemployment rate of 30 percent, combined with a bitter antagonism among Watts residents toward a largely white police force, created tensions that made the community an emotional tinderbox. Instead of easing these problems, new civil rights laws and modestly funded government programs had brought only frustration. Instead of optimism, Johnson reforms had produced despair among urban blacks who saw no way out of their poverty. One consequence was a Watts riot costing 34 lives, over $35

**Ghetto Riot 1964**
*The civil rights laws and modestly funded government programs of the 1960s brought more frustration than relief to urban ghetto dwellers.*

million in property damage, 856 injured, and more than 3,000 people arrested. A federal investigating commission described the bitterness and despair that had generated the rioting, warning that if the existing racial breach were allowed to continue, it "could in time split our society irretrievably."

As the commission had foreseen, Watts was "only a curtain-raiser" for what occurred during the next three summers. Between 1966 and 1968 Cleveland, Chicago, Detroit, Newark (New Jersey), Jacksonville (Florida), and other cities suffered similar racial eruptions, with widespread death, injury, and destruction: 43 people died in Detroit, for example, while another 2,000 suffered injuries and thousands of fires gutted the inner city.

Martin Luther King, Jr., who continued to preach nonviolence, now was out of step with black militants urging black nationalism and "black power." Rejecting King's call for love and understanding, dynamic new leaders appeared who alarmed even sympathetic whites. Stokely Carmichael of the SNCC and Malcolm X, at first a spokesman for the separatist-minded Black Muslims and later an advocate of a more orthodox (but still black-oriented) Islamic religion, urged their followers to separate themselves from their white oppressors. It was the whites' hatred and abuse, the militants said, that had forced blacks to fight back.

Whites did not really believe in equality and justice for all: on the contrary, white values created a self-serving institutional structure that made blacks a colonial people inside American society. Only an exclusively black, racially proud movement could hope to break these institutional shackles.

Blacks' turn toward militancy rested on a realistic appreciation that white America was unprepared to deal with the root causes of discrimination and black poverty. As one astute commentator put it, "It doesn't cost anything to move a few feet along a hamburger counter to make room for a Negro. But the cost—economic, social, psychological—of abolishing forever a Negro ghetto of half a million souls is only now becoming apparent." When King tried to desegregate housing in Chicago, angry white mobs pelted him with rocks. Despite the Johnson War on Poverty, blacks continued to earn about half of what whites made, while black unemployment remained at twice the rate of whites. The SNCC advised its members that "true liberation" for black Americans would mean forming "our own institutions, credit unions, co-ops, political parties, write your own histories." Soul singer James Brown expressed the defiant mood with his song "Say It Loud—I'm Black and I'm Proud."

In April 1968, in a tragic confirmation of the racial hatred that was an enduring part of America, a white escaped convict named James Earl Ray killed Martin Luther King, Jr., as he stood on the balcony of a Memphis motel. A fresh outburst of rioting shook the nation's ghettos, taking an additional thirty-nine lives and giving added meaning to the report that the National Advisory Commission on Civil Disorders had issued a month before: "Our nation is moving toward two societies, one black, one white—separate and unequal."

The commission was acutely aware of the entrenched poverty and despair of the ghettos, which the Great Society had barely begun to relieve. The rise of black separatism and the outbursts of ghetto rioting, which the commission attributed largely to the continuing effects of economic deprivation and white racism, frightened the progressive camp. Liberal whites and moderate blacks had united around the assumption that blacks desired—and should desire—peaceful integration into a hitherto white-dominated society. Thus warnings about a drift to "two societies" were not mere rhetoric: they arose from the fear that separatism, racial disorder, and the squalor that spawned them would, if not overcome, destroy the liberal dream of social justice and equality, thrusting the nation back into its segregated, violence-ridden past.

## The Johnson Foreign Policy

As a rising tide of troubles beset the Johnson administration at home, it was confronted with distracting problems abroad. Johnson's background and experience made him more comfortable with domestic than foreign affairs, and he was frustrated by his inability to control overseas events. Moreover, he had little patience with internal divisions over foreign policy. In his view, presidential direction of diplomacy was not a fit subject for domestic debate. "I am the only president you have," he was fond of saying. When the safety of the nation was at stake, he believed it unpatriotic for Americans to question the government's policy, especially in dealing with the "world-wide communist threat." The experience of the thirties helped shape Johnson's views on foreign affairs. Johnson feared that any hint of appeasement would undermine national security; every challenge to American power must be met with a vigorous response. His dealings with Panama and the Dominican Republic, for example, evoked memories of Theodore Roosevelt's "big stick" diplomacy. And in Southeast Asia Johnson became mired in a Vietnam war he could neither win nor end. The expansion of presidential control over foreign affairs since 1941, or the growth of the "imperial presidency," also influenced Johnson. FDR, Truman, Eisenhower, and Kennedy had all acted without public and congressional knowledge to ensure what they saw as the national security, and Johnson saw himself doing the same thing in the Caribbean and southeast Asia.

The violence Johnson perpetrated abroad soon tarnished and blocked the advances that LBJ achieved at home. Vietnam, one critic complained, is "poisoning and brutalizing our domestic life. . . . 'The Great Society' has become the sick society." The war split the country and blighted Johnson's presidency. By the time he left the White House, many Americans spoke of "the tragedy of LBJ"; but his was only part of the larger tragedy of a postwar liberalism that had failed in its drive to ensure social justice and halt communism in a single, simultaneous burst of progressive action.

**Policing Latin America**

Policy toward Latin America demonstrates LBJ's difficulties in overseas affairs. When, in January 1964, President Roberto Chiari of Panama broke relations with the United States and demanded renegotiation of the 1903 Panama Canal Treaty, Johnson took a hard line, saying that he would not knuckle under to a "banana republic" no more populous than St. Louis. When the Organization of American States proposed formal negotiations, Johnson contemptuously refused. Subsequently, however, the president did agree to a "review" of outstanding issues between the United States and Panama, which led to a new treaty giving Panama a greater voice in the management of the canal and a larger financial return.

Johnson's intervention in the Dominican Republic in the spring of 1965 had a less satisfactory outcome. In April a group of Dominican army officers revolted, hoping to replace an unpopular conservative regime with a more liberal one under Juan Bosch, a former head of government. Informed by the American embassy that American lives were in danger and that communists were playing a significant part in the uprising, Johnson immediately decided to send in the marines. The American troops, numbering over 20,000 quickly overcame the rebels, and the existing government stayed in power. Bosch justifiably complained that his had been "a democratic revolution smashed by the leading democracy of the world."

Johnson believed that a hands-off policy toward the Dominican Republic might have produced another Cuba. But he greatly overestimated and overstated the danger. Almost none of what the president said about the Dominican episode was true, and it helped create what became known as the credibility gap. "How do you know when Johnson is telling the truth?" a Washington joke went. "When he scratches his head, rubs his chin or knits his brow, he's telling the truth. When he begins to move his lips, he's lying." The invasion did little, if anything, to serve national security. Moreover, by raising doubts about the administration's capacity to pursue a rational foreign policy, it intensified a growing concern over the wisdom of Johnson's course in Vietnam.

**The Vietnam Disaster**

Like Eisenhower and Kennedy, Johnson felt compelled to stave off a communist victory in Vietnam. Unlike them, however, he responded to the growing peril in South Vietnam with a commitment of vast American resources. He and great numbers of Americans believed that a communist victory in South Vietnam would pave the way to Chinese communist domination of all Southeast Asia and would encourage Moscow and Beijing to take more aggressive steps that might provoke a nuclear war. The president also feared that failure in Vietnam would touch off a fierce domestic debate like the one of the early fifties over the "loss" of China. The spirit of Joe McCarthy made him fear right-wing Republicans again breaking Democratic-liberal control of the government. Thus Johnson vowed that he was "not going to lose South Vietnam." But he always regarded Vietnam as a frustrating obstacle to the enactment of his reform program at home. In order to dampen domestic challenge to his military plans, as well as to avert congressional balking over the expensive Great Society programs, Johnson waited much too long before asking for a tax surcharge to fight the war in Southeast Asia. Only in the seventies would the inflationary consequences of this decision become fully apparent.

In February 1965, after the Vietcong killed 8 Americans and wounded another 108 in an attack on an American base at Pleiku, 240 miles northeast of South Vietnam's capital, Saigon, the president ordered retaliatory air strikes. Three weeks later he authorized the continuous bombing of North Vietnam in the hope of forcing the North to the conference table. At the same time he sent additional combat units into South Vietnam to supplement the 16,000 men Kennedy had ordered there in 1962–63.

Johnson now acknowledged that American boys would fight in defense of United States military installations. (Thus he reversed Kennedy's intention that Americans act only as advisers, although some of these men died in combat.) But LBJ did not reveal that they were also authorized to undertake offensive operations. In short, he escalated American involvement without a debate or explicit congressional and public approval. It was a fatal error. Forgetting the lesson FDR had applied in World War II—that a major military commitment abroad required a stable supporting consensus at home—Johnson made himself vulnerable to later charges that Vietnam was his war. Since most Americans and a majority of the Congress would have supported his actions in early 1965, he could have saved his administration and the country considerable political grief by

**American Troops in Vietnam**
*LBJ's escalation of the war led to large United States casualties and some atrocities in Vietnam.*

making escalation of the fighting in Vietnam a genuine expression of the national will—for example, by having Congress declare war. This is not to say that American involvement would have been any wiser or that the war would have ended differently. But it might have reduced some of the alienation Americans felt toward their government over the war, and might have given Johnson greater political leeway eventually to jettison a failing enterprise.

Once he had committed American forces, Johnson sank ever deeper into a quagmire. By the end of April 1965, American forces in South Vietnam numbered almost 50,000. In July the administration committed itself to sending another 150,000 troops, who were to carry out an aggressive "search-and-destroy" strategy against the enemy. Although the American commander, General William Westmoreland, predicted that this would produce victory by 1967, during that year an end to the fighting was nowhere in sight. Worse yet, by then the number of American ground forces had risen to 400,000; as many as 543,000 were fighting in 1968. The cost in dead and wounded also grew alarmingly. By the end of 1968, more than 30,000 Americans had died and another 100,000 had been wounded. Repeated assertions from American political and military chiefs that they could see the light at the end of the tunnel evoked the cynical comment that "sometimes the light at the end of the tunnel is from an onrushing train."

Simultaneously the air war escalated in numbers and ferocity. In order to kill guerrillas in the South, disrupt supply lines from the North, and demoralize the North Vietnamese government and people, American planes assaulted "free fire zones" in South Vietnam and struck at North Vietnam's capital, Hanoi, and its main port, Haiphong. By 1968 the total tonnage of bombs dropped on Vietnam reached nearly 3 million tons—almost 50 percent more than had been dropped by United States air forces during World War II.

All this had astonishingly little effect in breaking the will of the Vietcong and North Vietnamese to fight. To be sure, tens of thousands of Vietnamese lost their lives and far more were wounded or driven from their homes. But according to numerous estimates at the end of 1967, the killing had "not discernibly weakened" the Saigon government's opponents. Where a series of corrupt South Vietnamese regimes generated little popular support, the communists had a sense of mission that allowed them to justify their sacrifices. The Tet, or Lunar New Year, offensive begun by the communists on January 30, 1968, underscored their continuing will and capacity to fight. Attacking most of South Vietnam's provincial capitals, briefly capturing the city of Hué, and assaulting the American embassy in Saigon, the communists demonstrated how far the United States remained from victory. Although American officials called the offensive "a complete failure" and discussed the possibility of sending another 206,000 troops to finish off the enemy, Johnson had to concede that further escalation was politically impossible. On March 31 he rejected the proposal for sending more troops, announced a reduction in the bombing of North Vietnam, proposed the start of peace talks, and revealed his decision not to run for reelection in 1968.

The war had been lost not so much through military defeat, but rather through an erosion of national will to continue fighting. No one knowledgeable of military realities would minimize the resources required for the United States to have broken communist resistance, but more than likely with an all-out effort the United States could have defeated North Vietnam. But Americans, understandably and wisely, did not wish to commit themselves to a struggle requiring not only vast additional forces but also a huge occupation army for the indefinite future. Although the North Vietnamese had exhausted themselves in the Tet offensive, public opinion in the United States was in no mood to take advantage of Hanoi's military vulnerability with another commitment of men to launch a fresh offensive.

**Opposition to the War**

Johnson withdrew from the presidential race because he believed he could not win. His record-breaking support in 1964 had disappeared in the debate over Vietnam. Far from being a nation of contented citizens thankful to their president for peace and prosperity, America by 1968 seethed with racial and political animosity.

Early in 1965, when Johnson had begun to expand American commitments in Vietnam, he had hoped that the war would be over in twelve to eighteen months,

**Antiwar Demonstrators**
*The Vietnam war provoked massive opposition in the United States and ultimately drove LBJ from office.*

before serious domestic opposition to the fighting could emerge. To his distress, protests erupted at once. In March 1965 students and faculty held the nation's first teach-in at the University of Michigan, where they presented the case against the war. Others followed across the country. Church, labor, civil rights, and congressional leaders, not to speak of ordinary middle-class Americans convinced that the war was morally wrong and destructive to the national well-being, took up the cry against the conflict. But instead of bringing about any change in administration policy, these protests only promoted a sense of betrayal among Johnson and his aides. Secretary of State Rusk, for example, railed at "the gullibility of educated men" and "their stubborn disregard of plain facts."

As the gap between opponents and supporters of the war widened, a minority among the opposition adopted more extreme tactics. Young men, many of them affluent university students, began to burn their draft cards and to chant "Hell No, We Won't Go!" Demonstrations and marches turned into violent clashes with the police. Angry college students seized campus buildings, roughed up university officials, and forced the temporary shutdown of several institutions of higher learning. Privately calling dissenters "crazies" and publicly denouncing them as "nervous Nellies" ready to "turn on their own leaders, and on their country, and on our own fighting men," Johnson drove them into a greater sense of alienation. Frustrated opponents of the violence in Vietnam and of American racism, which many saw reflected in the disproportionate numbers of blacks serving and dying in the war, seized on the administration's unbending attitude and began to advocate their own brand of self-righteous violence. Proclaiming violence to be "as American as cherry pie," and declaring that "to get rid of the gun it is necessary to take up the gun," radicals urged an all-out assault on the status quo, on an "Amerika" that had turned into a Hitlerlike "Fourth Reich."

## The Crisis of Modern Liberalism

During the sixties American liberalism reached its climax by enacting civil rights laws and social reforms that seemed to promise a substantial reduction in, if not an end to, discrimination and poverty. Resistance to "communist aggression," at least through the first half of the sixties, also satisfied liberals, who saw the resolution of the Cuban missile crisis as leading to advances in Soviet-American relations and reduced likelihood of a nuclear war. By the end of the decade, however, the limits to government effectiveness in overcoming poverty, riots in the country's urban ghettos, and the unproductive and demoralizing violence in Vietnam undermined liberal confidence and pushed the country in more conservative directions.

The expansion of federal power at home with only mixed results and the projection of so much American military might abroad with so little positive result left the country with a feeling that it had lost control of events. Kennedy's assassination caused not only a sense of personal loss, but also a feeling of national disintegration. Science and technology, particularly the computer, which in the fifties had promised impartial answers to the world's problems, began to seem not an answer to most problems but a threat to personal autonomy. The "military-industrial complex," against which Eisenhower had starkly warned in 1961, became a national obsession. And millions felt their hopes for social justice and progress betrayed as the Washington "experts" led the United States into an unwinnable war.

These crosscurrents generated a sense of alienation throughout American society. Alienation was most obvious among those young people, white and black, who protested against the war, denounced American institutions, and adopted lifestyles that shocked their elders; Marxism, which gave the question of alienation a revolutionary twist, attracted some. And although most upper-middle-class Americans rejected the young rebels' methods, they shared some of their children's alienation. Discontent with their jobs and family life, for example, drove elders restlessly to search for "fulfillment"; and worry over the dangers that technological progress posed to the individual knew no age boundaries. Alienation also extended to millions of ordinary, or "middle," Americans who felt threatened by the rapid social change around them. A "generation gap" was separating them from their children; traditional institutions and ideals such as the family, sexual morality, the work ethic, and patriotism came under attack; and black activism and expansive federal power challenged the familiar world of white power and community mores.

**The New Left**      The alienation of some young Americans expressed itself in the rise of the New Left movement. Impatient with thirties-era "Old Left" arguments over subtleties of Marxism and the inability of traditional left-wing ideas to alter enduring inequities in American society, the New Left offered a fresh radical perspective on long-standing problems. In 1962 Tom Hayden and Al Haber, University of Michigan students, formed Students for a Democratic Society (SDS) and issued Hayden's Port

Huron Statement, the New Left's manifesto. Condemning racism, poverty, and the Cold War, Hayden predicted that students, not workers, would be the catalyst for social changes. Much influenced by the dissident fifties sociologist C. Wright Mills, Hayden denounced social management by impersonal powerful elites, which described how some students felt about America's elite universities. Instead he called for decentralizing society through "participatory democracy," or power to the people. Two years later a group of students at the University of California, Berkeley, led by Mario Savio, captured national attention for New Left ideas with the Free Speech Movement. In the fall of 1964, when students alienated by Berkeley's bureaucratic impersonality challenged a new campus rule against political activism on campus, university police arrested them. Declaring "depersonalized, unresponsive bureaucracy...the greatest problem of our nation," Savio and 6,000 other students seized control of the administration building and stopped classes with a strike. In response University President Clark Kerr made the rules on free speech the same as those operating in the society at large. The success of direct action at Berkeley and the expansion of the Vietnam War spurred political activism on other campuses. The SDS steadily moved from antiwar protest and peaceful community organizing to disruptive and occasionally violent antiwar resistance. As it did so the SDS lost its optimistic, democratic tone. By the late sixties it had succumbed to fantasies of violent revolution, and divided into warring ideological factions.

**Counterculture**
Meanwhile other well-to-do white youths expressed their alienation by adopting a flamboyantly dissenting lifestyle. In the second half of the sixties the hippies, or flower children, as these young people were called, offered a penetrating commentary on contemporary life. Their protest exposed the most sensitive problems of the individual in modern society. In response to a dehumanizing bureaucracy, the young dissenters assaulted the nation's important institutions by pointedly rejecting the products of these institutions—the government's laws, the party's candidates, the corporation's goods, the university's degrees. Many more young people cheered them on. Rather than postpone gratification in the name of seeking a career, radicals (and millions of other youths) wanted the good life now. Feeling lonely, they emphasized community and loyalty and love; craftsmanship, nature, and the "whole earth" were sacred causes. A few rebels tried to build an entire life around these values in self-sufficient rural communes. Young radicals even reflected their society's preoccupation with power: the abuse of power, they claimed, lay at the root of America's social evils. "Power to the people," originally the SDS slogan, would bring a new era of justice. Although a small minority of their age group, they were so visible and so audible that they always seemed far more numerous than they were, clustering in parks to smoke marijuana and sing or crowding the sidewalks around college campuses.

In many ways these young dissenters were acting out just one more variation of the modern adolescent rebellion. All the standard elements of the past forty

**Janis Joplin** (1943–70)
*Joplin was a leading rock singer of the 1960s, known for her passionately extravagant style of singing and for her reckless personal life. She died of a drug overdose.*

years were there. Increasingly, fast-changing rock music raised a musical barrier between the generations. Trust no one over thirty, the rebels declared. Even their primary areas of rebellion—dress, language, drugs, and sex—were the familiar ones from the twenties. Yet as one historian put it, "the counter culture was foreshadowed by the 'revolution in morals' and the critique of Puritanism and materialism in America of the 1920's and, more recently, by the beats in the 1950's. But to produce a movement of this particular nature demanded the special circumstances of the sixties—the emergence of a generation of young people endowed with a superabundance of worldly goods, locked into an educational system for two decades or more, cordoned off in multiversities, roiled by the draft and the Vietnam War, troubled by its prospects in a world that seemed increasingly bureaucratized and technologically driven."

Yet there was also a mindlessness to the counterculture that made it a short-lived phenomenon. Rejecting history, rigorous study, almost every kind of traditional institution, and conventional notions of work and family, counterculture folks embraced mysticism, communal living, drugs, and sexual liberation. "Screw work," Yippie Jerry Rubin exulted, "we want to know ourselves." The goal was "to free oneself from American society's sick notion of work, success, reward, and status and to find and establish oneself through one's own discipline, hard work, and introspection." Despite such rhetoric, the counterculture tended to be elitist, parasitic, and self-indulgent. As the prominent writer and dissenter in the fifties and sixties Paul Goodman came to see, the movement attacked political

**A Barefoot Couple at a California Commune**
*The alienation of some young people in the 1960s gave rise to a counterculture reminiscent of earlier protest movements in America.*

and moral institutions not to change them but to replace them with a vague something called "interpersonal relations." It became clear to him that most counterculture rebels saw no room for the knowledge or standards necessary to a civilized society. The counterculture offended most American adults. To be sure, a minority of elders defended the right of their sons and daughters to a dissenting lifestyle, and they even found courage to act out their own feelings. Some marched for civil rights and peace. Others, acknowledging the need for a new intimacy in human relations, experimented with "encounter" and "sensitivity" groups and greater sexual freedom. A few joined the youthful dropouts. But a majority of adults opposed the new youth movement. By making public their private anxieties, the young rebels threatened the balance that older people were trying to maintain between adult responsibility and adult discontents. The more extreme the rebellion, the more widespread the opposition became. By 1970 the young radicals had lost almost all their adult sympathizers. Nevertheless some of the counterculture values infiltrated straight society in the seventies and eighties. The use of "recreational drugs," relaxed standards of what constituted appropriate viewing and language in films and on television, and the nationwide craze about "natural" foods were all, in one degree or another, survivals from the counterculture.

**Women's Liberation March**
*The late 1960s saw a powerful revival of women's demands for true equality and a greater measure of social justice. Rooted in the civil rights and antiwar causes, the new women's movement acquired a momentum of its own.*

**Rethinking Gender** The most lasting outgrowth of the rebellious sixties was a revived movement for women's rights, an emboldening of homosexuals to leave "the closet," and a greater sensitivity in society at large to questions of gender role.

After a promising search for new directions in the twenties, the women's movement had collapsed during the depression. In the forties women poured into the labor market to stay, and during the fifties they expanded the range of their public activities. But questions of basic rights remained dormant. Only in their private world away from work did women enjoy anything approximating the freedom of men. As dressing styles, leisure activities, and public behavior increasingly became "unisex," men continued to monopolize the best jobs. By the sixties, partly because one-third of American marriages ended in divorce, partly because of consumerism, and partly because of inflation, close to half of the women in America were employed. Most women received lower salaries or wages than men did for the same work, and an even larger proportion of women found themselves blocked somewhere along the ladder of promotion in their occupations. Meanwhile women's responsibilities at home scarcely changed. Widespread concerns about individual fulfillment, anxieties about powerlessness, and increasing doubts about the quality of American consumerism had particularly sharp application in the lives of women.

In 1963 Betty Friedan's *The Feminine Mystique* broke the silence by analyzing the evils of sexism. The drive for black rights, in which women took a significant part, contributed a vocabulary to communicate women's feelings of oppression; antiwar activity, especially draft counseling, also helped sensitize and politicize college-age women. The civil rights movement inspired the acronym of a new pressure group, the National Organization for Women (NOW), which appeared in 1966. ("What do you want?" the civil rights marchers chanted. "FREEDOM!" "When do you want it?" "NOW!") NOW issued a bill of rights calling for an Equal Rights Amendment to the Constitution; in turn, its supporters believed, the ERA would help them gain equal employment opportunity, maternity leave, community child-care facilities, tax deductions for child-care expenses, equal educational opportunity, and the right to an abortion.

One portion of the swelling movement declared themselves "radical feminists" and explored the myriad psychic and cultural ways in which women were bound into the role of "the second sex." Radicals urged the need for consciousness-raising activities that would draw women into their ranks and transform perceptions of women's personal problems as "common problems with social causes and political solutions." Through consciousness-raising, Robin Morgan wrote in *Sisterhood Is Powerful* (1970), "you begin to see how all-pervasive a thing is sexism—the definition of and discrimination against half the human species by the other half." Group action followed consciousness-raising. Organizing a day-care center, a women's health collective, or an abortion counseling center were some examples. At the same time women were urged to publicize sexism by bra burnings, invading all-male bars and clubs, protesting the Miss America Pageant by crowning a sheep, and holding protest marches.

Moderate and radical feminists joined in concentrating on women's economic plight. This reform agenda met far less male resistance. Gender, like race or culture, was irrelevant to the skills standards that prevailed in most white-collar occupations. Here women's demands for equal opportunity were an irrefutable claim. Both the federal courts and the national executive made commitments to enforce equal access to jobs and equal pay for equal work. Although extensive discrimination against women remained, an important start had been made.

Challenges in the sixties to conventional standards joined with the civil rights movement to encourage male and female homosexuals publicly to acknowledge their sexual preferences and demand gay rights or protection against discrimination. Sparked by a police raid in 1969 on a gay bar in New York City's Greenwich Village, the movement for gay rights or gay power took the form of marches and organized pressure for acceptance by private and public institutions. "Say it loud, gay is proud," marchers chanted in a parade through midtown Manhattan. Initially, the movement was largely confined to New York and San Francisco, where unconventional lifestyles were more commonplace than in other more traditional cities and towns. Like radical feminism, gay rights posed a challenge to heterosexual male primacy, which was deeply embedded in traditional American (and Western) culture. Pressure to end discrimination against gays made significant progress in the seventies, although the outbreak of the AIDS epidemic in the eighties revived and intensified feelings in the society against persons practicing alternative sexual lifestyles.

**Counterattack** The counterculture and radical protests provoked a national backlash aimed at inhibiting federal intrusion on behalf of minorities, restoring conventional values, and reestablishing white, middle-class citizens at the center of American life. This eruption of "middle America's" anger reached full force in 1968, and as late as the 1990s its power was not yet spent.

The period of acute crisis over federal intrusiveness had begun in 1957, when Congress passed the first civil rights law since Reconstruction, federal troops enforced school desegregation in Little Rock, and the Warren Court stepped up its activism. By 1965 the barriers against national power appeared to be smashed: federal officials were registering Southern black voters, and federal funds for the War on Poverty bypassed white middle Americans in favor of the people economically below them. Not only did the public welfare rolls swell enormously in the mid-sixties, but some agents of OEO even encouraged welfare recipients to demand more and to attack politically entrenched urban governments.

The first line of middle America's counterattack was against blacks' drive for full equality. Contrary to the hopes of those in the civil rights movement, millions of whites understood the American creed not as a common system of national values, but as the justification for their particular set of values. Turning inward, they continued to be concerned only with their own families, cultural identities, and special local ways. Attempts to draw Americans into a uniform system of national rules arrived like an enemy invasion. In most cases they could not grasp the legal and bureaucratic procedures behind such rules, and many were "functionally illiterate" in the face of tax forms, insurance claims, credit contracts, and similar fine print.

Across America, skin color was a primary means of establishing protective barriers. White wage earners, who increasingly had to work with people of other colors, still refused to accept them into their daily lives. During the fifties these insular feelings had exploded in anger throughout the South, where the civil rights movement had begun. But temperatures were also rising in the North, where every city suffered from housing shortages and where local resources were increasingly strained, partly as a result of new migrations. Rural blacks and whites who had been replaced by mechanical cotton pickers, consolidated farms, and mechanized coal mining poured into the city slums. So did Mexican Americans and Puerto Ricans, trying to escape their own grinding poverty. In the crowded, competitive northern cities, racial antagonisms turned into hate. When Martin Luther King, Jr., took his civil rights campaign north in 1964, the ferocity of the white reaction matched anything he had encountered in the South.

By itself the civil rights movement would not have provoked a white revolt against federal authority. But the movement was accompanied by a broader drive for power. Many of the Warren Court's decisions had interfered with the censorship of films, schoolbooks, and pornography by middle Americans. The Court's defense of the rights of accused alarmed these Americans, who feared street crime and thought that they could not walk in their neighborhoods if the police were hampered in the pursuit of suspects. The Court's outlawing of prayer and Bible reading in the public schools deeply offended the many Americans who continued to believe that religion belonged in the school as well as the home. And the Court's use in 1962 of the "one person, one vote" principle in redrawing state election districts undermined the customary way in which voters and politicians had sought to protect small towns against outside, urban intrusion. Liberals, however, praised the Court's decision as a remedy to the shift of urban tax revenues to rural areas and small towns which dominated state legislatures through unequal districting.

American liberals had convinced themselves that their understanding of equality, opportunity, and justice was everybody's American creed. As they used this creed to make national policy, they assumed that no one would seriously question the new policy's impartiality. Bursts of opposition, they believed, were only temporary interruptions in the march toward nationwide acceptance. But this nationalizing process had the opposite effect. Instead of creating a non-political consensus, it ignited fresh political conflicts. By 1965 not a great deal had actually changed. Only a small percentage of black children attended integrated classes. Many communities still found ways of keeping Christianity in and "alien" books out of their schools. Police procedures altered very little. Nevertheless, when conservative whites saw a solid phalanx in the national government arrayed against them, they prepared to fight for their traditional rights.

In northern and southern cities alike, advocates of traditional rights combated the racial integration of the schools, especially when integration meant busing black and white children. Numerous white Catholics in New Orleans, Philadelphia, and Boston openly resisted their church's policies of integration. Urban politicians attacked the local agencies of OEO and lobbied in Washington to disband it. They liked the federal dollars OEO offered cities but not the efforts to provide for maximum feasible participation of the poor. In the towns as well as the cities, bumper stickers reading "Impeach Earl Warren" and "Support Your Local Police" signaled a growing opposition to judicial restraints and supervisory review boards. The Crime Control Act of 1968, which generally endorsed strong police action, seemed a significant victory in this cause. Mayor Richard Daley of Chicago became an instant hero in many white communities when he reportedly instructed the police to maim looters and kill arsonists during a ghetto riot.

The second line of conservative America's counterattack was directed at the youth rebellion. "Side-burns . . . shall not extend lower than the bottom of the ear opening and shall be of uniform width," the regulations of the Louisville Fire Department stated. "Beards, goatees or any other extraneous facial hair will not be permitted." Opinion polls showed consistently large majorities favoring severe punishment for drug users, including marijuana smokers. Although the Vietnam War was unpopular throughout the United States by 1968, waving a Vietcong flag or burning an American one, as television showed some radicals doing, evoked widespread anger. By traditional values, affluent students had no right to insult their nation or squander its educational privileges. The New York police who cracked heads while breaking a campus strike at Columbia University in 1968, the townsmen who took a crowbar to the flower children, or the hard-hatted construction workers who roamed lower Manhattan beating up long-haired youths were expressing the feelings of innumerable fellow citizens. In May 1970, when four students at Kent State University were killed by the National Guard (summoned to confront a campus demonstration), a nationwide poll tallied four out of five Americans on the side of the guardsmen.

What happened at Kent State typified what was happening throughout the country at the end of the decade. University administrators relied more and more on the local police to control student unrest. Law enforcement agencies killed, jailed, or scattered the leadership of a small, militant black power organization, the Black Panthers. After 1967 the peace marches in Washington were battling, antagonistic affairs, and the peace organizations, always a quarreling lot, became increasingly fragmented. Occasionally a happy episode broke the pattern. In the summer of 1969 "the nation of Woodstock," perhaps 400,000 young people, gathered at White Lake, New York, for a rock festival and a holiday frolic. But a few months later in Altamont, California, an attempt to repeat the joys of Woodstock dissolved in violence.

**The Election of 1968**    These crosscurrents dominated the presidential campaign of 1968. At the beginning of that year, the forces of protest and reform seemed on the verge of capturing the national government. The summer before, a quarter-million Americans had marched quietly through Washington in behalf of peace in Vietnam. Both their number and their discipline gave the movement a new respectability. The inheritor of this strength was a thoughtful, enigmatic Democratic senator from Minnesota, Eugene McCarthy, who in November 1967 opened his campaign for president on a peace platform. In January and February 1968, as the Tet offensive seemed to expose the military failure of America's policy in Vietnam, McCarthy was touring New Hampshire in preparation for the first presidential primary. That March the idealistic candidate no one had taken seriously received almost as many votes as President Johnson himself.

A few weeks after the New Hampshire primary, Johnson quit the race. A second peace candidate, Robert Kennedy, announced for the presidency. The boyish Bobby Kennedy, who had been attorney general in John Kennedy's administration and then senator from New York, attracted an even more zealous following than his older brother had. The favorite of the youth movement, however, was still McCarthy. His willingness to fight a lonely battle and his cool, moral style converted tens of thousands of college students, "Clean for Gene" with shaves and neckties, into his campaign workers.

McCarthy, however, could not match Kennedy's broad appeal. Drawing on support from conventional party leaders and interest groups, RFK, like his brother before him, ran a well-organized, old-fashioned campaign. In a decisive

**Robert F. Kennedy**
*Robert Kennedy's concern for America's minorities made him attractive to liberals in the 1968 presidential campaign.*

showdown Kennedy won the California primary and seemed assured of the Democratic nomination. But in the midst of a victory celebration in a Los Angeles hotel, Sirhan B. Sirhan, a Jordanian immigrant, shot and killed Robert Kennedy; ostensibly he was angered by Kennedy's support of Israel. The shock of a second Kennedy assassinated only two months after Martin Luther King's murder, and in the train of so much public violence, spread the numbing sense that society was consuming itself through paroxysms of hate. Eugene McCarthy, now the sole leader of the peace movement, unaccountably allowed his own presidential drive to lose momentum.

In August 1968 the Democratic convention in Chicago nominated a very different Minnesota politician, the talkative, middle-of-the-road vice-president, Hubert Humphrey. As the delegates voted, policemen were banging their way through a park full of young demonstrators outside of convention hotels. Although Humphrey had a strong record on civil rights and other liberal causes, antiwar Democrats felt that he had hopelessly compromised himself on Vietnam, and they greeted his nomination with anger and despair.

The Republican nomination of Richard M. Nixon frustrated liberals. For the former vice-president, it was a remarkable political comeback from his defeats in the 1960 presidential campaign and the 1962 California gubernatorial election.

**Democratic National Convention, 1968**

*While Hubert Humphrey was being nominated, the Chicago police went on a rampage against youthful demonstrators outside the hall. Some victims of this "police riot" were delighted with the coverage they received; "the whole world is watching," they chanted. The convention riots reflected widespread anger and frustration over Vietnam and the Johnson administration's unresponsiveness to criticism.*

Effectively taking advantage of widespread weariness with social divisions and national self-reproach, Nixon in 1968 declared himself the candidate of the "silent majority" who yearned for a restoration of traditional values, public peace, and unity. Yet Nixon's choice of a running mate, Governor Spiro Agnew of Maryland, undermined this appeal. Agnew, an abrasive man who offended many with his tasteless comments about various ethnic groups, aroused fears of a divisive Nixon presidency that would offer no relief from the troubles of the previous four years.

Nixon and Agnew's campaign was partly calculated to offset the presidential candidacy of Governor George C. Wallace of Alabama, who was running as an independent. Wallace presented himself as the advocate of "poor folks" against "ivory tower" bureaucrats and of decent citizens against subversive youths, and he exuded patriotic virtues and conventional truths. Exploiting the white backlash against minorities and radicals, Wallace held 21 percent voter support in September, just 7 percent less than Humphrey.

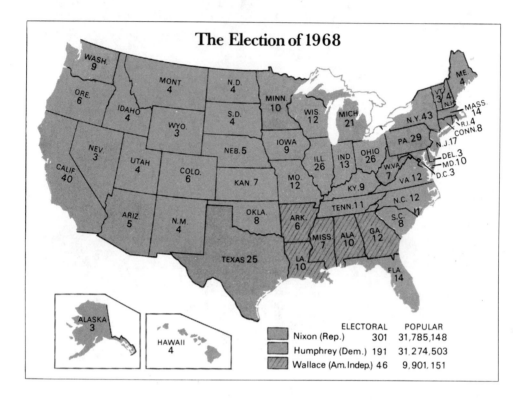

The abrasive Nixon and Wallace campaigns increased Humphrey's attractiveness to moderates. Moreover, when Humphrey announced that he would stop the bombing of North Vietnam—and when Johnson did just that a few days before the election—Humphrey closed the gap dramatically. But Johnson's failure in Vietnam was more than Humphrey could overcome. Moreover, Nixon's claim to have a secret plan for ending the war effectively countered Humphrey's attempt to seize the peace issue. Wallace's support receded as the election approached. In the end he took only 10 million votes; Nixon and Humphrey almost evenly divided the remaining 86 percent of the popular vote. With only 43.4 percent of the popular vote and a margin of less than seven-tenths of 1 percent, Nixon gained the White House.

"Of all the extraordinary developments of 1968," one commentator observes, "perhaps least expected was the durability of characters and institutions in the face of defiant challenge." Events in the sixties had strained American political and social institutions to their limits, but the election of 1968 demonstrated that they were highly resilient and unlikely to break. Events in the next six years further testified to this fact.

# CHRONOLOGY

| | | | |
|---|---|---|---|
| **1961** | Peace Corps organized. American-backed Bay of Pigs invasion of Cuba fails. Berlin Wall erected. | | American intervention in Dominican Republic. Johnson's Great Society programs enacted. Second major Civil Rights Act passed. Ghetto riots in Watts section of Los Angeles. |
| **1962** | Cuban missile crisis. | | |
| **1963** | Kennedy proposes major tax reduction and civil rights bills. Test Ban Treaty between United States and Soviet Union. Kennedy assassinated; Lyndon B. Johnson becomes president. | **1966** | National Organization for Women (NOW) founded. |
| | | **1968** | Martin Luther King, Jr., and Senator Robert Kennedy assassinated. Richard M. Nixon elected president. |
| **1964** | Johnson announces national War on Poverty. Free speech movement at Berkeley. Major Civil Rights Act passed. Tonkin Gulf Resolution. Johnson elected president. | **1969** | United States puts first man on the moon. |
| **1965** | Johnson sends American combat troops to Vietnam; bombing of North begins. | **1970** | Four students killed by the National Guard at Kent State University. |

## SUGGESTED READINGS

William E. Leuchtenburg, *A Troubled Feast: American Society Since 1945* (rev. ed., 1979), Lawrence S. Wittner, *Cold War America: From Hiroshima to Watergate* (2d ed., 1978), and Todd Gitlin, *The Sixties: Years of Hope, Days of Rage* (1987), are contrasting surveys of the sixties. Allen Matusow, *The Unraveling of America: A History of Liberalism in the 1960s* (1984), is a critical assessment. On John Kennedy and his administration, Theodore C. Sorensen, *Kennedy* (1965), and Arthur M. Schlesinger, Jr., *A Thousand Days* (1965), are appreciative assessments by insiders. Bruce Miroff, *Pragmatic Illusions: The Presidential Politics of John F. Kennedy* (1976), emphasizes Kennedy's limitations. In *The Promise and the Performance: The Leadership of John F. Kennedy* (1975), Lewis J. Paper tries to find a middle ground. Aida DiPace Donald, ed., *John F. Kennedy and the New Frontier* (1966), is a useful anthology. Herbert Parmet, *J.F.K.—The Presidency of John F. Kennedy* (1983), is a recent critical account. And Irving Bernstein, *Promises Kept: John F. Kennedy's New Frontier* (1991), is a much more positive picture. Thomas Brown, *JFK: History of an Image* (1988), describes JFK's hold on the public imagination. Richard E. Neustadt, *Presidential Power* (1990 ed.), is an analysis of leadership that reputedly influenced Kennedy. Tom Wicker, *JFK and LBJ* (1968), finds Kennedy wanting as a political leader alongside of Johnson. Arthur Schlesinger, Jr., *Robert Kennedy and His Times* (1978), is the fullest account of John Kennedy's younger brother. Also see the articles on the twentieth anniversary of Kennedy's death in *The New Republic*, November 21, 1983.

Initial accounts of Lyndon Johnson's personality and presidency can be found in Robert Novak and Rowland Evans, *Lyndon B. Johnson: The Exercise of Power* (1966); Eric Goldman, *The Tragedy of Lyndon Johnson* (1969); Doris Kearns, *Lyndon Johnson and the American Dream* (1976); and Ronnie Dugger, *The Politician: The Life and Times of Lyndon Johnson* (1982). For a hostile portrait of LBJ, see the first two volumes of what will eventually be a four-volume study, Robert A. Caro, *The Years of Lyndon Johnson* (1982, 1990). For a different picture of Johnson's prepresidential years, emphasizing his impact on the country's history, see Robert Dallek, *Lone Star Rising: Lyndon Johnson and His Times, 1908–1960* (1991). For the Johnson presidency, see Vaughn Davis Bornet, *The Presidency of Lyndon B. Johnson* (1983); Paul K. Conkin, *Big Daddy from the Pedernales: Lyndon Baines Johnson* (1986); Charles Murray, *Losing Ground: American Social Policy, 1950–1980* (1983); John E. Schwarz, *America's Hidden Success: A Reassessment of Twenty Years of Public Policy* (1983); and Marvin E. Gettleman and David Mermelstein, *The Great Society Reader* (1967).

The references in the previous chapter are useful on the civil rights movement in the sixties. Also of value are Taylor Branch, *Parting the Waters* (1988); Doug McAdam, *Freedom Summer* (1988); Michael Belknap, *Federal Law and Southern Order: Racial Violence and Constitutional Conflict in the Post-Brown South* (1987); Derrick Bell, *And We Are Not Saved: The Elusive Quest for Racial Justice* (1987); Juan Williams, *Eyes on the Prize: America's Civil Rights Years, 1954–1965* (1987); Charles E. Fager, *Selma 1965* (rev. ed., 1985); Clayborne Carson, *In Struggle: SNCC and the Black Awakening of the 1960s* (1981); Carl M. Brauer, *John F. Kennedy and the Second Reconstruction* (1980); Harris Wofford, *Of Kennedy and Kings* (1980); August Meier and Elliott Rudwick, eds., *Black Protest in the Sixties* (1970); Robert Conot, *Rivers of Blood, Years of Darkness* (1968), on the Watts Riot; and Stokely Carmichael and Charles Hamilton, *Black Power* (1967).

The violence of the sixties is analyzed in the *Report of the National Advisory Commission on Civil Disorders* (1968). The background to the violence of the decade is explored in Hugh Davis Graham and Ted Robert Gurr, *The History of Violence in America* (1969), and Richard Hofstadter and Michael Wallace, eds., *American Violence: A Documentary History* (1970), which also includes an important essay by Hofstadter. Nathan Glazer, *Remembering the Answers* (1970), explores the campus upheavals.

The literature of the youth rebellion, or counterculture, begins with Jack Kerouac's *On the Road* (1957) and more or less ends with Charles A. Reich's *The Greening of America* (1971). The world against which these youths rebelled is discussed in William H. Whyte, *The Organization Man* (1956), and Scott Donaldson, *The Suburban Myth* (1969). Theodore Roszak, *The Making of a Counter-Culture* (1969), and Richard Flacks, *Youth and Social Change* (1971), attempt to probe the rebellion's inner meaning. Philip E. Slater, *The Pursuit of Loneliness* (1970), contrasts the rebel culture with establishment culture. In *Young Radicals* (1968), Kenneth Keniston analyzes leaders in the rebellion. Kirkpatrick Sale, *SDS* (1973), is a sympathetic study of its most prominent campus organization. Seven fine books add historical perspective: John P. Diggins, *The American Left in the Twentieth Century* (1973); Rosabeth Moss Kantor, *Commitment and Community* (1972); James Weinstein, *Ambiguous Legacy: The Left in American Politics* (1975); Lawrence S. Wittner, *Rebels against War: The American Peace Movement, 1941–1960* (1969); Todd Gitlin, *The Whole World Is Watching: The Mass Media in the Making and Unmaking of the New Left* (1981); Maurice Isserman, *If I Had a Hammer...: The Death of the Old Left and the Birth of the New Left* (1987); and W. J. Rorabaugh, *Berkeley at War* (1989). Tom Wolfe's *The Electric Kool-Aid Acid Test* (1968), Joan Didion's *Slouching Towards Bethlehem* (1968), and Charles Perry, *The Haight-Ashbury* (1984), comment on the culture of Haight-Ashbury.

A fine general survey of women's history is Nancy Woloch, *Women and the American Experience* (1984). In addition to the books cited in earlier chapters, the following are valuable in studying feminism in the sixties. Betty Friedan, *The Feminine Mystique* (1963); Kate Millett,

*Sexual Politics* (1970), and Robin Morgan (comp.), *Sisterhood Is Powerful* (1970), all suggest the range and force of the women's movement. Peter G. Filene's *Him/Her/Self: Sex Roles in Modern America* (1975) is also useful. The best historical account of American women in the half-century after 1920 is William H. Chafe, *The American Woman* (1970). Sara Evans, *Personal Politics: The Roots of American Women's Liberation in the Civil Rights Movement and the New Left* (1979), should also be consulted.

Sources on the resistance to national liberalism and young radicalism are scattered. Arthur B. Shostak's *Blue-Collar Life* (1969) summarizes an array of studies on white urban wage earners and their families. Bennett M. Berger, *Working-Class Suburb* (1960), Herbert J. Gans, *The Levittowners* (1967), and William Kornblum, *Blue-Collar Community* (1974), add substantially to this analysis. Robert A. Caro, *The Power Broker: Robert Moses and the Fall of New York* (1974), Herbert J. Gans, *The Urban Villagers* (1962), and Sam Bass Warner, Jr., *The Urban Wilderness* (1972), include perceptive accounts of how government policies have damaged inner-city life. In *Small Town in Mass Society* (1958), Arthur J. Vidich and Joseph Bensman describe the defenses of townspeople against external authority. In *All Our Kin* (1974), Carol Stack explains the creative adaptations among poor black families. Peter Binzen, *Whitetown, U.S.A.* (1970), discusses urban dwellers in rebellion against government authority, and Numan V. Bartley, *The Rise of Massive Resistance* (1969), and Neil R. McMillen, *The Citizens' Council* (1971), trace an earlier rebellion in the South. The new explicitness about ethnic identities is explored in Michael Novak's *The Rise of the Unmeltable Ethnics* (1972).

References in the previous chapter are again of use in consulting additional materials on American foreign relations in the sixties. Walter LaFeber, *America, Russia and the Cold War, 1945–1984* (5th ed., 1985), contains a fine survey of the decade. On Kennedy's foreign policy, the following books are particularly useful. Richard J. Walton's *Cold War and Counterrevolution* (1972) takes a negative view of Kennedy's foreign policy, and the decline of Kennedy's Alliance for Progress is traced in Jerome Levinson and Juan de Onis, *The Alliance That Lost Its Way* (1970). On Cuba, see Peter Wyden, *The Bay of Pigs* (1979), and Graham T. Allison, *Essence of Decision: Explaining the Cuban Missile Crisis* (1971). Herbert S. Dinerstein, *The Making of a Missile Crisis: October 1962* (1976), tries to view the confrontation from Moscow's perspective. A recent study of great value is James G. Blight and David A. Welch, *On the Brink: Americans and Soviets Reexamine the Cuban Missile Crisis* (1989). The best account of the Test Ban Treaty is in Glenn T. Seaborg, *Kennedy, Khrushchev, and the Test Ban* (1981). On the Peace Corps, see Gerald Rice, *The Bold Experiment: JFK's Peace Corps* (1985). The Kennedy-Johnson policies in the Caribbean are discussed in Lester D. Langley, *The United States and the Caribbean, 1900–1970* (1980); Walter LaFeber, *Inevitable Revolutions: The United States in Central America* (1984); and Bryce Wood, *The Dismantling of the Good Neighbor Policy* (1985).

The Kennedy-Johnson policies in Vietnam are the subject of numerous books. George McTurnan Kahin and John W. Lewis, *The United States in Vietnam* (rev. ed., 1969), is a solid introduction to the war in Southeast Asia. Most writers on the war condemn the United States, and *The Indochina Story* (1970), by the Committee of Concerned Asian Scholars, is a particularly striking example. Donald S. Zagoria, *Vietnam Triangle: Moscow, Peking, Hanoi* (1967), and Gunther Lewy, *America in Vietnam* (1978), are two of the relatively few defenses of American policy. Henry Brandon, *Anatomy of Error: The Inside Story of the Asian War on the Potomac, 1954–1969* (1969), and Arthur M. Schlesinger, Jr., *The Bitter Heritage: Vietnam and American Democracy, 1941–1966* (1967), seek a middle ground. David Halberstam's fascinating *The Best and the Brightest* (1972) dissects the policymaking in Washington, and Frances Fitzgerald's excellent *Fire in the Lake* (1972) analyzes the consequences of this policy in Vietnam. J. William Fulbright, *The Arrogance of Power* (1967), expresses the opposition from Congress. A notorious massacre of civilians in Vietnam is exposed in Seymour M. Hersh, *My Lai 4* (1970). A number of recent works are particularly worth attention: Larry Berman,

*Planning a Tragedy* (1982); Arnold R. Isaacs, *Without Honor: Defeat in Vietnam and Cambodia* (1983); Stanley Karnow, *Vietnam: A History* (1983); Ronald Spector, *The United States Army in Vietnam* (1983); Bruce Palmer, Jr., *The 25-Year War* (1984); Wallace Terry, *Bloods: An Oral History of the Vietnam War by Black Veterans* (1984); R. B. Smith, *An International History of the Vietnam War: The Kennedy Strategy* (1985); George Herring, *America's Longest War* (2d ed., 1986); George Kahin, *Intervention: How America Became Involved in the Vietnam War* (1986); and Neil Sheehan, *A Bright Shining Lie: John Paul Vann and America in Vietnam* (1988).

Opposition to the war can be studied in Irwin Unger, *The Movement* (1974); Gloria Emerson, *Winners and Losers* (1976); Herbert Schandler, *The Unmaking of a President: Lyndon Johnson and Vietnam* (1977); Myra McPherson, *Long Time Passing: Vietnam and the Haunted Generation* (1984); Nancy Zaroulis and Gerald Sullivan, *Who Spoke Up? American Protest Against the War in Vietnam* (1984); James Miller, *Democracy in the Streets* (1987); David Caute, *The Year of the Barricades, 1968* (1988); Todd Gitlin, *The Sixties* (1988); and Melvin Small, *Johnson, Nixon, and the Doves* (1988).

# 33

# *An Elusive Stability*

## *The Modern Republic, 1969–1980*

◦

HE idealism, exuberance, and turmoil that had marked the 1960s had a last gasp in 1968. That tumultuous year accorded heady moments for advocates of democracy everywhere: Lyndon Johnson's decision not to run again, the protests and riots at the Democratic convention in Chicago, the student upheavals in American and French universities, and the Prague Spring—the exuberant months during which the government of Alexander Dubček and a majority of the Czech and Slovak people challenged Soviet limits on dissent. But the year ended in deep chagrin for those who had dreamed of fundamental change in the capitalist West and the communist East. The American presidential election pitted Hubert Humphrey against Richard Nixon, two of the country's most familiar political faces, and the antiliberal Nixon won. Established authority effectively cracked down on radical students in the United States and on students and workers in France. Soviet tanks crushed Czechoslovak independence and political dissent. Gloom and cynicism became rampant among liberals and leftists everywhere.

Beginning in 1969, America and most other Western industrialized nations endured a frustrating decade of inflation, external economic shocks, and perceived diminishing resources. America suffered the additional stress of a losing war, contracting international power and economic prowess, disillusionment with national institutions, incessant domestic recrimination, and humiliating political scandals—in short, deeply wounded national pride.

Essentially conservative principles governed international relations for most of the 1970s. Having crushed the Czechoslovak reach for "socialism with a human face," the Soviet Union and its Eastern European satellites embarked on what would prove to be two decades of increasing economic stagnation and neo-Stalinist political repression. This did not, however, prevent the Soviets from courting Third World clients and building up an impressive military machine.

China surmounted the worst of the Cultural Revolution, which had gravely damaged the nation's economic progress and social stability, and sought increasingly to renew economic and political ties with the noncommunist world. Often feeling itself on the defensive, always highly self-critical, and licking its wounds from the Vietnam War, the United States tried to play one communist power off against the other. Fifties anti-communist fervor and sixties hopes of spearheading democratic revolutions around the world now gave way, in American strategic thought, to plans for coolly balancing spheres of influence with the communist powers. Only late in the decade did Washington again make American ideals—human rights—the centerpiece of its foreign policy. And by that time the United States had unwittingly stumbled into a confrontation, in Iran, with militant Islamic fundamentalism that nothing in its historical tradition had prepared it to understand.

In these discouraging times the federal government—and especially the presidency—faced the daunting task of arresting what seemed like national decline and reasserting American self-confidence. Presidents of the 1970s seemed to face almost insoluble problems. All of them were commanded to spin the gold of American prosperity from the straw of worldwide stagnation, to control global affairs despite America's waning international authority, and to elevate the national spirit through political institutions in which Americans felt diminished faith.

For the American Republic, the possibility and even the desirability of economic expansion and technological advance became particularly nagging problems. Unprecedented shortages of basic raw materials and soaring costs of oil and natural gas; "stagflation" (sluggish economic growth combined with persistent inflation); defeat in Vietnam; the Watergate scandal and a president's ejection from office; the two worst economic downturns since the Great Depression; and the largest federal and trade deficits in the nation's history—all these shook confidence in the foundations of American strength and made the years from Richard Nixon's presidency to George Bush's a time of elusive stability.

## Narrowing Horizons

Sixties self-confidence glowed for perhaps the last time for Americans, on July 20, 1969, when astronauts Neil A. Armstrong and Edwin A. Aldrin, Jr., stepped onto the lunar surface, while Michael Collins orbited the moon in a command module. "That's one small step for a man, one giant leap for mankind," Armstrong intoned rather prosaically as untold millions in every nation stared in awestruck wonder at the television screens on which the landing was beamed instantaneously to Earth. Television cameras also recorded President Nixon talking to the astronauts by telephone and greeting them on the deck of the aircraft carrier that retrieved their spacecraft in the Pacific Ocean. The *Apollo* landing capped America's decade-long goal of putting a human being on the moon, which John F. Kennedy had proclaimed in 1961. Humanity's leap to the

**Moon Landing,** 1969
*In the aftermath of the turmoil of 1968, America's successful landing of astronauts on the moon gave the nation a welcome sense of triumph about its technology. Events in the 1970s, however, would dull the prestige of American know-how.*

moon was an extraordinary technological feat. And millions found themselves unexpectedly stunned by the photographs of a shimmering blue-and-white planet Earth, suspended against the black void of space, that the homeward-bound astronauts brought back with them—a vision that moved one of them to read aloud the ancient words of Genesis: "In the beginning God created the heaven and the earth... And God saw that it was good."

Although the flights of the first space shuttles in the 1970s also offered Americans a chance to savor the technological prowess that NASA had been mobilizing for years, Americans seldom experienced exhilarating moments of national pride comparable to those associated with the moon landing. The dominant theme of the decade was the discovery of human—and national—limits, not giant leaps for mankind. American power failed to avert defeat in Vietnam. The liberal social reforms of the Great Society proved to have neither eradicated poverty nor dampened racial antagonisms. Keynesian theory could not contain (nor even, at first, explain) the combination of lagging American productivity, galloping inflation, and flat economic growth that journalists inelegantly called stagflation. Best-selling books of the decade carried such titles as *The Limits of Growth, Small Is Beautiful,* and *Future Shock.* Perhaps the decade's most significant new idea was the realization of planet Earth's vulnerability to human greed—indeed, to human progress itself. Humbling and noble as such a discovery might be, it was not one deeply rooted in the American historical experience.

**Saving the Earth**

During the 1970s, as the civil rights movement and protest over the Vietnam War waned, civic-minded citizens' energies began focusing on the environment. Environmental consciousness had been slowly increasing since the publication of Rachel Carson's *Silent Spring* in 1962. Pointing to the dangers to humans, animals, and plants from the heavy use of the pesticide DDT, Carson reinforced fears about perils to the environment that had taken hold in the late 1940s and early 1950s over fallout from nuclear testing. To broaden public interest in the issue of environmental depredation and mobilize sentiment to combat it, Senator Gaylord Nelson of Wisconsin suggested the celebration of Earth Day. On April 22, 1970, millions of Americans took time from normal activities to help clean up the environment and encourage people everywhere to see the urgency of preserving the world's environment. The reasons for concern were numerous and growing: oil spills from offshore drilling sites, especially in the Santa Barbara Channel along the California coast; polluted rivers, lakes, and beaches; smog generated by automobile emissions and smokestack industries in many large cities; and threats to the Alaskan wilderness, the Florida Everglades, and the global ozone layer from proposals (respectively) to build an eight-hundred-mile oil pipeline, a jet airport in south Florida, and a supersonic passenger aircraft (SST).

The most positive attempts to reclaim some measure of lost control were the many efforts to repair the urban-industrial society's damage to the physical environment. Images of an uncontaminated Earth where man and nature once again dwelled in harmony had already touched deeply embedded emotions during the 1960s. During the 1970s a crescendo of cries arose demanding relief from the dangers of chemical sprays, industrial wastes, and automobile exhaust. Organic foods and recyclable products became increasingly popular. The national government responded to the public's demands by establishing a series of antipollution standards—beginning with the Clean Air Act of 1963—to protect the atmosphere and the waterways, and both state and local laws supplemented the ecology movement. Describing an "era of limits," E. F. Schumacher's *Small Is Beautiful* (1973) became the political bible for some, including California Governor Edmund G. "Jerry" Brown, Jr., who preached the politics of no-growth.

Some progress was made on the environmental front; yet here too the problems came to outweigh the prospects. As the economy faltered, the arguments that environmentalism cut into jobs, profits, and energy development sounded more and more persuasive. Learning that it would cost up to $70 billion in just five years to clean up the environment and that it would undercut their economic interests, American businesses and workers protested against environmentalism as an attack on the country's standard of living. "Why worry about the long run," an unemployed steelworker said, "when you're out of work right now." Critics of no-growth worried that in the interest of avoiding further plundering of the environment, the movement would keep disadvantaged individuals and entire developing societies below the threshold of self-sustaining prosperity, condemning them to perpetual poverty.

**Earth Day**
*In the 1970s rising public perception of a threat to the environment produced a movement to save Planet Earth, gathering much of the enthusiasm that young Americans had earlier poured into the civil rights and antiwar movements. Earth Day, first celebrated in 1970, became an occasion for large environmentalist rallies.*

Others feared that government would fail to meet the challenge of cleaning up the environment. Bureaucratic confusion between Washington's Environmental Protection Agency (EPA) and the regulatory offices in local governments hampered the enforcement of new laws. Unfolding revelations about the extensive dumping and the gruesome toxicity of industrial wastes dimmed hopes of ever undoing the damage. Outside Buffalo, chemicals buried for decades at a site called Love Canal oozed into backyards and basements of family homes, forcing the permanent evacuation of most residents. In 1979 a frightening crisis occurred at Three Mile Island near Harrisburg, Pennsylvania. Defective equipment and inadequate safety checks at a nuclear power plant almost caused a meltdown of the core reactor, which would have released radioactive gas into the earth, water, and atmosphere and inflicted gruesome consequences on surrounding populations. As it was, thousands of people had to flee their homes while plant operators cleaned up contaminants. The crisis at Three Mile Island dashed faith that government regulation could actually protect America from the worst environmental disasters, and the same fears focused on an inability to avert the ultimate threat to the human environment, a nuclear war. Graphic and pessimistic film versions of such catastrophes—*The China Syndrome* (1978) and *The Day After* (1983)—heightened these concerns.

**The No-Growth Era**  Twentieth-century progressive and liberal movements had assumed economic growth as a precondition for promoting a fairer distribution of social benefits. But in the 1970s this assumption could no longer be considered a given, as was demonstrated by both the advent of environmentalism and the rising cost of energy and natural resources. And American economic performance in the 1970s was generally dismal, precluding significant expansion of the nation's economic pie. As a result, hopes of expanding social justice that the Kennedy and Johnson administrations had kindled were doomed to disappointment. Unfortunately, the interest groups with legitimate claims to a larger share of national prosperity found themselves competing for available resources.

Between 1969 and 1980 the economies of industrial nations, and particularly that of the United States, are best described as sputtering engines. Energy shocks—the ability of petroleum exporters, chiefly in the Middle East, to band together to drive up oil prices—produced double-digit inflation in the West that, when coupled with declining worker productivity, played havoc with national economies. Government deficits, fueled by expanded social welfare programs or "entitlements," particularly Medicare and Medicaid in the United States, and environmental cleanup costs added to spiraling prices. The "peace dividend" that shrinking costs for the Vietnam War might have produced disappeared into the entitlement payments to certain special-interest groups, which no political leader could contain without risking electoral defeat. On top of all this, the decline of older "metal-bashing" industries and their replacement by high-technology manufacturing and services caused painful economic dislocation, especially in the Northeast and Midwest.

Demographic change was also connected to the economic stagnation of the 1970s. In the 1960s the entry of the baby boomers into the national market had helped stimulate demand and had produced a cheap entry-level labor supply. By the 1970s, however, the American population began to "gray": increasing numbers of Americans were reaching the end of their economically productive lives. Labor unions were generally still strong enough to shield most blue-collar workers from the worst ravages of inflation by bidding up wages almost fast enough to keep pace with price increases, and seniority often protected older workers faced with layoffs. But many young people who in the 1960s had been students or had taken entry-level jobs found their career paths blocked or slowed by a stagnant economy; this was one reason that the national birthrate dropped steadily. Indeed, the 1960s students who—now 1970s young adults—found themselves worst prepared for the changing times were those who had been the most idealistic and committed to the peace and freedom movements. Liberal arts and social sciences majors sometimes had difficulty breaking into the high-tech and financial-service careers that offered the greatest opportunities in the 1970s and 1980s. Most educated young people found life highly competitive as they struggled to get ahead under unexpectedly constricted conditions; little wonder that the assertive, materialistic "yuppie" replaced the laid-back, slightly starry-eyed idealist as the archetypal young person of the decade.

Educated women in the 1970s faced some special circumstances. Anti-discrimination laws offered them expanded opportunities; the Equal Rights Amendment (first proposed in the 1920s) finally breezed through Congress and many state legislatures in the early 1970s. A seemingly simple declaration that "equality of rights under the law shall not be denied or abridged . . . on account of sex," the ERA testified to the willingness of public authorities to open the way for women in the marketplace. In addition to finding greater job opportunities, women benefited from the Equal Credit Opportunity Act, which gave them equal access to bank loans and credit cards with men. Greater willingness of college and university graduate programs to enroll women and by voters to elect them to political office also expanded their chances of making careers in fields traditionally closed to them. Feminist consciousness-raising also continued apace in the 1970s. Many women responded to these widened opportunities by seeking jobs in fields that their mothers had never tried to enter. But frustration proved to be a frequent by-product. Women often found themselves competing bitterly with men for available jobs. By the end of the decade women earned, on the average, only 59 cents for every dollar that men earned—proof that equality of result was quite different from equality of opportunity. And whether they entered the marketplace voluntarily in search of a career or involuntarily because their family needed the income, most women found the pressures of juggling job and family particularly distressing. Women in the increasingly large pool of single mothers generally experienced the worst circumstances. In addition an anti-feminist campaign led by media celebrity Anita Bryant and veteran right-winger Phyllis Schlafly largely eliminated government funding of abortions for poor women and stalled passage of the ERA. By 1979 the proposed amendment had been ratified by thirty-five states, three short of the number required for passage. That year, to avoid the ERA's self-imposed deadline for ratification, Congress pushed the crucial date back to 1982.

Middle-class, well-educated young people of both genders were not the only—or most injured—victims of the 1970s slowdown. An underclass of poorly educated, often nonwhite people found itself increasingly excluded from even menial jobs by technological change and by competition from illegal immigrants willing to work for below-minimum wages. A rising tide of conservatism in the country dictated that welfare benefits not keep pace with inflation. The working poor, to whom unions offered little protection, thus faced declining real wages and lessened job security; for some, especially single mothers, going on welfare became a better economic choice.

The conservatism of the decade was also a function of the graying of the population and the growing influence of the so-called Sun Belt, the southern and western states. During the 1970s the number of Americans over sixty-five increased by 20 percent. In 1970 there were 81 Americans for every 100 under the age of five; by 1980 there were 156. While the populations of the older industrial ("Rust Belt") cities like New York, Philadelphia, Chicago, Cleveland, and Detroit contracted, such newer Sun Belt metropolitan centers as Atlanta, Miami, Dallas, Houston, Phoenix, Los Angeles, San Diego, and San Jose increased between 5 percent and 36 percent.

But despite worsening economic conditions, the United States still offered opportunities that attracted millions of immigrants from desperately poor Third World countries. Many took menial jobs that few Americans wanted—and because many of these immigrants were illegal and lacked the protection of Social Security, minimum wage, and unemployment-insurance safety nets, they toiled for substandard pay and under unregulated conditions. The 1970s saw the migration to the United States, principally from Asia and Latin America, of as many as 12 million people, some two-thirds of them illegal aliens. Asian immigrants made up the bulk of the legal aliens, and liberalization of immigration laws during the 1960s benefited Asian immigrants the most. Most Chinese and Korean newcomers, and many from Indochina, were middle-class or professional people, and often they enjoyed economic success. Filipinos, who were the largest number of Asian immigrants and generally poorer and less educated than other Asians, had a more difficult time.

Latinos were the most numerous immigrants to the United States in the 1970s, and they struggled hard to accommodate themselves to their new home. Many, having arrived illegally and unable to speak English, lived in poverty in California, Florida, and Texas. Although some Latinos, particularly Mexican Americans, benefited from affirmative-action programs enacted in the 1960s, most were only beginning to use group pressure to win a larger share of jobs.

The most effective Latino organization developed in California's "farm factories," where Mexican American labor supported a thriving commercial agriculture. Under the patient, persistent leadership of César Chavez, the United Farm Workers rallied national support through boycotts of nonunion lettuce and grapes. By the 1970s, these farm workers had built a solid union base in areas where exploitation had long been a way of life. By then, however, the majority of Mexican Americans were living in cities. Los Angeles, for example, a city of over 3 million, had the second largest concentration of Latino peoples in North America after Mexico City. Advocates of urban-dwelling Latinos demanded bilingual education in public schools and an end to the popular media image of Latinos as lazy ne'er-do-wells. In the 1960s younger Mexican Americans had begun calling themselves Chicanos (thus rejecting an identity as a hyphenated people), and proudly proclaimed themselves *La Raza Unida,* The Race United. Chicano studies courses and degree programs began to appear in university curriculums, reflecting an upsurge of ethnic pride.

But as has been common throughout United States history, the flood of new immigrants aroused the antagonism of numerous assimilated Americans, who saw the newcomers only as a threat to established ways of life. Chicanos and other

Latinos, for example, had a limited impact on most Americans despite their unprecedented assertiveness in the 1970s; "Anglo" citizens generally remained insensitive and even hostile to their needs. These suspicions overlooked the fact that, as in earlier times, many of those who endured the anguish of uprooting themselves were often ambitious, enterprising people, upwardly mobile and able to contribute constructively to American life.

Native Americans also found themselves at odds with a majority of their fellow United States citizens. In the 1950s, after a Republican-dominated Congress had declared an end to the national supervision of native Americans and had placed their reservations under individual states' laws, some tribes had suffered grievous losses. The Klamath Nation in Oregon promptly lost its rich lumber resources, and the demoralized Menominee Nation in Wisconsin saw its tribal economy disappear in a rush of panic sales. Not until the late 1960s did a significant improvement occur. Adapting the decade's protest tactics, groups of native Americans led by the Sioux Nations occupied sites that symbolized the burial of Indian heritages beneath white civilization: Alcatraz Island, Mount Rushmore, Fort Sheridan, and Wounded Knee, South Dakota. In 1973, at the site of the Wounded Knee massacre, Russell Means and Dennis Banks, founders of the American Indian Movement (AIM), mounted a violent confrontation with law enforcement agents.* Overlapping these public and often violent protests, striking victories occurred in the courts. In a wave of separate actions that began in 1969, sweeping from the Alaskan hinterland and northwestern fisheries to the Maine woods, various Indian nations transformed their endlessly violated nineteenth-century (and sometimes even older) treaties into a legal basis for claiming important economic rights in court. As a whole, however, the country's 800,000 native Americans continued to suffer more severely from poverty and disease than any other cultural group in the United States. The federal government neglected the situation, and the Indians themselves, divided into more than one hundred organizations seeking redress of different grievances, could not speak with one voice.

All the bitter social and political crosscurrents of the period and the momentum of federal power came together in the affirmative-action programs in the Nixon years. Affirmative action was one of the most effective weapons that the national government developed in combating racial and sex discrimination. It also gradually became one of the most controversial, for it often involved setting goals (critics called them quotas) for admitting women and minorities to higher-education institutions and labor unions, as well as for employing and promoting these victims of past discrimination in colleges and universities, local police and fire departments, and a host of white- and blue-collar jobs funded by federal contracts. Affirmative-action programs were largely created by federal officials

---

*For the Wounded Knee massacre, see chapter 22, pp. 104–105.

and judges, interpreting a vaguely worded section of the 1964 Civil Rights Act. Once set in motion, the policy won strong support from minority and women's organizations.

Affirmative action struck at the core of white male dominance in society and the economy, but it also raised thorny problems of deciding who should bear the burden of reversing past discriminatory patterns. Especially because a sluggish economy made the 1970s a period of intense competition for jobs and promotion, angry cries of "reverse discrimination" arose. Along with busing, affirmative action eventually proved to be one of the more divisive consequences of federal advocacy of disadvantaged groups' rights. But unlike busing, which Nixon and many other politicians felt free to denounce, affirmative action would not become a major political issue until the Reagan era. Undeniably, affirmative action speeded up the entry of minorities and women into upwardly mobile careers that modern social and economic change had set in motion. For example, only 20 percent of American women held jobs in 1920, but by 1980 more than half of them were employed. Critics worried that affirmative action was making the law more, not less, gender- and color-conscious, but supporters welcomed the widening of opportunities for pursuing a better-paying occupation or professional career.

## The Imperial Presidency: Nixon

The Nixon administration has come to be associated with the term *imperial presidency*. The phrase was coined by historian Arthur Schlesinger, Jr., a prominent advocate of strong Democratic executives like Jackson, FDR, and Kennedy, to attack the abuses of power by all presidents, especially by Nixon. Where earlier presidents from FDR to LBJ had violated constitutional and political standards on which the country's democratic system supposedly rested, Nixon's transgressions reached new heights, more directly threatening the nation's traditional political process than ever before.

Richard Nixon's five and a half years in the White House are a study in contradictions. Mistrustful and tending to see a "crisis" in every political squall, he nevertheless handled international affairs skillfully and shrewdly. A conservative Republican opponent of liberal social programs and relaxed moral standards, he dismantled some of Johnson's Great Society, resisted demands for further advances in civil rights, and appointed federal judges who would stem the tide of social permissiveness. Yet his administration also supported social reforms that pleased even his sharpest critics. An advocate of orthodox economic ideas, the president initially limited federal intrusion into the workings of the marketplace. But during his first term the country was wracked by a bad recession and rising prices, let loose by spending on the Vietnam War and Great Society programs—and Nixon tried to slow inflation and restore prosperity by using hitherto liberal policies. A staunch "Cold Warrior" with a record of unswerving hostility to communism, Nixon continued the war in Vietnam for another four years and carried it into Cambodia and Laos as well. But his administration

**Richard M. Nixon**
*Nixon's five and a half years in the White House were a study in contradictions. Here Nixon attempts to play the genial and responsive leader. Behind the scenes, he viciously railed against journalistic critics and political enemies.*

eventually negotiated "peace with honor" in Indochina, and Nixon startled the world not only by seeking détente with the Soviet Union, but also by opening the door to improved relations with the communist People's Republic of China, America's most embittered enemy in the 1950s and 1960s. "Law and order" conservatives, Nixon and Vice-President Spiro Agnew ridiculed "long-haired" radicals who rejected American conventions. Yet both men, greedy for money and indifferent to democratic traditions, violated fundamental canons of American law and politics, and both ended by being driven from office in disgrace.

**The Politics of Moderation**

Nixon took office in 1969 under a cloud. He had been elected with a minority of the popular vote, and he was a stiff, uninspiring speaker. Liberals loathed him, remembering his red-baiting as senator and vice-president, his alliance with Joseph McCarthy, and his transparent posturing to gain political ends. "He is the least 'authentic' man alive," one critic said. Countless intellectuals nursed a hatred for "Tricky Dick" Nixon unlike anything any other new president had faced in the twentieth century.

Yet Nixon initially surprised his critics, showing himself politically more moderate than they had expected. This was partly the result of any modern president's inability—regardless of his intent—to reverse the growth of federal power. Moreover, determined to have eight years in the White House and to make his mark on history, especially in foreign affairs, the new president worked hard to establish his credibility with moderates. In his inaugural address he called for a lowered political temperature in the United States and tried to position himself at the center of domestic affairs. "America has suffered from a fever of words," he said, "from inflated rhetoric that promises more than it can deliver; from angry rhetoric that fans discontents into hatreds.... We cannot learn from one another until we stop shouting at one another—until we speak quietly enough so that our words can be heard as well as our voices." Underscoring this appeal to the political center, Nixon appointed a number of moderate Republicans or independents to his cabinet. Daniel Patrick Moynihan, a Democratic adviser to the president on urban affairs, and Assistant Secretary of HEW James Farmer, a black civil rights leader, also helped give Nixon's program a centrist tone.

In addition the administration backed a number of reform measures that surprised liberals and strengthened Nixon's hold on moderates. At the start of his term, Nixon was not seen as a friend of the environmental causes that were generating widespread national concern. Nixon's appointment of Walter J. Hickel as secretary of the interior angered environmentalists, who saw the former Alaska governor as a friend of the oil interests and an anticonservationist. Nixon further alienated conservationists by successfully backing the Alaskan pipeline, which began construction in 1973, and by unsuccessfully supporting the SST, which Congress blocked in 1971. The president and Hickel, however, won the praise of environmentalists by banning the use of DDT in the United States (although not its sale abroad); by favoring passage of the National Environmental Policy Act of 1969, a law requiring impact studies for most public projects; by setting up the Environmental Protection Agency in 1970 to enforce the law; and by supporting enactment of the Clean Air Act, the Water Quality Improvement Act, and the Occupational Safety and Health Administration in 1970. And by largely leaving Great Society programs intact and successfully promoting other reforms, Nixon even managed to win some grudging liberal respect. Under him, Social Security benefits increased by 50 percent, the federal government assumed a greater role in medical education through increased grants, and the voting age dropped to eighteen on ratification of the Twenty-sixth Amendment in 1971.

Nixon also proposed a fundamental change in the country's welfare system. Instead of maintaining the cumbersome bureaucracy and varied levels of state support that were central features of existing programs, the administration developed the Family Assistance Plan to guarantee all welfare families a minimum annual income of $1,600 and to encourage many adults receiving such help either to work or to register for job training. The program also aimed to encourage families to stay together by reducing the favored treatment given to poor families headed by single women. Although Congress rejected the program, Nixon's plan demonstrated a commitment to helping the poor and streamlining the bureaucracy that might have done credit to a liberal Democratic administration.

Finally, at the beginning of 1971 Nixon called for a "New American Revolution." His program fell far short of what its name suggested, but it did include a plan, which Congress enacted in 1972, for sharing $30 billion in revenue between the federal and state governments during the next five years. Until the Reagan years of the 1980s, revenue sharing would constitute a major source of funds for local authorities.

On civil rights as well the Nixon White House managed to identify itself with significant gains. Because of his Supreme Court appointments, Nixon received partial credit for some of the Court's surprisingly liberal decisions, including *Roe* v. *Wade* (1973), a landmark case that ensured women's constitutional right to abortion. Justice Harry Blackmun, one of Nixon's appointees, wrote for a 7–2 majority that struck down forty-six state laws whose provisions had made pregnancy termination legally more difficult than in the nineteenth century. The Nixon administration also benefited politically when, in *Swann* v. *Mecklenburg Board of Education* (1971), the Court upheld the constitutionality of busing to achieve school desegregation. The administration sued to block the state of Georgia from maintaining separate school systems for blacks and whites. When the number of students in all-black schools declined by almost 75 percent in the first two years of Nixon's term, the White House rightly took substantial credit for promoting minority rights. Under Nixon, the federal bureaucracy and courts promoted affirmative action programs to open educational and employment opportunities for women and minorities who had suffered past discrimination. And in 1972 Nixon raised no objections as Congress sent to the states for ratification the ERA, which before the decade was over would galvanize furious conservative resistance.

The president's economic policies also showed the administration to be less doctrinaire than opponents had predicted. Serious economic problems had confronted the new president, in large part a legacy of Johnson's slowness to raise taxes to finance the Great Society and the Vietnam War. With inflation accelerating from 3 percent in 1967 to 5 percent in 1968, Nixon first tried standard conservative remedies: reduced federal spending and a slower growth of the money supply. But these policies only produced a sharp economic downturn without a corresponding drop in prices. Between 1969 and 1971 interest rates reached their highest levels in a century, the Dow-Jones Industrial Index lost over 30 percent of its value, and unemployment doubled to 6 percent, while inflation ran at about 5.5 percent—the worst since the Korean War. For the first time since 1893 the United States suffered a trade deficit, paying more for the goods it bought than it sold abroad; and the real gross national product declined in 1970, its first loss since 1958. Liberal economist Walter Heller sarcastically dubbed falling output and rising prices "Nixonomics."

To meet these difficulties, Nixon sharply reversed course, embracing Keynesian doctrines that once had been the exclusive preserve of liberal Democrats and that Republicans had scorned. Declaring frankly that "I am now a Keynesian,"

Nixon adopted the strategy of deficit spending to stimulate economic growth. (Ironically, by this time some leading economists were losing faith in Keynes.) He also devalued the dollar to boost American exports, and abandoned a promise never to cope with inflation by repeating the policies of the World War II Office of Price Administration. "Controls," he said, " . . . mean rationing, black markets, inequitable administration." But unable to bring inflation below 4 percent or reduce the trade deficit, in the summer of 1971 he introduced wage and price controls and in December he attacked the trade deficit by cheapening the dollar. These departures from traditional free-market ideas produced a strong economic rebound in the first half of 1972—the largest gain in real GNP for a quarter since 1965—and a smaller rate of price increases. Cynics noted that economic improvement arrived just on the eve of the presidential election. Certainly Nixon's policies provided no permanent relief from the unprecedented "stagflation" that persisted throughout his first term. The controls kept prices in line for a while, but they also produced underlying dislocation and shortages; when the controls came off in early 1973, inflation roared back worse than ever. Nevertheless price controls did permit temporary gains and strengthened impressions that Nixon was more a practical politician than a rigid conservative.

**The Appeal to Conservatives**

Yet just as Nixon was struggling to win over the political center, he was also vying to outflank George Wallace on the right by appealing to "middle Americans" fed up with street rioting and the counterculture's attacks on traditional values. Nixon aimed to create a Republican majority of middle Americans, chiefly white suburbanites. He selected an all-white, all-male Republican cabinet, including the outspoken conservative John Mitchell as attorney general. As his principal White House aides he chose a pair of hard, austere organization men, H. R. Haldeman and John Ehrlichman, who were strongly identified with middle America. Thus the new president left no doubt that his administration would reflect conservative views. And no administration figure expressed the right-wing outlook more strongly than Spiro Agnew. Nixon had been the harshly partisan voice of the Eisenhower presidency; now Agnew served the same function. He heaped scorn on "an effete corps of impudent . . . intellectuals," accused the television networks of bias, and locked horns with such influential liberal newspapers as the *New York Times* and the *Washington Post.* The vice-president attacked peace demonstrators as "ideological eunuchs," deplored the "spirit of national masochism," and flayed upper-middle-class snobs whose permissiveness was producing a generation of immoral "pot heads." He was praised for his efforts by such reactionaries as Senator Strom Thurmond of South Carolina, who compared him to John C. Calhoun, "the greatest vice-president in the history of America."

Several administration actions were calculated to appeal to the right. Despite some steps toward social reform, the White House clearly rejected starting new social programs, and it cut back on existing ones. Limiting the activities of such Great Society agencies as OEO and Model Cities, the administration in 1972 also began to withhold funds appropriated by Congress for social programs. At the same time, Nixon vetoed health, education, and welfare bills passed by the Democratic-controlled Congress, and he even failed to protest when Congress killed most of his own proposals for social advance.

The administration's occasional steps forward on civil rights were counter-balanced by undisguised efforts to accommodate southern segregationists—a political strategy aimed at ensuring Nixon's popularity in the South in the 1972 campaign. Nixon's Justice Department opposed an extension of the Voting Rights Act of 1965, asking instead for a law that would remove federal commit-ments to enforcement in the South. In addition, the administration won a delay in desegregating Mississippi's schools until October 1969, when the NAACP gained a favorable Supreme Court ruling on the issue. After the Court in 1971 ordered school busing to promote desegregation, the White House asked Congress for legislation restricting future busing. "For the first time since Woodrow Wilson," declared the NAACP, "we have a national administration that can be rightly characterized as anti-Negro." At the very least, black Americans saw the Nixon White House as indifferent to the fact that three times as many African Amer-icans as whites lived under the poverty line, and that black children were four times more likely than whites to be born in poverty. Black alienation deepened as antibusing riots exploded in Boston and Louisville and as all-white juries in Chattanooga and Miami acquitted whites accused of killing blacks.

Nixon's attempts to appoint two highly conservative southern jurists to the Supreme Court convinced administration critics of his fundamental antiblack bias. His first appointment—Warren Burger, a respected conservative, who replaced Warren as chief justice—had met little opposition. But shortly there-after in 1969, when Abe Fortas (a recent Johnson appointee) resigned his seat because of financial and political misdeeds, Nixon nominated South Carolina federal judge Clement Haynsworth. Although an able jurist, Haynsworth had been slow to recognize the legal rights of blacks; he had been overtolerant of Virginia's resistance to school desegregation and unfriendly to unions in labor disputes. But conflict-of-interest improprieties—judging cases in which he had a financial stake—persuaded the Senate to deny his confirmation, the first such action since 1930. Nixon's next recommendation suffered the same fate. G. Harrold Carswell, a federal Court of Appeals judge from Florida, lacked the stature among fellow jurists to qualify him for the Court. Even Senator Roman Hruska of Nebraska, Carswell's most outspoken supporter, could only say: "Even if he were mediocre, there are lots of mediocre judges and people and lawyers. They are entitled to a little representation, aren't they?" Nixon com-plained that both men were victims of bias against southerners and predicted that men with a similar outlook would one day sit on the high court. Unwilling to risk a third defeat, Nixon nominated Harry Blackmun, a moderate Minnesota jurist, who gained prompt confirmation. In 1971, when two more seats became available,

Nixon appointed Lewis F. Powell, Jr., the highly regarded former president of the American Bar Association, and Assistant Attorney General William H. Rehnquist of Arizona, the only one of Nixon's appointees who proved to be a consistent conservative.

How is one to assess Nixon's domestic record? Was he fundamentally a moderate forced by political needs to appease reactionaries? Or was he essentially a right-winger who adopted moderate positions to confound his critics and win reelection in a nation most notable for its affinity to middle-of-the-road leaders? Judging Nixon's career as a whole, it seems reasonable to conclude that he was at bottom a self-serving, unprincipled opportunist whose ambition for high office made him ready to accommodate extremists and moderates alike. His chief aim was the advancement of Richard Nixon, and he would let almost nothing stand in the way of his ambition. He is a case study in the attributes and dangers of the American self-made man.

**Foreign Affairs: "An Enduring Structure of Peace"**
Unlike most presidents, Nixon came to the White House better prepared to deal with foreign relations than with domestic affairs. Through extensive reading and travel he had prepared himself for major undertakings abroad, and during his term he devoted himself principally to solving world problems. He found a congenial partner in Henry Kissinger, a Harvard professor who became first his national security adviser and then his secretary of state. A brilliant analyst of world problems, Kissinger became known as a realist who understood the nature of power and how to defend American interests.

Nixon and Kissinger assumed that they were facing a new era in international relations, one in which the Soviet-American power struggle could no longer be Washington's all-consuming concern. "The rigid bipolar world of the 1940s and 1950s," Nixon said in 1971, had given way "to the fluidity of a new era of multilateral diplomacy." The number of independent nations had increased from 51 in 1945 to 127 in 1970, and the communist bloc had fragmented into what Nixon called "competing centers of doctrine and power." Thus had arisen "an increasingly heterogeneous and complex world." To meet these changed circumstances, Nixon and Kissinger aimed to encourage local and regional initiatives by groups of nations and to foster individual nations' independence and self-sufficiency. Through the recognition and acceptance of international diversity, they hoped to bring about widespread cooperation among nations that would lead to "an enduring structure of peace." This grand design—the "Nixon Doctrine," as the White House called it—included plans for détente, or improved relations with Russia and China. But Nixon and Kissinger believed that they could not realize their vision until they settled the war in Vietnam. Nixon also thought that American withdrawal from the conflict was a prerequisite to his reelection in 1972. Having asserted during the 1968 campaign that he had a secret plan to end the war, he needed to make good on his campaign rhetoric.

But achieving "peace with honor" in Vietnam proved unexpectedly difficult. Instead of a speedy conclusion to the fighting, which Nixon had promised, the struggle lasted four more years and the United States lost 27,000 more lives. The bloodshed went on because the administration sought an unrealizable objective: before quitting the war, Nixon wished to be sure that South Vietnam would survive as an independent state, so that the United States would not face renewed domestic recriminations over another Asian "loss." But as a client state ruled by unstable governments lacking widespread popular support, South Vietnam could not defend itself without the benefit of continuing American military aid, especially United States air and ground forces. This the Nixon administration could not give.

Washington tried to negotiate a settlement with the North Vietnamese in 1969. Despite the death that year of Ho Chi Minh, the driving force behind Vietnam's long struggle for independence from Western rule, Hanoi refused to talk. Nixon thereupon launched a program of Vietnamization: the United States would withdraw from the fighting as the South Vietnamese became capable of defending themselves. Although the administration reduced the number of American troops in Vietnam from half a million to 39,000 over the next three years, fierce fighting punctuated these withdrawals. In 1969 United States air forces secretly bombed North Vietnamese supply centers in Cambodia. In April 1970 American and South Vietnamese ground forces widened the war by striking at North Vietnamese units in Cambodia. The bombing and "incursion," as Nixon called the ground assault, did little to improve South Vietnamese capacity to resist. It did, however, destabilize Cambodia, in which a civil war between right-wing and communist forces killed as many as a million people. When the invasion provoked renewed campus demonstrations in the United States, which led to the death of four students at Kent State University in Ohio and two at Jackson State

**Kent State**
*Campus protests against Nixon's invasion of Cambodia in 1970 resulted in deaths at Kent State and Jackson State universities.*

in Mississippi and to the shutdown of some colleges and universities, Nixon defended his action as necessary to the survival of free institutions everywhere. If "the world's most powerful nation acts like a pitiful helpless giant," he said, "the forces of totalitarianism and anarchy will threaten free nations . . . throughout the world." Congress responded to the invasion by repealing the Tonkin Gulf Resolution of 1964.

The president's militancy, however, did not immediately bring Hanoi to the peace table, nor did it advance the cause of Saigon's independence. In March 1972, after further American efforts at negotiation with Hanoi came to nothing, the North Vietnamese launched a large-scale invasion of the South. Nixon answered with massive B-52 bomber attacks, by mining Haiphong harbor, and by imposing a naval blockade on North Vietnam. This round of fighting at last produced an American–North Vietnamese agreement to halt the war. But Saigon refused to go along with the settlement, which called for an American withdrawal while leaving North Vietnamese forces in place in the South. To force both Vietnams into an agreement, Nixon used the carrot and the stick. Promising the South Vietnamese an additional $1 billion in military supplies, and warning that Saigon would have to go it alone if it did not submit to Washington's demands, Nixon also committed himself to "swift and severe retaliatory action" should

**Kissinger in Hanoi**
*After four years of additional fighting, Nixon and Kissinger reached a settlement to the Vietnam War in 1973.*

Hanoi break the peace agreement. At the same time, he ordered twelve days of devastating air raids on the North in December 1972, during which the United States dropped more bombs than in the entire period from 1969 to 1971.

Unable to resist, both Vietnams agreed to a settlement in January 1973 that finally extricated the United States from its longest war in history. But "peace with honor" came at a high price. The war had cost over a million Vietnamese lives; 58,000 Americans were killed, and close to 300,000 were wounded. In the end these losses were in vain, for in the spring of 1975 Saigon fell to communist arms. Although Nixon had promised the South Vietnamese that they could "count on us," he had failed to reckon with public and congressional determination to halt America's "endless support for an endless war." Vietnamization and "peace with honor" were fig leaves covering a North Vietnamese victory. In the 1960s, Vermont Senator George Aiken had advised: "Declare victory and leave." Nixon had followed his advice, but rhetoric was no substitute for reality, and American defeat in the war was still reverberating in the United States twenty years later.

**Détente with China and the Soviet Union** While the Nixon administration wound down the war in Southeast Asia, it also tried to create a "structure of peace" through improved relations with Peking and Moscow. The brainchild of Nixon and Kissinger, détente principally aimed to inhibit Soviet and Chinese expansion, limit the costly arms race, and reduce Soviet and Chinese support for Third World revolutions that destabilized the world and threatened American interests. In 1969, at the start of Nixon's term, détente seemed an unlikely prospect—and not simply because Nixon had a reputation as a fierce anticommunist. Chinese and Soviet behavior in the late 1960s held out little hope for improved relations with the West. Beginning in 1966 Mao Zedong's communist government had sought to root out all "capitalist roaders" in China by unleashing the tumultuous Cultural Revolution. In a reign of terror conducted by mobs of youths called Red Guards, anyone suspected of moderation, traditionalism, or Western leanings was killed, imprisoned, or exiled to the countryside. Victimizing many of the country's best-educated and most productive members, the turmoil seriously damaged China's capacity to modernize its economy. In the Soviet Union, where Leonid Brezhnev and Alexei Kosygin had replaced Nikita Khrushchev in 1964, resurgent Stalinism seemed the order of the day—a trend confirmed by the heavy-handed Soviet intervention to stop Czechoslovak liberalization in August 1968. Yet the hostility between the two communist superpowers, coupled with each nation's desire to devote more attention to its internal affairs, made both China and Russia receptive to American offers of a better understanding. Competition for leadership of world communism and long-standing national tensions drove the two countries into an open split in the 1960s; even a Sino-Soviet war seemed possible. Moscow and Beijing each saw advantages in playing the United States off against the other.

Preliminary conversations in 1971 between Beijing and Washington indicated that both sides were ready for a major change in relations. To facilitate détente with China, Kissinger first met secretly with Premier Zhou Enlai; then, in the summer of 1971, the president broke the news that he would visit China. In February 1972 Nixon made good on his commitment to better relations with China by traveling to Beijing. His objectives were to end twenty-two years of mutual hostility and to ally China and the United States against Moscow's "geopolitical ambitions." "What brings us together," Nixon told Chairman Mao, "is a recognition of a new situation in the world and a recognition on our part that what is important is not a nation's internal political philosophy. What is important is its policy toward the rest of the world and toward us." One of the most significant acts of his presidency was Nixon's abandonment of his doctrinaire anticommunism in order to reach an accommodation with once-scorned "Red China." In the Shanghai communiqué at the close of the talks, the United States and the People's Republic announced their rejection of "foreign domination" over "any part of China or any independent country in this world." Obviously referring to the Soviet Union, they agreed to oppose the "efforts by any other country ... to establish ... hegemony." They also agreed to disagree about Taiwan: Nixon acknowledged that the island was a part of China but warned that the United States would not abandon it or allow it forcibly to be incorporated into the People's Republic.

In May 1972 Nixon and Kissinger followed their successful negotiations in Beijing with a visit to Moscow. Soviet leader Brezhnev, who sought to limit the range of Russian international involvements, willingly grasped a chance to lessen the tensions with his country's chief rival. Nixon and Kissinger shrewdly perceived that their acknowledgment of the Soviet Union as a unique state determined to follow its own destiny would produce meaningful agreements congenial to a new world order. "There must be room in this world for two great nations with different systems to live together and work together," Nixon declared in Moscow. As a consequence of this realism, as well as of Soviet eagerness to forestall a full-scale Sino-American rapprochement and to achieve greater economic well-being for its own people, the Kremlin agreed to sign the Strategic Arms Limitation Treaty (SALT I) with the United States, to expand Soviet-American trade, and to avoid international tensions that could play havoc with détente. The SALT agreement limited the building of antiballistic missile (ABM) systems, which were encouraging greater missile production to swamp the ABMs. The treaty also placed a five-year limit on the building and deployment of intercontinental ballistic missiles (ICBMs). The agreement, however, said nothing about MIRVs (multiple independently targeted re-entry vehicles), which enabled an attacker to use one missile to launch several warheads against different targets. Consequently, the treaty represented no more than a small step toward arms control. The trade agreement allowed the Soviets to buy $1 billion of surplus United States grain at below-market prices. Moscow was able to relieve a food shortage, and Washington was able to reduce trade deficits and crop surpluses.

**Nixon and Brezhnev**
*Nixon and Brezhnev engage in a bit of fun as they sign the SALT I Treaty in Moscow in May, 1972.*

**The Cold War Continues: Asia, Latin America, and the Middle East**

Yet these advances toward a new "structure of peace" did not mean the end of the Cold War. Despite Soviet promises to avoid tensions that could undermine détente, they and the Chinese continued to compete with the United States and with each other for influence in the Third World. At the same time the Nixon administration was improving relations with Beijing and Moscow, it was also demonstrating its reflexive anticommunism in Asia, Latin America, and the Middle East. This also helped perpetuate the East-West struggle. For example, Nixon saw the war between India and Pakistan in 1971 less as a regional conflict than as a battle between Soviet and Chinese client states in which the United States should side with Beijing. A nationalistic uprising in Pakistan's East Bengal region resulted in a bloody repression by the central government's authorities and moved India to intervene in support of the insurgent Bengalis. When Moscow lined up with India and Beijing with Pakistan, Washington threw its support behind the latter. Convinced that Pakistan was responsible for the crisis, which was essentially a local affair, administration critics complained that American policy was a throwback to the same kind of Cold-War orthodoxy that had sucked the nation into Vietnam. Moreover, the success of the rebels, who established the new nation of

Bangladesh, meant a fresh defeat for the United States in Asia. Similarly, the White House worked to topple Chile's democratically elected socialist regime under Salvador Allende, whom it considered pro-Soviet and dangerous to United States interests in Latin America. Although numerous American officials believed that Allende presented no serious threat to the United States, the Nixon administration helped bring about the military coup of September 1973 that overturned the Santiago government and cost Allende his life.

Many felt that Nixon and Kissinger also displayed an overblown concern with communism in the Middle East. "The difference between our goal and the Soviet goal in the Middle East," the president told Secretary of State William Rogers in 1969, "is very simple but fundamental. We want peace. They want the Middle East." Kissinger, although not entirely agreeing with Nixon's view that the Middle East was principally an arena of Soviet-American conflict, nevertheless thought it "essential to reduce the scope of Soviet adventurist policies" there. This focus on the Soviet danger helped tie the United States closely to Israel, which Nixon—like all presidents since Truman—viewed as "the only state in the Middle East which is pro-freedom and an effective opponent to Soviet expansion."

Washington's close identification with what Palestinians called "the Zionist entity" made it difficult for the United States to mediate between Israel and the Arab states, particularly Egypt, Jordan, and Syria, all of which had lost important territories to Israel in 1967. For almost eleven years after the Suez crisis of 1956, the Arabs and Israel had poised at the brink of war. Guerrilla attacks on Israel by Palestinians, who contended that the Jewish state had driven them from their homeland, kept the area in constant tension. In June 1967 these difficulties exploded in the Six-Day War, in which Israel seized the Sinai Peninsula from Egypt, the Golan Heights from Syria, and Jerusalem and the entire West Bank of the Jordan River from Jordan. Convinced that these Arab states would not risk further losses in another war with Israel and that the Soviets (whom Washington credited with excessive influence) would restrain the Arabs from another conflict, the Nixon administration failed to anticipate the Egyptian-Syrian surprise attack on Israel on the Jewish holy day of Yom Kippur in October 1973. The administration played a major part in arranging a cease-fire and used the conflict to adopt a more evenhanded approach to Arab-Israeli differences. Nevertheless, because the United States resupplied Israel with weapons during the fighting, the Arab states proclaimed an oil embargo against the West. Cutting oil production by 25 percent from the September 1973 output, Arab oil producers deprived the United States and its allies of needed supplies. Their action led to fuel shortages; long lines of grumbling drivers cued up at filling stations, and gasoline prices in the United States doubled during the fall of 1973.

Recognizing America's economic dependence on Arab oil and the unproductiveness of a narrow anticommunist view of Middle Eastern events, Nixon sent Kissinger to the area. The secretary of state shuttled between Israel, Egypt, and Syria trying to find diplomatic solutions to the region's conflicts. Between November 1973 and September 1975 Kissinger worked out a series of agreements that removed Israeli forces from newly captured Syrian territory and a part of the Golan Heights, reopened the Suez Canal (which had been closed since 1967), restored part of the Sinai Peninsula to Egyptian control, initiated indirect peace talks between Egypt and Israel, and ended the Arab oil embargo.

**The Election of 1972**      Nixon entered the 1972 campaign with a solid record of achievement overseas and an economy seemingly on the mend at home. Yet neither his accomplishments nor his popularity were so strong as to guarantee him a second term. At the beginning of 1972 his principal Democratic opponent, Senator Edmund Muskie of Maine, was running neck-and-neck with him in the polls; and George Wallace, who made a strong showing in the early Democratic primaries, was likely to cost Nixon votes on the right if he chose to run as an independent. Thus the president faced an uncertain reelection bid.

Circumstances, however, opened the way to a stunningly lopsided Nixon victory. In 1969 Senator Edward Kennedy, the youngest of the Kennedy brothers, had his presidential hopes dashed by his questionable behavior after an accident in which a young woman in his car drowned at Chappaquiddick on Cape Cod. Although apparently speeding and apparently negligent in attempting to save her or get help, he was largely unpenalized by the local authorities for the accident. The blow to his presidential ambitions, however, was decisive. In May 1972 an unbalanced young man in a crowd at a Maryland shopping mall shot Wallace, paralyzing him and forcing him out of the race. Muskie fell victim to a "dirty trick" by a Nixon campaign official. During the New Hampshire primary, when Muskie tearfully defended himself against a false accusation of disparaging French-Canadians in the state and objected to other slurs directed at his family, his candidacy was destroyed. Senator George McGovern of South Dakota, identified with the Democratic left wing and the counterculture, now became the nominee. He horrified middle Americans with talk of giving welfare recipients $1,000 a year, cutting the defense budget by some $30 billion, and withdrawing immediately from Vietnam with no apparent regard for the survival of the Saigon regime. Moreover, he stumbled badly when he had to replace his vice-presidential nominee, Senator Thomas Eagleton of Missouri, who revealed that he had been hospitalized three times for emotional disorders. Instead of being able to focus on Nixon's failings, McGovern had to appease conservative Democrats and defend his integrity and capacity for the presidency. Most voters gave him negative marks. Winning only 37.5 percent of the popular vote and a mere 17 electoral votes (from Massachusetts and the District of Columbia), McGovern fared even worse than had Goldwater against Johnson in 1964. Nixon's 60.7 percent of the popular count and 520 electoral votes made him the third most successful victor in a presidential contest in American history. But the Democrats kept control of Congress, and Nixon became the only president to begin two terms with the opposition dominant in both houses.

**Watergate**
Nixon's second term found him immersed in a series of scandals revealing the worst constitutional abuses by high officials in the country's history, and it ended in the most serious crisis that the office of the presidency had ever faced. Never conscionable about his political practices, as demonstrated by his vicious attacks on Alger Hiss and Helen Gahagan Douglas (his opponent in the 1950 Senate race), and by his behavior during the Eisenhower years, Nixon had an affinity for dirty tricks and a disregard for law that put his actions in the Watergate affair in line with much that he had done before.

Vice-President Agnew was the first high administration figure to leave office in disgrace. Early in 1973 the Justice Department reconstructed a long history of secret payments that engineering firms, in return for government contracts, had been making to Agnew throughout his rise in Maryland politics. Couriers had even sat outside the vice-president's office waiting to deliver the cash. After a frantic attempt to save his career, the vice-president suddenly resigned in October as part of a plea bargain with the Justice Department. Agnew received a light sentence for evading income tax but avoided the much more serious penalties for extortion and bribery. He was the first vice-president ever forced to resign because of wrongdoing. To replace him, Nixon appointed Congressman Gerald R. Ford of Michigan, an undistinguished conservative Republican. But Ford's role as minority leader, his reputation for honesty, and his popularity with fellow members of Congress assured him of prompt confirmation.*

The downfall of the vice-president was stunning enough. Yet Agnew was only the prologue. As he went down, President Nixon himself was beginning to topple. In June 1972 five men had been arrested for burglarizing Democratic headquarters at the Watergate Apartments in Washington, D.C. After a flurry of attention, the story had slipped from sight. Despite the clear connection between the burglars and the Republican Committee to Reelect the President (CREEP), McGovern had not been able to rouse much interest in the incident during the campaign. Then in the spring of 1973, as the *Washington Post* and Federal District Judge John J. Sirica pressed for more information about the break-in, one of the burglars decided to cooperate with the government investigators. As that culprit was confessing, John Dean, a close presidential adviser, acknowledged his own part in the White House coverup. Behind these two, a long line of penitents began to form.

The stories they told spread in two directions. One traced a variety of activities through the executive's most powerful offices: the use of campaign contributions to win government favors, the illegal handling of those funds,

---

*The Twenty-fifth Amendment, approved in 1967, had specified a procedure for filling a vice-presidential vacancy through presidential nomination and congressional confirmation.

**H. R. (Bob) Haldeman**
*An advertising executive best known for successfully selling an insect spray, Haldeman became one of Nixon's inner circle, known for his "tough guy" tactics. He was brought down by the Watergate scandal. In this photograph he attempts to answer the Senate Watergate Committee's questions.*

devious techniques for making the president a millionaire, and assorted tactics of political sabotage to ensure Nixon's reelection. In order to discredit Defense Department consultant Daniel Ellsberg for having leaked to the press a confidential Pentagon study of American involvement in Vietnam, the White House had also sanctioned the burglary of Ellsberg's psychiatrist's office. Although all this provided a sordid peep through the keyhole of national politics, it attracted far less attention than the second trail of evidence, which carried the burglary's planning and the subsequent suppression of evidence to Nixon's inner staff— Dean, Attorney General John Mitchell, and Haldeman and Ehrlichman. All these men had to resign and eventually served short prison terms. Would the trail lead to the president's desk?

Nixon fought to block the investigation for more than a year. In public the president repeatedly declared his innocence. When Haldeman and Erlichman quit in April 1973, Nixon announced that "there can be no whitewash at the White House." In private he plotted ways of obstructing a grand jury under the tenacious Judge Sirica and a Senate investigating committee under Sam Ervin of North Carolina, a conservative Democrat who saw himself as a staunch defender of the Constitution. Forced to accept a special Watergate prosecutor within the Justice Department, Nixon confronted a lawsuit for evidence he would not relinquish: secret tape recordings of conversations in the Oval Office. The existence of the taping system had come to light during testimony of a White House aide before the Ervin committee. In October 1973, in what became known as the "Saturday Night Massacre," Nixon forced Attorney General Elliot Richardson, the deputy attorney general, and Special Prosecutor Archibald Cox

**Nixon and Watergate**
*The Watergate crisis made Nixon the only president in United States history to resign.*

of the Harvard Law School, to resign. Cox's replacement, the conservative Houston lawyer Leon Jaworski, proved just as dogged and carried his demand for the evidence to the Supreme Court.

The evidence in question lay in the vault of tapes recording almost every conversation that had been held in President Nixon's private office. These tapes (which in 1984 Nixon said he wished he had destroyed) eventually wrecked his defenses. Someone tried erasing portions of the tapes. The White House issued an edited transcript of parts of them. Finally, the president decided to withhold them altogether. But in July 1974 the Supreme Court unanimously awarded the tapes to Judge Sirica's grand jury and, through the grand jury, to the public. As the House of Representatives was preparing to vote articles of impeachment against the president for obstruction of justice, defiance of a congressional subpoena, and the use of executive agencies to violate constitutional rights, Nixon acknowledged much of what the tapes would verify about his intimate involvement in the Watergate affair. Admitting the facts but denying guilt, Nixon resigned on August 9, 1974.

Nixon's political demise, although he never acknowledged it, was self-inflicted. Greedy for an unprecedented mandate, or at least one large enough to allow him close to a free hand in dealing with domestic and foreign affairs during a second term, Nixon overreached himself. Having succeeded repeatedly in past campaigns with the sort of underhanded tactics used in 1972, he was blind to the possibility that he might be brought down for his actions. His failure to destroy the tapes when they became public knowledge is a good case in point: he believed that the prestige and might of the presidency would insulate him from an effective congressional or judicial investigation of his misdeeds.

Nixon's resignation set the most astonishing of precedents. After receiving 97 percent of the electoral vote, the president—the indispensable leader—had been driven from office in midterm. Moreover, his replacement had been elected to no office higher than representative from the Fifth Congressional District of Michigan. Gerald Ford had a mandate for national leadership only from the two houses of Congress.

The Watergate scandal and its outcome greatly undermined the prestige of the "imperial presidency," and it meant a considerable—although temporary—resurgence of congressional power. In 1973 Congress overrode a presidential veto of a War Powers Act that called for the president to consult Congress in all possible instances before committing troops to foreign wars, to explain any unilateral commitment within two days, and to withdraw American forces after sixty days unless Congress approved their continued involvement abroad. In 1972 and 1974 Congress enacted campaign reform laws that restricted contributions to, and expenditures by, candidates for federal offices. Events in the 1980s demonstrated that these laws were more a case of symbolic than substantive reform. As another curb on political and constitutional abuses, Congress also strengthened the Freedom of Information Act of 1966, making it easier for citizens serving the public's "right to know" to obtain government documents.

Congress, however, was to prove generally ineffectual in exercising its revived authority. Despite the blow to the presidency inflicted by Nixon's resignation, more than forty years of expansive executive authority coupled with a reliance on presidents to ensure the national security in a dangerous world made it impossible for the legislative and judicial branches of government substantially to rein in the White House.

## The Custodial Presidency: Ford

The transition from Richard Nixon to Gerald Ford was remarkably smooth. Most Americans thought that a man, not the system, had failed. The news media interpreted Nixon's disgrace as a lesson proving that even the most exalted would suffer for the sin of pride.

The amiable, unaffected Ford—a study in contrast with the dour, withdrawn Nixon—eased the country's way through the first resignation by a chief executive. In his initial address Ford promised to represent all the people; and he began his presidency with a cautious, congressional style of leadership, offering a little for this group, a little for that one. Telling the country that its "long national nightmare is over," he implicitly promised a period of healing in which the abuses of imperial presidents like Johnson and Nixon would be things of the past. "I am acutely aware that I have received the votes of none of you," he said on taking office. "I am a Ford, not a Lincoln," he quipped on another occasion (perhaps his most successful venture into humor). Well before Nixon's resignation, only about one in four Americans was supporting the embattled president. At the start of Ford's term, three out of four citizens described themselves as behind the new chief.

**Gerald Ford**
*Ford was a weak interim president who filled out Nixon's term.*

But much of this goodwill evaporated when, a month into his term, Ford pardoned Nixon unconditionally for all federal crimes he had or may have committed as president. Ford's action angered many and rekindled feelings of alienation toward government officials. Under Nixon cynicism about Washington politics was widespread and intense, with four out of five Americans saying that, while he may have been lying, Nixon was no more corrupt than his predecessors. In 1974, 43 percent of the respondents in a national survey revealed that they had "hardly any" confidence in those running the executive branch of government. Revelations about the CIA and FBI during the two and a half years after Ford became president further weakened public faith in federal authority. Domestic spying on protest groups by both agencies, particularly an attempt by J. Edgar Hoover to discredit Martin Luther King, Jr., convinced millions of Americans that they could not trust their own government. A Senate committee investigating intelligence operations revealed that the CIA had conspired to kill Fidel Castro and overthrow Ngo Dinh Diem in South Vietnam and Allende in Chile. The fact that Diem and Allende lost their lives in the coups against them placed some responsibility for their deaths on the CIA.

A growing belief that the government wielded uncontrolled powers and that ordinary citizens could have little influence on government actions helped discourage many citizens from voting. Laziness and apathy toward politics, as had often been the case in the past, were also factors. Whereas between 60.6 percent and 63.3 percent of the electorate had participated in the five presidential elections between 1952 and 1968, the five succeeding campaigns of 1972 to 1988 drew only 50 to 55 percent of the voters to the polls. The nation's legislative branch received an even paltrier vote of confidence: in 1976 only 17 percent of Americans professed respect for Congress. This mood of alienation particularly damaged the Republican party, which was identified with Nixon and Watergate. In 1974 the party claimed only 18 percent of the registered voters, and in the congressional elections that year the Democrats substantially increased their hold on both houses. For all that, however, the Democrats commanded scarcely more public confidence than the Republicans. To most Americans the Democrats were now simply the lesser of two evils. Against this discouraging backdrop Ford set out to build a record that would warrant his election in 1976. But he fell far short of his goal. By no standard can he be described as an outstanding president. He was an uninspiring speaker who exercised little control over Congress and made no major gains in foreign affairs. Most citizens thought Ford "a nice guy" but doubted his command of serious issues.

**Energy Crisis**

One reason that Ford seemed so ineffectual was a worsening economic condition that fell on his unlucky head—a crisis that only in part stemmed from President Johnson's deficits.

The Arab oil embargo of 1973 had dramatically revealed the West's growing dependence on Third World petroleum producers and its vulnerability to the monopolistic practices of the Organization of Petroleum Exporting Countries (OPEC), a cartel of some of these producers. In 1974 OPEC unilaterally announced a fourfold increase in international oil prices. Driven by energy costs, inflation in the United States shot up to 11 percent, and other industrialized countries suffered similarly.

The energy crisis was one of the most momentous events of the postwar era, signaling the West's loss of control over the sources of cheap energy that for decades had sustained its economic growth and prosperity. Americans reacted with shock and disbelief. Much was said about the end of Western economic growth in the dawning new era of scarcity. Some talked wildly of seizing Middle Eastern oil fields. There were many scapegoats—Arab nabobs, greedy oil companies, obtuse politicians, even American manufacturers of gas-guzzling automobiles—but no heroes. Perceptive observers, however, realized that the answer would have to be found in conservation and the ultimate development of new energy sources. Meanwhile Western consumers would have to reconcile themselves to skyrocketing OPEC prices, financing new technologies, and enduring more stagflation.

Ford responded unimaginatively, offering no plan to meet what everyone soon called the energy crisis. Preoccupied with restraining price increases, Ford

**Gas Crisis**
*As OPEC squeezed United States oil supplies, long lines became a daily occurrence at gas stations across the country.*

handed out WIN (Whip Inflation Now) buttons, cut government spending, supported tight money (which drove up interest rates), and urged a tax increase to reduce federal deficits. All this merely depressed an already faltering economy. By the spring of 1975 unemployment reached 9 percent, where it remained for the rest of the year. A precipitous drop in stock prices and in the GNP showed that the country was caught in the worst economic downturn since the Great Depression. Instead of adopting a flexible policy to revive the economy, as Nixon had in 1971, Ford stuck with conservative ideas about wringing inflation out of the economy by slowing it down. Thus he vetoed numerous bills aimed at reviving the economy and helping the disadvantaged, and he refused loan guarantees to New York City, which, trapped between swelling social service costs and shrinking tax revenues, had reached the verge of bankruptcy. Although congressional overrides of Ford's vetoes and a presidential turn to a less hard-line approach stimulated a recovery by the end of 1975, the president was saddled with a reputation as being rigid and unimaginative in dealing with domestic affairs.

**The Ford Foreign Policy**

Ford fared little better in foreign affairs, where he had limited knowledge and experience. To give his administration credibility, Ford kept Kissinger on as secretary of state. "I became the focal point of a degree of support unprecedented for a nonelected official," Kissinger later wrote. "It was as if the public and Congress felt the national peril instinctively and created a surrogate center around which the national purpose could rally." Yet no such national purpose crystallized. Even Kissinger's prestige could not move Congress and the public to rescue a collapsing South Vietnam. Americans, so to speak, averted their glance as United States and South Vietnamese officials fled the country. The sight of South Vietnamese desperately trying to find space in departing American helicopters on the roof of the United States Embassy disgusted Americans at home but did little to stir them to action. Americans could do nothing to avert the horrors that befell Cambodia (or "Democratic Kampuchea," as it was renamed) when the fanatical Khmer Rouge guerrilla movement seized power and launched a genocidal onslaught against the nation's urban population. Nor could Kissinger persuade Americans that the United States should intervene against communist insurgents in the southern African nation of Angola. The only United States attempt at military reaction to these disasters—a commando raid on the American cargo ship *Mayaguez,* which the Khmer Rouge had seized—turned into a tragicomic fiasco when forty American troops died trying to rescue thirty-eight crew members who had already been released.

Ford's only significant success was in Soviet-American relations. He and Brezhnev outlined the framework of a SALT II agreement at a summit meeting in Vladivostok in November 1974. At Helsinki, Finland, in August 1975 the United States, the USSR, and thirty-three European nations formally recognized the boundaries established in Eastern and Western Europe after World War II. In exchange the Soviets promised a more liberal human rights policy and in particular promised to ease restrictions on Soviet Jews to emigrate. But the proposed SALT II treaty and Helsinki accords impressed relatively few voters and exposed Ford to right-wing Republican attacks (led by former California governor Ronald Reagan) as soft on communism.

The Ford-Kissinger record in foreign affairs was essentially one of treading water. The grievous losses in Vietnam followed by its capitulation to communism made Americans deeply resistant to any kind of bold foreign-policy initiatives. However cynical many Americans were about achieving genuine accommodation with the communists in Moscow and Beijing, citizens saw détente as the best means to limit future commitments overseas. Had it been a realistic possibility, the country probably would have supported a return to old-fashioned isolationism. But given the changed world in which Americans lived, they saw détente, with all its limitations—on which conservatives played effectively—as the best alternative to continuing Cold-War activism abroad.

**The Election of 1976** An undistinguished record during his more than two years as president seemed to make Ford an easy mark in the 1976 campaign. Reagan undermined Ford in a losing nomination battle by attacking the president's "weak" defense and foreign policies and his poor performance in managing the economy. But the Democrats, running their own undynamic candidate, almost lost the election. In a surprising turn of events, they nominated a one-term former Georgia governor, James Earl Carter, Jr. Because voters were soured on government officials and skeptical about "politicians," Jimmy Carter could turn to good advantage his obscurity and strong identification as a "born-again" Christian. Emphasizing his detachment from the Washington bureaucracy, and pledging that he would "never tell a lie," Carter touched responsive chords in a public eager for a less imposing, more open federal government. As a southern progressive who had a balanced view on civil rights, a track record as a successful middle-class businessman, and a hankering for less government regulation (red tape, in the public's mind), he seemed a compelling enough candidate in 1976 to bring most Democrats to his side.

Although Carter had begun his campaign against Ford with a 30 percent lead in the polls, most of his advantage dissolved by election day. His ineptitude as a candidate foreshadowed his inexpert performance as president. On the campaign trail he tried to be all things to all people, raising suspicions that he had no fixed opinion on any major public question. It seemed as though Ford would catch and pass Carter until the candidates held a televised debate in October, in which the president confirmed public perceptions of him as an uninformed bumbler. Ford's astonishing remark during the debate that "there is no Soviet domination of Eastern Europe" reinforced a widespread feeling that he was unqualified to be elected president of the United States. Finding little to choose in either candidate, some voters sported bumper stickers saying "Don't Vote. It Only Encourages Them." With the smallest proportion (53 percent) of eligible voters going to the polls since 1948, Carter won 51 percent of the popular vote to Ford's 48 percent. The division in the electoral college, 297 to 241, was the tightest since 1916.

## The Faltering Presidency: Carter

Like his three predecessors, Carter became an unpopular president. After a year and a half in office, his standing with the public had sunk even lower than Ford's at the corresponding point in the latter's term. Carter was a highly intelligent man (he had been trained as a nuclear engineer) and an exceptionally hardworking president. He was not short of political insight; in fact, Carter clearly understood the country's longing for a respite from imperious leaders. And thus he adopted an informal style that he believed would strike a resonant chord. At his inauguration he strolled down Pennsylvania Avenue hand in hand with his wife— "trusting us not to kill him," said one observer, remembering the killings and attempted killings of the two Kennedys, King, Wallace, and Ford. He attended town meetings in small communities, spending the night in local homes; he even gave a televised fireside chat wearing a cardigan sweater. Yet these gestures struck the public as too contrived. He was a poor administrator who got bogged down in the details of isolated issues and an unspontaneous, dull speaker who lacked what people (remembering John Kennedy) called charisma—the ability to inspire and excite the media and the public. Whereas TR, FDR, and JFK had impressed on the country the larger purposes of the Square Deal, the New Deal, and the New Frontier, Carter had no overall vision that kindled public imagination. Perhaps he is best compared to the inept and unlucky Herbert Hoover. Both were moralistic progressives with an engineer's passion for detail and limited command of larger matters; and overwhelmed by disasters not of their own making, both proved unable to inspire public hope.

Even Carter's image as a simon-pure moralist proved hard to maintain. Bert Lance, his budget director and a close friend from Georgia, resigned after questionable financial practices came to light. Congressional scandals known as Koreagate (bribes from the South Korean government to congressmen) and ABSCAM (kickbacks and bribes to various congressmen from federal agents disguised as Arabs) added to feelings that Carter could do nothing to stop corruption in high places. And when the press began to complain that an overprotective White House staff was insulating Carter from criticism, unhappy memories of Nixon revived.

**Domestic Affairs: The Unmanageable Economy**

Public confidence in Carter eroded chiefly because he could not restore a sound economy: for all the criticism of the "imperial presidency," Americans still expected their presidents to continue the Rooseveltian tradition of national economic management. Carter, like Nixon and Ford, had to wrestle with intractable problems of recession and inflation. On entering office, his first concern was to stimulate the economy and to reduce a nearly 8 percent unemployment rate. Since inflation had eased to 5.5 percent in 1976, only half of what it had been in 1974, Carter believed that he could concentrate on jump-starting the economy. As a major initiative in this direction, he proposed relaxing the regulation of industry and banks by the federal government. Carter·rightly believed that deregulation could reduce costs and help stem the tide of inflation. Accordingly, his administration began taking significant steps toward deregulation, notably in the trucking and airline industries, thus initiating a policy trend that would come fully into its own in the 1980s, with some long-term destructive consequences to the national economy. Moreover, because fuel costs were central to the recent price surge, Carter hoped to check the inflationary spiral through a national energy policy that would hold down oil and natural gas prices.

During his first year in office he pushed a number of bills through Congress directed at promoting economic expansion, and he pressed for a major energy law. The first half of his program succeeded. In 1977 Carter sponsored and the Congress approved tax cuts totaling $34 billion and enacted public-works and public-service measures costing $14 billion, including an unprecedented national youth employment law. Congress also raised the minimum wage by nearly 50 percent, increased farm price supports, and eased environmental regulations on industries struggling to make a profit. The economy responded to this stimulus: unemployment fell from 7.9 percent at the start of Carter's term to 5.8 percent in 1979.

But Carter's energy proposals largely failed. In April 1977 he asked Congress for a bill that would reduce energy consumption by increasing taxes on gasoline and fuel-inefficient automobiles. Industries were to be encouraged to substitute coal for oil; and natural gas and utility companies to switch to nuclear power. In March 1979, however, the near-catastrophe at the Three Mile Island nuclear power plant badly shook the nation's faith in nuclear power, focusing public attention on the dangers inherent in using nuclear energy. Well before this part of Carter's program came into question, the rest of his plans had been largely turned aside by a deadlock among competing interests. Although Congress agreed to create the Department of Energy in 1977, it stalled on the balance of Carter's proposal until 1978; then it passed an ineffectual National Energy Act promising little actual conservation and imposing no meaningful restraints on rising energy prices.

Without a plausible conservation program and dogged by higher government spending, the economy again began to overheat. Inflation soared to 9.6 percent in 1978 and kept on rising the next year. Shifting his attention to this problem, the president reduced the second of three proposed tax cuts by 20 percent and vetoed congressional appropriations for defense and public works that he feared would add to inflationary pressures. Futilely, he also promulgated "voluntary" guidelines on wage and price increases and promised to hold down government expenditures. But then the economy took another nosedive when the Federal Reserve raised interest rates to slow economic expansion and bolster the dollar, whose value had tumbled in relation to other currencies. By the end of 1980 unemployment had shot back up to 7.4 percent, while the prime interest rate stood at an astonishing 20 percent and the federal deficit approached record highs. Even worse, the cost of living increased by 13 percent during 1980, and there was little hope that these energy-driven price increases could soon be halted.

A second round of international oil shortages began in 1979 when a revolution broke out in Iran, one of the world's leading petroleum producers. World oil prices increased by another 50 percent; in the United States, gasoline now cost more than $1 a gallon. To meet the crisis—as well as to answer a growing clamor about his ineptness and erratic policy shifts—Carter proposed a new energy program in mid-July.

In announcing his new energy plan on national television, Carter prefaced his speech with a dramatic announcement that the country faced a "crisis of confidence" threatening to immobilize the national will and jeopardize American security. But having thus heightened a growing sense of crisis by complaining of a national malaise, Carter reinforced perceptions of his administration's inability to cope: his second plan was no more acceptable to Congress than his first had been, and many thought it unworkable. As he approached the election of 1980, ever-worsening stagflation opened Carter to attack from all along the political spectrum. Admitting the mediocrity of his performance in dealing with major domestic problems, Carter told a journalist after he left office that he deserved no more than a grade of "C."

**A Moral Foreign Policy**

Carter justifiably felt that he had done better in international affairs, although here too his administration suffered some setbacks. Unlike Nixon and Kissinger, Carter professed no ambitious new design for world peace resting on the realistic manipulation of power. Instead he mounted an idealistic campaign to discourage human rights abuses by right- and left-wing regimes alike, and he thoughtfully identified the major international problems that his administration should address. These included resolving differences with Panama over the canal, thus enabling the United States to conciliate Latin American sensitivities; reducing tension in the Middle East in order to avert another war and another energy crisis; further normalizing relations with China; and reaching an arms-control agreement with the Soviets that would reduce the chances of a nuclear war.

One of the great success stories of Carter's term was his negotiation of the canal treaties with Panama and securing of their Senate ratification. Skillfully directed by Secretary of State Cyrus Vance, the State Department concluded fourteen years of negotiations over America's future role in managing and defending the canal. Under the two treaties signed in 1977, Panama and the United States agreed to abolish American sovereignty over the Canal Zone. Control of the canal itself was to remain in United States hands until the year 2000, but the Panamanians would take over after that time, with the United States retaining the right to use and defend the waterway. The treaties provoked an outcry in Congress and among many Americans as a blow to national security and prestige. "It's ours," Senator S. I. Hayakawa of California said of the canal. "We stole it fair and square." But with the help of amendments strengthening American rights unilaterally to protect the canal, the agreement won Senate approval in the spring of 1978—by only one vote more than the two-thirds needed for passage. When the Carter administration also initially adopted a hands-off attitude toward a victorious left-wing Nicaraguan revolution that overthrew the reactionary and abuse-riddled Somoza government, United States standing in Latin America rose to a level not attained since the Kennedy years. However, when the Nicaraguan rebel government—the Sandinistas—curtailed civil liberties, aligned with Cuba, and began supplying revolutionaries in El Salvador, the Carter administration backed the government in San Salvador and cut off aid to Nicaragua. The president wanted no part of a return to backing repressive anticommunist regimes, but he wisely saw the dangers at home and abroad from indiscriminately supporting a radical leftist government that violated human rights and opened the door to Soviet adventurism in Central America.

In the Middle East as well, the Carter administration built on the Nixon-Kissinger initiatives of 1973–75 and achieved a signal triumph. To break the political stalemate in the region, the Egyptian and Israeli leaders, Anwar Sadat and Menachem Begin, agreed to convert the indirect discussions Kissinger had fostered into direct negotiations. They even visited each other's country. And when Egyptian-Israeli negotiations struck an impasse in 1978, Carter called in the two leaders for further talks. After two intense weeks with them at the presidential retreat in Maryland, Carter mediated the Camp David Accords. An outline

**Carter and Sadat**
*After weeks of intensive diplomacy, in the course of which Carter spent hours negotiating personally with Egypt's Anwar Sadat (shown here) and Israel's Menachem Begin, the president emerged with the Camp David Peace Accords, his greatest triumph.*

for an Egyptian-Israeli peace treaty and a framework for peace in the region, the accords proposed Egyptian recognition of Israel's right to exist in return for restoration of the entire Sinai Peninsula to Egyptian control, as well as autonomy for Palestinians living on the West Bank and in the Gaza Strip. After further negotiations, which took Carter to Cairo and Tel Aviv, Egypt and Israel signed a peace treaty in March 1979.

Although the two sides also agreed to begin discussing the future of the West Bank and Gaza—that is, the fate of the Palestinians—it was clear that such negotiations promised little significant gain. The Egyptian-Israeli accord represented the principal advance toward peace that could be achieved. Cairo's alienation from the rest of the Arab world made it almost impossible for other Arab countries to wage another all-out war with Israel. A civil war in Lebanon, beginning in 1975, provided plenty of opportunity for further bloodletting between Israel and its neighbors, but the peace treaty with Egypt placed limits on the extent of the fighting. Thus the Camp David agreements were a genuine step toward peace.

The Carter administration also extended the Nixon-Kissinger policy of seeking better Sino-American relations. In January 1979 the administration established normal diplomatic relations with Beijing and ended its official recognition of the Nationalist government on Taiwan. Although Washington also canceled a mutual defense pact with Taiwan, it maintained trade relations with the island and continued to sell it defensive weapons. The change in relations with Taiwan evoked strong criticism from conservative Americans; but the promise that the

United States government would not permit Taiwan to be politically attached to the mainland against its will blunted the conservative attack. The realization that in recognizing Beijing the United States was gaining a powerful anti-Soviet ally, doubling its trade with China, and unleashing it to curb Vietnam, Moscow's ally, made Carter's action popular in the United States.

At the same time that he improved relations with China, Carter also continued work begun under Ford for a second SALT agreement with the Soviets. But when the president openly encouraged Soviet dissidents struggling for human rights and asked for changes in the preliminary SALT II treaty negotiated by Ford and Kissinger, Moscow resisted further advances toward détente. By June 1979, however, the Soviets agreed to a SALT II treaty, apparently hoping thereby to discourage the development and deployment of new American weapons. Limiting the number of long-range missiles, bombers, and nuclear warheads on each side, the agreement promised to ease the arms race and open the way to further talks on reducing nuclear stockpiles.

The treaty, however, could not withstand a deterioration in Soviet-American relations brought on by aggressive Kremlin actions. Difficulties dated back to 1975–76, when Soviet-supported guerrillas, directly assisted by Cuban troops, seized control of Angola. Later, Soviet violations of the international Helsinki agreements of 1975 by which all parties promised to respect human rights, as well as the USSR's deployment of new SS-20 missiles aimed at Western Europe, raised strong American doubts about the sincerity of Moscow's commitment to détente. The last straw was a Soviet invasion of Afghanistan in the winter of 1979–80, to preserve a Marxist government under attack from Muslim rebels. American outrage over Afghanistan doomed the SALT II agreements. Although Carter tried unsuccessfully to save the treaty by delaying a Senate vote until the outcry cooled, he took other actions that reflected changed American attitudes. The United States and its NATO allies agreed to install new intermediate-range Pershing-2 and cruise missiles to counter the Soviet SS-20s; Carter proposed building an MX missile system that would make United States land-based ICBMs less vulnerable to Soviet attack by shuttling them around on underground railroad cars; and he halted grain and high-technology sales to the Soviets and induced American athletes to boycott the 1980 Olympic Games in Moscow.

This crisis in détente coincided with the worst foreign policy crisis of Carter's term, the seizure of American hostages in Teheran. Early in 1979 Ayatollah Ruhollah Khomeini, a revered and fanatical religious leader, drove the shah out of Iran—a severe blow to American interests. Despite the shah's police-state methods and disruptive modernization programs that alienated many Iranians, the United States had supported him, making his army the strongest in the region. Khomeini appealed strongly to ordinary Iranians by preaching a return to fundamental Islamic values and customs, which had eroded under the shah's regime. In November the White House allowed the exiled, dying monarch to come to the United States for medical treatment; in retaliation Khomeini encouraged the seizure of the American embassy by radical students howling for the shah's return, trial, and execution. The students imprisoned fifty-three Americans, most of whom were entitled to diplomatic immunity under international law. After negotiations failed to effect their release, American forces attempted a rescue operation in April 1980. But the mission had to be canceled when mishaps killed eight American troops and destroyed essential equipment. The resignation of Secretary of State Vance, who had opposed the mission and the drift toward a more anti-Soviet policy, raised questions about the wisdom of the operation and the administration's overall handling of foreign affairs. Entering the 1980 presidential campaign, Carter carried the burden of a faltering détente policy and a humiliating inability to subdue the defiant Iranians.

**The Outrage of America**
Americans looking back on the 1970s could not easily assume that all would come right with the world. Worldwide terrorism—hijackings, bombings, assassinations—and violent domestic crimes persuaded a majority of Americans that nobody was ever safe from random slaughter. Depictions of violence in countless TV shows reflected public taste. And the nation's official defenders of law and order, it seemed, were really specialists in deceit.

In 1971 the Pentagon Papers, leaked to the press by Daniel Ellsberg, exposed the government's secret maneuvers in Vietnam and its systematic lies about the Indochinese war. Each year brought more stories that discredited the agencies of law and order. President Johnson had approved a wiretap on Robert Kennedy; President Nixon had authorized one on his own brother. The director of the FBI, J. Edgar Hoover, had waged a personal vendetta against Martin Luther King, Jr. The bureau and military intelligence agencies had compiled mounds of dossiers on everybody from senators to singers, and the Internal Revenue Service had audited tax returns on the basis of citizens' political activities. Traditionally, Americans had enjoyed a bit of humbug now and then. But it was a deadly serious business for them to learn that President Eisenhower had instructed subordinates to "confuse" the public about widespread contamination from the government's nuclear tests.

Some Americans slipped into a sense of helplessness over inflation and recession, crime and violence, domestic poverty and global hunger. A feeling of the individual being trapped in a vast web of uncontrollable forces characterized the serious fiction of Joyce Carol Oates, John Cheever, and Joan Didion. The most popular movies alternated between fantasies of terror like *The Exorcist, Jaws,* and *Alien* and fantasies of escape like *Star Wars, Rocky, E.T., Die Hard, Batman,* and *Total Recall.*

To overcome the sense of helplessness about larger social issues, some Americans became preoccupied with personal improvement and fulfillment—what the journalist Tom Wolfe called "The Me Decade" and the historian Christopher Lasch condemned as "the culture of narcissism." Health foods, dieting, and physical fitness through jogging, bicycling, or regular workouts became a national mania. Meditation, Zen, yoga, encounter groups, and participation in religious cults gained large popular followings. Nostrums for achieving mental health, they were also evidence that some Americans had lost faith in traditional Western ideas and had turned to alien oriental religion for a sense of well-being.

Americans waxed highly indignant about corporate abuses of consumers. In 1965 a zealous young lawyer named Ralph Nader had inspired a consumer movement with the publication of *Unsafe at Any Speed,* a detailed analysis of the dangers built into automobiles manufactured in Detroit. A shabby attempt by General Motors to discredit him only enlarged his fame. Nader's young volunteers—"Nader's Raiders"—rapidly produced a variety of additional exposés. By the 1970s innumerable journalists, scientists, and local committees were spreading the gospel of consumer standards, and new legal guidelines covered such areas as automobile safety, credit contracts, product labeling, and food adulteration. Despite its popular base, however, the consumer movement never had a disciplined, focused strength.

The loss of faith in traditional institutions and alienation from established authority expressed themselves in postwar recriminations over Vietnam. Finding little, if anything, to celebrate in the failed war effort, most Americans wanted to forget this part of the country's past. Some surviving veterans were outraged by the country's general indifference to the sacrifice of their fallen and permanently disabled comrades. Tension over memories of the war reflected itself in a dispute about how best to memorialize the conflict. Clashes over what artist should create a monument in Washington, D.C., and over the monument itself betrayed the nation's continuing ambivalence about Vietnam. Demands that more be done to account for MIAs was another way of asking that Americans not forget the war. Even a decade later, the popularity of the *Rambo* movies, fantasies about a kind of military superman, testified to American longings for a renewed sense of power, even omnipotence, after defeat in the war. Other films like *The Deer Hunter* (1978), *Apocalypse Now* (1979), and their 1980s successors (*Platoon* and *Born on the Fourth of July*) expressed the anger Americans felt about the conflict—and in particular the bitterness of veterans who had fought in Vietnam.

## The New Conservatism

The 1970s were in many respects a reaction to the 1960s. By the end of the Johnson presidency in 1969, the country had run out of tolerance for upheaval and change; it felt exhausted by debate over the Great Society reforms, by social activism, and by agitation over Vietnam. Desperately the public yearned for tranquility and a chance for private gain. Less government activism in behalf of minorities, lower taxes, fewer government programs, and less government regulation appealed to most Americans as a wise alternative to the 1960s liberal agenda. California seemed to speak for the nation in 1978 when its voters approved Proposition 13, sharply reducing property taxes and government revenues for education and social programs. Conservatives across the country pressed the case for a balanced budget amendment to the United States Constitution. A group of conservative intellectuals came to prominence, led by veteran rightist William F. Buckley of the *National Review* and ex-liberal Norman

Podhoretz of *Commentary.* They decried cultural decadence, Soviet expansionism, crumbling Western self-confidence, affirmative action, feminism, unsuccessful and wasteful poverty programs, educational experimentation, and ebbing respect for authority.

Three strands came together in the conservative resurgence of the late 1970s. First were the traditional political-fiscal conservatives represented by business interests and by most congressional Republicans. The second strand consisted of "neoconservatives," mostly former liberals alienated by the failure (as they saw it) of their former political allies to advance American interests abroad and their affinity for wasteful, unsuccessful policies at home. Most vociferous were the so-called movement conservatives made up of a new Christian right—chiefly Protestant evangelicals and Catholic anti-abortionists—and assorted ideologues who had backed Barry Goldwater in 1964 and McCarthy in the 1950s.

Americans' instinctive Puritan sensibilities offended by the remnants of 1960s permissiveness fed the conservatism of the 1970s. Explicit sexuality and violence on television, in movies, and in popular music disturbed many and outraged some. Conservatives preached a return to the more wholesome values of family, religion, and patriotism. "All in the Family," an enormously popular television series, featured the character Archie Bunker, a heavy-handed blue-collar worker from Queens, New York, whose fulminations against "fags," "Hebes," "Spades," and "Spics" were meant to demonstrate the mindlessness of racial prejudice. Instead Archie came across as a lovable dolt: he touched resonant chords in the hearts of millions of Americans, who resented "bleeding-heart liberals" and "welfare cheats" too lazy to realize the American dream.

Other Americans tried to reassert tough, fundamental values. "Permissive" child rearing fell into disrepute, and parents pledged allegiance to maintaining clear authority and salutary discipline in the home. Hostility toward the rights of criminal suspects pervaded television dramas of the mid-1970s. With the Supreme Court's approval, infliction of the death penalty resumed in 1977; and by the end of the next decade hundreds of convicted criminals would face execution (usually after many years on Death Row as lawyers fought over their appeals, a lugubrious process that impressed some Americans as in itself "cruel and unusual punishment"). The well-organized Right-to-Life movement fought abortion. Deeply offended by abortion as "a death penalty for unborn babies," anti-abortionists used civil disobedience by blocking entrances to abortion clinics to stop the "killing." Conservatives also launched a well-publicized campaign against homosexuality, soon known as "gaybashing" and not always limited to verbal assaults. Especially appealing to Americans was fundamentalist Christian evangelism. Nearly one-third of all Americans, some 70 million people, described themselves as born-again Christians. Using cable television, "televangelist" preachers like Jim Bakker, Jerry Falwell, and Pat Robertson reached huge audiences. They collected millions of dollars from devoted followers and became aggressive political advocates of conservative causes. Falwell's Moral Majority, for example, campaigned loudly for prayer in schools and against abortion, the

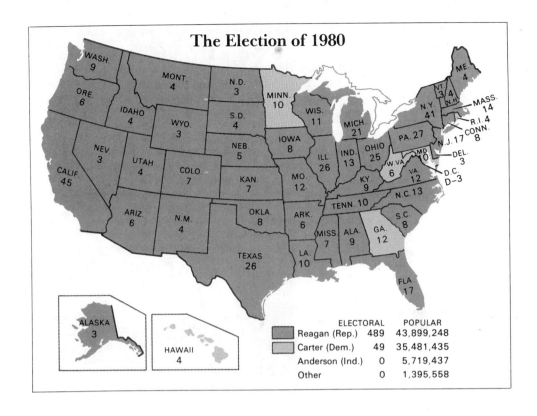

## The Election of 1980

| WASH. 9 | MONT. 4 | N.D. 3 | MINN. 10 | WIS. 11 | MICH. 21 | | | ME. 4 |
| ORE. 6 | IDAHO 4 | S.D. 4 | IOWA 8 | | | | N.Y. 41 | VT 3 / N.H. 4 |

(map of the United States with electoral votes per state)

| | ELECTORAL | POPULAR |
|---|---|---|
| Reagan (Rep.) | 489 | 43,899,248 |
| Carter (Dem.) | 49 | 35,481,435 |
| Anderson (Ind.) | 0 | 5,719,437 |
| Other | 0 | 1,395,558 |

ERA, and liberal political candidates. Amid the furor, antifeminists stymied passage of the ERA by the states.

**The Election of 1980**     Stagflation, frustration over the hostage crisis, and a rising conservative tide undermined Carter's reelection prospects. Senator Edward M. Kennedy challenged Carter for the nomination, but Kennedy's identification with unpopular liberal ideas, memories of Chappaquiddick, and Carter's incumbency defeated his bid. Carter's chances of winning another term depended chiefly on the effectiveness of the Republican campaign. To no one's surprise, the Republicans chose Ronald W. Reagan, a former movie actor and two-term governor of California. Reagan was sixty-nine years old, and a Republican victory would make him the oldest person ever elected to the White House. Further, he had a close association with right-wing groups that many feared would jeopardize social programs and threaten peace. The Democrats seized upon these two issues and emphasized them throughout the campaign.

But Reagan quieted voters' concerns by running a vigorous campaign that appealed to a broad cross section of the electorate. In his nomination speech he displayed the wit and charm that had endeared him to voters in California, emphasizing the themes that made him seem a pragmatic, steady man who could overcome the disarray that (according to opinion polls) 75 percent of Americans saw besetting their country. At the opening of his campaign he made a series of

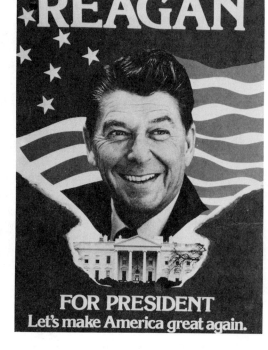

**Reagan Campaign Poster**
*Reagan exploited economic problems at home and frustration with foreign affairs to defeat Carter in 1980 and usher in more than a decade of conservative administration dedicated to making America "stand tall" again.*

blunders, rekindling suspicions that he was a slightly befuddled reactionary. Later, however, Reagan repaired the damage by appointing a new campaign manager. He then put Carter on the defensive, using television to depict himself as a pleasant, reasonable leader who wanted peace as much as anyone else. He was particularly effective in a nationally televised debate with Carter a week before the election.

Reagan almost perfectly expressed the national mood. A former New Deal Democrat who had supported Harry Truman's reelection in 1984, Reagan had taken up the conservative cause in the 1950s. In 1964 he captured national attention with a speech for Barry Goldwater that emphasized many of the conservative ideas that would flower during the 1970s. As governor of California after 1966, he had demonstrated his pragmatism by signing an abortion rights bill and a withholding-tax law favored by liberal Democrats. Reagan's divorce and remarriage would have killed his chances for the presidency a generation before; now even his most conservative backers were unfazed. For all his identification as a conservative, Reagan benefited from the country's shift to more liberal cultural values in the 1960s.

Reagan decisively defeated Carter, receiving 50.7 percent of the popular vote to Carter's 41 percent; most of the remaining votes went to John Anderson, a thoughtful liberal Republican congressman who had run as an independent. Reagan gained 489 electoral votes to the president's 49, which came from victories in only six states and the District of Columbia. But because only 55.1 percent of the electorate had gone to the polls, Reagan had actually captured the White House with a mere 28 percent of the eligible vote. Gaining 12 Senate seats, the Republicans won their largest majority in the upper house since 1928, 53 to 47. Although the Democrats retained control over the House of Representatives, 243 to 192, the Republicans reduced the Democratic margin by 33 seats, and the Republican-southern Democratic coalition that had frustrated Kennedy was reborn.

## CHRONOLOGY

**1969** Nixon takes office.

**1970** Establishment of the Environmental Protection Agency (EPA).
U.S. forces bomb and invade Cambodia.

**1971** Twenty-sixth Amendment, giving eighteen-year-olds the right to vote.
Wage and price controls introduced.
Classified documents about the Vietnam War, the Pentagon Papers, leaked to the press.

**1972** Nixon visits China and the Soviet Union.
SALT I treaty signed.
Congress sends Equal Rights Amendment (ERA) to the states for ratification.
Watergate break-in.
Nixon reelected president.

**1973** American withdrawal from Vietnam.
*Roe* v. *Wade* establishes women's constitutional right to abortion.
United States supports overthrow of Allende in Chile.
Senate Watergate Committee begins hearings.
Vice-President Agnew resigns; Gerald Ford appointed to succeed him.
Yom Kippur war and Arab oil embargo.

**1974** Worst economic recession since 1930s.

Nixon resigns the presidency; Ford becomes president.
Ford pardons Nixon.

**1975** Government in South Vietnam falls; Laos and Cambodia overrun by communist guerrillas.
*Mayaguez* incident.
Helsinki accords.

**1976** James Earl ("Jimmy") Carter, Jr., elected president.

**1977** Establishment of the Department of Energy.

**1978** Panama Canal treaties ratified.

**1979** United States formally recognizes the People's Republic of China.
SALT II treaty signed.
Accident at Three Mile Island nuclear power plant.
President Carter mediates an Egyptian-Israeli peace settlement.
Iranian hostage crisis begins.
Reverend Jerry Falwell establishes the Moral Majority.

**1979–1980** Iranian revolution pushes up oil prices an additional 50 percent; United States experiences the worst stagflation yet.

**1980** Boycott of Moscow Olympic Games in response to Soviet invasion of Afghanistan.
Rescue mission in Iran fails.
Ronald W. Reagan elected president.

SUGGESTED READINGS

Three interesting books attempt general interpretations of contemporary U.S. politics: David Knoke, *Change and Continuity in American Politics* (1976); Everett Carll Ladd, Jr., and Charles D. Hadley, *Transformations of the American Party System* (rev. ed., 1978); and Kevin P. Phillips, *The Emerging Republican Majority* (1969). Accounts of Richard Nixon include a favorable one in Earl Mazo and Stephen Hess, *Nixon* (1968), and an unfavorable one in Garry Wills, *Nixon Agonistes* (1970). More recent treatments are Stephen E. Ambrose, *Nixon: The Education of a Politician, 1913–1962* (1987) and *Nixon: The Triumph of a Politician, 1962–1972* (1989), and Roger Morris, *Richard Milhous Nixon: The Rise of an American Politician* (1989). In *Kissinger* (1974), Marvin and Bernard Kalb raise Nixon's reputation in foreign affairs by deflating claims that Kissinger dominated the president. Tad Szulc, *The Illusion of Peace: Foreign Policy in the Nixon Years* (1978), is harsher still on Kissinger. Kissinger defends himself in his memoirs, *White House Years* (1979) and *Years of Upheaval* (1982). Seymour Hersh, *The Price of Power: Kissinger in the Nixon White House* (1983), raises disturbing questions about Kissinger's actions. Harland B. Moulton's *From Superiority to Parity: The United States and the Strategic Arms Race, 1961–1971* (1973) discusses some preliminary moves toward détente. On the Middle East, William B. Quandt, *Decade of Decision: American Policy Toward the Arab-Israeli Conflict, 1967–1976* (1977), and Robert W. Stookey, *America and the Arab States* (1975), are especially useful. Recent interest in the office of the chief executive has generated a variety of books, including George E. Reedy, *The Twilight of the Presidency* (1970); Arthur M. Schlesinger, Jr., *The Imperial Presidency* (1973), which is sharply critical of Nixon; and Otis L. Graham, Jr., *Toward a Planned Society: From Roosevelt to Nixon* (1976), which also faults Nixon for disrupting the evolution of national planning. Domestic policies and developments in the 1970s are assessed in Daniel P. Moynihan, *The Politics of a Guaranteed Income* (1973); Barry Commoner, *The Politics of Energy* (1979); Lester C. Thurow, *The Zero-Sum Society* (1980); James A. Reichley, *Conservatives in an Era of Change: The Nixon and Ford Administrations* (1981); Peter Carroll, *It Seemed Like Nothing Happened: The Tragedy and Promise of America in the 1970s* (1982); and Herbert Stein, *Presidential Economics* (1984). The Watergate affair elicited its own special group of studies. Carl Bernstein and Bob Woodward, the *Washington Post* reporters who helped to expose the affair, tell a fascinating tale of investigation and deception in *All the President's Men* (1974). Their sequel, *The Final Days* (1976), deals with Nixon during the year before his resignation. Among the many memoirs by participants, John Dean's *Blind Ambition* (1976) is particularly enlightening. Jonathan Schell, *The Time of Illusion* (1976), also illuminates the Watergate period. The conservative senator who led an early investigation into the mess is the subject of Dick Dabney's *A Good Man: The Life of Sam J. Ervin* (1976). The first authoritative account by an historian is Stanley I. Kutler, *The Wars of Watergate: The Last Crisis of Richard Nixon* (1990).

On minority groups, the essays in Michael V. Namorato, ed., *Have We Overcome?* (1979), assess the state of black rights, and Anthony Downs, *Opening Up the Suburbs* (1973), discusses race and social policy. Five other valuable books on issues of race in the 1970s are Thomas Sowell, *Affirmative Action Reconsidered: Was It Necessary in Academia?* (1975), the observations of a black conservative; Manning Marable, *Race, Reform and Rebellion: The Second Reconstruction in Black America, 1945–1982* (1984), and his *Black American Politics: From the Washington Marches to Jesse Jackson* (1985); Joe R. Feagin, *Discrimination American Style: Institutional Racism and Sexism* (1986 ed.); and William Julius Wilson, *The Ghetto Underclass: Social Science Perspectives* (1989), the work of a sociologist. Matt S. Meier and Feliciano Rivera, *The Chicanos: A History of Mexican Americans* (1972), is a general account of an increasingly important minority in American life. Also useful is Julian Samora, *Los Moiados: The Wetback Story* (1971). More recent works of importance are James D. Cockcroft, *Outlaws in the Promised Land:*

*Mexican Immigrant Workers and America's Future* (1986), and Frank D. Bean and Marta Tienda, *The Hispanic Population of the United States* (1988). On immigration in general, see John Crewdson, *The Tarnished Door: The New Immigrants and the Transformation of America* (1983); David M. Reimers, *Still the Golden Door: The Third World Comes to America* (1985); and Gil Loescher and John A. Scanlan, *Calculated Kindness: Refugees and America's Half-Open Door* (1986). Wilcomb E. Washburn, *Red Man's Land, White Man's Law* (1971), details a record of mass injustice; D'Arcy McNickle, *Native American Tribalism* (1973), helps to explain the culture of recent protests; and Vine Deloria, Jr., *Behind the Trail of Broken Treaties* (1974), expresses the spirit of 1970s militancy. For a general survey and extensive bibliography, see Wilcomb Washburn's *The Indian in America* (1975).

Recent constitutional and political questions are addressed in Alexander M. Bickel, *The Supreme Court and the Idea of Progress* (1970), and in two books on Earl Warren: G. Edward White, *Earl Warren: A Public Life* (1982), and Bernard Schwartz, *Super Chief—Earl Warren and the Supreme Court* (1983). Martin P. Wattenberg, *The Decline of American Political Parties, 1952–1980* (1984), Walter Dean Burnham, *The Current Crisis in American Politics* (1983), and Theodore Sorenson, *A Different Kind of Presidency: A Proposal for Breaking the Political Deadlock* (1984), deal with problems in American political institutions.

Environmental issues are the subject of Ronald Inglehart, *The Silent Revolution* (1977); Robert Stobaugh and Daniel Yergin, eds., *Energy Future* (1979); Daniel Martin, *Three Mile Island* (1980); Edith Efron, *The Apocalyptics* (1984); Lester Milbrath, *Environmentalists: Vanguard for a New Society* (1984); and Sam Hays, *Beauty, Health, and Permanence: Environmental Politics in the United States, 1955–1985* (1987).

The literature on the Ford–Carter years is limited. On Ford, see his own account, *A Time to Heal: An Autobiography* (1979), and two books by journalists: J. F. ter Horst, *Gerald Ford and the Future of the Presidency* (1974), and Richard Reeves, *A Ford Not a Lincoln* (1975); John Osborne, *White House Watch: The Ford Years* (1977); Reichley's book cited above; and James L. Sundquist, *The Decline and Resurgence of Congress* (1981). The election of 1976 is covered in Elizabeth Drew, *American Journal: The Events of 1976* (1977), and Jules Witcover, *Marathon* (1977).

Carter's term is recounted in his memoirs, *Keeping Faith* (1982), and in the memoirs of his two principal foreign policy advisers: Cyrus Vance, *Hard Choices: Critical Years in America's Foreign Policy* (1983), and Zbigniew Brzezinski, *Power and Principle: Memoirs of the National Security Advisor, 1977–1981* (1983). Defense questions are analyzed in Strobe Talbott, *Endgame* (1979); and James Fallow, *National Defense* (1981). Foreign affairs issues are studied in Walter LaFeber, *The Panama Canal* (rev. ed., 1986); William Quandt, *Camp David* (1986); Anthony Lake, *Somoza Falling* (1989); A. Glenn Mower, Jr., *Human Rights and American Foreign Policy: The Carter and Reagan Experiences* (1987); Richard S. Newell, *The Struggle for Afghanistan* (1981); R. K. Ramazani, *The U.S. and Iran* (1982); and Warren Christopher et al., *American Hostages in Iran* (1985). Carter, the man and the president, is also studied in James T. Wotten, *Dasher: The Roots and the Rising of Jimmy Carter* (1978); William Lee Miller, *Yankee from Georgia: The Emergence of Jimmy Carter* (1978); Betty Glad, *Jimmy Carter: In Search of the Great White House* (1980); and Clark Mollenhoff, *The President Who Failed* (1980). The 1980 election is the subject of Elizabeth Drew, *Portrait of an Election: The 1980 Presidential Campaign* (1981). On Reagan's prepresidential career, see Lou Cannon, *Reagan* (1982), and Robert Dallek, *Ronald Reagan: The Politics of Symbolism* (1984).

# 34

# Conservatism in Power
## The Modern Republic Under
## Reagan and Bush

*I*N THE 1980s conservatism again surged to the fore in America's political cycle, as it had in the 1920s and the 1950s. And just as in these two earlier decades, America's political mood now reflected a public reaction against crusading civic activism: demands for government intervention to cure the nation's economic and social ills left most citizens cold. The 1980s, like the 1920s and 1950s, also witnessed a resurgent faith in American institutions and values. A seven-year economic expansion in the United States and the dramatic collapse of communism in Eastern Europe and the Soviet Union at the decade's end convinced a majority of Americans that despite some flaws theirs was the world's best possible economic and political system.

Yet for all the similarities to earlier decades, 1980s conservatism had its distinctive, contradictory features. Favoring a balanced budget amendment and maximum independence from foreign economic control, the Reagan administration produced the largest federal and trade deficits in United States history, leaving the nation dependent—for the first time since before World War I—on foreign investment to maintain growth. While the country celebrated democracy, free enterprise, and limited government, growing numbers of citizens stayed away from the polls, and those who still voted chose Democratic Congresses that kept intact liberal-inspired domestic social programs. The public favored substantial increases in defense spending but shied away from sustained military intervention abroad that risked substantial losses in blood and treasure.

In the post–Vietnam War era, a growing public aversion to international commitments had cast a haze of uncertainty over the nation's foreign policy. Americans of the 1970s had viewed world affairs with a greater impatience and a lower tolerance for the ceaseless volatility of life around the globe. During the oil embargo of 1973–74, a number of writers and officials had suggested a little gunboat diplomacy to seize the resources America wanted. Later some ordinary Americans had responded to the Iranian hostage crisis with demands to "nuke Iran." By the 1980s, the nation was ready to applaud quick foreign interventions that achieved their goals swiftly and with minimal loss of life. Thus Reagan's invasion of the Caribbean island of Grenada in 1983 to topple a Marxist regime and George Bush's successful military ouster of Panama's corrupt dictator Manuel Noriega in 1989 escaped public debate. On the other hand, such impatience would also generate a kind of public indifference. As Third World revolutions continued to unravel America's network of global connections, a powerful urge welled up to stay clear of these eruptions. Fear of "another Vietnam" haunted the country, and the public dreaded the prospect of long-term military intervention anywhere. In the summer and fall of 1990, when Bush challenged Iraq's invasion of Kuwait and threat to Saudi Arabia by sending 400,000 troops into the Persian Gulf—the largest overseas deployment of United States forces since Vietnam—the public's initial enthusiasm for the president's assertive policy waned as it contemplated the likelihood of a war with thousands of casualties. A six-week war, in which the United States and its Western and Arab allies won a stunning victory over Iraq with minimal American casualties, reestablished America's faith in its technology and military. But neither the public nor the president was willing to commit United States forces to a longer, murkier struggle to overthrow Iraq's dictator or to establish justice for Iraq's minority peoples.

## Reaganism

The conservative mood that sent first Ronald Reagan and later George Bush to the White House was part of a worldwide swing to the right. More specifically, around the globe rich and poor nations alike were turning away from state-dominated approaches to social and economic management and espousing the virtues of free enterprise. The accession to power of Prime Minister Margaret Thatcher in Great Britain led the way in 1979, and conservative governments in Canada, West Germany, and Italy followed her lead. The triumph of capitalism was nowhere more obvious than in East Asia, where South Korea, Taiwan, Hong Kong, Singapore, and above all Japan gave free rein to private corporate enterprise. In addition nominally socialist governments in France, Spain, and Australia relied increasingly on conservative policies to expand their economies. Third World countries, particularly in Latin America, submitted to pressures from the World Bank to clear the way for market forces. And as capitalism boomed, centrally planned economies spun into permanent eclipse. When people in communist-bloc countries considered that Singapore, a country with 2 million people, exported more industrial products than all the socialist societies of Eastern Europe, pressures against command economies increased perceptibly, and even the ruling Marxist-Leninist parties lost faith in their collectivist ideology.

**Reagan's America**     Despite the drift to the right that the Reagan and Bush presidencies embodied, the problems of America's modern state looked very similar to its earlier problems in broad outline. The issue of a strong economy remained at the center of American life, as did the obligation of public officials to oversee it. Governments at all levels—national, state, and local—had grown so luxuriantly that together they sucked in one-third of the nation's personal income in taxes and paid out one-third of the nation's personal income in salaries, wages, and other disbursements. Nevertheless government in America expanded at a much slower pace than in most other industrialized countries. Canada, Japan, and most Western European nations, for example, boasted superior social services (including health insurance) and paid more attention to modernizing their infrastructures—roads, bridges, tunnels, rail lines—than did the United States. Most Americans, without easing their demands for prosperity and services, insisted on lower taxes and smaller bureaucracies. Especially in hard times, the voters wanted more services for less money.

The 1980s revolt against taxes and rules was part of a general reaction against elite authority that included, but spread well beyond, government power. Confidence in all major institutions—corporations, universities, medicine, law—had dropped drastically during the 1970s. In the 1980s, despite President Reagan's praise for traditional habits, the country remained irreverent toward its leaders. Interest in mysticism, astrology, and other supernatural forces thrived, and unorthodox routes to good health increasingly competed with traditional medicine. Fears spread that the United States was losing its technological edge to Japan and other competitors, and that the educational system was in serious decay, as evidenced by steadily declining college entrance examination scores. The worldwide computer revolution, in which desktop personal computers and photocopying and fax machines reshaped the means of information processing and the role of middle management, added burdens that America's educational system seemed barely capable of handling. The rise of this technology also heightened fears of greater government capacity to monitor its citizens and added to a sense of disenchantment with impersonal expertise. (Ironically, in centrally planned, Soviet-style societies, the computer and photocopying and fax machines helped small groups of dissenters disseminate opposing ideas and challenge the authority of communist regimes. China in 1989 would be a major case in point.) Genetic engineering, with its unsettling capacity to tamper with nature, particularly disturbed Americans. All this increasing technological sophistication helped strengthened ordinary people's attraction to personal concerns. Innumerable Americans, for example, began to search for family and ethnic roots that could give life meaning apart from the hierarchical world of skills and careers.

Increasing skepticism about "the system" went hand in hand with widespread caution about the future. In diverse ways Americans resisted long-term commitments. More and more pairs of people substituted tentative living arrangements for marriages, and the practice spread from the young to older age groups. By the late 1970s courts were struggling to devise a new subdivision of the law that would cover these ad hoc partnerships. At the nation's bicentennial, the birthrate had reached its lowest level in American history, although it would rebound in the 1980s with the expansion of the economy. Large percentages of voters avoided party labels and declared themselves independents.

Commentators used such labels as "privatism" and "narcissism" to describe these trends. The prominence of "yuppies" (young urban professionals) preoccupied with the pursuit of careers and pleasure became a hallmark of the 1980s. New attendance records and multimillion-dollar salary scales in professional sports, the unprecedented box office returns for movies filled more than ever with explicit sex, foul language, and gory violence, and the proliferation of specialized cable channels like MTV testified to the dominant role of mass entertainment in American life. More and more Americans were trying to fashion lives that would maximize personal pleasure and personal growth by minimizing their formal ties in an imponderable society. A "restless energy, love of challenges, and appreciation of the good life are characteristic of much that is most vital in American culture," wrote sociologist Robert Bellah and his associates in *Habits of the Heart,* a widely discussed examination of 1980s Americans' futile search for deeper meaning and commitment in their lives. On examination the "values" and "priorities" by which these modern Americans lived were "not justified by any wider framework of purpose or belief. What is good is what one finds rewarding." As a successful Californian articulated this bland live-and-let-live philosophy, "I guess I feel that everybody on this planet is entitled to have a little bit of space and things that detract from other people's space are kind of bad."

The decade's prominent conservative critics decried the trends toward narcissism and away from traditional values. University of Chicago philosophy professor Allan Bloom attacked the drift in American universities away from classical education and the great texts that had formed the core of general education for generations. In *The Closing of the American Mind* (an unexpected best-seller despite its ponderous philosophical ruminations), Bloom challenged the country's universities to abandon 1960s experimentation and innovations giving minorities and women equal representation in college curricula and urged a return to old-fashioned, more coherent ideas of what and how to teach undergraduates. John Silber and William Bennett, formerly liberal academics offended by the educational "permissiveness" of the 1960s and 1970s, became politically prominent as they campaigned to restore more "wholesome" values in elementary, secondary, and higher education.

In the midst of all its prosperity, the country confronted human and technological failings in the 1980s that defied easy answers. First Lady Nancy Reagan led an antidrug crusade, television ads exhorted young people to "just say no," and "DARE" bumper stickers challenged everyone to keep off drugs. Still, an epidemic of cocaine and crack (its cheaper derivative) swept the country's inner cities. Able to earn large sums of money from the drug trade, impoverished ghetto youngsters vied to get in on the action. Crime, prostitution, and premature death from overdoses and gang wars were direct consequences of the growing drug use.

Equally alarming was the spread of AIDS (acquired immune deficiency syndrome). First diagnosed in the United States in 1981, the disease struck particularly hard at male homosexuals and at drug addicts using unsterilized needles for their "fixes." By 1988 nearly half the gay community of San Francisco had been infected and some 32,000 Americans had died of the disease. The threat of AIDS produced something of a sexual counterrevolution in the 1980s among frightened straights and gays alike; promiscuity and sexual experimentation evidently declined, and middle-class Americans grew warier still of drug use. Although the federal government, under the leadership of Surgeon General Dr. C. Everett Koop, launched an educational program to promote safe sex and discourage drugs, it was slow to finance research programs that might develop anti-AIDS drugs. Political considerations dictated the government's cautious response: Koop found it hard to mobilize public support for spending scarce federal funds to fight an illness afflicting principally gays and poor drug-users.

Reagan's America was also notable for the large number of immigrants who flocked into the United States. During the decade approximately 10 million people arrived, chiefly from Latin America and Asia—the greatest number of newcomers in one decade in American history. The flood of people suggested how attractive the United States remained as a dynamic, expanding society, for immigrants generally felt optimistic about their chances for a better life and contributed significantly to the country's prosperity.

As usual, however, interactions between citizens and newcomers provoked tensions. About one-third of the new arrivals were "illegals." Did employers deliberately seek out *illegal* immigrants to do menial jobs at substandard pay? "No," replied an "undocumented" Latino. "But . . . they end up using us and are happy. They would take anyone who would do the job. People in the U.S. don't want these jobs. They're for people like us. We have to do anything that comes along to stay alive." To end the abuse of illegal-immigrant workers and prevent more from coming, Congress in 1987 passed the Simpson-Mazzoli bill. This law allowed people who had entered the United States illegally before 1982 to gain amnesty and apply for citizenship, while threatening to prosecute businesses that hired illegal aliens. But it soon became clear that the law could do little to prevent undocumented immigrants from getting into the United States, especially from Mexico and Central America.

Legal or illegal, most of the immigrants met difficulties in their new country. Although Asians excelled at finding work, opening businesses, and competing in schools, they could not escape racial antagonism. Whites vying with them for a living sometimes resorted to physical intimidation—for example, terrorizing Vietnamese fishermen in Texas and Louisiana. Korean grocers in a black Brooklyn neighborhood found themselves boycotted by residents who resented their economic success; Miami suffered repeated clashes between exiles from Castro's Cuba and poor blacks. Latinos in California, Texas, Florida, and New York faced discrimination in housing, jobs, and general acceptance by "Anglos." Bilingual education programs, which Latinos in particular demanded, aroused growing insistence that Latinos learn English and abandon their cultural distinctions. Although blatant chauvinism formed a significant part of the argument against bilingualism, opponents also argued with some justification that non–English speaking children needed maximum classroom immersion in English in order to improve their chances of finding work, as well as to avoid "Balkanizing" the country into ethnic enclaves. Since some Latinos, especially immigrants from Mexico, required government support to make ends meet, controversy over bilingualism added to the antagonism felt by second- and third-generation middle-class Americans who had no direct memory of (or sympathy for) the problems of newcomers to the United States.

The 1980s also saw an ugly resurgence of racism on many college campuses. For students of this era the civil rights struggle of the 1960s was irrelevant ancient history; and all too often black students found themselves isolated and patronized on largely white campuses. Arguments over replacing traditional Western civilization courses with new requirements emphasizing "multiculturalism" added to the tensions. At bottom the issue was how the United States would fit into the coming twenty-first-century global society and economy, with an increasingly large nonwhite minority population within the republic. In California, for example, the 1990 census revealed that 43 percent of the state's population consisted of nonwhite minorities.

**The Reagan Revolution**

Reagan's entrance into the White House in 1981 gave conservatives a fresh opportunity to direct national affairs and test the validity of their ideas. The release of the embassy hostages in Teheran on the day of his inauguration gave Reagan even greater popularity and influence than incoming presidents usually enjoyed. Then, in March, Reagan's gallant response to an attempt on his life by a mentally unbalanced young man increased his public standing still further. "Honey, I forgot to duck," the wounded president told his wife, and at the hospital he asked whether the surgeon was a Republican or a Democrat. Such courage and humor at a moment of personal danger endeared him to the public.

To restore the nation's economic health and ensure its safety, Reagan proposed a conservative program of less government, lower taxes, balanced budgets, and peace through military strength. "In this present crisis," he said in his inaugural address, "government is not the solution to our problem; government is the problem.... It is no coincidence that our present troubles parallel and are proportionate to the intervention and excessive growth of government.... It is time to reawaken this industrial giant, to get government back within its means and to lighten our punitive tax burden." At the same time, he intended to "rebuild" American military strength and close "a window of vulnerability" by modernizing the country's nuclear arsenal. The objective was to face down the Soviet Union, the malevolent adversary that "underlies all the unrest that is going on. If they weren't engaged in this game of dominoes, there wouldn't be any hot spots in the world." Finally, Reagan wanted to restore conservative social values:

traditional ideas about family, flag, and religion that "permissive liberals" and "their programs" had undermined. Reagan and conservative supporters wanted to limit abortion on demand, restore prayer in schools, and revive respect for the military and national patriotic symbols. Clearly, Reagan launched his presidency intending to make dramatic changes in American policies at home and abroad.

To reduce the country's 13 percent inflation, 20 percent prime interest rate, $56 billion in projected federal deficits, and 7.4 percent unemployment rate, Reagan asked Congress to enact a series of measures described as supply-side economics. He proposed a 30 percent reduction in taxes over three years and substantial cuts in domestic social programs. The tax cut was supposed to produce a dramatic expansion of the economy, which in turn would lessen unemployment and increase federal revenues; more could then be spent on defense, and the deficit would shrink. Ridiculed during the nomination campaign as "voodoo economics" by his rival—and later his running mate—George Bush, the Reagan plan seemed unlikely to ease inflation and unemployment at the same time. In fact, much of what Reagan proposed was a throwback to Republican thinking in the 1920s—tax cuts (principally for the most affluent) would stimulate investment and a "trickle-down effect" would extend prosperity to the mass of Americans. (But reliance on benefits "trickling down" had also marked Kennedy's tax cut of the early 1960s.) Most professional economists—whether Keynesians advocating "demand-side" policies or monetarists and "new classical" theorists opposed to government intervention in general—dubiously shook their heads about supply-side economics from the start.

Reagan's proposal generated considerable skepticism in Congress. An old-fashioned fiscal conservative senator like Robert Dole of Kansas called the whole scheme "a riverboat gamble"; another congressman, contemplating the deficits that supply-side policy might produce, muttered, "God help us if this doesn't work." Yet the country and Congress were ready to try something new to break the stranglehold of stagflation. And Reagan, a master of the modern electronic media, used his speech-making skills to sell the public on his economic program. Communicating in simple, straightforward language and promising dramatic results, Reagan made his program irresistible to the country and ultimately to Congress. In the spring and summer of 1981, Congress consequently agreed to cut federal spending on domestic social programs by $41 billion: welfare payments, food stamps, Medicaid, medical care for the indigent, and public housing programs were among those hardest hit. At the same time, Congress agreed to a program of military Keynesianism—a $1.6 trillion expansion of defense spending that would serve not only the national security but also the domestic economy. Congress also passed the Economic Recovery Tax Act, reducing personal income taxes across the board by 25 percent over three years. Lowering the maximum tax from 70 percent to 50 percent, the act favored the country's wealthiest citizens. David Stockman, Reagan's budget director, confirmed that the tax change was indeed a reversion to the "trickle-down" theory. The program had been thrown together haphazardly—with much sleight-of-hand yet without a realistic grasp of the data or the likely consequences, as a chastened Stockman later confessed:

> None of us really understands what's going on or all these numbers. You've got...such complexity now in the interactive parts of the budget between policy action and the economic environment and all the internal mysteries of the budget, and there are a lot of them. People are getting from A to B and it's not clear how they are getting there. It's not clear how we got there.

The new administration attacked economic stagnation by speeding up the policies of deregulation begun under Carter—the limiting of government controls over banks and savings-and-loans, corporations, environmental agencies, hospitals, and anything else that seemed to hold back free enterprise and economic expansion. Reagan capitalized on the unpopularity of unions to break a strike of the country's air traffic controllers, firing many of them for breach of contract—thereby encouraging corporations to intensify their resistance to union demands for higher pay for less work. Supported by public opinion, such unionbusting worked: organized labor's political influence and membership slid precipitously during Reagan's first term.

The president won most of what he had asked from Congress, and the news media labeled his initial triumph the Reagan Revolution. No other president since FDR, a national magazine said, had "done so much of such magnitude so quickly to change the economic direction of the nation." Yet there was far less of a revolution here than met the eye. Reagan proved himself remarkably adept at manipulating the symbols and shibboleths of which the modern presidency is the custodian. Indeed, he used his skill at manipulating images to create the impression that his economic policies were far more of a revolution than in fact they were. Politically, Americans in the 1980s were pulled in two directions, and the constitutional system let them act on contradictory impulses simultaneously. On the one hand, the majority was plainly fed up with special interests, frustrated by the decline of United States power and prestige, and conservative on sociocultural issues. On the other hand, most voters also wanted to continue (if not expand) those social-service programs from which they benefited. When the chips were down on abortion (the decade's most nagging moral issue), most Americans favored the pro-choice, not the pro-life position, whatever revulsion they might feel about abortion itself. A majority of voters therefore pulled the Republican lever for presidential candidates while continuing to send Democratic incumbents back to Congress. *Both* were really conservative, status quo–oriented decisions.

The so-called Reagan Revolution produced unsettling initial results. The stock market's response to Reagan's "riverboat gamble" was quick and loud—it tumbled. Investors panicked at the thought of skyrocketing deficits and an untried theory. Between 1981 and 1983 the economy went into a sharp decline. Unemployment climbed to 10.8 percent, the highest level since the Great Depression; capital spending, which was supposed to expand, dropped in each of the three years; and deficits soared higher than ever, reaching $195 billion in 1982–83.

These disappointing consequences of the Reagan Revolution's first shots drove the administration in the summer of 1982 to abandon some of its supply-side dogma. The White House persuaded the Federal Reserve to expand the money supply and lower interest rates to 10.5 percent (half of what the prime rate had been in 1981). The result was an impressive recovery. A great "bull market" took off on the stock exchange in August 1982, and the surge would last for the rest of the decade. Meanwhile unemployment fell to 8.2 percent of the work force, and during 1983 the GNP grew at 3.3 percent—the quickest pace in five years. Energy conservation in the United States and excess oil production abroad helped cut inflation to less than 4 percent. By the summer of 1984, with the national economy booming, unemployment had dropped even further (to 7.1 percent) and annual inflation remained under 5 percent.

This recovery, Reagan declared, proved that "our economic game plan is working." But many economists disagreed. They acknowledged that the administration had achieved an immediate improvement, but they were pessimistic about long-term economic prospects and reluctant to credit "Reaganomics" with restoring economic health. Economists worried in particular about the nation's massive deficits, for cuts in entitlement programs did not match tax cuts to help bring the budget into balance. Confronted by elderly middle-class voters who threatened the political life of any representative or senator who agreed to reductions in Social Security or Medicare, Congress refused to cut either. The costs of entitlements combined with the large jump in defense spending meant deficits of $200 billion or more for at least the next five years. Economists predicted that competition for loans between business and government would push up interest rates again, rekindle double-digit inflation, and stall the recovery. Economists also worried that business spending on new plants and equipment had shown no gain for three years. Since the supply-side policy aimed chiefly at expanding the economy's productive capacity, economists remained unconvinced that the Reagan program was working. The recovery, they believed, resulted essentially from government actions long advocated by liberal Keynesians: lower interest rates produced by easier monetary controls, and government deficits triggered by tax cuts and defense spending. (Again, the 1960s Kennedy tax cut and military buildup seemed the closest parallel.) Slackened international demand had also created an "oil glut" that undercut OPEC and stabilized energy prices. All this had given consumers the additional spending power to create a "demand-side" recovery through purchases of homes, automobiles, and other goods. Above all, what economic critics did not anticipate was the extent to which foreign investors, particularly the Japanese, would be willing to finance American deficits by buying corporate and government bonds. The infusions of vast sums of foreign money into the American economy sustained America's economic recovery and keep annual inflation under 5 percent until 1990.

Reagan's social-service spending cuts were severe and painful, although not drastic enough to offset the tax cut and the additional money poured into the

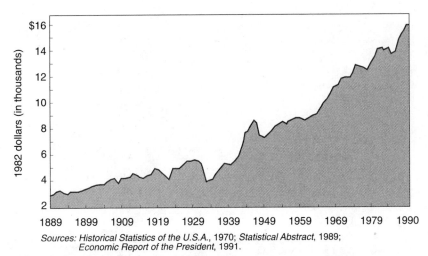

Sources: *Historical Statistics of the U.S.A.*, 1970; *Statistical Abstract*, 1989; *Economic Report of the President*, 1991.

**U.S. Real GNP per Capita, 1889-1990 (1982 prices)**

military buildup (hence the decade's ballooning budget deficits). The poor and the young bore the brunt of the Reagan Revolution. More Americans fell below the poverty level than at any other time since Lyndon Johnson launched his War on Poverty in 1965. Under Reagan the country's neediest citizens had to subsist with shrunken government benefits: fewer food stamps, public-service jobs, student loans, legal services, child nutrition programs, and housing subsidies; lower unemployment compensation, urban mass-transit subsidies, and welfare payments to mothers with dependent children. Reagan's cuts hit especially hard at nonprofit social-service and education agencies, at advocacy groups for the poor, and at municipal governments—these, rather than the federal agencies, employed most of those who provided social services for the poor. "Welfare for the rich" was how Reagan critics summed up (with considerable justification) the administration's fiscal policy. The tax cuts gave only 8.5 percent of the overall reduction to the 31.7 million taxpayers earning $15,000 or less annually (and who tended to suffer from reduced government services), whereas the 5.6 percent of Americans with annual incomes of $50,000 or more pocketed 35 percent of the federal government's lost revenue. And corporations made a windfall gain by reducing their share of each federal tax dollar from 13 cents to 8 cents.

But however much damage it did to America's underclass, the Reagan administration found itself largely stymied in carrying out conservatives' social agenda. Reagan advocated constitutional amendments against abortion and for public-school prayer; he opposed the ERA, affirmative action, and busing; and he proposed allowing segregated private schools to claim tax-exempt status. But the administration attained none of its social goals except for the defeat of the ERA—which came in 1983, when rural-dominated legislatures in a few states rejected the amendment and the extended deadline for its ratification by the states expired. Reagan's failure came in part because the White House neglected

**Tammy and Jim Bakker**
*The Bakker's PTL movement (meaning "Praise the Lord"—or, some said, "Pass the Loot")
featured these enthusiastic preachers on a television program reaching into millions of homes.
"Televangelists" such as the Bakkers preached a simple "feel good" religion, heavily laden with
appeals for financial support. Jim Bakker went to prison after reports of his financial and
sexual misconduct surfaced. His cynical behavior proved deeply offensive to many genuinely
religious persons.*

to make the same strong effort on behalf of its social aims that it had made for its economic and defense programs. Reluctant to alienate minorities and pro-gressive-minded women—political constituencies that as a whole objected to the conservative program—Reagan gave only erratic backing to the causes that he and the conservative evangelical movement "The Moral Majority" believed essential to the restoration of a healthy nation.

Indeed, to diminish the hostility of women and minorities, Reagan appointed the first woman to serve on the Supreme Court, Sandra Day O'Connor, and he gave token support to civil rights. After his administration came under attack for fostering a renewed atmosphere of racism and sexism in the country—the United States Civil Rights Commission, for example, criticized the White House for reducing the number of minorities and women in high government posts—the Justice Department filed a desegregation suit against Alabama's public higher-education system. Reagan also proposed tougher antidiscrimination provisions in the fifteen-year-old Fair Housing Act.

**Anti-Sovietism**    The hallmark of Reagan's first-term defense and foreign policies was anti-Sovietism. Like all other presidents since 1945, Reagan had a legitimate concern about Soviet expansionism. But more reminiscent of John Foster Dulles in the 1950s than of recent administrations, Reagan came into office seeing little room for reasonable compromise with Moscow, and he openly hoped for the day when the West "will transcend communism." Soviet leaders, he said, were ready "to commit any crime, to lie, to cheat" to further their cause; the Soviet Union was an "evil empire" and the Soviet-American conflict a "struggle between right and wrong, good and evil." In September 1983, when a Soviet fighter plane shot down a South Korean passenger aircraft that had strayed into Soviet airspace, killing 269 civilians, Reagan declared that this action confirmed what he had been preaching about Soviet barbarism for more than thirty years.

Reagan's moralistic absorption with countering Soviet power and defeating "the communist threat" often made it difficult for him to deal realistically and constructively with foreign affairs. Supported by a minority of American defense specialists, Reagan feared a preponderance of Soviet nuclear capabilities and insisted on a compensatory buildup of the United States nuclear arsenal. The president pointed to the Soviets' eclipsing of the United States in land-based ICBMs and claimed the USSR had gained an advantage in Europe by targeting SS-20 missiles on NATO allies. But other knowledgeable Americans disputed these conclusions. Emphasizing the "futility of any war fought with these weapons," the veteran Soviet-affairs analyst George Kennan asserted that the United States and the Soviet Union had achieved "levels of redundancy" in destructiveness "of such grotesque dimensions as to defy rational understanding." And the nuclear physicist Hans Bethe, conceding that the Soviets held an advantage in land-based ICBMs, argued that this did not give Moscow any overall superiority. He noted that since the United States had "invulnerable nuclear-powered submarines" and bombers carrying cruise missiles—against which the Soviets had no effective defense—the United States still had the capacity to retaliate against any first strike and thus had no reason to feel inferior to Moscow in nuclear weaponry. The greatest threat to American national security, Bethe said, arose not from the United States' lag behind the USSR in strategic weapons, but from "the grotesque size and continuing growth of both nuclear arsenals." Both sides had enough nuclear weapons to make the rubble bounce.

But Reagan, who continued to see a "window of vulnerability" in America's inferior land-based arsenal, pressed forward with a buildup of weapons. A key element in his plans was the Strategic Defense Initiative (SDI), a tremendously expensive scheme that critics quickly dubbed "Star Wars," suggesting that it more resembled a popular science-fiction movie than a realistic defense program. Reagan's SDI proposal in March 1983 promised an outer-space shield of laser weapons that would make the United States all but invulnerable to nuclear-armed missile attack. Despite the skepticism of most scientists, who maintained that technological difficulties could not be overcome to create such a shield, and the prospect that SDI would extend the arms race into space, the administration went ahead with its plans.

In response to Reagan's buildup and SDI program, a "nuclear freeze" movement arose in the United States and Western Europe, calling on the two superpowers mutually to cease producing and deploying more nuclear weapons. The president offered a series of arms-control proposals for drastically cutting the number of intermediate and long-range missiles on both sides, but the Soviet Union—as well as most American critics of the administration—dismissed them as ploys to appease the freeze movement. And indeed, however eager Americans were for a strong defense, they also worried about the possibility of a nuclear war. Warnings that one 16-megaton nuclear bomb exploded above Manhattan would turn everything—people, buildings, streets—from the tip of Battery Park to 110th Street into molten ash disturbed great numbers of Americans. In November 1983 a chilling television film depicting a nuclear exchange and the resultant extinction of human life itself, *The Day After,* attracted 100 million fascinated yet horrified viewers in the United States.

Americans had good reason to worry. In late 1983 a new arms race, embracing outer-space Star Wars weapons as well as land-based missiles, seemed likely. Supported by their electorates, several NATO governments (notably West Germany and Great Britain) had reiterated their support for the deployment of Pershing-2 missiles to counter the SS-20s; and as the weapons began arriving in Europe, nuclear arms talks between Moscow and Washington collapsed.

But although prospects for arms control and reduced Soviet-American tensions seemed more remote than ever, in fact the Reagan policies may have made the Soviets less reluctant to work out differences with the United States. During his first three years in office, Reagan apparently convinced Soviet leaders that the nuclear-freeze movement would not deter him from deploying Pershing and cruise missiles, developing SDI, and keeping NATO intact. In sum, he confronted Moscow with an increasingly expensive arms race that it could not win, planting the seeds of the accommodationist strategy that a new Soviet leader, Mikhail Gorbachev, would begin to implement in 1985.

**Anticommunism in the Third World**  Reagan's foreign policies, however, scarcely offered realistic solutions to other problem areas around the globe. Central America generally and El Salvador in particular were cases in point. At the start of Reagan's term, the administration described the situation in El Salvador as a "textbook case of indirect aggression by communist powers through Cuba." In the administration's view the Salvadoran insurrection had "no true domestic causes"; it stemmed not from indigenous poverty and political repression, but from "a virus imported from eastern Europe." Such an analysis, as one Latin American expert pointed out, ignored local realities.

To combat this communist threat in El Salvador, the administration largely overlooked the failings of the ruling junta, particularly its shocking human rights violations, and urged a program of economic and military aid. It asked Congress to fund arms shipments to El Salvador, to allow American military advisers to train local government forces, and to permit the CIA's covert subversion of the Marxist government of neighboring Nicaragua, the presumed fountainhead of the entire insurgency.

Seizing an opportunity to take direct action that would have been impossible on the Central American mainland, in October 1983 Reagan launched an invasion of the tiny Caribbean island of Grenada to crush a Marxist coup, using as a pretext an alleged threat to the lives of American medical students there. Matching the achievement of Prime Minister Margaret Thatcher's conservative British government, which in 1982 had restored a measure of national pride by waging a successful little war against Argentina for control of the Falkland Islands, Reagan's quick and relatively painless defeat of pro-Cuban Marxist forces on Grenada was accounted a major foreign policy and domestic political success.

But matters took a different course in Central America. In the spring of 1984 the administration's secret assistance to Nicaraguan counterrevolutionaries mining their country's harbors came to light. A loud outcry in Congress brought the operations to a halt. More important, the secret operation sparked an amendment by Representative Edward Boland of Massachusetts forbidding American intelligence agencies from using funds, "directly or indirectly," to aid the contras, Nicaraguan rebels fighting to overthrow the Marxist Sandinistas. Trying to circumvent this congressional opposition would later entangle Reagan in his worst political crisis.

Overall, Reagan's Central American policy was simplistic and counterproductive. "The administration," wrote the *New York Times* Mexico City bureau chief, "has not found the right answers [because] it has not asked the right questions." Reagan seemed not to realize that political instability was indigenous, but instead blamed it on "external forces: . . . Moscow, Havana, Managua." Other critics, who acknowledged the real presence of a Marxist threat to United States interests in Central America, especially if it took the form of a Soviet base in Nicaragua, nevertheless felt that Reagan's military response to the problem was inappropriate. After three and a half years of the Reagan policy, Central American difficulties remained as intractable as ever.

In the Middle East, Reagan initially focused on building a "strategic consensus"—that is, an anti-Soviet combination of Israel and moderate Arab states—to ensure the region's defense against communism. But this plan was unrealistic. Moderate Arab leaders refused to believe that the Soviet threat to the area was a more urgent concern than the issue of autonomy for Palestinians packed into squalid Middle Eastern refugee camps and led by the Palestine Liberation Organization (PLO), a turbulent and often violent coalition of resistance groups. Unwilling to accept this proposition, until September 1982 the White House made no major effort to address Arab-Israeli tensions over the Palestinian question and Israel's continued occupation of the West Bank of the Jordan River.

Only in June 1982 was the administration shocked into adopting a more realistic Middle Eastern policy. Israel invaded Lebanon to drive out Palestinian guerrillas who had repeatedly staged attacks on the Jewish state, but it succeeded only in worsening the already-bloody Lebanese civil war and exacerbating Arab-Israeli antagonisms. Prodded by his new secretary of state, George Shultz, who had replaced the militant and rigid anti-communist Alexander Haig, Reagan advanced a comprehensive peace plan on September 1. Although neither Israel nor the moderate Arab states accepted Reagan's plan as a basis for negotiations, the proposal at least focused on problems specific to the region rather than on some more general Soviet threat.

The difficulty of finding realistic answers to Middle Eastern problems was further underscored by the administration's inability to bring peace to Lebanon. Sending 1,500 American marines to Beirut in 1983 as part of a multinational peacekeeping force, the administration hoped to end civil strife between warring Lebanese and Palestinian factions. Divided between Yasir Arafat and more radical leaders, the PLO struggled within itself over an appropriate strategy for defeating Israel. The peacekeeping force also aimed to arrange the departure from Lebanon of Israeli forces, as well as of the Syrian troops that had been occupying northern Lebanon since 1976. Instead the lightly armed and poorly guarded peacekeepers became targets of violence. Hundreds of American troops lost their lives (many of them in an attack by a suicide truck bomber) before the rest were withdrawn in March 1984.

Reagan's rather ignominious withdrawal from Lebanon quieted American fears of "another Vietnam" with substantial loss of American lives and no significant gains for American foreign policy. By leaving Lebanon, the Reagan administration spared itself the kind of domestic turmoil that had torn the nation apart during the Southeast Asian conflict. Unable to master the irreconcilable differences in Lebanon and vulnerable to a loss of political credibility at home as casualties mounted in Beirut, Reagan declared unilaterally (and unfoundedly) the operation a success and ended it. It was a wise decision. Like Vietnam, Lebanon was not a country in which the United States had a long-term strategic interest. By contrast Reagan did not back off from United States involvement in Central America generally or Nicaragua in particular, where the triumph of Marxist regimes and the potential introduction of Soviet bases would seriously threaten United States national security.

One of Reagan's genuine successes was to repair the damage that his own initial tilt toward Taiwan had done to Sino-American relations. Common concern about Soviet intentions, as well as growing commercial ties, gradually brought the administration and the mainland government together, and both sides acknowledged a more realistic understanding of their mutual interests. In 1984 Reagan made a successful visit to Beijing, where he signed new agreements for the sale of nuclear power plants to the People's Republic and promised to reduce arms shipments to Taiwan. Success in this limited area, however, did not remove the uneasiness that many Americans felt about Reagan's ability to cope with the varied and complex problems facing the United States overseas.

**The Election of 1984**     Yet Reagan's meager foreign accomplishments were balanced by the dramatic improvement in the domestic economy during 1983 and by his extraordinary ability to maintain his popularity with the American public. "The Great Communicator," journalists called him. In a league with FDR and JFK in delivering a set speech, he was particularly effective on television and the radio. How he spoke outweighed what he said. "With Ronald Reagan, the blithe spirit entered the White House," the columnist Joseph Kraft observed. "He exudes charm, gentility, and good feeling. Even . . . massive inattention to the substance of policy has, with him, a positive side. He walks away from failure—changes policies in the middle of the deba-cle—in seeming innocence that anything much has happened." Congresswoman Patricia Schroeder of Colorado, a liberal Democrat, called Reagan the "Teflon" president: "He sees to it that nothing sticks to him." Indeed, only the label stuck.

By his fourth year in the White House, Reagan seemed to be the most reassuring president since Eisenhower. One *New York Times* columnist called Reagan "president feel good." After more than two decades of tumultuous change and shattering disillusionment, however, it was above all reassurance and positive views of itself that the nation craved. The change in mood reflected itself in television ads that celebrated domestic products "Made in the U.S.A." and crowed "The pride is back." At the summer Olympics in Los Angeles in 1984, which the Soviet Union and most other communist countries boycotted in retaliation for United States absence from Moscow in 1980, Americans carried off the lion's share of the medals. When the games went off without a hitch—and with no terrorist attack of the kind committed by PLO commandos in Munich in 1972 against Israeli athletes—the country prided itself on a job well done.

As Reagan began his 1984 reelection campaign, he could point to lower inflation and an expanding economy, but he had no clear design for reducing unprecedented deficits that might halt the economic upturn, and he had few gains to show for his sporadic efforts in behalf of the conservative social agenda. Least of all could he claim to have trimmed back the federal bureaucracy, which continued to expand, although at a much slower pace.

Reagan entered the 1984 campaign with most of the advantages: incumbency, domestic prosperity, and the country at peace. Although the economy had its weaknesses—midwestern farmers struggled to avoid foreclosures on their farms, and laid-off workers in smokestack industries were hard pressed to find new jobs—most middle-class Americans enjoyed flush times. The GNP grew at nearly 7 percent during 1984, inflation ran at only 4 percent, and unemployment, although still at 7.1 percent, was at a four-year low and falling.

The Democrats struggled futilely to find a winning formula. Scandals had driven EPA and Defense Department officials from office, but what the Demo-crats called the "sleaze factor" scarcely dented Reagan's popularity. Identifying no clear issue on which they could go after the administration, the Democrats appeared to the public as nay-sayers who could only cater to special interests— labor unions, women, blacks, the elderly, and Latinos. Many such formerly stalwart Democratic constituents as blue-collar workers and Italian and Slavic "ethnics" now in fact leaned toward Reagan. Although the Reverend Jesse Jackson stirred some interest as the first serious black candidate for a major party

**Geraldine Ferraro**
*The first woman and first Italian-American to be nominated on a presidential ticket by a major party, the Democrats' vice-presidential candidate Geraldine Ferraro in 1984 drew both intense admiration and criticism. Here she greets supporters while antiabortionists demonstrate against her in the background.*

nomination in the country's history, he constituted no real challenge to the nomination of former Vice-President Walter Mondale. Trying to take advantage of Reagan's shaky standing with women voters, Mondale picked Congresswoman Geraldine Ferraro of New York as his running mate. But whatever advantages Ferraro could muster for Mondale by being the first major-party woman vice-presidential candidate were blunted by revelations about her husband's questionable business dealings in the corruption-ridden New York City construction industry. During the campaign Mondale attacked Reagan's unprecedented peacetime deficit of $175 million; but when he proposed raising taxes to solve the problem, Reagan tied him to Carter's failed presidency and labeled Democrats in general as "tax and tax, spend and spend" politicians.

Reagan enjoyed one of the greatest landslide victories in American history. His nearly 54.5 million votes was the highest total ever, and his 58.8 percent share of the popular ballots fell just short of the 60.4 to 61.1 percent totals achieved by Harding, FDR, LBJ, and Nixon. Reagan's 525 electoral votes was also the greatest ever recorded by a candidate; Mondale took only his native Minnesota and the District of Columbia. Reagan's coattails, however, were not long enough to give Republicans control of the House or increase their numbers in the Senate. Republicans gained 14 House seats, but they remained on the short end of a 253-to-182 count. They also lost two Senate seats, reducing them from a 10- to a 6-seat margin in the upper house. The country's shift to the political right, the booming economy, and Reagan's personal appeal left the Democrats with only their most die-hard supporters backing Mondale—staunch liberals, the disadvantaged, the unemployed, many Jews, most blacks, and some Latinos. The rest of the country decisively sided with Reagan. The election also made clear the at least temporary eclipse of liberalism as established under FDR and carried forward by Presidents Truman, Kennedy, and Johnson.

## Reagan Under a Cloud

Reagan's reelection by a landslide should have given him pause. Most two-term presidents had a bad second term, and if recent history was any guide, a second term for a president with a lopsided electoral victory was likely to be a disappointment. FDR in 1936, LBJ in 1964, and Nixon in 1972 had all received huge mandates from the voters for four more years in the White House. And overconfident of their popularity, each fell victim to political miscalculations, overreached himself, and suffered humiliating defeats that undermined his historical reputation. Although Reagan (like Eisenhower) fared somewhat better than Roosevelt, Johnson, and Nixon—he won some domestic and foreign-policy victories and ended his second term with an unprecedented 68 percent favorable rating—he also stumbled badly on a number of issues. Within two years of leaving the White House, substantial questions would arise about how history would judge his presidency.

As president, however, Reagan never really lost his hold on the popular imagination. Although most Americans understood that at the age of seventy-five he was not a hands-on president who attended to the details of governing, they loved his old-fashioned patriotism. In 1986 the hoopla surrounding the hundredth anniversary of the Statue of Liberty accorded Reagan the role of relighting the torch—inspiring one columnist who witnessed the scene to liken him to an American king, brilliantly managing the ceremonials of government but leaving the actual administration of national affairs to subordinates.

**The Debt-Ridden Economy**

Reagan would not have enjoyed such popularity without a growing economy. Some 14.5 million new jobs became available between 1983 and 1988, spurred by the federal government's continuing deficit spending and by foreign investment to finance American debt. With inflation holding under 5 percent annually, unemployment dropping to 5.4 percent, its lowest level in the 1980s, and a stock market that hit its all-time high in 1987, the administration celebrated the wonders of Reaganomics.

The White House also took satisfaction from the Tax Reform Act of 1986. "Revenue neutral" (that is, neither raising nor lowering overall government income), the tax reform put an end to loopholes that hitherto allowed some of the country's wealthiest citizens to pay little or no taxes, the elimination of the income tax for 6 million poor wage earners, and a reduction of the highest bracket from 50 percent to 33 percent. An end to tax inequities pleased liberals

(President Carter had unsuccessfully sought a similar reform), while lower overall income-tax rates appealed to fiscal conservatives as promising higher savings rates, greater investment, and additional economic expansion. No one, however, spoke much about the fact that large increases in Social Security, state, and local taxes generally kept citizens' overall tax burden higher than reductions in federal income taxes alone suggested. Lower-income workers, whose higher contributions to Social Security took a significant bite out of their incomes, suffered particularly.

Behind the facade of apparent prosperity, however, severe structural problems had developed in the nation's economy. American corporations did not increase their productivity very much, and most of the new jobs in the country were in the service sector, not in industrial manufacturing. The combination of tax cuts, defense outlays of over $1.6 trillion, and domestic entitlement programs made for annual budget deficits of over $200 billion. Reagan had slowed increases in spending on domestic social programs, but he had not abolished some of them, as he had promised—and meanwhile he had tripled the national debt, incurring cumulative obligations larger than all the deficits run by previous presidents. By the end of his term the United States government owed $2.7 trillion and was paying nearly $200 billion a year in interest on it, the second largest item in the budget after defense. To put the country's fiscal house in order, Congress in 1985 passed the Gramm-Rudman Act mandating deficit reductions; supposedly these reductions would bring a balanced budget by 1993. Gramm-Rudman aimed to force Congress to cut the domestic social programs that the Reagan Revolution had failed to eliminate or reduce. If Congress and the president failed to meet the Gramm-Rudman targets, automatic cuts in domestic and defense spending were to occur. Financial gimmicks like off-budget accounting, which excluded some federal outlays from budget calculations, and inclusion of surplus Social Security funds, which could not be used to reduce the deficits, masked the full extent of the actual federal debt in the last three years of Reagan's term.

The nation's increasing economic vulnerability became evident in another way, too. A creditor nation since World War I, the United States under Reagan turned into the world's largest debtor. Running trade imbalances, especially with Japan and with oil-exporting countries, that reached almost $170 billion in 1986, the American economy had to borrow ever-larger sums abroad to meet its financial obligations. Such heavy borrowing pushed American interest rates up; it also drew foreign money to the United States and away from Third World countries, which found it harder to service their own heavy overseas debts. By 1988 Third World countries owed $1.2 trillion to the banks and governments of advanced industrial nations. Although reluctant to default on their loans, developing nations found it impossible to pay without diverting funds from desperately needed domestic investments. The Reagan administration and American banks saw no way out of this crisis except through temporary moratoriums on payments and repackaging of debts.

Besides, the American banking community had its own increasingly deep problems. By the late 1980s many savings-and-loan institutions were collapsing, principally in the Southwest. Dogmatically convinced that regulation equalled inefficiency and that free-market policies would benefit everyone, the Reagan administration—specifically, the Federal Home Loan Bank Board—as well as state regulators largely left the savings industry to police itself. Congressmen and senators, who collected handsome campaign contributions from freewheeling savings-and-loans officers, made no serious effort to rein in the business. As a result, billions of dollars disappeared in bad loans—often in unwise speculation, and sometimes after unscrupulous bank directors lined their own pockets. By 1990 the trouble spread from savings-and-loans to major banks with hitherto sterling reputations. Hundreds of savings institutions ended in bankruptcy, and the federal government had to repay savers for their federally insured accounts. In 1990 the government estimated that the bailout might cost the nation's taxpayers as much as $500 billion over thirty years.

A free-for-all atmosphere also reigned in the arcane world of corporate finance. The Reagan administration virtually abandoned any attempt at antitrust policy, and industrial consolidators flourished in an atmosphere recalling conditions of the Gilded Age or the 1920s. Billions of dollars circulated in the "junk-bond" market, a new financial device that offered high-interest returns on the risky loans floated to finance buy-outs of vulnerable corporations by wheeler-dealers like T. Boone Pickens, Carl Icahn, and Frank Lorenzo. Having bought up a controlling share of stock in a corporation, these "raiders" would sell off parts of the newly acquired firm to reduce their obligations and attempt to streamline operations in what remained; unionbusting was a favorite technique. Fearing hostile takeovers, established and hitherto conservatively run corporations sometimes ran up debts recklessly to make themselves look less attractive to would-be raiders, or played the same speculative game by swallowing weaker companies. Some economists defended the 1980s consolidators, noting that the risk of a hostile buy-out imposed a salutary discipline on corporate management, but most observers worried about the efficiency of the resulting conglomerate corporations and about the feverish speculation that the junk-bond market generated. The late 1980s saw the arrest and conviction of various prominent Wall Street manipulators, including stockbroker Ivan Boesky and Michael Milken, the young tycoon who had almost singlehandedly invented the junk-bond market. Milken's brokerage house went bankrupt and the junk-bond market collapsed in 1989 amid revelations of the dishonest practices of certain high-flying investors and corporate "insiders," leaving many corporations saddled with crushing debts. Despite federal prosecutors' eventual intervention against the likes of Boesky and Milken, the 1980s corporate raiding and junk-bond speculating were symptomatic of the Reagan administration's encouragement to deregulated capitalist enterprise. They also reflected easygoing public attitudes toward money-making—attitudes that made media celebrities of such businessmen as Chrysler Corporation's Lee Iacocca and New York real estate speculator Donald Trump. Both men published best-selling accounts of their exploits, and even the collapse of Trump's paper empire in 1990 kept the tabloid press agog with his financial and marital crises.

When the stock market crashed on October 19, 1987, losing over 500 points and nearly 20 percent of its value in one day, many in the country predicted a general economic collapse. But the drop in the market was apparently more the consequence of technical factors (notably, unregulated buying and selling of shares on the basis of computer programs) than of the economy's structural problems. In addition the Federal Reserve, unlike in 1929 when it reduced the money supply and tightened credit, now moved quickly to expand the supply of funds. The market soon regained equilibrium, but investor confidence had been shaken.

Overall, Reagan's economic legacy was a polarization of wealth and poverty that boded ill for the country's future. Despite substantial economic expansion, wealth concentrated in fewer and fewer hands during the 1980s. The increase in jobs, for example, did not necessarily mean more evenly distributed prosperity, but more Americans living close to an economic edge. Well-paid blue-collar jobs in manufacturing disappeared; many of the new jobs that opened up were low-paying (often minimum wage) service positions in fast-food restaurants and retail stores. Even more significantly, low-level computer-punching jobs in the new high-tech financial and information services firms replaced unionized industrial labor. The Reagan tax cuts largely went to the country's most affluent: during the 1980s the share of the national income received by the richest one-fifth jumped from 41.6 percent to 44 percent, and the top 1 percent increased their income from 9 percent to 11 percent of the total. The 60 percent of Americans in the middle saw a slight drop in income, while the poorest 20 percent gave up most of the gains that went to the people at the top. Stated another way, the income of the richest 20 percent of American families in the 1980s went up 19 percent, while the poorest 20 percent lost 9 percent of their income.

However affluent they might feel, middle-class Americans had to struggle to keep up. Particularly for young families, the cost of buying a home escalated frighteningly. For many, achieving a higher standard of living meant becoming a two-income family. Consequently, by 1983, 50.5 percent of adult women held jobs, the highest percentage ever in American history. In 1988, 57 percent of married women with children under six were in the labor force. Personal indebtedness offered another way to maintain middle-class living standards, and in the heady years 1982–86 consumer debt rose by 9.5 percent annually—twice the rate of the 1970s, and considerably ahead of the growth of most families' income. Credit cards, auto loans, mortgages, and home equity loans all played a role in the borrowing binge. The expansion slowed after the 1987 stock-market crash, but the heavy load of debt and interest that weighed down most middle-class families left them disturbingly vulnerable should real estate values tumble or a recession drive up unemployment. By 1990 both such ominous developments were occurring.

The numbers of Americans struggling to subsist increased substantially—approximately 12 percent at the start of the decade to between 14 and 15 percent at the end of it. But the demographics of poverty were now changing. In the first half

**A Homeless Person**
*In the 1980s, deep cuts in federal programs and soaring rents made hundreds of thousands—possibly millions—homeless.*

of the century poverty had been concentrated primarily among the elderly; by the 1980s, the hardest hit were children and households headed by single women, particularly minority children and women. Forty percent of the poor were children, although they made up only 27 percent of the population. Twelve percent of whites and nearly 36 percent of blacks—and nearly half of all black children—lived in poverty. Children, of course, did not vote at all, and demoralized, impoverished adults tended to vote less frequently than the elderly, for whom maintaining Social Security and Medicare payments was the highest priority. Reagan had to conciliate the elderly; he could ignore the poor and the young, allowing the cuts in welfare and social programs that deprived them of the means to stay above the poverty line. Cuts in federal housing programs and soaring rents drove many of these people into homelessness; estimates of this forlorn, almost uncountable population varied wildly, from 350,000 to 4 million. A significant number of the homeless were former mental patients who had been "deinstitutionalized"—transferred from hospitals to neighborhood programs that in turn simply abandoned them to the streets. But most victims were formerly self-supporting workers. They crowded into makeshift shelters recalling the depression Hoovervilles and into squalid "welfare hotels" maintained by urban governments. "After you're living here a while you begin to lose hold of your dream," said a formerly middle-class mother displaced by her husband's chronic unemployment. "You start to tell yourself that it's forever. 'This is it. It isn't going to change. It can't get worse. It isn't going to get better.' So you start to lose the courage to fight back."

Debt and impoverishment were not the only matters that troubled observers of the American economy. With good reason, the nation's mounting technological failures continued to cause public concern. In 1990 the Energy Department estimated that $28.6 billion would be needed in the next five years to clean up radioactive and toxic wastes at seventeen nuclear weapon production sites in twelve states; others put the eventual cost at $100 billion or even $200 billion. An even more dramatic and shocking catastrophe had struck in 1986 when the space shuttle *Challenger* exploded shortly after launching, killing the seven astronauts, including teacher Christa McAuliffe, who was aboard as part of a publicity campaign for NASA. Was the explosion a result of human error or of unmanageable technological problems? Americans wondered—the more so after NASA suffered such later embarrassments as the misdesigned Hubble space telescope. And in 1988 the accidental shooting down of an Iranian civilian jetliner by an American naval vessel in the Persian Gulf cast the same cloud of doubt over America's vaunted military technology and the human judgment necessary to operate it. Were all these failures symptoms of a national loss of basic technical competence, on which the nation had so long prided itself?

Doubts about the military—more specifically, about the Defense Department—had been agitated by revelations of waste and corruption in Pentagon procurement procedures that cost the country hundreds of millions of dollars. This Pentagon scandal, as well as another involving corruption in the Housing and Urban Development Department that surfaced after Reagan left office, resembled earlier exposés that had forced more than one hundred prominent Reagan officials to resign. Some of these culprits were indicted and convicted of influence peddling, including two of the president's closest advisers, Lyn Nofziger and Michael Deaver. Attorney General Edwin Meese also left office under a cloud. All these scandals made the phrase *sleaze factor* a permanent part of the vocabulary associated with the Reagan presidency, fueling public anger and cynicism over waste and corruption in high places.

**The Court's Turn Rightward**  From the moment it took office, the Reagan administration had been determined to encourage the federal courts, and above all the Supreme Court, to abandon the activist role that the Warren Court had spearheaded in the liberal 1960s. Frequently Reagan spoke out against what he considered "legislating" by the Court, meaning interpreting the Constitution or federal law broadly to break new ground in public policy. Instead, he and Attorney General Meese urged the Court to make "original intent"—the supposed initial aims of the Founders embodied in the Constitution—the standard by which they judged cases. "Judicial restraint," the administration's watchword, hearkened back to early-nineteenth-

**Graduation Day at Columbia University**
*Diversity in American universities became a hallmark of the 1970s.*

century criticism at the Marshall Court's broad interpretations of the Constitution. Administration critics objected that "original intent" was open to interpretation and did not necessarily conform to the Reagan administration's views. And on the social issues where the federal judiciary had generally been rather liberal, the administration's conservatism revealed itself in the cases it argued before the Supreme Court. Between 1981 and 1984 the White House asked the Court to rule against busing to achieve desegregation, against women's right to an abortion, against denials of tax exemptions to segregated private schools, and against the use of racial quotas in hiring. The Supreme Court had given conservatives some hope that the administration would win these cases. In 1978 it permitted federal and state authorities to refuse the use of public funds for abortions. That same year, in *Bakke* v. *University of California* (1978), the Court had placed limits on racial quotas in admitting students to graduate programs. But it by no means ended affirmative action as a device for righting historic wrongs against minorities and women; on the contrary, the *Bakke* decision approved the use of race in judging an applicant's file if "it does not insulate the individual from competition with all other candidates for the available seats." Educators believed that *Bakke* left the bulk of affirmative-action programs intact. Still, it had drawn a line that encouraged conservatives.

The Court initially disappointed the Reagan administration by responding unpredictably to the cases it brought. In 1981–83 the justices consistently refused to move in the direction that the administration asked. Only in 1984 did it shift ground, siding with the administration by limiting liberal precedents on law-and-order issues. Specifically, it relaxed the Miranda rule on illegally obtained evidence by putting public safety needs above the requirement that police warn suspects against self-incrimination before questioning them, *U.S.* v. *Leon* (1984). In addition it took another step in a conservative direction on affirmative action; it gave priority to seniority over race in job layoffs, allowing a last-hired, first-fired rule to take precedence over considerations of racial equity, *Fire fighters Local 1784* v. *Stotts* (1984). It acted conservatively as well on the issue of sex discrimination, limiting cuts in federal aid to discriminatory school programs rather than to the whole school, *Grove City* v. *Bell* (1984). The Court also signaled a new openness toward government involvement with religious observance by allowing Pawtucket, Rhode Island, to include a Nativity scene in an official Christmas display. Yet for all these conservative decisions, the Court did nothing to undermine affirmative-action hiring programs.

The Supreme Court's 1983–84 term had given conservatives hope that a conservative majority—Chief Justice Burger and associate justices Rehnquist, O'Connor, Byron White, and Lewis Powell—would consistently reverse or at least cut back liberal Warren Court decisions. But conservatives could not rely on Powell's centrist "swing" vote. In its 1984–85 term the Court confounded expectations that it would build on its conservative decisions of the previous year. Instead of relaxing constitutional church-state barriers, as it seemed to be doing in the Pawtucket case, the Court handed the Reagan administration a sharp setback by affirming the separation of church and state. The Court also struck a blow against states' rights by overruling a nine-year-old precedent under which state governments enjoyed immunity from various forms of federal regulation. Instead the Court required state and local governments to pay their employees according to federal minimum wage and hour standards.

In 1986–87 Reagan had the opportunity to make two appointments to the bench, and he moved to render the Court decisively conservative. In 1986, Warren Burger's retirement after 17 years prompted Reagan to promote William Rehnquist from associate to chief justice and to make United States Appeals Court judge Antonin Scalia a new associate justice. Although highly conservative, Scalia had excellent credentials as a jurist and won unanimous Senate consent for his appointment. Rehnquist's confirmation was more controversial. Senate hearings raised anew questions about his performance as a Justice Department official under Nixon. The Senate confirmed his appointment by the minimum 65 votes needed; 13 liberals voted against him and 22 other senators abstained.

The following year Powell retired, and Reagan nominated as his replacement Robert H. Bork, another Appeals Court judge. Known as a combative conservative who favored the maximum judicial restraint, Bork aroused bitter opposition from abortion rights, civil rights, and civil liberties advocates. Bork was an outspoken advocate of the conservative belief that elected representatives, not unelected judges, should be making public policy and taking responsibility before the electorate for the policies thus made. Three and a half months after his nomination and a fiery battle between supporters and opponents, the Senate rejected Bork 58 to 42. The case against Bork partly rested on mudslinging and distortion. But the bulk of what was used against him came from his own mouth. As a law professor he had left a paper trail of opinions on controversial questions.

Bork's defeat was probably only a hollow victory for liberals. Other conservative jurists with similar views would later be confirmed, in part because they were more cautious about revealing their views. Reagan next nominated Douglas H. Ginsburg, yet another staunch conservative Appeals Court judge—who had to withdraw after admitting that he had smoked marijuana once as a student in the 1960s and a few more times in the 1970s. (Thus Reagan gained the dubious distinction of being only the third president, along with Grover Cleveland and Nixon, to have two successive Court nominees fail to win appointment.) But his third recommendation succeeded—Anthony M. Kennedy, another Appeals Court judge. Some conservatives opposed Kennedy as too centrist, but his reputation as a fair, balanced, although essentially conservative, jurist assured him of quick confirmation by the Senate.

In 1990, two years after Kennedy joined the Court, it seemed more decidedly conservative than in the recent past. In its 1987–88 term, however, the Court defied Reagan by upholding the federal law on independent prosecutors, which was put in place during Watergate as a curb on presidential power. At the same time, the Court rejected administration arguments for strict limits on the use of statistical evidence to prove that employers discriminated against members of minority groups or women. It upheld the right of states and cities to ban sex discrimination by large private clubs where business lunches took place. It expressed its more conservative impulses, however, by upholding federal grants to religious groups teaching teenagers about chastity and counseling against abortions.

The Court's turn to the right was more evident in 1988–89. It gave states greater leeway to restrict abortions, and made it harder for plaintiffs to win job discrimination lawsuits by shifting the burden of proof from employers to show that there wasn't bias to employees to demonstrate that there was. The Court also invalidated a Richmond, Virginia, ordinance channeling 30 percent of public-works funds to minority-owned construction companies. The Court said that the program violated the constitutional rights of white contractors to equal protection of the law. On questions of criminal law (particularly the death penalty) and on the immunity of state and local governments from lawsuits, the Court also showed itself to be more conservative than in the past. Only on First Amendment rights did the Court reject popular conservative sentiment, by protecting the right to burn the American flag as an expression of free speech, and it echoed its 1985 church-state decisions by declaring the display of a Nativity scene in a Pittsburgh courthouse unconstitutional.

By 1990–91 a decade of conservative appointments had moved the federal judiciary rightward. Bush continued the transformation. In 1990 he named conservative New Hampshire judge David Souter to succeed highly liberal Justice William Brennan; and in 1991 he nominated an equally conservative black federal judge, Clarence Thomas, to assume the seat of Thurgood Marshall, the nation's first black justice, who in 1954 had argued the *Brown* case and since 1967 had been a stalwart of the Court's liberal wing. Meanwhile Bush vetoed (on the grounds that they would establish hiring quotas) civil rights bills by which the Democratic-controlled Congress had tried to counter Court limitations on affirmative action.

**The Iran-Contra Fiasco**

The Reagan administration's greatest second-term domestic success thus was putting a conservative stamp on the federal judiciary. Its worst defeat was the Iran-contra affair, which revealed serious errors of judgment among several top administration officials, including the president himself.

The seeds of the scandal lay in the Reagan administration's frustrations with combating Middle East terrorists and Nicaragua's Marxist government. In 1985–86 Iranian-supported terrorists seized additional hostages in Lebanon (including some American citizens), hijacked a TWA jet flying from Athens to Rome, and took over the Italian cruise ship *Achille Lauro* in the Mediterranean. The American public was outraged by the protacted detention of the hostages; by the killing of one American passenger on the TWA flight, the beating of others, and the imprisonment on the plane of thirty-nine Americans for seventeen days; and by the callous murder of a handicapped elderly American by the *Achille Lauro* terrorists. When American fighter planes eventually forced down the Egyptian jet carrying the *Achille Lauro* hijackers in Italy, where most of them were put on trial, some American frustration was relieved. An air strike against Libya in retaliation for an American soldier's death in a West Berlin terrorist bombing also gave the country some satisfaction, for Libya's ruler Muammar Qaddafi, who long had trumpeted support for Middle Eastern terrorist groups, impressed the Reagan administration and most Americans as beyond the pale of international standards. Yet neither the seizure of the *Achille Lauro* kidnapers nor the attack on Libya alleviated Americans' sense of helplessness about the hostages in Lebanon.

The administration also felt its hands tied in its dealings with the Nicaraguan Sandinista regime. Nicaragua's support of Salvadoran rebels fighting the elected pro-American government of José Napoleon Duarte in San Salvador, its ties to Cuba and to European communist regimes, and its repression of political opponents all outraged Reagan. To him the contras were "freedom fighters" comparable to America's eighteenth-century revolutionaries. Ignoring pleas from Venezuela, Mexico, Panama, and Colombia to negotiate differences with Managua, Reagan clapped an economic embargo on Nicaragua in 1985. Under these circumstances, the Boland Amendment that Congress had passed in 1984, forbidding United States support for the contras, seemed to the president a contemptible impediment.

Reagan made clear to national security advisers that he was eager for them to bring American hostages home from Lebanon and to aid the contras. But he gave them no specific instructions. Thus encouraged, CIA Director William Casey, two successive national security advisers (Robert "Bud" McFarlane and Admiral

John Poindexter) and the advisers' principal subordinate, Marine Lieutenant Colonel Oliver North, tried to strike an arms-for-hostages deal with Iran. Talking to what they thought were "moderates" in Iran eager to acquire arms for use in that country's protracted war against Iraq, the advisers arranged to send missiles to Teheran. Despite his pledges never to negotiate or make a deal with terrorists to win the release of hostages, Reagan signed a secret intelligence "finding" that hid the operation from the secretaries of state and defense and from Congress. At the same time, McFarlane, Poindexter, and North secretly raised money from foreign and private United States sources to circumvent the Boland Amendment and ship arms and other war supplies to the contras. Collecting the profits made from arms sales to Iran (which made possible the release of just one American hostage), the Reagan officials used the money to dispatch additional supplies to Nicaragua. Some of the profits, however, went into the pockets of the operatives running what they called "the Enterprise."

The operation did not remain a secret for long. In the fall of 1986 a Lebanese newspaper set off an outcry in the United States when it published a story about the arms-for-hostages negotiations. This leak by the pro-Iranian newspaper was perhaps a response to a United States tilt toward Iraq in the Gulf war. Under pressure from Congress and the public, Reagan asked Attorney General Meese to investigate allegations about "unauthorized" actions of administration officials in the Middle East and Central America. North and a secretary spent a weekend trying to cover up things by destroying documents. The record, however, was too abundant for them to succeed. By the end of the year enough became known about the Iran-contra machinations to compel Poindexter's resignation and North's firing. Reagan appointed former Texas senator John Tower to lead one inquest (and Congress initiated another one), and Meese designated prominent attorney Lawrence Walsh as special prosecutor to root out wrongdoers.

The investigations and subsequent judicial proceedings lasted three and a half years. Although North and Poindexter were ultimately convicted of lying to Congress and destroying government documents, questions remained open about how much Reagan and Vice-President Bush knew about and participated in the affair—Irangate, as journalists began to call it. Reagan's insistent denials of direct involvement did not convince the public; an opinion poll in January 1989, as he left office, showed more than 50 percent of those questioned believing that Reagan had lied when he denied knowing that money from Iranian arms sales went to help the contras. In 1990 the publication of additional excerpts from North's diaries renewed suspicions that Bush, too, knew about Iran-contra operations as they developed. None of these concerns, however, significantly affected Bush's public standing, either when he ran for president in 1988 or later. Perhaps reluctant to bring down another president and vice-president, especially because their presumed offense had been an attempt to outmaneuver such unpopular countries as Iran and Nicaragua, the public was ready to forget the affair without substantial penalties for the guilty parties. When in 1990 North's conviction was struck down on appeal, there was little outcry.

## The Cold War Ends

During Reagan's first term foreign affairs had taken a backseat to domestic issues. Priorities were reversed in the second term. Dramatic changes in the Soviet Union led to Reagan's first summit meetings with Soviet leaders and to productive arms-control negotiations; meanwhile fresh hostage crises boiled up in the Middle East and the Iran-contra affair dragged on. As a result, foreign policy became front-page news and the focus of administration energies. Developments in 1985–88 paved the way for a major shift in East-West relations. By 1989 it became apparent that the Cold War was ending and an undefined new era opening in international relations.

**Reagan and Gorbachev**    Entering the fifth year of his presidency in 1985, Reagan was the only president since Herbert Hoover not to have met at the summit with his Soviet counterpart. Reagan's instinctive distrust of Moscow and his desire to concentrate on domestic questions and to build up American military strength played a major part in preventing any productive changes in Soviet-American relations. But Moscow shared responsibility for the impasse, displaying little readiness for a new round of détente in the early 1980s. Bogged down in a war in Afghanistan since 1979 and led by unimaginative old men, the Kremlin seemed content to avoid fresh discussions with the United States. Neither the ailing Yuri Andropov, a former head of the KGB (the Soviet secret police) who held power for less than two years after Leonid Brezhnev died in 1982, nor Konstantin Chernenko, a doddering old Communist party apparatchik who died in March 1985 after only thirteen months in office, altered course at home or abroad.

A new era in Soviet and world history began in March 1985, when Mikhail Gorbachev, a relative youngster at the age of fifty-four, became Communist party chief. Gorbachev's initial aim was to shore up the existing Soviet system and perhaps split NATO, as his predecessors had tried to do. But events beyond his control overtook him—notably the rotten state of the one-party, command-economy system in the Eastern bloc. Probably he had to make far more concessions to the West and to domestic opponents than he had ever expected. A brilliant political tactician, he shifted ground repeatedly to ease tensions abroad and accommodate changing conditions at home. Gorbachev realized that the Soviet Union needed to end its disastrous intervention in Afghanistan and modernize its creaking economy. The latter goal in turn required slashing defense spending, replacing the heavy hand of Communist party rule and tolerating a degree of political pluralism, moving toward a market economy—and improving Soviet-American relations. Accordingly Gorbachev began discussing a possible summit conference to be held in Geneva November 1985. Gorbachev's principal concern was to disarm some of Reagan's suspicions and revive arms-control negotiations, particularly the Strategic Arms Reduction Talks (START), which had collapsed in 1983 and resumed in 1985 only to reach a quick impasse over SDI. Sensing a genuine opportunity to reduce arms and improve relations—and

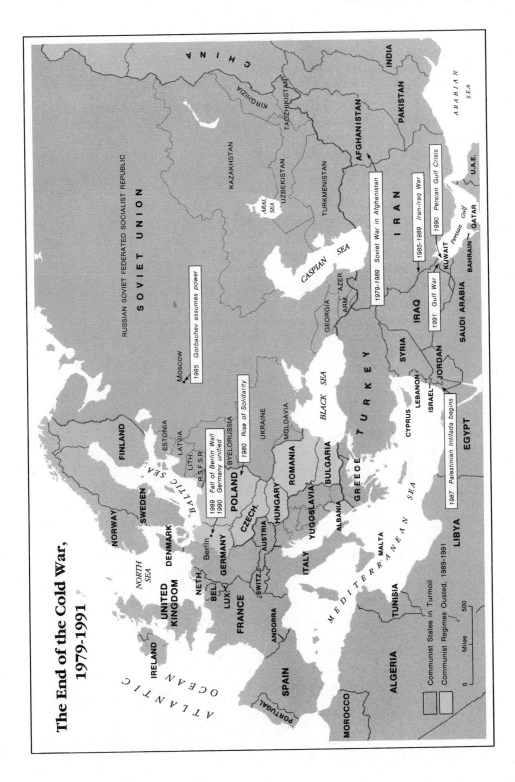

**The End of the Cold War, 1979-1991**

1985 *Gorbachev assumes power*

Moscow

1979-1989 *Soviet War in Afghanistan*

1985-1989 *Iran-Iraq War*

1990 *Persian Gulf Crisis*

1991 *Gulf War*

1989 *Fall of Berlin Wall*
1990 *Germany unified*

1980 *Rise of Solidarity*

1987 *Palestinian Intifada begins*

Communist States in Turmoil

Communist Regimes Ousted, 1989-1991

Miles
0          500

eager not to go down in history as the only president in half a century not to negotiate seriously with Moscow—Reagan agreed to meet Gorbachev. For all his ideological baggage, Reagan had a pragmatic streak that allowed him, like Gorbachev, to respond to changing realities at home and abroad.

Geneva became the first of four dramatic and highly productive Soviet-American summits. The two leaders at Geneva agreed in principle to cut strategic weapons by 50 percent; even more important, convictions rose in both Moscow and Washington that significant changes in relations were possible. Indeed, at a meeting in Reykjavik, Iceland, in 1986, Reagan got carried away by a naive vision of dramatically altering world history in a single stroke; he recklessly proposed that both sides at once give up all nuclear weapons, and had to be reined in by his alarmed advisers and allies. Nevertheless the Reykjavik talks opened the way to a major arms-control agreement on land-based intermediate-range nuclear forces (INF), missiles with a 600- to 3,400-mile range. Signing an INF agreement in Washington in December 1987, Reagan and Gorbachev eliminated a whole class of weapons. This was the first such agreement in the post-1945 era. The Soviets demonstrated their eagerness for the agreement by accepting on-site inspections of bases to assure that missiles were being destroyed—something the Kremlin had resisted for decades. Satisfying one of Reagan's favorite sayings, "trust but verify," the INF agreement was indeed a turning point in the post–World War II era.

Reagan's view of the Soviet Union had undergone a remarkable change since the time of his verbal assaults on the "evil empire." At a final summit conference in Moscow in June 1988, Reagan spoke glowingly of a shared Soviet-American aversion to bureaucracies and celebrated the loosening of Communist party dictatorship by then under way in the USSR. It was, he said, "a time when the first breath of freedom stirs the air . . . one of the most exciting, hopeful times in Soviet history." Reagan was not mistaken: the Soviet Union was in the throes of the most profound changes in its foreign and domestic policies since the Russian Revolution—its withdrawing from Afghanistan, relaxing its grip on Eastern Europe, and struggling desperately to switch from a socialist to a market economy and improve its standard of living. Inviting the Soviet people to transform their society by adopting American-style freedom, Reagan closed out his presidency believing that the USSR wished to convert itself into a kind of Eastern European United States. If he was too evangelical about the attractions of American institutions—and especially about the Soviet capacity to become a Western-style pluralistic, capitalistic society in either the short or the long term—Reagan had correctly sensed an opportunity to move away from cold-war tensions. Whatever the eventual shape Soviet society would assume, the likelihood of a superpower war had fallen dramatically, offering Moscow and Washington relief from the heavy burden of enormous defense spending. Convinced as Reagan might be that the United States would grow its way out of the $200 billion deficits his presidency had spawned—and most observers were highly skeptical that it would—ending the arms race was a realistic way to help deficit reduction along.

"IT'S A HELL OF A NOTE IF GORBACHEV CAN IMPRESS PEOPLE JUST BY SEEMING TO BE A PERSONABLE GUY"

©1985 HERBLOCK

**Imagery in Politics**
*Like John F. Kennedy, Ronald Reagan created a public personality that captivated millions of Americans, although Reagan never enjoyed the admiration that intellectuals, journalists, and editorial cartoonists (like the* Washington Post's *Herblock) showered upon Kennedy. By the late 1980s, Soviet leader Mikhail Gorbachev exerted a comparable fascination over the Western press and media.*

As Reagan ended his second term, his abandonment of earlier Cold-War orthodoxies angered some of his conservative supporters, who continued to see Communist Russia as intent as ever on worldwide subversion and expansion. The majority of Americans, however, viewed the president's flexibility in dealing with the Soviets as an act of wisdom. Where 68 percent generally approved the president's overall job performance during his eight years, 71 percent specifically supported his handling of foreign relations. Such endorsement was especially surprising—and demonstrated the importance of the Soviet-American dimension of his foreign policy—in the light of his dismal performance in the Iran-contra affair, the worst crisis of his presidency.

Reagan's popularity after eight years in office was a tribute to his astuteness as a politician, to his consistent ability to address majority concerns. Most Americans liked his emphasis on individualism, on free enterprise and less government, and on equal opportunity without special favors for reasons of race or gender. Throughout his presidency, Reagan remained the optimistic, self-made American who preached traditional values of hard work, family, morality, religion, frugality, and country. Never mind that his own rather lazy work habits, loose family ties, lax church attendance, and self-indulgence contradicted much of what he preached. He had "the gift of gab," as he himself liked to say, and a great capacity to sell himself to people. In a sense he was the consummate expression of the modern, post-1920 consumer culture hymning old-fashioned values—very much the heir of the presidents he admired, Coolidge and Hoover. And Reagan succeeded: during the last six years of his presidency the economy boomed and the United States reestablished itself as the world's preeminent power, obviously far more attractive, prosperous, and stable than the Soviet Union or any other communist country. In this sense Reagan's America had "won" the Cold War. Whatever the problems with deficits, trade imbalances, and other grave structural weaknesses in the economy, the future once more seemed on America's side. Few other presidents in the century had managed to end eight years in the White House on as positive a note as Ronald Reagan.

**The 1988 Election** Despite Reagan's success, the Democrats entered the 1988 campaign with renewed hopes of recapturing the White House. Since 1986 the Republicans had largely been on the defensive and seemed ripe for national defeat. A number of portents encouraged the Democrats: in the 1986 congressional elections they had added 5 seats to their House majority, giving them a 258 to 177 advantage, and they had won a dramatic reversal in the Senate, turning a 6-seat Republican majority into a 10-seat Democratic majority. Reagan administration corruption, including the Iran-contra scandal, was a potent political charge. The Democrats also expected to capitalize on the increase in crime and illegal drugs, the rise in poverty, and a deterioration in the country's schools during the Reagan years. There was irony in the fact that Reagan, the staunch proponent of shrunken government, had restored confidence in federal authority. Forty-eight percent of Americans in 1988, compared to 32 percent in 1980, favored expansive government, historically associated with Democratic rather than Republican administrations. And perhaps the Democrats' most important advantage was the Twenty-second Amendment, which barred Reagan from a third term.

Yet the Democrats failed to reckon with their own limitations—namely, their continuing identification in the public mind with wasteful government and foreign-policy irresolution. More important, the Democrats underestimated the continuing appeal of a Republican party that seemed to have brought prosperity, low taxes, a strong defense, and the defeat of communism in the Cold War. The Democratic nomination fight among a group of candidates whom Republicans derided as "the seven dwarfs" generated little national enthusiasm. The most dynamic of them, Jesse Jackson, could not attract enough support for traditional liberal ideas that had once made the Democrats so popular. Liberalism, indeed, had by now sunk so low in the electorate's eyes that Republicans sneered at the "L" word, as if it were some unutterable obscenity no respectable office seeker would use in public. In this inauspicious atmosphere, the Democrats nominated Governor Michael Dukakis of Massachusetts, a man who struck most people as a bloodless technocrat. He confirmed this impression in a televised debate with George Bush by giving a long-winded, deadpan response to a reporter's loaded what-if question about inflicting the death penalty on someone who had raped and murdered his wife.

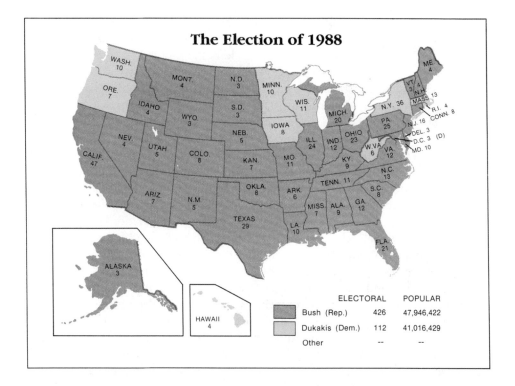

**The Election of 1988**

| | ELECTORAL | POPULAR |
|---|---|---|
| Bush (Rep.) | 426 | 47,946,422 |
| Dukakis (Dem.) | 112 | 41,016,429 |
| Other | -- | -- |

Vice-President Bush turned to good advantage his eight-year association with Reagan's popular presidency. He easily defeated Senate minority leader Robert Dole and television evangelist Pat Robertson for the nomination, then branded Dukakis weak on crime and defense and a friend of higher taxes. Repeatedly denying that he would raise taxes to deal with projected large budget deficits, Bush assured voters that when it came to taxes they should simply "read my lips—no new taxes." Bush's only real weakness was his selection of handsome but inept Indiana Senator J. Danforth Quayle as his running mate. Generally perceived as a man of limited talents and experience who had made his way in life through family connections, Dan Quayle alarmed most Americans as a poor choice to be next in line for the presidency. But largely keeping Quayle on the sidelines, Bush managed to limit the damage that his running mate could do to his candidacy. He distanced himself to some extent from hard-line conservatives by speaking of his wish for a "kinder, gentler America." The campaign, however, was largely devoid of serious issues and was punctuated by highly charged, deceptive television ads. "Trivial, superficial, and inane," Richard Nixon (of all people) called it. Bringing only 50.2 percent of the potential electorate to the polls, Bush beat Dukakis 53.4 percent to 45.6 percent in the popular count and 426 to 112 in the electoral column. The congressional divisions remained essentially the same, with the Democrats losing one seat in the Senate and gaining one in the House.

**1989–1991: Stasis at Home, Revolution Abroad**

No one watching the election campaign of 1988 had much reason to think that either candidate would effectively address the domestic problems worrying Americans: drugs, crime, environmental deterioration, decaying schools, deficits, bank failures, homelessness, poverty, racial tensions. All seemed to be insoluble puzzles that no political leader had the wit to solve. George Bush promised to be the "education president," predicted that continued economic growth would reduce and eventually eliminate government deficits, and urged voluntarism ("a thousand points of light") rather than government activism as the way out of the country's domestic difficulties. But two years into his presidency, there were few signs of progress against domestic ills.

The 1980s economic expansion continued slowly until the summer of 1990, when it went into a recession. The problems were familiar: inflation back up to 5 percent; the national debt exceeding $3 trillion; the 1989–90 budget deficit at $220 billion (just a shade below its peacetime high of $221 billion in 1986), and the world's largest annual trade imbalance. The savings-and-loan bailout threatened to cost present and future taxpayers $500 billion; and the country's aging infrastructure and battered environment remained unattended problems. It was politics as usual. A familiar litany of grievances rounded out the list: crime, drugs, poor educational performance, a diminished ability to compete in international markets, and governmental paralysis as the White House and Congress wrangled endlessly over how to reduce the deficit without inconveniencing any voters. Just as in 1980, polls showed that more than two-thirds of Americans felt the country was "fundamentally on the wrong track." It was difficult to pin down exactly what bothered people, but historian Paul Kennedy's best-selling 1987 book *The Rise and Fall of the Great Powers,* with its warnings against the erosion of American power as a consequence of "imperial overstretch" and unwise use of national resources, touched a raw nerve.

The midterm elections of 1990 hardly broke the stalemate. In June, Bush conceded that the prospect of continuing large deficits made him ready to "increase revenues," upsetting other Republicans, who feared he was giving up the party's politically advantageous opposition to higher taxes. On the eve of the elections, Congress finally screwed up the courage to vote a small tax increase. Public disgust over entrenched politicians' pusillanimity and subservience to special interests was supposed (so the pollsters predicted) to result in a "throw the rascals out" purge of incumbents by an outraged electorate, but the result was anticlimactic. A smaller-than-usual number of voters chose a new Congress with just one fewer Republican Senate seat and nine fewer Republican House seats than before; almost all of those incumbents who ran for reelection went back to Washington. The biggest losers were state governors who had had to raise taxes and cut services. On the other hand, Bush's standing in the opinion polls suffered only slight damage.

By mid-1991 Americans still struggled with uncertainties in national and international affairs. A sense of contingency always hangs over unfolding public events and social change, but the normal sense of uncertainty seemed heightened by 1991 because of conservative leaders' failures thus far to fulfill their promises of stable prosperity and a secure social order.

The great economic boom of the 1980s had by then run its course. A recession began in July 1990, driving unemployment back up to 7 percent and saddling state and local governments with huge deficits that they struggled to meet by imposing new taxes and cutting social programs. By June 1991 the federal deficit seemed certain to exceed $300 billion, and everyone wondered where the money would come from to pay for bank failures, environmental cleanups, and the medical, educational, and welfare programs needed by the old, the young, and the indigent. Democrats and especially the party's dominant liberal wing complained with some justification that the administration had no domestic agenda.

Nor did the Democrats know what to do. For the most part liberals continued to prefer their traditional remedy of greater government activism in meeting domestic needs. But the party of FDR now had little new to offer, either in candidates or programs. Lacking any worthy would-be Democratic presidential candidate to attack, Bush confined himself to lambasting LBJ's Great Society. The Democrats themselves had no credible educational policy to offer when Bush endorsed national achievement testing and the "parental choice" idea (under which public and private schools would compete for students). Democrats found themselves branded with favoring racial hiring quotas when they tried to pass a civil rights bill in 1991. Progressive intellectuals and minority scholars alike were forced onto the defensive as a backlash gathered force on the nation's campuses against "political correctness"—that is, the alleged tendency of tenured, radical professors to impose their worldview on the curriculum and to skew hiring decisions in their favor. Exaggerated as this conservative case against "the liberal establishment" may have been, it contained enough truth to bother the American public and to bolster Republican charges that the Democrats had become captive to minority special interests and to left-wing ideologies. Meanwhile the nation's tangible problems festered, largely unattended.

And yet as Americans worried about the country's failure to address current problems effectively, they took deep satisfaction from events abroad that demonstrated a worldwide attraction to American political and economic institutions. Throughout the communist world, in South Africa, and in Latin America mass movements demanding free elections and democratic governments challenged, and in many instances overwhelmed, undemocratic regimes.

By 1989 the downfall of Marxism-Leninism seemed an irresistible tide in the Soviet Union and its Eastern European sphere of influence. Gorbachev's *perestroika* policy since 1985 had aimed at making Communist party leadership more accountable to the populace and sought to modernize the economy. But Gorbachev's halting attempt to introduce a market economy produced only economic chaos. And as Gorbachev allowed seventy years of repressive rule to crumble, dissenters challenged the Communist party's exclusive hold on power, uncensored political debate became the order of the day.

**Revolts Against Communism**
*The fall of the Berlin Wall in November 1989 amid anticommunist uprisings throughout Eastern Europe symbolized the end of the Cold War (right). The massacre of demonstrators in Beijing's Tiananmen Square (opposite, above) on June 4, 1989, discredited Chinese communism. In the USSR, a similar bloodbath was averted in August 1991 when soldiers refused to fire on Muscovites gathered to prevent an assault on the Russian parliament building and the arrest of Russia's President Yeltsin (opposite, below). By thus foiling a coup aimed at ousting Soviet President Gorbachev, the Russian people dealt a fatal blow to the remnants of the Soviet autocracy and opened the way to a democratic reorganization of the USSR.*

Preoccupied by internal confusion and needing a rapprochement with the West, Gorbachev surrendered Stalin's East European empire. The year 1989 initiated astonishing change. Dissidents led mass movements that peacefully ousted Marxist regimes in East Germany, Poland, Czechoslovakia, Hungary, and Bulgaria, and a bloody revolt overthrew Romania's tyrannical dictator, Nicolae Ceaușescu. The Berlin Wall, a symbol of communist repression since 1961, came down; in October 1990 the two German states achieved reunification while remaining within NATO. Communism toppled in remote, impoverished Albania and in several Yugoslav republics in 1990–1991. By late 1990 the Warsaw Pact, soon to be dissolved, concluded an arms-limitation agreement with the West that substantially reduced the size of armies and number of weapons. In July 1991 Bush and Gorbachev concluded an agreement cutting United States and Soviet long-range missile forces by about 30 percent. Ethnic strife—particularly in the USSR and Yugoslavia—clouded prospects for democracy and peace in Eastern Europe, and the transition to capitalism promised to be painful. Yet the cause of liberty received powerful reinforcement in the Soviet Union in August 1991 when popular resistance in Moscow, led by the elected president of Russia, Boris Yeltsin, blocked a hardliners' coup that had tried to depose Gorbachev. The Cold War at last seemed over, and the containment policy first proposed by George Kennan in 1947 appeared vindicated.

No such rapid collapse of communism occurred in Asia; rather, a slow erosion. In the spring of 1989 China seemed on the verge of fundamental transformation when a million students and workers jammed Beijing's Tiananmen Square to demonstrate for freedom and acclaim the "Goddess of Liberty," a plaster replica of America's Statue of Liberty. But on June 4 the authorities struck back with a ruthless, sickeningly violent military crackdown.

At least as long as Deng Xiaoping, the octogenarian paramount leader of Chinese communism, lived, authoritarianism seemed secure on the mainland. But so was the nation's impetus toward free-market economic reform. Vietnam, too, appeared headed toward a restoration of free enterprise if not toward political liberalization, and signs multiplied that a settlement might be possible in Cambodia's endless civil war among Vietnamese- and Soviet-backed government forces, Chinese-backed Khmer Rouge guerrillas, and various weak Western-backed resistance groups. Even North Korea—perhaps the world's most closed and repressive communist regime—came under Soviet pressure to lessen tensions with its booming South Korean rival.

Ending the Cold War removed Africa from the arena of East-West conflict. Moscow cut its ties to such African clients as Ethiopia, Angola, and Mozambique, permitting Washington to pay more attention to the continent's intractable problems. Beginning in 1989 a more moderate white South African government began curtailing apartheid, released Nelson Mandela (its most formidable black opponent) from twenty-seven years' imprisonment, and allowed a black-led resistance movement to take power in Namibia. Diminished South African fears of international communism played a part in bringing about this change; so did the international economic sanctions, in which the United States had participated (without enthusiasm from the Reagan administration). Washington accepted with relief South Africa's abandonment of the hard line, and Mandela's triumphant tour of the United States in the summer of 1990 became a celebration of the man and of his desire for democracy in South Africa. But democracy's prospects in that land clouded as bloody tribal conflict erupted soon after the straitjacket of apartheid loosened, and it was not clear how much influence the United States might have in the country's future. In 1991, however, the South African government announced its intention to abolish apartheid, and Bush lifted economic sanctions.

Latin America also gave the United States some grounds for hope as the Cold War ended. Doubtless told by Moscow that further support would not be forthcoming, the Sandinista regime in Nicaragua agreed to hold honest elections in 1989; it lost, and Violetta Chamorro, a representative of the country's political moderates, took office peacefully. Washington in turn disengaged somewhat from El Salvador's civil war. Chile's iron-fisted dictator Augusto Pinochet, the rigid anticommunist who had seized power in 1973 in a CIA-sponsored coup, gave way to a democratically elected successor. In Cuba, Fidel Castro still clung to power, but future Soviet subsidies for his battered regime seemed doubtful; in any case he stirred little Latin American admiration, and his revolution appeared increasingly anachronistic. Obsession with Marxist revolutionaries no longer haunted United States hemisphere policy; at last, drugs and endemic Latin economic problems seemed fully to focus Washington's attention. George Bush's warm relations with Mexico and his generally friendly public reception when he toured several Latin American capitals in December 1990 would scarcely have seemed likely a few years earlier.

**War With Iraq**
Amid this exhilarating series of western triumphs, anyone would have seemed mad in mid-1990 to predict that within half a year the United States would go to war. Astonishingly, that prophesy came to pass. Yet the outbreak of fighting between Iraq and an American-led coalition in late January 1991 was directly related to the recent end of East-West hostilities.

On August 2, 1990, the Iraqi dictator Saddam Hussein sent his army into the small neighboring emirate of Kuwait. Once a Soviet client, Hussein had found himself freed of Moscow's restraining influence. Washington no longer saw Moscow's hand in every outbreak of trouble abroad and had sent confusing signals to Baghdad, perhaps convincing Hussein that the world would acquiesce in his annexation of one of the Middle East's richest oil producers. But belying media stereotypes of him as a "wimp," Bush responded vigorously to what he and other western leaders immediately branded as a threat to world stability. Iraqi success, they reasoned, would upset the precarious Middle Eastern balance of power; they also feared that Iraq's ruthless dictator would gain control of a dangerously large share of the world's oil output. Hussein kindled uncomfortable memories of 1930s-style military aggression, which the United Nations had been created to avert. Should his seizure of Kuwait succeed, Hussein might well attack the Saudis and tempt other Third World dictators to use force in settling disputes with weaker neighbors. Within a few days of the Iraqi attack, Bush and the Pentagon organized Operation Desert Shield, an enormously complicated airlift that by January 1991 brought more than 400,000 American troops and their equipment to the deserts of northern Saudi Arabia, facing Hussein's dug-in forces in Kuwait and southern Iraq. Meanwhile American diplomats fanned out around the world to enlist support.

At first Bush's strategy worked brilliantly. The American public rallied around their president (as it usually does in any moment of crisis). The United States assembled a coalition of anti-Iraqi Arab states that included Egypt, Syria, Saudi Arabia, and the small Persian Gulf monarchies. At the United Nations, the Soviet Union and China backed United States efforts to have the Security Council approve a series of increasingly tough resolutions demanding Iraq's withdrawal from Kuwait on pain of embargo and (later) of war. In the end, only Cuba, the Palestine Liberation Organization, and several quasi-democratic Arab states (where local public opinion could influence official policy) eventually stood by Iraq.

But as time passed, Americans' enthusiasm for an armed showdown with Iraq slowly ebbed. Abstract arguments about defending the world order stirred diminishing enthusiasm, and the administration occasionally blundered by crudely claiming that American jobs were at stake or that Hussein was "worse than Hitler." Critics insisted that war would be fought over nothing nobler than the price of gasoline or George Bush's political credibility. Beginning in November 1990 Congress dithered over the merits of letting economic sanctions squeeze Hussein out of Kuwait, as opposed to empowering the president to commit United States forces in support of forcibly evicting the Iraqis, which the Security Council had authorized as a last resort. Finally, as the United Nations' January 15, 1991, deadline for an Iraqi pullout approached and Hussein's government maintained a stubborn defiance, the House and Senate mustered the somber dignity to debate the issue of war versus embargo. On January 12, by agonizingly close and largely partisan votes (most Democrats opposing), both houses agreed to war if the president deemed it necessary.

On January 16 Desert Storm—the allied offensive—erupted. Dire predictions that war would become a Vietnam-like quagmire and that tens of thousands of American soldiers would perish in clouds of poison gas proved groundless. For almost six weeks a largely American air assault blasted the Iraqi troops in Kuwait and pounded thousands of targets in Iraq itself. Hussein's efforts to lure Israel into the fray, thereby turning the war into a revolutionary Arab-Israeli conflict, failed. Then in a 100-hour ground assault, American, British, French, and Arab forces brilliantly outmaneuvered, encircled, and crushed Hussein's once-formidable army. The entire operation, including the prewar buildup, cost about 350 American lives (almost half of them in accidents unrelated to the fighting); estimates of Iraqi war dead ranged to 100,000 or more. Spectacularly successful American military technology proved its worth: "smart bombs" that honed in on targets, Stealth fighters that eluded radar detection, and Patriot missiles that shot

**American Soldier and Iraqi Captives**
*Tens of thousands of Iraqi soldiers surrendered in the lightning Allied onslaught. Here a trooper of the 101st Airborne Division, which launched a helicopter attack deep behind Iraqi lines, guards a group of newly captured enemy soldiers.*

# The Middle East

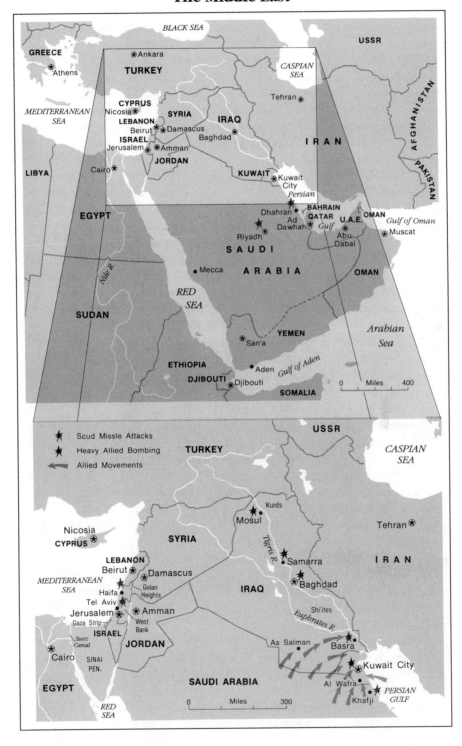

down almost every Iraqi rocket fired at Saudi Arabia and Israel. Iraq emerged from the war barely able to function as a modern society.

The American-led victory in Iraq, Bush exulted, banished forever the "Vietnam syndrome" that had left the nation fearful of any foreign entanglements that might lead to war. Certainly the conflict's swift and almost painless conclusion produced a wave of flag-waving euphoria across the land, and Vietnam veterans—who had never received such recognition for their sacrifices in a losing cause—at last found themselves marching alongside returning Gulf War troops in joyful welcome-home ceremonies. For the first time since World War II the public could admire victorious military commanders who had planned and executed a successful war strategy: the tough but humane General Norman Schwarzkopf and the cooly professional chief of staff, General Colin Powell, the son of Jamaican immigrants. After two decades of gnawing doubt about the nation's principles, resolve, and technological prowess, most American citizens at last felt that they could take pride in the nation's assertion of its power abroad.

However, the conduct of foreign policy, especially when it leads to war, generally entails frustrating moral ambiguities and compromises with high principles. The war with Iraq was no exception. The United States had assembled a war coalition and gained United Nations backing for the sole purpose of reversing Iraq's annexation of another sovereign country. Once that objective had been achieved with the liberation of Kuwait, Bush felt impelled to end the war. Unfortunately enough of the Iraqi army survived to keep Hussein in power and to hammer mercilessly the Kurdish and Shi'ite Arab minority populations that had dared to rise up against his rule at the end of the war. Most members of the United Nations had no interest in empowering the organization to reorder the internal affairs of another sovereign state, even one as oppressive as Saddam Hussein's Iraq. Although it had hoped that Hussein would be overthrown by a less despotic military junta or a coalition of opposition leaders, the United States lacked adequate knowledge of Iraqi internal affairs to sponsor a successor regime, and it feared a destabilizing scramble for Iraqi territory among Turkey, Iran, and neighboring Arab countries. In the end Washington felt obliged to accept Hussein's political survival and merely trust that continued economic sanctions would keep his regime weak. The only aid that United States forces extended to tens of thousands of hapless Kurds was to create refugee camps in Iraq's northern borderland and hand them over to unarmed United Nations guards, whom (it was hoped) Hussein would not risk attacking. Shi'ite rebels in southern Iraq received not even that much foreign succor. Congress and the American public sympathized with the plight of Hussein's rebellious subjects, but they supported Bush's decision to avoid further involvement in Iraq's internal affairs.

Similarly, even its impressive military victory did not give the United States enough leverage to force Israel and its Arab neighbors to make peace. Mutual distrust remained too deep to permit either side to accept compromises imposed by outside powers. After several assiduous months of postwar shuttle diplomacy, however, Secretary of State Baker managed to win agreement to a peace conference. In August 1991, its outcome remained uncertain.

**The Great Republic After Two Centuries**

The years 1989–91, so filled with dramatic events abroad, marked the two-hundredth anniversary of the launching of the American Republic and the framing of the Bill of Rights. The coincidence of these dates presented a striking opportunity to reflect on the nation's history and its recent experience.

Mobilizing their citizens for war or other great sacrifices, modern democracies tend to invoke a sense of transcendent moral purpose; mere national or individual self-interest hardly seems sufficient. Nowhere is this pattern more apparent than in the history of the American people, ever since John Winthrop preached to his fellow Puritans that they must think of themselves as a City Upon a Hill, an example of godly order for all humanity. Jefferson and Paine had evoked a secularized version of Winthrop's charge, justifying the American revolution by appealing to the high principle of liberty and challenging Americans to rally all humanity to its standard; the United States Constitution was designed to create a mechanism by which power could be created consistent with individual liberties. Conscious that the embattled American Republic stood as the world's only democracy, Lincoln made the survival of "government of the people, by the people, and for the people" the great principle to which he dedicated the nation during the Civil War. Wilson and Franklin Roosevelt led Americans in two world wars by proclaiming that America's cause was that of peoples everywhere struggling for liberty and self-determination, and on that conviction rested America's opposition to the Soviet system through four decades of Cold War. Martin Luther King, Jr., spoke to the conscience of every reasonable American in asking that the Republic fulfill its overdue obligation to African-American citizens, so that justice might "roll down like the waters, and righteousness like a mighty stream."

True, American society has often fallen short of its own ideals. Americans of every generation have behaved in ways that would make them seem utterly unprincipled: dispossessing the native population and enslaving Africans, repeatedly despoiling the environment and exploiting the poor in the name of the untrammeled individual's right to profit, and persistently pursuing special interests over the common good. Every generation's moment of high purpose has seemingly given way to sourly disillusioned times, bereft of ideals. So it was when the founding generation of New England Puritans passed from the scene, when the Revolution gave way to rampant entrepreneurship, when Reconstruction dissolved into a Gilded Age of greed and racism, when wars to make the world safe for democracy appeared to have brought forth the Ku Klux Klan, McCarthyism, Watergate, and the Iran-contra scandal.

History, of course, is never simply a succession of brief, shining moments of goodness succeeded by sloughs of despondency. Good and evil, virtue and greed, self-sacrifice and self-interest always intertwine inextricably. Self-indulgence or selflessness may seem (in retrospect) to have predominated at any one time, but actually both impulses are always at work. The highly dramatic and fast-paced events of 1989–91 confirmed these principles. Communism's collapse and the Eastern bloc peoples' striving to replace Marxist-Leninist institutions with democracy and market economies testified, by any measure, to the greater efficiency of the western model for organizing a modern society. At America's behest, the willingness of the overwhelming majority of the world's nations to oppose Iraqi aggression against a vulnerable neighbor vindicated the principle of collective security essential to a stable international order. But disillusionment followed swiftly as everyday international politics brought the war with Iraq to an end on morally ambiguous terms. The collapse of communism found the United States ambivalent about offering the material aid that might better ensure its former adversaries' secure transition to liberty. Politics-as-usual at home meant seemingly endless bickering over the allocation of diminished financial resources. Republican virtue seemed as elusive as ever, and—as usual—moral shortsightedness competed with idealism for the nation's soul.

Had America won the Cold War? The answer depended on how heavy a price one thought the Republic had paid in terms of corrupted political values, economic dislocation, and neglected domestic social problems. Nevertheless the worldwide impulse to acknowledge the United States as an exemplar of human freedom and economic progress suggested that the nation still deserved Churchill's accolade to it during World War II: the Great Republic.

## CHRONOLOGY

**1981** Reagan cuts domestic social programs and wins a 25 percent tax cut.
AIDS first observed in the United States.

**1982** Worst recession since the Great Depression, with 10.8 percent unemployment.

**1983** Economic recovery combined with record deficit of $195 billion.
Reagan announces the Strategic Defense Initiative.
American troops sent to Lebanon.
Invasion of Grenada.
Collapse of U.S.-Soviet arms talks.

**1984** American forces withdrawn from Lebanon.
Congress condemns covert administration help to rebels mining Nicaraguan harbors.

Unemployment declines to 7.1 percent.
Reagan reelected president by a landslide.

**1985** Gorbachev assumes power in the Soviet Union and proclaims glasnost and perestroika.
Additional American hostages seized in Lebanon, a TWA jet and the *Achille Lauro* hijacked in the Middle East.
Reagan administration national security advisers negotiate missiles-for-hostages deal with Iran.
Reagan and Gorbachev meet in Geneva.

**1986** Profits from Iran missile sales channeled to the contras.
Tax Reform Act passed.

**1986** William Rehnquist confirmed as chief justice and Antonin Scalia as associate justice of the Supreme Court.
Reagan meets Gorbachev in Reykjavik.
Iran-contra operations become public.
Investigations of Iran-contra affair by Tower Commission, special congressional committee, and special prosecutor.
Immigration Reform and Control Act passed.
Democrats recapture control of the Senate in congressional elections.

**1987** Reagan and Gorbachev meet in Washington, D.C.
INF Treaty signed.
Reagan nominees Robert Bork and Douglas H. Ginsburg fail to win appointment to the Supreme Court.
Stock market falls over 500 points.

**1988** Reagan meets Gorbachev in Moscow.
Savings-and-loan crisis deepens.
Defense Department procurement scandal revealed.
Attorney General Meese leaves office under a cloud.
Bush elected president.

**1989–**
**1990** Supreme Court adopts more conservative positions on abortion and affirmative action but endorses right of flag burning.
Oliver North and John Poindexter convicted; North's conviction later overturned.
Massacre of Chinese students demanding democracy in Beijing's Tiananmen Square.
Communist regimes ousted in Eastern Europe; Soviet Union moves toward a market economy, greater democracy, and national splintering.
Berlin Wall torn down, East Germany collapses, and Germany achieves unification.
Nelson Mandela released from prison in South Africa and visits the United States.
Bush abandons no-tax-increase pledge.
Bush sends American forces into the Persian Gulf to reverse Iraq's annexation of Kuwait.

**1991** American, Western, and Arab forces defeat Iraq in a six-week war and liberate Kuwait.
Communist regimes overthrown in Albania and Ethiopia.
Russian President Yeltsin blocks hardliners' coup that attempted to depose Soviet President Gorbachev.

---

## SUGGESTED READINGS

Scholarly literature on the 1980s is as yet limited. On Reagan and the first years of his presidency, see the works by journalists Lou Cannon, *Reagan* (1982); Ronnie Dugger, *On Reagan* (1983); and Laurence I. Barrett, *Gambling with History* (1983). Initial early accounts by scholars are William E. Leuchtenburg, "Ronald Reagan," a chapter in *In the Shadow of FDR* (1983); Robert Lekachman, *Greed Is Not Enough: Reaganomics* (1983); and Robert Dallek, *Ronald Reagan: The Politics of Symbolism* (1984). More recent books include several memoirs that reveal administration infighting: Alexander M. Haig, Jr., *Caveat: Realism, Reagan, and Foreign Policy* (1984); David Stockman, *The Triumph of Politics: The Inside Story of the Reagan*

*Revolution* (1986); Michael Deaver, *Behind the Scenes* (1987); Donald Regan, *For the Record* (1988); Larry Speakes, *Speaking Out* (1988); Nancy Reagan, *My Turn* (1989); and Ronald Reagan, *An American Life* (1991). More recent works by academics and journalists are Paul D. Erickson, *Reagan Speaks: The Making of an American Myth* (1985); Michael Rogin, *Ronald Reagan, the Movie* (1987); Garry Wills, *Reagan's America* (1987); and Jane Mayer and Doyle McManus, *Landslide: The Unmaking of the President, 1984–1988* (1988).

For domestic developments, see Jonathan Lash, *A Season of Spoils: The Story of the Reagan Administration's Attack on the Environment* (1984); Joan Claybrook, *Retreat from Safety: Reagan's Attack on American Health* (1984); Austin Ranney, ed., *The American Elections of 1984* (1985); Robert Bellah et al., *Habits of the Heart: Individualism and Commitment in American Life* (1985); Jeffrey H. Birnbaum and Alan S. Murray, *Showdown at Gucci Gulch: Lawmakers, Lobbyists, and the Unlikely Triumph of Tax Reform* (1987); Leslie W. Dunbar, ed., *Minority Report: What Has Happened to Blacks, Hispanics, American Indians, and Other Minorities in the Eighties* (1984); The Staff of the Chicago Tribune, *The American Millstone: An Examination of the Nation's Permanent Underclass* (1986); Reynolds Farley and Walter Allen, *The Color Line and the Quality of Life in America* (1987); Harrell R. Rodgers, Jr., *Poor Women, Poor Families* (1986); William Julius Wilson, *The Truly Disadvantaged: The Inner City, the Underclass, and Public Policy* (1987); Larry Brown and H. F. Pizer, *Living Hungry in America* (1987); Marian Wright Edelman, *Families in Peril* (1987); Jonathan Kozol, *Rachel and Her Children: Homeless Families in America* (1988); E. Fuller Torrey, *Nowhere to Go: The Tragic Odyssey of the Homeless Mentally Ill* (1988); Randy Shilts, *And the Band Played On: Politics, People, and the AIDS Epidemic* (1987); John Langone, *AIDS: The Facts* (1988); Joan Moore and Harry Pachon, *Hispanics in the United States* (1985); David Reimers, *Still the Golden Door: The Third World Comes to America* (1985); Al Santoli, *New Americans* (1988); Frank Levy, *Dollars and Dreams: The Changing American Income Distribution* (1987); Benjamin Friedman, *Day of Reckoning: The Consequences of American Economic Policy Under Reagan and After* (1988); and Kevin Phillips, *The Politics of Rich and Poor: Wealth and the American Electorate in the Reagan Aftermath* (1990).

For defense and foreign policies in the 1980s, see Harvard Nuclear Study Group, *Living with Nuclear Weapons* (1983); National Academy of Sciences, *Nuclear Arms Control* (1985); Stephen Cimbala, *The Reagan Defense Program* (1986); Paul Stares, *Space and National Security* (1987); Carl Feldbaum and Ronald Bee, *Looking the Tiger in the Eye: Confronting the Nuclear Threat* (1988); John Newhouse, *War and Peace in the Nuclear Age* (1989); and two books by Strobe Talbott, *Deadly Gambits: The Reagan Administration and the Stalemate in Nuclear Arms Control* (1984) and *The Master of the Game: Paul Nitze and the Nuclear Peace* (1988). Relations with Latin America are covered in Walter LaFeber, *Inevitable Revolutions* (2d ed., 1984); Karl Bermann, *Under the Big Stick* (1985); Bradford Burns, *At War with Nicaragua* (1987); Leslie Cockburn, *Out of Control* (1987); Robert Pastor, *Condemned to Repetition: The United States and Nicaragua* (1987); Lars Schoultz, *National Security and U.S. Policy Toward Latin America* (1987); Abraham F. Lowenthal, *Partners in Conflict: The United States and Latin America* (1987); Roy Gutman, *Banana Diplomacy, 1981–1987* (1988); Bob Woodward, *Veil: The Secret Wars of the CIA* (1987); Jane Hunter et al., *The Iran-Contra Connection* (1987); and Steven Emerson, *Secret Warriors: Inside the Covert Military Operations of the Reagan Era* (1988). For Soviet-American relations and other foreign policy issues, see Seweryn Bialer and Michael Mandelbaum, eds., *Gorbachev's Russia and American Foreign Policy* (1988); Richard J. Barnet, *The Alliance: America, Europe, Japan* (1983); Cheryl A. Rubenberg, *Israel and the American National Interest* (1986); Jerry Hough, *The Struggle for the Third World* (1986); Bruce Jentleson, *Pipeline Politics: The Complex Political Economy of East-West Trade* (1986); and Christopher Coker, *The United States and South Africa, 1968–1985* (1986).

# APPENDIX

# *Declaration of Independence*

IN CONGRESS, JULY 4, 1776

THE UNANIMOUS DECLARATION OF THE THIRTEEN
UNITED STATES OF AMERICA

When, in the course of human events, it becomes necessary for one people to dissolve the political bands which have connected them with another, and to assume, among the powers of the earth, the separate and equal station to which the laws of nature and of nature's God entitle them, a decent respect to the opinions of mankind requires that they should declare the causes which impel them to the separation.

We hold these truths to be self-evident: That all men are created equal; that they are endowed by their Creator with certain unalienable rights; that among these are life, liberty, and the pursuit of happiness; that, to secure these rights, governments are instituted among men, deriving their just powers from the consent of the governed; that whenever any form of government becomes destructive of these ends, it is the right of the people to alter or to abolish it, and to institute new government, laying its foundation on such principles, and organizing its powers in such form, as to them shall seem most likely to effect their safety and happiness. Prudence, indeed, will dictate that governments long established should not be changed for light and transient causes; and accordingly all experience hath shown that mankind are more disposed to suffer, while evils are sufferable, than to right themselves by abolishing the forms to which they are accustomed. But when a long train of abuses and usurpations, pursuing invariably the same object, evinces a design to reduce them under absolute despotism, it is their right, it is their duty, to throw off such government, and to provide new guards for their future security. Such has been the patient sufferance of these colonies; and such is now the necessity which constrains them to alter their former systems of government. The history of the present King of Great Britain is a history of repeated injuries and usurpations, all having in direct object the establishment of an absolute tyranny over these states. To prove this, let facts be submitted to a candid world.

He has refused his assent to laws, the most wholesome and necessary for the public good.

He has forbidden his governors to pass laws of immediate and pressing importance, unless suspended in their operation till his assent should be obtained; and, when so suspended, he has utterly neglected to attend to them.

He has refused to pass other laws for the accommodation of large districts of people, unless those people would relinquish the right of representation in the legislature, a right inestimable to them, and formidable to tyrants only.

He has called together legislative bodies at places unusual, uncomfortable, and distant from the depository of their public records, for the sole purpose of fatiguing them into compliance with his measures.

He has dissolved representative houses repeatedly, for opposing, with manly firmness, his invasions on the rights of the people.

He has refused for a long time, after such dissolutions, to cause others to be elected; whereby the legislative powers, incapable of annihilation, have returned to the people at large for their exercise; the state remaining, in the mean time, exposed to all the dangers of invasions from without and convulsions within.

He has endeavored to prevent the population of these states; for that purpose obstructing the laws for naturalization of foreigners; refusing to pass others to encourage their migration hither, and raising the conditions of new appropriations of lands.

He has obstructed the administration of justice, by refusing his assent to laws for establishing judiciary powers.

He has made judges dependent on his will alone, for the tenure of their offices, and the amount and payment of their salaries.

He has erected a multitude of new offices, and sent hither swarms of officers to harass our people and eat out their substance.

He has kept among us, in times of peace, standing armies, without the consent of our legislatures.

He has affected to render the military independent of, and superior to, the civil power.

He has combined with others to subject us to a jurisdiction foreign to our constitution, and unacknowledged by our laws, giving his assent to their acts of pretended legislation:

For quartering large bodies of armed troops among us;

For protecting them, by a mock trial, from punishment for any murders which they should commit on the inhabitants of these states;

For cutting off our trade with all parts of the world;

For imposing taxes on us without our consent;

For depriving us, in many cases, of the benefits of trial by jury;

For transporting us beyond seas, to be tried for pretended offenses;

For abolishing the free system of English laws in a neighboring province, establishing therein an arbitrary government, and enlarging its boundaries, so as to render it at once an example and fit instrument for introducing the same absolute rule into these colonies;

For taking away our charters, abolishing our most valuable laws, and altering fundamentally the forms of our governments;

For suspending our own legislatures, and declaring themselves invested with power to legislate for us in all cases whatsoever.

He has abdicated government here, by declaring us out of his protection and waging war against us.

He has plundered our seas, ravaged our coasts, burned our towns, and destroyed the lives of our people.

He is at this time transporting large armies of foreign mercenaries to complete the works of death, desolation, and tyranny already begun with circumstances of cruelty and perfidy scarcely paralleled in the most barbarous ages, and totally unworthy the head of a civilized nation.

He has constrained our fellow-citizens, taken captive on the high seas, to bear arms against their country, to become the executioners of their friends and brethren, or to fall themselves by their hands.

He has excited domestic insurrection among us, and has endeavored to bring on the inhabitants of our frontiers the merciless Indian savages, whose known rule of warfare is an undistinguished destruction of all ages, sexes, and conditions.

In every stage of these oppressions we have petitioned for redress in the most humble terms; our repeated petitions have been answered only by repeated injury. A prince, whose character is thus marked by every act which may define a tyrant, is unfit to be the ruler of a free people.

Nor have we been wanting in our attentions to our British brethren. We have warned them, from time to time, of attempts by their legislature to extend an unwarrantable jurisdiction over us. We have reminded them of the circumstances of our emigration and settlement here. We have appealed to their native justice and magnanimity; and we have conjured them, by the ties of our common kindred, to disavow these usurpations, which would inevitably interrupt our connections and correspondence. They, too, have been deaf to the voice of justice and of consanguinity. We must, therefore, acquiesce in the necessity which denounces our separation, and hold them, as we hold the rest of mankind, enemies in war, in peace friends.

We, therefore, the representatives of the United States of America, in General Congress assembled, appealing to the Supreme Judge of the world for the rectitude of our intentions, do, in the name and by the authority of the good people of these colonies, solemnly publish and declare, that these United Colonies are, and of right ought to be, FREE AND INDEPENDENT STATES; that they are absolved from all allegiance to the British crown, and that all political connection between them and the state of Great Britain is, and ought to be, totally dissolved; and that, as free and independent states, they have full power to levy war, conclude peace, contract alliances, establish commerce, and do all other acts and things which independent states may of right do. And for the support of this declaration, with a firm reliance on the protection of Divine Providence, we mutually pledge to each other our lives, our fortunes, and our sacred honor.

JOHN HANCOCK [*President*]
[*and fifty-five others*]

# Constitution of the United States of America

## PREAMBLE

*We the people of the United States, in order to form a more perfect union, establish justice, insure domestic tranquillity, provide for the common defense, promote the general welfare, and secure the blessings of liberty to ourselves and our posterity, do ordain and establish this Constitution for the United States of America.*

## Article I

**Section 1.**   All legislative powers herein granted shall be vested in a Congress of the United States, which shall consist of a Senate and a House of Representatives.

**Section 2.**   The House of Representatives shall be composed of members chosen every second year by the people of the several States, and the electors in each State shall have the qualifications requisite for electors of the most numerous branch of the State Legislature.

No person shall be a Representative who shall not have attained to the age of twenty-five years, and been seven years a citizen of the United States, and who shall not, when elected, be an inhabitant of that State in which he shall be chosen.

Representatives and direct taxes shall be apportioned among the several States which may be included within this Union, according to their respective numbers, *which shall be determined by adding to the whole number of free persons, including those bound to service for a term of years, and excluding Indians not taxed, three-fifths of all other persons.* The actual enumeration shall be made within three years after the first meeting of the Congress of the United States, and within every subsequent term of ten years, in such manner as they shall by law direct. The number of Representatives shall not exceed one for every thirty thousand, but each State shall have at least one Representative; *and until such enumeration shall be made, the State of New Hampshire shall be entitled to choose three, Massachusetts eight, Rhode Island and Providence Plantations one, Connecticut five, New York six, New Jersey four, Pennsylvania eight, Delaware one, Maryland six, Virginia ten, North Carolina five, South Carolina five, and Georgia three.*

When vacancies happen in the representation from any State, the Executive authority thereof shall issue writs of election to fill such vacancies.

The House of Representatives shall choose their Speaker and other officers; and shall have the sole power of impeachment.

---

NOTE: Passages that are no longer in effect are printed in italic type.

**Section 3.**  The Senate of the United States shall be composed of two Senators from each State, *chosen by the legislature thereof,* for six years; and each Senator shall have one vote.

*Immediately after they shall be assembled in consequence of the first election, they shall be divided as equally as may be into three classes. The seats of the Senators of the first class shall be vacated at the expiration of the second year, of the second class at the expiration of the fourth year, and of the third class at the expiration of the sixth year,* so that one-third may be chosen every second year; *and if vacancies happen by resignation or otherwise, during the recess of the legislature of any State, the Executive thereof may make temporary appointments until the next meeting of the legislature, which shall then fill such vacancies.*

No person shall be a Senator who shall not have attained to the age of thirty years, and been nine years a citizen of the United States, and who shall not, when elected, be an inhabitant of that State for which he shall be chosen.

The Vice President of the United States shall be President of the Senate, but shall have no vote, unless they be equally divided.

The Senate shall choose their other officers, and also a President *pro tempore,* in the absence of the Vice President, or when he shall exercise the office of President of the United States.

The Senate shall have the sole power to try all impeachments. When sitting for that purpose, they shall be on oath or affirmation. When the President of the United States is tried, the Chief Justice shall preside: and no person shall be convicted without the concurrence of two-thirds of the members present.

Judgment in cases of impeachment shall not extend further than to removal from office, and disqualification to hold and enjoy any office of honor, trust or profit under the United States; but the party convicted shall nevertheless be liable and subject to indictment, trial, judgment and punishment, according to law.

**Section 4.**  The times, places and manner of holding elections for Senators and Representatives shall be prescribed in each State by the legislature thereof; but the Congress may at any time by law make or alter such regulations, except as to the places of choosing Senators.

The Congress shall assemble at least once in every year, and such meeting *shall be on the first Monday in December, unless they shall by law appoint a different day.*

**Section 5.**  Each house shall be the judge of the elections, returns and qualifications of its own members, and a majority of each shall constitute a quorum to do business; but a smaller number may adjourn from day to day, and may be authorized to compel the attendance of absent members, in such manner, and under such penalties as each house may provide.

Each house may determine the rules of its proceedings, punish its members for disorderly behavior, and with the concurrence of two thirds, expel a member.

Each house shall keep a journal of its proceedings, and from time to time publish the same, excepting such parts as may in their judgment require secrecy; and the yeas and nays of the members of either house on any question shall, at the desire of one-fifth of those present, be entered on the journal.

Neither house, during the session of Congress, shall, without the consent of the other, adjourn for more than three days, nor to any other place than that in which the two houses shall be sitting.

**Section 6.** The Senators and Representatives shall receive a compensation for their services, to be ascertained by law and paid out of the treasury of the United States. They shall in all cases except treason, felony and breach of the peace, be privileged from arrest during their attendance at the session of their respective houses, and in going to and returning from the same; and for any speech or debate in either house, they shall not be questioned in any other place.

No Senator or Representative shall, during the time for which he was elected, be appointed to any civil office under the authority of the United States, which shall have been created, or the emoluments whereof shall have been increased during such time; and no person holding any office under the United States shall be a member of either house during his continuance in office.

**Section 7.** All bills for raising revenue shall originate in the House of Representatives; but the Senate may propose or concur with amendments as on other bills.

Every bill which shall have passed the House of Representatives and the Senate, shall, before it become a law, be presented to the President of the United States; if he approve he shall sign it, but if not he shall return it with objections to that house in which it originated, who shall enter the objections at large on their journal, and proceed to reconsider it. If after such reconsideration two-thirds of that house shall agree to pass the bill, it shall be sent, together with the objections, to the other house, by which it shall likewise be reconsidered, and, if approved by two-thirds of that house, it shall become a law. But in all such cases the votes of both houses shall be determined by yeas and nays, and the names of the persons voting for and against the bill shall be entered on the journal of each house respectively. If any bill shall not be returned by the President within ten days (Sundays excepted) after it shall have been presented to him, the same shall be a law, in like manner as if he had signed it, unless the Congress by their adjournment prevent its return, in which case it shall not be a law.

Every order, resolution, or vote to which the concurrence of the Senate and House of Representatives may be necessary (except on a question of adjournment) shall be presented to the President of the United States; and before the same shall take effect, shall be approved by him, or being disapproved by him, shall be repassed by two-thirds of the Senate and House of Representatives, according to the rules and limitations prescribed in the case of a bill.

**Section 8.** The Congress shall have power

To lay and collect taxes, duties, imposts and excises, to pay the debts and provide for the common defense and general welfare of the United States; but all duties, imposts and excises shall be uniform throughout the United States;

To borrow money on the credit of the United States;

To regulate commerce with foreign nations, and among the several States, and with the Indian tribes;

To establish an uniform rule of naturalization, and uniform laws on the subject of bankruptcies throughout the United States;

To coin money, regulate the value thereof, and of foreign coin, and fix the standard of weights and measures;

To provide for the punishment of counterfeiting the securities and current coin of the United States;

To establish post offices and post roads;

To promote the progress of science and useful arts by securing for limited times to authors and inventors the exclusive right to their respective writings and discoveries;

To constitute tribunals inferior to the Supreme Court;

To define and punish piracies and felonies committed on the high seas and offenses against the law of nations;

To declare war, grant letters of marque and reprisal, and make rules concerning captures on land and water;

To raise and support armies, but no appropriation of money to that use shall be for a longer term than two years;

To provide and maintain a Navy;

To make rules for the government and regulation of the land and naval forces;

To provide for calling forth the militia to execute the laws of the Union, suppress insurrections, and repel invasions;

To provide for organizing, arming, and disciplining the militia, and for governing such part of them as may be employed in the service of the United States, reserving to the States respectively the appointment of the officers, and the authority of training the militia according to the discipline prescribed by Congress;

To exercise exclusive legislation in all cases whatsoever, over such district (not exceeding ten miles square) as may, by cession of particular States, and the acceptance of Congress, become the seat of government of the United States, and to exercise like authority over all places purchased by the consent of the legislature of the State, in which the same shall be, for erection of forts, magazines, arsenals, dock-yards, and other needful buildings;—and

To make all laws which shall be necessary and proper for carrying into execution the foregoing powers, and all other powers vested by this Constitution in the government of the United States, or in any department or officer thereof.

**Section 9.** *The migration or importation of such persons as any of the States now existing shall think proper to admit shall not be prohibited by the Congress prior to the year 1808; but a tax or duty may be imposed on such importation, not exceeding $10 for each person.*

The privilege of the writ of habeas corpus shall not be suspended, unless when in cases of rebellion or invasion the public safety may require it.

No bill of attainder or ex post facto law shall be passed.

No capitation, or other direct, tax shall be laid, unless in proportion to the census or enumeration herein before directed to be taken.

No tax or duty shall be laid on articles exported from any State.

No preference shall be given by any regulation of commerce or revenue to the ports of one State over those of another; nor shall vessels bound to, or from, one State, be obliged to enter, clear, or pay duties in another.

No money shall be drawn from the treasury, but in consequence of appropriations made by law; and a regular statement and account of the receipts and expenditures of all public money shall be published from time to time.

No title of nobility shall be granted by the United States: and no person holding any office of profit or trust under them, shall, without the consent of the Congress, accept of any present, emolument, office, or title, of any kind whatever, from any king, prince or foreign state.

**Section 10.**   No State shall enter into any treaty, alliance, or confederation; grant letters of marque and reprisal; coin money; emit bills of credit; make anything but gold and silver coin a tender in payment of debts; pass any bill of attainder, ex post facto law, or law impairing the obligation of contracts, or grant any title of nobility.

No State shall, without the consent of Congress, lay any imposts or duties on imports or exports, except what may be absolutely necessary for executing its inspection laws: and the net produce of all duties and imposts, laid by any State on imports or exports, shall be for the use of the treasury of the United States; and all such laws shall be subject to the revision and control of the Congress.

No State shall, without the consent of Congress, lay any duty of tonnage, keep troops or ships of war in time of peace, enter into any agreement or compact with another State, or with a foreign power, or engage in war, unless actually invaded, or in such imminent danger as will not admit of delay.

# Article II

**Section 1.**   The executive power shall be vested in a President of the United States of America. He shall hold his office during the term of four years, and, together with the Vice-President, chosen for the same term, be elected as follows:

Each state shall appoint, in such manner as the legislature thereof may direct, a number of electors, equal to the whole number of Senators and Representatives to which the State may be entitled in the Congress; but no Senator or Representative, or person holding an office of trust or profit under the United States, shall be appointed an elector.

*The electors shall meet in their respective States, and vote by ballot for two persons, of whom one at least shall not be an inhabitant of the same State with themselves. And they shall make a list of all the persons voted for, and of the number of votes for each; which list they shall sign and certify, and transmit sealed to the seat of government of the United States, directed to the President of the Senate. The President of the Senate shall, in the presence of the Senate and House of Representatives, open all the certificates, and the votes shall then be counted. The person having the greatest number of votes shall be the President, if such number be a majority of the whole number of electors appointed; and if there be more than one who have such majority, and have an equal number of votes, then the House of Representatives shall immediately choose by ballot one of them for President; and if no person have a majority, then from the five highest on the list said House shall in like manner choose the President. But in choosing the President, the votes shall be taken by States, the representation from each State having one vote; a quorum for this purpose shall consist of a member or members from two-thirds of the States, and a majority of all the States shall be necessary to a choice. In every case, after the choice of the President, the person having the greatest number of votes of the electors shall be the Vice-President. But if there should remain two or more who have equal votes, the Senate shall choose from them by ballot the Vice-President.*

The Congress may determine the time of choosing the electors and the day on which they shall give their votes; which day shall be the same throughout the United States.

No person except a natural born citizen, *or a citizen of the United States at the time of the adoption of this Constitution,* shall be eligible to the office of President; neither shall any person be eligible to that office who shall not have attained to the age of thirty-five years, and been fourteen years a resident within the United States.

In case of the removal of the President from office or of his death, resignation, or inability to discharge the powers and duties of the said office, the same shall devolve on the

Vice-President, and the Congress may by law provide for the case of removal, death, resignation or inability, both of the President and Vice-President, declaring what officer shall then act as President, and such officer shall act accordingly, until the disability be removed, or a President shall be elected.

The President shall, at stated times, receive for his services a compensation, which shall neither be increased nor diminished during the period for which he shall have been elected, and he shall not receive within that period any other emolument from the United States, or any of them.

Before he enter on the execution of his office, he shall take the following oath or affirmation:—"I do solemnly swear (or affirm) that I will faithfully execute the office of the President of the United States, and will to the best of my ability preserve, protect and defend the Constitution of the United States."

**Section 2.**   The President shall be commander in chief of the army and navy of the United States, and of the militia of the several States, when called into the actual service of the United States; he may require the opinion, in writing, of the principal officer in each of the executive departments, upon any subject relating to the duties of their respective offices, and he shall have power to grant reprieves and pardons for offenses against the United States, except in cases of impeachment.

He shall have power, by and with the advice and consent of the Senate, to make treaties, provided two-thirds of the Senators present concur; and he shall nominate, and by and with the advice and consent of the Senate, shall appoint ambassadors, other public ministers and consuls, judges of the Supreme Court, and all other officers of the United States, whose appointments are not herein otherwise provided for, and which shall be established by law; but Congress may by law vest the appointment of such inferior officers, as they think proper, in the President alone, in the courts of law, or in the heads of departments.

The President shall have power to fill up all vacancies that may happen during the recess of the Senate, by granting commissions which shall expire at the end of their next session.

**Section 3.**   He shall from time to time give to the Congress information of the state of the Union, and recommend to their consideration such measures as he shall judge necessary and expedient; he may, on extraordinary occasions, convene both houses, or either of them, and in case of disagreement between them, with respect to the time of adjournment, he may adjourn them to such time as he shall think proper; he shall receive ambassadors and other public ministers; he shall take care that the laws be faithfully executed, and shall commission all the officers of the United States.

**Section 4.**   The President, Vice-President and all civil officers of the United States shall be removed from office on impeachment for, and on conviction of, treason, bribery, or other high crimes and misdemeanors.

# Article III

**Section 1.**   The judicial power of the United States shall be vested in one Supreme Court, and in such inferior courts as the Congress may from time to time ordain and establish.

The judges, both of the Supreme and inferior courts, shall hold their offices during good behavior, and shall, at stated times, receive for their services a compensation which shall not be diminished during their continuance in office.

**Section 2.**    The judicial power shall extend to all cases, in law and equity, arising under this Constitution, the laws of the United States, and treaties made, or which shall be made, under their authority;—to all cases affecting ambassadors, other public ministers and consuls;—to all cases of admiralty and maritime jurisdiction;—to controversies to which the United States shall be a party;—to controversies between two or more States;— *between a State and citizens of another State;*—between citizens of different States;— between citizens of the same State claiming lands under grants of different States, and between a State, or the citizens thereof, and foreign states, citizens or subjects.

In all cases affecting ambassadors, other public ministers and consuls, and those in which a State shall be party, the Supreme Court shall have original jurisdiction. In all the other cases before mentioned, the Supreme Court shall have appellate jurisdiction, both as to law and fact, with such exceptions, and under such regulations, as the Congress shall make.

The trial of all crimes, except in cases of impeachment, shall be by jury; and such trial shall be held in the State where said crimes shall have been committed; but when not committed within any State, the trial shall be at such place or places as the Congress may by law have directed.

**Section 3.**    Treason against the United States shall consist only in levying war against them, or in adhering to their enemies, giving them aid and comfort. No person shall be convicted of treason unless on the testimony of two witnesses to the same overt act, or on confession in open court.

The Congress shall have power to declare the punishment of treason, but no attainder of treason shall work corruption of blood, or forfeiture except during the life of the person attainted.

# Article IV

**Section 1.**    Full faith and credit shall be given in each State to the public acts, records, and judicial proceedings of every other State. And the Congress may by general laws prescribe the manner in which such acts, records, and proceedings shall be proved, and the effect thereof.

**Section 2.**    The citizens of each State shall be entitled to all privileges and immunities of citizens in the several States.

A person charged in any State with treason, felony, or other crime, who shall flee from justice, and be found in another State, shall on demand of the executive authority of the State from which he fled, be delivered up, to be removed to the State having jurisdiction of the crime.

*No person held to service or labor in one State, under the laws thereof, escaping into another, shall, in consequence of any law or regulation therein, be discharged from such service or labor, but shall be delivered up on claim of the party to whom such service or labor may be due.*

**Section 3.**  New States may be admitted by the Congress into this Union; but no new State shall be formed or erected within the jurisdiction of any other State; nor any State be formed by the junction of two or more States, or parts of States, without the consent of the legislatures of the States concerned as well as of the Congress.

The Congress shall have power to dispose of and make all needful rules and regulations respecting the territory or other property belonging to the United States; and nothing in this Constitution shall be so construed as to prejudice any claims of the United States, or of any particular State.

**Section 4.**  The United States shall guarantee to every State in this Union a republican form of government, and shall protect each of them against invasion; and on application of the legislature, or of the executive (when the legislature cannot be convened), against domestic violence.

## Article V

The Congress,whenever two-thirds of both houses shall deem it necessary, shall propose amendments to this Constitution, or, on the application of the legislatures of two-thirds of the several States, shall call a convention for proposing amendments, which, in either case, shall be valid to all intents and purposes, as part of this Constitution, when ratified by the legislatures of three-fourths of the several States, or by conventions in three-fourths thereof, as the one or the other mode of ratification may be proposed by the Congress; provided *that no amendents which may be made prior to the year one thousand eight hundred and eight shall in any manner affect the first and fourth clauses in the ninth section of the first article;* and that no State, without its consent, shall be deprived of its equal suffrage in the Senate.

## Article VI

All debts contracted and engagements entered into, before the adoption of this Constitution, shall be as valid against the United States under this Constitution, as under the Confederation.

This Constitution, and all the laws of the United States which shall be made in pursuance thereof; and all treaties made, or which shall be made, under the authority of the United States, shall be the supreme law of the land; and the judges in every State shall be bound thereby, anything in the Constitution or laws of any State to the contrary notwithstanding.

The Senators and Representatives before mentioned, and the members of the several State legislatures, and all executive and judicial officers, both of the United States and of the several States, shall be bound by oath or affirmation to support this Constitution; but no religious test shall ever be required as a qualification to any office or public trust under the United States.

## Article VII

The ratification of the conventions of nine States shall be sufficient for the establishment of this Constitution between the States so ratifying the same.

Done in convention by the unanimous consent of the States present, the seventeenth day of September in the year of our Lord one thousand seven hundred and eighty-seven and of the Independence of the United States of America the twelfth. In witness whereof we have hereunto subscribed our names.

[Signed by]
G° WASHINGTON
*Presidt and Deputy from Virginia*
[*and thirty-eight others*]

# Amendments to the Constitution

## Article I*

Congress shall make no law respecting an establishment of religion, or prohibiting the free exercise thereof; or abridging the freedom of speech, or of the press; or the right of the people peaceably to assemble, and to petition the government for a redress of grievances.

## Article II

A well-regulated militia being necessary to the security of a free State, the right of the people to keep and bear arms shall not be infringed.

## Article III

No soldier shall, in time of peace, be quartered in any house without the consent of the owner, nor in time of war, but in a manner to be prescribed by law.

## Article IV

The right of the people to be secure in their persons, houses, papers, and effects, against unreasonable searches and seizures, shall not be violated, and no warrants shall issue but upon probable cause, supported by oath or affirmation, and particularly describing the place to be searched, and the persons or things to be seized.

## Article V

No person shall be held to answer for a capital, or otherwise infamous crime, unless on a presentment or indictment of a grand jury, except in cases arising in the land or naval forces, or in the militia, when in actual service in time of war or public danger; nor shall any person be subject for the same offence to be twice put in jeopardy of life or limb; nor shall be compelled in any criminal case to be a witness against himself, nor be deprived of

---

*The first ten Amendments (Bill of Rights) were adopted in 1791.

life, liberty, or property, without due process of law; nor shall private property be taken for public use without just compensation.

## Article VI

In all criminal prosecutions, the accused shall enjoy the right to a speedy and public trial, by an impartial jury of the State and district wherein the crime shall have been committed, which district shall have been previously ascertained by law, and to be informed of the nature and cause of the accusation; to be confronted with the witnesses against him; to have compulsory process for obtaining witnesses in his favor, and to have the assistance of counsel for his defence.

## Article VII

In suits at common law, where the value in controversy shall exceed twenty dollars, the right of trial by jury shall be preserved, and no fact tried by a jury shall be otherwise re-examined in any court of the United States, than according to the rules of the common law.

## Article VIII

Excessive bail shall not be required, nor excessive fines imposed, nor cruel and unusual punishments inflicted.

## Article IX

The enumeration in the Constitution, of certain rights, shall not be construed to deny or disparage others retained by the people.

## Article X

The powers not delegated to the United States by the Constitution, nor prohibited by it to the States, are reserved to the States respectively, or to the people.

## Article XI
### [*Adopted 1798*]

The judicial power of the United States shall not be construed to extend to any suit in law or equity, commenced or prosecuted against one of the United States by citizens of another State, or by citizens or subjects of any foreign state.

## Article XII
### [*Adopted 1804*]

The electors shall meet in their respective States, and vote by ballot for President and Vice-President, one of whom, at least, shall not be an inhabitant of the same State with themselves; they shall name in their ballots the person voted for as President, and in distinct ballots the person voted for as Vice-President, and they shall make distinct lists of all persons voted for as President, and of all persons voted for as Vice-President, and of the number of votes for each, which lists they shall sign and certify, and transmit to the seat of government of the United States, directed to the President of the Senate;—The President of the Senate shall, in the presence of the Senate and House of Representatives, open all the certificates and the votes shall then be counted;—the person having the greatest number of votes for President shall be the President, if such number be a majority of the whole number of electors appointed; and if no person have such majority, then from the persons having the highest numbers not exceeding three on the list of those voted for as President, the House of Representatives shall choose immediately, by ballot, the President. But in choosing the President, the votes shall be taken by States, the representation from each State having one vote; a quorum for this purpose shall consist of a member or members from two-thirds of the States, and a majority of all the States shall be necessary to a choice. And if the House of Representatives shall not choose a President whenever the right of choice shall devolve upon them, before *the fourth day of March* next following, then the Vice-President shall act as President, as in the case of the death or other constitutional disability of the President.

The person having the greatest number of votes as Vice-President shall be the Vice-President, if such a number be a majority of the whole number of electors appointed; and if no person have a majority, then from the two highest numbers on the list the Senate shall choose the Vice-President; a quorum for the purpose shall consist of two-thirds of the whole number of Senators, and a majority of the whole number shall be necessary to a choice. But no person constitutionally ineligible to the office of President shall be eligible to that of Vice-President of the United States.

## Article XIII
[*Adopted 1865*]

**Section 1.**   Neither slavery nor involuntary servitude, except as a punishment for crime whereof the party shall have been duly convicted, shall exist within the United States, or any place subject to their jurisdiction.

**Section 2.**   Congress shall have power to enforce this article by appropriate legislation.

## Article XIV
[*Adopted 1868*]

**Section 1.**   All persons born or naturalized in the United States, and subject to the jurisdiction thereof, are citizens of the United States and of the State wherein they reside. No State shall make or enforce any law which shall abridge the privileges or immunities of citizens of the United States; nor shall any State deprive any person of life, liberty, or property, without due process of law; nor deny to any person within its jurisdiction the equal protection of the laws.

**Section 2.**   Representatives shall be apportioned among the several States according to their respective numbers, counting the whole number of persons in each State, excluding Indians not taxed. But when the right to vote at any election for the choice of Electors for President and Vice-President of the United States, Representatives in Congress, the executive and judicial officers of a State, or the members of the legislature thereof, is denied to any of the male inhabitants of such State, being twenty-one years of age and citizens of the United States, or in any way abridged, except for participation in rebellion, or other crime, the basis of representation therein shall be reduced in the proportion which the number of such male citizens shall bear to the whole number of male citizens twenty-one years of age in such State.

**Section 3.**   No person shall be a Senator or Representative in Congress, or Elector of President and Vice-President, or hold any office, civil or military, under the United States, or under any State, who, having previously taken an oath, as a member of Congress, or as an officer of the United States, or as a member of any State legislature, or as an executive or judicial officer of any State, to support the Constitution of the United States, shall have engaged in insurrection or rebellion against the same, or given aid or comfort to the enemies thereof. Congress may, by a vote of two-thirds of each house, remove such disability.

**Section 4.**   The validity of the public debt of the United States, authorized by law, including debts incurred for payment of pensions and bounties for services in suppressing insurrection or rebellion, shall not be questioned. But neither the United States nor any State shall assume or pay any debt or obligation incurred in aid of insurrection or rebellion against the United States, or any claim for the loss of emancipation, of any slave; but all such debts, obligations, and claims shall be held illegal and void.

**Section 5.**   The Congress shall have the power to enforce, by appropriate legislation, the provisions of this article.

# Article XV
*[Adopted 1870]*

**Section 1.**   The right of citizens of the United States to vote shall not be denied or abridged by the United States or by any State on account of race, color, or previous condition of servitude.

**Section 2.**   The Congress shall have power to enforce this article by appropriate legislation.

# Article XVI
*[Adopted 1913]*

The Congress shall have power to lay and collect taxes on incomes, from whatever source derived, without apportionment among the several States, and without regard to any census or enumeration.

# Article XVII
*[Adopted 1913]*

**Section 1.**   The Senate of the United States shall be composed of two Senators from each State, elected by the people thereof, for six years; and each Senator shall have one vote. The electors in each State shall have the qualifications requisite for electors of [voters for] the most numerous branch of the State legislatures.

**Section 2.** When vacancies happen in the representation of any State in the Senate, the executive authority of such State shall issue writs of election to fill such vacancies: Provided, that the Legislature of any State may empower the executive thereof to make temporary appointments until the people fill the vacancies by election as the Legislature may direct.

**Section 3.** This amendment shall not be so construed as to affect the election or term of any Senator chosen before it becomes valid as part of the Constitution.

## Article XVIII
*[Adopted 1919; Repealed 1933]*

**Section 1.** *After one year from the ratification of this article the manufacture, sale, or transportation of intoxicating liquors within, the importation thereof into, or the exportation thereof from the United States and all territory subject to the jurisdiction thereof, for beverage purposes, is hereby prohibited.*

**Section 2.** *The Congress and the several States shall have concurrent power to enforce this article by appropriate legislation.*

**Section 3.** *This article shall be inoperative unless it shall have been ratified as an amendment to the Constitution by the legislatures of the several States, as provided by the Constitution, within seven years from the date of the submission thereof to the States by the Congress.*

## Article XIX
*[Adopted 1920]*

**Section 1.** The right of citizens of the United States to vote shall not be denied or abridged by the United States or by any State on account of sex.

**Section 2.** The Congress shall have the power to enforce this article by appropriate legislation.

## Article XX
*[Adopted 1933]*

**Section 1.** The terms of the President and Vice-President shall end at noon on the 20th day of January, and the terms of Senators and Representatives at noon on the 3d day of January, of the years in which such terms would have ended if this article had not been ratified; and the terms of their succesors shall then begin.

**Section 2.** The Congress shall assemble at least once in every year, and such meeting shall begin at noon on the 3d day of January, unless they shall by law appoint a different day.

**Section 3.** If, at the time fixed for the beginning of the term of the President, the President-elect shall have died, the Vice-President-elect shall become President. If a

President shall not have been chosen before the time fixed for the beginning of his term, or if the President-elect shall have failed to qualify, then the Vice-President-elect shall act as President until a President shall have qualified; and the Congress may by law provide for the case wherein neither a President-elect nor a Vice-President-elect shall have qualified, declaring who shall then act as President, or the manner in which one who is to act shall be selected, and such persons shall act accordingly until a President or Vice-President shall have qualified.

**Section 4.** The Congress may by law provide for the case of the death of any of the persons from whom the House of Representatives may choose a President whenever the right of choice shall have devolved upon them, and for the case of the death of any persons from whom the Senate may choose a Vice-President whenever the right of choice shall have devolved upon them.

**Section 5.** Sections 1 and 2 shall take effect on the 15th day of October following the ratification of this article.

**Section 6.** This article shall be inoperative unless it shall have been ratified as an amendment to the Constitution by the Legislatures of three-fourths of the several States within seven years from the date of its submission.

# Article XXI
## [*Adopted 1933*]

**Section 1.** The eighteenth article of amendment to the Constitution of the United States is hereby repealed.

**Section 2.** The transportation or importation into any State, Territory, or Possession of the United States for delivery or use therein of intoxicating liquors, in violation of the laws thereof, is hereby prohibited.

**Section 3.** This article shall be inoperative unless it shall have been ratified as an amendment to the Constitution by conventions in the several States, as provided in the Constitution, within seven years from the date of submission thereof to the States by the Congress.

# Article XXII
## [*Adopted 1951*]

**Section 1.** No person shall be elected to the office of President more than twice, and no person who has held the office of President, or acted as President, for more than two years of a term to which some other person was elected President shall be elected to the office of President more than once. But this article shall not apply to any person holding the office of President when this article was proposed by the Congress, and shall not prevent any person who may be holding the office of President, or acting as President, during the term within which this article becomes operative from holding the office of President or acting as President during the remainder of such term.

**Section 2.** This article shall be inoperative unless it shall have been ratified as an amendment to the Constitution by the legislatures of three-fourths of the several States within seven years from the date of its submission to the States by the Congress.

# Article XXIII
## [*Adopted 1961*]

**Section 1.** The District constituting the seat of Government of the United States shall appoint in such manner as the Congress may direct:

A number of electors of President and Vice-President equal to the whole number of Senators and Representatives in Congress to which the District would be entitled if it were a State, but in no event more than the least populous State; they shall be in addition to those appointed by the States, but they shall be considered for the purposes of the election of President and Vice-President, to be electors appointed by a State; and they shall meet in the District and perform such duties as provided by the twelfth article of amendment.

**Section 2.** The Congress shall have the power to enforce this article by appropriate legislation.

# Article XXIV
## [*Adopted 1964*]

**Section 1.** The right of citizens of the United States to vote in any primary or other election for President or Vice-President, for electors for President or Vice-President, or for Senator or Representative in Congress, shall not be denied or abridged by the United States or any State by reason of failure to pay any poll tax or other tax.

**Section 2.** The Congress shall have the power to enforce this article by appropriate legislation.

# Article XXV
## [*Adopted 1967*]

**Section 1.** In case of the removal of the President from office or of his death or resignation, the Vice-President shall become President.

**Section 2.** Whenever there is a vacancy in the office of the Vice-President, the President shall nominate a Vice-President who shall take office upon confirmation by a majority vote of both Houses of Congress.

**Section 3.** Whenever the President transmits to the President pro tempore of the Senate and the Speaker of the House of Representatives his written declaration that he is unable to discharge the powers and duties of his office, and until he transmits to them a written declaration to the contrary, such powers and duties shall be discharged by the Vice-President as Acting President.

**Section 4.** Whenever the Vice-President and a majority of either the principal officers of the executive departments or of such other body as Congress may by law provide, transmit to the President pro tempore of the Senate and the Speaker of the House of Representatives their written declaration that the President is unable to discharge the powers and duties of his office, the Vice-President shall immediately assume the powers and duties of the office as Acting President.

Thereafter, when the President transmits to the President pro tempore of the Senate and the Speaker of the House of Representatives his written declaration that no inability exists, he shall resume the powers and duties of his office unless the Vice-President and a majority of either the principal officers of the executive department[s] or of such other body as Congress may by law provide, transmit within four days to the President pro tempore of the Senate and the Speaker of the House of Representatives their written declaration that the President is unable to discharge the powers and duties of his office. Thereupon Congress shall decide the issue, assembling within forty-eight hours for that purpose if not in session. If the Congress, within twenty-one days after receipt of the latter written declaration, or, if Congress is not in session, within twenty-one days after Congress is required to assemble, determines by two-thirds vote of both Houses that the President is unable to discharge the powers and duties of his office, the Vice-President shall continue to discharge the same as Acting President; otherwise, the President shall resume the powers and duties of his office.

# Article XXVI
*[Adopted 1971]*

**Section 1.** The right of citizens of the United States, who are 18 years of age or older, to vote shall not be denied or abridged by the United States or by any State on account of age.

**Section 2.** The Congress shall have power to enforce this article by appropriate legislation.

# Presidential Elections*

| Election | Candidates | Parties | Popular Vote | Electoral Vote |
|---|---|---|---|---|
| 1789 | **George Washington** | No party designations | | 69 |
| | *John Adams* | | | 34 |
| | *Minor Candidates* | | | 35 |
| 1792 | **George Washington** | No party designations | | 132 |
| | *John Adams* | | | 77 |
| | *George Clinton* | | | 50 |
| | *Minor Candidates* | | | 5 |
| 1796 | **John Adams** | Federalist | | 71 |
| | *Thomas Jefferson* | Democratic-Republican | | 68 |
| | *Thomas Pinckney* | Federalist | | 59 |
| | *Aaron Burr* | Democratic-Republican | | 30 |
| | *Minor Candidates* | | | 48 |
| 1800 | **Thomas Jefferson** | Democratic-Republican | | 73 |
| | *Aaron Burr* | Democratic-Republican | | 73 |
| | *John Adams* | Federalist | | 65 |
| | *Charles C. Pinckney* | Federalist | | 64 |
| | *John Jay* | Federalist | | 1 |
| 1804 | **Thomas Jefferson** | Democratic-Republican | | 162 |
| | *Charles C. Pinckney* | Federalist | | 14 |
| 1808 | **James Madison** | Democratic-Republican | | 122 |
| | *Charles C. Pinckney* | Federalist | | 47 |
| | *George Clinton* | Democratic-Republican | | 6 |
| 1812 | **James Madison** | Democratic-Republican | | 128 |
| | *DeWitt Clinton* | Federalist | | 89 |
| 1816 | **James Monroe** | Democratic-Republican | | 183 |
| | *Rufus King* | Federalist | | 34 |
| 1820 | **James Monroe** | Democratic-Republican | | 231 |
| | *John Q. Adams* | Independent Republican | | 1 |

*Candidates receiving less than 1% of the popular vote are omitted. Before the Twelfth Amendment (1804) the Electoral College voted for two presidential candidates, and the runner-up became vice-president. Basic figures are taken primarily from *Historical Statistics of the United States, 1789–1945* (1949), pp. 288–90; *Historical Statistics of the United States, Colonial Times to 1957* (1960), pp. 682–83; and *Statistical Abstract of the United States, 1969* (1969), pp. 355–57.

| Election | Candidates | Parties | Popular Vote | Electoral Vote |
|----------|-----------|---------|-------------|----------------|
| 1824 | John Q. Adams (Min.)* | Democratic-Republican | 108,740 | 84 |
| | *Andrew Jackson* | Democratic-Republican | 153,544 | 99 |
| | *William H. Crawford* | Democratic-Republican | 46,618 | 41 |
| | *Henry Clay* | Democratic-Republican | 47,136 | 37 |
| 1828 | Andrew Jackson | Democratic | 647,286 | 178 |
| | *John Q. Adams* | National Republican | 508,064 | 83 |
| 1832 | Andrew Jackson | Democratic | 687,502 | 219 |
| | *Henry Clay* | National Republican | 530,189 | 49 |
| | *William Wirt* | Anti-Masonic ⎫ | 33,108 | 7 |
| | *John Floyd* | National Republican ⎭ | | 11 |
| 1836 | Martin Van Buren | Democratic | 762,678 | 170 |
| | *William H. Harrison* | Whig ⎫ | | 73 |
| | *Hugh L. White* | Whig ⎬ | | 26 |
| | *Daniel Webster* | Whig ⎪ | 736,656 | 14 |
| | *W. P. Mangum* | Whig ⎭ | | 11 |
| 1840 | William H. Harrison | Whig | 1,275,016 | 234 |
| | *Martin Van Buren* | Democratic | 1,129,102 | 60 |
| 1844 | James K. Polk (Min.)* | Democratic | 1,337,243 | 170 |
| | *Henry Clay* | Whig | 1,299,062 | 105 |
| | *James G. Birney* | Liberty | 62,300 | |
| 1848 | Zachary Taylor (Min.)* | Whig | 1,360,099 | 163 |
| | *Lewis Cass* | Democratic | 1,220,544 | 127 |
| | *Martin Van Buren* | Free Soil | 291,263 | |
| 1852 | Franklin Pierce | Democratic | 1,601,274 | 254 |
| | *Winfield Scott* | Whig | 1,386,580 | 42 |
| | *John P. Hale* | Free Soil | 155,825 | |
| 1856 | James Buchanan (Min.)* | Democratic | 1,838,169 | 174 |
| | *John C. Frémont* | Republican | 1,341,264 | 114 |
| | *Millard Fillmore* | American | 874,534 | 8 |
| 1860 | Abraham Lincoln (Min.)* | Republican | 1,866,452 | 180 |
| | *Stephen A. Douglas* | Democratic | 1,375,157 | 12 |
| | *John C. Breckinridge* | Democratic | 847,953 | 72 |
| | *John Bell* | Constitutional Union | 590,631 | 39 |
| 1864 | Abraham Lincoln | Union | 2,213,665 | 212 |
| | *George B. McClellan* | Democratic | 1,802,237 | 21 |
| 1868 | Ulysses S. Grant | Republican | 3,012,833 | 214 |
| | *Horatio Seymour* | Democratic | 2,703,249 | 80 |
| 1872 | Ulysses S. Grant | Republican | 3,597,132 | 286 |
| | *Horace Greeley* | Democratic and Liberal Republican | 2,834,125 | 66 |

*"Min." indicates minority president—one receiving less than 50% of all popular votes.

| Election | Candidates | Parties | Popular Vote | Electoral Vote |
|----------|-----------|---------|-------------|----------------|
| 1876 | **Rutherford B. Hayes** (Min.)* | Republican | 4,036,298 | 185 |
|      | *Samuel J. Tilden* | Democratic | 4,300,590 | 184 |
| 1880 | **James A. Garfield** (Min.)* | Republican | 4,454,416 | 214 |
|      | *Winfield S. Hancock* | Democratic | 4,444,952 | 155 |
|      | *James B. Weaver* | Greenback-Labor | 308,578 | |
| 1884 | **Grover Cleveland** (Min.)* | Democratic | 4,874,986 | 219 |
|      | *James G. Blaine* | Republican | 4,851,981 | 182 |
|      | *Benjamin F. Butler* | Greenback-Labor | 175,370 | |
|      | *John P. St. John* | Prohibition | 150,369 | |
| 1888 | **Benjamin Harrison** (Min.)* | Republican | 5,439,853 | 233 |
|      | *Grover Cleveland* | Democratic | 5,540,309 | 168 |
|      | *Clinton B. Fisk* | Prohibition | 249,506 | |
|      | *Anson J. Streeter* | Union Labor | 146,935 | |
| 1892 | **Grover Cleveland** (Min.)* | Democratic | 5,556,918 | 277 |
|      | *Benjamin Harrison* | Republican | 5,176,108 | 145 |
|      | *James B. Weaver* | People's | 1,041,028 | 22 |
|      | *John Bidwell* | Prohibition | 264,133 | |
| 1896 | **William McKinley** | Republican | 7,104,779 | 271 |
|      | *William J. Bryan* | Democratic | 6,502,925 | 176 |
| 1900 | **William McKinley** | Republican | 7,207,923 | 292 |
|      | *William J. Bryan* | Democratic; Populist | 6,358,133 | 155 |
|      | *John C. Woolley* | Prohibition | 208,914 | |
| 1904 | **Theodore Roosevelt** | Republican | 7,623,486 | 336 |
|      | *Alton B. Parker* | Democratic | 5,077,911 | 140 |
|      | *Eugene V. Debs* | Socialist | 402,283 | |
|      | *Silas C. Swallow* | Prohibition | 258,536 | |
| 1908 | **William H. Taft** | Republican | 7,678,908 | 321 |
|      | *William J. Bryan* | Democratic | 6,409,104 | 162 |
|      | *Eugene V. Debs* | Socialist | 420,793 | |
|      | *Eugene W. Chafin* | Prohibition | 253,840 | |
| 1912 | **Woodrow Wilson** (Min.)* | Democratic | 6,293,454 | 435 |
|      | *Theodore Roosevelt* | Progressive | 4,119,538 | 88 |
|      | *William H. Taft* | Republican | 3,484,980 | 8 |
|      | *Eugene V. Debs* | Socialist | 900,672 | |
|      | *Eugene W. Chafin* | Prohibition | 206,275 | |
| 1916 | **Woodrow Wilson** (Min.)* | Democratic | 9,129,606 | 277 |
|      | *Charles E. Hughes* | Republican | 8,538,221 | 254 |
|      | *A. L. Benson* | Socialist | 585,113 | |
|      | *J. F. Hanly* | Prohibition | 220,506 | |
| 1920 | **Warren G. Harding** | Republican | 16,152,200 | 404 |
|      | *James M. Cox* | Democratic | 9,147,353 | 127 |
|      | *Eugene V. Debs* | Socialist | 919,799 | |
|      | *P. P. Christensen* | Farmer-Labor | 265,411 | |

*"Min." indicates minority president—one receiving less than 50% of all popular votes.

| Election | Candidates | Parties | Popular Vote | Electoral Vote |
|---|---|---|---|---|
| 1924 | **Calvin Coolidge** | Republican | 15,725,016 | 382 |
| | *John W. Davis* | Democratic | 8,386,503 | 136 |
| | *Robert M. La Follette* | Progressive | 4,822,856 | 13 |
| 1928 | **Herbert C. Hoover** | Republican | 21,391,381 | 444 |
| | *Alfred E. Smith* | Democratic | 15,016,443 | 87 |
| 1932 | **Franklin D. Roosevelt** | Democratic | 22,821,857 | 472 |
| | *Herbert C. Hoover* | Republican | 15,761,841 | 59 |
| | *Norman Thomas* | Socialist | 881,951 | |
| 1936 | **Franklin D. Roosevelt** | Democratic | 27,751,597 | 523 |
| | *Alfred M. Landon* | Republican | 16,679,583 | 8 |
| | *William Lemke* | Union, etc. | 882,479 | |
| 1940 | **Franklin D. Roosevelt** | Democratic | 27,244,160 | 449 |
| | *Wendell L. Willkie* | Republican | 22,305,198 | 82 |
| 1944 | **Franklin D. Roosevelt** | Democratic | 25,602,504 | 432 |
| | *Thomas E. Dewey* | Republican | 22,006,285 | 99 |
| 1948 | **Harry S Truman** (Min.)* | Democratic | 24,105,812 | 303 |
| | *Thomas E. Dewey* | Republican | 21,970,065 | 189 |
| | *J. Strom Thurmond* | States' Rights Democratic | 1,169,063 | 39 |
| | *Henry A. Wallace* | Progressive | 1,157,172 | |
| 1952 | **Dwight D. Eisenhower** | Republican | 33,936,234 | 442 |
| | *Adlai E. Stevenson* | Democratic | 27,314,992 | 89 |
| 1956 | **Dwight D. Eisenhower** | Republican | 35,590,472 | 457 |
| | *Adlai E. Stevenson* | Democratic | 26,022,752 | 73 |
| 1960 | **John F. Kennedy** (Min.)* | Democratic | 34,226,731 | 303 |
| | *Richard M. Nixon* | Republican | 34,108,157 | 219 |
| 1964 | **Lyndon B. Johnson** | Democratic | 43,129,484 | 486 |
| | *Barry M. Goldwater* | Republican | 27,178,188 | 52 |
| 1968 | **Richard M. Nixon** (Min.)* | Republican | 31,785,480 | 301 |
| | *Hubert H. Humphrey, Jr.* | Democratic | 31,275,166 | 191 |
| | *George C. Wallace* | American Independent | 9,906,473 | 46 |
| 1972 | **Richard M. Nixon** | Republican | 45,767,218 | 520 |
| | *George S. McGovern* | Democratic | 28,357,668 | 17 |
| 1976 | **Jimmy Carter** | Democratic | 40,276,040 | 297 |
| | *Gerald R. Ford* | Republican | 38,532,630 | 241 |
| 1980 | **Ronald W. Reagan** | Republican | 43,899,248 | 489 |
| | *Jimmy Carter* | Democratic | 35,481,435 | 49 |
| 1984 | **Ronald W. Reagan** | Republican | 54,451,521 | 525 |
| | *Walter F. Mondale* | Democratic | 37,565,334 | 13 |
| 1988 | **George H. W. Bush** | Republican | 47,946,422 | 426 |
| | *Michael S. Dukakis* | Democratic | 41,016,429 | 112 |

*"Min." indicates minority president—one receiving less than 50% of all popular votes.

# Presidents and Vice-Presidents

| Term | President | Vice-President |
|------|-----------|----------------|
| 1789–1793 | George Washington | John Adams |
| 1793–1797 | George Washington | John Adams |
| 1797–1801 | John Adams | Thomas Jefferson |
| 1801–1805 | Thomas Jefferson | Aaron Burr |
| 1805–1809 | Thomas Jefferson | George Clinton |
| 1809–1813 | James Madison | George Clinton (d. 1812) |
| 1813–1817 | James Madison | Elbridge Gerry (d. 1814) |
| 1817–1821 | James Monroe | Daniel D. Tompkins |
| 1821–1825 | James Monroe | Daniel D. Tompkins |
| 1825–1829 | John Quincy Adams | John C. Calhoun |
| 1829–1833 | Andrew Jackson | John C. Calhoun (resigned 1832) |
| 1833–1837 | Andrew Jackson | Martin Van Buren |
| 1837–1841 | Martin Van Buren | Richard M. Johnson |
| 1841–1845 | William H. Harrison (d. 1841) John Tyler | John Tyler |
| 1845–1849 | James K. Polk | George M. Dallas |
| 1849–1853 | Zachary Taylor (d. 1850) Millard Fillmore | Millard Fillmore |
| 1853–1857 | Franklin Pierce | William R. D. King (d. 1853) |
| 1857–1861 | James Buchanan | John C. Breckinridge |
| 1861–1865 | Abraham Lincoln | Hannibal Hamlin |
| 1865–1869 | Abraham Lincoln (d. 1865) Andrew Johnson | Andrew Johnson |
| 1869–1873 | Ulysses S. Grant | Schuyler Colfax |
| 1873–1877 | Ulysses S. Grant | Henry Wilson (d. 1875) |
| 1877–1881 | Rutherford B. Hayes | William A. Wheeler |
| 1881–1885 | James A. Garfield (d. 1881) Chester A. Arthur | Chester A. Arthur |
| 1885–1889 | Grover Cleveland | Thomas A. Hendricks (d. 1885) |
| 1889–1893 | Benjamin Harrison | Levi P. Morton |
| 1893–1897 | Grover Cleveland | Adlai E. Stevenson |
| 1897–1901 | William McKinley | Garret A. Hobart (d. 1899) |
| 1901–1905 | William McKinley (d. 1901) Theodore Roosevelt | Theodore Roosevelt |

| Term | President | Vice-President |
| --- | --- | --- |
| 1905–1909 | Theodore Roosevelt | Charles W. Fairbanks |
| 1909–1913 | William H. Taft | James S. Sherman (d. 1912) |
| 1913–1917 | Woodrow Wilson | Thomas R. Marshall |
| 1917–1921 | Woodrow Wilson | Thomas R. Marshall |
| 1921–1925 | Warren G. Harding (d. 1923) Calvin Coolidge | Calvin Coolidge |
| 1925–1929 | Calvin Coolidge | Charles G. Dawes |
| 1929–1933 | Herbert C. Hoover | Charles Curtis |
| 1933–1937 | Franklin D. Roosevelt | John N. Garner |
| 1937–1941 | Franklin D. Roosevelt | John N. Garner |
| 1941–1945 | Franklin D. Roosevelt | Henry A. Wallace |
| 1945–1949 | Franklin D. Roosevelt (d. 1945) Harry S Truman | Harry S Truman |
| 1949–1953 | Harry S Truman | Alben W. Barkley |
| 1953–1957 | Dwight D. Eisenhower | Richard M. Nixon |
| 1957–1961 | Dwight D. Eisenhower | Richard M. Nixon |
| 1961–1965 | John F. Kennedy (d. 1963) Lyndon B. Johnson | Lyndon B. Johnson |
| 1965–1969 | Lyndon B. Johnson | Hubert H. Humphrey, Jr. |
| 1969–1974 | Richard M. Nixon (resigned 1974) | Spiro T. Agnew (resigned 1973); Gerald R. Ford |
| 1974–1977 | Gerald R. Ford | Nelson A. Rockefeller |
| 1977–1981 | Jimmy Carter | Walter F. Mondale |
| 1981–1985 | Ronald W. Reagan | George H. W. Bush |
| 1985–1989 | Ronald W. Reagan | George H. W. Bush |
| 1989– | George H. W. Bush | J. Danforth Quayle |

# Growth of U.S. Population and Area

| Census | Population | Percent of Increase over Preceding Census | Land Area, Square Miles | Population per Square Mile |
|---|---|---|---|---|
| 1790 | 3,929,214 | | 867,980 | 4.5 |
| 1800 | 5,308,483 | 35.1 | 867,980 | 6.1 |
| 1810 | 7,239,881 | 36.4 | 1,685,865 | 4.3 |
| 1820 | 9,638,453 | 33.1 | 1,753,588 | 5.5 |
| 1830 | 12,866,020 | 33.5 | 1,753,588 | 7.3 |
| 1840 | 17,069,453 | 32.7 | 1,753,588 | 9.7 |
| 1850 | 23,191,876 | 35.9 | 2,944,337 | 7.9 |
| 1860 | 31,443,321 | 35.6 | 2,973,965 | 10.6 |
| 1870 | 39,818,449 | 26.6 | 2,973,965 | 13.4 |
| 1880 | 50,155,783 | 26.0 | 2,973,965 | 16.9 |
| 1890 | 62,947,714 | 25.5 | 2,973,965 | 21.2 |
| 1900 | 75,994,575 | 20.7 | 2,974,159 | 25.6 |
| 1910 | 91,972,266 | 21.0 | 2,973,890 | 30.9 |
| 1920 | 105,710,620 | 14.9 | 2,973,776 | 35.5 |
| 1930 | 122,775,046 | 16.1 | 2,977,128 | 41.2 |
| 1940 | 131,669,275 | 7.2 | 2,977,128 | 44.2 |
| 1950 | 150,697,361 | 14.5 | 2,974,726* | 50.7 |
| †1960 | 178,464,236 | 18.4 | 2,974,726 | 59.9 |
| 1970 | 204,765,770 | 14.7 | 2,974,726 | 68.8 |
| 1980 | 226,504,825 | 10.6 | 2,974,726 | 76.1 |
| 1990 | 249,632,692†† | 10.2 | 2,974,726 | 83.9 |

*As remeasured in 1940.

†Not including Alaska (pop. 226,167) and Hawaii (632,772).

††As released by U.S. Census Bureau, December 26, 1990. Critics of the census count have estimated that this figure may have undercounted the U.S. population by as much as 5 million persons.

# ILLUSTRATION CREDITS

The following abbreviations are used for some sources from which several illustrations were obtained:

AP/WW–AP/Wide World Photos. BA–The Bettmann Archive. BB–Brown Brothers. CP–Culver Pictures. DPH/SI–Division of Political History, Smithsonian Institution. GC–Granger Collection, New York. LC–Library of Congress. NA–National Archives. NW–North Wind Picture Archives. SI–Smithsonian Institution. UPI/BN–UPI/Bettmann Newsphotos. WH–The White House.

**Part 4**  p. 1, LC.

**Chapter 20**  pp. 9, 11, 12, 26, 28, 32, 33, LC; p. 36, R. B. Hayes Presidential Center, Fremont, Ohio.

**Chapter 21**  pp. 43, 56, LC; p. 61 (top), DPH/SI; p. 61 (bottom), NW; p. 65, LC; p. 67, DPH/SI.

**Part 5**  p. 71, LC.

**Chapter 22**  p. 77, SI; p. 78, LC; p. 83 (top), NA; p. 83 (bottom), LC; p. 86, LC; p. 87, LC; p. 105, Texas State Archives; p. 106, Nebraska State Historical Society; p. 109, LC; p. 110, University of Washington; p. 112, LC; p. 119, LC.

**Chapter 23**  p. 137, Pennell Collection, University of Kansas; p. 141, DPH/SI; p. 143, LC; p. 150, DPH/SI; pp. 153, 161, NW; p. 163, DPH/SI; p. 175 (top), BB; p. 175 (bottom), DPH/SI.

**Chapter 24**  p. 184, UPI/BN; pp. 189, 192, LC; p. 199, CP; p. 201, BB; p. 203, UPI/BN; p. 208, LC; p. 213, *Colliers,* June, 1905.

**Chapter 25**  p. 222, LC; p. 226, BB; p. 229, Lewis W. Hine Collection, United States History, Local History and Genealogy Division, The New York Public Library, Astor, Lenox and Tilden Foundations; pp. 234, 236, LC; p. 241, CP; pp. 243, 245, 247, LC.

**Chapter 26**  p. 262 (top), LC; p. 262 (bottom), CP; p. 266, LC; p. 274 (top), GC; p. 274 (bottom), BA; pp. 281 (top and bottom), 284, LC.

**Chapter 27**  p. 291 (top), U. S. Air Force Photographic Collection, National Air and Space Museum, SI; p. 291 (bottom), NA; p. 294, NA; p. 295, CP; p. 298 (top), LC; p. 298 (bottom), NA; p. 301, LC; p. 303, LC; p. 306, The Museum of Modern Art, New York; p. 309, BA; p. 311, LC; p. 317, NA; p. 320, LC; p. 321, GC.

**Part 6**  p. 328, Steve McCurry/Magnum.

**Chapter 28**  p. 336, BA; p. 338, LC; p. 342, BA; p. 350, SI; p. 351, BA; p. 354, CP; p. 356 (top), CP; p. 356 (bottom), BB; p. 359, BB; p. 364, CP; p. 368 (top), National Baseball Library, Cooperstown, New York; p. 368 (bottom), BA.

**Chapter 29**  p. 377, LC; p. 379, GC; p. 383, BA; p. 391 (top), Baker Library, Harvard Business School; p. 391 (bottom), LC; p. 392, AP/WW; p. 398, LC; p. 402, AP/WW; p. 408, LC; p. 414, BA; p. 418, NA.

**Chapter 30**   p. 428, U.S. Navy, NA; p. 429, BA; p. 430, U.S. Army photograph; p. 431, BB; p. 434, U.S. Air Force; p. 437, LC; p. 440, NA; p. 444, Imperial War Museum, London; p. 454, DPH/SI; p. 460, BB; p. 466, Pictorial Parade, Inc.

**Chapter 31**   pp. 482, 483, 484, 488, UPI/BN; p. 493, DPH/SI; p. 495, Dwight D. Eisenhower Library; p. 496, LC; p. 499, Charles Moore/Black Star; p. 500, UPI/BN; p. 501, Estate of Edwin Marcus; p. 506, NA; p. 508, WH; p. 509, DPH/SI; p. 510, AP/WW.

**Chapter 32**   p. 520, LC; p. 526, AP/WW; p. 529, Swanson Collection of Caricature and Cartoon, LC; p. 535, DPH/SI; pp. 537, 542, UPI/BN; p. 546, Donald McCullam/Magnum; p. 548, Charles Harbutt/Actuality Inc.; p. 551, UPI/BN; p. 552, AP/WW; p. 553, Leonard Freed/Magnum; p. 558, NYT Pictures; p. 559, UPI/BN.

**Chapter 33**   p. 567, NASA; p. 569, UPI/BN; p. 575, R. Freeman/Magnum; p. 581, UPI/BN; p. 582, LC; p. 585, Nixon Presidential Materials Project, NA; p. 589, UPI/BN; p. 590, Courtesy Scrawls and *The Palm Beach Post;* p. 592, WH; p. 594, AP/WW; p. 600, Bill Fitz-Patrick, WH; p. 606, DPH/SI.

**Chapter 34**   p. 620, UPI/BN; p. 626, AP/WW; p. 631, Reuters/Bettmann; p. 633, Eugene Richards/Magnum; p. 641, *Herblock at Large* (Pantheon Books, 1987); p. 646, UPI/BN; p. 647 (top), AP/WW; p. 647 (bottom), AP/WW; p. 650, Bill Gentile/Sipa Press.

# INDEX

Abolitionism, 237. *See also* Antislavery
Abolitionists: and freedmen, 10; values, 234; tradition, Debs and, 246
Abortion, 577, 617, 619, 633, 635. *See also* Anti-abortion movement
*Abrams* v. *U.S.* (1919), 325
ABSCAM scandal, 597
Accused, rights of, 540, 556
Acheson, Dean, 450, 451, 461
*Achille Lauro,* 636
Adams, Charles Francis, Jr., 87
Adams, Henry, 208, 259; opinion of Grant administration, 53
Adams, John Quincy, 74
Adams, Samuel Hopkins, 199
Adams, Sherman, 490
Addams, Jane, 188, 195, 240
*Adkins* v. *Children's Hospital* (1923), 349
Administrative systems: Reconstruction period, 11–14; progressive era, 194–198, 209–210, 219–220; World War I, 295–299, 304; New Deal, 404; federal bureaucracy, since World War II, 490–491. *See also* Bureaucracy; Government
Advertising: Gilded Age and progressive era, 98; in 1920s, 353
Affirmative-action programs, 573–574, 577, 633, 634, 636; Reagan's opposition to, 619
Afghanistan, 601, 638, 640
AFL-CIO, 514. *See also* American Federation of Labor (AFL); Congress of Industrial Organizations (CIO)
Africa, 648; imperialism in, 256; nationalism in, 525. *See also* North Africa; South Africa
African Americans. *See* Blacks
Afrika Korps, 427
Agassiz, Louis, 29
Aging. *See* Elderly
Agnew, Spiro, 559, 578, 588
Agrarianism, 129; Gilded Age, 100, 102–103, 112–114, 129, 159; and Populism, Gilded Age, 114–117
Agribusiness, 90, 110
Agricultural Adjustment Act (1933), 386, 400
Agricultural Adjustment Administration

(AAA), 386
Agriculture: in South, Reconstruction period, 6; breakup of plantation system, 17–19; tariff problem, Gilded Age, 47; Gilded Age, 90, 113; depression, 1880s, 115; cooperatives, progressive era, 185–186; in 1920s, 347; Great Depression and New Deal, 378–379; and New Deal legislation, 386, 400–404; in 1930s, 401–403; New Deal legacy, 404; in 1950s, 479–480. *See also* Agrarianism
Agriculture, Department of, 185, 387
Aguinaldo, Emilio, 265
AIDS (Acquired Immune Deficiency Syndrome), 555, 614
Airline industries, 597
Air traffic controllers, strike of, 617
Air travel, 485
Air war: World War I, *291;* World War II, 412, 416, *418;* Vietnam War, 581–583; war with Iraq, 649–652
Alabama: Reconstruction period, 7, 34; Gilded Age, 62, 66; civil rights, 499, 524, 540, 620
*Alabama* C.S.S., 44
Alaska: purchase of, 45; admittance to Union, 494; Indians, 573; pipeline, 576
Albania, 645
Albee, Edward, 487
Alcatraz Island, 573
Alcohol: Indians and, 105
Aldrich, Nelson B., 159, 212
Aldrin, Edwin A., Jr., 566
Alexander, E. P., 6
*Alien,* 602
Alienation, sense of, 549–550, 579, 593; in 1970s, 603
Allende, Salvador, 586
Alliance for Progress, 526
Alliance movement, 116–117
Alliances: farming, late nineteenth century, 114–118; World War II, 442–443; of U.S. with other countries, 501–502; CENTO, 503; SEATO, 504; NATO, 622, 638, 646; of U.S. and Latin America, 526; U.S.-Taiwan mutual defense pact, 600
"All in the Family," 604
Alsace-Lorraine: as settlement issue, Paris Peace Conference, 318